THE CATHOLIC UNIVERSITY OF AMERICA
CANON LAW STUDIES
No. 86

THE CANON LAW OF WILLS

AN HISTORICAL SYNOPSIS AND COMMENTARY

A DISSERTATION

Submitted to the Faculty of Canon Law of the Catholic University of America in Partial Fulfillment of the Requirements for the Degree of

DOCTOR OF CANON LAW

BY

JEROME DANIEL HANNAN, A.M., LL.B., S.T.D., J.C.L.,
Priest of the Diocese of Pittsburgh

THE CATHOLIC UNIVERSITY OF AMERICA
WASHINGTON, D. C.
1934

Nihil Obstat:

VALENTINUS T. SCHAAF, O.F.M., J.C.D.,
Censor Deputatus.

Washingtonii, D. C., die II Maii, 1934.

Imprimatur:

HUGO C. BOYLE, D.D.,
Episcopus Pittsburgensis.

Pittsburghi, die III Maii, 1934.

Printed by
THE PAULIST PRESS
New York, N. Y.

TO

THE MOST REVEREND

HUGH CHARLES BOYLE, D.D.,

BISHOP OF PITTSBURGH

PATRON OF CLERICAL SCHOLARSHIP

TABLE OF CONTENTS

THE CANON LAW OF WILLS

FOREWORD

THE conclusions that will be presented in the subsequent pages are the result of a serious attempt to compare the principles of Roman law, modern law, and canon law, with a view to establishing a rather complete juridical theory of wills under the canons. Much of the system thus developed bears the very evident character of being pioneering deduction. The Code provides no explicit guidance on many of the problems that inevitably arise in the administration and execution of wills. It says nothing explicitly of the shares of the natural heirs, of the age required in the testator, of the degree of mental capacity requisite, of the effect of undue influence, of the formalities of revocation, of definiteness as to beneficiary, or of the essential character of a bequest for Masses. Conclusions touching these phases of testamentary law are necessary in practice. In the course of this study they have been drawn from the Decretals, the particular councils of the Church, the rescripts of the Sacred Congregation of the Council, the principles of Roman and modern law, and the implications contained in the Code itself. It is because these foundations supply the groundwork for our conclusions, that they are found scattered through the various chapters of this work. They have been studied not for themselves, but with a view to justifying, or at least illuminating, conclusions that could not be substantiated by any definite or explicit canon in the Code.

Where references to the statutes of the States are given, and when Anglo-American decisions are cited, they have been carefully scrutinized with a view to ascertaining their precise significance. Certain phases of Anglo-American law have been presented in summary form based on the excellent text on *Wills* by Rood, especially where the canon law on mental soundness and undue influence is illustrated by the principles of American decisions. To present an array of references to these decisions would have been to attempt a rather lame imitation of an authoritative work upon which it is impossible for this study to improve.

An attempt is made to present a thorough view of the statutes, and the theories behind the statutes, that often defeat bequests to charity. These statutes are shown to be of three kinds. Some invalidate all charitable bequests made within a definite period antecedent to the testator's death. A second group restricts the amount of property that a charitable institute may possess. A third prohibits the bequeathing to charity of more than a prescribed ratio of the decedent's estate. The topical index provides the necessary guidance in discovering the sections of the text where each class of statute is reviewed. The same is true of judicial decisions that are here investigated to illustrate the theories on which tribunals in the United States have declared charitable bequests invalid on still other grounds. It is pointed out that fundamentally these decisions have rested on the juridical opinion that charitable trusts are governed by the same rule as private trusts, and that the former fail if they labor under the defects by which the latter would be defeated. Chief among these defects, the text points out, are the indefiniteness of the beneficiary and the perpetuity of the trust which the testator seeks to establish. After reviewing the vicissitudes of charitable bequests defeated on these grounds in various States, the text establishes the fact that all the States, except Maryland, now acknowledge the distinction between charitable and private trusts and are prepared to support the former even though the beneficiary be indefinite and the trust be established in perpetuity.

Various phases of the subject of wills are rather explicitly contained in the legislation of the Code. It was the aim of this present study to trace the history of those provisions and to present the views of the authoritative commentators touching them. Chapter V collects the rather copious juridical material applying to the wills of clerics drawn from historical sources, particular legislation, and the Code. Chapter VII presents the historical attitude of the canons towards formalities and analyzes the views of modern commentators on the significance of Canon 1513, § 2. Chapter XI reviews the functions of the bishop as testamentary executor as revealed in history; while Chapter XII investigates the scope of his powers as conceded under the provisions of Canons 1514-1517.

Gratitude is due for the inspiration and cooperation of which the present investigator was the beneficiary in the course of a rather arduous program of research. Eminent among those whose advice and counsel were most stimulating are the Most Reverend Hugh Charles Boyle, D.D., Bishop of Pittsburgh; the Dean of the School of Canon Law, Rev. Valentine T. Schaaf, O.F.M., J.C.D.; Rev. Louis H. Motry, S.T.D., J.C.D.; Rev. Edward G. Roelker, S.T.D., J.C.D.; Rev. Francis J. Lardone, S.T.D., J.U.D.; and the Dean of the School of Civil Law, John McDill Fox.

THE CANON LAW OF WILLS

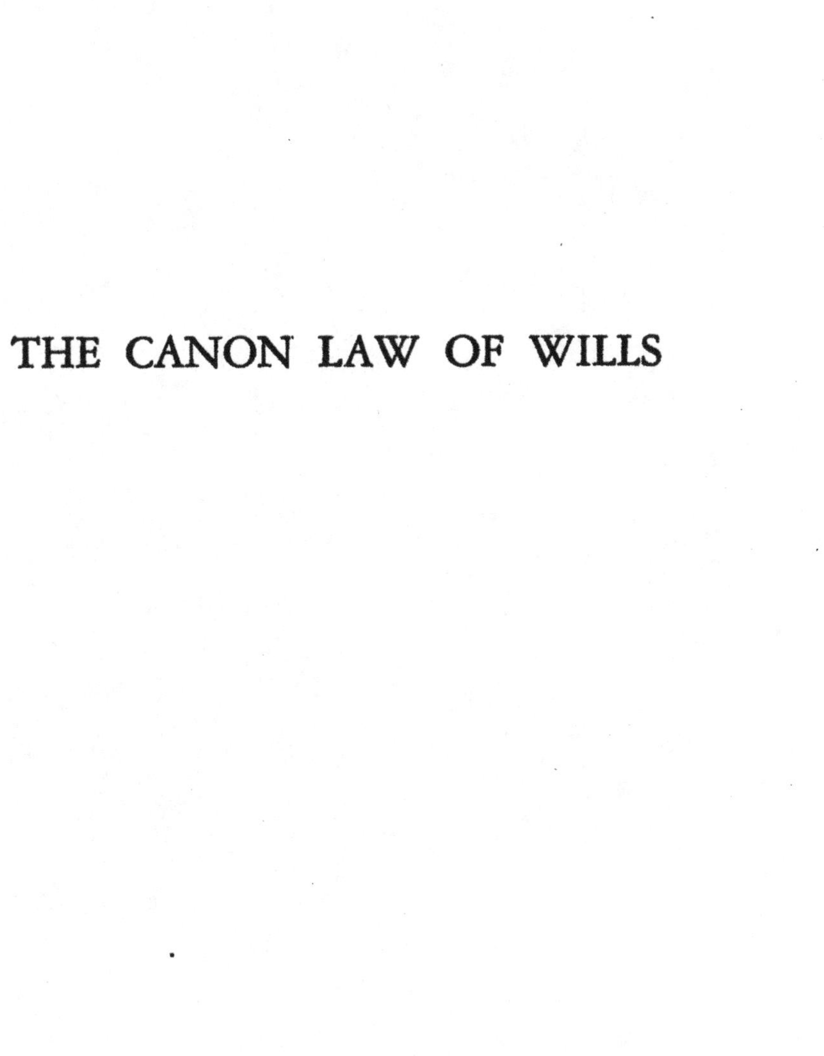

CHAPTER I.

THE NATURE AND THE ORIGIN OF WILLS

ARTICLE 1.

THE RIGHT TO HAVE A WILL ENFORCED.

1. The general nature of wills is the subject matter of the first chapter of this study. At the moment, however, a preliminary notion must be obtained of the right which a man possesses to have his last will enforced. Lacking such a right, it would be futile for him to make a will, and for us to study the nature of his act. Clarity in the process of investigating that right, however, requires that a definition of the testamentary act be known and that a will be carefully distinguished from certain other acts which might easily be confused with it. For that reason the definition of a will is given herewith as a disposition of a man's will concerning what he wishes done after his death.[1] At one time, a will disposed of many things besides property. But now the disposition usually concerns the material goods that were in a man's possession during his life. When the text reviews the history of the testament, the will that disposed of intangible things will be revealed in its full significance. Suffice it for the moment to note that a will today is usually a donation without delivery conditioned on, and revocable until, the death of the donor. A testament was not always conditioned on death, however, and this will be only too obvious when the development of this legal instrument is understood. Consequently, it was not always revocable. Testaments at first took effect as soon as they were executed. They could not be revoked. They were not secret.[2]

2. A trust differs from a will. It may be the creature of a will. It may also be constituted by a contract *inter vivos*, a *contractus innominatus*, *"do ut des."* The trustee is the donee and the donation

[1] Redfield, *Wills*, I, 4.

[2] Maine, *Ancient Law*, p. 169.

is perfected before the death of the donor. Prior to the death of the latter, the trustee becomes the actual owner of the property, with the obligation of distributing it as requested by the grantor. The obligation arises, as is evident, not from a testamentary act. The property passes not from a dead man but from a living man. It passes to a trustee and thence to a beneficiary. It matters nothing that the conveyance from the trustee to the beneficiary does not occur until after the death of the grantor. Consequently, this transaction must not be confused with the notion of a testament when an attempt is made to arrive at a knowledge of the source whence derives a man's right to have his will enforced. For it is not seriously doubted by any one that a man has a right to dispose of his property as he pleases during his life, or that this right derives from the natural law.

3. A *donatio mortis causa* also differs from a will. The more intimate nature of this act will be discussed at greater length in a more appropriate study. At the moment, it suffices to observe that this kind of donation is also made prior to the death of the donor. It differs from ordinary gifts in that it is revocable. However, until revoked, it remains valid, conditioned on the death of the donor. And at the latter's death, ownership vests irrevocably and at once in the donee.[3] By the disposition of the donor a specific person has received a specific gift. The gift, moreover, has been made during the donor's life under a definite condition. That condition is the death of the donor. When the condition is fulfilled, a *donatio mortis causa* vests just as any other conditional gift. It can not be said that the property vests in no one at the death of the testator. *De facto* it vests at once in the donee. It seems a warranted conclusion, then, that the *donatio mortis causa* is a transaction by which the donee is entitled by the natural law to claim the gift at once when the donor dies. It differs from no other donation once the condition has been fulfilled.[4]

On the other hand, property bequeathed or devised in a will is not given as a conditional gift to the beneficiary. It is not to be

[3] Vermeersch-Creusen, *Epitome,* II, 834; Cocchi, *Commentarium,* VI, 189; De Meester, *Compendium,* 1464.

[4] D'Annibale, *Theol. Mor.,* II, 341.

given to the beneficiary at all until *after* the death of the testator. The testator does not give the property to the beneficiary; he merely provides that it shall be given to him. Even when a *specific* legacy is included in a will, that is, when a specific object is given to a specific person, the testator contemplates that he will be dead before the actual conveyance of the bequest.

It is otherwise with the *donatio mortis causa,* as has been indicated. Under this transaction, the gift vests as soon as the donor dies. His death need not operate *positively,* as it must in the case of the testament. Under a *donatio mortis causa,* the death of the donor removes the force impeding the vesting. On the other hand, under a testament the testator's death sets his will in operation. Through that will, even if it be an oral will, he effects his purpose, but *positively* not negatively.

It was necessary to emphasize this distinction in order to prepare for an argument which will be advanced shortly in support of the position that a man's right to have his will enforced does not proceed from the natural law.

4. Extrinsic authority among canonists would indicate that **the right to have a will enforced derives from the natural law.**[5] Reiffenstuel even contends that this view is practically unanimous. Nevertheless, Schmalzgrueber, Zallinger, Pufendorf, Pothier, and Beusch contradict it.[6] Schmalzgrueber deprives the opposing school of what seems to be its main argument, the historical argument, when he denies that the use of testaments is as old as human nature. For it is from this assertion that is derived the notion that the right to have a will enforced derives from the *ius gentium.* And the *ius gentium* is at once translated into the *ius naturale.* This argument and its sequelae will receive more intense scrutiny when the history

[5] Reiffenstuel, *Ius Can. Univ.,* III, 26, 28; Wernz, *Ius Decretalium,* III, 274; Lehmkuhl, *Theol. Mor.,* I, 1143; Pirhing, *Ius Can.,* III, 26, 2; Pichler, *Candidatus,* III, 26, 4, 47; Santi, *Praelectiones,* III, 26, 2; Cavagnis, *Inst. Iur. Pub.,* III, 356.

[6] Schmalzgrueber, *Ius. Eccl.,* III, 26, 4, 5; Zallinger, *Inst. Iur. Nat.,* I, 120; *idem, Inst. Iur. Eccl.,* Prolegomena, § 47 and III, 326; Pothier, *Donations Testamentaires,* c. 1; Beusch, c. 1, n. 89, cited by Tanquerey, *Theol. Mor.,* II, 296; Pufendorf, *De Iure Nat. et Gent.,* CVIII.

of testaments is considered. For the moment, observe that some confusion may exist as to terminology. It is not always certain that they who rely on the natural law as the source of a man's right to have his will enforced are thinking of the will as we know it. This opinion is very old, and it is possible that since it was valid when adopted, its invalidity has been obscured by the brilliance of the names traditionally supporting it through modifications completely changing the nature of the testament. When that opinion arose, grants in view of death were made in virtue of a right arising out of the natural law, because they were made during the life of the donor. Failure of close analysis would obscure the fact that the word, "will," did not always mean a provision requiring positive administration after the death of the testator. Consequently, nothing would be more probable than that a theory adopted when a will was really a grant *inter vivos* continued to be accepted when a will became a grant to be made after death.

5. **The right to acquire for others derives from the natural law.** This is not seriously questioned by any one. But Cavagnis [7] advances this proposition to prove that the testator has a right to have his will enforced. Careful analysis will probably reveal that it affords no basis for such a conclusion. If a man acquires property for another, he is the agent of the other. The principal can claim the goods at any time, even after the death of the agent, without the interposition of a will. On the other hand, the mere fact that a man may happen to think that he will give the property to another is no indication that he is acquiring it for any one but himself. And he has a right *de iure naturae* to give that property to whomsoever he wishes as long as he lives. That is beyond dispute. But if he has acquired the property for another, he can give it to no one but his principal, either before or after death.

6. **The natural right of the widow and the orphan** has always been strenuously defended by the Church. Conceivably this defense has had some influence on the origin of the opinion that the right to have a will enforced also proceeds from the natural law. But the two rights are not interdependent. Had the world never heard of the

[7] *L. c.*

testament, it must have known of the rights of widow and children. **So, too, of the claims of creditors.** But the natural right in these cases resides in the beneficiaries, not in the person making a will. While their right to be provided for derives from the natural law, it is not so certain that the testator's right has the same origin. The one does not follow as a corollary of the other.

The Encyclical Letters of Pope Leo XIII and Pope Pius XI, touching the social order, do indeed speak of man's right to transmit property by inheritance, but it is obvious from the context that they refer to the rights of the family to be preserved out of the personal estate of its chief. Indeed, as head of the family, the father does have a right that his family be not deprived of the means of sustenance which he has acquired for it. But it is significant that the Encyclicals speak only of the right to transmit by inheritance, not of the right to have a will enforced.[8]

[8] The Encyclical, *Rerum Novarum,* 15 May, 1891, says this: "That right of property, therefore, which has been proved to belong naturally to individual persons must also belong to a man in his capacity of head of a family; nay, such a person must possess this right so much the more clearly in proportion as his position multiplies his duties. For it is a most sacred law of nature that a father must provide food and all necessaries for those whom he has begotten; and, similarly, nature dictates that a man's children, who carry on, as it were, and continue his own personality, should be provided by him with all that is needful to enable them honorably to keep themselves from want and misery in the uncertainties of this mortal life. Now, in no other way can a father effect this except by the ownership of profitable property, which he can transmit to his children by inheritance."—Translation of the International Catholic Truth Society, pp. 17, 18.

The Encyclical, *Quadragesimo Anno,* 15 May, 1931: "Provided that the natural and divine law be observed, the public authority, in view of the common good, may specify more accurately what is licit and what is illicit for property owners in the use of their possessions. . . . History proves that the right of ownership, like other elements of social life, is not absolutely rigid . . . 'It is plain, however, that the state may not discharge this duty in an arbitrary manner. Man's natural right of possessing and transmitting property by inheritance must be kept intact and cannot be taken away by the state from man' (cited from the Encyclical, *Rerum Novarum*) . . . However, when civil authority adjusts ownership to meet the needs of the public good it acts not as an enemy, but as the friend of private owners; for thus it effectively prevents the possession of private property, intended by Nature's Author in His Wisdom for the sustaining of human life, from creating intolerable burdens and so rushing to

7. A natural right arises when positive law countenances wills. For the natural law by its implications sanctions positive precepts which provide for the peaceful distribution of property. This conclusion derives from the principles of distributive justice. Once canon law or secular law has instituted a law of wills, every man governed by that law has a right to have his will enforced. This right is a natural right arising out of a quasi-contract between the testator and the legislator. Moreover, under a legal system granting testamentary rights to its subjects, each subject has a natural right, implying an obligation in commutative justice, to be unhampered in the making of his will as against all persons subject to the same laws. But this natural right is posterior to the positive legislation authorizing disposition by testament. If one speaks of this right as a natural right, there is no room for controversy. The precise problem, however, is this: whether a man has a natural right anterior to positive law.

So it happens that when the Church makes reference in her rescripts to the necessity for a just cause to modify the wills containing bequests to charity, it is reasonable to suppose that the natural right to which allusion is made is the right that derives from positive enactment or custom. This conclusion is warranted the more because, as these references are incidental, they do not explicitly analyze the source of this right, but simply recognize its existence and assign it as the reason why the will demands respect.[9]

8. There are three juridical arguments for the contention that the right to have a will enforced does not derive from the natural law. There is another argument, the historical, which is lengthy enough to justify a separate article, and will not be considered at this time.

The first juridical argument is that **a dead man is not a subject of rights *de iure naturae*.** A dead man, consequently, has no right derived from nature to have his will enforced. Only by the fiction that he still lives in his representative does the civil and the canon law support his right to its fulfillment.

its own destruction."—Translation of the National Catholic Welfare Conference, 1931, pp. 17, 18.

[9] See the reply of the Sacred Congregation for the Propagation of the Faith to the Vicar Apostolic of Cochin-China (1807)—*Coll. S. C. P. F.*, 689.

Second, a dead man is incapable of ownership. His will, operative only when his property ceases to belong to him, attempts ineffectually to dispose of property that is not his. Only by the fiction that his representative succeeds as the agent of a living man does the civil and the canon law enable his will to have its effect.[10]

Third, if the deceased had the right *de iure naturae* to dispose of his property after his death, that right should logically be unrestricted as to time. If the right exists one moment after his death, there seems to be no cause which would prevent it from existing a million years after it. That he has a natural right so extensive as this is not seriously contended anywhere.[11]

9. The right of the secular or the canon law to abolish succession by testament, each within its own sphere, is substantiated by the denial that the right of testamentary disposition proceeds from the natural law. However, men generally need not fear that their wills lack sufficient sanction. To avoid chaos the secular and the canon law provide for the due recognition of these dispositions. And in at least all civilized nations, wills can validly be made. Nevertheless, any interference by positive law, within its proper sphere and according to the laws of equity, seems warranted, whether it be to deny testamentary capacity to all or certain classes of its subjects; or to curtail, modify, or infringe upon it. That the moralist would concur with this view seems justified by Ballerini's conclusion that the derivation of the testamentary right from the natural law could be safely denied.[12]

This conclusion, however, does not justify such extensive control of the rights of those who have a vested claim on the deceased. These rights do not depend on the right of testamentary disposition. They would be valid even though the right of testamentary disposition were rescinded by positive law. They are independent of the latter and must be protected by it.

10. Scholion. The testamentary right is not a necessary adjunct of the right of private property. That it is such an adjunct is suggested in much of the reasoning that derives the testa-

[10] See Schmalzgrueber, *l. c.;* Rood, *Wills,* 6.

[11] Blackstone, *Commentaries,* II, 1, 10.

[12] Ballerini-Palmieri, *Theol. Mor.,* III, 697.

mentary right from the natural law. Undoubtedly, the right of free disposition is essential to any adequate concept of private ownership. But the right of testamentary disposition is not essential to it. Indeed, two arguments would suggest quite the reverse.

First, the testamentary right can not be identified with the right of free disposition, for the testator himself sets his testamentary disposition at odds with his ownership. Indeed, ownership actually defeats, during the testator's life, the disposition involved in testamentary acts, because the testator actually retains ownership while seeming to dispose of his property. Testamentary disposition, therefore, is only a fictitious disposition. One does not give and retain at the same time. It is futile, then, to argue that private ownership demands the right of testamentary disposition, for private ownership actually defeats any *real* disposition in that fashion.

Second, at the moment when the real disposition is expected to be effective, private ownership has ceased to reside in the person who attempts to make the disposition. He is dead. It would seem not to be of the essence of private ownership that property owned should continue to be at the free disposal of the proprietor at a time when he is no longer capable of exercising the right of ownership over it.

It appears, then, that the testamentary right should not be given a foundation in the natural law as a derivative of the right of ownership. It is a right easily distinguished from any rights in property actually owned and from rights of disposition that are capable of being exercised during life.

Article 2

The History of Intestate Succession

11. The ius gentium seems called on to supply the chief argument in support of the view that the testamentary right derives from the natural law. Lest the distinction between the *ius gentium* and the *ius naturale* be obscured and the issue confused, some attention should be given at this point to the nature and the origin of the *ius gentium* and the manner of its historic association with the *ius naturale*.

The *ius gentium* arose from the practice of the Roman pretors of disposing of suits brought before their tribunals by foreigners who were considered unworthy of the privileges of the Quiritary law which governed Romans.[13] But the *peregrini* were too numerous to be outlawed. Their disputes must be settled in an orderly manner. Consequently, when the necessities of foreign trade brought before the pretor suits between foreigners or between a foreigner and a Roman citizen, he assumed jurisdiction from two motives: viz., the preservation of order and the promotion of foreign trade.

But to adjudicate such matters the pretor was compelled to discover principles upon which to rest his decision. He refused to employ the principles of the Quiritary law, inasmuch as foreigners were regarded as beneath such a privilege. He would not use the principles of the law of the foreigner, inasmuch as that would imply a degradation of his office. He adopted the expedient of selecting rules of law that seemed common to Rome and the community from which the immigrant had come.

In the beginning the immigrants came only from the neighboring Italian tribes, and it was from the rules of law used by these nations that the pretors at first constructed the foreign code, not named then the *ius gentium,* but corresponding to the later concept implied by that name. It was named the *ius honorarium,* the pretorian law, or the edictal law. The pretor was probably not too scientifically informed on the laws of the other nations. Probably he included in his system his own concepts of what was reasonable and fair. The *ius naturae,* operating through his conscience, would very probably enable him to identify its principles with many of the rules of law common to other peoples.[14]

It is not necessary to conclude that the pretor attached superiority to the system thus devised as an eclectic code. The opposite might seem to be the case, considering his affection for the forms, rights, and ceremonies of the Roman law. It is not necessary to believe that he recognized the excellence of the common principles that really sprang from the heart of all men into their laws. A complete revolution of attitude was probably necessary before his system could

[13] Sherman, *Roman Law,* I, 33.

[14] Sherman, *op. cit.,* I, 40, 50, 56, 60, 61; Maine, *op. cit.,* p. 47.

challenge his reverence. But such a revolution undoubtedly did occur and under the matured jurisprudence of the jurisconsults the *ius gentium* was elevated to the position of a model, perhaps imperfectly developed in their estimation, but one nevertheless to which all positive law should be made to conform.[15]

12. This change of view was brought about by the influence of the Greek theory of the *ius naturae*. Stoic philosophy had adopted the proposition that man's end in life is to live according to nature. It conceived, and correctly, that there are simple, harmonious rules established by the very nature of man, according to which the thoughts, observances, and aspirations of humanity must be directed. In the moral sphere, these rules were conceived to be manifestations of a single, eternal principle, just as in the physical sphere the uniformity of physical reactions manifested the same principle.[16]

On the subjugation of Greece this philosophy made its way into Rome where it subdued the leading classes, among whom were the lawyers. The association of Roman lawyers with Stoic philosophy lasted through many centuries. The golden age of Roman jurisprudence, the time of the Antonines, was precisely the time when Stoic philosophy was exercising its greatest influence in high places. Thus the belief gradually grew among the Roman jurisconsults that the old *ius gentium* was really the lost code of nature.[17] Thus the *ius gentium* and the *ius naturae* came at least vaguely to be identified. Though Ulpian attempts to distinguish between them, Justinian uses the terms as if there were no distinction.[18] Probably the correct distinction is that one is the philosophical, the other the legal aspect of the same law.

13. There is greater difficulty in establishing the derivation of a right from the *ius gentium* than in proving that it arises out of the

[15] Maine, *op. cit.*, pp. 48-50.

[16] *Cf.* Cicero's *De Republica,* III, 22, where it is said that there is a true law conformable to justice, diffused through all hearts, unchangeable, eternal, which by its commands summons to duty, by its prohibitions deters from evil.

[17] Maine, *op. cit.*, pp. 51-54.

[18] Ulpian, D. 1, 1, 1, 4, Justinian says that the law which natural reason appoints for all mankind is called the *ius gentium* because all nations use it—I. 1, 2, 1.

ius naturae. Greater patience, more profound research, and an intelligent correlation of statistical information is involved in the former enterprise. It has been shown that the right to have one's last will enforced does not derive from the *ius naturae.* It remains to establish that it does not arise out of the *ius gentium.*

It may be stated as a general hypothesis that in some societies at least, first a state of jurisprudence exists in which testamentary privileges are unknown. Only late in the development of these societies have wills been given effect. To establish that proposition, several preliminary points must be examined. As will appear in the course of this argument, a will in its earliest form was an instrument used to convey an inheritance, not to make a multitude of diverse dispositions.

14. An inheritance is a form of universal succession, and a universal succession is an entry into the whole body of rights and duties of another, into his *universitas iuris.* To grasp the nature of the early form of the will, it is necessary to understand the significance of an inheritance and a *universitas iuris.*

The *universitas iuris* is the legal personality of an individual, the sum total of all his rights and duties, the whole set of legal relations which he bears to the rest of the world. In this set of relations, the duties may, in a given case, overbalance the rights. A man may owe more than he can claim. In that case he is insolvent. His personality, or *universitas iuris,* is insolvent. And the person who succeeds to his personality is also insolvent. And that consideration leads at once to the notion of a universal succession.

A true universal succession takes place *uno ictu.* One person might acquire the whole body of rights and duties of another by a series of acts, v. gr., by a number of purchases. He might come into possession of them by one act but in different capacities, v. gr., partially as purchaser, partially as legatee. In neither case would he take by universal succession. A universal succession occurs only when the whole body of rights and duties pass at the same moment in virtue of one and the same capacity in the person who succeeds.[19]

Bankruptcy is a modified form of universal succession under the

[19] Maine, *op. cit.,* pp. 172-174.

laws of the United States. The assignee succeeds to the *universitas iuris* of the bankrupt. He is insolvent. But he makes payments only to the extent of the assets of the assignor. Under a true universal succession, he would be liable beyond the assets.

Adrogation was a form of universal succession in Roman law. This was a legal process by which a person *sui iuris* (that is, subject to no *paterfamilias* but enjoying the full rights of a *paterfamilias* himself) was adopted by another independent Roman citizen.[20] The person adrogated lost his own independence, and became subject to the paternal power of the adopting father. His property passed from his control into the control of the *paterfamilias* who adrogated him.[21]

15. The *hereditas* was the most important form of the universal succession in Roman law. It occurred at death. The universal successor was the *heres,* the heir. He assumed the legal personality of the deceased as to rights and obligations. His character was the same whether he inherited through intestacy (*ab intestato*) or under a will (*ex testamento*).[22]

The heir was not necessarily an individual. Several co-heirs, all together, could constitute legally the continuation of the personality of the intestate or the testate decedent. But in any event, in the earlier jurisprudence, complete identity of personality between the successor and the person to whom he succeeded was required.

A will was invalid that did not provide for the uninterrupted continuity of the personality, that is, that failed to provide for the instantaneous devolution upon the heir of the whole body of the tes-

[20] *Sui iuris*—I. 1, 11, 1; Gaius, I, 99. The person adopted was previously a *paterfamilias*—I. 3, 10, 1; Gaius, 3, 83. *Cf.* D. 1, 7, 12 and Sherman, *op. cit.*, II, 501.

[21] Sherman, *op. cit.*, II, 502; Gaius, 3, 84.

[22] Sherman, *op. cit.*, II, 662. Gaius uses both terms, *ab intestato* and *ex testamento*—2, 100. *Cf.* also I. 2, 9, 6.

The technical term for the inheritance was *hereditas,* but it was also called the *universum ius defuncti, bona defuncti,* and *familia*—*Cf.* I. *l. c.;* and D. 10, 2, 2, pr.

As to what inheritance is in its nature observe the following: *hereditas nihil aliud est quam successio in universum ius quod defunctus habuerit*—D. 50, 17, 62. The character of the *heres* is thus described: *heredem eiusdem potestatis iurisque esse, cuius fuit defunctus, constat*—D. 50, 17, 59.

tator's rights and duties. Clearly the object of first importance was not the execution of the testator's intentions, but the continuation of the personality of the deceased. It was the concern for this continuation of personality that brought the will into being. The later right that attached to the will of providing for the fulfillment of the testator's wishes was an addition. It probably would not have existed without the previous concern for the preservation of the *universitas iuris*. It is of some importance, then, to learn why such stress was laid upon it.

16. The importance of status in primitive society explains the concern of the laws to preserve the personality of the head of the family. In primitive social organizations men are treated according to status rather than on the basis of their individual personality. They are thought of by the law or by custom principally as members of a particular group within the organization. Every man is regarded first as a member of the tribe or state; then as a member of an order or caste; then as a member of a *gens* or clan; and finally as a member of a family. The family was the most nearly personal aspect in which the law regarded him. He was not looked upon as himself. Society was composed not of individuals, but of groups of men united by the reality or the fiction of blood relationship.[23]

Primitive tribes were really federations of families, in which the family was practically a little state with the patriarch at its head. Public law dealt not so much with the individual as with the family, or rather with its head, who was the public officer of the group. His rights and duties, in the contemplation of law, were identified with those of the corporation.

17. When the head of a family died, he was regarded by the law as not dying at all. For was he not the family? The person who succeeded him would be the family, identified with it in every respect, in the place of the man who died. The person representing it for the future bore a different name, and that is all. Creditors would have the same remedies against the succeeding chieftain as against his predecessor, for their claims were against the family. The rights also of the family remained the same. Only for the future it must sue under a different name.

[23] Maine, *op. cit.*, pp. 177, 178.

The corporation sole illustrates the position of the chieftain in primitive society. As will appear in a subsequent portion of this treatise, certain Catholic bishops in the United States are regarded by the law in this capacity. Under this concept, the office is viewed apart from the particular person who from time to time may be its incumbent. As the office is perpetual, the series of persons who occupy it are invested with the principal quality of corporations, viz., perpetuity. The office never dies. The capacities of a previous incumbent are instantly filled by his temporary or permanent successor.

The fact of death may be conceived to have been eliminated in primitive society. The family, by a fiction, lived on. If any decedent attempted before his death to violate this fiction, even indirectly, the instrument was probably repudiated as invalid. He must not be permitted to separate his actual from his posthumous existence. The testament could not be used to disinherit those who had a right to be invested with the leadership of the family.[24]

18. Adoption takes the place of the will in Hindu law. Both contrivances were methods adopted at first merely to prevent the disruption of the family when there is no succession of kindred to carry it on. The persons appointed by adoption or by testament were by a

[24] Maine, *op. cit.*, pp. 178-184. *Cf.* also Sherman, *op. cit.*, II, 505. The use of the word *familia* as synonymous with the *hereditas* indicates that what passed in the testament was the aggregate of rights and duties comprised in the *patria potestas*.

This view explains the intimate connection in primitive society that existed between the testament and the *sacra* or family rites. As late as Cicero's time, adoption was permitted only when due provision had been made for the performance of the funeral rites in the family from which the adopted person was taken, and no testament could make a conveyance of an inheritance without a strict apportionment of the expenses of these ceremonies.

Among the Hindus, the right to inherit a dead man's property is exactly co-extensive with the duty of performing his obsequies. If they are not properly performed by the person designated, the family is irreparably disrupted, and no one can inherit the property.

The patriarch therefore embodied in himself the function of family priest. The rites at the death of one and the succession of another chieftain afforded liturgical evidence of the continuation of the family.—Maine, *op. cit.*, pp. 185-187.

fiction of law placed in the position of an heir, succeeding by blood, to continue the personality of the family. Of the two, adoption was probably the first device that suggested itself.

To Rome belongs the distinction of having developed the testament. But among Roman lawyers it was never looked upon as a means of separating the property and the family, but rather as a contrivance to make better provision for the members of the family than could be made under the rules of intestate succession.[25]

Whatever testamentary law was known to the barbarian invaders came from Rome. This is the one consistent conclusion that can be derived from a critical analysis of their Codes. The ancient nucleus of these Codes, the system by which the tribe was governed in its home, shows no trace of the testament.[26] For example, under the *Lex Salica* the deceased's lands descend to his sons. His chattels might descend to the women folk. But all succession was *ab intestato* and no land could descend to women.[27] Indeed, the nations that grew out of the invasions knew nothing of the real testament until the twelfth century. In the meanwhile, a sort of testamentary disposition grew up from the custom by which the *sacra,* or dead man's share, was given to a trustee prior to the decedent's death, not to be buried with him, as the ancient custom had been, but to be distributed in works of charity and religion.[28]

19. Three conclusions are warranted from the discussion that has been presented as to the origin of the testator's right to have his will enforced.

First, intestate succession probably preceded succession by testament amongst most peoples. This conclusion would seem to invalidate the argument that the right to have one's will enforced proceeds from the *ius gentium.*[29]

[25] Maine, *op. cit.,* pp. 187-189.

[26] Maine, *op. cit.,* p. 190.

[27] Pollock-Maitland, *English Law,* II, 250, 251; 257, 258.

[28] Huebner, *German Private Law,* p. 754; see also Pollock-Maitland, *op. cit.,* II, 316-318.

[29] Indeed, it may be fairly concluded that whatever testamentary law is to be found in the world has derived from Hellenico-Roman concepts; except perhaps the testament in Bengal, which probably was developed independently.—Maine, *op. cit.,* p. 191.

Second, succession *ab intestato* derives from the theory that the family is above the vicissitudes of death. It is not based on the notion that this plan best distributes the property of a decedent. It would seem an invalid argument, therefore, to use the institution of universal succession *ab intestato* as a foundation for the opinion that it is from the natural law that testamentary rights derive. On the contrary, it should be concluded that the institution of the family as a patriarchal unit derives as such from the natural law, for succession *ab intestato* was a means to its preservation. It is difficult to see how this conclusion can be admitted in view of the fact that the institution has been abandoned practically everywhere.

Third, the original testament passed obligations to the heir as well as rights and assets. It seems faulty reasoning that would conclude that one phase of the original testament derives from the *ius gentium*, and not the other which was inextricably bound up with it. Yet, it seems impossible to hold that the right to pass on one's obligations beyond the capacity of assets derived from the natural law since this theory has been almost everywhere abandoned also. If the right of the testator to bequeath his obligations is thought to have rested only on the authority of positive law, was the right to bequeath assets based on any firmer foundation?

20. Scholion I. Succession under the Mosaic system is difficult to study. It is significant that the Levitical law makes no provision for testamentary disposition. A natural right might well have been safeguarded here if anywhere. A reference to the right of inheritance is found, indeed, but it is in connection with slaves, and the text would seem to deny liberty of testamentary disposition.[30]

On the other hand, in the jubilee year every one returned to his possessions. This made the system of ownership a closed one. The right to have one's will enforced would have been futile under it. The aim seems to have been, as among so many other peoples, to perpetuate the rights of the family, and to guarantee that at the worst

[30] Lev. XXV, 45, 46: "And of the strangers that sojourn among you, or that were born of them in your land, these you shall have for servants: And by the right of inheritance shall leave them to your posterity, and shall posssess them forever."

its possessions could not be estranged for a period exceeding fifty years.

A certain automatic adoption resulting in a tentative right of succession appears in the history of Abraham. Abraham, it will be recalled, complained that the son of his steward would be his heir, and alleges as the reason the fact that the boy was born in his house. So far from demonstrating that Abraham here was making a will, this narrative indicates that the original aim among all peoples was to perpetuate the house as a unit, property and all. For Abraham had relatives at Haran whom he could have remembered by will. If the right to have one's will enforced is from the *ius gentium,* why did Abraham feel constrained to ignore his blood relatives in favor of the relatives of his house?[31]

Indeed, the blessing given by Isaac to Jacob indicates that he was appointing his son his universal successor. Jacob was to be lord of his brethren. But Isaac's blessing should not be construed as necessarily indicating that he was free to bestow it on whom he pleased. Jacob was a supplanter, as his name indicates. And Esau had a birthright, which he had sold. Both facts indicate a right of succession to the family rights that should devolve by right on the oldest son. The blessing itself seems to be a solemn religious act of institution for a new patriarch, "with corn and wine," as Isaac himself describes it. Isaac was confronted with a legal difficulty when he discovered his mistake. He solved it by giving Esau a blessing, too. In the issue, Jacob succeeded as patriarch but without the allegiance of Esau. Isaac's second blessing amounted to an emancipation.[32]

The gift of Jacob to Joseph as the former was dying can hardly be construed as a will. From the text it appears to be an actual gift, as if he had handed a deed to his property to Joseph.[33]

The later Rabbinical jurisprudence granted testamentary capacity, it is true. But it could be exercised only when there were no kindred to claim the decedent's estate. Besides, the Roman testa-

[31] Gen. XV, 3.

[32] Gen. XXVII, 28-40.

[33] Gen. XLVIII, 22.

ment was not unknown to the lawyers who made the concession.[34]

21. **Scholion II. Positive law with great assurance deprives persons of testamentary capacity.** This corroborates the view that this capacity is a creature of positive law. The freedom with which positive law acts in this matter will be more manifest when the problem of testamentary capacity presents itself. For the moment, suffice it to observe that fairly universally positive law denies this right to definite and determined classes of its subjects. Even when the testament does appear, and even where it has sanctions in the positive law, great numbers of persons are excluded from its privileges. Sometimes, more than half the population is excluded from the use of it. At Roman law, for instance, slaves, foreigners, the *filius familias* (that is, one who was under subjection to the *paterfamilias*), and women were deprived of its benefits.[35]

The laws of nations struggled to maintain caste even by the instrumentality of the testament. Consequently, it may be surmised that the testament was not allowed to contravene the avowed purpose of the law. It is difficult to see how the practice of permitting a will to serve the purposes of caste should be taken as an evidence

[34] Maine, *l. c.*

[35] Moyle, *Inst.*, I, 251-253 (footnotes); Sherman, *op. cit.*, II, 680; D. 28, I, 6 pr.; I. 2, 12.

Besides, many others were affected by an incapacity that came indirectly by a prohibition against bequeathing certain kinds of property, particularly the *res nec mancipi*. That is, property not transferable by *mancipatio*. It included principally land lying outside of Italy. The theory was that this property belong to the State. *Cf.* Sherman, *op. cit.*, II, 570.

In England, no will of lands was permitted till the reign of Henry VIII (32 Henry VIII, c. 1; 34, 35 Henry VIII, c. 5). Even then the right was hemmed in with numerous restrictions which were not removed until after the Restoration (12 Charles II, c. 24). A will of lands did not become ambulatory until 1837.—See Blackstone, *op. cit.*, II, 1, 12, 13; Pollock-Maitland, *op. cit.*, II, 315.

This indirect disfranchising illuminates and strengthens the view that the practices of nations, if they afford any hint as to what those nations thought of testamentary disposition, indicate rather an emphasis on caste. For all of these restrictions are in the interests of caste. They suggest, therefore, that the laws of nations constantly concentrate on social organization rather than on the personal freedom of the individual.

that nations universally sponsored the sort of will by which devises and bequests are made today.

Only by infusing into the minds of ancient legislators the concepts of modern jurisprudence can they be made to speak for the natural right of men to have their wills enforced. These legislators, who manifested such little regard for individual prerogative, make very poor witnesses for an individual's right as an individual to speak after his death. If there was any institution which they regarded as proceeding from the very nature of man, it was not individual liberty, but the sanctity of the caste. If they were wrong, at least they can not be painted as agreeing with the legislative concepts of today. When they admitted the testament, it was in form a free act of the testator. Nevertheless, to the testament adhered for centuries, in ever diminishing degree, the original notion of perpetuating the caste.

22. It is the will itself that now must engage the attention. It was Rome that gave the will to the world. A kind of will had been authorized under the Laws of Solon at Athens.[36] And the imperfect will of Bengal may have developed without Roman influence. But both these forms hallow the claims of caste. And neither would have converted the jurisprudence of the world. That was the missionary task of the Roman form. An examination of the Roman will reveals that it, also, enthroned patriarchal rights at first. But under a constant trend towards freedom, it was revolutionized, eventually becoming the instrument of free disposition. To this examination the subsequent article addresses itself.

Article 3.

The Origin and Development of the Roman Testament.

23. The first Roman testaments were executed in the *comitia calata*, that is, in the *comitia curiata*. This was the parliament of the patricians of Rome, assembled for private business.[37] This procedure has led to the constantly repeated conclusion that every Roman testament of this primitive Roman era was a distinct legislative

[36] Maine, *l. c.;* Blackstone, *op. cit.*, II, 32, 491; Redfield, *op. cit.*, I, 2.

[37] I, 2, 10, 1; see Gaius, 2, 101; Sherman, *op. cit.*, II, 683.

enactment. The precision and solemnity should rather be traced to the caste organization of the Roman state. Members of the same *gens* originally had certain rights in the estate of families belonging to it. The heirs first in line of precedence under the Roman canons of descent were the direct descendants of the *paterfamilias* who had never been emancipated from his power. If there were no such persons who could succeed to the inheritance, the father or brothers of the decedent were next in line. Mark well, the family to which the *paterfamilias* belonged is preferred to the families originated by his emancipated sons, who originally could in no case inherit from their father. If there were no *agnati* (the general name of the class of persons belonging to the family of the *paterfamilias* by descent from his male ancestors), the *gentiles* originally were next. These persons were members of the *gens*, that is, the fictitious extension of the family consisting of all the Roman patricians bearing the same name as the decedent. It was argued that they were all *agnati* of the decedent, that is, descended through the male line from the same common ancestor. Because of this theory, they excluded the *cognati*, who were relatives of the *paterfamilias* through female descent. This preference for the *gentiles* is said to have ceased at an early date. But it was adequate cause for a procedure that continued long after the preference had been forgotten.[38]

The *comitia curiata* was an assembly in which the *gentes* were exclusively represented. It was constituted on the assumption that the *gens* was the constituent unit of the Roman state. It is natural to suppose that every testament was submitted to this assembly in order that those who might be injured by its dispositions (that is, the *gentiles* who had the right to succeed in default of *agnati*), might veto the instrument, or by allowing it to pass, renounce their claim.

The same procedure, it may be observed, appears among the primitive Germans. When a man had no heir, the tribal council appointed one for him. When, somewhat later in their legal development, they permitted the decedent to name his own heir if he had no legal successor, the approbation of the same council was nevertheless necessary to the validity of the appointment. For the council

[38] *XII Tables*, 5, 4, 5; Gaius, 3, 1-9 and 3, 17; Ulpian, *Reg.* 26, 1-5; I. 3, 1-8; Sherman, *op. cit.*, II, 671; Maine, *op. cit.* p. 193.

was composed of those who had the right to succeed by escheat in default of an heir.[39]

24. But the Roman testament that has had so wide an influence is not the one made in parliament. It is a later form, one that was introduced very probably to enable plebeians to make a will. In any event, its origin has all the evidence of an attempt to evade the law. It was a conveyance *inter vivos*, a sale of the *familia* (not, it must be observed, of property, but of the whole family). The effect of adrogation, already noticed, was really a sale of the *familia* by the adopted person to the person adopting him. But the sale of the *familia* known as the testament, though irrevocable, was not to be effective until after the death of the testator. The legalization of this form of sale is probably contained in the following text of the *XII Tables: Pater familias uti de pecunia tutelave rei suae legassit, ita ius esto.*[40]

As late as the early years of the Empire, the *comitia* still held its meetings. But the publicity of reciting wills in the assembly proved distasteful, and eventually few wills, or none, were presented at its semi-annual sittings. Indeed, wills seem not to have been made in the presence of the *comitia* even in the days of Cicero.[41]

25. **The plebeian will** had supplanted it. The characteristics of the plebeian will can be understood only by reference to the procedure from which it derived. This procedure was the *mancipatio*, the Roman conveyance. The origin of *mancipatio* is traced to the time when writing was little used. Then intricate ceremonial was necessary to impress upon the memory legal and public acts worthy of remembrance.

The *mancipatio* required the presence of the parties to the transaction, *i.e.*, the vendor and the vendee. There were needed also five witnesses and the *libripens*. The latter brought with him the scales to weigh the uncoined copper money of ancient Rome. The testament that was a fictitious sale of the *familia* was made with the formalities of the *mancipatio*. From those formalities it derives its name. It was long to be known technically as the testament *per aes*

[39] Maine, *op. cit.*, p. 194; Huebner, *op. cit.*, pp. 740, 750.

[40] *XII Tables*, 5, 3; I. 2, 22; Sherman, *op. cit.*, II, 685, 696.

[41] Cicero, *De oratione*, 1, 53; Sherman, *op. cit.*, II, 683.

et libram, that is, "with the copper and the scales." It was an ordinary *mancipatio* in which the testator was the vendor, and the appointed heir was the vendee (or technically the *emptor familiae,* the purchaser of the family). The *emptor familiae* pretended to pay a price by striking the scales with a piece of money. The testator then ratified the transaction with a definite formula called the *nuncupatio,* or the publication of the sale. The *emptor* thenceforth was the heir in the strict sense of the primitive Roman law. He had purchased the corporation sole known as the *familia,* the property, the slaves, the ancestral privileges, with all the duties and obligations incumbent on it.[42]

26. The *emptor familiae* took the inheritance subject to legacies. The *familia* was bought with whatever obligations the testator attached at the moment of transfer, and all other obligations that had previously attached to it. This doctrine seemed warranted by the extreme generality of the clause of the *XII Tables* which legalized this form of testamentary disposition. Observe the relaxation of the original rigorous view of the character of the heir. Since the heir was now bound by legacies created at the moment he purchased the *familia,* written records of the transaction became increasingly important to guard against the refusal of the heir to satisfy the claims of the legatees.[43]

27. The pretor began to recognize wills made without the symbolic ceremony of the *mancipatio*. Each pretor, it must be understood, issued an edict at the beginning of his term of office in which he indicated what acts he would sustain during his incumbency even though they might not be legal under the Quiritary law. In some particular year, it is probable that the pretor inserted in his edict the provision that he would uphold testaments lacking some of the formalities of the *mancipatio.* The convenience of the new form was probably quickly recognized. Subsequent pretors included the provision in their edicts. Eventually it became incorporated as a legal form in the Perpetual or Continuous Edict. This was the accumulation of rules of procedure gathered through the constant proclama-

[42] Gaius, 2, 102-104; I. 2, 10, 1; Sherman, *op. cit.,* II, 685; *Cf.* also Gaius, 1, 119; Maine, *op. cit.,* pp. 197-201.

[43] Sherman, *l. c.;* Maine, *op. cit.,* p. 201.

tion of edicts from year to year, stabilized at length in the reign of the Emperor Hadrian, who forbade further additions to be made.[44]

The pretor based his formalities on the solemnities of the testament *per aes et libram*. But he retained only those elements that seemed necessary to him to guarantee against fraud. He demanded the seals of seven witnesses on a written document. This number was probably obtained by adding together all the persons who were required to be present under the *mancipatio*.[45]

28. But the pretor could not grant under the pretorian form all that was signified by the *familia*. This was communicable only by compliance with the decrees of the Quiritary law. Nor could the pretor place the heir in the relation to the rights and duties of the inheritance which the testator had enjoyed. What he did was to confer upon the designated heir the enjoyment of the property bequeathed, and to acquit him of any further obligation of payment when once he had discharged the testator's debts.

Technically, the pretor gave the heir *bonorum possessio*. This was really only a possession in fact, protected by the pretor. But after he had possessed the property for a year, the principle of *usucapio* operated on it. This was a principle similar to prescription and adverse possession. Thus, at the end of the year the heir had acquired a legal title to the estate, his property ceased to be *res nec mancipi*, and his ownership came to be Quiritary instead of merely bonitary possession.

The recognition of the pretorian will became impregnable after the rescript of Marcus Aurelius. This decree gave the heir instituted in such a will an *exceptio doli* (similar to a plea of *non assumpsit*), by which the person attacking his claim was authoritatively deprived of a verdict and was assumed to be fraudulently harassing the possessor of the property. Thus the heir during the year of his factual possession could interpose in the pretor's court this defense against the relatives of the deceased, should they seek to dispossess him.[46]

[44] Sherman, *op. cit.*, I, 44, 50, 56, 60, 61; Maine, *op. cit.*, pp. 60, 61; 202, 203.

[45] Sherman, *op. cit.*, II, 686; Maine, *op. cit.*, pp. 202-204; Gaius, 2, 119, 120; I. 2, 10, 2; Ulpian, *Reg.* 28, 6.

[46] Gaius, 2, 120; Moyle, *op. cit.*, I, 249.

29. The testament *per aes et libram* continued to be used contemporaneously with the pretorian will.[47] But in the days of Gaius, the *emptor familiae* could be a party who was not to be the actual beneficiary at all. He became the heir with the obligation of surrendering the *familia* to another after the death of the testator. The testament thenceforward assumed the property of secrecy. The actual formality of conveyance soon lost all meaning. The *nuncupatio* became the real testament, at first made orally, later written. The *nuncupatio,* it will be recalled, was the dispositive portion of the testament *per aes et libram* in which the testator imposed obligations on the *emptor.* At length, the emphasis on this element of the procedure became so great, that the other element was almost ignored. The testament came to be looked upon as revocable, not as an irrevocable sale. While the jurisconsults were effecting this development of the testament *per aes et libram,* it is improbable that the pretors were lagging far behind in perfecting the pretorian will. It seems probable that this form also made allowance for the institution of an heir who was not to be the real beneficiary, and became also a secret will and revocable. In any event, just before the codification of Justinian, the subjects of the Eastern Roman Empire employed a form of testament that had the simplicity of form of the pretorian will but, like the will *per aes et libram,* required the formalities to be performed in the presence of the testator and all the witnesses, and passed Quiritary rights to the inheritance and not merely the *bonorum possessio.*[48]

30. Meanwhile, Theodosius II had put his hand to the pretorian will, requiring subscription, as well as sealing, by the witnesses.[49] He provided, too, that the testator should sign the will, or summon an eighth witness to sign in his place, unless it is stated on the face of the will that it was written entirely by the testator himself.[50]

[47] Sherman, *op. cit.,* II, 685.

[48] D. 28, 1, 21, 3; I. 2, 10, 3 (as to the performance of the formalities in the presence of the testator and all the witnesses).

[49] C. 6, 23, 21; Moyle, *op. cit.,* I, 250.

[50] C. 6, 23, 28, 6; Moyle, *l. c.*

31. The *testamentum tripartitum* of Justinian was the fully developed Roman will. It is this form that possessed characteristics of both the testament *per aes et libram* and the pretorian will. Indeed, some of its most important features were derived also from the decrees of the emperors. Because it derived from the three sources indicated, viz., the old *ius civile*, the *ius honorarium* (the law of the pretor), and the imperial law, it was called *tripartitum*. It is this form that is usually meant when reference is made to the Roman will. It was a written will, shown to seven witnesses, and then subscribed (signed at the end) by the testator in the presence of the witnesses, who then affixed their signatures and seals to the document.[51]

But no one who has followed its development can fail to appreciate that its parent was the universal succession accomplished through an instrument of conveyance, the fictitious sale, which aimed at perpetuating the *familia* more effectually than intestate succession. It can scarcely be concluded, therefore, that this form of testament, which required so many years of gradual growth, flows out of the *ius gentium* in its present form. For the present form is practically a contradiction of the original.[52] Nothing is clearer than that the original Roman testament grew out of a desire to guard the natural rights of others rather than to grant freedom to individuals to express their wishes as to what they desired to be done after their death.[53]

[51] I. 2, 10, 3-5; D. 28, 1, 21, 2; D. 28, 1, 20, 8; D. 28, 1, 22, 3-4; D. 28, 1, 24; C. 6, 23, 12; C. 6, 23, 21. Sherman, *op. cit.*, II, 687.

[52] "The making of a written will in England and the United States," says Sherman, "demands the observance of all these formalities so essential to the making of this fully developed Roman will,—the only change being a reduction of the number of witnesses from seven to usually three. Blackstone observes that the publication of a will in the presence of witnesses (*the nuncupatio*) was introduced into English law by Bracton, who 'has implicitly copied the rule of the Civil Law' "—Sherman, *l. c.;* Blackstone, *op. cit.*, II, 32, 502.

As to the United States this is substantially true, but various States depart in some measure from the rule, requiring only two witnesses.

[53] The Romans had a great horror of intestacy. The horror that is found in the Middle Ages doubtlessly was derived from the attitude of the Romans (see Pollock-Maitland, *op. cit.*, II, 321). No adequate reason appears for

32. Scholion I. Patricians used an alternative form of will in place of the testament made in the parliament. The alternative form was made just before they set out on a military expedition (*in procinctu*). It is probable that it differed from the form *calatis comitiis* in greater simplicity of publication. It was announced to only three or four witnesses instead of the whole assembly.[54]

33. Scholion II. Oral or nuncupative wills were legal in the time of Justinian. These were either private or public. A private oral will was made verbally before seven witnesses.[55]

A public oral will was declared by a public act before a magistrate.[56]

34. Scholion III. In the laws of the German invaders a counterpart of the Roman development is found. It was characteristic of most of the German systems that, besides the *allod* or domain of each family, they recognized other kinds of property, the concepts of which arose by separate and distinct transfusions of Roman principles. The primitive property was strictly reserved to the kindred,

the extreme, morbid, and almost irrational horror of intestacy unless it be a traditional attitude inherited with the testament itself.

The necessity for a will in Roman civilization will appear from the following consideration. After it became possible at Roman law for a son to be emancipated, he was regarded as outside his father's family. He was the head of a new family. The laws of succession, therefore, excluded him from participating in his father's estate, for they aimed at the continuance of the legal family, to which the emancipated son no longer belonged. The same was true of a married daughter, who passed from the *patria potestas* of her own father into that of her husband.

Thus, the bonds of blood were severed by the bonds of law. The legal institution that aimed at perpetuating the family really did violence to the claims of blood. In this state of affairs, the law permitted resort to a fiction, the *mancipatio,* to avert the injustice. Indeed, in given circumstances, the father could be regarded as failing in an obligation of the natural law if he neglected to protect a dependent son, even though the latter were emancipated, or a dependent daughter, even though she had passed into the *patria potestas* of her husband. But to argue from this obligation to a natural right to have any sort of will enforced is hardly warranted.—Maine, *op. cit.,* pp. 214, 215; Sherman, *op. cit.,* II, 469, 470.

[54] Gaius, 2, 101; I. 2, 10, 1; Sherman, *op. cit.,* II, 684.

[55] I. 2, 10, 14; C. 6, 23, 21, 2; C. 6, 23, 26; Sherman, *op. cit.,* II, 688.

[56] C. 6, 23, 19; Sherman, *op. cit.,* II, 688.

scarcely capable of being alienated by an act *inter vivos*. The male children were co-proprietors with their father. The family estate could not be conveyed without the consent of all the members. But the other forms of property, of more recent origin and of lesser dignity, could be much more easily alienated. Because they lay outside the strict family endowment, women and the descendants of women could succeed to the non-allodial forms. It was on these that the imported Roman testament was allowed to operate. And well into the Middle Ages, until the twelfth century, even these dispositions were not revocable. The Germans placed the emphasis on the sale even in such wills as they legalized, just as the Romans did at a certain stage of their development. The German plan was that the testator should make a conveyance to a *salman*, a figure possibly borrowed from the *fiduciarius* of the Roman law. When a man had no heirs, even the allodial property could be conveyed to the *salman*, with the approval of the tribal council. The *salman* was obliged to hand the estate over to the real heir after the death of the testator.[57] The *salman* held something of the position of the heir at Roman law at that period in its history when the heir could be compelled to hand over the whole estate to another.

A further examination of the European law of testaments is appropriate at this point, for the practices and customs of the nations that grew out of the invading tribes came into most intimate contact with the developing canon law of wills.

Article 4.

The Development of the European Testament.

35. The departure from the Roman law of testaments that occurred in Europe shortly after the invasion of the German tribes, warrants this study of the manner in which testamentary disposition was introduced among them. It is warranted, too, by the interdependence of their legislators and the legislators of the canonical system.

[57] Maine, *op. cit.*, pp. 191, 192.

36. Under the primitive German law, only he who had no heir could create one.[58] This creation was accomplished by the herital contract, though the appointment was probably reserved originally to the tribal council. When the decedent eventually came to be permitted to make the appointment himself, he still required the approbation of the members of the tribal council or the king. For, these persons were affected by a diversion of property that otherwise would escheat to them.

The herital contract was consummated among the Lombards when the testator handed a spear to the appointed heir by the hand of a third party in the presence of the folk court. Among the Franks, though it was probably one act originally, it appears in the Salic law as three consecutive acts.[59] The first act was a transfer in the minor court of the folk, accomplished symbolically by the handing of a reed to the *salman* with a designation of the amount of the estate and the name of the heir. The second act was the seisin (that is, the assumption of possession with the intention of holding the property as the owner of it). It was the *salman* who thus took possession. The third act was the delivery of the reed to the heir within a year.[60]

37. The herital contract became gradually a mere gift effective on the death of the donor. The executor (or *salman*) came to have unlimited powers conferred on him, on condition that at the death of the donor he would make due conveyance to the designated heir.[61]

The procedure was simplified under the *Lex Ripuaria,* so that the gift *mortis causa* could be made by the delivery of a document (*traditio chartae*). The executor was still employed as intermediary, especially when the donor was so ill, as he usually was, that he could not deliver the document to the heir in person.[62]

[58] Huebner, *op. cit.*, pp. 740, 750.

[59] It was called among them *affatomie.* Among the Lombards, it was known as *gairethinx* (from *thinx,* court, and *ger,* spear).

[60] Huebner, *op. cit.*, pp. 740-742; Brissaud, *French Law,* pp. 685-689.

[61] Huebner, *op cit.*, p. 742.

[62] Huebner, *op. cit.*, p. 754. The author observes that when the grantor could not place the document of transfer upon the altar in person, to signify that the altar was to be his heir, the executor did it for him.

38. The right to dispose of a portion of the non-allodial property was gradually introduced. The procedure thus far discussed was applied at first only when the donor had no heirs. By degrees, it was made applicable also to certain portions of the non-allodial property, even when he had heirs. This concession grew up on the theory that he had a right to dispose of the dead man's portion.

The dead man's portion in pagan days was the share of his property that was buried with the corpse or burnt with it as part of the funeral rites. Under the new concept, however, it was no longer buried with the corpse, but was distributed to religious and charitable uses for the benefit of the dead man's soul. From the ninth century onward this portion was one-third the non-allodial property.[63]

Brissaud remarks that executors appear as such in Frankish deeds of the eighth century, and in almost every disposition made after that period in view of death—*op. cit.*, p. 692.

An example of procedure by executor appears in the Capitularies under the reign of Louis, the son of Charlemagne (819). It was ordained by that ruler that any man is authorized to make a lawful transfer of his property at the place where he resides to a pious place or to any person. If he resides outside the limits of his county, he is to employ two witnesses who belong to his native jurisdiction, and to constitute executors with a legal title (*fideiussores vestiti*) to convey the gift.—*M. G. H. Legum*, § II, *Capitularia Regum Francorum*, tom. I, 282.

[63] Brissaud thinks that the division of the estate into thirds: one-third for the children, one-third for the wife, and one-third for the decedent's soul, owes its origin to the German law—*op. cit.*, p. 691. But it seems not to have been outside the influence of canon law, for in the Constitutions of the Apostles there appears a provision that ordains that the goods of a decedent are to be distributed to the poor for a memorial of him—VIII, 42—Mansi, I, 590 B; Funk, I, 554, 555. And the Council of Nice prescribed that a certain portion of the estate is to be devised to God, c. 15—Mansi, II, 1044 D. In Ireland, it was prescribed that the testament should contain a provision for the Church, and that the estate was to be divided between the kingdom, the Church, and the heirs—*Cap. Coll. Can. Hibern.*, lib. 31, c. 22—Mansi, XII, 129 A; Wasserschleben, p. 115. It is noted in the same connection that the Church takes only what is God's portion and gives the heir what is his—*op. cit.*, lib. 41, c. 6—Mansi, XII, 135 E; Wasserschleben, p. 160.

As to the origin of this method of division in England, where it may, after all, have originated, Pollock and Maitland tell of a certain householder of whom St. Bede speaks in his history. This man died one evening but returned to life the next morning. He arose and went to the village church. After remaining

The portion due the dead man's soul became a vested claim by the twelfth century. It was regarded by canon law as a claim just as certain as the claims of creditors. In the Council of Cashel, (1172), where the Irish bishops pledged allegiance to Henry II, the faithful are commanded to make a will dividing their estates into three parts, if they have a wife and children; or into two parts, if they have either no wife or no children surviving them. Their own souls are to be the beneficiaries of one-third or one-half, respectively.[64]

a while in prayer, he divided all his substance into three parts. One of these he gave to his wife; another to his sons; and the third he reserved to himself. Forthwith he distributed the reserved portion among the poor. The authors regard it as a remarkable coincidence that this tale should be told of a Northumbrian, "for in after days it was in Scotland and the northern shires of England that the custom which secured an *aliquot* share to the wife, and an *aliquot* share to the children, and left the dying man free to dispose of the residue of his goods, struck its deepest roots"—Pollock-Maitland, *op. cit.*, II, 314; II, 257, 258; 338-340. See Blackstone, *op. cit.*, II, 32, 491, 492.

When in the fourteenth and fifteenth centuries widows and children went into the secular courts to sue for their portions, the judges could not determine with certainly what was the origin of their right to their one-third—Pollock-Maitland, *op. cit.*, II, 351. But this proportionate division was still recognized as the law under Charles I—Blackstone, *op. cit.*, II, 32, 492.

[64] C. 6—Harduin, VI, B, 1630. Many other councils in England and Ireland defended the soul's right to this portion. *Ita:* Council of Worcester (1240), c. 50—Harduin, VII, 345; Constitutions of the Bishop of Salisbury (1256)—Mansi, XXIII, 823 A; Council of Lambeth (1261)—Harduin, VII, 543; Council of London (1268), c. 24—Harduin, VII, 631 B; Synod of Oxford (1287), c. 50—Harduin, VII, 1114; English Provincial Council (1509)—Mansi, XXXI A, 401 A; Council of Dublin (1348)—Mansi, XXVI, 114 E.

The *Diploma* of Stephen, King of England (1134), evidently moved by the spirit of canon law, ordained that the Church should supervise the proper distribution of the estate of a deceased bishop so that the usual share would be given for the benefit of his soul. And the Constitution of Thurstan, Bishop of York (1134), decreed that the income of a prebend be distributed for one year for the benefit of the soul of the canon who had been its incumbent. *Diploma*—Mansi, XXI, 495 E; Constitution of Thurstan—Mansi, XXI, 495 B.

But in the province of Toulouse, a council under Simon de Montfort permitted no more than one-fifth of the disposable estate to be bequeathed to charity—*Conventus Apamiensis,* c. 10—Mansi, XXII, 857 E.

Bracton says that if a man had neither wife nor children the whole of his disposable estate was to be distributed for the good of his soul—*De Legibus Angliae,* 2, 26, 2. This notion is thoroughly in harmony with the principle that

39. The method by which the new nations disposed of their bequests was not testamentary disposition. Until the twelfth century, it was a *donatio mortis causa.*[65] These gifts were often made shortly before death, and hence they came to be known as "the last words" of the decedent. To these "last words" the whole Christian world was accustomed by the time of Pope Alexander III, as appears from his legislation requiring the presence of the pastor at the making of wills.[66]

a man's right to have his will enforced proceeds from the positive, and not from the natural, law. But it contradicts the opinion that the right derives from the natural law. For, even if it be assumed that the confiscation of the whole of a decedent's estate for works of charity is nothing more than the assertion of a claim due under the natural law; nevertheless, when it extends to the whole of his disposable estate under every consideration, at the very least it nullifies any right which he may have had under the natural law to have his will enforced.

[65] Moreover, it seems that certain kinds of land had gradually come to be disposed of in this fashion. This land was known as book-land in England. The owner disposed of it without consulting the heir on the theory that, being land given into the jurisdiction of the possessor, it was accompanied by a prerogative from the crown in virtue of which the possessor was authorized to appoint subordinate owners—Pollock-Maitland, *op. cit.*, II, 250. The transfer in this case was really an execution of a power of appointment which the owner had in virtue of the instrument giving him the land, enabling him to name pious causes as grantees. But the land-book, or the indenture of transfer, was called a testament—Pollock-Maitland, *op. cit.*, II, 315-318.

[66] C. 10 X, *de testamentis et ultimis voluntatibus,* III, 26. *Cf.* also the *Responsiones* of Egbert, Archbishop of York, made in 748, in which reference is made to these "last words," c. 2—Mansi, XII, 492 E.

Pollock and Maitland say of these "last words": ". . . those last words which we find the Church protecting are essentially words spoken by one who knows himself to be passing away. And we seem to see that they are as a rule spoken, not written words. . . . Some portion of his chattels, no doubt, the dying man may give to pious uses . . . But . . . there is much in future history, much in continental history, to suggest that even here we have to deal with gifts which were thought of as gifts *inter vivos.* . . . The sick man distributes . . . a portion of his chattels. He makes that portion over to his confessor for the good of his soul; he makes what—regard being had to the imminence of death—is a sufficient delivery of them to the man who is to execute his last will. The questions that we wish to ask—Are his words revocable and are they ambulatory?—are not practical questions. Not in one

40. Land was also given to charity as a *post obit* gift or as a gratuitous gift with the reservation of usufruct. There was little difference between the two forms. What difference there was consisted chiefly in formalities. The notion was that the beneficiary became the legal owner by both transactions, while the grantor retained a life estate. When the gift was made with usufruct reserved, there was usually an accompanying act of seisin performed by the beneficiary, and a nominal annual rent to be paid by the donor as life tenant. The latter might receive as an alternative a life estate in another plot of ground instead of that which he had just conveyed. These two forms of donation were known not only in England but also on the Continent and were defended by a decree of Innocent III.[67]

These *post obit* gifts were what is sometimes described as the Anglo-Saxon will. They were clearly not Roman wills. There was no institution of the heir. The donation itself is irrevocable, as the Roman testament itself had been in its earlier stages. It is not ambulatory, that is, it does not provide that property to be acquired after the transaction shall pass in virtue of it. "In England after the Conquest," say Pollock and Maitland, "there was no sudden change. A man could still make the *post obit* gift of land. Occasionally in such cases it was thought well that the donor should put himself under the obligation of paying a small rent to the abbey while he lived, but there was no necessity for a duplex process of feoffment and re-feoffment." [68] That is, there was no necessity for the execution of a contract by which the land would be given back to the original grantor as a life estate or in usufruct.

case in a thousand does a man live many hours after he has received the last sacrament."—Pollock-Maitland, *op. cit.*, 318-321.

[67] C. 3, X, *de successionibus ab intestato*, III, 27. *Cf.* Huebner, *op. cit.*, p. 744; Pollock-Maitland, *op. cit.*, II, 316-318. It is the seisin by the beneficiary in these gratuitous gifts to which Innocent III probably refers under the name *scotage*. This was a remedy prescribed by him especially for the case in which a certain principality would not recognize wills made outside its territory. By the act of *scotage* a handful of earth of that principality was to be placed on the extremity of a sacred cloth and placed on the altar by the grantor in the presence of witnesses—c. 2, X, *de consuetudine*, I, 4.

[68] *Op. cit.*, II, 324.

41. But during the ninth, tenth, and eleventh centuries,[69] **the *post obit* gift and "the last words" seem to coalesce in England.**[70] The result is a written will, formless in the main, written in the vernacular, and containing in advance the grantor's "last words." Traces of revocability are rare. Occasionally provision for the residuary estate indicates that these wills are sometimes ambulatory. Finally, the grantor provides in these documents for the payment of debts. But generally, it would seem, he is not making a real will, but only charging his estate with an irrevocable gift. This seems the more probable from the fact that the document of conveyance was often handed to the grantee in lieu of the gift itself. Appeal is often made to the bishop to see to it that the transfer is properly made. So also the king is called upon to lend his authority, and a handsome gift is provided for him in return for his intervention.[71]

42. But in the twelfth century the king's court in England condemned the *post obit* gift of land and every dealing with land that is of a testamentary character.[72] But it spared the customs of the

[69] This is the period in which, according to Brissaud, the Church had exclusive jurisdiction over gifts *mortis causa* on the Continent—Brissaud, *op. cit.*, p. 696.

[70] Pollock-Maitland, *op. cit.*, II, 321, 322. Huebner says that the will takes the place of gifts *mortis causa* on the Continent beginning with the twelfth century.—*Op. cit.*, p. 755. Brissaud notes that after the twelfth century dispositions *mortis causa,* which up to that time had been religious acts, became half-secularized.—*Op. cit.*, p. 696.

[71] Pollock-Maitland, *l. c.*

[72] *Cf.* Magna Carta, 9 Henry III, c. 36 (apud Blackstone, *op. cit.*, II, 18, 270, footnote): "Non licet alicui de caetero dare terram suam alicui domui religiosae, ita quod illam resumat tenendam de eadem domo; nec liceat alicui domui religiosae terram alicujus sic accipere, quod tradat illam ei a quo ipsam recepit tenendam: si quis autem de caetero terram suam domui religiosae sic dederit, et super hoc convincatur, donum suum penitus cassetur, ut terra illa domino suo illius feodi incurratur." Blackstone regards this decree as an attempt to prevent the evasion of a prohibition against mortmain conveyance. It is part of his thesis to show that mortmain statutes are very old. But the decree can just as easily be regarded as legislation against an attempt to continue the old gratuitous gift with reservation of usufruct.

On the Continent, too, the executor's power was limited to chattels after the twelfth century—Brissaud, *op. cit.*, p. 695.

boroughs and permitted certain of the newer interests in land to be regarded as chattels, v. gr., a tenancy for a term of years.[73]

This was really a compromise effected by the judges of Henry II to protect the expectant heir whose rights had been constantly waning, among them the right to be interrogated prior to the alienation of property in which he had an interest. The effect of the compromise was that there could be no testamentary disposition of lands for the future, but the consent of the heir would no longer be required for alienation *inter vivos*.[74]

The *post obit* gift itself did not disappear until late in the century. After that, if a tenant in fee "would become a tenant for life, there must be a feoffment and a re-feoffment, two real transfers of a real seisin." During the thirteenth century, "men not infrequently professed to dispose of their lands by their last wills or by charters executed on their death beds. It is a common story in monastic annals that so and so bequeathed land to our church and that his heir confirmed the bequest. . . . But as a matter of fact no validity was ascribed to these legacies or imperfect gifts. What had happened . . . was either that the heir had made a feoffment, or that the monks having already taken seisin, he had released his right to them, and such a release would have been just as effectual if there had been no will." [75]

However, it was found possible to devise land by a subterfuge. Land was conveyed to uses during the life of the testator, who then in his will nominated the uses to which it was to be put. The first recorded case of this kind appeared in 1383. The law courts, of course, held that the title of the grantee (who was a trustee) was absolute. Thus those in whose favor the uses were declared in the will depended entirely on the good faith of the grantee. But the chan-

[73] Pollock-Maitland, *op. cit.*, II, 315-318; Redfield, *op. cit.*, I, 2.

[74] Pollock-Maitland, *op. cit.*, II, 250, 255.

[75] Pollock-Maitland, *op. cit.*, II, 329-331; *cf.* also Blackstone, *op. cit.*, II, 1, 12. No will of lands was permitted till the reign of Henry VIII (32 Henry VIII, c. 1 and 34, 35 Henry VIII, c. 5). *Cf.* footnote 35, this chapter. An attempt was made in the thirteenth century to revive the devise of land by the *forma doni* (that is, in virtue of the original grant of land with the power of appointment of a successor). The courts wavered, and then decided against it.—Pollock-Maitland, *op. cit.*, II, 329, 330.

cellor held that the grantee was bound in conscience to devote the emoluments of the estate to the uses prescribed.

The Statute 15 Richard II, c. 5, was enacted to prevent the enjoyment of these uses (or equitable estates) by corporations. It enacted that land *purchased* to uses should be amortised by license from the crown or else sold to private persons. It also decreed that for the future, uses are to be subject to the statutes of mortmain (forbidding corporations, especially the religious corporations, to hold land in fee), and therefore forfeit like the lands themselves, if license was not obtained from the crown.

But devises to uses continued, certainly to private persons, perhaps also to corporations. Thus when the Statute of Uses was passed in 1535, 27 Henry VIII, such devises were the rule and intestacy as to lands exceptional. The purpose of the Statute of Uses was manifestly to put a stop to such devises. But it was met with a flood of protest so strong that the Statute 32 Henry VIII, c. 1, was passed, permitting the devise of all lands, tenements, and hereditaments held on the basis of rent in money or kind (free and common socage), and of two-thirds of the land held on the basis of rent by military service. This was made to apply only to estates held in fee simple by the Statutes 34, 35 Henry VIII, c. 5 (1542, 1543). In 1660 all lands were reduced to the basis of tenure by free and common socage, and hence became devisable without restriction—12 Charles II, c. 24.[76]

From the twelfth century to the sixteenth, land descended to the eldest son, who was excluded from the *chattels* in his father's estate. Thus unity of succession was destroyed. In the exigency of the situation, canon law now developed the last will for chattels and it really assumes a testamentary character. When a man died intestate, his chattels fell to the bishop for proper distribution.[77]

43. There are ten conclusions that summarize what has been learnt in the discussion just presented of the development of the will among the growing nations of Europe. These conclusions are:

[76] The mortmain statutes of course did not apply to lands taken for charitable uses by bishops or private persons. Or to charges impressed on lands held by heirs and devisees in favor of charitable causes.—*Cf.* Rood, *op. cit.*, 94, 95; Blackstone, *op. cit.*, II, 18, 267-273; II, 23, 375.

[77] Pollock-Maitland, *op. cit.*, II, 325, 326.

First, in the beginning nothing could be conveyed except by intestate succession, unless a man was without an heir.

Second, if he had no heir, he could at first ask the folk court to appoint one; later, he was permitted to appoint one himself in the presence of the folk court through an intermediary *salman*.

Third, the appointment was gradually simplified into an act by which the *salman* was entrusted with the duty of instituting the heir at the death of the principal. However, the *salman* took seisin of the property before the testator's death.

Fourth, there was a further simplification by which the *salman* took only a document to be handed the heir in due time.

Fifth, it came to pass that even when the grantor had heirs he could dispose of the soul's portion, considered to be one-third the nonallodial property.

Sixth, none of these grants was a real testament.

Seventh, gradually a relaxation of the law permitted certain lands to be conveyed away in view of death, but by instruments that were actually not testaments but conveyances.

Eighth, the conveyance of land by testamentary disposition was forbidden in the twelfth century and the relaxation of the old law corrected.

Ninth, thenceforth the will proper appears for the testamentary disposition of chattels.

Tenth, the church courts assumed jurisdiction over these wills in England, though their influence over testamentary dispositions on the Continent was not so great after real wills appeared as it had been prior to that time. The diversity between these tendencies offers a probable explanation of the distinction that exists between the formalities required in England and on the Continent. The influence of canon law was all on the side of simplification; the influence of Roman law was in the direction of the *testamentum tripartitum* of Justinian. More on this divergence of laws will follow in due time, viz., when a study is made of the jurisdiction of canon law over wills. For the moment, this summary notice of the two distinct tendencies explains why in England and the United States the form of the will may be said roughly to be the canon law will, while on the Continent it is more nearly the will of Roman law.[78]

[78] See cc. 10, 11, X, *de testamentis et ultimis voluntatibus,* III, 26; Pollock-Maitland, *op. cit.,* I, 122, 123; 128, 131, 133; II, 336, 337.

CHAPTER II

RIGHTS OF SUCCESSION GROWING OUT OF THE TESTAMENT

44. A glance at the province of testamentary succession reveals the fact that no longer is the testament the sole means by which a decedent indicates what he wishes done after his death. Many new forms have arisen out of the constant tendency of human nature to escape the limitations set upon it by law. The very liberality of the law has permitted it to recede before the repeated aggressions that gave birth to these devices. Many of them have proved their usefulness for a later day, and so have survived the incident that brought them into being.

It is the aim of the present chapter to study these forms as they exist in the secular law and in canon law. It will consequently be divided into four articles: the first of which will review the testamentary devices of the secular law; the other three, the same devices as accepted by canon law.

Article 1

Testamentary Devices in the Secular Law

45. As attempts were made to defeat the rigorism of intestate succession, and even of testamentary inflexibility, subterfuges were adopted. They were either institutions or instruments.

The institutions were devices contrived to effect the will of the decedent in contravention of the legal provisions.

The instruments were documents, extra-legal in their origin, that gained at first legal toleration and finally legal recognition.

The institutions were chiefly the *donatio inter vivos* with the reservation of usufruct and the *donatio mortis causa.*

The documentary devices were principally the legacy, the codicil, and the *fideicommissum* (the written trust).

46. Among many primitive peoples the earliest wills were allowed only in default of an heir *ab intestato*. They needed the approval of the folk or the *gens*, because the larger group was conceived as having a definite interest in the succession. However, this requirement could be defeated if the decedent had already conveyed his property to a beneficiary before his death. He could so convey it that it vested at once in the grantee, reserving, if he pleased, some rights in the gift. On the other hand, he could so convey it that it should vest only at the moment of his death. Of the former method of conveyance, little need be said in a treatise on testamentary dispositions. The second, however, is really a testamentary disposition because under its provisions death is a necessary condition for the vesting of the bequest.

47. It is a *donatio mortis causa*, this gift that vests when the donor dies. The *testamentum per aes et libram* was a *donatio mortis causa* in a wide sense. True, there was a fictitious sale involved, and the conveyance was not therefore technically a gift. Moreover, the whole family (the *familia*) was sold or conveyed. And, at first, it was not revocable, while a *donatio mortis causa* can be revoked at any time prior to death. But it was a conveyance to be effective at death, and its power to displace the rigorous requirements of the intestate succession and of the *testamentum calatis comitiis* seems to consist in this that the conveyance forestalled their operation. A decedent who had no property could not well be brought under the rigor of the primitive law.[1]

Among the growing European nations, the *donatio mortis causa* afforded a similar escape from the inflexibility of the law of succession. It has already been indicated that at first one-third the non-allodial estate could be bequeathed by a *donatio mortis causa*, and eventually even certain kinds of land.[2]

48. The legacy is probably the most important of the instruments providing testamentary disposition excepting, of course, the testament itself. Legacies resemble gifts *mortis causa*. Indeed, it has even been stated that the one essential difference between them is that a gift *mortis causa*, unlike a legacy, does not depend for its own validity upon the validity of a will.

[1] Sherman, *op. cit.*, II, 685; Gaius, 2, 102-104; I. 2, 10, 1.
[2] *Cf.* §§ 37-40.

Legacies originally grew out of the desire to escape the necessity of bestowing universal succession on one's heir. They were made possible, it seems, by the extreme liberality of the *XII Tables* in permitting the testator to attach obligations to the *familia* at the very moment when the conveyance was made to the *emptor.*[3] That meant that the testator must take the estate subject to legacies. Thus it became increasingly necessary to make written records of the bargain struck between the testator and the *emptor* to protect the legatees against the heir.[4] And in the days of Gaius, when it was possible to transfer the *familia* through an intermediary, the actual conveyance became a mere formality. The list of obligations became the real will, and as such revocable (since the irrevocable formality, the conveyance, was of no further significance). Thus the legacy grew in importance, so that from the day of its first appearance, few testaments were made without one or more of them. Indeed, most wills now are no more than a bundle of legacies.

Justinian defines a legacy as a "kind of gift left by a deceased person." [5] Unless contained in a will or codicil, a legacy was invalid at Roman law. This, of course, is explainable under the theory of its origin just discussed. A legacy did not convey a universal succession, but only a portion of it.[6] A legacy was required to speak imperatively. If it merely prayed the heir to fulfill the decedent's request, it was no more than a *fideicommissum.*[7] Latin was the language in which it was necessary to write a legacy, under pain of invalidity, until the time of Constantius who permitted it to be made in

[3] *Cf.* § 26, supra; *XII Tables,* 5, 3; I. 2, 22.

[4] Sherman, *op. cit.*, II, 685; Maine, *op. cit.*, p. 201.

[5] I. 2, 20, 1; *cf.* Sherman, *op. cit.*, II, 706.

The *Digest* gives the following definition: "*legatio est delibatio haereditatis, qua testator ex eo, quod universum haeredis foret, alicui quid collatum velit*"—D. 30, 116.

[6] I. 2, 9, 6; Ulpian, *Reg.*, 25, 15; D. 50, 16, 164, 1; D. 30, 26, 2. When a *fractional* portion of the universal succession was thus conveyed it was called *legatum partiarium*—D. 50, 16, 164, 1. One could bequeath a universal succession that he had received from another without any provision for his heirs—D. 32, 29, 2; D. 31, 88, 2.

[7] Ulpian, *Reg.*, 24, 1.

any language.[8] A legacy lapsed, if the heir did not accept the inheritance. This was due to the fact that the *nuncupatio* was originally secondary to the *emptio familiae.*[9] This was not true of legacies granted in a codicil. Even though the heir refused to accept the inheritance, the legacy was still valid.

49. A codicil was an informal will that originated in the time of Caesar Augustus, and indeed was patronized by him and his successors.[10] At first, it required no formalities [11] but was enforced as a trust to be discharged.[12] However, a century prior to Justinian the presence of five witnesses came to be required for its validity; and they were to sign the codicil.[13]

The codicil was devised to simplify the granting of legacies, and to escape the necessity of instituting the heir. It was a further step away from the notion of universal succession. Therefore, it is not surprising that the heir could not be appointed or disinherited by a codicil.[14] Though a decedent could leave trust bequests by codicil without a will (*codicilli non confirmati*), he could leave legacies by this device only if he confirmed it in advance in his *testamentum,* (*codicilli confirmati*).[15]

Therefore, a codicil in Roman law was not a supplementary will as it is in the law of England and the United States. In the latter systems, the codicil must have the same formalities that are required in a will. This was not required by Roman law, so that a man might die intestate and leave behind a codicil, an event impossible under English and American law.[16] On the other hand, a legacy in the Anglo-American system means just what it did under the Roman law,

[8] Moyle, *op. cit.,* I, 292; C. 6, 37, 21.

[9] *Cf.* §§ 24-26, 29, supra; I. 2, 23, 11; Sherman, *op. cit.,* II, 705.

[10] I. 2, 25 pr.; Sherman, *op. cit.,* II, 705 (note), 714.

[11] I. 2, 25, 3.

[12] I. 2, 25 pr.

[13] C. 6, 36, 8, 3.

[14] I. 2, 25, 1, 2; Gaius, 2, 273; Cocchi, *op. cit.,* VI, 189; Vermeersch-Creusen, *op. cit.,* II, 834; Schmalzgrueber, *op. cit.,* III, III, 26, 62; Reiffenstuel, *op. cit.,* III, 26, 707.

[15] I. 2, 25, 1; Gaius, 2, 270 a; 273.

[16] *Cf.* Sherman, *op. cit.,* II, 715.

though, of course, it does not depend for its validity upon the institution of an heir and his acceptance of the succession.

50. The Roman ***fideicommissum*** (trust bequest) resembled a legacy so closely that eventually Justinian fused the two.[17] This device also arose as the result of the constant trend towards simplification in testamentary dispositions. A gesture, if unmistakable, was sufficient to constitute a *fideicommissum.*[18] The *fideicommissum* was usually oral, or incorporated in a codicil. This is a natural inference from the fact that codicils were clothed with binding force almost simultaneously with the intervention of Augustus in favor of these trust bequests.[19]

51. The greater flexibility of these testamentary trusts as compared with legacies appears from five contrasts. The first is that the trust bequest was valid if only the intention of the decedent was evident.[20] The second, the trust bequest did not depend on a will for its validity. It could be imposed on the heirs by one who died intestate.[21] The third, from the beginning the trust bequest could be written in Greek.[22] The fourth, a legacy could be imposed only on the testamentary heir, but a trust bequest could be charged on any person who benefited in any way from the decedent's estate.[23] The fifth, originally any person was capable of receiving goods under a trust bequest, whereas under a legacy, to have due capacity to receive it, one must have the *testamenti factio passiva,* that is, the capacity to be an heir.[24]

A *fideicommissum* at first gave rise to only a moral obligation. Since it departed so widely from legal technical requirements, it could not be enforced by a legal action. But eventually it was favored with the protection of the pretor. It was Caesar Augustus who first gave it legal recognition. This he did either because his good offices had

[17] I. 2, 20, 3; C. 6, 43, 2.
[18] Ulpian, *Reg.,* 25, 2, 3.
[19] I. 2, 23, 1; Moyle, *op. cit.,* I, 312; Buckland, *Roman Law,* pp. 349, 350.
[20] Ulpian, *Reg., l. c.*
[21] Gaius, 2, 270; Bry, *Droit Romain,* I, 399.
[22] Gaius, 2, 281; Bry, *l. c.*
[23] Moyle, *op. cit.,* I, 312.
[24] Moyle, *l. c.;* Bry, *l. c.*

been invoked very frequently or because he saw that many trust bequests were failing and that the moral obligation was too often slighted. He ordered the consuls to provide for their fulfillment. This extraordinary jurisdiction soon became ordinary, and eventually a special pretor was appointed to maintain the necessary defense.[25]

The method of proving a *fideicommissum* under the provision of Justinian was to administer an oath to the heir. He must swear he never heard of it, if he expects to be relieved of the obligation. Should he refuse to take the oath, he must make payment. If he admits the trust bequest, he can not defeat it by legal subtleties.[26]

An act closely akin to the Roman trust bequest is the first evidence of testamentary disposition among the invading German tribes. To what degree the German instrument was influenced by the Roman device remains uncertain. It seems clear, however, that the *salman* among the German nations came into existence as a protest against the rigors of intestate succession just as the *fideicommissum* was a gesture in the direction of greater testamentary freedom among the Romans.[27]

And the trust or use under the English common law arose as an evasion of unjust and discriminatory statutes. It was the religious corporations which, when they found themselves unable to obtain a quiet title to land because of the statutes of mortmain, devised a new method of conveyance by which lands were conveyed, not to themselves directly, but to nominal feoffees *to the use* of the religious houses.[28]

Article 2

The Donatio Mortis Causa in Canon Law

52. Canon law sanctions *donationes mortis causa*. Hence in those matters where canon law governs to the exclusion of the sec-

[25] I. 2, 23, 1; Gaius, 2, 278; Bry, *l. c.;* Buckland, *l. c.*

[26] I. 2, 23, 12.

[27] *Cf.* §§ 35, 36, supra.

[28] Blackstone, *op. cit.*, II, 18, 271, 272.

ular law, such a donation is valid, even though it be forbidden by the latter.[29]

53. The canonical definition of this device must therefore be stated with some accuracy. It may be defined as a voluntary, revocable, executed transfer, intended as a gift, of a future interest, vesting at death, in any kind of property to any amount, accompanied by delivery and acceptance, made by one who possesses testamentary capacity.[30]

54. Since it must be voluntary, it is rendered invalid by all those influences which destroy the freedom of testamentary disposition.[31] **It is revocable,** because the interest conveyed does not vest until the death of the grantee.[32] **It must be an executed transfer,** for an intention to make the gift is not sufficient. The intention must be put into effect. Even the promise of the grantor, whether oral or written, or the performance of acts preparatory to the making of the gift, whether singly or combined, can not take the place of the actual execution of the gift.

If the disposition is intended as a will, and not as a gift, it is not a *donatio mortis causa.* This distinction, though important for the

[29] Because they resemble legacies, Justinian completed a movement begun prior to his time, and regarded them as on the same legal level—I. 2, 7, 1; C. 8, 56, 4; Sherman, *op. cit.*, II, 660, 711; Bargilliat, *Praelectiones,* 1481; Ferreres, *Insts. Can.*, II, 486.

On account of the temptation which the gift *mortis causa* seems to offer towards compassing the death of the donor, the Belgian and French Codes forbid it—De Meester, *op. cit.*, 1464; Vromant, *De Bonis Temporalibus,* 148; Cance, *Droit Canonique,* III, 144; Vermeersch-Creusen, *op. cit.*, II, 835. Cocchi says it is not admitted by modern codes—*op. cit.*, VI, 189. The State of Louisiana also forbids it—Civil Code, art. 1570.

[30] This definition has been taken from Rood, *op. cit.*, 15. Certain modifications have been made in it to bring it within the more comprehensive scope of the canonical concept. These modifications will appear in the course of the explanation of the terms. See definitions in Cocchi, *l. c.*, De Meester, *l. c.;* Cance, *l. c.*, Vermeersch-Creusen, *op. cit.*, II, 834.

[31] What these influences are will appear presently in the discussion of the requisite freedom for the validity of a will; and in the same place it will be seen what is meant by testamentary capacity.

[32] American decisions permit revocability but require that the title must pass when the transfer is made—Rood, *op. cit.*, 20-22; 38, 39.

disposition of interests governed by the secular law, serves the canonical system, touching bequests to charity and religion, only for the purposes of legal precision.[33]

It vests automatically *at the death* of the grantor, if it has not been revoked before that event.[34]

Under the canonical concept any kind of property in any amount can be conveyed by a *donatio mortis causa.* But under American decisions, land can not be thus conveyed, though the value of chattels that may be transferred is not limited.[35]

55. Delivery is necessary in order that the quality of the act may be clear. Otherwise, it would be merely a promise to give, or an oral will.[36] Under the canons governing bequests to charity, the proposed beneficiary would indeed have a claim under a promise or an oral will, but it could not be said to be precisely in virtue of a gift *mortis causa.* Constructive delivery suffices in any event. Indeed, it

[33] Under secular systems a disposition might be sustained as a *donatio mortis causa* while it might fail as a will, for instance, if it lacked the necessary subscription by witnesses—Rood, *op. cit.*, 19.

[34] This would sufficiently explain why the donee has perfect title without probate even under American decisions. Rood uses this fact as an argument that the title passes at the moment of the execution rather than at the death of the donor—*op. cit.*, 21.

Vromant holds that the donee has only a *ius ad rem* at the death of the testator when the gift is made without specification of any particular object bequeathed. Even if a specific object is given, he thinks it more probable that only a *ius ad rem* passes at the donor's death. But this is because he identifies *donatio mortis causa* with a legacy, and applies his view of the right of the legatee to the right of a donee—*op. cit.*, 148.

[35] However, deeds of land in which it is expressly provided that they are not to take effect during the grantor's life, nor to be recorded till after his death, have been sustained. The basis for this doctrine is that they grant a vested estate which can be sold by the grantee at any time, though the enjoyment of it is postponed. Such deeds are not revocable.

Moreover, land can also be conveyed to trustees, with the provision that they dispose of it according to any future will of the grantor, with residue to be conveyed to the grantee. This provides for implicit revocation, should the grantor wish it, by a future will—Rood, *op. cit.*, 24, 25.

[36] However, Justinian enacted that a promise to make a gift could be enforced by an action at law—I. 2, 7, 2; Sherman, *op. cit.*, II, 657 (note).

is recognized by Roman law and the American decisions.[37] And the ecclesiastical executor, the Ordinary, in determining whether constructive delivery has been made, need not follow the rules of interpretation which might be adopted by secular judges. Any sufficient evidence of a transfer of ownership would be sufficient to sustain a gift *mortis causa.*[38] Thus, under the canons the following kinds of delivery would be regarded as sufficient, though they would not be so under the American decisions: the delivery of the donor's receipt for stock in the possession of a third party; of his pass book containing the record of his checking account (the courts say that this book does not give control of the account, which they hold as necessary to adequate delivery); of a check on such an account (secular decisions say that the check just ahead of it may exhaust the account, and consequently the donee receives nothing); of a promissory note (the courts say this is not delivery of the money, for it is only a promise to pay).[39]

Delivery may be made, however, to a third party in trust for the donee, or as agent for the donee. The gift is valid even if it does not come to the donee until after the death of the donor. However, if

[37] Constructive delivery according to the division of Roman law was 1—*symbolical,* when the means of taking possession were transferred in lieu of the thing itself, v. gr., a title deed, the keys of a house—I. 2, 1, 45; 2—*traditio longa manu, i. e.,* the placing of the gift before the grantee with the implicit or explicit statement that it is now his—D. 46, 3, 79; 3—*traditio brevi manu,* if the gift is in the possession of the grantee when the title is transferred to him, or if at his request the grantor gives the property to a third party as his agent—D. 23, 3, 43, 1; 4—*constitutium possessorium,* when the grantor says that he will hold the property as possessor for the grantee—D. 41, 2, 18 pr. See Sherman, *op. cit.,* II, 643; Rood, *op. cit.,* 26-28.

[38] An American decision illustrates to what extent a judge may go in construing sufficient delivery. A woman was found dead with a slate by her side stating, "I wish Dr. L. S. Ellis to take possession of all, both personal, real and mixed, *Rachel Hill.* I am so sick, I believe I shall die; look in the valise." In the valise by her side were found the securities in question and an envelope addressed to Dr. L. S. Ellis, containing the following memorandum: "I wish you to take possession of all my effects, to do with them as you see fit. Dunlap has the Higgins and Parr papers, the rest you will find in my valise. I have paid Dunlap $34. Push them according to your judgment. . . . *Rachel Hill.*" These facts were held to constitute a valid gift *causa mortis.*—Ellis v. Secor (1875), 31 Mich. 185, 18 Am. Rep. 178.

[39] Rood, *op. cit.,* 29.

the intermediary was acting as the agent of the donor, the gift can not be sustained where delivery is made after the latter's death. This is the secular view; but under the canons the disposition could be supported, not as a *donatio mortis causa* but as a will.[40] And in the absence of definite evidence to the contrary, the agent should be regarded as the agent of the beneficiary, not of the donor; or, at least, as trustee for the beneficiary. Of course, the gift must belong to the donor at the time he makes the gift. It would not suffice if he acquired it at some time following the disposition, unless the gift were re-executed.[41]

56. Acceptance is essential to the completion of the gift. The law compels no one to accept a gift he does not want.[42] But if the gift is beneficial to the donee, his acceptance is presumed, though the delivery was made to an intermediary as agent for him and was not known to him until after the death of the donor. But if the donee dies before the donor, the heirs of the former can not claim the gift, because the gift never vested.[43]

57. Revocation of a gift *mortis causa* occurs automatically under the rulings of the American courts when the donor recovers from his illness or by his escape from the danger of death. Their view derives from the fact that secular law regards the peril of death essential to the validity of a gift *mortis causa*. This is not so, of course, under the canons. But an explicit revocation made upon the patient's convalescence would be valid even in the latter case. So, too, would be an implicit revocation; if, for example, the donor took the property and used it as his own; or entered a suit to recover it; or sent a messenger for it, even though the donor should die before the agent arrived at his destination. But an intention to revoke is not sufficient revocation. Moreover, under the American decisions, a revocation can not be made in a will, for a will is conceived as speaking only after the death of the donor, *i. e.*, after the vesting of the gift. But under the canons, an explicit and clear revocation in a will would be

40 Rood, *op. cit.*, 31.

41 Rood, *op. cit.*, 33.

42 Rood, *op. cit.*, 32; Cocchi, *l. c.;* Vermeersch-Creusen, *l. c.*

43 Vromant, *op. cit.*, 148; Reiffenstuel, *op. cit.*, III, 26, 705; Rood, *op. cit.*, 41.

regarded as a revocation *de praesenti,* only the change in beneficiary referring to the time when the will speaks.[44]

58. The words, "*per actum mortis causa,*" of Canon 1513, paragraph 1,[45] could be understood as referring exclusively to the *donatio mortis causa,* to the exclusion of all other kinds of testamentary disposition. Four arguments justify this interpretation: one based on the text itself; one on a comparison of the text with the second paragraph of Canon 1513; one on a comparison of the text with Canon 1529; and the fourth, on the history of canon law.

59. From the text it appears that in Canon 1513, § 1, the words "*per actum mortis causa,*" refer exclusively to a *donatio mortis causa;* and this for two reasons. First, the terminology, *mortis causa,* is legally distinctive. To introduce a wider meaning into these words would be an innovation, and of this there is not sufficient indication in the text.

Second, "*actum*" is placed in designation of a procedure that may occur "*inter vivos*" or "*mortis causa,*" according to the very terminology of the canon. Consequently, the word, "*actum,*" should be interpreted in the same sense in both positions, since there is no sufficient reason to modify the significance in one case and not in the other. There is no doubt that the word means *donatio* in connection with the words, "*inter vivos*"; consequently, this should be its significance also in connection with the words, "*mortis causa.*"

The second argument is based on the second paragraph of Canon 1513. It is this. *Legislator quod voluit expressit, quod noluit tacuit.* In the second paragraph, the legislator employs the terminology, "*in ultimis voluntatibus.*" If he wished a wider significance to be attributed to the phraseology of the first paragraph, the obvious terminology was both ready and at hand. He could have explicitly mentioned last wills. That he did not employ this terminology, indicates that he did not wish to use it.

The third argument derives from a comparison of the text with

[44] See Rood, *op. cit.*, 37-40.

[45] Canon 1513, § 1. "Qui ex iure naturae et ecclesiastico libere valet de suis bonis statuere, potest ad causas pias, sive per actum inter vivos sive per actum mortis causa, bona relinquere."

Canon 1529.[46] It becomes apparent that if there was to be an exception to the canon law of contracts as expressed in Canon 1529, it was juridically necessary to state it, *i. e., "iure canonico caveatur."* Canon 1513 seems to serve this purpose in its first paragraph, which consequently appears to refer exclusively to *contracts,* and not to wills. Moreover, since the whole spirit of the canons is to treat contracts and wills separately, it would seem juridically inconsistent that they should be joined in this first paragraph of Canon 1513. Not only has canon law traditionally treated these two kinds of dispositions separately, but it has treated them differently. The Ordinary has been the executor of testamentary dispositions, and the only invasion of his province made by the canons of the general law has been in regard to the formalities of wills. This is not true of contracts. Even in the present general law, while there is a provision for the substantive law of contracts in Canon 1529, there is no provision for the substantive law of wills, except the traditional one, that touching formalities. The rest is left to the Ordinary as executor (and that office, touching wills, includes the legislative and the judicial power).

The fourth argument derives from the history of canon law. It views the disabilities which canon law was traditionally compelled to face. These were the mortmain statutes aimed directly at pious causes; and rigorous formalities which, by invalidating wills, indirectly affected them. Against such statutes the canons were vigilant. But in all the history of canon law there was never an attempt made to interfere with the secular law where it incapacitated certain particular groups and rendered them incapable of making an enforceable will, except where that law was easily recognized as a statute of mortmain. The canonical struggle has been against mortmain statutes forbidding men generally to make grants to pious causes. Is it to be concluded that the first paragraph of Canon 1513 takes up a new position, and confers capacity for the first time in its history for the making of wills? [47] Or is it not rather to be concluded that canon

[46] Canon 1529. "Quae ius civile in territorio statuit de contractibus tam in genere quam in specie, sive nominatis sive innominatis, et de solutionibus, eadem in iure canonico in materia ecclesiastica iisdem cum effectibus serventur, nisi iuri divino contraria sint aut aliud iure canonico caveatur."

[47] Canon 23. "In dubio revocatio legis praeexistentis non praesumitur, sed

law in Canon 1513, § 1, is re-stating the canonical position on the problem of mortmain, granting capacity to all men to make donations to pious causes, exclusive of testamentary dispositions strictly so-called, provided there exists no natural or ecclesiastical incapacity? This would seem to be true, especially from a consideration of the authorities cited as sources of the text in question. For the Constitution, *Inter Cunctas,* of Martin V,[48] and the Encyclical, *Quanta Cura,* of Pius IX,[49] are both defenses of the right of ecclesiastical persons to hold and to receive property. Alone these citations would not perhaps be conclusive of the mind of the legislator. But in connection with the arguments herewith advanced they seem to lead to the inescapable conclusion that the *"actum mortis causa"* of the first paragraph of Canon 1513 should not be extended to include every kind of disposition in view of death, but only the *donatio mortis causa.*

60. Nevertheless, the correct conclusion is that the terms of this paragraph include all testamentary dispositions. This position will be defended with two arguments. Then a refutation will be offered to the argument derived from the history of canon law.

The first argument derives from a consideration of the text. The text does not speak of *donatio mortis causa* but of *"actum mortis causa."* Clearly there is a variation from the strict and the accepted terminology designating a specific kind of disposition. This variation seems sufficient to indicate an enlargement in the scope of the terms, sufficient to include all testamentary dispositions.

The second argument derives from the Civil Code of Louisiana in which it is provided that "no disposition *mortis causa* shall henceforth be made otherwise than by last will or testament."[50] Clearly this

leges posteriores ad priores trahendae sunt et his, quantum fieri possit, conciliandae."

[48] 22 February, 1418—Harduin, VIII, 911. Articles 31-33 condemn the propositions of John Wycliff touching the right of ecclesiastical persons to have possession of property: v. gr., the proposition condemned in Article 32: "Ditare clerum est contra regulam Christi."

[49] 8 December, 1864—*Fontes,* n. 542.

[50] Art. 1570.

Code understands the disposition *mortis causa* to include dispositions by will, and there is no reason, in the light of this provision, to insist that the provision in the first paragraph of Canon 1513 shall be restricted to the *donatio mortis causa.*

The refutation of the argument derived from the history of canon law proceeds in the following fashion. It is true that Canon 1513 is primarily a defense of the freedom of the individual to leave his property to pious causes. Thus far, it is a defense against the mortmain attacks of secular law. To this extent also, it is an exception to Canon 1529 so far as contracts are concerned. But there is good reason to join testamentary dispositions with contracts in Canon 1513, because now at least the canons wish to legislate as to the capacity of individuals to make dispositions to pious causes either by gift or by legacy. There seems to be no real distinction between the capacity of the individual to make a gift and his capacity to make a bequest, so far as the recipient is concerned. And it is on the recipient that Canon 1513, § 1, places the emphasis. It certainly does not wish to contend merely for the individual's right to make gifts *inter vivos* to pious causes; it defends his right to make any kind of gift to them, not excluding testamentary disposition.

Why does canon law now for the first time touch the matter of capacity for testamentary disposition? The answer seems fairly obvious. No longer is Roman law the official source relied on to supply omissions in the canonical system. So long as Roman law was a sort of secondary canon law, the canonical legislator knew just what measures would supply a deficiency in his law. But when Roman law was dislodged from that privileged position, the legislator no longer knew what other secular laws might decree as to testamentary capacity. Lest the restraints prove capricious or even unjust, it was within his prudent province to lay down a general rule. And what general rule for testamentary capacity would be found better than the same rule that he made for the capacity to make gifts to pious causes *inter vivos*?[51]

[51] See Vermeersch-Creusen, *l. c.*; Cocchi, *l. c.*; Cance, *l. c.*; De Meester, *l. c.*

Article 3

The Testament in Canon Law

61. The terms, "*in ultimis voluntatibus,*" in the second paragraph of Canon 1513, designate every act by which one institutes an heir or disposes of his estate in whole or in part by an act to be effective at his death.[52]

62. The chief division of testamentary acts is *ratione formae.* This division embraces those acts the development of which has been studied in the preceding articles of this treatise: viz., *the donatio mortis causa, the testament, the legacy, the codicil, and the trust bequest (fideicommissum).*

63. *Ratione formae* the testament itself is divided *extrinsece,* or *ratione effectus legalis* into *testamentum formatum, non-formatum,* and *privilegiatum; intrinsece,* or *ratione formae intrinsecae,* into the *written, holographic, nuncupative, and mystic* testament.

A *testamentum formatum* is one that is fortified with all the solemnities required by law; *non-formatum,* one that lacks them; *privilegiatum,* one that is exempt from them.

A *written* will is one consigned to writing of whatsoever kind by whomsoever written; a *holographic* will is one written entirely in the handwriting of the testator; a *nuncupative* will is one that is not written, by whatsoever other means it is expressed; a *mystic* will is one sealed by the testator and delivered to a notary in the presence of witnesses who endorse it with the notary.[53]

64. By division *ratione materiae* testamentary dispositions in general, but more particularly legacies, are *devises* or *bequests; general, specific, demonstrative,* and *residuary.* A *devise* conveys land; a *bequest,* chattels. A *general* legacy grants a portion of the estate by measure, fractional or quantitative, v. gr., one-third of the estate, five thousand dollars. A *specific* legacy grants definite objects, v. gr., a watch and fob, the ten shares of stock in the safe de-

[52] Canon 1513, § 2. "In ultimis voluntatibus in bonum Ecclesiae serventur, si fieri possit, sollemnitates iuris civilis; hae si omissae fuerint, heredes moneantur ut testatoris voluntatem adimpleant."

[53] The holographic and the mystic will derive from the French and Spanish codes—Rood, *op. cit.,* 48.

posit vault. A *demonstrative* legacy demonstrates the fund from which a general legacy is to be paid, v. gr., five thousand dollars out of the proceeds of the sale of a house. A *residuary* legacy grants whatever portion of an estate remains after all other legacies have been paid.

65. The division *ratione modi*, or according to the method by which the gift is made, regards these dispositions as *absolute, conditional, ad diem, ex die, sub demonstratione, sub causa, sub modo.*

A legacy *ad diem* is for a definite period of enjoyment; one *ex die* postpones the right of enjoyment for a time; when it is *sub demonstratione,* it describes the legacy (which could thereby become either a specific or a demonstrative legacy); when it is *sub causa,* the motive of the donor is explained; and when *sub modo,* the purpose of the legacy is described.

These distinctions are helpful because the various features they present might easily be confused with conditions imposed on the legacy. Conditions, if unfulfilled, invalidate the legacy. The various appendages just described do not cause invalidity if they happen to lack verification. They are incidental rather than essential.[54]

Conditions imposed on testamentary dispositions may be divided by reason of the time when the condition is to be verified or by reason of the relation of the fulfillment of the condition to the vesting of the gift.

By reason of the time when the condition is to be verified, it may be *de praeterito, de praesenti,* and *de futuro.* Conditions *de praeterito* must be verified at the time the disposition is made; so, too, conditions *de praesenti.* But conditions *de futuro* depend on future fulfillment, v. gr., the failure of a prior heir, the death of a preferred beneficiary, the attainment of a determined age, the completion of a certain act.

By reason of the relation of the fulfillment of the condition to the vesting of the gift, these conditions are *precedent* or *subsequent.* A condition *precedent* must be verified before the beneficiary becomes the owner of the gift; a condition *subsequent* does not postpone the vesting of the title in the beneficiary, but must be fulfilled after he enters into ownership.

[54] Cocchi gives this list of modes—*l. c.*

66. ***Ratione finis,*** **that is, by reason of their destination, testamentary dispositions are** *pious* or *profane,* as their purpose is to promote works of charity and religion from a supernatural motive, or merely to confer a natural benefit on the beneficiary.

67. The most general form of testamentary disposition is the testament itself. A testament may be defined as a lawful and voluntary solemn juridical act, essentially revocable, valid without the acceptance of the beneficiary, by which a person enjoying due competence provides for what he wills to be done after his death with his estate, in whole or in part, determined fractionally or specifically.[55]

A testament is a *lawful* act, because it is invalid if it is not made according to law and if it commands any act prohibited by law.

It must be *voluntary,* for freedom of disposition is of the essence of the instrument or act.

It is *solemn,* because it must be attended with certain requisite formalities, at least sufficient for proving it.

Since it is enforceable at law, it is well described as a *juridical* act.

It is *revocable,* because a testament is not a gift or a unilateral contract, but an expression of a schedule of distribution which the deceased expects to be carried out after his death under the supervision of the law. Hence the schedule can be modified at any time until the death of the testator.

Because it is not a contract it does not require acceptance on the part of the beneficiary.

Competence is required to make a will. Not every one is competent. Limitations on competence may be imposed by the natural law, by secular law, and by canon law. What those limitations are, it will be the province of later chapters to investigate.[56]

Under modern law, both canon and secular, a man may by testament dispose of all or only a portion of his estate. But under the Roman concept, due to the necessity of instituting the heir prior to

[55] See Vermeersch-Creusen, *l. c.;* De Meester, *l. c.;* Cocchi, *l. c.;* Vromant, *op. cit.,* 149; Schmalzgrueber, *op. cit.,* III, III, 26, 1; Wernz, *op. cit.,* III, 274, ad 2um.

[56] *Cf.* Chapters IV, V.

the validity of the testament, no one, except a soldier, could die partially testate and partially intestate.[57]

68. The property that is subject to testamentary disposition may be described by the following general rule. The power of testamentary disposition extends to all interests in real or personal property, corporeal or incorporeal, which, if not disposed of, would devolve to the heirs of personal representatives of the testator. The converse of this proposition is equally true, namely, that an interest that is not transmissible to others can not be devised.[58]

A joint interest in land or chattels can not, therefore, be subject to disposition by will. For it is of the nature of a joint interest that it should pass to the surviving co-owners at the death of one of them. This provision of secular law seems valid also in canon law. For the joint interest is contractual, and therefore governed as to its effects by the civil law as prescribed by Canon 1529.[59]

69. The following interests in property may be bequeathed. Contingent and executory interests in realty or personalty which would devolve to heirs or personal representatives. These interests are an expectancy which one already possesses in the contemplation of the law itself; not, however, the mere possibility that one may inherit from another. A mere possibility that one will inherit can not be bequeathed.

A naked legal title without possession can be bequeathed, v. gr., the right to property which has been taken out of the owner's possession by unlawful means. Similarly, mere possession without ownership can be transmitted by testament, and the devisee can recover the property from any one who can not show a title superior to that of the testator. That is, the beneficiary can claim it from any one who can not prove that he, and not the testator, was the real owner of the property.

[57] D. 50, 17, 7; Sherman, *op. cit.*, II, 678.

[58] Rood, *op. cit.*, 78.

Generally speaking, under American statutes and decisions a document making any other provision except a disposition of property is not regarded as a will, but some States authorize the appointment of guardians by will.—Rood, *op. cit.*, 68.

[59] Canon 1529. *Cf.* footnote 46, this chapter. *Cf.* Cocchi, *op. cit.*, VI, 211.

A *chose in action* (that is, a *ius ad rem*) may be bequeathed, v. gr., the right to renew a copyright. But if suit is brought to claim the right, it is brought not in the name of the legatee but in the name of the personal representative of the deceased.

Chattels real, v. gr., a lease of land for years, or a mortgage on land, were always regarded as personalty and subject to testamentary disposition. So also with crops to be grown within the current term of the court.

70. Personalty can be bequeathed even before the owner has come into possession or ownership. But as to real estate acquired between the date of the will and the death of the testator, there is no agreement among the States.

This divergence of legal opinion derives from the heritage of the common law. Prior to the prohibition against devises in land, such devises were made, as has been indicated heretofore,[60] *in forma doni*, that is, in virtue of a power of appointment contained in the original grant. It was therefore contended that a man could not use a power before he had it. Consequently he could not appoint a successor before he had power to appoint him. And he had no power to appoint him before he had the land to which the power of appointment attached.

This rule was accepted as part of the common law by some of the States. Others enacted statutes similar to those of the Statutes 32 and 34 Henry VIII, permitting the devise of land acquired after the making of the will but before the testator's death.

In both England and the United States there is agreement that such land may be devised if the testator really intended that it should be so. The point of departure is the testator's intention. Some States imply an intention in the absence of any expression in the will excluding such land. Other States require an explicit statement in the will that such land is to be included.[61]

[60] *Cf.* §§ 39, 42 supra.

[61] Rood, *op. cit.*, 80-88.

References to statutes will be made consistently from the Codes noted in the bibliography. Unless otherwise noted, references to California Statutes will be taken from the Probate Code; references to Louisiana Statutes, from the Civil Code; and references to New York Statutes, from the Decedent's Estate Law.

As to the attitude of the canons on such devises, it would be based on the intention of the testator. Only in those States which require a clear expression of intention would there be possible conflict between the interpretation of the Ordinary and the secular courts. In the other States, the land would be transferred unless a contrary intention was manifest. But judgment even on that contrary intention would be reserved by the canons to the Ordinary in proper cases.[62] As a practical matter, however, the problem should arise infrequently, as it occurs only when there is a general devise or a residuary devise of all the testator's real estate. Most devises to pious causes are specific, and do not increase with the accretions to a decedent's estate.[63]

Certain States provide by statute that the testator may dispose of *all* his estate, real and personal. It is held that these statutes sufficiently provide for the transfer by general devise of all the real property the testator had at death. The States that thus provide are: Arkansas (§ 10492); Missouri (§ 505); New Mexico (§ 154-101); Oregon (§ 10-501).

The same effect is given to the statutes of those States which empower the testator to devise all that he may have at the time of his death. These States are: Arizona (§ 3636); Colorado (§ 5184); Illinois (c. 148, § 1); Mississippi (§ 3550); Texas (Art. 8281).

The States requiring that the intention of the testator be clear as to the inclusion of this land are: District of Columbia (tit. 29, § 45); Kansas (§ 22-257); Maine (c. 88, § 5); Michigan (§ 13480); Minnesota (§ 8749); Nebraska (§ 30-203); Nevada (§ 9924); New Hampshire (c. 297, § 7); Ohio (§ 10579); Vermont (§ 2749); Washington (§ 1411); Wisconsin (§ 238.03); Wyoming (§ 88-103).

In the rest of States, more than half of all, the will disposes of everything the testator had at death unless the contrary is expressed in it. These States are: Alaska (§ 587); Alabama (§10580); California (§ 121); Connecticut (§ 4875); Delaware (§ 3244); Florida (§ 5459); Georgia (§ 3905); Idaho (§ 14-325); Maryland (Art. 93, § 346); Massachusetts (c. 191, § 19); Montana (§ 7014); New Jersey (p. 5870, § 26); New York (§ 14); North Carolina (§ 4164-4165); North Dakota (§ 5684); Oklahoma (§ 1578); Pennsylvania (§ 8317); Rhode Island (§ 4296); South Carolina (§ 8915); South Dakota (§ 642); Tennessee (§ 8089); Utah (§§ 101-1-37, 101-2-15); Virginia (§ 5236); West Virginia (§ 4039).

[62] Canon 1515, § 1. "Ordinarii omnium piarum voluntatum tam mortis causa quam inter vivos exsecutores sunt."

[63] It should be remarked that under the Roman law a testator could be-

71. The schedule of distribution may divide the estate into fractions, v. gr., one-third to A, one-third to B, and one-third to C. Or it may name a specific object. Or it may name some objects and divide the remainder fractionally.[64]

queath by legacy the property of another person, provided he knew it was not his own—I. 2, 20, 4; Gaius, 2, 202.

If the testator bequeathed to a legatee something he owed to a creditor, the heir, and not the legatee, must pay the creditor its value—I. 2, 20, 5. The law implied this obligation in the acceptance of the inheritance. But secular law in the United States does not imply this obligation. Under the law here the heir is not conceived as taking the inheritance, but only that portion of it which he acquires free of obligation. Should the legatee of such a bequest be a pious cause, it could not receive what is owing to another, and there is no law that requires any other person to do what the testator failed to do, *i. e.*, make the gift his own before bequeathing it.

A bequest to the legatee of his *own* property was not valid at Roman law in the sense that the heir would be obliged to pay the legatee its value. Nevertheless, if it came to belong to the legatee only after the death of the testator, the heir would be so obliged—I. 2, 20, 6; D. 30, 82. This provision is without warrant in the laws of the United States. If a bequest were made here of the property of a pious cause to the pious cause itself, the value of the legacy could not be collected. For, what was a juridical interpretation of the testator's intention under the Roman law can not be employed to impose an obligation under a different system. The testator is presumed to have written what he wished to write. If he set down a specific object as a bequest, he did not mean its value. Of course, if the object really belonged to the testator, it passes to the legatee, even though the testator thought it belonged to the legatee; for though the legacy might seem futile, the will of the testator clearly indicated that the legatee was to be the owner. The fact that it actually belonged to the testator without his knowledge is incidental to his main purpose—I. 2, 20, 11; Blat, *De Rebus*, tom. 2, 425.

[64] For the sake of greater precision certain other terms might be properly defined herewith. The person who makes a will is a *testator,* if he is a man; if she is a woman, she is known as the *testatrix.* When a person dies after having made a valid will, he is said to die *testate;* if he has made no will, he dies *intestate.* Property is commonly disposed of by will by the use of the words, *give, devise,* and *bequeath.* Of these three, the word *give* has the widest significance. Every transfer of property, whether of chattels or of land, if it is a voluntary transfer without the receipt of anything in return (*i. e., without consideration*) may be called a *gift.* A *devise* is a gift of land by will. The person making the gift is called the *devisor;* the person receiving it, the *devisee.* When any kind of property except land is given by will, the gift is called a

72. It has already been indicated that *ratione formae* wills may be written, holographic, nuncupative, and mystic. Adequate explanation of these terms will be given when the formalities of testamentary dispositions are discussed. It is pertinent to observe here, however, that where the law requires one of these forms, it sometimes tolerates one or more of the others in specific cases or under special circumstances. Thus a nuncupative will is frowned on under English and American statutes, but it is sometimes permitted, especially where the amount bequeathed is small, or where the person making the bequest is a soldier or sailor in active service and in peril of death. The circumstances in which it is tolerated vary from State to State. Such a form, exempt from the usual legal requirements, is a privileged will.[65]

After the decree of Pope Alexander III, demanding no more than the requirements of the natural law for the validity of bequests to pious causes, canonists have held that such bequests are privileged

legacy or a *bequest*. The beneficiary in this case is called the *legatee*. However the use of the wrong word by the testator will not invalidate his gift—Rood, *op. cit.*, 45.

[65] There were four kinds of special or privileged wills at Roman law in the days of Justinian. They were: first, the will of a blind person who was permitted to make his will in the presence of seven witnesses by declaring before a notary what he wished to be included in it. The notary was to be asked to put the declaration in writing. The witnesses were to hear the declaration and see the notary write it. Then the document was to be signed by the notary and the witnesses, all of whom attached their seals—C. 6, 22, 8.

The second special form was that of illiterate persons living in the country. If they were unable to read or write, they were permitted to make their wills with the aid of only five witnesses, if seven could not be found—C. 6, 23, 31, 2, 3. The witnesses were to be told the contents of the will and the name of the heir—C. 6, 23, 31, 4.

The third form was that of soldiers and sailors. They could make a valid will without any formality—Gaius, 2, 109; I. 2, 11. This privilege was first granted by Julius Caesar, and was made part of the fixed testamentary law by Trajan—D. 29, 1, 1 pr.

The fourth form was the will of parents conferring a benefit on those very descendants who would have taken without the will. Such a will could be very informally executed; a mere memorandum was enough, provided that the date, the names and the shares of the heirs were set down by the testator—C. 3, 36, 16; *Nov.*, 107, 1, 2.

by canon law, as the wills of soldiers and sailors, or of parents to their children, were privileged at Roman law.[66]

73. *Ratione modi* testamentary dispositions have been said to include *conditional* bequests. Similar to conditional bequests are alternative bequests. An alternative bequest is one where two provisions are made depending on conditions mutually exclusive of each other. One provision become effective, if a certain event occurs; the other, in case an alternative event happens.

74. The whole will may be conditional, as well as some bequest contained in it. The condition on which the will may depend may be the approval of a third person to be expressed after the death of the testator. Under the American decisions, however, a testator may not appoint another to make his will for him. Under the provisions of the canons, however, even this is possible.[67] Therefore, should a bequest be made to pious causes by an executor authorized to make a will for a decedent, that bequest would be sustained as valid under the provisions of canon law.

A similar power is recognized by American decisions, but the two must be carefully distinguished. The American courts recognize the right in a decedent to create a power in his executor to declare a will operative or inoperative according to his discretion. This act of the

[66] The decree of Pope Alexander III is c. 11, X, *de testamentis et ultimis voluntatibus,* III, 26. It reads: "Relatum est auribus nostris, quod, quum ad vestrum examen aliqua super testamentis relictis ecclesiae causa deducitur, vos secundum humanam, et non divinam legem in ea vultis procedere, et, nisi septem vel quinque idonei testes intervenerint, omnino deinde postponitis iudicare. *Unde quia huiusmodi causae de iudiciis ecclesiae, non secundum leges, sed secundum canones debent tractari, et his, divina scriptura testante, duo aut tres idonei testes sufficiunt, discretioni vestrae per apostolica scripta* Mandamus quatenus, quum aliqua causa talis ad vestrum fuerit examen deducta, eam non secundum leges, sed secundum decretorum statuta tractetis, et tribus aut duobus legitimis testibus requisitis [sitis contenti] quoniam scriptum est: 'In ore duorum vel trium testium stat omne verbum.'" *Cf.* Wernz, *op. cit.,* III, 274, 279; Cocchi, *op. cit.,* VI, 192.

[67] Under the sanction of Pope Innocent III, contained in c. 13, X, *de testamentis et ultimis voluntatibus,* III, 26, which declares: "In secunda vero quaestione dicimus, quod qui extremam voluntatem in alterius dispositionem committit non videtur decedere intestatus." *Cf.* Barbosa, *Ius Pontificium,* III, 26, 13, 1, 2; Phillips, *Compendium,* 407.

executor is not quite the same as if he actually made a will for the decedent, for he is limited to granting or denying approval to a will already made by the testator.[68]

75. Another restriction in American law, important for charitable bequests, is that an executor can not be empowered to appoint the legatee. The testator must at least designate the class of persons he intends to benefit under the legacy. The executor may be permitted to select the individuals from the class. Thus, if it is evident that a bequest is not for the benefit of the person given the power of appointment, and the class of persons to be benefited is not indicated, the provision is entirely void.[69] Consequently, a direction to an executor to distribute a thousand dollars to whatever charitable cause he chose would be invalid under the American law. But it would be sustained under the canons.

76. The condition made in a testamentary provision may not always be a real condition. It may be merely an explanation of the motive which led the testator to make the will (*testamentum sub causa*).[70]

77. It is sometimes a matter of doubt whether a condition affects the whole will. The courts follow the more lenient interpretation, restricting the condition to as few legacies as possible. In the case of a legacy to a pious cause a similar function of interpretation would devolve upon the Ordinary.[71]

78. Parol evidence is not competent to show that a will absolute on its face was made on condition, or that a will conditional on its face was meant to be absolute; or that in spite of the fact that a condition turned out contrary to the expressed statement in the will, the testator nevertheless re-affirmed the provisions of the testament.

[68] Rood, *op. cit.*, 63, 64.

[69] Rood, *op. cit.*, 63, 64 (footnote).

[70] For instance, consider the expression, "If any accident should happen to me that I die away from home, my wife, J. A. L., shall have everything I possess." This was held to express merely the inducement for the making of the will. The will was regarded as valid even though the testator died not away from home but at home, after a safe return—Rood, *op. cit.*, 65 (footnote). *Cf.* Likefield v. Likefield (1885), 82 Ky. 589, 56 Am. Rep. 908.

[71] In virtue of Canon 1515, § 1. "Ordinarii omnium piarum voluntatum tam mortis causa quam inter vivos exsecutores sunt."

For that would be allowing an oral will to contradict a written one. This is the doctrine in the American courts under the statutes that permit oral wills only under exceptional circumstances.[72] It is sound doctrine also under the canons. This seems clear from a decision of the Sacred Congregation of Bishops and Regulars in 1869. Though an oral will is valid under the canons for the purpose of making bequests to pious causes, nevertheless where there is a written will, it speaks for itself and needs no oral supplement to contradict its plain provisions.[73]

In case of doubt, the American courts permit parol evidence to show the circumstances under which the will was made, so that the language may be correctly interpreted.[74] This, too, is the correct doctrine under the canons, as is clear from the discussion in the case just noted. It is evidenced also by a decree of the Sacred Congregation of the Council, where parol evidence was accepted as to the habits of the testator in order to arrive at the significance of his will.[75] Two witnesses were permitted, in another decree of the same Sacred Council, to clarify the testator's intention by their parol testimony.[76]

So, under the American rule, parol evidence was admitted to show that the testator, though he had written the will prior to the occurrence of the event contradicting the condition, nevertheless executed the will in spite of the adverse event; or that the testa-

[72] Rood, *op. cit.*, 66.

[73] The decision to which reference is made here, turned on the will of a certain Archbishop, who had omitted a certain item of his estate from his will. Parol evidence was offered to show that he had intended his whole estate to be divided between two pious causes. But the parol evidence was not admitted, and it was said that such evidence aids in interpreting patent ambiguity in the will, but not to establish what does not appear on its face. The Archbishop was considered to have died intestate as to the item omitted—S. C. EE. RR., 13 August, 1869—*A. S. S.*, V (1869), 92.

[74] Rood, *l. c.*

[75] S. C. C., 27 February, 1875—*A. S. S.*, VIII (1874), 575.

[76] This was a case where the testator had founded two chaplaincies with a definite endowment. The oral testimony was admitted to show that the testator wished the amount specified to be given to each, not one-half to each—S. C. C. *in Causa Ariminen.*, 24 July, 1858—Pallottini, XI, 561.

tor, though he had executed the will prior to the occurrence, nevertheless retained the will and kept it carefully even afterwards.[77]

79. Conditional wills may be such by reason of a condition precedent or a condition subsequent. A condition subsequent does not suspend the vesting of the bequest, but simply imposes an obligation on the beneficiary, a charge upon him, which may or may not defeat the estate if left unfulfilled. But in any case, the estate vests pending fulfillment.[78]

80. Scholion I. The Contract to Devise. If a competent person, for a sufficient consideration (that is, for something to be paid or borne by the other party in return), obliges himself to give his estate or any part of it, whether by will or otherwise, to another, such a contract is neither a *donatio inter vivos* nor a *donatio mortis causa,* but a bilateral contract. However, to prove the existence of the contract, it is not enough to show a declaration of purpose to make a will. Nor does it suffice to prove that the decedent led the claimant to expect that his services would be rewarded by remembrance in the former's will.

Moreover, even a promise without consideration offers no ground for a claim unless it is made under the seals of the parties (the seal may be made with a pen, if it is indicated that it is meant to be a seal). The affixing of the seals raises a presumption of consideration which can not be attacked.

A contract to remember a person in a will for services rendered gives ground for a suit *quantum meruit* (that is, for as much as is deserved). This is true also where instead of services, the claimant gave value of some other sort to the decedent. If a definite object or sum was mentioned, the suit will be for the specific article or sum. If the object itself can not be recovered, its value can. Since this is a contract, it is governed by all the rules of law demanding that contracts be in writing. Otherwise, no suit can be maintained, unless the contract is established by partial performance on the part of the

[77] Rood, *l. c.* (footnote).

[78] Rood, *op. cit.,* 595-597, 623.

An impossible condition is considered not annexed—Schmalzgrueber, *op. cit.,* I, V, 35, 31.

claimant. But it is within the discretion of the courts to determine whether the part performance is sufficient.[79]

Even where a pious cause is the claimant under such a contract, it would seem that it has no good claim unless the contract is fortified with the formalities required by secular law or by part performance. The pious institute should be concerned, therefore, that any promise, by which it is to be remembered in another's will, should be made in writing under the seals of both parties.[80]

So, where the secular law forbids as invalid all pacts touching future hereditary succession and all renunciations of right to succeed (for a consideration, of course), such pacts and renunciations are invalid also in canon law.[81]

81. Scholion II. Joint, Double, Mutual, and Simultaneous Wills. Since a will can not be the wish of more than one person, it can not be a joint instrument. It would be by the most unlikely of coincidences that both testators would die at the same time. And even in that event the deaths would be not the same death, but separate deaths, and the joint will would be really two or more separate and distinct wills.

An agreement between two persons to inherit of each other was

[79] Rood, *op. cit.*, 51-57.

[80] Canon 1529. *Cf.* footnote 46, this chapter.

Even if a promise to remember a pious institute in one's will were to be regarded as a testamentary disposition, it would be essentially revocable as such. The mere fact that the promised will was not made is evidence in itself of revocation.

[81] Vermeersch-Creusen, *op. cit.*, II, 850.

Since the civil formalities touching contracts are actually adopted by canon law, there is no doubt that they bind in conscience, at least in those matters where canon law governs—Cance, *op. cit.*, III, 161.

The secular law of contracts which the canons adopt is the law at the time of the making of the contract and of the place where the contract is made, whether it be common law, statute law, or judicial law—Ferreres, *op. cit.*, II, 500.

If the formalities required for validity by the secular law are verified, the contract binds under canon law, even though it might be impossible to prove the validity of the contract to the satisfaction of the secular tribunal—Vermeersch, *Theol. Mor.*, II, 447.

invalid at Roman law, but it is valid under the canons if fortified with the oaths of the parties.[82]

Under the American decisions, it seems that it is possible for two persons to execute the same instrument expressing what is to be done with their property after their death, but the instrument will be sustained as the separate and distinct will of each, unless this be forbidden on the face of the will, or unless it be difficult to construe it as a sole will for each.

However, if one of the parties revokes the instrument, it can not be supported as his will, even if the other party executed it in consideration of his doing the same. The mere fact of simultaneous execution, however, is not a presumption that each was executed in consideration of the other. But where they have been thus executed, the death of one of the parties without revoking the will is sufficient partial performance to bind the survivor not to revoke.[83]

This problem might arise where a charitable or religious institute was a beneficiary under a joint will. If no one of the testators revoked, it would take its share from the estate of each at the time when each one died. But if any one of them revoked the instrument, it could not collect from his estate, because even under the canons, a will is essentially revocable, And as to the contract, the canons adopt the provisions of the secular law as to its effects.

If the instrument was made by each in consideration of the other's making it, the death of one without revocation binds the other not to revoke. In that event, the will of the survivor would become an irrevocable promise to which the law will give effect. The problem now lies in the fact that the religious institute was not a party to the contract, but only a beneficiary under it. There is no doubt that under the canons it has an enforceable claim to the gift, for it is only the substantive law of contracts that the canons adopt, not the adjective law. They accept all that pertains to the validity and the consequences of the contract; not the rulings of the courts in granting or refusing actions to claimants under the contracts. But even under

[82] Schmalzgrueber, *op. cit.*, I, V, 35, 24-27.

Under the provisions of Canon 1529 such a pact would be invalid where the secular law forbids it.

[83] Rood, *op. cit.*, 70-72.

the secular law, the pious institute has its claim: in the probate court, if the will has not been revoked by the decedent who survived the other; by a bill in equity for specific performance, if he did attempt to revoke.[84]

ARTICLE 4

LEGACIES AND TRUSTS IN CANON LAW

82. The terms, *"in ultimis voluntatibus,"* of Canon 1513, § 2, include, as well as testaments and gifts *mortis causa,* legacies, and trusts. The manner in which legacies sprang into being has been noted heretofore.[85]

83. A definition of legacies adequate to the canonical purpose remains to be given here. And the definition may safely include within its scope particular devises, that is, in a sense, legacies of land. Within these limits a legacy may be defined as a testamentary disposition, contained in a will, making a donation bequeathed by a competent testator, to be executed after his death by his heir or some other person designated by him, at the demand of the legatee or of the law.[86]

It is a testamentary disposition because it possesses the quality of speaking after the death of the testator.

It is a component part of a will, disposing of a portion of the estate. This is the distinctive quality of a legacy. If the disposition stood independently, it would be a testament and not a legacy. But the name *devise* is applied even to a testament disposing of land. Because it is a component part of a will, a legacy must possess the essential qualities of a will. It must be lawful, voluntary, solemn, juridical, and revocable.

It requires no acceptance on the part of the legatee. Like the will, it is a gift to be executed after the death of the testator, and consequently is not a contract.

[84] Woerner, *Administration,* I, 37.

[85] §§ 46-48.

[86] See Vermeersch-Creusen, *Epitome, l. c.;* Cocchi, *l. c.;* Vromant, *op. cit.,* 150; Schmalzgrueber, *op. cit.,* III, III, 26, 146, 147.

Under the canons, it is not necessary that an heir be instituted or that he claim the inheritance in order that legacies contained in the will may be sustained. It suffices that there be a sufficient fund from which the payment may be made. It then becomes the duty of the person who is the heir, or of some other person appointed by the testator, to distribute the property of the deceased to the legatees.[87] If the legatee should be ignorant of the legacy, the law can demand that it be paid to him.

84. The time at which the legacy vests in the legatee is a moot question among canonists. Under the Roman law, where acceptance of the inheritance by the heir was required, it vested at the moment when the heir performed this act. As to the canons, Wernz believes that the title now vests in the legatee by action of law as soon as the testator dies.[88] Others say that this is impossible when the legacy is merely a general one, that is, with no special designation of an object *in individuo*. But even as to the latter sort of legacy, they insist that the legatee obtains under the legacy only a *ius ad rem.*[89]

The latter opinion seems the more acceptable as to legacies. But its validity appears precisely from a contrast that is evident between a legacy and a *donatio mortis causa*. A legacy is not a contract with a condition precedent; while that is precisely what a *donatio mortis causa* is. It is a gift made on condition that the ownership be taken

[87] Originally under the Roman law, if the legatee outlived the testator and the legacy was unconditional, the legacy became due at the testator's death—Ulpian, *Reg.*, 24, 31. This was a contingent right (*dies cedit*), dependent upon the acceptance of the heir. When the heir accepted the inheritance, the legatee's right was no longer merely contingent, but vested, and the legacy was payable (the right was now *dies venit*). Since the right was now a vested right, the legatee could transmit it to his heirs—D. 31, 32 pr.

The due date of the contingent right (*dies cedit*) was postponed by the *Lex Papia Poppaea* until the day of the opening of the will—Ulpian, *Reg.*, 17, 1. But the old law was restored by Justinian—C. 6, 51, 1, 1. However, if the legacy was conditional, the contingent right accrued only on the fulfillment of the condition—Ulpian, *Reg.*, 24, 31; C. 6, 51, 1, 1.

[88] *Op. cit.*, III, 286.

[89] Vermeersch-Creusen, *l. c.;* Cocchi, *l. c.;* Vromant, *l. c.*

As was noted, Vromant holds the same view as to the time at which a donatio mortis causa vests—*op. cit.*, 148. But that seems to be due to his concept that the latter is only an informal legacy.

by the beneficiary only when the donor dies. Therefore, the death of the donor actually fulfills the condition on which the vesting of the gift, the subject matter of the contract, depends. While this is the case with a *donatio mortis causa,* it is not so with a legacy. In a sense, the subject matter of a legacy lacks an owner after the death of the testator. Pending distribution the ownership of it is in no one. It is sequestered in the custody of the law. This means that the legatee has a *ius ad rem* against the agent of the testator for his claim under the will.

However, in the case of a devise (that is, a legacy of land), which under the common law vests without the interposition of the testator's personal representative, it is clear that the vesting is authorized by the law at some discernible moment after the death of the testator.[90] In other words, the law makes automatic distribution of the real estate to the devisee at a moment that is juridically distinct from and posterior to the testator's death. Thus under the common law, the devisee obtains a *ius in re* in the moment, or fraction of a moment, that next succeeded the testator's death.

85. While in the case of a *donatio mortis causa,* the beneficiary has no right to the gift unless he accepted it, due to the contractual nature of a legacy, the legatee has a right to it until he refuses it.[91]

86. The Definition of a Codicil. When the Romans wished to grant legacies that would be valid without the acceptance of the inheritance by the heir, they resorted to the simpler form of codicil.[92] Consequently, a codicil was a kind of informal will. As such, of course, it is included within the meaning of the words of Canon 1513, § 2, viz., "*in ultimis voluntatibus.*" This is true whether the codicil be regarded under the original Roman, or under the Anglo-American, aspect. Consequently, for the purposes of canon law, it may be either a less solemn will by which one disposes of his goods by an informal memorandum (the Roman notion); or it may be a testamentary disposition appended to a will, fortified with all the formalities required in the will (the Anglo-American idea). As to definition, the canoni-

[90] See Rood, *op. cit.,* 756 d.

[91] Vermeersch-Creusen, *l. c.;* Cance, *op. cit.,* III, 145.

[92] *Cf.* § 49, supra.

cal definition of the testament[93] may be applied to the codicil with the omission of the word, *solemn*.[94]

87. Codicils were clothed with binding power almost simultaneously with the intervention of Augustus in favor of *fideicommissa*. It is a warranted conclusion that the flexibility of the codicil was intimately associated with the rise of the *fideicommissum*.[95] There can be no serious doubt that Canon 1513, § 2, includes these trust bequests (*fideicommissa*) within the meaning of the terms, "*in ultimis voluntatibus*."

Indeed, during the earlier centuries of contact with the growing German nations, the "*ultimae voluntates*" with which canon law dealt were almost exclusively trust bequests or something very like them. Such were "the last words" pronounced in the presence of the confessor (who then became trustee)[96] and such were the wills executed by the *salman* (or trustee), the official who rose out of the attempt of the new nations to escape the rigors of intestate succession.[97]

88. What then does a *fideicommissum* mean in canon law? It may be defined in the same manner as a legacy, except that the words *contained in a will* must be omitted. A *fideicommissum* is really a legacy that is dependent on the fidelity of the executor rather than on the formality of the will. The beneficiary of a trust is called a *fideicommissarius*. He corresponds to the *cestui que trust* of the English law of equity. The trustee may be called a *fiduciarius*, that is, one upon whom rests the obligation of discharging the duty imposed by the trust.[98] These terms apply to public trust bequests as

[93] *Cf.* § 67, supra.

[94] Vermeersch-Creusen, *l. c.*; Cocchi, *l. c.*; Vromant, *op. cit.*, 149; Schmalzgrueber, *op. cit.*, III, III, 26, 62; Reiffenstuel, *op. cit.*, III, 26, 707.

[95] *Cf.* § 50, supra.

[96] *Cf.* §§ 39-41, supra; Pollock-Maitland, *op. cit.*, II, 321, 322; Phillips, *l. c.*; the *Responsiones* of Egbert, Archbishop of York, c. 2—Mansi, XII, 428 E.

[97] *Cf.* §§ 35-38, supra; Brissaud, *op. cit.*, p. 692; Huebner, *op. cit.*, 740-742.

[98] Vermeersch-Creusen, *op. cit.*, I, 178; II, 836. See the decree of the Sacred Congregation of the Council, 23 April, 1927—*A. A. S.*, XX (1928), 362. There a private letter imposing the trust relation was regarded as binding on the *fiduciarius*. *Cf.* also Cocchi, *l. c.*, De Meester, *op. cit.*, 1469; Vromant, *op. cit.*, 151; c. 13, X, *de testamentis et ultimis voluntatibus*, III, 26.

well as to the secret ones. In the Moral Theology of Ballerini-Palmieri,[99] a public trust is called fideicommissary, and from this it has been implied that a secret trust is not fideicommissary, but only fiduciary. This leads Bondoni to suppose that the obligation of Canon 1516 [100] applies only to secret trust bequests.[101] But the distinction between the words, *fideicommissary* and *fiduciary,* is not to be sought in the public or secret nature of the trust bequest, but in the persons involved in the transaction. The fideicommissary is the beneficiary of the trust bequest; the fiduciary is the person charged with payment.[102]

89. The beneficiary of a trust bequest may be the testator himself. This would be the case if he provided a fund from which Masses were to be said for himself, though, of course, he would be beneficiary of only the *fructus specialis.*[103]

90. The trustee may be a moral person, that is, a community or a corporation.[104]

91. **There is a noteworthy distinction between a trustee and an executor.** A trustee takes a *ius in re,* that is, the legal title vests in him, and he in turn conveys the title to the beneficiary according to

[99] *Op. cit.,* III, 691 ff.

[100] Canon 1516. *Cf.* footnote 93, Chapter XII.

[101] In *Ius Pontificium,* VI (1926), 87 ff.

[102] The word *fiduciary* is derived from the early Roman contract of pledge known as *fiducia.* The creditor was secured by a transfer of title from the debtor, subject to an agreement (*fiducia*) that as soon as the debt was paid, the title would be re-transferred. This transfer of title was a great hardship on the debtor, for if the goods were sold by the creditor, he could not recover them. All he could do was sue the creditor for damages. Because of the hardship it implied, it was abolished by Constantine.

[103] Vromant, *op. cit.,* 152. It is important to remember that the fruits of the Mass are applied to the whole Catholic world, as well as to the special intention for which it is celebrated at any given time. On this ground trust bequests for Masses have been upheld in the United States as public trusts, when otherwise they would have been regarded as private trusts (*i. e.,* for the benefit of the deceased alone), invalid on the ground of perpetuity and of the inability of the beneficiary to enforce the trust.

[104] Vromant, *l. c.* In the United States chartered corporations can be trustees, but not unincorporated associations—Rood, *op. cit.,* 202, 439.

the terms of the trust. An executor, on the other hand, assumes merely the ministry of executing the will.[105]

Moreover, an executor is appointed only by a will, be it oral or written; while a trustee may be appointed by a disposition *inter vivos*. It seems that the first executors were trustees, as the *salman* among the German tribes and the earliest trustees under the Roman law. This was due very probably to the necessity of conveying the title to them. The state of the law was such that otherwise the law would not have recognized them as ministers of the testator's will. When they came to have a legal place, it is only natural to expect that the formality of conveying title, at least in a trust bequest, would be regarded as superfluous.

Indeed, under the French and Belgian Codes, while a trust bequest to be discharged during the life of the person who institutes it or at the discretion of the trustee, is valid; a trust bequest is invalid, since it is regarded as an attempt to determine the succession to the heir. This provision derives from a protest that occurred at the time of the French Revolution against a system that permitted the concentration of wealth in the hands of a few families. That system was based on the *fideicommissary substitution* of the Roman law.[106]

[105] Vromant, *op. cit.*, 153; Wernz, *op. cit.*, III, 283.

[106] *Cf.* Art. 896; Vromant, *l. c.;* De Meester, *op. cit.*, 1469.

A *substitution* was the provision for an alternative heir in case the heir originally appointed did not or could not take the inheritance. Besides this simple form, there was also *pupillary substitution*, *quasi-pupillary substitution*, and *fideicommissary substitution*. The first occurred when the head of a family (the *paterfamilias*) appointed an heir to succeed a minor child in case the child should die before attaining the age of puberty (for prior to that age, the child could not make a legal will of his own).

The second form, *quasi-pupillary*, occurred when the substitution was made for an insane heir—I. 2, 15 (ordinary form); 2, 16 (pupillary form); 2, 16, 1 (quasi-pupillary form); Sherman, *op. cit.*, II, 692-694.

Fideicommissary substitution occurred by means of a trust (*fideicommissum*)—Gaius, 2, 277; I. 2, 23, 11. All the other forms of substitution depended on the heir's failure to enter into an inheritance. But the last form demanded that the heir should take title to it. Ordinarily, the heir held the property for life, and when he died the property was to descend to a definite person indicated in advance by the testator. Thus it became possible validly

92. The prohibition against fideicommissary substitution is part of the Civil Code of Louisiana, but the General Statutes provide that it shall be lawful for any one to make a *donatio inter vivos* or *mortis causa* of any kind of property to trustees for educational, charitable, or literary purposes, or for the benefit of educational, charitable, or literary institutions, notwithstanding the provisions of the Civil Code (Art. 1520) and of the General Statutes (§ 1296) against fideicommissary substitution.[107]

93. There is an obvious similarity between the fideicommissary substitution of Roman law and the *executory devise* of English common law. The executory devise postpones by will the vesting of a fee until after the completion of a life estate, or until a certain event has happened, or until the death of the first heir in fee. When it was settled that by an executory devise a fee could be limited on a fee, the courts resorted to a measure similar to that of the French codes, but not so drastic. The courts adopted the rule against perpetuities and it may be stated thus: *every gift is void at its creation which by any possibility might vest later than twenty-one years and nine months after the termination of some life or lives in being at the time of the death of the testator.* But the time is now shortened in many States. A private trust that violates this rule, is invalid from the beginning. A trust for a public cause, however, is exempt from the rule, as will appear when the problem of charitable trusts presents itself.[108]

94. The *fiduciarius* can be the intermediary between the testator and a moral person which is to be burdened with the obligation imposed by the will and to which the capital fund is to be paid.[109]

to prolong the order of succession by naming in the will an almost limitless series of persons to take one after the other, and thus property could be entailed in the same family from one generation to another—Sherman, *op. cit.*, II, 695.

[107] § 1303 (Gen. Stat.). And when it speaks of *donatio mortis causa*, this permission means legacies, because no disposition *mortis causa* in the strict sense is allowed in that State—Art. 1570.

[108] Rood, *op. cit.*, 570-575, 610 (from Rood has been taken the statement of the rule against perpetuities); Blackstone, *op. cit.*, II, 11, 172-175.

[109] Vromant, *op. cit.*, 347; Couly, in *Le Canoniste Contemporain*, XLV (1922), 205. Under this arrangement an unincorporated moral person can take

95. This situation suggests the relation that exists between a trust and an endowment (a *fundatio*). There are two similarities between them and three contrasts. The similarities are: first, both can be constituted by donation, whether *inter vivos* or *mortis causa*, as well as by a testament (including a codicil); second, an endowment, just like the trust, imposes a burden in favor of a work or person distinct from the person, moral or physical, that is burdened.[110]

The three contrasts are: first, an endowment is entrusted by its very essence to a moral person, while a trust is imposed on either a moral or a physical person; second, the formal element in an endowment is its perpetuity, which is not *per se* a property of a trust; for instance, if a fund is given to a moral person to be distributed at once to the poor, it is a trust and not an endowment; third, it is of the essence of an endowment that the capital should be preserved, invested, and the income devoted to the purpose served by it; while it is only *per accidens* that a trustee would invest the capital of the trust inasmuch as the essential idea of a trust is that the capital is ultimately to be distributed.[111]

96. An heir who would repel a *fiduciarius* because of the civil invalidity of a *fideicommissaria substitutio*, and would refuse to give him whatever funds were to constitute the capital of the trust, would be bound in place of the trustee to perform the duties attached to the trust.[112]

97. Trusts and legacies are frequently instituted in behalf of pious causes. A pious disposition of one's property is a donation of goods to the cause of religion or of Christian virtue.[113]

charitable bequests in most States, as will appear in the course of this study. The responsibility to the courts rests, in this case, on the trustee (the *fiduciarius*) for the proper discharge of the obligations.

110 Vromant, *l. c.;* Couly, *l. c.;* Goyeneche, in *Com. pro Rel.*, III (1922), 269.

111 Vromant, *l. c.;* Couly, *l. c.;* De Meester, *op. cit.*, 1499.

112 In case the trust were profane, and the secular law invalidated the *obligation*, but not the trust itself, as is the case under the Italian law, the trustee may accept the legacy in good conscience without any obligation of fulfilling the trust. But if the trust itself is invalid, it will depend on the prevailing wish of the testator as to whether the heir or the *fiduciarius* should receive the legacy under these circumstances—Vermeersch, *Theol. Mor.*, II, 564.

113 Vermeersch-Creusen, *op. cit.*, II, 834; Cocchi, *op. cit.*, VI, 189; De Meester, *op. cit.*, 1464; *cf.* Vromant, *op. cit.*, 146; Blat, *op. cit.*, 425.

More extensively it may be described as a donation that is made for the good of the soul of the testator, for the honor and glory of God, to adore Him, to render Him gratitude, to obtain the remission of sin or of the punishment due to it, to increase grace or the reward in Heaven due to saintliness.

A gift to a church, a monastery, or a religious institute for its maintenance or for the support of the poor is consequently a gift to a pious cause. So also is a donation for the manumission of a slave, the ransom of a captive, the conversion of heretics or infidels, the granting of dowries to poor girls, and the endowment of orphan asylums and trade schools, provided it is made with a supernatural motive.[114] Schmalzgrueber thinks that if they are granted from a pious motive, the following donations should also be regarded in this category; for the building of roads, bridges, public monuments, and fortifications.[115] But Blat insists that they are not pious unless given to pious institutes at least approved by ecclesiastical authority.[116]

In any event it is not a pious gift if made merely out of a spirit of humanitarianism to a lay institute (that is, to an association not duly instituted by ecclesiastical authority, whether founded by laymen or clerics).[117]

98. Thus, according to Blat, a gift to a secular hospital, to the Red Cross, to a civic welfare fund, to a non-sectarian school, or to the Salvation Army, would not be a pious gift under any consideration, because these beneficiaries are not approved by ecclesiastical authority. This view seems the only one consistent with the actual situation. The canons would hardly attempt to regulate property that was not in the hands of persons subject to the jurisdiction of the Church.

Moreover, according to all canonists a gift made from a spirit of philanthropy merely is not a pious gift, even if given to an institute

[114] Schmalzgrueber, *op. cit.*, III, III, 26, 42; Reiffenstuel, *op. cit.*, III, 25, 65, 66; III, 26, 137; Pirhing, *op. cit.*, III, 26, 19; Soglia, *Iur. Priv.*, II, 4, 122; Abbas Panorm., *Decretalium,* VI, 11, 7.

[115] *L. c.*

[116] *L. c.*

[117] Reiffenstuel, *l. c.;* Vromant, *l. c.;* Cance, *op. cit.*, III, 144; Vermeersch, *Theol. Mor.*, II, 564.

approved by competent canonical authority, unless that institute be also incorporated canonically. Thus a gift to the Society of St. Vincent de Paul from a motive merely of altruism would not be a pious gift.[118]

A will is not a pious one simply because it contains pious legacies. Nor is the will of a cleric a pious will just because it is his will.[119]

118 Cappello, *Summa*, 55; Maroto, *Iur. Can.*, I, 475; Vromant, *De Fidelium Assoc.*, 37.

119 Zallinger, *op. cit.*, III, 26, 292.

The definition of a charitable bequest given by Judge Gray is enlightening as to the secular court's view in the United States. He says, "A charity in a legal sense may be more fully defined as a gift, to be applied consistently with existing laws, for the benefit of an indefinite number of persons, either by bringing their hearts under the influence of education or religion, by relieving their bodies from disease, suffering, or constraint, by assisting them to establish themselves for life, or by erecting or maintaining public buildings or works, or otherwise lessening the burthens of government. It is immaterial whether the purpose is called charitable in the gift itself, if it is so described as to show that it is charitable in its nature."—Jackson v. Phillips, 14 Allen 539 (Mass.); quoted in Webster v. Sughrow (1898), 69 N. H. 380, 45 Atl. 139; Hoeffer v. Clogan (1898), 171 Ill. 462; 49 N. E. 527; and *In re* Lennon's Estate (1907), 152 Cal. 327, 92 Pac. 870. *Cf. Restatement of Trusts,* The American Law Institute, Tentative Draft No. 5, §§ 358-364, where charitable purposes are said to include the relief of poverty; the advancement of education; the advancement of religion; the promotion of health; governmental and musicipal purposes; and other purposes the accomplishment of which is beneficial to the community.

CHAPTER III

THE RIGHTS OF HEIRS AGAINST LEGATEES

99. As the law grew more liberal towards the testator, the increased freedom worked a hardship on the heir. This hardship might be that he inherited only a shell, or that he was burdened with liabilities and no assets to meet them, or that he was disinherited. To remedy this inequitable position, the law at length gave the heir the right to decline the inheritance. But this proved to be fruitful of a hardship on the legatees. When the heir declined to accept the inheritance, the legatees were deprived of their gifts under the will. It became the concern of the law and of the legatee to make it the interest of the heir to accept the inheritance. Consequently, various measures were enacted guaranteeing definite portions of the estate to him, withdrawing them from the right of the testator to make testamentary disposition of them. These guarantees were supported, as was necessary, by proper legal action granted the heir in case they were violated.

It is the province of the present chapter to investigate the legislative process just outlined. It will be divided into five articles, The first article will examine the development of the reservation of the Falcidian twenty-five per cent for the benefit of the heir. The second will study the guarantee, known as the *legitima portio,* and the legal action that sanctioned it, known as the *querela inofficiosi testamenti.* The third will consider the guarantees given the heir in modern systems. The fourth will investigate the manner in which these guarantees affect the rights of surviving spouses. And the fifth will review the consequences of these guarantees for bequests to charity and religion.

Article 1

The Falcidian Fourth

100. Limitation of Liability at Roman Law. Even before legacies and trusts came to be legally recognized, an estate might be impoverished by gifts and debts. The estate could be a *damnosa* *hereditas*, since the heir, as universal successor, inherited not only the assets of the decedent, but also his liabilities.[1] Originally it was impossible for family heirs (*sui heredes*)[2] to decline the inheritance. They were *sui et necessarii*. But finally the pretor gave the family heir the right to decline (the *beneficium abstinendi*.)[3] But any meddling with the inheritance was construed as an acceptance.[4]

There was another kind of *heres necessarius*, the slave.[5] He was liberated when he was made heir. But he dare not decline the inheritance. And usually he was made heir by an insolvent master who wished by this device to evade the stigma of bankruptcy.[6] However, the slave was given the special benefit of the *separatio bonorum*. By this privilege, the property he acquired after his liberation constituted a separate fund, which was free from the claims of his master's creditors.[7]

101. All other heirs were called *heredes extranei*. Among them were included actual strangers to the blood, but also persons who, though not strangers to the blood, were either emancipated from the decedent's *patria potestas* or descended through the female line.[8] The *heredes extranei* always had the right to refuse the inheritance.[9] That they might the more safely decide whether they would accept the inheritance, they were granted by the pretor a period of deliberation.[10] Formal acceptance was known as *cretio*.[11] But this came to

[1] An exception was made in favor of a soldier whose liability was limited to the extent of the assets. *Cf.* Gaius, 2, 163; I. 2, 19, 6; C. 6, 30, 22 pr. Moreover, the strictly personal obligations and rights of the deceased were extinguished by death. *Cf.* D. 43, 20, 1, 43; C. 3, 33, 14.

[2] They were those who were under the *patria potestas* of the decedent. *Cf.* Gaius, 2, 152 and 156; 3, 2-4; I. 2, 19 pr.; I. 3, 1, 2.

[3] Gaius, 2, 158 and 163; I. 2, 19, 2 and 5.

[4] Gaius, 2, 163; I. 2, 19, 5; D. 29, 2, 71, 3-8.

[5] Gaius, 2, 154; I. 2, 19, 1.

[6] Gaius, 2, 153-155; I. 2, 19, 1.

[7] *Cf.* Gaius, 2, 155; Sherman, *op. cit.*, II, 665.

[8] Gaius, 2, 161; I. 2, 19, 3.

[9] Gaius, 2, 162; I. 2, 19, 5.

[10] D. 28, 8, 1, 1. It was usually a period of one hundred days. *Cf.* Gaius, 2, 170; *Cf.* D. 28, 8, 2-5.

[11] Gaius, 2, 164-173; Ulpian, *Reg.*, 22, 34.

be abolished a hundred years before Justinian;[12] so that in the later imperial law, only constructive acceptance existed. This was any interference with the estate. Only when the heir touched the estate in any administrative fashion was he presumed to accept it.[13]

After Justinian introduced the *beneficium inventarii*[14] the system of admitting a period of deliberation became obsolete. The *beneficium inventarii* was then at the service of all classes of heirs.[15] However, the *heres extraneus* must choose either one of the privileges, not both: that is, either the right of deliberation or the *beneficium inventarii*. It was to his advantage to choose the new privilege, because, should he choose the right merely of deliberation, he was afterwards bound, upon acceptance, to the unlimited liability of the earlier Roman law.[16]

This advantage can be understood only in the light of the *separatio bonorum*, a further privilege granted by Justinian to accompany the *beneficium inventarii*. Under the *separatio bonorum*, the property inherited was not merged with the prior property of the heir, but each remained a distinct fund, the inherited fund being constituted by the inventory, and it was made solely responsible for the debts disclosed.[17] The inventory thus became an established institution, for, though theoretically it was optional, penalties were attached for acceptance without it. Consequently, the prudent heir was anxious to profit by its advantages.[18]

[12] C. 6, 30, 17. It had been partially abolished by Constantine. *Cf. Cod. Theod.*, 8, 18, 1, 1.

[13] Gaius, 2, 167-169; I. 2, 19, 7.

[14] C. 6, 30, 22 (531 A. D.). The inventory was made before a notary and in the presence of witnesses representing the legatees and the creditors; it was to begin within a month of the date when the heir was first informed of his rights; it was to be completed within two months of the date it was begun, unless the time was lawfully extended. *Cf.* C. 6, 30, 22, 2, 3.

[15] C. 6, 30, 22, 1 a -4; I. 2, 19, 5-6. Thus it could be demanded by the three classes: those who had the right to abstain from acceptance, (the *heredes sui*); those who had the right to deliberate (the *heredes extranei*); and by implication also the *heredes necessarii*.

[16] I. 2, 19, 6; C. 6, 30, 22, 14.

[17] Gaius, 2, 163; I. 2, 19, 6.

[18] One of the penalties was that full responsibility for all the debts due under the estate devolved upon him if he accepted without an inventory, be-

102. After the *beneficium inventarii* was granted the heir, he in turn became a creditor of the estate, but his claim was subject to that of other creditors, being preceded in order by debts incurred for funeral expenses, the expenses of inventory and administration, claims secured by mortgage, unsecured claims, and bequests.[19]

103. **Restrictions on Bequests at Roman Law.** If the estate were burdened with too many legacies, the heir had the right, as just indicated, under the *ius abstinendi* and the *beneficium inventarii* to refuse the inheritance. The *XII Tables* had permitted unrestricted testamentary disposition so far as legacies were concerned.[20] But this unrestrained freedom often left so small a portion of the inheritance for the heir that he would not accept. To remedy this situation, the *Lex Furia* imposed a penalty of four times the value of the legacy on any legatee who accepted more than one thousand asses from any individual testator.[21] Testators evaded this law by making their bequests to many legatees. The *Lex Voconia* attempted a further remedy, by ordaining that no legatee should accept a legacy greater than the joint portion of the heirs.[22] But given a sufficiently large number of legatees, each of whom would receive a portion equal to that of the heir, this might leave little enough for him. Consequently, the *Lex Falcidia* stepped into the breach (40 B. C.) and provided that at least one-fourth the inheritance must be given to the heir.[23] The percentage was to be figured on the value of the estate at the moment of the testator's death [24] after deduction of debts, funeral expenses, and the cost of administration.[25]

104. The counterpart of the Falcidian fourth is found in the

cause without this investigation the law could not be informed as to the degree in which the decedent's estate was capable of meeting them. *Cf.* C. 6, 30, 22, 1, 12 and 14.

In American law, the inventory is *prima facie* evidence of the amount of the assets and of their value. *Cf.* Rood, *op. cit.*, 845.

19 C. 6, 30, 22, 9; *Cf.* also C. 6, 30, 22, 4-8 and 11.

20 *XII Tables*, 5, 3; I. 2, 22, 1.

21 Gaius, 2, 225; Ulpian, *Reg.*, 1, 2.

22 Gaius, 2, 226.

23 Gaius, 2, 227; D. 35, 2, 1.

24 I. 2, 22, 2.

25 I. 2, 22, 3.

Pegasian fourth. As one-fourth of the estate was granted the heir by the *Lex Falcidia*, so by the *Senatusconsultum Pegasianum* a similar portion was granted the *fiduciarius* or trustee when a trust bequest was made to him.[26] As part of the same decree, however, it was enacted that the heir named by the testator could be obliged to accept the inheritance for the benefit of persons for whom he had been constituted trustee, and that when such compulsion became necessary he forfeited the portion guaranteed him by this law.[27]

105. These provisions were both approved by Justinian, viz., the Falcidian and the Pegasian fourth, together with the sanctions attached to the latter. He added a further measure, that if the trustee inadvertently paid out the percentage which he was entitled to retain, he had an action for the recovery of it.[28]

Article 2

The Legitima Portio and Its Sanction

106. Family claims and the rights of children were soon protected against the great freedom of testamentary disposition permitted by the *XII Tables*. The first reaction in this direction was the doctrine of *disinherison*.[29] Under the restraint of this measure, if the testator desired to disinherit any child or grandchild who was under his power as *paterfamilias* (that is, any of the *heredes sui*, not the *heredes extranei*), he must do it by express mention in his will. If he merely omitted their names, the instrument was void.[30]

Prior to the time of Justinian, however, express designation was

[26] I. 2, 23, 5; Moyle, *op. cit.*, I, 315. This measure was enacted during the reign of Vespasian.

[27] I. 2, 23, 6.

[28] I. 2, 23, 7; Gaius, 2, 283.

[29] This is the name given it in the Civil Code of Louisiana, Art. 1617.

[30] Gaius, 2, 123; I. 2, 13 pr. An heir not formally designated or disinherited was called *praeteritus* (passed over)—D. 28, 2, 3, 2-4. He could obtain a share in the inheritance on petition to the pretor but his possession would be only *bonitary* (*de facto* possession), not Quiritary. He would have *bonorum possessio contra tabulas*—I. 3, 9, 3. After a year had passed, however, by the doctrine of *usucapio* his possession became legal or Quiritary ownership.

required only of sons; a general clause of exclusion sufficed to disinherit grandchildren and daughters.[81] Justinian required specific mention of all.[82] Posthumous children, born after the making of the will, could not be disinherited by an anticipatory act until the *Lex Junia Velleia.*[83] Of course, even after permission was granted, it was necessary to mention them according to the provisions touching the others.[84]

107. The Legitimate Share at Roman Law. But the necessity of expressly mentioning disinherited heirs did not deter testators from depriving them of their due. To make this act less of a hardship, it was ordained that the testator must give at least a certain determined portion of his property (the *legitima portio*) to the heir even when he disinherited him. It was to be measured on the basis of what the heir would have received if the testator had died without a will. Of this legitimate share the heir could not be deprived unless it could be proved that he had been guilty of some legally specified offense against the testator.[85]

[81] Gaius, *l. c.;* 2, 127, 128; I. *l. c.*

[82] I. 2, 13, 5; C. 6, 28, 4.

[83] Gaius, 2, 139; I. 2, 13, 1; D. 28, 2, 29, 11-13.

[84] This necessity of an express mention of children in order to disinherit them seems to be reflected in the Anglo-American notion of the necessity of giving the natural heir at least a small sum by will. This is a safe practice, because it clearly shows that the person was not forgotten. But all that is required by the Anglo-American provisions is that a person who should be remembered be not forgotten.

[85] For the grounds on which the heir might be deprived of this portion, *Cf. Nov.*, 22, 47 pr.; C. 1, 5, 13.

In the law of Louisiana a child may be completely disinherited if he has (1) struck or raised his hand to strike a parent; (2) been guilty of crime, cruelty, or grievous injury against his parents; (3) attempted the life of either parent; (4) accused a parent of any capital crime except high treason; (5) culpably refused sustenance to a parent; (6) neglected to care for an insane parent; (7) refused to ransom a parent; (8) used violence or coercion to prevent a parent from making a will; (9) refused bail for a parent; (10) married as a minor without the consent of his parents. *Cf.* Art. 1621. All descendants may be disinherited for the first nine acts just enumerated committed against the testator. A child can disinherit a parent for the same crimes or offenses, except the first two and the last, and in addition, for having attempted the life of the other parent. *Cf.* Art. 1623. A disinherison must be made with the

108. The Ratio of the Legitimate Share to the Estate. Restriction of testamentary freedom by the legitimate share was introduced by custom. Traces of it are found as early as the time of Caesar Augustus.[36] The *portio legitima* was originally fixed at one-fourth of what the heir would have received if the testator had died without a will, that is, if there were four children, each one was entitled to one-sixteenth of the estate.[37] Justinian modified this rule and provided that the portion should be one-third, if the testator was survived by less than five children; one-half, if by five or more.[38]

109. The heirs entitled to this *portio*[39] were the children or grandchildren who would have inherited from the testator, had he died intestate.[40] If there were no descendants surviving the testator, his parents were entitled to it. In case the latter did not survive, the decedent's brothers and sisters could claim it, but only when the testator had conferred the inheritance on an infamous person.[41]

110. An action to claim the ***legitime*** was granted towards the beginning of the Empire against a will which disregarded it. The effect of the action was not to award the *legitime,* but was even more extensive. The will was entirely invalidated, and intestate sucession substituted for it. The action was called the *querela inofficiosi testamenti.*[42]

same formalities as a will; and the remaining heirs are burdened with the necessity of proving the existence of the reason assigned in the document of disinherison. *Cf.* Art. 1624. But natural fathers and mothers can not dispose in favor of adulterous or incestuous children, except such an amount as may be necessary for their sustenance and educational or professional training.—Art. 1488.

At English common law, illegitimate children could inherit from neither parent. But in this country they can inherit from their mother; and in a few States, from both parents—Rood, *op. cit.*, 770.

[36] Sherman, *op. cit.*, II, 697 (footnote).

[37] I. 2, 18, 6, 7; D. 5, 2, 8, 6.

[38] *Nov.*, 18, 1. (536 A. D.)

[39] Called the *legitime* by the Civil Code of Louisiana.—Art. 1617.

[40] I. 2, 18 pr. and 1; I. 2, 13, 5.

[41] I. 2, 18, 1. Legal infamy was a legal penalty for certain crimes, avocations, reprehensible conduct. *Cf.* D. 3, 2; D. 48, 1, 7; Gaius, 4, 182.

[42] Gaius cites no provision of this kind earlier than Trajan. *Cf.* D. 5, 3, 7; I. 2, 18; I. 3, 1, 14; D. 5, 2, 8, 16; D. 5, 2, 24.

Parents had this action, in proper circumstances, against their children. So also brothers and sisters could sue on its warrant when they had a claim based on the succession of an infamous person to the estate of their kin.[43]

111. These provisions preventing a testator from disposing of his whole estate to the detriment of those to whom he owed a duty of nature came late. But not too late. They arose out of a necessity, the consequence of a relaxed attitude of law towards testamentary disposition. But they have exerted great influence wherever Roman law has had any share in framing testamentary law, notably in France and Louisiana.

Article 3

The Heir's Guarantees in Modern Law

112. The right of the family heirs at early German law was as strict as that which they enjoyed at early Roman law.[44] Gradually, however, they also admitted a relaxation, first as to the non-allodial property, and later as to certain kinds of land.[45]

But a stabilized ratio seems early to have been developed as to the amount of non-allodial property that could be taken from the testator's wife and children. This proportion was one-third, if a wife and children survived; one-half, if only a wife or only children survived.

This ratio survived in England till the days of Charles I. Bracton, in the middle of the thirteenth century, describes this division as being the law of his time, adding that before division was made, proper deduction was allowed for funeral expenses and the cost of supporting the widow until she received the dower portion out of her deceased husband's estate. The third *Magna Carta* of Henry III, c. 18 (1224), supports this contention, and so does Glanvil towards the end of the twelfth century.

By degrees, however, it was swept away by contrary custom. But it required statutes to counteract its influence in other portions of the

[43] I. 2, 18, 1.

[44] *Cf.* §§ 36-38, supra.

[45] *Cf.* §§ 39, 40, supra.

kingdom. The effect of these statutes was to permit a man to dispose freely of all his chattels without restriction. But even in Blackstone's time, traces of the old arrangement still survive.[46]

113. The constant insistence on the rights of the wife and children that is observed in the laws and customs of the Middle Ages, makes it fairly evident that the testator, if he was survived by neither wife nor children, might dispose as he pleased of his whole estate. Bracton says that this is so.[47] From this it follows that the portion of the children was confined to the children themselves and that no right of representation was allowed, that is, no child of a deceased child could claim any share in it.[48] Nor was there a restriction placed on the testator in favor of grandchildren, parents, brothers, or sisters, as it was in the Roman law. On the other hand, the Middle Ages provided for the wife, who seems to have been neglected by the measures enacted under the Roman system.

114. Guarantees for the Heirs in the United States. Both legal systems probably have had some influence on the laws of those States which place limitations on the amount of one's estate that may be given to charity. There seems to be no doubt that the provisions of the Louisiana Code derive from the guarantees of the Roman law.[49]

[46] Blackstone, *op. cit.*, II, 32, 492, 493; Rood, *op. cit.*, 100. The statutes to which reference is made in the text were: 4 and 5 William and Mary, c. 2; 2 and 3 Anne, c. 5, for the province of York; 7 and 8 William III, c. 38, for Wales; and 11 George I, c. 18, for the City of London. The right of the widow to her wardrobe was never denied. The husband is not mentioned in the various enactments providing for the three-fold distribution, because he was the owner of his wife's property from the moment of their marriage. So, when a wife died, there was no possibility of a bequest of chattels. They were already in the complete power of her husband. But in Ireland, one-third of her property could be bequeathed to the Church with the consent of her husband. *Cap. Coll. Can. Hibern.*, lib. 41, c. 10—Wasserschleben, p. 161.

[47] *De Legibus Angliae*, 2, 26, 2; *Cf.* footnote 64, Chapter I.

[48] Pollock-Maitland, *op. cit.*, II, 361.

[49] Consider the following provisions. Art. 1493: "Donations *inter vivos* or *mortis causa* can not exceed two-thirds of the property of the disposer if he leaves at his decease a legitimate child; one-half, if he leaves two children; and one-third, if he leaves three or a greater number. Under the name of children are included descendants of whatever degree they may be." These provisions are more liberal than even the dispositions of Justinian who raised

115. Other States have similar provisions. California provides that no testator leaving statutory heirs may give more than one-third of his estate to charity. But only the amount in excess of the one-third fails, the remainder of the bequest being sustained.[50] It excepts from this restriction gifts to the State, or to any State institution, or to any educational institution that is exempt from taxation under the State Constitution.[51] Every gift is exempted, too, that is contained in a will executed at least six months prior to the death of the testator if the latter is survived by no spouse, parents, children, or grandchildren, or if all such heirs have waived their rights by a document executed six months prior to the testator's death.[52]

116. Georgia, Idaho, and Montana prohibit the disposition of more than one-third the testator's estate to charity, if the wife or children survive.[53] Iowa permits no more than one-fourth to be willed away from a surviving spouse, child, child of a deceased child, or parent.[54] Massachusetts provides that the income of grants, gifts, bequests, and devises made to or for the use of any one church shall not exceed ten thousand dollars a year.[55] Mississippi permits bequests of personality to charity, but not a devise of realty; allowing neither to be granted to religion.[56]

117. New York's provision reads that persons having a husband, a wife, a child, a descendant, or a parent may not devise or bequeath to benevolent, charitable, literary, scientific, religious or missionary societies, associations, corporations or purposes, in trust or otherwise, more than one-half his or her estate, after payment of debts, and such devise or bequest is valid to the extent of one-half and no more. The validity of such devise or bequest may be contested only by a surviving husband, wife, child, descendant, or parent.[57]

the heir's quarter to one-third, if less than five children survived; to one-half, if five or more survived.

[50] § 41. For method of citing State laws, *cf.* bibliography.

[51] § 42.

[52] § 43.

[53] Georgia (§ 3851); Idaho (§ 14-326); Montana (§ 7015).

[54] § 11848.

[55] C. 68, § 9.

[56] §§ 3564, 3565; Greely v. Houston (1927), 148 Miss. 799, 114 So. 740.

[57] § 17.

118. These States, however, are generally speaking more liberal towards the freedom of testamentary disposition than foreign statutes. And in most of the States, as is apparent, there is little interference with the testator's wish to disinherit his children, provided only that his intention be manifest.[58]

119. Where a child has been born to a testator after he made his will, or where it appears that some child has been overlooked through error, or where marriage has ensued since the will was made, revocation, total or partial, is decreed by many of the States. As to the last provision, it is sometimes required that a child be born to the

[58] The following statements of law in this matter are summarized from the digest of the statutes of various foreign nations as they appear in Martindale and Hubbell, II, *s. v.* "Wills."

In the Philippines, the children receive two-thirds, one-third being placed at the disposal of the testator. If there are no children surviving, the wife receives one-half the estate. Not all the estate, however, is included in this arrangement.

In Brazil, not more than one-half the estate can be willed away from lineal ascendants and descendants except a life estate to the surviving spouse in the remaining half. Nothing need be left to the spouse.

In Italy, Sweden, Germany, Czecho-Slovakia and Hungary, one-half may be bequeathed if heirs survive, and in the last two countries the heirs are the children and the parents. In Italy, two-thirds may be bequeathed if there are no children.

Switzerland provides that one-fourth of the intestate share of a descendant can be bequeathed; one-half of a parent's share; three-fourths of a brother's or a sister's; and one-half of the spouse's, if she is the sole heir; otherwise none of her share can be taken.

Spain, Cuba, and Denmark permit one-third to be taken from the necessary heirs, the spouse, the children, and the descendants. Spain includes the ascendants as privileged also.

Norway allows only one-fourth to be bequeathed if there is surviving issue, unless the estate exceed a specified sum.

Chile allows one-fourth, if there are surviving descendants; one-half, if there are none.

France, Netherlands, and Rumania permit one-fourth, one-third, one-half according to the number of children and parents surviving.

Russia allows departure from the intestate arrangement only in favor of the communist party or its affiliates, and heirs under the age of eighteen years can not be deprived of more than one-fourth the estate in any event.

Netherlands also requires a royal decree for the validity of every bequest to charitable institutions.

marriage in order that the case come under the statute. In the absence of a statute, however, it is the ruling of the courts that the birth of a child does not revoke a previous will. But wherever a statute provides revocation for a child that has been overlooked by the testator, it includes also a posthumous child, whether such a child is expressly mentioned or not.[59]

120. Pretermitted Children. In many of the States, permission to take from the estate of the decedent as if he had died intestate is granted to children who were living at the time the will was made but who are neither mentioned nor provided for in it.[60]

[59] Rood, *op. cit.*, 383, 385.

[60] For method of citing State laws, *Cf.* bibliography. Arizona (§ 3642; Arkansas (§ 10507); California (the heirs of the pretermitted child may take his share should the child die before the parent, *Cf.* §§ 71 and 90); Idaho (§ 14-320); Kansas (holds only for child reported dead but actually living at the death of the parent, *Cf.* § 22-243); Maine (c. 88, § 9); Massachusetts (includes the issue of the child pretermitted; *Cf.* c. 191, § 20); Michigan (§ 15550); Minnesota (§ 8745); Missouri (§ 514); Montana (includes the issue of the pretermitted child; *Cf.* § 7009); Nebraska (§ 30-227); Nevada (includes the issue of the pretermitted child; *Cf.* § 9919); New Hampshire (c. 297, § 10; New Mexico (§ 154-112); Ohio (as to child reported dead but living at the death of the parent; *Cf.* § 10563); Oklahoma (including the issue of the pretermitted child; *Cf.* § 1570); Rhode Island (including the issue of the prepermitted child; *Cf.* § 4313); South Carolina (§ 8295); South Dakota (including issue of the deceased child; *Cf.* § 636); Tennessee (§ 8131); Utah (§ 101-1-31); Washington (§ 1402); Vermont (§ 2977); Wisconsin (§ 238.11); Alaska (§ 569).

In California, the presumption of intestacy as to the pretermitted child is conclusive (*iuris et de iure*), and can not be attacked by proof to show that the testator had not forgotten the child. The presumption can be overthrown by proof in Arkansas and Missouri. Only if the omission occurred by mistake does Vermont regard the testator partially intestate, *i. e.*, as to the child omitted.

If the child was omitted intentionally, the will is not even partially revoked in Maine, Massachusetts, Oklahoma, Rhode Island, South Dakota and Wisconsin. If there was an advancement made to the child during the life of the parent, there is no revocation in California, Maine, Massachusetts, Nevada and Washington. These exceptions modify the provisions of these States touching the matter at hand. States that have no restricting statutes on this subject would be just as liberal where there is a manifest intention to exclude a child from the inheritance, or where advancements have been made during the testator's life.

Posthumous Children and Children Born After the Will. In nearly all the States, a similar permission is granted to children born after the making of the will.[61] But Iowa extends this favor not to a child born merely after the will was made, but only to one born after the testator's death.[62] Only a few States provide for complete revocation of the whole will. Connecticut, Georgia, and Indiana have this provision without qualification of any kind. Qualifications are attached by other States. In some there is a distinction based on the existence or non-existence of children at the time the will was made; in others, the will is not revoked unless the child reaches the age of majority or has been married before he died.

Thus, Arizona, Mississippi and Texas provide that the will is

[61] Alabama (§§ 10585, 10586); Arizona (§ 3641, posthumous children; § 3642, after-born); Arkansas (§ 10506); California (§§ 71 and 90); Colorado (§ 5189); Connecticut (§ 4880); Delaware (§§ 3251, 3252; 3262); Georgia (§ 3923); Idaho (§ 14-319); Illinois (after-born, c. 39, § 10; posthumous, c. 39, § 9); Indiana (§ 3457); Kansas (§§ 22-240, 22-243); Louisiana (Art. 1705); Maine (posthumous, c. 88, § 8; other after-born children would be included among pretermitted children, c. 88, § 9); Massachusetts (c. 191, §§ 20, 21); Michigan (§ 15549); Minnesota (posthumous, § 8744; other after-born children included among pretermitted children, § 8745); Mississippi (posthumous, § 3551; after-born, § 3552); Missouri (§ 514); Montana (§ 7008); Nebraska (§ 30-226); Nevada (§ 9918); New Hampshire (c. 297, § 10); New York (including a child adopted after the will was made—§ 26); New Mexico (included among children and descendants pretermitted—§ 154-112); North Carolina (§ 4169); North Dakota (includes a child adopted after the will was made—§ 5666); Ohio (§§ 10561-10564); Oklahoma (§ 1569); Oregon (§ 10-508); Pennsylvania (§ 8333); Rhode Island (pretermitted children, § 4313; posthumous, § 4314); South Carolina (§ 8924); South Dakota (§ 636); Tennessee (§§ 8131, 8386); Utah (§ 101-1-30); Texas (posthumous, Art. 8291; after-born, including descendants of such child, Arts. 8292, 8294); Washington (if the child was living at the death of the parent—§ 1402); Vermont (after-born included among pretermitted children, § 2977; posthumous, § 2976); Wisconsin (§ 238.10); Alaska (§ 569).

The provisions as to presumptions and exceptions, which were applied to children overlooked by the testator, are applied also to children born after the will was made in California, Arkansas, Missouri, Vermont, Maine, Massachusetts, Nevada, Oklahoma, Rhode Island, South Dakota, Washington and Wisconsin. See the end of the preceding footnote.

[62] § 11858. So also Nova Scotia, c. 146, § 17 (noted in Martindale and Hubbell, *s. v.* "Wills.")

revoked only when those two conditions are fulfilled, viz., the making of the will at a time when there were no children and the fortune of the child born after the making of the will to reach his majority or to be married before his death.[63] Only the latter condition is required in Kentucky, Virginia, and West Virginia, viz., that the child must live to majority or be married before death. Consequently, in these States the revocation takes place even if there were children living at the time the will was made.[64] But these last three States permit the testator to exclude the children born subsequent to the making of the will.

New Jersey allows for express exclusion of such children; and then on the hypothesis that they were not excluded, provides that the whole will shall be revoked if there were no children at the time the will was made; but only partially, that is, *pro tanto,* if there were children at that time.[65]

121. **A will made prior to marriage is in some instances revoked by the Anglo-American law** to protect the rights of the heir. At common law, it was established towards the end of the sixteenth century, and never afterwards doubted until comparatively recent times, that the marriage of a woman acted as an absolute revocation of a will she had previously made, so that it could not be revived even by the death of her husband. This was a corollary of the law touching the rights of the husband in the property of his wife. A woman's personal property became her husband's as soon as she married. Consequently, it were futile to speak of her making a testament concerning it.

Moreover, during the marriage, the woman lacked testamentary capacity. Even as to the property which her husband did not reduce to possession, and as to land, which she retained in her own right, she could make no new will nor change a prior one. Consequently, if a will she had made prior to marriage were allowed to remain valid, it would be irrevocable for the period of the duration of the marriage. It was in view of these considerations that the law revoked her will for her the moment she entered the married state.

[63] Texas provides that the will remains ineffective meanwhile. *Cf.* Art. 8293.

[64] Kentucky (§ 4847); Virginia (§ 5242); West Virginia (§ 4059).

[65] P. 5865, §§ 20, 21.

But if she had been given a power by some one over property that could in no way come into the possession of her husband, and if that power included the making of a will, a will made in the exercise of it could be revoked by the wife even during the period of the marriage. Consequently, it was not revoked when she entered the married state.[66]

But now in most of the States a married woman controls her property after marriage as well as prior to it. She also possesses all rights of disposing of it as she pleases even by will.[67] Nevertheless, many States regard her marriage such a change in her status as to revoke her will.[68] But a woman's will is not revoked by marriage in

[66] Rood, *op. cit.*, 372.

[67] The express authority is granted married women to make wills in the following States: Alabama (§ 8276); Alaska (§ 489); Arizona (§ 2174); Connecticut (§ 5165); Delaware (§ 3050); District of Columbia (tit. 14, § 21); Florida (§ 5458); Indiana (§ 3450); Iowa (§ 10446); Kansas (right may be conferred by the court; *cf.* § 67-416); Kentucky (§ 4827); Maine (c. 74, § 1); Maryland (Art. 45, §§ 4, 5); Massachusetts (c. 191, § 1); Michigan (§ 13057); Minnesota (§ 8735); Montana (§§ 5782-5812); Nebraska (§ 30-201); Nevada (§ 9905); New Mexico (*M & H*); North Carolina (§ 4129); North Dakota (§ 5641); Oklahoma (§ 1537); Oregon (§ 10-502); Rhode Island (§ 4199); South Dakota (§ 605); South Carolina (§ 8574); Tennessee (§ 8098); Utah (§ 101-1-3); Vermont (§ 2744); Washington (§ 6891); West Virginia (§ 4732); Wyoming (§ 69-104); Hawaii (§ 3318); Ontario (*M & H*); Quebec (*M & H*).

The symbols *M & H.* indicate Martindale and Hubbell's law digests, *s. v.*, "Wills."

In the other States the complete emancipation of a married woman touching her separate estate makes inevitable the conclusion that she has testamentary capacity even during the period of the marriage. Consult: Arkansas (*M & H*); California (Civil Code, § 162); Colorado (§§ 5576-5578); Georgia (§ 2993); Idaho (§§ 31-903, 31-904); Illinois (c. 68, § 9); Louisiana (Arts. 2334, 2384); Mississippi (§ 1940); Missouri (§ 2998); New Hampshire (c. 288, §§ 1, 2); New York (c. 14, § 51); Ohio (§ 7998); Pennsylvania (§§ 14569, 14570); Texas (Art. 4614); Virginia (§ 5134); Wisconsin (§ 246.03). New Jersey seems not to permit married women to make a will. *Cf.* p. 5862, § 3.

[68] Alabama (§ 10584); Arkansas (§ 10503); Colorado (§ 5188); Florida (if the will disposes of all her property; *cf.*, Colcord v. Conroy, 1898, 40 Fla. 97, 23 So. 561); Georgia (§ 3923); Idaho (§ 14-313); Illinois (unless it is stated in the will that it is made in contemplation of marriage; *cf.* c. 39, § 10); Kansas (Shorten *et al.* v. Judd, 1898, 60 Kan. 73; 55 Pac. 286); Indiana (revives if the testator survives the spouse and issue and the wife of

Maine, Maryland, New Jersey, or Ohio.[69]

However, in the States that revoke a woman's will at her marriage, the interpretation of the statute is very rigorous. The statute operates as an absolute revocation. Consequently, the will does not revive when the husband dies. Moreover, the statute is not subject to repeal by implication. It is not repealed, therefore, by statutes giving married women power to make wills, or to deal with their property, or providing that wills shall be revoked only in a certain way. Moreover, the will of a widow is subject to revocation when she marries. The one exception seems to be the will made by a married woman who marries a second time after the death of her previous husband. This will seems to escape revocation.

122. **As to the revocation of a man's will at his marriage,** it seems not to have been maintained in England at any time that his marriage was sufficient to revoke his will. Coupled with the birth of issue, it was regarded as sufficient cause, but even that situation was so construed only towards the end of the seventeenth century, and was restricted to bequests of personalty.

After a century of doubt, it was established in the Court of Exchequer that these circumstances operated as a revocation not only of a bequest of personalty but also of a devise of land. But if the testator had a son surviving from a former marriage, it was held that

issue—§§ 3456, 3458); Kentucky (§ 4832); Massachusetts (unless in contemplation of marriage; *cf.* c. 191, § 9); Minnesota (§ 8742); Missouri (§ 510); Montana (§ 7002); Nebraska (to the extent of the husband's interest; *cf.* Vandeveer v. Higgins, 1899, 59 Neb. 333; 80 N. W. 1043); Nevada (§ 9915); New York (only to the extent of the interest of surviving spouse and children; *cf.* § 35); North Carolina (§ 4134); North Dakota (§ 5668); Oklahoma (§ 1563); Oregon (§§ 10-505); Pennsylvania (only to extent of interest of surviving spouse and children; *cf.* § 8333); Rhode Island (§ 4306); South Carolina (§ 8922); South Dakota (§ 630); Utah (only as to the interest of the surviving spouse and children; *cf.* § 101-1-24); Washington (if the spouse is living at the death of the testator and it is clear that no provision was meant to be made in the will; *cf.* § 1399); Virginia (§ 5232); West Virginia (unless made in contemplation of marriage; *cf.* § 4044); Alaska (§ 566); Prince Edward Island (*M & H*).

[69] Maine (*M & H*); Maryland (Roane v. Hollingshead, 1892, 76 Md. 369; 25 Atl. 307); New Jersey (Vreeland's Ex'r. v. Ryno's Ex'r., 1875, 26 N. J. E. 160); Ohio (§ 10560).

as this son was entitled to all the land under the laws of descent, a second marriage revoked only bequests of personalty when issue was born. The reason advanced was that the issue of the second marriage could have no rights to the land in any event. So, too, a will made by the man touching any property that would not pass to the wife or issue was not revoked.[70]

123. If the will was made in contemplation of marriage and provided for the wife and issue, it was admitted that it was not revoked. Nor was it revoked, if it disposed of only a portion of the estate. But it did not suffice that other property was acquired after the will was made. Nor that the whole estate was given under the will to the widow, from whom his issue, being her issue also, might expect to inherit. Nor that an ante-nuptial agreement had been made.

Revocation, therefore, operated by force of law and not by the law's interpretation of the testator's wish. Consequently, no amount of evidence of his desire that the will be sustained sufficed to prevent revocation. If he wished the provisions of the will to be valid, he must re-execute it after marriage. Statutory revocation is not defeated by even the proven intention of the testator.

124. Marriage alone is sufficient to revoke a man's will in some of the States, even without birth of issue: viz., in Colorado, Connecticut, Georgia, Kansas, Kentucky, North Carolina, Oregon, Rhode Island, Virginia, and Alaska.[71] Unless it was made in contemplation of marriage it is revoked by marriage in Illinois, Massachusetts, West Virginia.[72] Such a circumstance saves the will in South Caro-

[70] Rood, *op. cit.*, 375.

[71] Rood, *op. cit.*, 376-380. Colorado (§ 5188); Connecticut (§ 4880); Georgia (§ 3923); Kansas (Shorten *et al.* v. Judd, 1898, 60 Kan. 73, 55 Pac. 286); Kentucky (§ 4832); North Carolina (§ 4134); Oregon (§ 10-505); Rhode Island (§ 4306); Virginia (§ 5232); Alaska (§ 566).

[72] Illinois (c. 39, § 10); Massachusetts (c. 191, § 9); West Virginia (§ 4044). This exception, viz., the will's being made in contemplation of marriage, exempts from revocation the wills of both husband and wife in the following provinces of Canada: Alberta, British Columbia, New Brunswick, Newfoundland, Nova Scotia, Ontario and Saskatchewan. In Ontario the will is also saved if the surviving spouse elects to take under it. This summary touching the Canadian provinces derives from the digests of Martindale and Hubbell.

lina only if it be so stated on the face of the instrument itself.[73] Marriage alone is not sufficient to revoke the will in Florida.[74] Maryland regards the will as revoked when a child is born.[75] But elsewhere the will is not revoked unless the wife or issue survive.[76]

Article 4

Rights of Surviving Spouses

125. Closely associated with the principle that prompted the law to revoke the will of an unmarried person on the occasion of his or her marriage is the right of dower and of curtesy. **Curtesy** was a right by which a man who married a woman seised of an estate of inheritance, that is, of lands and tenements in fee-simple or fee-tail, and who had issue by her born alive and capable of inheriting the estate, on the death of his wife could hold her lands for life.[77]

126. Dower, on the other hand, was the right of a woman who married a man seised of an estate of inheritance, that is, of lands and tenements in fee-simple or fee-tail to have at his death one-third of all the lands and tenements whereof he was seised at any time

[73] § 8922.

[74] Herzog v. Trust Co. (1914), 67 Fla. 54; 64 So. 426.

[75] Roane v. Hollingshead (1892), 76 Md. 369, 25 Atl. 307.

[76] It is revoked by the wife's surviving without provision being made for her in Nevada (§ 9914), Utah (§ 101-1-24), and Washington (§ 1399). By the survival of issue with no provision for the issue and disposition of the whole estate made in the will; *cf.* Missouri (§ 509). In Indiana it is revoked unless there is no spouse surviving, or issue, or the wife of issue (§§ 3456, 3458). The widow takes as if her husband died intestate in Delaware (§ 3263). The will is revoked *pro tanto* for the widow, and for the child born or adopted; *cf.* Pennsylvania (§ 8333). If the wife survives, the will is revoked unless there is a provision for her by the will, or a marriage settlement, or the will shows an intention that it shall not be revoked; *cf.* Arizona (§ 3638), California (same principle is applied to the wife's will if the husband survives; *cf.* § 70); and Idaho (§ 14-312). The same attitude of the testator towards spouse and issue as that required for the spouse in the last three States saves the will from revocation in Arkansas (§ 10502); Montana (§§ 7001, 7002); New York (§ 35); North Dakota (§ 5666); Oklahoma (§ 1562); South Dakota (§ 629), and Wisconsin (*M & H*).

[77] Blackstone, *op. cit.*, II, 8, 126.

during the coverture (that is, during the period of the marriage), to hold for herself for the term of her natural life.[78]

127. Neither spouse can or ever could, by a devise or otherwise, defeat the estate of the other in dower or curtesy.[79] But under the English Dower Act (4 and 5 William IV, c. 105) the husband can sell or devise his land free from his wife's dower and without her consent.[80]

128. The common law rule of dower is retained by some of the States. By express enactment, they guarantee the widow the possession during the term of her life, of one-third of all the real property of which her husband was seised during the period of the marriage, provided she had not relinquished her right of dower or debarred herself for the reason and in the manner set forth in the statute.[81]

A great diversity of provisions is found elsewhere. Alabama, for instance, grants the wife a right in one-half the realty if the estate is solvent, otherwise in one-third; but if the wife have private property equal to the dower, she can not claim it, and in any event she is entitled only to the quantity in excess of her own property.[82]

Virginia grants her a life estate in one-third without qualification; in the remaining two-thirds subject to the rights of heirs, creditors, and devisees.[83]

[78] Blackstone, *op. cit.*, II, 8, 129.

[79] Rood, *op. cit.*, 99.

[80] Rood, *op. cit.*, 99 (footnote); Woerner, *op. cit.*, 113.

[81] Woerner, *op. cit.*, 106.

So Alaska (§ 462); Delaware (§ 3303); District of Columbia (tit. 14, § 29); Georgia (§ 5247); Hawaii (§ 3017); Illlinois (c. 41, § 1); Iowa (§ 11990 ff.); Maryland (Art. 45, § 6); Massachusetts (c. 189, § 1); Kentucky (§ 2132); Michigan (§ 13072); Missouri (§ 318); Montana (§ 5813); New Hampshire (c. 306, §§ 3-5); New York (as to marriages contracted prior to September 1, 1930; *cf.* c. 51, § 190); North Carolina (§ 4100); Ohio (§ 8606); Rhode Island (§ 5781); South Carolina (wife may take instead one-sixth in fee; *cf.* § 8586; Jeffries v. Allen, 1891, 34 S. C. 189, 13 S. E. 365); Tennessee (§ 8351); West Virginia (§ 4096); Wisconsin (if death occurred after August 31, 1921; *cf.* § 233.01).

The provisions in Alaska, Georgia and Tennessee seem to touch only the property which the husband owned at the time of his death.

[82] §§ 7427-7430.

[83] § 5117.

Arkansas grants the common law dower if children have been born to the marriage, and permits in addition one-third of the personal estate of the husband to be taken absolutely. If there be no children, the wife may have one-half the realty and personalty in fee. But she may have no more than a life estate in one-half of the realty, if it came to her husband by inheritance from his kindred. And if there are creditors, she is restricted to one-third the realty and the personalty in fee.[84]

The dower right in Pennsylvania is the share the widow would have if her husband died intestate, but extends to lands he sold after the marriage unless she relinquished her claim as to them.[85] Utah grants one-third the realty in fee;[86] Vermont adds one-third the personalty in fee, or one-half if there be but one child;[87] Kansas grants one-half the realty in fee;[88] and Delaware, in case of intestacy, grants a life estate in one-half the realty if there are children, a life estate in all the realty if there are no children, and all the realty in fee if there are no kindred of the husband.[89]

129. But twenty-one States have no dower right as such, either because it never existed there or because it was abolished.[90] In

[84] C. 50. Florida makes the same provision as to personalty irrespective of creditors, except that the wife takes one-half the personalty even when there is a child, provided there is no more than one. *Cf.* §§ 5493, 5494.

[85] § 8344.

[86] § 101-4-3.

[87] § 3401.

[88] § 22-108.

[89] 33 D. L. 617; Oregon permits a life estate in one-half the realty in any event (§ 10-301).

[90] Arizona (*M & H*); California (Civil Code, § 173); Colorado (*M & H*); Connecticut (as to marriages contracted after April 20, 1877; *cf.* § 5154); Idaho (§ 31-915); Indiana (§ 3377); Kansas (§ 22-127); Louisiana (*M & H*); Maine (abolished by the act taking effect May 1, 1895, except as to persons then married; it took effect as to them January 1, 1897; *cf.* c. 89; § 8); Minnesota (§ 8622); Mississippi (§ 1942); Nebraska (§ 30-104); Nevada (*M & H*); New Mexico (§ 68-308); New York (as to marriages performed after August 31, 1930); *cf.* c. 51, § 190); North Dakota (§ 4414); Oklahoma (§ 1618); South Dakota (§§ 175, 702); Texas (*M & H*); Washington §§ 1343, 6897); Wyoming (§ 88-4001).

thirty-two States the right of common law curtesy is not known.[91]

130. But a life estate is taken in Rhode Island by the husband in his wife's realty. This is the rule also in Tennessee, New Hampshire, New York, North Carolina, Missouri, and Alaska.[92] The right is contingent upon the wife's dying intestate in Alabama and the District of Columbia. Consequently in these jurisdictions the expectancy is defeated by the wife's devising any portion of her realty away, but only to the extent of the devise. But in Alabama, the husband receives in addition one-half the personalty in fee.[93] This is practically the arrangement in Wisconsin also, but there the provisions add that the expectancy is defeated also by the existence of an heir by a former marriage or by the husband's re-marriage.[94] Delaware limits the life estate to one-half the realty when there is an heir to the marriage.[95] New Jersey and Oregon have the same restriction whether there is issue to the marriage or not, though prior to January 1, 1929, New Jersey observed the common law rule.[96] Pennsyl-

[91] Alabama (§ 7376); Arizona (*M & H*); California (Civil Code, § 173); Colorado (§ 5151); Connecticut (as to marriages contracted after April 20, 1877); Florida (*M & H*); Georgia (§ 3670); Idaho (§ 31-915); Indiana (§ 3377); Iowa (§ 11990 ff.); Kansas (§ 22-127); Louisiana (*M & H*); Maine (c. 89, § 8); Maryland (Art. 45, § 7); Michigan (§§ 13057, 13096); Minnesota (§ 8622); Nebraska (§ 30-104); Nevada (*M & H*); New Mexico (§ 68-308); New York (as to a wife dying after August 31, 1930; prior to that, the husband obtained a life estate in the realty of which his wife died seised; *cf.* c. 51, § 189); North Dakota (§ 4414); Ohio (§ 8614); Oklahoma (§ 1618); South Carolina (§ 8577); South Dakota (§§ 175, 702); Texas (*M & H*); Utah (§ 101-4-9); Washington (§§ 1343, 6897); West Virginia (§ 4113; Wyoming (§ 88-4001).

The symbol *M & H* in the last two footnotes refers to the digests in Martindale and Hubbell, *s. v.*, "Dower" and "Curtesy," respectively.

[92] Rhode Island (§ 4200); Tennessee (§ 8098); New Hampshire (c. 306, § 9); New York (if the wife died prior to September 1, 1930; *cf.* c. 51, § 189); North Carolina (§ 2519); Missouri (§ 518); Alaska (Session Laws, 1923, c. 40—life estate valid in all the property, real and personal, of which the wife died seised. *Cf.* § 482, Compiled Laws).

[93] Alabama (§ 7376); District of Columbia (tit. 14, § 42).

[94] § 233.23.

[95] D. L. 617.

[96] New Jersey (Laws 1927, c. 71, p. 128; 1928, c. 209, p. 380); Oregon (§ 10-330).

vania provides for curtesy the same rule as for dower, viz., the husband may elect the share he would have taken if the wife had died intestate.[97]

Curtesy and dower are governed by the same provisions also in Vermont, Iowa, and Kansas. In Vermont, one-half the realty is taken by the husband in fee if there is only one child; otherwise one-third in fee.[98] Though Iowa and Kansas do not recognize curtesy as such, they have a provision in lieu of it. In virtue of this provision in Iowa the husband takes one-third the realty and the personalty in fee[99] and in Kansas, one-half the realty in fee.[100]

131. The homestead exemption bears a noteworthy resemblance to the devices of dower and curtesy. This exemption belongs to the head of the house during life, and at death passes to the surviving spouse. And it is an institution that exists in most of the States.

It is a privilege by which the homestead is exempt from nearly all claims for debts and from the claims of devisees. When it passes at death to the surviving spouse, in most States it is provided that it shall endure for the period during which the children are minors and for the life of the surviving widow. Some States allow it to the surviving husband, who in any case enjoys it until his children come of age. But it is granted in fee in only a few States, the remaining States restricting it to a life estate.

There is frequently found the requirement that the homestead be recorded publicly as such, but this is not conceived to be necessary when it is transferred at death to the surviving spouse. Where there is no homestead as such, some States actually authorize the probate judge to set aside a sufficient amount of property to make up the quantity or value allowed by law.

As to the quantity of the property exempted and its value, there is diversity among the States. The value ranges from five hundred dollars to eight thousand dollars. The acreage most frequently allowed

[97] § 8353. A uniform rule for curtesy and dower obtains also in Illinois (c. 41, § 1); Kentucky (§ 2132); Massachusetts (c. 189, § 1); Maryland (Art. 45, § 7); Virginia (§ 5139 a).

[98] § 2964 (§ 3414, Laws of 1917).

[99] § 11990 ff.

[100] § 22-108.

is one hundred and sixty acres in rural districts and one-fourth of an acre in towns and cities.

No homestead exemption as such exists in Connecticut, Delaware, District of Columbia, Indiana, Maryland, Pennsylvania, and Rhode Island.[101]

[101] For method of citing State laws, *cf.* bibliography. Connecticut allows an exemption in the discretion of the court (§ 4954). Indiana provides five hundred dollars for funeral expenses and permits the widow and the minor children to occupy forty acres for one year (§§ 3105, 3112). Maryland makes an allowance of one hundred and fifty dollars if there are minor children surviving; seventy-five dollars, if there are no children (Art. 93, §§ 317, 318). Pennsylvania provides an exemption of five hundred dollars for the widow and the minor children (§ 8446). In Rhode Island, the court can arrange for the support of the family for a period of six months (§ 6485).

Herewith also are presented some of the peculiarities of the homestead exemption as it exists in the various States. Unless otherwise noted, it is understood to be a life estate for the wife and for the children during their minority. If it is for the life of either the husband or the widow, that fact will be indicated by the phrase, "either spouse"; if it vests in fee, that will be signified by the phrase, "in fee"; the figures in dollars indicate the limit beyond which the exemption does not extend.

Alabama (in fee if the estate is insolvent or there is no other realty in the State; $2,000.00; *cf.* §§ 7918-7920); Alaska ($2,500.00; *cf.* § 1104); Arizona ($4,000.00; *cf.* §§ 1731-1737); Arkansas ($2,500.00; *cf.* c. 84); California (Code Civil Procedure, § 1464); Colorado (either spouse; $2,000.00; *cf.* §§ 5924-5931); Florida (in fee to the widow and the heirs, or to the widow, if there be no issue; $1,000.00; *cf.* const., Art. 10, § 2; Laws 1927, § 5484); Georgia ($1,600.00; *cf.* §§ 3392-3396); Idaho (in fee to the surviving spouse, if it belongs to the community property; otherwise it may be granted for a time to the family by the probate judge; $5,000.00; *cf.* §§ 15-507, 15-508); Illinois (as long as either spouse occupies it; $1,000.00; *cf.* c. 52, §§ 1, 2); Iowa (either spouse; $500.00; *cf.* §§ 10136, 10145); Kansas (const., Art. 15, § 9; Statutes 1923, § 22-102); Kentucky (either spouse; $1,000.00; *cf.* §§ 1707, 1708); Louisiana (either spouse; $2,000.00; *cf.* const., Art. 11, §§ 1, 2); Maine ($500.00; *cf.* c. 95; §§ 68-71); Massachusetts ($800.00; *cf.* c. 188, §§ 1-4); Michigan ($1,500.00; *cf.* const., Art. 14, §§ 2-4; also Laws 1929, § 14608); Minnesota (either spouse; *cf.* §§ 8340, 8341); Mississippi (either spouse; $3,000.00; *cf.* §§ 1765-1770); Missouri ($3,000.00 within the city, $1,500.00 in the country; *cf.* §§ 608, 612); Montana (either spouse; $2,500.00; *cf.* §§ 10151-10153); Nebraska (either spouse; $2,000.00; *cf.* §§ 40-101, 40-117); Nevada ($5,000.00; *cf.* §§ 3315, 3318); New Hampshire (either spouse; $500.00; *cf.* c. 214, §§ 1, 2); New Jersey ($1,000.00; *cf.* § 4963); New Mexico ($1,000.00; *cf.* §§ 48-111 to 48-114); New York

132. Election is permitted a spouse in many States. This means that she is either permitted or commanded to choose the share the law gives her rather than the provision made in the will, within a limited period of time. It is usually the wife only who is given this choice. In some States the share that the law allots is the dower portion. In other States, she may take either the dower portion or the share she would have received if her husband had died intestate. In a third group of States, she may take only what she would have received in case of intestacy. There are certain similarities, however, in the provisions of the various States around which the diversities may be classified. First of all, however, it is important to have some knowledge of the share of the surviving spouse in case of intestacy on the part of the other.

133. The Intestate Share of the Spouse. One of the most fre- divisions is this: one-third to the spouse, if there are children surviving; one-half, if there is one child or no children; the whole estate, if there is no surviving kindred. Some States extend this division to both realty and personalty; some restrict it to personalty only. Some grant the whole estate to the spouse when there are no surviving children or parents; others require a failure of brothers and sisters and their descendants; still others will not grant the entire estate until there is a total failure of kindred of the decedent.[102]

($1,000.00; *cf.* C. P. A., §§ 674, 675); North Carolina ($1,000.00; *cf.* const., Art. 10, §§ 2, 3, 5); North Dakota (either spouse; $5,000.00; *cf.* §§ 5605, 5627); Ohio (either spouse; $1,000.00; *cf.* § 11730); Oklahoma (either spouse; $5,000.00; *cf.* §§ 1643, 1223-1225); Oregon (either spouse; $3,000.00; *cf.* §§ 3-202; 11-402); Porto Rico (either spouse; $500.00; *cf.* §§ 1000, 1001); South Carolina ($1,000.00; *cf.* §§ 9085-9088); South Dakota (either spouse; $5,000.00; *cf.* §§ 449, 466); Tennessee ($2,000.00; *cf.* § 7719); Texas (either spouse; $5,000.00; *cf.* Arts. 3833, 3496, 3501); Utah (either spouse; if the estate is insolvent the exemption can not be allowed for longer than one year; *cf.* § 102-8-1; const., Art. 22, § 1); Vermont ($1,000.00; *cf.* § 2706); Virginia ($2,000.00; *cf.* §§ 6531, 6536, 6537); Washington (either spouse; $2,000.00; *cf.* §§ 552, 561); West Virginia (for minor children only; $1,000.00; *cf.* §§ 3911, 3915); Wisconsin (for life if the children are living, otherwise in fee; $5,000.00; *cf.* §§ 272.02, 272.20); Wyoming ($2,500.00; *cf.* §§ 89-2986, 89-2987).

[102] So it is in Arkansas (touching only personalty, all of which goes to spouse on failure of kindred—Laws, 1925, p. 441); California (extends to

134. Another rather common plan of distribution is to give all the personalty to the spouse, if there are no children; and various

realty; one-half to spouse if one child; whole to spouse only on failure of grandchildren of brother or sister of decedent; *cf.* §§ 221-224); Connecticut (realty included; whole to spouse on failure of parents and all up to $2,000.00, plus one-half the remainder on failure of issue; holds for marriages contracted after April 20, 1877; *cf.* § 5156); District of Columbia (the whole estate to spouse on failure of kindred; *cf.* tit. 25, § 242); Idaho (includes realty; whole goes to spouse on failure of parents of the decedent; one-half to spouse if only one child; *cf.* § 14-103); Maine (realty included; division as indicated for Arkansas; *cf.* c. 89, § 1); Maryland (realty included; whole to spouse on failure of descendants of brothers and sisters of decedent; *cf.* Art. 46, §§ 1, 2; Art. 93, § 125); Massachusetts (realty included; if no issue, $5,000.00 clear goes to spouse in addition to one-half whole estate; *cf.* c. 190, § 1); Michigan (realty divided according to the plan outlined in general, except that if there are children, the husband takes no interest in it at all; as to personalty, either spouse takes one-half if there be but one child and the widow takes one-half plus $3,000.00 if there are no children; *cf.* §§ 13440, 15726).

Missouri (realty included; but if there are children, the spouse takes a child's share; *cf.* §§ 306, 319-321); Montana (realty included; one-half of the estate goes to the spouse if there be but one child; *cf.* § 7073); Nebraska (realty included; one-half goes to the spouse if there be but one child; all, on failure of blood relatives of the decedent; *cf.* §§ 30-101, 30-102); New Hampshire (realty included; $5,000.00 clear to the spouse before division when there are no children; *cf.* c. 306, §§ 10-13); New York (realty included; if there are no children, $500.00 clear before division if both parents are living; if one parent is dead, $5,000.00 goes clear to the spouse; if both parents dead, $10,000.00 clear; *cf.* §§ 83, 98).

North Carolina (as to personalty, in case there are children, instead of the one-third, the widow takes a child's share if there are more than two; the husband takes the share of a child if there be more than one child; *cf.* § 137); North Dakota (realty included; spouse takes one-half if only one child, and the same if there be no children, except that the spouse takes the first $15,000.00 in that event, and the first $25,000.00 if there are no parents surviving the deceased; *cf.* § 5743 in Compiled Laws and in Supplement); Oklahoma (realty included; one-half goes to spouse if one child; the whole estate, if no brothers or sisters or their descendants survive; except from the rule property acquired by joint industry, in which only a life estate goes to surviving spouse, the property to be distributed at death to the heirs of both spouses; *cf.* § 1617); Pennsylvania (realty included; $5,000.00 clear before division, if there are no children, which amount is not given, however, to a spouse electing against a will; *cf.* §§ 8342-8344).

South Carolina (realty included; *cf.* § 8906); South Dakota (includes

proportions of it, if there are children surviving, such as one-third,[103] or one-half.[104]

realty; one-half goes to spouse if there be but one child; if no children, $20,000.00 clear before division is given to spouse; if there be no descendants of brothers or sisters, all the personalty is taken by the spouse; *cf.* § 701); Utah (the same provisions obtain here as in South Dakota, except the amount taken when there are no children; in Utah it is $25,000.00; *cf.* §§ 101-4-5); Washington (the same provisions as in South Dakota touching separate realty, except there is no preferred amount distributed to the spouse prior to division when there are no children; *cf.* § 1341); Wisconsin (one-half is taken by the spouse if there be but one child, and the whole estate, including realty, if there be no issue; if there is more than one child, only dower and curtesy are taken; *cf.* §§ 237.01, 318.01, 318.04).

[103] So in Arizona (§ 978); Minnesota (the same plan for the whole estate; *cf.* §§ 8720, 8726); New Jersey (Sup. §§ 146-169); Ohio (except that one-half the first $400.00 goes to the spouse in any event; *cf.* § 8592); Texas (Art. 2571); Virginia (§ 5273); West Virginia (§ 4089).

These States have separate provisions for the realty except Minnesota. Arizona and Texas retain the same proportion for realty as for personalty, when there are children, but in Arizona it is a life estate; when there are no children, they grant one-half the estate to the parents of the deceased; and if there are no parents surviving, then the whole estate to the surviving spouse, but Texas grants the whole estate only on failure of descendants of brothers and sisters. New Jersey, when there are no children, gives the surviving spouse all the realty acquired during the marriage (Laws, 1926, c. 41, p. 77); if there be no kindred surviving, all realty goes to the spouse (C. S., p. 1917).

Ohio has a similar provision, giving a life estate, if there be no children, in all realty that has descended in the decedent's family or has been acquired by devise and deed of gift, but granting an estate in fee in all other realty (§ 8573). Virginia gives the realty to the spouse when there survives no brother or sister or descendant of brother or sister (§ 5264); in West Virginia, the spouse shares with the brothers and the sisters when the parents of the decedent have died before him (§ 4080).

[104] Alaska (§ 595); Colorado (§ 5151); Kansas (wife takes one-half; *cf.* Dodge v. Beeler, 1874, 12 Kan. 524; husband takes child's share; *cf.* Delashmutt v. Parrent, 1889, 40 Kan. 641, 20 Pac. 504; § 22-118); Kentucky (exempts only $750.00 unless there is no kindred; §§ 1393, 1401); Oregon (§ 10-102); Washington (§ 1364).

Colorado and Kansas make this same provision, *i. e.*, one-half, for realty. Kentucky and Oregon give the spouse all the realty, if no kindred survive, but in Oregon the failure of lineal descendants suffices; otherwise the realty is governed by the principles of dower and curtesy.

Alabama gives one-half the personalty to the widow if there be but one

135. Georgia and Mississippi give the whole estate to the spouse if there are no children, otherwise the child's share,[105] while some States give only the dower and curtesy rights in the realty unless there is a failure of kindred.[106] New Mexico allows one-fourth of the estate to the spouse, if children survive, the whole of it, if there are no children.[107] Louisiana allows all the community property to the spouse, if no kindred survive; Nevada, if no parent of the decedent survive.[108]

136. Arizona, California, Idaho, Louisiana, Nevada, New Mexico, Texas, and Washington have special provisions for community property. Community property is that acquired by the husband after marriage, not out of his ancestral property, but by his labor or profession. One-half of this property belongs of right to the survivor. It is only about the one-half that belonged to the decedent that a

child; but gives a child's share if there are two, three, or four children; one-fifth, if there are more than four children; the husband takes only one-half the personalty in any event; *cf.* §§ 7374, 7376. Iowa allows the whole estate up to $7,500.00 to the surviving spouse and one-half the remainder; the whole estate, if there be no surviving kindred; *cf.* §§ 12017, 12026. Tennessee gives all the personalty to the spouse if there are no children; otherwise, a child's share; *cf.* § 8389. This is the rule also in Delaware as to a surviving husband (§ 3382; 30 D. L. 568); but a widow takes $3,000.00 and one-half the remainder, if there are no children, and one-third if there are children; however, she takes the whole estate if there be no surviving kin.

[105] Georgia (the widow to receive no less than one-fifth in any event; §§ 3930, 3931); Mississippi (§ 1404).

[106] North Carolina (§ 1654, rule 8); Tennessee (§ 8382); Virginia (when there are no descendants of a brother or sister, the whole estate goes to the spouse; *cf.* § 5264). In Florida, the spouse takes the whole estate if there are no children or descendants (§ 5483). Hawaii gives only dower and curtesy rights if there are children; if there are none, the surviving spouse takes one-half the estate; if there are no kin, the whole estate (c. 187).

[107] §§ 38-106, 38-109.

[108] Louisiana grants the spouse one-half the decedent's share (which is one-half the whole community property) of this property, if father or mother survive, when there are no children; and if there are children, only the usufruct in this same portion (Arts. 915, 916). Nevada grants in addition one-half the separate estate of the decedent, if there be one child; one-third, if more than one child survives (§ 9859).

question arises. It is solved in different ways by the various States.[109]

137. The provisions of the remaining States are so peculiar that they must be stated just as they are without attempt at classification.[110]

138. The method of holding property known as joint tenancy (which in the case of ownership by husband and wife is known as ten-

[109] In Arizona and Texas, the decedent's half descends to the spouse, if there are no children; Arizona (§ 985); Texas (Art. 2578). In California, the spouse takes it, if the decedent did not dispose of it by will; *cf.* § 201. Washington allows this, if there be no will and no issue; *cf.* § 1342. Idaho says that of the decedent's half, any amount less than an aggregate $25,000.00 can be bequeathed only to the descendants or the parents of either spouse; *cf.* § 14-113. In Nevada, the husband takes it, unless he has deserted his wife; the widow takes it only if there is no will and no issue; *cf.* §§ 3364, 3365. New Mexico has the same provision except that the widow takes only one-half of the decedent's half when there is no will and no issue, the remaining half being distributed among the descendants of the deceased; *cf.* §§ 38-104, 38-105.

[110] Illinois arranges that one-third the whole estate, realty and personalty, be taken by the spouse if there are children; if there are no children, one-half the realty and all the personalty; the whole estate, if there are no brothers or sisters of the decedent and no descendants of them (c. 39, § 1).

Indiana grants in lieu of the dower claim one-third the realty in fee to the widow unless the estate exceeds $10,000.00 in value; then one-fourth, unless it exceeds $20,000.00; then one-fifth: all as against creditors; with only one child, she takes one-half the realty; in lieu of curtesy to the husband, one-third of the realty is granted, subject to the debts of the wife contracted before her marriage. But in case of intestacy, the widow, if there is only one child, is entitled to one-half the whole estate; to one-third the estate, if there is more than one child. The surviving husband, in case of intestacy is entitled to only one-third, if there are any children at all. If there are no children, either spouse is entitled, in case of intestacy, to the whole estate, if it is less than $1,000.00; otherwise, to three-fourths; and in any event to the whole estate, if neither parent of the deceased survives. *Cf.* §§ 3337-3348.

Rhode Island grants a life estate in the realty and one-half the personalty, if there are children; if there are no children, $3,000.00 clear, and after that deduction, one-half the personalty. *Cf.* §§ 5549-5554. In Vermont, the court assigns the share of the personalty, which is not to be less than one-third (§§ 3278, 2833); there is no right granted in the realty except dower and curtesy rights unless there be no issue to the marriage; if there be no issue, the surviving spouse is entitled to $4,000.00 and one-half the remainder (§ 2966).

Wyoming grants one-half the estate if there are children; $20,000.00 and three-fourths of the remainder, if there are no children; and the whole estate, if there are no brothers or sisters or descendants of them. *Cf.* § 88-4001.

ancy by the entireties) is recognized in some of the States, even where the phenomenon of community property is not accepted.[111] The special feature of this method of holding property by joint tenancy is that each of the proprietors holds an undivided half during life, and that at the death of either of them the whole passes automatically to the survivor. This differs from a tenancy in common because under the latter method the undivided share of one of the owners may be devised to his heirs. Indeed, in certain States, it is definitely stated that a conveyance to husband and wife creates an estate by the entireties, viz., Indiana, Maryland, and Wisconsin.[112] New York provides that such an estate may be divided by proper petition to the court.[113] A last will, of course, does not touch such an estate. The law acts on it in such a way as to deprive the testator of capacity in regard to it.[114]

[111] It should be clear, however, that in the United States, the ordinary arrangement by which husband and wife hold property is that of an entire separation of the property of each, with certain rights contingent upon death.

[112] Indiana (§ 13384); Maryland (Jordan v. Reynolds *et al.*, 1907, 105 Md. 288, 66 Atl. 37; *cf.* also Brewer v. Bowersox, 1901, 92 Md. 569, 48 Atl. 1060); Wisconsin (§ 230.45).

[113] C. 14, § 56.

[114] The regulations of foreign countries touching the manner in which husband and wife hold property are not unimportant. The general rule is that the husband has usufruct and the administration of all the wife's property, except her wardrobe.

Germany allows marriage pacts, arranging for the manner of tenure of property, but they must be proved to the satisfaction of the court. In their absence, gifts expressly excluded from the husband's power are exempt from the husband's control, as are the wife's independent earnings. Since they remain the wife's, they are subject to bequest by her when she dies. Switzerland's provisions are like Germany's except that they do not exempt gifts from the husband's control. In Austria, the husband has the administration and the usufruct of all the wife's property. *Cf.* Civil Codes of Germany, Arts. 1366-1372; Switzerland, Arts. 194-214; Austria, § 1238.

France also permits marriage pacts; but the community property system obtains. All goods become community property except realty possessed before marriage and property obtained by gift on the express condition that it should not become community property. Of this separate property the spouse may make legal disposition. At the death of either spouse, the community property is divided between the surviving spouse and the heirs of the deceased. *Cf.* Civil

139. Compulsory election means a statutory obligation imposed on a spouse, by which she (or he) is compelled either to dissent within a given time from a provision in a decedent spouse's will or accept the provision of the law. It is evident, then, that election is necessary only when the law demands it. For what the law grants is taken automatically by the surviving spouse, unless she is required to dissent from the dispositions in the will.

This, however, does not imply that she takes the intestate provisions of the law in any event, or that the decedent can not bequeath away any of the estate in any other fashion than that in which the intestate law distributes it for him. Only those portions of the

Code, Arts. 1401-1408. Belgium practically agrees with these provisions in every particular. *Cf.* Civil Code, Arts. 1401-1497.

In Italy, the husband has the administration and the usufruct of a determined amount of the wife's property, known technically as the dowry, and this is to be restored to her at her husband's death. It remains the property of the wife and consequently capable of being given by will. The wife retains the full ownership also of all other property not included in the dowry. *Cf.* Civil Code, Arts. 1389, 1391, 1418, 1427. Austria's provisions are very similar to this, if the husband demands a dowry. *Cf.* Civil Code, § 1245. In Spain the income from the property of the husband and wife constitute a common fund for all family expenses. *Cf.* Civil Code, Art. 1315. *Cf.* also Prümmer, *Theol. Mor.*, II, §§ 18-26; Genicot, *Theol. Mor.*, I, § 473.

Under the ancient Roman system the wife passed into the family of her husband and became one of his heirs, just as if she were his daughter. This is the consequence of the form of marriage known as *cum manu; cf.* Gaius, 1, 115, b; Sherman, *op. cit.*, II, 470. But all her property was absorbed in her husband's; *cf.* Gaius, 3, 82; 2, 86; Ulpian, *Reg.*, 19, 18. But as early as the *XII Tables* (450 B. C.), "free" marriage was known, in which the husband and wife remained independent of each other. By the second century A. D., the form of marriage *cum manu* had fallen into desuetude; and by the fourth century, it no longer existed; *cf.* Sherman, *op. cit.*, II, 469.

There was no right of succession in the husband or the wife under the newer form. But a surviving wife or husband was called by the pretor to the inheritance, if there was no heir at all; *cf.* I. 3, 9, 6; D. 38, 11; C. 6, 18. But Justinian ordained that if the widow had no dowry (that is, a marriage fund to support her), she was entitled to share as follows in her husband's estate: one-fourth in fee unless there were more than three children, in which event she took a life estate in a child's share, the fee being in the children. He gave the same right to the husband, but soon repealed this provision; *cf. Nov.*, 117, 5 (A. D. 542); *Nov.*, 53, 6 (A. D. 537).

estate of which he is forbidden by law to dispose are taken by the persons to whom the law assigns them. The surviving spouse, as one of the favored persons, may claim the share granted by law. This can be done in two ways: either by formal protest against and renunciation of the will (known as election); or by the claiming of the lawful share in addition to the gift made in the will.

The provision of the State of Tennessee will clarify the difficulties involved in this privilege. It ordains that the surviving spouse may within one year, if the provision of the will is unsatisfactory, or fails because of debts, sue for dower or curtesy rights (and if the provision fails because of debts, she may sue without formal protest). *Cf.* §§ 8358, 8359. If the provision is merely unsatisfactory, formal dissent is necessary, and then the widow is entitled to support for one year for herself and her family (§ 8231). In both cases, dower and curtesy rights are granted the survivor, and in addition the intestate shares of personalty provided by the law (§§ 8359, 8360).

140. A vested right resides in the surviving spouse to dower, curtesy, homestead rights, and community property, wherever the statutes grant this right. This right exists independently of any testamentary disposition of the decedent, and can not be defeated by such disposition. It is evident, therefore, that when a problem arises as to whether a surviving spouse is compelled to make election, it must be solved according to the principles on which other cases of election are solved, as in the case of creditors and legatees.

In the absence of a statute requiring election by the spouse, the rule and presumption is that the testator did not wish to put the beneficiary to an election, but to make an additional gift out of the property of which he was free to dispose. This presumption can be overthrown only by explicit or implicit manifestation of contrary intent which must be contained in the will itself.

Certain statutes, however, have reversed the presumption, so that provision for the spouse under the will of the decedent is presumed to be in lieu of dower, unless it be otherwise indicated in the will.[115]

[115] Minnesota, for instance, decrees that no devise is considered to be in addition to the statutory provision unless it be clear from the will that such is the intent (§ 8722). Ohio has the same provision (§ 10572). South Carolina's

These statutes derogate the common law and must therefore be interpreted strictly. And even where the will declares that the provision is in lieu of all the rights of the spouse in the estate, it does not affect the exemption granted for her support pending the date of distribution. To be excluded, that item must be clearly specified in the will. And to defeat the spouse's rights, the will can not convert realty into personalty, or personalty into realty.[116]

141. The question of election, therefore, is pertinent only when the surviving spouse is both beneficiary under the will and by statute. It does not arise where the beneficiary under the will seeks to take at the expense of the rights of the spouse guaranteed by law. There the surviving spouse simply claims against the beneficiary who is not entitled to the gift.[117]

142. Wherever a spouse is put to an election, she may not take under both the will and the statute, unless it is clear that the testator wished her to receive both gifts. The statutes of Pennsylvania, Delaware, Kansas and Nebraska provide that she can be cited to make an election.[118] Certain States also put the surviving husband to an election when he is beneficiary under his decedent wife's will.[119]

143. If the spouse refuses to make an election, the court is confronted with the problem of deciding which of the two benefits should accrue. Most States requiring an election regard such refusal as a

doctrine is that where the will states that the gift is in lieu of dower, the widow must elect between the two provisions. *Cf.* Otts v. Otts (1908), 80 S. C. 19, 61 S. E. 109.

[116] Rood, *op. cit.*, 757 f.

[117] However, in Georgia it is possible to exclude the wife and the children from the whole estate; though a will which attempted this would be scrutinized most searchingly by the court. *Cf.* § 3832.

[118] Pennsylvania (§ 8338); Delaware (§§ 3307-3308); Kansas (§ 22-247).

[119] For instance, Colorado (§§ 5184, 5185); Illinois (c. 41, § 10); Indiana (§§ 3343, 3345, 3358); Iowa (§ 12007); Maine (c. 89, § 13); Massachusetts (c. 191, § 15); Minnesota (§ 8722); Mississippi (§§ 3561-3563); Nebraska (§ 30-107); New Hampshire (c. 306, §§ 12, 13); Ohio (§ 10566); Oklahoma (Laws, 1925, c. 26); Oregon (§ 10-330, as to dower; curtesy, *M & H*); Pennsylvania (§ 8338); Tennessee (§§ 8359, 8360); Texas (*M & H*); Virginia (§ 5276); West Virginia (§ 4091); Wyoming (§ 88-101); Ontario (*M & H*).

waiver of the privilege to dissent from the will. The testamentary disposition remains valid so long as it is not renounced. Consequently, on failure of the spouse to make election within the time specified by statute, the court regards the testamentary provision as supplanting the statutory provision.[120] But Kansas and Utah provide that the spouse takes under the statute and not under the will, that is, they presume that she renounces the dispositions of the will.[121]

[120] So Colorado (§§ 5184, 5185); Connecticut (§ 5161); Indiana (§ 3357); Illinois (c. 41, § 10); Iowa (§ 12010); Kentucky (§ 1404); Maine (c. 89, § 13; Maryland (Art. 93, §§ 310, 311); Massachusetts (c. 191, § 17); Minnesota (§ 8722); Mississippi (§§ 3561, 3563); New Hampshire (c. 306, §§ 10-13); Oregon (§ 10-319); Pennsylvania (§ 8338); Alberta (*M & H*); Nova Scotia (*M & H*); Saskatchewan (*M & H*).

[121] Kansas (§§ 22-238, 22-245 to 22-247); Utah (§ 101-4-4).

The following States also put the widow to her election: Alabama (§ 10593); Arkansas (§ 3527); Florida (§ 5493); Hawaii (§ 3030); Missouri (§§ 328, 329); Montana (§ 5819); New Jersey (§ 2048); New York (*M & H*); Oregon (§ 10-317); Rhode Island (§ 4311); Wisconsin (§ 233.13).

In Alabama and Kentucky when she elects against the will, the widow takes dower and the distributable share of the personalty. *Cf.* Alabama, § 10593; Kentucky, § 1404. In Colorado, either spouse has an election of one-half the estate (§§ 5184, 5185). In Connecticut, the statutory amount (§ 5161); the same in Indiana (§§ 3343, 3347, 3358); Illinois (c. 41, § 10); Maryland (Art. 93, §§ 310, 311); Minnesota (§ 8722); New Hampshire (c. 306 §§ 10-13); Nebraska (§§ 30-107, 30-108). Massachusetts allows this amount but provides that in case election is made no more than a life estate in any amount over $10,000.00 is taken, and that the maximum amount that can be taken by election in any event is the intestate share which the spouse takes when there is no issue. This limitation of course restricts the amount in case there should be no surviving kindred of the decedent. *Cf.* c. 191, § 15.

Mississippi has a similar provision, decreeing that no more than one-half the estate is to be taken by the spouse electing. *Cf.* § 3561. This is the case also in Pennsylvania (§ 8344). Virginia grants dower and the distributable share of the personalty, but provides that no more than one-half the personal estate shall be taken when it passes by election (§ 5276). West Virginia allows the share of realty and personalty that would be taken by the surviving spouse had the decedent left issue (§ 4091). Maine grants the realty by descent to the one electing, but the allowance of personalty rests with the court (c. 89, § 8). Wyoming permits one-half the realty and the personalty to be taken (§ 88-101), but Wisconsin grants the widow no more than one-third the estate (§ 233.14).

The other States permitting election grant the wife her dower rights and the husband his curtesy.

144. A brief notice as to the effect of divorce is pertinent at this point. In a few courts, and under special circumstances, it has been decided that divorce revokes a will made prior to it. But the general doctrine is that divorce does not revoke the will, not even as to the provisions made for the person from whom the divorce is obtained.[122] Of course, the rights of homestead exemption, dower, and curtesy, are extinguished by divorce, as well as the right to share in the property of an intestate spouse. But the property is divided at the time of the granting of the divorce according to rules that attempt an equitable appraisal of the rights of the parties.

Article 5

The Effect of Legal Guarantees on Pious Bequests

145. The importance of the foregoing review of statutory provisions in the various States is of some canonical importance. Whenever a will seeks to dispose of a portion of an estate, or of an entire estate, for the benefit of religious or charitable causes, it may be checked by the provisions just examined. There ensues in such a case a conflict of law. The conflict results because the portion of the will making bequests to religion or charity is governed also by the canons.

146. The problems that might arise out of such a conflict may be grouped into four classes.

Class A. A larger portion of the estate may be bequeathed than the statutes allow.

Class B. A will in which bequests to charity are contained may be revoked by the birth of a child or the failure to mention a child; or the bequest may abate to the extent necessary to provide the child with his intestate share, even though the will be not revoked in its entirety.

Class C. A will containing bequests to charity may be revoked by the subsequent marriage of the testator.

Class D. Charitable bequests may be forced to abate by the enforcement of claims of homestead exemption, dower, curtesy, election, and rights in community property.

122 Rood, *op. cit.*, 391.

It is appropriate that at this point an examination of the solutions possible under such conflicts be suggested.

147. The problems under Class A arise, as just observed, when the will attempts to bequeath more to charity, education, or religion than the statute permits. Two questions immediately present themselves in this connection: the first, can such a provision be harmonized with the decrees of the canons? the second, how far can it be harmonized with them?[123]

148. Can a provision of the secular law forbidding bequests to charity beyond a certain proportion of the estate be harmonized with canon law? This is the first question proposed as to the difficulties under Class A.

[123] Since the matter of bequests to charity belongs exclusively to the canonical forum, when the laws can not be harmonized, the canon law must prevail; *cf.* Bargilliat, *op. cit.*, § 1481. Charity is understood to mean pious causes in the sense already outlined in this treatise; § 95. Only bequests to such causes belong to the exclusive supervision of the canons. That the canons govern these bequests exclusively will be manifest when the matter of the authority of the Ordinary is presented for discussion. Suffice it to say here that the imperial constitutions of Rome (C. 1, 3, 28, 1, 2; C. 1, 2, 15; C. 1. 3, 45) and the decrees of Pope Gregory the Great (c. 4, C. XIII, q. 2; c. 14, C. XVI, q. 1; c. 3, X, *de testamentis et ultimis voluntatibus,* III, 26) crystallized this juridical concept of an ecclesiastical right deriving ultimately from the divine law and the mission of the Church.

That the canon law prevails is evident, moreover, from a scrutiny of Canon 1529, where the canons explicitly recognize and adopt the provisions of secular law in the matter of contracts: "Quae ius civile in territorio statuit de contractibus tam in genere, quam in specie, sive nominatis sive innominatis, et de solutionibus, eadem iure canonico in materia ecclesiastica iisdem cum effectibus serventur, nisi iuri divino contraria sint aut aliud iure canonico caveatur." This provision clearly indicates that in contracts that pertain to the canonical forum exclusively, the canon law must prevail.

Vermeersch thinks that even canon law as established by custom prevails over secular law in its proper sphere (Vermeersch-Creusen, *op. cit.*, II, 850), though De Meester (*op. cit.*, 1481, 3) and Cocchi (*op. cit.*, VI, 211) think otherwise as to custom. In any event, particular canon law prevails in its proper field over secular law, general or particular (Vermeersch-Creusen, *l. c.;* Cocchi, *l. c.;* Cance, *op. cit.*, III, 161; Blat, *op. cit.*, 445).

Proposition 42 condemned by the Syllabus of Pope Pius IX read: "In conflictu legum utriusque potestatis ius civile praevalet"; *cf.* the Encyclical, *Quanta cura,* 8 December, 1864—*Fontes,* n. 543.

149. Such legislation seems to be class legislation, and consequently to offend against the fundamental principles of sound jurisprudence. It can hardly be freed from this defect on the ground that no particular form of charitable enterprise is affected. It is discriminatory legislation, beyond a doubt. And there is no juridical or practical necessity that could even excuse such discrimination.

Should the legislation be couched in other language it might escape the defect. For instance, if it prescribed that a testator might not bequeath more than a certain portion of his estate to strangers beyond a certain degree of kindred, it would seem to be free of stigma. By such language it could accomplish the same purpose that it is presumed to intend. And what seems under the present language to be a condemnation of generosity to charity, would under the new phraseology appear clearly to be what presumably it is meant to be, a guarantee of the rights of kindred.

150. Suppose, however, that this modification of language had been effected, and that the legislation was so worded as not to be discriminatory; that it bore on its face the clear purpose of protecting the kindred of the testator, without any sinister implications. Could it, then, be reconciled with the canons? It would seem that at least in principle it could be reconciled. For it is the common opinion of canonists that *heredes necessarii* can always claim their legitimate share of the decedent's estate.[124]

151. To what extent can these provisions be reconciled with the canons, granted that in principle reconciliation is possible? To answer that question two other considerations must be understood: viz., who are the *heredes necessarii* and what is the legitimate portion?

152. Who are the *heredes necessarii?* Originally the *heredes necessarii* were those who were under the *patria potestas* of the decedent.[125] In other words, they were his children and his grandchildren.[126] Now, prior to the time of Justinian the daughters and the

[124] Cocchi, *op. cit.*, VI, 191; Vermeersch-Creusen, *op. cit.*, II, 835; De Meester, *op. cit.*, 1465; Cance, *op. cit.*, III, 146; Soglia, *op. cit.*, II, 4, 122; Lehmkuhl, *op. cit.*, I, 1147; Genicot, *op. cit.*, I, 602; c. 43, C. XVII, q. 4; cc. 16, 18, X, *de tastamentis et ultimis voluntatibus*, III, 26.

[125] *Cf.* Art. 1 of this chapter. *Cf.* also Gaius, 2, 152 and 156; Gaius, 3, 2-4; I. 2, 19 pr.; I. 3, 1, 2.

[126] Gaius, 2, 123; I. 2, 13 pr.

grandchildren could be disinherited by a general exclusion in the will; if not so disinherited, they took their share of the inheritance.[127] To be disinherited sons had to be mentioned by name.[128]

Justinian required specific mention of them all.[129] Thus the heirs entitled to the legitimate portion were the children and the grandchildren who would have inherited had the testator died intestate; and if there were no descendants, his parents stood in their place.[130] It was these persons who had the action called the *querela inofficiosi testamenti* by which the will was revoked when it did not give them their legitimate share.[131] Now it would seem that canonists would be prepared to accept these heirs as necessary heirs, *heredes necessarii*, especially in view of the fact that canon law drew so largely on Roman law in questions of testamentary disposition.

153. On the other hand, the division of the decedent's property into thirds which Brissaud traces to German law [132] was accepted by the canon law principles of the Middle Ages.[133] This plan included the spouse as a necessary heir. For she was to receive one-third of the estate in the event that there were children surviving; and one-half if there were none. Thus it would seem that canon law should accept the spouse also as a necessary heir, unless there is to be a correction of the law. Now a correction is odious, and is to be proved, not presumed.[134]

154. A more difficult question touches the amount that must be regarded as contained in the *portio legitima*. It has just been

[127] Gaius, 2, 123; I. 2, 13 pr.

[128] Gaius, *l. c.;* also 2, 127-128; I. *l. c.*

[129] I. 2, 13, 5; C. 6, 28, 4.

[130] I. 2, 18 pr. and 1; I. 2, 13, 5.

[131] I. 2, 18; 3, 1, 14; D. 5, 2, 8, 16; D. 5, 2, 24.

[132] Brissaud, *op. cit.*, p. 691. *Cf.* §§ 38, 39 supra.

[133] Council of Cashel (1172), c. 6—Harduin, VI B, 1630; Council of Worcester (1240), c. 50—Harduin, VII, 345; Constitutions of the Bishop of Salisbury (1256)—Mansi, XXIII, 823 A; Council of Lambeth (1261)—Harduin, VII, 543; Council of London (1268), c. 24—Harduin, VII, 631 B; Synod of Oxford (1287), c. 50—Harduin, VII, 1114; English Provincial Council (1509)—Mansi XXXI A, 401 A; Council of Dublin (1348)—Mansi, XXVI, 114 E.

[134] Canon 23. "In dubio revocatio legis praeexistentis non praesumitur, sed leges posteriores ad priores trahendae sunt et his, quantum fieri possit, conciliandae."

noted that the amount approved by the canonical jurisprudence in the Middle Ages was one-third of the chattels for the children; one-third for the wife; and one-third for the soul of the testator. If there was no issue surviving, then the wife was to receive one-half, and one-half was at the disposal of the testator for the good of his soul.

155. On the other hand, the early legitimate share under Roman law had been one-fourth of the intestate share of the *heres necessarius*;[135] but this was modified by Justinian so that the share was one-third, if there were less than five children; and one-half, if there were five or more.[136] Thus the testator had even greater freedom of testamentary disposition under the system of the Roman law, as to the share which might be disposed of by will, than under the canonical system of the Middle Ages. Of course, by a provision of the secular law, the testator in the Middle Ages was forbidden to dispose of his land by will. But then he could not leave it to the necessary heirs, either. So that it can not be argued that the rule adopted by the canonical jurisprudence of that day is useless now. The rule was adopted in contemplation of the only fund from which the heirs could profit, and in the face of that situation, it provided that one-third was to be at the disposal of the testator, or one-half if there were no children.

156. To what extent can the secular provisions be harmonized with the canon law principles? An attempt can now be made to answer the question.

The conclusion that ought to be drawn is probably this: there is no conflict with the canons in any secular system that permits the free disposal of one-third the whole estate of the decedent when he is survived by children or descendants or parents and his spouse; and of one-half, if only the spouse or a child or a descendant or a parent survive. Thus the canons can be harmonized with the provisions in California, Georgia, Idaho, Montana, New York, and Louisiana, except in so far as they would forbid more than one-third to be willed away if only a spouse, or only a child, or only parents survived; for, in such cases, under the rule advanced, the testator

[135] *Cf.* Art. 2 of this chapter. *Cf.* also I. 2, 18, 6, 7; D. 5, 2, 8, 6.

[136] *Nov.*, 18, 1 (536 A. D.).

should be permitted to dispose of one-half.[137] New York's doctrine, of course, is in perfect harmony, for its provisions permit one-half to be distributed by will in any event.

Massachusetts, forbidding bequests to any one church in excess of an annual income of ten thousand dollars aims at the beneficiary and not at the protection of the heirs.[138] But if the rightful share of the heirs happened to coincide at any time with the reduction made by the law in any bequest to charity, harmony could be established for the particular case even under the Massachusetts doctrine.

Iowa restricts the disposable portion to one-fourth the estate and is out of harmony with the rule,[139] and so is Mississippi, which forbids all bequests and devises to religion, but permits bequests of personalty to charity. The reason that prompted the canons to tolerate the restrictions on realty in feudal times do not exist in Mississippi. Indeed, realty can be freely devised in that State to secular and non-religious interests.

157. Thus, the law in the Philippines, Brazil, Italy, Sweden, Germany, Czecho-Slovakia, Hungary, Spain, Cuba, and Denmark are in harmony with the rule.[140] But France, Norway, Rumania, and Switzerland are not. Netherlands would be at variance should the royal decree be refused. And Russia's doctrine seems the most extreme of all.

158. In those systems which forbid more than a certain proportionate share to be taken from the heirs, it may happen that the beneficiaries of legacies totaling an excessive amount are both secular interests or persons, on the one hand, and pious causes, on the other. The question then arises as to which shall make contribution to the heirs, and whether all shall suffer equally.

The obvious intention of the testator would seem to be that the public cause should benefit rather than private persons. Thus his property will benefit the larger number of persons. Moreover, the presumption is that he wished to aid those in distress rather than

[137] *Cf.* §§ 115-117 supra. California (§ 41); Georgia (§ 3851); Idaho (§ 14-326); Montana (§ 7015); New York (§ 17).

[138] C. 68, § 9.

[139] § 11848.

[140] See § 118, this treatise.

those less needy; and finally he is presumed to have sought the promotion of supernatural rather than merely natural interests. For these three reasons, the bequests to pious causes must be sustained, even though the bequests to secular interests should fail entirely.

Iowa is the only State in which this precise problem would occur, for the doctrine of that State is the only one expressed in general terms. However, in the foreign countries that have enacted such restrictions, the terms are always general. The restriction is not aimed solely at pious causes. And so the situation just described might be of frequent occurrence there.

159. The Ordinary would seem warranted, therefore, in compromising with the heirs, where pious bequests are threatened, provided that the pious causes are not deprived of the one-third or the one-half part of the estate. If more than one charitable or religious institution were interested, the Ordinary would make a proportionate abatement in their shares, corresponding with the proportion established among them in the will itself, paying them out of the net amount that remains after the transaction. This would be no act of commutation, since the heirs are entitled under the canonical interpretation of the natural law to the amount that the Ordinary surrendered to them.[141]

160. The conclusion expressed herewith does not seem to be opposed to any official canonical pronouncements. There have been decrees of the Sacred Congregation of the Council which declared that the heir can not come into court and plead that the estate is insufficient to pay the pious legacies unless he can show from an inventory that the testator willed more than one-half his estate to pious causes.[142] To conclude from these decrees that the testator may be-

[141] It was once thought that the right of the testator to distribute one-third of his chattels for his soul was not merely a right but a duty, and that charity really had a vested claim in that portion. Consequently, when he died intestate, distribution of that one-third portion was made by the Ordinary as an interpretative disposition by the decedent himself. But here it is contended that the testator, though not obliged to bequeath these shares, must be left free to do so.

[142] *In Causa Camerinen.*, 30 May, 1761—Pallottini, XI, 543; *in Causa Burgen*, 15 March, 1777—Pallottini, XI, 543; *in Causa Ianuen.*, 24 November, 1787; *in Causa Bononien.*, 21 November, 1835—Pallottini, XI, 543.

queath one-half his estate to charity in any case is to extend their significance. First of all, the legacies are not being disputed on the ground that they have deprived the necessary heirs of their legitimate portion. Rather, the basis of the defense is lack of funds to pay. Consequently, the Sacred Congregation is not refusing the plea of heirs alleging their right to their legitimate portion, but of heirs alleging their inability to pay. There is nothing to indicate that the heirs are necessary heirs; and even if they are, they are making the wrong plea, and cases are decided on the pleadings of the parties.

What the Sacred Congregation is saying is that one-half a man's estate ought to be sufficient to pay his debts, not that the necessary heirs are not entitled to more than one-half on occasion. That was not the point of the decrees. The point is in the adequacy of the estate to meet the claims of creditors. The decrees raise a presumption in the absence of inventory that one-half a man's estate is adequate to meet his obligations.

161. Class B. The problem in Class B arises out of the failure to name a child in a will, or the birth of a child after the making of the will. The consequence of these circumstances is sometimes the revocation of the whole will; sometimes of only such portion as is necessary to provide for the child.[143] The canons are silent as to the power of the secular law to revoke a will, except that bequests to charitable causes contained in the will can not be revoked. Because such legacies are governed exclusively by canon law, secular law is incapable of invalidating them even when they are contained in a will that the law revokes.[144]

162. When the will is only partially revoked, the child obtains the share that the law gives him by contribution from the other beneficiaries under the will. Here the conclusions reached in the first problem must be recalled.[145] The right of the pious causes to one-

[143] *Cf.* §§ 119, 120, this treatise.

[144] S. C. C. *in Causa Ianuen.*, 28 September, 1737, § *Momenta*—Pallottini, XI, 560; *in Causa Anconitana*, 28 September, 1771, § *Quae*—Pallottini, XI, 561; Pirhing, *op. cit.*, III, 26, 28; Reiffenstuel, *op. cit.*, III, 26, 161; Santi, *op. cit.*, III, 26, 23; Soglia, *op. cit.*, II, 4, 123; Zallinger, *op. cit.*, III, 26, 292; Phillips, *op. cit.*, 407.

[145] *Cf.* §§ 156-158, this treatise.

third or one-half the estate must be maintained according to circumstances. Furthermore, as already established herein, profane legacies must abate before pious legacies are touched. In harmony with these two principles, it should be possible to solve all problems arising under a will where beneficiaries are compelled to make contribution.

163. If there are no other legatees who might contribute, investigation must be made to see whether the necessary heirs have received their intestate share as determined by the canonical rule just established.[146] If they have received it, it is they who must contribute to the child, for he is one of their number. The pious legacies are not called upon to surrender any portion of their bequests. It seems fairly obvious that the intention of the testator was so strongly fixed on the works of charity that he expected the heirs to save them intact, at least when they were properly provided for.

This is not true of other legatees. They are not in the same privileged position as works of charity. The testator can hardly be presumed to have intended to benefit them while his natural heirs were obliged to surrender a portion of their benefits.

164. If the necessary heirs received less than the proper share, and there are no legatees except the pious causes, the latter can be called on to make contribution. The child is one of the necessary heirs, even if he was omitted from his father's will. But the contribution should be no more than the amount necessary to make the sum total of all property taken by the necessary heirs equivalent to two-thirds or one-half the original estate, according to circumstances.

When the pious causes are called upon to make contribution, the Ordinary can make the necessary compromise with the child or its legal guardian out of court, but only within the bounds of the accepted rule. It is the Ordinary's duty also to make proportionate distribution among the works of charity that may be affected, with equitable deductions from the share of each of them.

165. **Class C. The problem in Class C is raised by the statutory revocation of a will upon the marriage of the testator.** In certain States marriage itself revokes the will of both a man and a woman; in others, the will is revoked by the marriage and the survival of necessary heirs to the marriage; in still others, it is only par-

[146] *Cf.* § 156, this treatise.

tially revoked, to the extent, namely, that it is required to provide for the necessary heirs.[147]

The solution of the problem is almost the same as that of the previous one. According to the same principles, a legacy to a pious cause is not invalidated by such a revocation as is contemplated in the present situation, whether the revocation occur at the time of the marriage or by the survival of necessary heirs. Only in the event that the necessary heirs are deprived of their legitimate share and there are no other legatees whose contributions would be adequate, can the pious cause be called upon. And when it is called upon, the amount of its contribution is measured by the rule advanced in the solution of the previous problem.

166. Class D. The fourth and final problem concerns the rights of dower, curtesy, homestead exemption, election, and community property. There is no conflict as to the rights of dower, curtesy, and homestead exemption. For these are all life estates, and a life estate in a plot of ground is only a very small portion of the value of an estate in fee. However, where other property has been left to the heirs these rights should be given a value where an attempt is made to determine whether the heirs have received their legitimate portion. Moreover, where the homestead exemption is expressed in money values, it must be reckoned just as any other liquid portion of the estate, whether personalty or realty. If in any particular case the value set by statute should happen to exceed two-thirds, the excess would be available for pious legacies. In a proper case, the excess above one-half would be available according to the rule that has been here adopted.[148]

167. Where the right of election extends only to dower or curtesy, the same conclusion applies as that advanced in the case of dower itself. Where it extends to personalty, it is a claim usually not to the full intestate share that would devolve on the spouse if no kindred of the decedent survived, but generally to no more than one-half the personalty.[149]

[147] *Cf.* §§ 121-123, this treatise.

[148] *Cf.* § 156; and Art. 4 in general, of this chapter.

[149] *Cf.* §§ 133-135, 140-143, this treatise.

In Colorado, the widow takes one-half the estate (§§ 5184-5185); Massachu-

But difficulties can arise in certain States that permit the spouse to elect the statutory share of personalty, where that share is the whole amount of the personalty where no issue survives;[150] or where no parents survive;[151] or on the failure of brothers or sisters or their descendants;[152] or of blood relatives or kindred.[153] For in these cases, given the proper situation, the spouse could elect the whole of the personalty contrary to the wishes of the testator to grant bequests to pious causes. The difficulty is increased because all these States, except Alabama and Kentucky, include the realty in their provisions. If there were realty exempted, it might be sold and the proceeds given to the pious causes. Where it is impossible to save the provisions of the statute by any device, it must yield to the right of the pious cause to receive what the testator intended.

168. The distinction between separate property and community property, though known to later Roman law, was not found in German law. It seems not to have been considered by canonists in connection with the law of testaments. Perhaps the reason is that community property belonged half to each spouse, divisible at death. Thus when the rule was made that the husband should grant one-third the value of his chattels to his children, one-third to his wife, and one-third to his soul, it contemplated community property as well as separate property. For there seems no good reason why a separate rule should be made as to the portion of his share of the community

setts provides that the spouse's share in default of issue (but with surviving relatives) shall be the maximum (c. 191, § 15); Mississippi has a similar provision, decreeing that no more than one-half the estate shall go to the spouse electing (§§ 3561, 3563); so, too, Pennsylvania (§ 8344); Virginia (§ 5276) and Wyoming (§ 88-101). West Virginia allows the share that would be taken if the decedent had left issue (§ 4091). Wisconsin grants one-third in any event (§ 233.14).

150 As in Alabama (§§ 7374, 7376, 10593); Kentucky (§§ 1393, 1401, 1404); Connecticut (up to $2,000.00 plus one-half the remainder; § 5161); Minnesota (§§ 8720, 8722, 8726).

151 Connecticut, *l. c.*, as to the amount over $2,000.00.

152 Illinois (c. 39, § 1; c. 41, § 10); Maryland (Art. 46, §§ 1, 2; Art. 93, § 125; Art. 93, §§ 310-311).

153 Nebraska (§§ 30-101, 30-102, 30-107, 30-108); New Hampshire (c. 306, §§ 10-13).

property which a testator might be permitted to bequeath to charity. Consequently, the same rule will be retained. The statutes of States recognizing community property vary.[154] Some are more liberal towards testamentary freedom than the rule just stated; others, less liberal. With the former there is no conflict.[155] Nevada and New Mexico are not in conflict when the husband is the decedent, for they allow him to dispose of one-half the property; but the decedent wife can not dispose of any of it. The whole belongs to the husband at her death.[156] But even in these two States it may be possible in a given case to pay pious legacies out of the separate property of the decedent. The amount available, however, should equal one-third or one-half the decedent's whole estate, if that much is required to meet the obligation of the bequests.

The same plan may possibly be followed in Idaho where the surviving spouse takes one-half the community property, and only the portion of the other half in excess of $25,000.00 is capable of being bequeathed; and in Texas, where one-half the community property descends to the surviving spouse, if there are children, otherwise the whole of it.[157]

169. There is no conflict as to the spouse's intestate share in the Civil Codes of foreign countries noted herein,[158] for the wife's property insofar as it is in the control of the husband, is controlled by him only as to the administration and income, and it remains her property, at her disposal at the dissolution of the marriage by death.

170. The rule stated [159] need not be applied to property held by joint tenancy or by the entireties,[160] that is, by husband and wife in such a way that at the death of either the whole property passes

[154] *Cf.* § 136, this treatise.

[155] Thus Arizona, California, and Washington permit one-half of the whole community property to be bequeathed; *cf.* California (§ 201); Arizona (§ 985); Washington (§ 1342).

And Louisiana gives one-half the property to each spouse for free disposal (Arts. 915, 916).

[156] Nevada (§§ 3364-3365); New Mexico (§§ 38-104, 38-105).

[157] Idaho (§ 14-113); Texas (Art. 2578).

[158] *Cf.* footnote n. 114 of this chapter.

[159] *Cf.* § 156, this treatise.

[160] *Cf.* § 138, this treatise.

to the other automatically. And this for two reasons. First, the property is held under this device as if by a corporation sole, and the goods of a corporation sole are not divided by death. In other words, the husband and the wife are really regarded as one and the same person, and this person continues to exist even after the husband or the wife dies. Second, when the husband and the wife take property by this device they deliberately surrender their right to make testamentary disposition of it. When it is conveyed to them by gift in this manner, either the donor wished that neither should have testamentary disposition of the undivided half; or the husband and the wife can be presumed to have acquiesced in this condition raised by the law at the moment they accepted the gift or during the time of proprietorship. For they could have agreed among themselves to a division of title even after coming into possession.[161]

The rule established is of more than theoretical importance, for it enables the Ordinary as executor to know how far he can admit the restrictions of secular law as to the rights of heirs without recurrence to the Sacred Congregation of the Council. Any infringement on the will of the testator not warranted by a general rule of law becomes in effect a commutation, a procedure which the Sacred Congregation reserves to itself.

171. Scholion I. The canons are concerned, as they have always been, not only for the rights of heirs but also for those of creditors. These rights occupied the attention of the Councils of the Middle Ages,[162] which expressly mention funeral expenses ;[163]

[161] "The properties of a joint estate are derived from its unity, which is four-fold; the unity of interest, the unity of title, the unity of time, and the unity of possession; or in other words, joint tenants have one and the same interest, accruing by one and the same conveyance, commencing at one and the same time, and held by one and the same undivided possession." Blackstone, *op. cit.*, II, 12, 180-187.

[162] Council of Cashel (1172), c. 6—Harduin, VI B, 1630; Council of Worcester (1240), c. 50—Harduin, VII, 345; Council of Lambeth (1261)—Harduin, VII, 543; Council of Avignon (1282), c. 10—Harduin, VII, 882; Council of Bourges (1286), c. 30—Harduin, VII, 960; Synod of Oxford (1287), c. 50—Harduin, VII, 1114; Council of Cologne (1536), c. 11—Harduin, IX, 2026; Mansi, XXXII, 1289 B.

[163] Constitution of Henry Chichley, Archbishop of Canterbury (1416)—

and the Council of Cashel (1172) includes wages.[164] More recent Councils have been equally solicitous for the payment of these claims.[165]

Blackstone and Rood, therefore, seem somewhat inaccurate in supposing that the Statute of Westminster 2nd, 13 Edward I (1285), indicates that the Ordinary was accustomed to divert the funds of decedents' estates from creditors who had claims against them.[166] Rood, indeed, admits that it has been thought that this statute was only declaratory of the common law as it had existed prior to this enactment, and that it was fashioned to remove doubt as to the method of proceeding. Pollock-Maitland explain the background of the statute and tell that the king's court was just at that time beginning to give the creditor an action against the executor. The purpose of the statute, they say, seems to be that creditor may have a similar action in the ecclesiastical court.[167]

The same authors trace the process by which the executor gradually became liable for the debts of the deceased. In the time of Glanvil (that is, of Henry II), the liability rested on the heir. It was similar to the obligation of the Roman law heir prior to the granting of the *separatio bonorum* under Justinian.[168] It was an unlimited obligation. By the time of Bracton (that is, of Henry III), the heir's legal liability was limited to the amount of the dead man's estate. But even in Bracton's eyes, the moral liability of the heir was unlimited. At first, then, it was the heir that was sued for debts, and he was sued in the secular courts. But gradually the idea grew that the executor could be sued for the debts. At first, it was thought proper to do this only when the testator had enjoined his executor

Mansi, XXVIII, 962 A; Council of Worcester (1240), *l. c.;* Synod of Oxford, *l. c.;* Council of Cologne (1536), *l. c.*

[164] *L. c.*

[165] Synod of Mount Lebanon (1736), pars. 2, c. 9, n. 3—*Coll. Lacensis,* II, 155 a; the Greco-Melchite Council (1835), c. 5—*Coll. Lacensis,* II, 583 a; Council of Westminster (1852), tit. 25, c. 8—*Coll. Lacensis,* III, 942; Council of Cashel (1852)—*Coll. Lacensis,* III, 838; Council of Halifax (1857), tit. 15, c. 4—*Coll. Lacensis,* III, 746.

[166] Blackstone, *op. cit.,* II, 32, 495; Rood, *op. cit.,* 97.

[167] *Op. cit.,* II, 360.

[168] *Cf.* § 101, this treatise.

to pay his debts. The debt was regarded by a fiction of the law as a legacy to the creditor. Thus, the creditor was permitted to go into the ecclesiastical court and sue for his debt. But it soon became plain that the justices of the secular courts were jealous of this new jurisdiction which was being exercised in the ecclesiastical courts. It was probably in the midst of this controversy that the statute in controversy was enacted in favor of the ecclesiastical courts. But the secular courts were eventually triumphant; and the creditor was ultimately compelled to seek his action in the secular tribunals.[169]

172. Scholion II. The Falcidian fourth and the Pegasian fourth[170] passed into the administration of wills during the Middle Ages. At that time, the executor took the place of the heir, and the commission was payable to him. But it could not be deducted from a legacy made to a pious cause, unless the executor were a monastery. Even the heir was forbidden to make such a deduction.[171]

The custom of awarding this commission seems to have carried into those systems which adopted the Roman law theory of the will after the twelfth century. There is no evidence of it in the canonical development of wills in England. Hence, it is unknown in the Anglo-American system.[172] But the Anglo-American systems allow the executor a smaller commission. It would seem that this commission should not be deducted from a legacy to a pious cause. The reasoning would be the same as that applied to the Falcidian fourth. It would seem manifest that the testator did not wish the pious cause to lose any portion of the bequest which he made to it. Consequently, when this commission is paid, it should not be charged against pious bequests, but against the estate generally.

[169] Pollock-Maitland, *op. cit.*, II, 346.

[170] See Art. 1, this chapter.

[171] S. C. C. *in Causa Bonien.*, 21 November, 1835—Pallottini, XI, 542; *in Causa Ferrarien.*, 30 November, 1830, § *Oratorum*—Pallottini, XI, 542; *in Causa Pergulana*, 27 June, 1857, § *Qui*—Pallottini, XI, 543 (the last case holds this to be the rule in all cases, not only when the heir attempts to frustrate the pious legacy); Pirhing, *op. cit.*, III, 26, 92; Soglia, *op. cit.*, II, 4, 123; C. 1, 3, 48, 1, 2; *Nov.*, 131, 1, 2.

[172] But the Civil Code of Louisiana (which derives indirectly from the Roman law system) expressly abolishes it (Art. 1616).

CHAPTER IV

THE CAPACITY OF THE TESTATOR

173. Canon 1513, § 1. "Qui ex iure naturae et ecclesiastico libere valet de suis bonis statuere, potest ad causas pias, sive per actum inter vivos sive per actum mortis causa, bona relinquere."

This paragraph of Canon 1513, while it states the qualifications required of the donor in a positive fashion, really states who is not disqualified. It does not state that the natural law gives any one the right to make a bequest to pious causes. But it does ordain that any one not disqualified by the natural or the ecclesiastical law may make such a bequest. It thus provides implicitly that the disqualifications of secular law are inoperative where bequests or gifts to pious causes are involved.

The distinction just noted is not without importance, because unless it be well understood, this canon might be used as an arguement to demonstrate that the right to have one's will enforced proceeds from the natural law. On the contrary, the canon simply states the rule of canon law as to the capacity required to make bequests to charity. It is a decree by which canon law asserts testamentary capacity.

174. But precisely because it is a capacitating provision, it might seem that it should not apply to any person who was not baptized. Only members of the Church, constituted such by baptism, are subject to the provisions of the canons.[1]

Pious causes, however, are subject to the jurisdiction of the canons. Now, Canon 1513, § 1, capacitates the pious cause to re-

[1] Canon 12. "Legibus mere ecclesiasticis non tenentur qui baptismum non receperunt, nec baptizati qui sufficienti rationis usu non gaudent, nec qui, licet rationis usum assecuti, septimum aetatis annum nondum expleverunt, nisi aliud iure expresse caveatur."

Canon 87. "Baptismate homo constuitur in Ecclesia Christi persona cum omnibus christianorum iuribus et officiis, nisi, ad iura quod attinet, obstet obex, ecclesiasticae communionis vinculum impediens, vel lata ab Ecclesia censura."

ceive the gift. It is not merely an act by which capacity is given to the donor to make the gift. Granted, then, that a gift was made to a pious cause by an unbaptized person, the gift is valid not only in the internal but also in the external forum. The law which has exclusive jurisdiction over the recipient determines by Canon 1513, § 1, that the act is legal. Consequently, it is beyond the province of secular law to hinder the pious cause from profiting by the bounty of the testator, unbaptized though he may have been and disqualified, perhaps, by the provisions of the secular law. He remains disqualified, in such a situation, for all secular gifts. In that sphere, the secular law is competent. But he is qualified for all gifts to charity.

175. But because the secular law is, in many particulars, an expansion of the natural law, it will happen that its rules often coincide with the dictates of the natural law. To that extent, the incapacity of the secular law will be at the same time an incapacity of the natural law. Therefore, an incapacity of this kind, created by secular law, is recognized by canon law. In order to know what are the disqualifications arising out of the natural law, it is a convenient approach to study the incapacities decreed by the secular law. That study will occupy the attention of the present chapter. There will be four articles: the first discussing the disqualification of age; the second, of mental unsoundness; the third, of undue influence; and the fourth, incapacities that seem the creatures of purely positive law, remotely connected, if at all, with the demands of nature.

Article 1

The Disqualification of Age

176. A child is able to exercise the power of choice at birth, but not of intelligent choice. Some years of development are required before intelligence begets discretion. Prior to the attainment of discretion, the child lacks one of the elements essentially necessary to the performance of a really human act. The making of a last will is essentially a human act; any last will that is not such can not be sustained.

When is a child considered to have sufficient discretion to make a will? This is an important problem, and its solution presupposes a knowledge of the rights a child may have in property. No one can dispose of that which is not his own. What kind of property, then, may a child own?

177. The child had no rights to property under the Roman law of early times. This followed as a corollary of the concept of the family as an economic unit. Whatever the child or grandchild acquired became the property of the family, which is another way of saying that it belonged to the *paterfamilias*. The child or grandchild under the *patria potestas* was as incapable of owning property as a slave.[2]

Some enjoyment of the family property might be allowed him, subject, however, to recall at the will of the *paterfamilias*. Even a slave might be granted a similar temporary enjoyment, for the purpose, v. gr., of carrying on some business transaction. Such property in the hands of the *filius familias* was known by the slave name, *peculium* or *peculium profectitium.*[3]

178. Property Rights of the *Filius Familias*. During the early Empire, however, the *filius familias* was empowered by imperial constitutions to hold as his own property his military pay, which thus came to be called the *peculium castrense.*[4] Later Constantine authorized him to hold as his own the salary he received as a State official, the *peculium quasi castrense.*[5] Finally, he was permitted by the authority of Justinian to hold for himself the property that came to him from his mother, his maternal relatives, or strangers, that is, the *bona materna* or the *bona adventicia.*[6] The last class of property, however, was subject to the life estate of the *paterfamilias*. Even if the child was emancipated, the *paterfamilias* was still entitled to a life estate in one-half this property.[8] But when he was emancipated, the child took *none* of the *peculium profectitium*.

[2] Gaius, 2, 87; 3, 163; Sherman, *op. cit.*, II, 509.

[3] D. 15, 1, 1, 5; D. 15, 1, 39.

[4] D. 49, 17, 1; Paul, *Sent.* 3, 4 a, 3; Sherman, *op. cit.*, II, 512.

[5] C. 12, 30, 1 (A. D. 320).

[6] C. 6, 60, 1.

[7] C. 6, 61, 6; I. 2, 9, 1.

[8] I. 2, 9, 2; Sherman, *op. cit.*, II, 446, 514.

But the *filius familias* could not dispose of it even with the consent of the *paterfamilias; cf.* D. 28, 1, 6 pr. Not even by a gift *mortis causa;* though

179. Property Rights of Minors in the United States. The *peculium profectitium*, or whatever corresponds to it, does not belong to the child under American law. On the other hand, the *bona adventicia* belong exclusively to him, though the father is the natural and logical administrator of that property. The earnings of the child are not his own, unless the father willingly gives them to him. Consequently, the property that would correspond to the *peculium castrense* and the *peculium quasi castrense* belong to the father.[9]

180. Thus in the United States, the property available for disposal by will is the *bona adventicia* only, with interest. In some countries, the child would have at his disposal the property corresponding to the *peculium castrense* and the *peculium quasi castrense*, that is, generally speaking, his salary or savings from his salary.

181. The Will of a *Filius Familias*. Under the Roman law, it was not until the period of the Empire that a person under a *paterfamilias* could make a will at all. It was then he was given authority to dispose of his *peculium castrense* and *quasi castrense*.[10]

as to the *peculium profectitium*, he could make such gifts with the consent of the *paterfamilias*; *cf.* D. 39, 5, 7, 4; D. 39, 6, 25, 1.

[9] Schouler, *Domestic Relations*, §§ 252, 267; Blackstone, *op. cit.*, I, 16, 453.

In Switzerland (Art. 295), Belgium (Art. 387), and Italy (Art. 229), the earnings also belong to the father. In England, the father has a right to them at least until the child reaches the age of sixteen and probably till the latter's majority; Slater, *Theol. Mor.*, I, 353, 354.

The earnings belong to the child in France (Art. 387), Germany (Art. 1651), and Mexico (Arts. 428-429).

Abroad, the father has ordinarily the use of the child's property until the latter comes of age or is emancipated. This is true in England. In France (Art. 384), it terminates when the child reached the age of eighteen. The same privilege is found in German law (Art. 1649); in Spanish law (Art. 160); in Italian law (Arts. 228, 229); in Switzerland (Arts. 290-294); in Belgium (Art. 384); and in Louisiana (Art. 223). In Austria, however, the father has only the administration of the child's property, and not even this right over property which the child has earned while living away from home (§§ 149, 151); and as to such earnings, the same provision is made by Italy (*l. c.*), Belgium (*l. c.*), and Spain (Art. 159).

[10] Ulpian, *Reg.*, 20, 10; Gaius, 2, 106; I. 2, 12 pr.; D. 45, 3, 18 pr.; C. 3, 28, 37 pr. and 1 a. Moyle says that Justinian granted the power of disposing by will of the *peculium quasi castrense*; *op. cit.*, I, 253. But the surviving *paterfamilias* retained a life estate in the *bona adventicia*.

182. The age at which a child, under Roman law, was regarded as possessing sufficient discretion to make a will is directly pertinent to the subject at hand. In the discussion so far, reference has been made to the *filius familas* as the person incapacitated. But the incapacity was due not necessarily to lack of discretion, for he might be a man of fifty years of age, if his *paterfamilias* lived to a sufficiently ripe age. On the other hand, a child of five years might be a *paterfamilias,* that is, the heir of the family, independent of any family power, *sui iuris.* The *filius familias* prior to the period of the Empire could make no will at all; and even after that, only as to the *peculium castrense* and *quasi castrense.* At what age could the *paterfamilias* make a will? It was when he reached the age of puberty that he was considered competent, that is, when a boy was fourteen years old; a girl, twelve.[11]

183. The rule that at the age of puberty children could make wills was adopted by the ecclesiastical courts, and the age was accepted as fourteen or twelve respectively, according to the rule of Justinian. This is especially true of England where children at that age could make wills without the consent of their guardian, though they were prohibited from making wills at an earlier age even with that consent. When it was made lawful to devise lands by the Statute 34 and 35 Henry VIII, c. 5 (1542-1543), the age set for

[11] I. 2, 12, 1; I. 1, 22 pr.; C. 5, 60, 3.

These ages were fixed by Justinian, following the Proculian school—Sherman, *op. cit.,* I, 74.

A woman, even when she was *sui iuris* was *in tutela,* that is, under perpetual guardianship, until she married; *cf.* Gaius, I, 144; 190. Hadrian empowered women to make a will with the authority of their guardian, but without *coemptio.* The next step in woman's emancipation was made when the pretor gave *bonorum possessio* to her legatee under a will she had made without the authority of her guardian; *cf.* Gaius, 2, 118-122.

When her guardian refused to consent to her making a will, she had recourse to a subterfuge, the details of which were something like the following; she compelled him to sell her by *mancipatio,* or more specifically, *coemptio,* by which sale she was conceived as passing into the *manus* of the buyer, viz., by a fictitious marriage. There was an accompanying understanding that the person who bought her would manumit her. Then she could have a more compliant guardian; Gaius, I, 115 a. The guardianship of women was abolished in 410; *cf.* C. 8, 58, 1. Thenceforward a woman could make a will as freely as a man.

making such devises was twenty-one. The same age was set for personalty by the Statute of Wills, 1 Victoria, c. 26, § 7 (1837). Such is the law in England today.[12]

184. In the United States, the age limit seems to be lowest in Georgia, where only those under fourteen years of age are considered lacking the discretion necessary.[13] Louisiana sets the age at sixteen.[14] The age of eighteen is favored by many States with many variations in the privileges allowed at that time. Some States make no distinction as to sex or the kind of property that may be bequeathed, simply bestowing testamentary capacity on those who have attained this age.[15] The right is restricted at this age to women in some jurisdictions,[16] and to married women, in others.[17] A restriction is made as to property in other States, which permit bequests of personalty at eighteen, but devises of realty only at twenty-one.[18]

[12] Rood, *op. cit.*, 106; Blackstone, *op. cit.*, II, 32, 497.

[13] § 3839. But Maryland allows wills touching personalty to be made by children of fourteen and twelve respectively (Art. 93, § 331).

Fourteen is the age in Spain (Art. 663); Portugal (Arts. 365 and 1764); Panama (Art. 695); and Mexico. Chile requires the age of puberty; Japan, fifteen. Hungary permits a will to be made by children of twelve years, but if the child is under eighteen he can make his will only in the presence of a notary. Austria also allows a child under eighteen to make a will before a notary (Art. 569). And in Norway, a will made by a child under eighteen is valid, if confirmed by royal decree. *Cf.* digests of the laws of these countries in Martindale and Hubbell, *s. v.*, "Wills."

[14] Art. 1477. France and Belgium set the same age for one-half the estate; Art. 904. Germany allows wills at this age if made before a magistrate; Art. 2228. *Cf.* Martindale and Hubbell, *s. v.*, "Wills."

[15] California (§ 20); Connecticut (§ 4875); Idaho (§ 14-301); Montana (§ 6974); Nevada (§ 9905); North Dakota (§ 5640); Oklahoma (§ 1536); South Dakota (§ 604); Utah (§ 101-1-1).

This is the age also in the Philippine Islands, in Italy (Art. 763); Argentina, Denmark, Netherlands, and Norway, *cf.* Martindale and Hubbell for the law of these countries, *s. v.*, "Wills."

[16] Illinois (c. 148 § 1); District of Columbia (tit. 29, § 21); Minnesota (§ 8735); Oregon (§ 10-501). This provision holds in Maryland as to realty (Art. 93, § 331).

[17] Maine (c. 88, § 1); Nebraska (§ 38-101); Wisconsin (§ 238.01).

[18] Alabama (§§ 10577, 10582); Arkansas (§§ 10492, 10493); New York (§§ 10, 15); Rhode Island (§§ 4292, 4295); South Carolina (§ 8915; *cf.* Posey

Colorado's provisions are the same except that the age for bequeathing personalty is seventeen.[19] The exception in Kansas is based on marriage, and married persons have testamentary capacity at eighteen.[20] Marriage itself seems to endow the parties with testamentary capacity in other States, without any further specification of age.[21] The remaining eighteen States require simply the age of twenty-one for all wills, all persons, and all kinds of property.[22]

The age disability can be removed in some jurisdictions by the action of the court.[23]

185. Two problems arise under Canon 1513, § 1, touching the

v. Posey, 1848, 3 Strobhart 167, Ann. Cases, 12 A 622); Virginia (§§ 5227, 5228). The right to bequeath personalty at eighteen is given only to males in Missouri (§§ 505, 506).

19 § 5184.

20 §§ 22-201; 38-101.

21 Arizona (§ 3636); Iowa (§ 11846); New Hampshire (c. 297, § 1); Texas (Art. 8281).

Sweden makes the same provision but allows a person at sixteen to dispose of his own earnings even if unmarried; otherwise, he must have attained the age of twenty-one.

22 Delaware (§§ 3050, 3240); Florida (§ 5457; *cf.* Beekman v. Beekman, 1907, 53 Fla. 858, 43 So. 923); Indiana (§ 3449); Kentucky (§ 4826); Massachusetts (c. 191, § 1); Michigan (§ 13478); Mississippi (§ 3550); New Jersey (§§ 2616, 5862, 5871); New Mexico (§ 154-101); North Carolina (§ 4128); Ohio (§§ 8023, 10503); Pennsylvania (§ 8307); Tennessee (§ 8098); Vermont (§ 2744); Washington (§ 1394); West Virginia (§§ 4039, 4040); Wyoming (§ 88-101).

Alaska (§ 563) has the same provisions and the following provinces of Canada: Alberta, British Columbia, New Brunswick, Nova Scotia, Ontario, Prince Edward Island, Quebec, and Saskatchewan. *Cf.* Martindale and Hubbell, *s. v.*, "Wills."

23 *E. g.*, Alabama (at the age of eighteen; § 8280); Arkansas (at eighteen for men, sixteen for women; *M & H*); Kentucky (Simmons v. Stewart, 1923, 198 Ky. 330, 248 S. W. 892); Louisiana (at fifteen, by emancipation by the father before a notary and two witnesses; Art. 366); Mississippi (§§ 353-357); Oklahoma (§ 1756); Tennessee (§§ 10370-10374); Texas (at nineteen; Arts. 5291-5293).

France provides similarly (at fifteen, if the parents are living; at eighteen, if parents deceased; Art. 480 ff). So, too, Austria (§ 174) and Switzerland (Art. 18). *Cf.* Martindale and Hubbell, *s. v.*, "Infants."

wills of minors. One concerns the age at which a will may be made; the other, the property of which disposition may be made.

186. As to the first, puberty seems to be the lowest limit beyond which modern secular jurisprudence does not recognize testamentary capacity. Indeed, this doctrine rests on the Roman law and on the law of the English ecclesiastical courts. Is this the age limit to be adopted under Canon 1513, § 1? [24] The answer seems to be suggested in Canon 88, § 3.[25] Persons who have completed their seventh year are legally presumed to possess discretion; those under that age are presumed to lack it. On the other hand, the canons recognize clearly that there is something of discretion lacking in those who have not reached the age of puberty. Canon 2230 exempts such persons from all ecclesiastical penalties stated by the general law.[26] Canon 1067 constitutes as a diriment impediment for marriage the age below sixteen for men, and fourteen for women.[27] And Canon 555 invalidates the year of the novitiate, if it is begun before the fifteenth year is completed.[28]

Thus it would seem that the canons require the age of discretion in those whom they would regard as capable of transacting the business of adults whether for good or evil. Nevertheless, there seems no good and sufficient reason to depart from the ordinary significance of the terms of Canon 1513, § 1. Hence the provision of

[24] Canon 1513, § 1. *Cf.* § 173 for the text of this canon.

[25] Canon 88, § 3. "Impubes, ante plenum septennium, dicitur infans seu puer vel parvulus et censetur non sui compos; expleto autem septennio, usum rationis habere praesumitur. Infanti assimilantur quotquot usu rationis sunt habitu destituti."

[26] Canon 2230. "Impuberes excusantur a poenis latae sententiae, et potius punitionibus educativis, quam censuris aliisve gravioribus vindicativis corrigantur; puberes vero qui eos ad legem violandam induxerint vel cum eis in delictum concurrerint ad normam can. 2209, §§ 1-3, ipsi quidem poenam lege statutam incurrunt."

[27] Canon 1067, § 1. "Vir ante decimum sextum aetatis annum completum, mulier ante decimum quartum item completum, matrimonium validum inire non possunt."

[28] Canon 555, § 1. "Praeter alia quae in can. 542 ad novitiatus validitatem enumerantur, novitiatus ut valeat, peragi debeat: 1°. Post completum decimum quintum saltem aetatis annum; 2°. Per annum integrum et continuum; 3°. In domo novitiatus."

Canon 18 must be followed.[29] Consequently, it must be concluded that any person above the age of seven years, completed, is presumed by the canons endowed with sufficient discretion to be able to make a gift to pious causes even by will; but this presumption yields to proof in the individual case.

187. Parental Consent. Nevertheless, Canon 89 must be observed by the minor.[30] Consequently, in making a will or a bequest to pious causes, every person who has not completed his twenty-first year, that is, until the day after his twenty-first birthday,[31] must do it only with the consent of his parents or guardian. There is no exemption for the making of wills from the general provisions of the law.

He is bound by this obligation whether he be married or emancipated by civil process, until he has reached the age of majority as determined by the canons. The law does not exempt him, when it might easily do so, especially as the latter part of Canon 89 does exempt those whom canon law withdraws from the power of the father. If the legislator had any other exemption in mind, certainly the statement of the one would have suggested the other.

188. But the consent of the parent or guardian does not seem to be necessary for the validity of the will. The failure to obtain the consent would seem rather to render the will rescindible.[32] Thus the will is capable of tacit ratification either by the minor him-

[29] Canon 18. "Leges ecclesiasticae intelligendae sunt secundum propriam verborum significationem in textu et contextu consideratam; quae si dubia et obscura manserit, ad locos Codicis parallelos, si qui sint, ad legis finem ac circumstantias et ad mentem legislatoris est recurrendum."

[30] Canon 88, § 1. "Persona quae vicesimum primum aetatis annum explevit, maior est; infra hanc aetatem, minor."

Canon 89. "Persona maior plenum habet suorum iurium exercitium; minor in exercitio suorum iurium potestati parentum vel tutorum obnoxia manet, iis exceptis in quibus ius minores a patria potestate exemptos habet."

[31] Canon 34, § 3, 3°. "Si terminus *a quo* non coincidat cum initio diei, ex. gr., *decimus quartus aetatis annus, annus novitiatus, octiduum a vacatione sedis episcopalis, decendium ad appellandum*, etc., primus dies ne computetur et tempus finiatur expleto ultimo die eiusdem numeri."

[32] Canon 11. "Irritantes aut inhabilitantes eae tantum leges habendae sunt, quibus aut actum esse nullum aut inhabilem esse personam expresse vel aequivalenter statuitur."

self after he attains the age of majority, or by the parent. If the will is not revoked by either, tacit ratification will be presumed.

But what shall be said of tacit ratification, if the parent or guardian knew nothing of the will until after the decease of the minor testator. Does the will become irrevocable by his death, on the ground that he is no longer capable of revoking it? It would seem that this is faulty reasoning, for the right to rescind resides primarily in the parent or guardian.

Nevertheless, for two reasons it would seem that in such circumstances the will can not be attacked. The first reason is that to attempt to rescind the will would be to attack a bequest to charity, which can not be modified or renewed by the donor, as it could be if he were still alive. His death seems to bring his gift indisputably within the province of Canon 1513, § 1. If the will on the face of it demonstrates that it is as reasonable as if the parent or guardian had intervened, indisputable evidence is thereby afforded that the testator was not incapacitated by the law of nature. Nor is he incapacitated by the canons, for their only provision requires that he have the consent of his parents before performing the act of testamentary disposition.

The second reason is that at death the guardian ceases to have a ward. Hence the basis of his authority is gone. The will is subject not to him, but to public authority, and to the interpretation of the ecclesiastical judge, who is the Ordinary.[33] It then becomes the duty of the Ordinary to determine whether the minor showed sufficient discretion in making the will. The minor should be expected to make due provision for his parents as explained when the rights of heirs were discussed [34] and failure to do so would result in an official obligation of the Ordinary to correct this fault.

189. As to the property of which a minor may make testa-

[33] Canon 1515, § 1. "Ordinarii omnium piarum voluntatum tam mortis causa quam inter vivos exsecutores sunt."

When a free-born woman made a will without the authority of her guardian (after Hadrian had authorized such a will to be made with the guardian's consent), the pretor upheld it by granting a *bonorum possessio* to the legatee under it; Gaius, I, 115 a; 2, 118-22.

[34] *Cf.* § 156, this treatise.

mentary disposition, the simplest answer is that he may give away what is his own. As was indicated, gifts from friends and property he has inherited belong to him in the United States, but not his earnings. In foreign countries, the earnings usually belong to the child.[35] The provisions of secular law govern as to what property the child may acquire in ownership; and consequently indirectly as to what funds are at his disposal for distribution to pious causes.

The statutes of various States restricting the amount of property that may be bequeathed to charity affect the bequests of minors as well as those of adults, wherever the former are permitted to make a will under the age of twenty-one.[36]

Article 2

The Disqualification of Mental Unsoundness

190. A testamentary disposition must be made with an understanding of the relation of the act to objective reality. Otherwise, it can not be said to be the act of a human being. What constitutes a sufficient understanding of this relation is necessarily difficult to determine. Intelligence ranges through many degrees. Certainly even though the person who performed the act lacked the understanding of an average man, his action could nevertheless be an intelligent act. Nevertheless there are certain symptoms which clearly indicate that the person acting does not grasp the significance of what he is doing, at least not sufficiently that it might be said he was acting as a human being. It is clear on occasion that certain actions are not intended to have their normal meaning.

Even a vague understanding of the implications of the deed rescues it from being irrational. In a case where it is doubted whether the testator had sufficient understanding of the consequences of his bequests to charity, the decision rests with the Ordinary. In rendering his judgment, the Ordinary will weigh the symptoms, calling to his aid the testimony of experts, if need be, according to the prescription of Canon 1792.[37] But the Ordinary is not bound to follow their

[35] *Cf.* §§ 179, 180, this treatise.

[36] *Cf.* §§ 114-118; 156-159, this treatise.

[37] Canon 1792. "Peritorum opera utendum est quoties ex iuris vel iudicis

testimony, even should all agree.[38] Since a great deal of discretion rests with the Ordinary himself, he should have a knowledge of the symptoms by which a man might betray his incapacity to make a will. The conclusions of the secular system may profitably be reviewed, therefore, not as conclusive, but as illuminating.[39]

191. **They who are habitually deprived of the use of reason are regarded by the canons as infants,** that is, as children who have not reached the age of seven years.[40] But this provision means they are merely presumed to lack the use of reason, and this presumption, of course, yields to proof. The significance of the presumption is not that men are presumed to lack the use of reason until it has been proved that they possess it. Rather the presumption is just the contrary. Consequently, they who attack a will because of an alleged infirmity of mind in the testator, must prove that he was habitually insane or that he was actually insane at the moment he made the will. Granted that sufficient proof is brought forth that he was habitually insane, a presumption is raised that he was insane at the moment the will was made. But this presumption can be overthrown by contra-

praescripto eorum examen et votum requiritur ad factum aliquod comprobandum vel ad veram alicuius rei natura dignoscendam."

[38] Canon 1804, § 1. "Iudex non peritorum tantum conclusiones, etsi concordes, sed cetera quoque causae adiuncta attente perpendat."

[39] Under Roman law it was not always clear whether *furiosi* could make a will, but at length they were forbidden to do so except in a lucid interval; *cf.* C. 6, 22, 9; I. 2, 12, 1. Moreover, they were always under the necessity of exercising their legal rights through a guardian. This restriction applied to the two classes of mentally incompetent persons. One class was that of the imbeciles; *the stulti, the fatui, the insani, the simplices, the mente capti; cf.* D. 22, 3, 25, 1; D. 26, 10, 3, 18; D. 27, 1, 6, 19; I. 1, 23, 4. The other class was that of the insane: *the furiosi* (maniacs) and *the dementes* (lunatics); *cf.* D. 26, 5, 8, 1; C. 5, 4, 25. There was no legal difference between *the furiosi* and *the dementes; cf.* Sherman, *op. cit.*, II, 445.

Guardianship of *furiosi* is an institution of very ancient origin, as it is found in the *XII Tables;* 5, 7. Later guardianship was extended to the imbecile as well; *cf.* I, 1, 23, 3-4; D. 27, 10, 1 pr.; D. 27, 10, 14; D. 27, 1, 1, 5; C. 5, 34, 2; C. 5, 70, 1.

[40] Canon 88, § 3. "Impubes, ante plenum septennium, dicitur infans seu puer vel parvulus et censetur non sui compos; expleto autem septennio, usum rationis habere praesumitur. Infanti assimilantur quotquot usu rationis sunt habitu destituti."

dictory proof. It may be shown that, though the testator was habitually insane, he had a lucid interval at the moment he made the will. This procedure agrees with the judiciary practice in the United States.

192. Roman law had already recognized a distinction between two general forms of insanity. One was deficiency; the other, derangement. Deficiency is found in those deprived of the use of reason; derangement in those in whom reason is distorted, operating from premises so false as to be absurd.

193. The consequences of mental deficiency will be first considered. The lack of reasoning power may be permanent or temporary. But where it is temporary, the person laboring under it does not come within the scope of Canon 88, § 3, unless the affliction can be regarded as habitual for the period of its duration. Nevertheless, a will made while one lacked the use of reason would be made by one unable, at least for the time being, to dispose of his goods according to the law of nature. And persons thus incapable are not qualified under Canon 1513, § 1.

194. Temporary lack of reason is found in those who are asleep, under the influence of intoxicating drink,[41] in the throes of feverish delirium, or suffering from physical or nervous shock. Persons laboring under such a temporary disability are incapable under the natural law of making reasonable disposition of their property, and consequently they are unable, during the period of the deficiency, to make a valid bequest even to pious causes.

195. Permanent lack of reason may be found in persons who have never possessed it and in those who, though they once enjoyed it, have lost it.

The feeble-minded are those who have never had the use of reason, or at least not sufficient use of it to enable them to dispose properly of their goods. Certainly, idiots can not make a will, even with the consent of their guardians, unless they have sufficient understanding to know what sort of an instrument is being drawn up. And by the definition of an idiot, he is regarded as lacking that degree of understanding.

Where the deficiency does not prevent the testator from under-

[41] Cocchi, *op. cit.*, VI, 192; De Meester, *op. cit.*, 1465; Wernz, *op. cit.*, III, 276.

standing what is being done, he should be regarded as an *impubes*, capable of making a will with the consent of his guardian. For the sole test of ability to make bequests to charity is the ability to reason.

Persons who once enjoyed the power of reasoning but have lost it are in the same position as idiots, so far as their capacity to make bequests is concerned. But there is a real problem where these persons are concerned, because their faculties ebb away slowly, and it is sometimes difficult to determine in a particular case whether the afflicted person was sufficiently competent to have testamentary capacity. For, even under the American decisions, one almost destitute of reason may make a will.[42]

196. The general rule satisfying the natural law for the testamentary dispositions of both types of the feeble-minded can perhaps be stated as the following. At the time at which the will is made, the testator must understand the meaning and the general effect of the act he is performing, with a memory sufficiently strong to gather all the elements together mentally, without prompting, and to hold them in his mind long enough to enable him to grasp their more evident relations and to make a rational judgment concerning them. The elements that memory should be capable of holding before his mind are: the persons whom the testator should favor; their merits and their needs; the proportion in which he has aided them in the past relative to one another; and the amount, value, and condition of his property.

It is the *power* to remember that the courts consider, not the actual *fact* of remembering. Thus a will may be construed as valid even though one of the elements was forgotten, if the court is satisfied that the testator had the power to remember it, had it not been for inadvertence.

197. Wills have been held valid, in accordance with this rule, or void, according to circumstances. The decisions have been rendered in cases where wills were executed by persons whom age had rendered mentally feeble or forgetful; who were on their death beds and close to death; who were habitual drunkards and somewhat muddled by drink when the will was made; who were suffering great pain in

[42] Rood, *op. cit.*, 111.

addition to physical weakness induced by previous pain; or who never had much sense. It is possible that in spite of these handicaps, the testator retains as much mental competence as the courts demand.[43]

198. The mentally deranged form the second general class of the insane. The derangement from which they suffer may be permanent, recurrent, or temporary. It may affect the person's judgments only in certain matters. It may be caused by disease of the brain or of the nervous system, as paresis, which "is a syphilitic disease of the nervous system, progressive and incurable, characterized in typical cases by 'delusions of grandeur' that make the patient think that he is a notable personality, very wealthy, etc., but capable of simulating any known mental disorder."[44] It may be the result of a drug habit or of disease in other portions of the body. Or it may be the consequence of abnormal mental reactions to the realities of life, as *dementia precox,* which is marked by early dementia, or general disintegration of the mind, and is usually preceded by "peculiar bizarre behavior, loss of interest in the outside world, lack of correspondence between intellectual states and their emotional expression, hallucinations and delusions;"[45] or as *paranoia,* which is "a

[43] Rood, *l. c.*

Blackstone included among those unable to make wills on the ground of lack of reason persons who were *born* deaf, blind, *and* dumb. This was because they had always lacked the common inlets of understanding. But this theory no longer commands respect. Such persons are to be judged by the rule just stated; *cf.* Blackstone, *op. cit.,* II, 32, 497; Rood, *op. cit.,* 114. If the testator can find means of expressing his will, and has sufficient understanding of what he is doing, the will is valid. The difficulty for a person who is deaf, dumb, and blind, lies in the giving of adequate expression to his will in terms that will make it acceptable in the external forum.

There may be some connection between the Roman law and the theory which Blackstone advances. A deaf-mute could not make the will *per aes et libram; cf.* D. 28, 1, 6; Ulpian, *Reg.,* 20, 13. Justinian removed the testamentary incapacity except as to those who were deaf-mutes from birth, but required that a mute should write the whole will with his own hand; *cf.* C. 6, 22, 10; I. 2, 12, 3; Moyle, *op. cit.,* I, 253. A blind man could make a will under Roman law, provided he did it in the presence of a notary, or if a notary could not be obtained, in the presence of an additional witness; *cf.* C. 6, 22, 8.

[44] Moore, *Dynamic Psychology,* p. 423.

[45] Moore, *op. cit.,* p. 416.

form of insanity that has its roots in the intellectual life and leads the patient to false interpretations of the actions of others and to the weaving of schemes and speculations that have no foundation in reality." [46]

199. The symptoms of these derangements indicate their presence in the individual case. They are discernible in the conduct, in the beliefs, and in the preferences which the afflicted persons disclose. If these seem extravagant and unwarranted, there is evidence to suspect that the person is not in his right mind. If they become so extreme as to be absurd, they leave little room to escape the conclusion that the person is insane.

200. The conduct of the person may often be a symptom of his distorted mentality. Abnormal conduct is one of the means by which his affliction can be discerned. Measuring a man's conduct by propriety and accepted norms of action can be of some help as a test. Yet perfectly sane persons may act contrary to these norms. The better test is a comparison of the present and past conduct of the same person. A rather prolonged departure, without adequate external cause, from the state of feeling and the modes of thinking usual to him when he was in health, is a genuine feature of a disordered mind. Has he who was refined, mild, kind, and affectionate, become vulgar, scurrilous, abusive, and hateful? Or was he always so? Has anything occurred which might produce this change without inducing a distortion of mind?[47]

Men are presumed sane. Consequently an attempt must be made to explain even abnormal conduct as the conduct of a sane man. The man's temperament may explain what otherwise would seem preposterous. The circumstances that attended the absurd conduct may have been unusual. Dignified men have been known to act as small boys at football games. As to the will itself, is there evidence of deliberation in the drafting of it, even though the provisions are absurd. For men may be cynical and perverse without being insane.[48] Finally, the subject's own recognition of his oddities is a circumstance almost sufficient to preclude the judgment of distorted mental facul-

[46] Moore, *op. cit.*, p. 423.
[47] Rood, *op. cit.*, 119.
[48] Rood, *op. cit.*, 124.

ties. For insane persons usually do not know of their eccentricity.[49]

201. Preferences as a basis for determining mental derangement must also be approached with caution, even when they seem monstrous. Even a sane man may delight in what is repugnant to the sensibilities of most men or he may despise what others hold sacred. It would not be reasonable to suppose that preferences are due to insanity when they can just as easily be attributed to the person's peculiar habits, temperament, experience, and education. Even the basest depravity does not incapacitate a person as to testamentary dispositions.

Illustrations of these preferences in sane men can be drawn from the decisions of the courts. Sanity was the verdict in the case of a man who lived in a small room, wore shabby clothing, almost never washed, ate with his fingers, and rejoiced in his constant repetitions of vulgar jokes. The same verdict was reached in the case of a man who annoyed the poor, offering frequently to give them a ride to market, and then driving off at a furious pace in the wrong direction, setting them down eventually many miles away from their destination. This was true also in the case of a man who ate with his cats and dogs, played a violin while his wife lay dead in the house, and slept in the box in which she was to be buried. The opposite, however, was held in the case of a woman who kept dogs in kennels in her drawing room and furnished her cats with plates and napkins.[50]

Dislike of relatives is no proof of insanity in itself, but it may be accepted as evidence of it, if the dislike came as the result of a sudden aversion of feeling without any accountable external circumstance.[51]

202. Beliefs affords symptoms of mental derangement. It is from these particularly that partial insanity is often detected in a person otherwise apparently sane. When they are discerned in a person otherwise sane, they are known as delusions.[52]

[49] Rood, *op. cit.*, 120.

[50] Rood, *op. cit.*, 121. For the first case *cf. In re* Knight's Estate (1895), 167 Pa. 453, 31 Atl. 682. For the second, *cf.* Frere v. Peacocke (1846), 1 Rob. Ecc. 442. For the third, *cf.* Bennett v. Hibbert (1893), 88 Ia. 154, 55 N. W. 93.

[51] Rood, *op. cit.*, 122, 123.

[52] The following is a test of insanity based on beliefs given in the leading case

Absurdity of belief may be difficult to establish. The ideas that are common at any given period of history may be wrong, but the belief that contradicts them will seem contemporaneously to be absurd. But as long as men must be judges, they must judge by the state of the knowledge accepted by the public opinion of their time, unless the person who is at variance with it can show reasons that convince their intelligence. It would be unsafe, perhaps, to judge a man insane, or under a delusion, simply because his notions on certain subjects seem contrary to general beliefs. It would be wise to demand certain corroborating evidence.

Apparent absurdity of belief as the sole basis for a judgment of insanity is not a safe test. The opinions of Galileo and Columbus seemed absurd enough, but they were not used to convict those men of insanity. If they were called insane, it was only as an insult; not because any one really believed that they were.[53]

If sufficient external explanation of an absurd belief can be found, such as would explain its presence in a sane man, it is not to be regarded as indicating insanity. Investigation should be attempted with a view to discovering whether there was any influence at work capable of producing this belief in a mind that might be

of Dew v. Clark (1826), 3 Addams Ecc. 79, at p. 90: "Whenever the patient once conceives something extravagant to exist which still has no existence whatever but in his own heated imagination; and whenever, at the same time, having once so conceived, he is incapable of being, or at least of being permanently, reasoned out of that conception, such a patient is said to be under a delusion in a peculiar, half-technical sense of the term; and the absence or presence of delusion, so understood, forms, in my judgment, the true and only test of absent or present insanity. In short, I look upon delusion in this sense of it, and insanity, to be almost, if not altogether, convertible terms; so that a patient, under a delusion, so understood, on any subject or subjects in any degree, is for that reason essentially mad or insane on such subject or subjects in that degree."

[53] Thus belief in spiritism is not admitted by the courts as an evidence of insanity. And a will granting the greater part of the estate of a testatrix to a society for the promotion of Christian Science, revoking a previous will, was held valid, even though the beneficiary under the previous will was a sister of the testatrix and it seemed that the latter had been led to make the new will by the erroneous belief that she had recoverd her health through the society and that her sisters had persecuted her for her belief. Rood, *op. cit.*, 125-130; *cf. In re* Brush's Will (1901), 35 Misc. Rep. 689, 72 N. Y. Supp. 421.

superstitious, suspicious, credulous, prejudiced, or illogical, but not insane. If any such influence can be found, the belief must not be regarded as an insane delusion.[54]

203. Lucid Intervals. Granted, however, that the Ordinary is convinced that a state of mental derangement actually existed in the testator, what is its effect? Does the fact that a person suffers insane delusions invalidate a will either in whole or in part?

Some persons suffer these delusions only at intervals. It seems clear enough that in a lucid interval, that is, at a time when he is free from the delusions and in possession of his faculties, he can make a valid will. This conclusion seems valid even though the disease that may be at the root of the evil has not been cured, and even if it is constantly growing worse. The secular courts would admit as much, and it seems to be the correct principle also under the canons. For by their provisions a man who has lucid intervals and is not *habitually* deprived of the use of reason, is capable of making a valid will during one of those intervals.

Some persons suffer insane delusions on definite subjects only, being perfectly normal as to other matters. Whether such a delusion be continuous or recurrent, a person thus afflicted can make a valid will, provided the delusion does not touch the subject matter of the will or the beneficiaries under it or the heirs.[55]

204. Actionable Interest Necessary to Contest the Will. If

[54] On this doctrine, verdict was for sanity in spite of an erroneous belief entertained by the testator that his wife was unfaithful (*cf.* Scott's Estate, 1900, 128 Cal. 57, 60 Pac. 527); that a child was illegitimate (*cf.* Clapp v. Fullerton, 1866, 34 N. Y. 190, Redfield Cas. 105); that a son who had taken sides with a neighbor belonging to the same lodge was conspiring with the latter to defraud the testator of his land (*cf. In re* White's Will, 1890, 121 N. Y. 406, 24 N. E. 935); that a brother was a rogue (*cf.* Stevens v. Leonard, 1900, 154 Ind. 67, 56 N. E. 27). In each case, there was sufficient evidence of the falsity of the belief, yet because it was false it was not necessarily an insane delusion. It was not ground for declaring the will invalid.

[55] Judge Cooley said of the effect of such singular delusions: "A man may believe himself to be the Supreme Ruler of the universe, and nevertheless make a perfectly sensible disposition of his property, and the courts will sustain it when it appears that his mania did not dictate its provisions." Fraser v. Jennison (1879), 42 Mich. 206, at p. 232, 3. N. W. 882.

a testator has omitted a person from his will because of an insane delusion, the latter can not attack the will unless he is entitled to succeed *ab intestato* or on some other title, should the will be declared invalid. In other words, he must have an actionable interest in the estate that has been bequeathed away from him.

If a nephew failed to be remembered by his uncle because of such a delusion, he would have no right of action as long as there were sons to take *ab intestato*. The same would be true in the case of a pious cause, which the testator had intended to remember prior to suffering an insane delusion in regard to it. The pious cause would have no redress. For even if the will were declared invalld, the pious cause would not benefit by the declaration.

If the pious cause was written beneficiary in a previous will, the case would be different. The courts will not permit a course of succession, thus established by will, to be interrupted by an insane delusion.[56]

205. On the other hand, insane delusions in favor of a beneficiary defeat the legacy. Thus a legacy bequeathed to a charitable cause under a delusion that the testator was morally bound to leave his property to it was held invalid on the ground that it was made under the influence of an insane delusion.[57]

In view of what has been said already, it would seem that it was not necessary to consider this an insane delusion. Indeed, it probably would not have been considered such if there had not been other evidence helping to show that the legacy was the fruit of an insane mind. Surely such a belief can be founded on reasonable arguments; and it is not inconceivable that a sane man might have exactly the same notion. If such a bequest were contested on the ground of error, there might be better ground for attack; what the result of such an attack would be will appear from the discussion on error that will be presented in the scholion following this article.[58]

[56] So it would be, too, if the insane delusion resulted in the disinheriting of a son who would succeed otherwise *ab intestato;* for the insane delusion would thus interrupt the course of succession.

[57] Rood, *op. cit.*, 136. *Cf.* American Bible Society v. Price (1886), 115 Ill. 623, 5 N. E. 126.

[58] Clearer examples of insane delusion are the following: that the Lord had

206. The Proof of Sanity in Probating a Will. Where proof of sanity or insanity is required, the presumption of sanity makes a *prima facie* case for the validity of the will, unless the will is contested. If the will is contested, the burden of proof rests upon the person who defends the will. He is aided, of course, by the presumption of sanity, but if there is evidence to nullify that presumption, even without proving insanity, the will is regarded as insufficiently proved.

A few courts hold that even where there is no contest, the person offering the will to the court must prove that the testator had capacity; a few others place the burden of proof on the person who contests the will, that is, he must show by the preponderance of evidence that the testator was insane. If he fails, the will is regarded as valid.[59]

207. The Ordinary should regard the will as made by one capable of testamentary disposition, unless the will is contested. Then if evidence is offered to nullify the presumption of sanity, he should require proof of the testator's sanity from the person claiming legacies under it. This is the more common rule in the secular courts, and it seems to be the more reasonable.

However, a person who is known to suffer delusions is presumed to be insane as to everything that he does, and the bequest must be adjudged void, unless it is proved that the delusions did not affect it.[60]

Ordinaries should seek the testimony of alienists, as has been already indicated.[61] But it seems that as well as alienists, laymen should be called on, to testify as to whether they judged the testator sane, provided they substantitate their belief with reasons, which the Ordinary should weigh for what they are worth.[62]

208. The time at which soundness of mind in the testator must be proved to have existed, is the time when the will was made.

commanded the testator to make the will, directing the disposition made in it; that the beneficiary was a supernatural person sent by God to redeem the world from its sins.

[59] Rood, *op. cit.*, 137 a.

[60] Card. Lega, *De delictis et poenis*, n. 38; Sole, *De delictis et poenis*, § 23, n. 1.

[61] *Cf.* § 190, this treatise.

[62] Laymen are thus admitted in the secular courts of the United States. Rood, *op. cit.*, 137 a.

But it is admissible to show the state of mind of the testator for a period long preceding the time of the making of the will. His mental capacity in the days following close on the making of the will, may also be shown. But even official adjudication of insanity made by the court a short time before or after the date of the will is not conclusive evidence that the will was invalid for insanity.

The Ordinary, therefore, should not accept an adjudication of insanity as conclusively invalidating a bequest to charity. It may be accepted as weighty evidence, but not as conclusive.[63]

209. **Scholion I. Spendthrifts.** To the class of the mentally incompetent, Roman law added by analogy persons who were unable to take proper care of their property. They were known as prodigals (spendthrifts). Such persons were provided with curators (guardians), after judicial investigation of their character.[64] Because they were regarded as mentally weak, they were deprived of the right to make a will, unless it had been made prior to the judicial sentence. In that case, it was not invalidated.[65]

The incapacity of spendthrifts is not known in the United States, except insofar as it might be construed real mental derangement or deficiency. And it is only to this extent that the Ordinary need consider it where a spendthrift has made bequests to pious causes. In Roman law the analogy was the creature of positive law. It did not flow from a natural incapacity. The spendthrift, consequently, must be regarded as capable, under Canon 1513, § 1, of making bequests to charity and religion.

210. **Scholion II. Error** might be regarded as a sane delusion. It is the result not of a deficiency of mental power or of a diseased functioning of the mind. Rather, it is a lack of functioning through inadvertence, ignorance, or misunderstanding. Nevertheless, the capacity of a sane man laboring under error possesses some analogies to that of an insane man.

The general rule in the United States as to a will made under the influence of error is that error does not invalidate the will unless it is a mistake as to the form of the instrument or as to the existence of

[63] Rood, *op. cit.*, 137 a and b.

[64] Ulpian, *Reg.*, 12, 2 and 3; I. 1, 23, 3.

[65] I. 2, 12, 2.

a child who might be beneficiary *ab intestato*. As to errors of law or fact that may have induced the testator to make the will or certain of its provisions, they are not fatal.

The general rule of canon law in the same problem practically coincides with this. An act is invalidated only by an error as to its substantial nature or as to a matter that is a *conditio sine qua non.*[66] But whatever is given to a pious cause under a false notion of obligation can not be reclaimed.[67] However, this is consistent with the general rule, for an error as to obligation is not an error as to the substance of the act, but only as to the inducement that led to the gift.

211. **Error touching the form of the instrument** may occur either as to the whole instrument itself or as to a part of it. When it occurs as to the whole instrument, it is probably due to the testator's mistaking the instrument for something other than a will or for another will. When it occurs as to a portion of the will, it may be due to the insertion of clauses in the executed draft contrary to the wishes of the testator. Invalidating effect is not allowed, however, to the omission of words and phrases. The courts will not permit parol evidence to be introduced to show that the testator erroneously omitted words and phrases that he had intended to include.[68]

The testator might easily sign the wrong will where mutual wills were being made. Each testator might sign the will of the other. In these circumstances, neither will would be valid in the United States. Each one is absurd. And the courts do not feel competent to read above each signature what was contained in the will of the other person. They think they might with quite as much warrant fill in a blank sheet signed by the testator.

[66] Canon 104. "Error actum irritum reddit, si versetur circa id quod constituit substantiam actus vel recidat in conditionem *sine qua non;* secus actus valet, nisi aliud iure caveatur; sed in contractibus error locum dare potest actioni rescissoriae ad normam iuris.

[67] S. C. C. *in Causa Neapolitana,* 20 December, 1732, § *Quo*—Pallottini, XI, 570; *in Causa Bosanen.,* 13 March, 1762, § *Denique*—Pallottini, XI, 570.

[68] This is the rule of the canonical decrees also. The will of a testator known outside the testament aids in interpreting what is contained in the will, but does not establish what does not appear there; *cf.* S. C. EE. RR., 13 August, 1869—*A.S.S.,* V (1869), 92; S. C. C. *in Causa Ariminen.,* 24 July, 1858—Pallottini, XI, 561.

But the canons would justify the Ordinary in reading above the signature what was contained in the will of the other person. Of course, competent evidence must be demanded by him to show that the wills were mutual wills, made in consideration of each other, and not subsequently revoked. Where pious causes are involved, even a gesture suffices to indicate a person's will, if it can be fairly established that it really expressed the will of the testator.[69]

212. Inserted Phrases. Parol evidence is admitted by the English courts to show that words and phrases were introduced into the will contrary to the testator's wish and that he did not know their import when he signed the instrument. The rule in the United States seems to be the other way, for the courts contend that to admit parol proof of this would be to make the testator's will for him. Of course, if the error was obvious on the face of the instrument, even these courts would strike out the insertions.

The more lenient rule would seem to be the correct one under the canons. The purpose of the Ordinary is to discover the real intent of the testator. If parol evidence is beyond suspicion and sufficiently strong to demonstrate that the testator did not wish his will to mean what the inserted words and phrases meant, the Ordinary should know this, that he might be able to strike them from the instrument.

Here there is no question of an attempt to supply what is not in the will. Here there is an action by an external agent by which a testator is led to sign a document signifying something he did not intend. That action can certainly be proved, whereas what the testator wished to write in his will can not be argued from what he omitted.

The two cases would be much more similar if the testator read the will before he signed it or if he had it read to him after the words had been inserted. His acquiescence would seem to indicate acceptance. That should be the decision of the Ordinary, it would seem, under the rules just noted in the decrees of the Sacred Congregations. So, too, he can not admit parol evidence to fill in blank spaces left where amounts, names, or descriptions should be filled in.

[69] Barbosa, *Coll.*, III, 26, 11, 2; De Luca, *Theatrum, De Testamentis*, XIV, 7; Gasparro, *Iur. Civ.*, II, 4, 60; Cocchi, *op. cit.*, VI, 192; Reiffenstuel, *op. cit.*, III, 26, 154; Schmalzgrueber, *op. cit.*, III, III, 26, 46.

213. Error as to the existence of a child might cause the testator to omit that child from his will. Much has already been said on this matter when statutory revocation for this cause was discussed.[70] Suffice it to say here that any sort of provision for a child prevents the presumption of error in some States, even though the testator erroneously thought he owned the property that he devised and though the child consequently receives nothing. Some decisions allow parol evidence to disclose whether the omission was intentional. Others require that intention to disinherit appear at least implicitly on the face of the will.

As a general rule, if the testator feels that he can conscientiously omit a child in his will, he should say so in the instrument itself. Otherwise, he should make some sort of provision for the child.[71]

The statutes revoking a will for this cause conflict with the canons only where in revoking the will *in toto* they invalidate pious bequests contained in it. As to the harmonizing of these statutes with the canons when revocation is made only in part, *cf.* §§ 161-164.

Article 3

Undue Influence

214. Besides correct judgment one requires free will in order to perform a human act. Consequently, whatever hinders the freedom of an act prevents it in that degree from being a human act. Now both physical violence and intimidation affect the freedom of an agent who performs an act under their influence, and both consequently affect the validity of the act.

Since a will must be made by a human act, it must be the result of a free act of the will. Consequently any element that infringes upon that freedom affects the validity of the will. In order to invalidate the will, however, the influence must completely destroy the freedom of choice. If it merely impels the testator to choose a provision that he would not otherwise have chosen, it does not render the will invalid. However, the law recognizes that where that influence has been exerted unjustly, the external agent should not be

[70] *Cf.* §§ 119, 120 supra.

[71] Rood, *op. cit.*, 153-165.

allowed to profit by his injustice. Consequently it frequently invalidates the act; at other times, an action is given the victim by which he may revoke it.

The influence may be brought to bear by actual force or by intimidation. For the purposes of this discussion, actual force will be called violence. Intimidation will be called duress when reference is made to the cause; dread, when reference is made to the effect on the victim.

215. **Violence prevents completely the free exercise of the will.** It renders a testament invalid. Thus, if the testator's hand were violently seized and compelled to subscribe the will, the will would undoubtedly be invalid. The testator simply did not choose that act at all. Under Canon 1513, § 1, a bequest made to pious causes in this fashion could not be sustained. The canons assert the validity of only those bequests which are valid under the natural law.[72]

216. There is a *violentia secundum quid,* a technical name for duress that is overwhelming. The effect of it is to compel the victim to act without choice as completely as if he had been physically forced to perform the action. A will made under its influence would consequently be invalid.[73]

217. **Usually, however, duress impels the victim to act out of a dread of the consequences.** This dread may be defined as confusion of mind caused by the threat of present or imminent danger. Thus it is not merely the emotional experience of fear. It is fear influencing the intellect and acting on the will, impelling it to do or omit something for the purpose of avoiding the imminent peril.

The evil that is feared is not yet a matter of fact; otherwise, it could not be avoided, and would be a source of sadness or despondency rather than of dread. Nevertheless, the evil is so nearly a matter of fact that it can not easily be avoided. For if it could be easily escaped, it would not cause dread.

Evil threatening a third party may also cause sufficient dread to impel the choice of an action that otherwise would not be performed. This is especially evident in the case where a child is threatened in order to compel the mother to perform the desired act.

[72] Prümmer, *op. cit.,* I, 63-65.

[73] Prümmer, *l. c.*

218. By reason of its source, duress can be interior or exterior. It is interior when it is the reaction on the mind of nature and the world at large. It is exterior, when it is deliberately exercised by an external free agent, that is, by a person acting with free will.

219. By reason of the intensity of its influence, dread may be classified as grave, trivial, and reverential. Reverence at times partakes of the nature of the two former types, but of itself it is more akin to trivial or insignificant dread.

Dread may be either absolutely or relatively grave. Duress that would intimidate even a brave man causes dread that is absolutely (that is, in its very nature) grave, because it proceeds not from the weakness of its victim, but from the power of the threat to intimidate. If it is not so overpowering as to intimidate a brave man, duress may nevertheless be sufficiently overbearing as to dominate the actions of less resolute persons, and the dread that is then inspired is known as *relatively* grave. Thus a timorous child may be influenced as much by the dread of paternal chastisement as a courageous man would be by the threat of a severe flogging. The dread of parental chastisement is, of course, *reverential.* It derives its effect not so much from intimidation as from affection for the parent and a consciousness of duty. Reverential dread may become grave, however, especially where there is a possibility that the superior may exceed the bounds of his authority. Dread of constant rebuke from a parent or of an irreconcilable attitude that the parent threatens to assume might transform reverence into grave dread in persons of a timorous nature.

220. Duress may be justly exercised even when it causes grave dread, v. gr., the threat of a father to bring the seducer of his daughter to court if the latter does not marry her. It is only when the bounds of justice are exceeded that duress in the juridicial sense is conceived to exist. Otherwise the person intimidated is regarded as having done no more than he should freely have chosen to do.

221. Even grave dread does not make an act involuntary, unless it be overwhelming, that is, unless it destroys the use of reason. This seldom happens, except perhaps in the case of abnormal dread suddenly induced in extraordinarily fearful men and women. But unless the dread is overwhelming, there remains to the performer sufficient deliberation and freedom for a human act. But though the act is voluntarily performed under ordinary duress, it is performed with repugnance, and is to that extent also involuntary.[74]

222. Positive law, whether human or divine, usually ceases to bind when the subject of the law is threatened with the alternative of imminent grave evil if he refuses to break the law. Thus, a person who knows the combination of his employer's safe is no longer bound by the law of fidelity when his life is threatened to compel him to surrender it to the thief. But one could not deny his faith even under the threat of death, for the denial would be intrinsically evil.[75]

Positive law also binds whenever the public good is at stake, even though grave evil impends. A soldier's and a policeman's duty exemplify this statement. It is applicable *a fortiori* to the duty of avoiding scandal. Thus when the evil that threatens would induce an act showing contempt to the faith or to ecclesiastical authority or would cause grave harm to the spiritual life of others, the evil must be resisted and the peril risked.

223. Acts or contracts which are the result of duress causing grave dread are indeed valid but rescindible; but some of them are actually declared by positive law to be invalid.[76]

[74] St. Thomas says that what is done under duress, "esse simpliciter voluntaria et involuntaria secundum quid"—*Summa Theol.*, 1, 2, q. 6, a. 6.

[75] *Cf.* Canon 2205, § 2. "Metus quoque gravis, etiam relative tantum, . . . plerumque delictum, si agatur de legibus mere ecclesiasticis, penitus tollit.

§ 3. "Si vero actus sit intrinsece malus aut vergat in contemptum fidei vel ecclesiasticae auctoritatis vel in animarum damnum, causae, de quibus in § 2, delicti imputabilitatem minuunt quidem, sed non auferunt."

[76] Canon 103, § 2. "Actus positi ex metu gravi et iniuste incusso vel ex dolo, valent, nisi aliud iure caveatur; sed possunt ad normam can. 1684-1689 per iudicis sententiam rescindi, sive ad petitionem partis laesae sive ex officio."

Examples of invalidation by the canons are the following:

Canon 169, § 1, 1°. "Suffragium [in ecclesiastical elections] est nullum, nisi fuerit: Liberum, et ideo invalidum est suffragium, si elector metu gravi aut dolo, directe vel indirecte, adactus fuerit ad eligendam certam personam aut plures disiunctive."

Canon 185. "Renunciatio [the resignation of an ecclesiastical office] ex metu gravi, iniuste incusso, dolo aut errore substantiali vel simoniace facta, irrita est ipso iure."

Canon 542: 1°. "Invalide ad novitiatum admittuntur: . . . Qui religionem ingrediuntur vi, metu gravi aut dolo inducti, vel quos Superior eodem modo inductus recipit."

Observing, then, for the moment that acts performed under duress are rescindible under the canons, and noting that the latter prescribe nothing particularly touching bequests made under duress, it is appropriate to pass at this point to a consideration of the secular law in the United States, reserving to a subsequent discussion the procedure to be followed under the canons.

224. The American decisions regard duress as an invalidating factor. They speak of it as if it destroyed the free agency of the testator, substituting the will of a third person for the will of the testator himself. But it seems pretty clear that the duress to which they refer is not the extraordinary, overwhelming duress that destroys temporarily reasonable choice, but the duress which inspires grave dread. Most of the wills that have come before the courts have been made freely enough, but under the influence of the threats or the vexations of others.

The courts could have regarded the will as merely rescindible with practically the same effect as was obtained by holding it to be invalid. For the courts, being the constituted authority for the purpose of giving effect to wills, had it in their power to rescind it. This invalid will can not be validated by mere subsequent ratification. It must be re-executed. However, only that part of the will is invalid which was made under duress.

225. But with this difference as to the effect on wills, what the courts regard as undue influence would coincide fairly well with what the canons mean by *metus gravis*.[77]

Canon 572, § 1, 4°. "Ad validitatem cuiusvis religiosae professionis requiritur ut: . . . Professio sine vi aut metu gravi aut dolo emittatur."

Canon 1087, § 1. "Invalidum quoque est matrimonium initum ob vim vel metum gravem ab extrinseco et iniuste incussum, a quo ut quis se liberet, eligere cogatur matrimonium." § 2. "Nullus alius metus, etiamsi det causam contractui, matrimonii nullitatem secumfert."

Canon 1307, § 3. "Votum metu gravi et iniusto emissum ipso iure nullum est."

Canon 2238. "Poenae remissio, vi aut metu gravi extorta, ipso iure irrita est."

[77] Moore's Exrs. v. Blauvelt (1862), 15 N. J. Eq. 367: "What constitutes undue influence can never be precisely defined. It must necessarily depend, in each case, on the means of coercion or influence possessed by one party over the other; upon the power, authority, or control of the one—the age, the sex,

It is not undue influence where the testator has been inspired by affection, gratitude, pity, flattery, hatred, anger, prejudice; by appeals to these emotions; by modest persuasions; or by arguments addressed to his understanding. Thus bequests to a second wife to the exclusion of a daughter by the first marriage; to one child who had treated the parent with marked kindness to the exclusion of the other children; even to a mistress, have been upheld as having been made with freedom sufficient to make them really the will of the testator. However, in the case of flattery, if it was immoderate, the legacy great, the testator a person of weak judgment, the will would probably be regarded as void.

226. **To determine whether the pressure was sufficient** to cause the testator to make a will which he did not wish to make, the court should be guided by the circumstances attending the making of the will. A comparison should be made between the powers of the testator to resist the external influence and the nature and intensity of the influence. The conduct of the testator and of the person suspected should be examined to see what it was prior to the making of the will, at the time the will was made, and subsequent to the making of it. The will itself should be analyzed with a view to determining whether it coincides with what the testator would likely have wished or with what the person suspected would have desired. These examinations suggest what evidence may be admitted to determine the extent of the coercion.

227. **The following evidence is competent in secular courts to establish duress, and the ecclesiastical judge may also admit it.** First, evidence which shows the mental and physical powers of the deceased. Second, that which indicates the degree and the intensity of the influence exercised over him by the suspected person. Third,

the temper, the mental and physical condition and dependence of the other. Whatever destroys the free agency of the testator constitutes undue influence. Whether that object be effected by physical force, or mental coercion, by threats which occasion fear, or by importunity which the testator is too weak to resist, or which extorts compliance in the hope of peace, is immaterial. In considering the question of undue influence, therefore, it becomes essential to ascertain, as far as practicable, the power of coercion upon the one hand, the liability to its influence upon the other."

that which demonstrates the kind of will the testator should have been expected to make. Fourth, that which describes the conduct of the person suspected.

228. **To demonstrate the kind of will the testator should have been expected to make,** the following points may be admitted in evidence. First, that the person suspected has received a disproportionate interest in the estate. Second, that the testator has not given sufficient reason for so great a disproportion or for other unusual characteristics of the will. Third, that when the will was made, the testator was friendly or hostile to the persons favored or not favored. Fourth, that when the will was made, the testator had or had not the intention of disposing of the property as his will disposed of it.

229. **The real intention of the testator may be discerned in:** first, previous or subsequent wills even though they lacked the legal formalities; second, previous or subsequent statements of the testator, if they were uttered close to the time of the making of the will; third, letters and memoranda made by the testator at about that time; fourth, the opportunities he had to revoke the will after the influence had been removed. These instruments and documents are admissible, of course, merely to show the state of the testator's mind, and not to prove any matter contained in them.

230. **The conduct of the person suspected may be shown** by evidence that exhibits: first, threats made that the testator would be obliged to make such a will as was made; second, the failure of the suspect to notify other relatives of the testator's illness; third, the attempts made by the suspect to keep the will secret; fourth, officious conduct on the part of the suspect in procuring the execution of the will; fifth, attempts made by the suspect to prevent others from communicating with the testator; sixth, the kind of treatment meted out to the testator by the suspect at about the time the will was made; seventh, the actual feeling this person had for the testator at about that time.

Mere declarations of the testator that he was subjected to undue influence can not be admitted, since they are mere hearsay testimony, unless they are so closely associated with the making of the will as to be a part of it (*res gestae*). They may be admitted also to show the state of mind of the testator, even though not so intimately associated with the making of the will.

231. **Undue influence can not be presumed.** On the other hand, it need not be proved in the secular courts by direct and positive testimony. This would seem applicable to the rule also that should be followed in ecclesiastical procedure.

A *prima facie* case is made against the will if three points are are established. First, if the will contradicts the known previous intention of the testator, or is contrary to what would be his natural desires. Second, if the testator is shown to have been under the influence of the person suspected when he made the will. Third, if it is evident that his power of resistance was unable to cope with the devices of coercion. This *prima facie* case, of course, can be rebutted by arguments advanced to disprove any one of the elements just noted.

The chief of these elements is probably the first, viz., the character of the will itself. At least it would seem to be so for the Ordinary. For, a person may be physically and mentally weak, and at the same time subject to the influence of a strong will, and nevertheless be free from undue influence. There are still honest people with strong wills exercising control over persons with weak wills. If, in spite of this influence, the will itself is not suspect, it would seem that it should be regarded as having been made freely.

232. This becomes all the more apparent where confidential relations exist. In some cases the secular courts have held that because a beneficiary under a will had enjoyed the confidence of the testator a presumption of undue influence arose. Thus, an attorney, a guardian, a physician, a priest, a confidential agent, if beneficiaries under the will of the person whose confidence they enjoyed, would be compelled to prove that they exercised no coercion over him when he made his will.

The general rule, however, raises no more presumption against persons in the confidence of the testator than against others who might have an opportunity of influencing him, provided that they had nothing to do with the making of the will itself. If they had, there arises a *prima facie* of influence which the beneficiaries must adequately rebut in order to take under the will.

The ecclesiastical judge would not regard this conduct as sufficient to make out a *prima facie* case, but would be governed in this case by the rule established above in the preceding section.[78]

233. Ecclesiastical Procedure. In passing, rules for the ecclesiastical judge have been suggested in the preceding sections. He must, of course, be satisfied that there is a *prima facie* case suggesting that the testator actually made a will that he would not have made except for the desire to escape an imminent evil. If the *prima facie* case is not adequately rebutted, he must find against the will. A will like any other act performed under duress can be rescinded on petition by the party injured or *ex officio*.[79]

In the case of a will executed under duress, the person whose freedom was outraged is dead. He can no longer petition for the rescinding of his will. It is not to be conceded that the person who seems to have been his real choice should be allowed to petition for the rescinding, for it can not be shown that a person has been injured who had no certain rights. And a prospective beneficiary under a will has no certain rights under it.

On the other hand, it can not be said that the persons who would have taken *ab intestato* have been injured, if they would not have been beneficiaries even if the testator had been allowed to exercise the utmost freedom of choice. And even if they should be the persons who would have taken both under the will and *ab intestato*, nevertheless they can not petition for the rescinding of the will be-because their loss is not caused by the duress but by the voluntary act of the testator. They can not sue against the testator, for he did not injure them.

It is the testator who has suffered the duress, and he can no longer sue for the rescinding of the will. Indeed, in any case, the rescinding of a will executed under duress will never occur under the canons on the petition of the person injured. As long as he lives, he need only revoke the will, and has complete remedy there.

The ecclesiastical judge may none the less *ex officio* rescind a will or bequest made under duress. And the parties who would have

[78] This whole matter is discussed in this manner by Rood, *op. cit.*, 175-191.

[79] Canon 103, § 2. *Cf.* text of this Canon in footnote 76, this chapter.

benefited or who will benefit *ab intestato* may bring the knowledge of undue influence to his attention.[80]

234. There are at least three cases when it becomes the office of the canonical executor, that is, the Ordinary, to rescind a bequest when it is juridically clear that it was made under duress.

One is when the bequest would have been made to a pious cause other than that mentioned in the will, had duress not been employed. It is clearly within the competence of the Ordinary to award it to the pious cause which should have been beneficiary. This may be done even though the secular courts have made the award to the pious cause mentioned in the will, provided that the Ordinary is certain that undue influence was used and that it was this and nothing else that prevented the testator from carrying out his good intentions toward the cause whose hopes were defeated. The case, of course, would be much stronger, if the expectant institute had been named beneficiary in a will revoked by the one made under duress.

The second case is where a pious cause is the beneficiary of a bequest made under duress, though it would not have been made to any pious cause, had the testator been free. The Ordinary should exempt the executor from making payment, or accept whatever compromise the latter is willing to make. The basis of the compromise is that the persons mentioned in a will, on account of its voluntary nature in spite of duress, have rights as good as those who might have been omitted in any event.

The third case is where under duress, property is transferred to a joint account, which accrues to the survivor, thus depriving a pious cause of its expected bequest. The principles applied to the first case are to be called on to solve this problem as well.

These solutions are valid only where there is genuine duress, not mere suggestion, persuasion, appeal to reason, or even argument from religious belief. If the testator could choose freely and was not coerced, there is no duress.

235. **Scholion I. Fraud is very closely related to coercion;** but by fraud the testator is deceived, not coerced. For fraud is a

[80] It must be remembered that under the secular laws, these wills are invalid. They may be attacked by any party in interest, v. gr., by persons who will take *ab intestato*.

"trick, a secret device, a false statement, or pretense, by which the subject of it is cheated." [81]

The invalidating effects of fraud are wider than those of error, though fraud is successful only through the error of the testator. These are correlatives, fraud in the schemer, error in the testator. Fraud's effects are wider because it involves an injustice that is not present in simple error. Simple error might be compared to interior dread, while fraud is very similar to duress. As an instance of the divergence in the application of the law to mere error and to fraud, observe that if it can be definitely proved that the insertion of a clause or phrase in a will was done fraudulently, there is probably no court that would not admit parol evidence to demonstrate that fact, even though some secular courts would not admit such evidence if the introduction of those clauses was due to simple error.

236. **In order that the deception be fraud in the juridical sense,** there must be the intention to deceive in the schemer, and the effect in the will must be due to the deception. If there was no intention to deceive, nothing but simple error intervened. If the same effect would have been accomplished without fraud, the latter is not the effective element, and therefore does not invalidate the bequest.

237. **Fraud is not to be presumed,** but all the circumstances attending the making of the will, including the testator's declarations may be introduced as evidence in the secular courts to prove it. For instance, it will be relevant to show the disproportionate share of the estate that was bequeathed to the person who had the opportunity of practising fraud; the opportunity may be described; and it may be demonstrated that the testator was blind, or unable to read the will, or susceptible to any kind of imposition. It will be remembered that these are the elements that make out a *prima facie* case of duress. They also make out a *prima facie* case of fraud, subject, of course, to rebuttal.

238. **Where the deceit has consisted in a promise** to perform certain acts which the promisor never intended to perform, the secular courts will impress the bequest with a trust *ex maleficio* for the benefit of the objects or persons whom the testator thought would be the beneficiaries of the act that was promised.[82]

[81] Rood, *op. cit.*, 169.

[82] Rood, *op. cit.*, 169-174.

Article 4

Disqualifications of the Purely Positive Law

239. Persons otherwise capable under the natural law of making a will may be disqualified by the purely positive law. Disqualifications may thus arise either as developments out of the social organization of the time or as penal sanctions for other laws. In both cases they are generally corrollaries of the loss of the *ius commercii*, which for all practical purposes was the right to dispose of one's property as seemed fitting to him.

240. **Disqualifications of the purely secular law do not invalidate bequests made to pious causes.** But if the positive law works a forfeiture of property prior to the testator's decease, of course he has nothing to bequeath by will. On the other hand, disqualifications arising out of canon law would invalidate bequests even to pious causes.[83]

241. **The disqualifications arising out of social organization** are those imposed on persons because of their status. Thus under the Roman system persons were disqualified who were not *sui iuris*, and this class included those who had lost their independence through the *minima capitis diminutio* (which was really a loss of financial responsibility).[84] The following were also disqualified because of status: *impuberes*,[85] women,[86] slaves,[87] aliens, including citizens who

[83] Canon 1513, § 1. *Cf.* § 173, this treatise.

[84] I. 2, 12; D. 49, 17, 1; C. 12, 30, 1.

[85] I. 2, 12, 1; 1, 22 pr.; C. 5, 60, 3.

[86] Women who were married *cum manu* were under the *patria potestas* of their husbands and so were not *sui iuris; cf.* Gaius, I. 115 b. But even women who were *sui iuris* could make a will prior to Hadrian only by *coemptio; cf.* Gaius, I, 115 a. Justinian enabled them to make a will as freely as men; *cf.* C. 8, 58, 1. This power was granted to married women as well, for by the second century A. D. the form of marriage *cum manu* had fallen into desuetude; *cf.* Sherman, *op. cit.*, II, 469. *Cf.* footnote n. 11, this chapter.

[87] Except slaves of the State who, under the Empire, could dispose by will of one-half of their personal belongings; *cf.* Ulpian, *Reg.*, 20, 16.

had lost their citizenship (*media capitis diminutio*),[88] and citizens who had lost their liberty (*maxima capitis diminutio*).[89]

242. In England, a list of persons incapacitated is given by Swinburne, writing on wills in 1590. That list comprises all those persons just enumerated, including serfs as well as slaves, but not unmarried women.[90] But Rood declares that prisoners of war were never disqualified under the English common law.

Ecclesiastics are mentioned by Swinburne, and this disqualification is traceable to the imperial constitution of Theodosius the Younger (434).[91] But again Rood claims that the ecclesiastic was never disqualified under the common law of England.

243. **The second group of persons incapacitated are those penalized for an offense.** Under the Roman imperial constitutions heretics generally were forbidden to make a will or to take a benefit under a will. Property which they bequeathed or which was bequeathed to them escheated to the State, except where it passed to Christian children converted from Manicheism.[92] Jews and Samaritans were at first merely forbidden to disinherit their children who had become Christians;[93] but eventually they were deprived of the

[88] Sherman, *op. cit.*, II, 432; Moyle, *op. cit.*, I, 251, 252 (footnote). Even persons whose origin was in the provinces subject to Rome were aliens. But the emperors consistently bestowed citizenship on the residents of various provinces until at length Caracalla (212) granted this boon to all the free subjects of the Empire. An alien could always make a testament according to the law of his own State.

[89] The will of a Roman citizen taken prisoner by the enemy was invalid until the *Lex Cornelia* (81 A. D.). This law regarded the captive as dying at the very moment of capture. Hence, if he had made a will prior to the moment when he was captured, the will was valid, but distribution did not take place until his real death; this was due to the *ius postliminii*, by which, if he returned from captivity, he could be restored to all his rights; *cf.* I. 1, 12, 5; Gaius, 1, 129; D. 28, 1, 12; Sherman, *op. cit.*, II, 437.

[90] *Wills*, Book I, part 2; cited by Rood, *op. cit.*, 138 (footnote).

[91] *Codex Theod.*, 5, 3, 1; C. 1, 3, 20; *Nov.*, 131, 13. Bishops, priests and religious were included. They were probably regarded as being similar in function to the *curiales* whose property, if they died intestate, went to the college of *curiales*, and not to their heirs; *cf. Codex Theod.*, 5, 2, 1.

[92] *Codex Theod.*, 16, 5, 65, 3; C. 1, 5, 4, 5; *Codex Theod.*, 16, 5, 7; *Nov.*, 144, 1.

[93] *Codex Theod.*, 16, 8, 28.

right to make or take under a will unless the heirs they designated were Christians.[94] The following persons were also disqualified by way of penalty: apostates,[95] adulterers,[96] libellers and lampooners,[97] the infamous (that is, those officially declared to be depraved),[98] and all others who for treason or felony were deprived of liberty (*maxima capitis diminutio*) or of citizenship (*media capitis diminutio*).[99]

244. Under the laws of particular councils, usurers were incapacitated.[100] Notaries were forbidden to draw up wills for them unless a priest was present, and the priest was ordered to ascertain that the usurer had made restitution of his ill-gotten gains or had given bond for the payment of them before the instrument was executed.[101] Some councils merely insist on the necessity of adequate restitution before the faithful may assist a usurer in the making of his will.[102] A cleric who would unlawfully assist was placed under suspension.[103] And the Council of Bourges (1286) commanded pastors to announce each Sunday that usurers may not make valid wills until they have given ample security for adequate restitution of their forbidden profits.[104]

245. In England, Swinburne lists all these persons herewith enumerated as disqualified in penalty, except Jews, adulterers, and the infamous. Rood, however, insists that the disqualification of usurers, libellers, and heretics was never part of the common law.[105]

[94] *Nov.*, 144, 1.

[95] C. 1, 7, 4.

[96] D. 22, 5, 14.

[97] D. 28, 1, 18, 1.

[98] D. 28, 1, 6.

[99] I. 1, 12, 1; D. 50, 17, 209. But Roman law provided for a full pardon by the emperor by which the person might be restored to his original status as a citizen; D. 48, 19, 27 pr.; D. 48, 23, 1; C. 9, 51, 1.

[100] Council of Pergamo (1311), rub. 24—Mansi, XXV, 923 C.

[101] Second General Council of Lyons (1274), c. 27—Mansi, XXIV, 100 B; Council of Ravenna (1286), c. 6—Mansi, XXIV, 621 C.

[102] Constitutions of Autun (prior to 1300), c. 100—Mansi, XXXII, 306 D; Synod of Cologne (1300), c. 12—Mansi, XXV, 21 B; Council of Florence (1346)—Mansi, XXVI, 61 E; Council of Benevento (1378), c. 10—Mansi, XXVI, 623 C.

[103] Council of Pergamo, *l. c.*

[104] C. 17—Mansi, XXIV, 636 A.

[105] *L. c. Cf.* Blackstone, *op. cit.*, II, 32, 499.

In addition, under the common law, a suicide could not make a will of personalty because this was forfeit to the crown;[106] while under the Roman law his goods were forfeit only when the suicide was committed as a means of escaping punishment for a crime of which forfeiture of property was a part.[107]

246. The Capacity of Married Women. As has been indicated, there is propably no State in the United States where a woman, even a married woman, may not make a will with as much freedom as a man.[108]

The reason for the disqualification of married women under the English common law was not sex, for single women and widows from a very early date were allowed practically unlimited freedom in disposing of goods capable of being given by will.[109] At present, however, the rule is practically the same in England as it is in the United States.[110]

[106] Blackstone, *l. c.*

[107] D. 48, 21, 3.

[108] *Cf.* § 121 supra.

[109] It was due in part to the husband's right to all the chattels of his wife (*cf.* § 121 supra). She might make a will if her husband consented to all its provisions, but it was really his will more than hers, since he could revoke it at any time before probate. But another reason for the married woman's incapacity was that she was conceived to have no existence apart from her husband, and consequently no separate disposing power.

As to realty, the wife's heirs succeeded to it after the husband's death by the laws of descent. She could make no devise, unless she resorted to the device of uses, as men were doing prior to the Statute of Uses, 27 Henry VIII (1535), that is, she might bequeath the use after having conveyed the property to a trustee to hold it for those uses which she would name in her will. When Henry VIII passed the Statute of Wills, 32 Henry VIII, c. 1 (1540), enabling all and every person and persons having any interest in lands to devise it, the ecclesiastical courts interpreted it as giving married women a right to make devises. But this interpretation was contradicted by a Statute passed three years later, 33-34 Henry VIII, c. 5, s. 14 (1542, 1543). This was probably due to a survival of the idea that a married woman is not a separate person.

But the wife of a felon-convict, of a man transported or forbidden to return to England, or of an alien non-resident could make a will as if she had no husband; Rood, *op. cit.*, 144-149.

[110] Under the Married Woman's Property Act, 45 and 46 Victoria, c. 75 (1882).

247. When married women were forbidden to make bequests, they did not own their chattels. These belonged to the husband. Consequently, the wife could not have disposed of these under the regulations of Canon 1513, § 1. Not only did the secular law deprive her of the right to make a will. It actually gave her chattels to her husband. However, married women always retained title to their realty; and the secular law, in this hypothesis, could not have prevented her from devising what was her own to charity.

The problems herewith noted are discussed hypothetically. As indicated, they are not likely to become practical in the United States or England, where marriage would seem no longer to incapacitate a woman as to the making of a will.

248. **At one time, treason, felony and suicide created an incapacity** by causing a forfeiture of the goods of the guilty person. Of course, forfeiture incapacitated him indirectly. He could not bequeath to charity goods forfeited to the State, for they were no longer his. However, lands were never forfeit without an attainder in due course of law, though this formal procedure was not required in the case of chattels, except in the case of felony. Now, however, attainders, corruptions, and forfeitures no longer exist in England, having been abolished under the Statute, 33 and 34 Victoria (1870), c. 23.

Under the Constitution of the United States,[111] the States are forbidden to pass any bill of attainder. And even attainder of treason against the United States works forfeiture only during the life of the traitor.[112]

No conviction works a forfeiture under the statutes of most of the States.[113] But some of the States provide that convicts may not make a will. In the absence of such a statute, even prisoners sentenced to death are competent. Where the States deprive a convict of the right to make a will, it would seem that they have not taken his property from him, but merely incapacitated him. Consequently, should he make a bequest to charity, the bequest should be upheld by the ecclesiastical judge under the provisions of Canon 1513, § 1.

[111] Art. I, § 10.

[112] Art. III, § 3.

[113] Rood, *op. cit.*, 141-143.

On the contrary, when the Congress of the United States attaints a man for treason, it not only incapacitates him as to the making of a will, but actually takes his property from him for the period of his life. Consequently, he has nothing of which to dispose. Even if he made a bequest to charity, it would be invalid under Canon 1513, § 1.

249. Aliens generally have unlimited freedom of disposition by will in the United States and England.[114]

Canon 1513, § 1, would endow an alien with the right to dispose of any property which he held by right at the time of his death even to alien pious causes.

250. The remaining disqualifications of secular positive law seem to have little application today.[115] Or the disqualification of usury of the ecclesiastical law.

Nevertheless, the disqualification which the Roman law placed upon ecclesiastics was adopted by ecclesiastical law. It is important enough to receive treatment in a special chapter. Consequently, the next chapter will consider the history of this disqualification, and the degree in which it is applicable today.

[114] This was always true at common law, except that where the alien was an enemy and domiciled outside the jurisdiction, his property was subject to seizure and confiscation unless it was removed or conveyed to a citizen or a neutral within a reasonable time after war was declared. And the crown always had the right to take by forfeit any lands devised to aliens.

[115] Viz., slavery, serfdom, captivity in war, heresy, apostasy, adultery, libel, infamy, and suicide.

CHAPTER V

THE DISQUALIFICATION OF RELIGIOUS VOWS

ARTICLE 1

SAFEGUARDS FOR THE PATRIMONY OF THE CLERIC AND THE CHURCH

251. The disqualification based on ecclesiastical status was probably accepted by Roman law in accordance with its traditional notion of the *familia* and the *patria potestas*. Ecclesiastics were regarded as passing through a sort of *adrogatio* by which they ceased to be persons *sui iuris* to become *filii familias* under the *patria potesta* of the Church.

252. Ecclesiastical legislation, however, was beforehand in this matter, and the secular legislation seems rather to be patterned after the canonical.

253. The question of testamentary capacity in a cleric is intimately connected with the rights of the cleric in the property of the Church. It was always regarded as a logical corollary of the natural and the divine law that the clergy should receive their support from the possessions of the Church. And canonical legislation provided for this.[1] Nevertheless, since the property of the Church was regarded traditionally as the patrimony of the poor,[2] the clergy

[1] The property of each diocese was divided into four parts, of which one was destined for the support of the bishop's office; one, for repairs to church buildings; one, for the poor; and the fourth, for the clergy; cc. 28-31, C. XII, q. 2; Canon of Pope Sylvester, c. 4—Harduin, I, 291 B; Letter of Pope Gelasius to the Bishop of Lucania, c. 27—Mansi, VIII, 45 B; *idem* to the Bishop of Sicily—Mansi, VIII, 46 A; *idem* to the Archdeacon Justin—Mansi, VIII, 124 A (*MPL,* LIX, 140); the Council of Orléans (511), c. 5—Mansi, VIII, 352 D; the Second Capitulary of Theodulf, Bishop of Orléans (797)—Mansi, XIII, 1009 D; Sixth Council of Paris (829), lib. 1, c. 15—Mansi, XIV, 549 A; Council of Worms (868), c. 7—Mansi, XV, 871 A; Council of the Kingdom of Dalmatia (1199), c. 3—Mansi, XXII, 702 A.

[2] Council of Chalons (813), c. 6—Mansi, XIV, 95 A; Council of Rennes (1273), c. 2—Mansi, XXIV, 34 B; Council of Rheims (1408)—Mansi, XXVI, 1059 E.

were regarded as sharing in it as beggars with the poor.[3] Consequently, it was in harmony with this theory that the early Fathers attempted to prevent the clergy from having possessions of their own.[4] **But the property that *de facto* a cleric might have as patrimony was always regarded as belonging to him,** though the example of Saints Paulinus and Hilary was frequently cited to encourage him, when he assumed the clerical state, to give up, as they had done, everything he owned.[5]

254. On the other hand, whatever he received after ordination to the priesthood belonged to the Church, excepting, of course, inherited patrimony. This was regarded as the canonical rule as early as Pope Pius I (153). But as to priests, evidences of this traditional rule do not appear after the seventh century.[6] As to bishops, however, at least one document of the thirteenth century attests its survival until that time.[7]

[3] Council of Aix-la-Chapelle (816), cc. 35 and 108—Mansi, XIV, 193 A and 215 C.

[4] Cc. 5, 6, 8, 9, 18, C. XII, q. 1.

[5] Council of Aix-la-Chapelle (816), cc. 35 and 108—Mansi, XIV, 193 A and 215 C.

Cf. the decision of Pope Gregory the Great ordaining that the heiress of a bishop is not to be disturbed because what she took from his estate he had owned prior to his becoming a prelate; *Ad Deusdedit*—Mansi, XII, 38 (*MPL*, LXXVII, 1246). But if the cleric died intestate and without relatives, his property descended to the Church; Council of Tribur, cited in c. 7, C. XIII, q. 5.

[6] C. 3, X, *de peculio clericorum*, III, 25; c. 3, C. XII, q. 3 (*i. e.*, Council of Agde, 506, c. 6—Mansi, VIII, 326 B); c. 4, C. XII, q. 5 (*i. e.*, Council of Seville, 590, c. 5—Mansi, X, 452 B); c. 1, C. XII, q. 4; c. 2, C. XII, q. 3; Ninth Council of Toledo (655), c. 4—Mansi, 27 B; *Cap. Coll. Can. Hibern.*, lib. 2, cc. 21 and 26—Mansi, XII, 120 B and C; Wasserschleben, pp. 18, 19.

[7] Fragments of the Decrees of Gregory IX, c. 8—Mansi, XXIII, 112 B. *Cf.* also Council of Rheims (630), c. 20—Harduin, III, 573, 574; Hefele, III, 263.

Pope Gregory the Great appointed, in one of his letters, an administrator to preserve distinct after a bishop's death the two classes of property, that which he had acquired before and that which had come to him after he had become bishop; *Ad Anthemium Campaniae Subdiaconum*—Mansi, X, 142 D (*MPL*, LXXVII, 1010). On another occasion, he ordered an investigation with a view to determining the date at which the property of a deceased bishop had been acquired, implicitly indicating that if the property had been acquired while

255. As early as the Third and Fourth Councils of Carthage, however, it was conceded that gifts which were clearly meant for the cleric personally might be joined to his own funds (as a kind of *peculium adventitium*).[8]

the bishop was still a deacon, the bequest made by him should be sustained; *Ad Deodatum Episcopum*—Mansi, X, 334 A. *Cf.* also the letter *Ad Mariamnum* —Mansi, VI, 1 (*MPL*, LXXVII, 793). The Ninth Council of Toledo (655) suggests that the bishops should leave to their churches whatever they purchased even with their own funds; c. 1, C. XII, q. 4.

[8] *Cf.* § 178, this treatise. Third Council of Carthage, c. 49—Mansi, III, 892 A (*i. e.*, c. 1, C. XII, q. 3); Fourth Council of Carthage (419), c. 38—Mansi, IV, 432 B. This seems also to be conceded by the Council of Mayence (847), c. 8—Mansi, XIV, 905 E; and by the *Capitula of Hincmar*, c. 18—Mansi, XV, 480 E.

Of course, there was never any question as to the property which was given him for the Church. For instance, the Canons of the African Church regard one who buys land in his own name from the funds of his church as an invader of the property of the Lord; c. 32—Mansi, III, 727 D; *cf.* c. 6, C XII, q. 2 (where Pope Anacletus says that whoever takes money from Christ or the Church is a murderer); *cf.* also cc. 18, 19, C. XII, q. 2.

For that reason, the sale or exchange of ecclesiastical property was always hedged about by the canons with numerous safeguards. Bishops were required to have the primate's permission; Canons of the African Church, c. 26—Mansi, III, 726 A; Fifth Council of Carthage (438), c. 4—Mansi, III, 969 B; Breviary of Fulgentius Ferrandus, c. 47—Mansi, VI, 471 A. In an urgent case, the consent of the neighboring bishops sufficed under the ruling of the Fifth Council of Carthage. The consent of the bishop's clergy was sometimes regarded as adequate; Council of Carthage (419), c. 39—Mansi, IV, 432 C; Council of Carthage (*circa* 436), c. 32—Mansi, III 954 B; Statutes of the Ancient Church, c. 48—Mansi, VII, 896 A. Pope Hilary, in writing to the Bishops of Gaul, required previous discussion in council; *cf.* epistle 8, c. 5—Mansi, VII, 936 D (*MPL*, LVIII, 26). Again, the concurrence of two bishops of the same province is regarded as sufficient safeguard; Council of Agde (506), c. 7—Mansi, VIII, 325 C; *Capitula* of Hadrian, c. 26—Mansi, XII, 875 D. And after the Protestant revolt, the Council of Cosenza (1579) required the permission of the Holy See for a three-year lease of the property belonging to a pious foundation; session 4 —Mansi, XXXV B, 950 D.

The priest, of course, was required to have the consent of his bishop; Council of Ancyra (314), c. 14—Harduin, I, 278; Council of Carthage (419)—*l. c.;* Council of Carthage (421) *l. c.;* Fourth Council of Orléans (541), c. 34—Harduin, II, 1438; Council of Narbonne (589), c. 8—Mansi, IX, 1016 C; Constitution of the Bishop of Salisbury (*circa* 1217), c. 41—Harduin, VII, 101.

Indeed, alienation of endowments is often forbidden absolutely, even by

256. The canons early recognized the danger that the cleric might inadvertently confuse ecclesiastical property with his own. They were consequently emphatic in reminding clerics to exercise proper care in keeping the respective goods distinct from one another. One of the special prohibitions concerned the temptation of the cleric to be generous to his relatives at the expense of the Church.[9] Even bishops were sometimes cautioned to keep accurate inventory of the items belonging to the different funds.[10] A bishop who failed in

exchange; c. 1, C. XVII, q. 4; c. 2, C. X, q. 2; Letter of Pope Gelasius to Justin the Archdeacon—Mansi, VIII, 130 A (*MPL,* LIX, 140); Letter of Pope Gelasius to Caesarius, Bishop of Arles—Mansi, VIII, 212 B; Fourth Synod of Rome (for Rome), cc. 4, 6, 7, 8—Mansi, VIII, 267 B; Council of Carthage (525)—Mansi, VIII, 644 A; *Cap. Coll.* of Martin of Braga, c. 14—Mansi, IX, 850 E; Council of Auvergne (*circa* 549), c. 13—Mansi, IX, 144 A; Fourth Council of Toledo (589), c. 3—Mansi, IX, 993 D; Council of Rheims (630), c. 13—Harduin, III, 573; 17th Council of Toledo (694), cc. 2 and 6—Mansi, XII, 104 D and 105 B; *Capitula* of Hadrian, c. 33—Mansi, XII, 876 A.

Deposition was the penalty imposed for alienation without profit to the church; c. 19, C. XII, q. 2; *Statuta Complutensia,* c. 52—Mansi, IV, 535 A. Or excommunication, as in Ireland—*Cap. Coll. Can. Hibern.,* lib. 17, cc. 3 and 5 —Mansi, XII, 123 E; Wasserschleben, pp. 50, 51. Two years of penance with loss of benefice was the penalty in Narbonne for clerics who alienated church property without permission of the bishop; Council of Narbonne (589), c. 8—Mansi, IX, 1016 C.

[9] Canons of the Apostles, cc. 26, 39, 40—Harduin, I, 18, 19; 37; Council of Antioch (341), c. 25—Harduin, I, 605 B; *Cap. Coll.* of Martin of Braga (6th cent.), c. 15—Mansi, IX, 851 C; *Capitula* of Hadrian (773), c. 35—Mansi, XII, 861 A; Council of Worms (868), c. 45—Mansi, XV, 877 D; Council of Oxford (1222), c. 36 (church property can not be sold or pledged to relatives)—Mansi, XXII, 1161 E; Council of Mount Lebanon, pars 3, c. 4, n. 27, 5 (citing canons 39 and 40 of the Canons of the Apostles)—*Coll. Lacensis,* II, 315 d.

[10] Canons of the Apostles, cc. 26 and 72—Harduin, I, 18 and 27; Council of Antioch (341), c. 25—Harduin, I, 605 B; Fourth Council of Carthage (436), c. 31—Mansi, III, 953 E; Breviary of Fulgentius Ferrandus, c. 72 (from the Council of Laodicea)—Mansi, VIII, 894 B; Statutes of the Ancient Church, c. 14—Mansi, VII, 894 B; *Capitula* of Hadrian, c. 35—Mansi, XII, 861 A; Third Council of Tours (813), c. 10—Mansi, XIV, 84 E; Second Council of Chalons (813), cc. 6 and 8—Mansi, XIV, 94 E; Harduin, IV, 1033; Second Council of Aix-la-Chapelle, lib. 3, c. 8—Mansi, XIV, 733 A; Second Council of Mayence (847), c 8—Mansi, XIV, 906 A; *Capitula* of Hincmar (874), lib. 4, c. 4 (he is not to build his house or buy a farm with ecclesiastical goods)—Mansi,

this point was worthy of public rebuke at the hands of the other bishops of the province;[11] or of excommunication, as in the Province of York, under Egbert (748).[12]

257. The problem of protecting ecclesiastical property from the claims of the incumbent's heirs persisted after his death. That accounts for the rather insistent legislation requiring bishops to establish beyond question the amount and kind of property in their hands that belonged to them personally.[13] And claimants were commanded not to touch even the property that was personal to the deceased bishop without due authority.[14]

258. Should a bishop chance to bequeath property that did not

XV, 496 B; Council of Mount Lebanon (approving c. 25 of the Council of Antioch), (1736), pars. 3, c. 4, n. 27, 5—*Coll. Lacensis,* II, 316 d.

[11] Council of Orléans (511), c. 5—Mansi, VIII, 352 D.

[12] *Responsiones,* c. 71—Mansi, XII, 420 A.

[13] Cc. 19 and 20, C. XII, q. 1 (cited as c. 15, Council of Agde, 506); Canons of the Apostles, cc. 39 and 40—Harduin, I, 19 and 37 (*cf.* cc. 20, 21, C. XII, q. 1); Council of Antioch (341), c. 24— Harduin, I, 604 D; *Cap. Coll.* of Martin of Braga (6th cent.), c. 15—Mansi, IX, 851 A; *Capitula* of Hadrian (773), cc. 24 and 36—Mansi, XII, 861 A and 865 D; Council of Tarragona (1239), c. 16—Mansi, XXIII, 518 A; Council of Mount Lebanon (approving c. 39 of the Canons of the Apostles and canon 24 of the Council of Antioch), (1736), pars 3, c. 4, n. 27, 5—*Coll. Lacensis,* II, 315 d and 316 b.

The Roman Council of 1725 has a special regulation in this matter requiring an inventory of the property of churches and pious institutions to be made within a year, and decreeing that a prelate in danger of death or undertaking a journey must give an inventory of the property of his see to his confessor, who in turn must transmit it to the prelate of the most important monastery in the diocese, where it is to be kept until the bishop's return or until the installation of his successor; tit. 12, c. 1—Mansi, XXXIV B, 1809 E.

[14] Coucil of Ancyra (314), c. 14—Harduin, I, 278; Letter of Pope Gelasius to Justin the Archdeacon and to Faustus—*MPL,* LIX, 145; Fourth Council of Orléans (541), cc. 9, 35, 36—Mansi, IX, 114 D, 119 B; Council of Ponthion (France), (876), c. 10—Mansi, XVIII, 312 C.

A fortiori, it was forbidden to plunder it; Council of Chalcedon, c. 22—Mansi, VII, 367 A; Council of Pavia (876), c. 18—Mansi, XVII A, 328 C; Council of Ponthion (876), c. 14—Mansi, XVII A, 312 D; Council of Trosley (France), (909), c. 14—Mansi, XVIII A, 302 E; Council of London (1257)—Mansi, XXIII, 950 E.

belong to his patrimony, it was to be reclaimed by his successor;[15] or compensation could be claimed from his patrimony;[16] for such a bequest was invalid.[17]

259. The estate of a decedent bishop was protected against the unwarranted claims of even his metropolitan [18] and his successor. The latter is cautioned to make due distribution to the diocesan clergy of whatever portion of the property was due them under the early plan of four-fold distribution.[19]

The estate of a cleric was similarly guarded against claims which the bishop might be prompted to make against it.[20]

And the cathedral chapter (that is, the canons at the cathedral church) are reminded to abstain rigorously from any meddling with the deceased bishop's estate.[21] Priests and deacons are given a

[15] *Cf.* the first four authorities cited in footnote 14, just cited; also, c. 42, C. XII, q. 2 (from the Council of Ancyra).

[16] Council of Albon (France), (517), c. 17—Mansi, VIII, 561 B.

[17] C. 12, X, *de rebus eccl. alienandis,* III, 13; 17th Council of Toledo (694), c. 4—Mansi, XII, 105 A; *Capitula* of Hadrian, c. 32—Mansi, XII, 876 A.

[18] Council of Chalcedon, c. 26—Mansi, VII, 367 E; the Trullan Synod (692), c. 35—Mansi, XI, 959 B; Fifth Council of Orléans (549), cc. 8 and 16—Harduin, II, 1445, 1446; Fifth Council of Paris (615), c. 8—Harduin III, 552; Hefele, III, 253; Council of Rheims (630), c. 21—Harduin, III, 574; Council of Mount Lebanon (1736), pars 3, c. 4, n. 27, 5—*Coll. Lacensis,* II, 317 a.

[19] Pope Gelasius—Mansi, VIII, 141 C.

[20] Fifth Council of Paris (615), cc. 8 and 9—Harduin, III, 552; Hefele, III, 253; *cf.* also Fifth Council of Orléans (549)—*l. c.*

The bishop is also warned not to merge the property of filial churches with that of the cathedral church; Council of Carthage (421), c. 10—Mansi, IV, 450 E; Breviary of Fulgentius Ferrandus, c. 38—Mansi, VI, 470 B; Fifth Council of Paris (615)—*l. c.;* Council of Tortose (Spain), (1429)—Mansi, XXVIII, 1155 E; Provincial Council of England (1509)—Mansi, XXXI A, 402 C.

Should a bishop chance to claim any such property and take it over, the penalty inflicted by Boniface VIII (1299), is interdict *ab ingressu ecclesiae;* c. 9, *de officio Ordinarii,* I, 16, in VI°.

Clement V in the Council of Vienne condemned the practice of claiming the property left in a vacant benefice when the incumbent had been a religious, and of demanding the fruits of the benefice for the first year of vacancy; c. *un., de excessibus praelatorum,* V, 6, in Clem.

[21] C. 40, *de electione et electi potestate,* I, 6 in VI° (decreed by Boniface

similar warning.[22] But this warning should be understood in the

VIII under penalty of suspension from office and from benefices until restitution is made).

Cf. also c. 38, C. XII, q. 2, where there is a prohibition against the usurpation of a bishop's estate; cc. 46-47, C. XII, q. 2, excommunicating laymen who seize the estate of a bishop or of a cleric. Even prior to this, the same penalty was inflicted on those who seized the bishop's estate before his will had been read, and the Fifth Council of Paris included the estate of a priest within the sanction (615); *cf.* c. 7—Mansi, X, 541 A; Harduin, III, 552; Hefele, III, 252; Council of Rheims (630), c. 16—Mansi, X, 596 D; Harduin, III, 573; Hefele, III, 263; Council of Chalons (650), c. 7—Mansi, X, 1191 A.

For the censure of excommunication inflicted on those who seized the estate of a deceased bishop or cleric; *cf.* also the Tenth Epistle of Pope Leo IX to the people of Osimo—Mansi, XIX, 672 C; the Council of Nîmes (1096), c. 5—Mansi, XX, 935 C; Council of Poitiers (1100), c. 15—Mansi, XX, 1124 C; Council of Rheims (1131), c. 3—Mansi, XXI, 458 C; Second General Council of the Lateran (1139), c. 5—Mansi, XXI, 527 B; Forty-first Letter of Pope Adrian to Berengarius, Archbishop of Narbonne—Mansi, XXI, 826 B; Council of Merton (1258)—Mansi, XXIII, 981 A; Council of Lambeth (1261)—Mansi, XXIII, 1069 A; Council of Cologne (1266), c. 7—Mansi, XXIII, 1138 B; Second Council of Milan (1569), tit. 3, c. 15—Harduin, X, 753.

The Council of London (1257) commanded the king not to touch the estate of a deceased bishop; Mansi, XXIII, 950 E. It also protested against the conduct of the king's bailiffs in forbidding executors to administer the estate of a bishop pending the hearing of a charge lodged against him in the secular tribunals; c. 23—Mansi, XXIII, 957 C.

The excommunication decreed by the Councils of Merton (1258) and Lambeth (1261) were directed chiefly against bailiffs who confiscate the property of vacant sees and vacant monasteries while pretending to guard it in the interests of the king's equity; *locis citatis.*

Interdict was proclaimed by the Council of Magdeburg (1266) against patrons who seized, at the death of the occupant, benefices to which they had the right of presenting a nominee; excommunication, by the Council of Vienne; while all invaders are placed under interdict by a number of councils of the thirteenth century, the Council of Salzburg laying under interdict the place to which the confiscated property is conveyed; Council of Magdeburg, c. 14—Mansi, XXIII, 1164 C; Council of Vienne (1267), c. 10—Mansi, XXIII, 1173 C; Council of Buda (1279), c. 49—Mansi, XXIV, 292 E; Council of Salzburg (1281)—Mansi, XXIV, 401 D; Council of Reggio (1285), c. 18—Mansi, XXIV, 583 D; Council of Würzburg (1287), c. 26—Mansi, XXIV, 861 B; Synod of Cologne (1300), c. 11—Mansi, XXV, 20 E; Council of Mayence (1310)—Mansi, XXV, 327 E.

[22] Council of Chalcedon, c. 22—Mansi, VII, 367 A (c. 43, C. XII, q. 2); cc. 38, 42, C. XII, q. 2; Council of Tarragona (516), c. 12—Mansi, VIII, 543 D;

light of other canons which provide that the deceased bishop's estate is to be distributed to the clergy according to certain claims which they were given under the law. The claims were not to be paid, however, except in an orderly fashion, for instance, after a due inventory had been made and an administrator appointed.[23]

260. Custody of the Estate. Mere warning would probably have been inadequate. Consequently rather elaborate precautions were taken by the canons to provide a method of control that would guarantee justice to all concerned. The first act in the process was the custody of the estate.[24] Various plans for the proper custody were devised. For instance, the metropolitan is commanded to appoint an administrator.[25] Or the archdeacon is appointed to be custodian.[26] On the other hand, two honest persons are regarded elsewhere as suitable custodians;[27] or honest men in general.[28] The cathedral chapter is commanded, under late legislation, to appoint the administrator.[29] The metropolitan is to make the appointment in

Council of Aix-la-Chapelle (816), c. 88 (approves the Council of Chalcedon, c. 22)—Mansi, XIV, 202 D; Council of Worms (868), c. 75 (also approves the Council of Chalcedon, c. 22)—Mansi, XV, 882 B.

[23] C. 38, C. XII, q. 2 (*cf.* also Mansi, VIII, 615 A); Council of Valentia (524), c. 2—Mansi, VIII, 620 D.

[24] Council of Antioch (341), c. 24—Harduin, I, 603; Council of Valentia (524), c. 2—Mansi, VIII, 620 D; Fifth Council of Paris (615), c. 7—Mansi, X, 541 A; Harduin, III, 552; Hefele, III, 252; Council of Ponthion (876), c. 14—Mansi, XVII A, 312 D; Council of Pavia (876), c. 18—Mansi, XVIII A, 328 C; Council of Nîmes (1096), c. 5—Mansi, XX, 935 C; *Diploma* of Stephen, the King of England—Mansi, XXI, 495 E; Council of Tarragona (1239), c. 16—Mansi, XXIII, 518 A; Council of Aquileja (1596), c. 8—Mansi, XXXIV B, 1390 B; Council of Florence (1573), rub. 15, c. 2—Mansi XXXV A, 738 D; Council of Sienna (1599), c. 26—Mansi, XXXVI B, 552 B; Council of Petrokow (1577), c. 24—Mansi, XXXVI B, 634 D; Council of Mount Lebanon (1736), pars 3, c. 4, n. 27, 5 (approving the Council of Chalcedon, cc. 22, 25, 26 and the Trullan Synod, c. 35)—*Coll. Lacensis,* II, 317 a.

[25] Council of Valentia (524)—*l. c.;* Council of Aquileja (1596)—*l. c.*

[26] Fifth Council of Paris (615)—*l. c.*

[27] Council of Nîmes (1096)—*l. c.;* Council of Tarragona (1329), c. 26—Mansi, XXV, 847 A.

[28] *Diploma* of Stephen, the King of England—*l. c.*

[29] Council of Florence (1573)—*l. c.;* Council of Sienna (1599)—*l. c.*

case the chapter fails to do so, and in one instance he is commanded to intervene within eight days of the bishop's death.[30]

Pope Gregory the Great was especially solicitous that this custody be scrupulously maintained. In one letter he required a bishop to visit the diocese of a neighboring prelate and to provide that no misappropriation of property should occur.[31] On another occasion, he commissioned an administrator for this purpose;[32] in a third case, he requested an inventory of the chattels of a deceased prelate from a neighboring bishop into whose hands he had given the custody of the decedent's estate;[33] and where he feared that the deceased prelate might have appropriated ecclesiastical property without warrant, he ordered an inquiry to provide for restitution should his fears be verified.[34]

261. **The second act in the administration of a deceased bishop's estate was the inventory.** Reference has already been made to a case that came to the notice of Pope Gregory, where he anxiously sought an inventory of the deceased prelate's property. The device of the inventory is noted in canonical legislation, however, as early as the Council of Antioch.[35] Various instrumentalities are designated at various times for the completion of this rather important task. In one instance, the inventory was ordered to be drawn up under the supervision of the nearest bishop and presented to the metropolitan.[36] The priests and deacons of the decedent's diocese are the designated agents in another case.[37] The administrator may also be charged with this responsibility. The procedure he follows is to draft the inventory in the presence of a notary within ten days of the prelate's decease.[38]

In the case of a priest's property, it was the bishop who was to

[30] Council of Sienna (1599)—*l. c.*

[31] *Ad Agnellum*—Mansi, X, 59 B (*MPL*, LXXVII, 870).

[32] *Ad Anthemium*—Mansi, X, 142 D (*MPL*, LXXVII, 1010).

[33] *Ad Constantinum*—Mansi, X, 162 A.

[34] *Ad Cyprianum Dioconum*—*MPL*, LXXVII, 753 (c. 2, C. XII, q. 5).

[35] Council of Antioch (341)—*l. c.*

[36] Council of Valentia (524)—*l. c.*

[37] Council of Tarragona (516), c. 12—Mansi, VIII, 543 D.

[38] Council of Tarragona (1239)—*l. c.;* Council of Tarragona (1329)—*l. c.*

provide for due custody and inventory.[39] In one case, however, the archpriest is charged with this duty.[40] Indeed, the priest is required to make an inventory himself during his life.[41] A new copy of the inventory is to be made every ten years, and a copy of it sent to the bishop.[42]

262. **Disposition of the estate was forbidden until after the deceased prelate's will was read.**[43] Distribution was made in the case of an archbishop by his successor; in the case of a bishop, by the metropolitan; in the case of a priest, by the bishop.[44] Consequently, relatives of a deceased bishop were required to present their claims to the metropolitan and not to seize his estate on their own authority.[45]

263. **The bishop or priest himself is reminded that in making his will he must observe scrupulously the distinction** between ecclesiastical property and his own personal estate. This warning is discerned in both the canonical legislation and in the secular legislation of the empire. The canons are insistent on the point far back into antiquity.[46]

[39] Second Council of Orléans (533), c. 6—Mansi, VIII, 836 D.

[40] Statutes of Autun (1468), c. 29—Mansi, XXXII, 343 E.

[41] Ninth Council of Toledo (655), c. 4—Mansi, XI, 27 B.

[42] Council of Benevento (1599), tit. 34, c. 1—Mansi, XXXVI B, 446 B. And the same council commands the heirs of the cleric to surrender to the bishop all documents pertaining to the benefice as such; *l. c.*, c. 2—Mansi, XXXVI B, 446 D.

[43] Fifth Council of Paris (615)—*l. c.;* Council of Rheims (630)—*l. c.;* Council of Chalons (650)—*l. c.;* Ninth Council of Toledo (655), c. 7—Mansi, XI, 28 B.

[44] Ninth Council of Toledo (655)—*l. c.*

The property of a see was to be preserved inviolate during the vacancy; Council of Meaux (845), c. 21—Mansi, XIV, 823 C; Council of Pavia (892), c. 3—Mansi, XVIII A, 122 A; Council of Clermont (1095), c. 31—Mansi, XX, 818 D; Synod of Constance (1156)—Mansi, XXI, 839 E.

[45] Council of Valentia (524), c. 3—Mansi, VIII, 621 C; Ninth Council of Toledo (655), c. 1—Mansi, XI, 25 E.

[46] C. 3, C. XII, q. 3; Thomassin, *Vetus et Nova Disciplina,* III, 1, 16, 5; *ASS,* III (1867), 277. *Cf.* also Council of Antioch (341), cc. 24 and 25—Harduin, I, 603 and 605; Council of Agde (506), cc. 6, 33, 48—Mansi, VIII, 326 B, 330 C, and 333 A; Canons of the Apostles, cc. 39, 40—Harduin, I, 19 and 37 (cc. 20, 21, C. XII, q. 1); Third Council of Carthage, c. 49—Mansi, III,

Article 2

The Estate of an Intestate Cleric

264. The Heir of the Intestate Cleric. Though there was always a strong feeling that even the personal estate of a cleric should be devoted to the interests of the Church or of charity, nevertheless he was never forbidden to dispose of it according to his own wish.[47] The Church, however, was so far regarded as the natural heir of the deceased cleric, that should he die without distributing his personal estate, it was presumed that he wished his church to be the beneficiary.[48] But under the earlier councils, the estate of a bishop was distributed, when he died intestate, to the clergy of his diocese;[49] or to the poor.[50]

265. Escheat to the Bishop. After it was well established that the estate of a cleric dying intestate belonged to the church which he served, a further step was taken. This was escheat to the bishop, for

892 A (c. 1, C. XII, q. 3); Breviary of Fulgentius Ferrandus, cc. 31 and 35 (approving c. 24 of the Council of Antioch)—Mansi, VI, 469 C and 470 A; *Cap. Coll.* of Martin of Braga (6th cent.), c. 15—Mansi, XI, 851 B; *Cap. Coll. Can. Hibern.*, lib. 41, cc. 2-5—Mansi, XII, 135 A; Wasserschleben, pp. 158, 159; *Capitula* of Hadrian, c. 32—Mansi, XII, 876 A; First Council of Mayence (847), c. 8—Mansi, XIV, 905 E; *Capitula* of Hincmar, c. 18—Mansi, XV, 480 E; Letter of Pope Gelasius to Honorius—Mansi, VIII, 133 A; (*MPL*, LIX, 147); Council of Germany (1225), c. 5—Mansi, XXIII, 4 B; Council of Clermont (1268), c. 4—Mansi, XXIII, 1206 D; Statutes of Cahors (1289)—Mansi, XXIV, 1023 D; Council of Würzburg (1289), c. 12—Mansi, XXIV, 1192 C; Synod of Cologne (1300), c. 5—Harduin, VII, 1217; Council of Bayeux (1300), c. 58—Harduin, VII, 1234; Council of Florence (1346)—Mansi, XXVI, 45 E; Greco-Melchite Council (1812), c. 19—*Coll. Lacensis*, II, 588 c.

[47] C. 12, X, *de testamentis et ultimis voluntatibus*, III, 26.

[48] C. 1, X, *de successionibus ab intestato*, III, 27; c. 7, C. XII, q. 5; c. 18, X, *de verborum significatione*, V, 40; De Héricourt, *Les Lois Ecclesiastiques*, D. III, 126.

[49] Council of Agde (506), c. 33—Mansi, VIII, 330 D; Council of Valentia, c. 2—Mansi, VIII, 620 D.

[50] Council of Celichychth (816), c. 10 (prescribing that at least one-tenth of the estate be thus distributed)—Mansi, XIV, 359 B; Council of Ponthion (876), c. 14—Mansi, XVII A, 312 D; Council of Pavia (876), c. 18—Mansi, XVII A, 328 C; *cf. the Diploma* of Stephen, the King of England (1134)—Mansi, XXI, 495 E.

the benefit of the diocese, instead of to the cleric's church. The bishops were probably influenced in claiming the estate by the fact that a monk's property became, at death, the property of the abbot for the uses of the community. It was not difficult to argue that the cleric held in the organization of the diocese a place similar to that held by the monk in his community. Moreover, it would seem a bit rigorous to restrict the usefulness of the cleric's estate to that small portion of the diocese in which he had labored. It seemed more reasonable that it should be available for diocesan work.

Thus, the notion of the cleric's intimate union with his benefice gradually yielded to the idea that his union was with his diocese. Instead of the idea of mystical espousals between the cleric and his church, there developed the notion of *adrogation* to the diocese. The mystical spouse no longer claimed his personal estate when he died without a will. His church was no longer his beneficiary. His estate passed rather, by analogy, to the *paterfamilias* into whose *patria potestas* he had entered by ordination.

The new theory seems to have arisen towards the end of the twelfth century. At that time, the Council of Rouen (1189) ordained that the bishop should distribute the property of an intestate cleric to worthy causes.[51]

266. Towards the end of the thirteenth century, a movement arose in favor of the relatives of the intestate decedent. The Council of Nîmes (1287) and the Statutes of Cahors (1289) both provide that the personal estate of an intestate cleric shall be distributed first to relatives; if there be no relatives, then to the church which the cleric had served; and if he had had no charge, then to the bishop for the benefit of the poor.[52]

267. The *Ius Spolii*. The growth of the idea that the cleric is under the *patria potestas* of his bishop naturally suggested the further notion that the cleric everywhere is bound to the Holy See. His

[51] C. 15—Mansi, XXII, 584 B; so also the Council of Worcester (1240), c. 51 —Mansi, XXIII, 541 E; Council of London (1342), c. 8—Harduin, VII, 1662; Reforms of the Clergy of Liége (1446)—Mansi, XXXII, 36 C; Provincial Council of England (1509)—Mansi, XXXI A, 402 C.

[52] Council of Nîmes—Mansi, XXIV, 543 E; Statutes of Cahors—Mansi, XXIV, 1023 D.

status as a cleric removes him from every lay connection and incorporates him in a new familiy of which the Holy Father is the chief *paterfamilias*. He is no longer a juridical member of the family to which he belongs by blood.

Since the descent of his estate is determined not by blood but by juridical enactments based on his juridical status, it was sound legislation that placed his new family in the position of his heir rather than the natural family of which he was no longer a member. No natural rights were violated, because the natural family itself has rights in a decedent cleric's property only in virtue of positive enactments. The cleric is governed by the positive enactments of canon law. For him, canon law takes precedence over the secular law. It is only by toleration or concordat that the cleric at any time is permitted to be ruled by the laws of the civil State. Neither are any vested rights infringed, except those which might arise under the positive secular law. By these, as has been indicated, the cleric *per se* is not bound.

268. Consequently from the fourteenth century, at least, the Holy See began to reserve to the Apostolic Camera the property of clerics who died intestate. The beginnings of this reservation appear in the pontificate of Innocent IV (1243-1254).[53] This right (called the *ius spolii*) was resigned so far as it concerned the Kingdom of Naples in 1694 by Innocent XII in his constitution, *Inscrutabili,*[54] and Pius VII transferred the right in such estates to the Sacred Congregation for the Propagation of the Faith.[55]

[53] Wernz, *op. cit.*, III, 186; Pollock-Maitland, *op. cit.*, II, 359; Ferraris, *Bibliotheca Prompta*, VII, 282; Paul III, const., *Romani Pontifices*, 3 January, 1542—*Bullarium Romanum*, VI, 317; Julius III, const., *Cum sicut nobis*, 26 June, 1550—*Fontes*, 84. The second of these constitutions allowed the successor of the deceased to take all the vestments, the income of the benefice that had accrued since death, and a lump sum of fifty ducats. The constitution, *Romani pontificis providentia*, of Pope St. Pius V, provided that the church over which the cleric had been placed should have all the furniture and equipment; indeed, the whole estate, if the income of the benefice was less than thirty ducats (30 August, 1567)—*Bullarium Romanum*, VII, 609; *Fontes*, n. 123.

[54] 30 January, 1694—*Bullarium Romanum*, XX, 590.

[55] *Motu Proprio*, 19 June, 1817—*Coll. S. C. P. F.*, 724.

269. But the right of the Apostolic Camera to these estates seems not to have been recognized in France, Spain, Belgium, Portugal,[56] or Germany.[57] In France and Castile, moreover, relatives succeed to these estates.[58] Indeed, this privilege was sometimes granted by the Holy See in particular cases.[59]

In the fifteenth century, it appears that the cleric's estate in Liége and Cologne was distributed by his bishop.[60] The contrary is stated, however, in the Constitution of Cardinal Compeggio, Apostolic Delegate to Germany (1524), which ordains that the bishop is not to take over the patrimony or the property acquired by the cleric through personal industry (known as quasi-patrimony).[61]

270. As early as 1577 a new plan of distribution can be observed in the decrees of the Council of Petrokow, which ordains that after payment has been made of the debts, the funeral expenses, and the wages of domestics, the estate of the intestate cleric is to be divided into three parts, one of which is to be distributed to the church which he served; one, to his successor; and the third to pious causes for the repose of the soul of the deceased.[62]

271. The Council of Prague (1860) calls it the ancient custom of the province to divide the estate of an intestate cleric into three parts, of which one is given to the church which the decedent served (or to the seminary, in the case of a bishop); one to the poor of the locality which he served; and the remaining third to relatives. If the relatives are poor, they may have two-thirds; if there are no

[56] *Catholic Encyclopedia, s. v., "Jus Spolii."*

[57] Schmalzgrueber, *op. cit.*, III, III, 27, 58.

[58] Schmalzgrueber, *l. c.*

[59] Schmalzgrueber, *op. cit.*, III, III, 25, 9 and 36.

[60] Reforms of the Clergy of Liége (1446)—Mansi, XXXII, 36 C; Council of Cologne (1536), pars 13, c. 11—Mansi, XXXII, 1289 B. Both decrees provide that the administrator is to pay the debts of the decedent before turning the estate over to the bishop for distribution. *Cf.* also the Statutes of Autun (1468), c. 29—Mansi, XXXII, 343 E.

[61] C. 23—Mansi, XXXII, 1089 C. The same provision is found in the Council of London (1342), c. 8—Harduin, VII, 1662; the Council of Tortose (Spain) (1429)—Mansi, XXVIII, 1155 E; the Provincial Council of England (1509)—Mansi, XXXI A, 402 C.

[62] Mansi, XXXVI B, 719 B. The bishop is named executor.

heirs, the church of the cleric receives two-thirds.[63] The same plan was adopted by the Council of Vienna (1858).[64]

This three-fold division Wernz says is not to be condemned. But his cautious language refers only to the estate which the cleric probably derived from the income of his benefice.

For he notes that the heirs ordinarily take the patrimonial property, as well as the quasi-patrimony (that is, the estate the cleric has acquired by personal industry) and the parsimonial savings (that is, what the cleric was entitled to spend out of the income of his benefice, but saved instead).

If there are no heirs, then the church to which he was attached takes his estate. If he had no benefice, then his estate escheats to the treasury of the diocese or of the Holy See, unless by tolerated custom it is permitted to escheat to the State.

Wernz admits that the heirs may be permitted to take the whole estate, including the accumulated income from the benefice, provided they assume the same obligation of generosity to charity which rested on the cleric in virtue of that property. But even this obligation, he continues, does not bind them, if it has been abrogated by contrary custom or by apostolic privilege.[65]

272. Abrogation of the *Ius Spolii*. Clearly, at the time that Wernz wrote, and in general prior to the Code, the disposition of the personal estate of an intestate cleric was determined largely by custom. And custom seems pretty generally to have derogated the laws by which his estate escheated to the Apostolic Camera.

In the United States, the intestate cleric's property never escheated to the Church, not to the church he served, or his diocese, or the Holy See. Moreover, the New Code makes no mention of the

[63] Tit. 8, c. 5—*Coll. Lacensis,* V, 594 d.

[64] *Cf.* Council of Vienna (1858), tit. 7, c. 5—Mansi, XLVII, 838; *Coll. Lacensis,* V, 216, 217. It was also provided that if the decedent had more than one benefice, the one-third allotted to his benefice was to be distributed proportionately to the rate of income the cleric had received from each; if he had possessed only one at a time, the one-third should be given to the one he had held last, unless it was very rich; in which case it was to be distributed to the others.

[65] Wernz, *op. cit.,* III, 186 and 288.

escheat of such property. It would seem, therefore, that the *ius spolii* has been abrogated, in accordance with Canon 6, n. 6.[66]

273. There is no room then to doubt that in the United States, the provisions of the positive secular law regulate the distribution of an intestate cleric's personal estate. A particular law, of course, could intervene. But there seems to be no such law in any of the provinces or dioceses of the country. The silence of the canons indicates that the distribution of an intestate cleric's estate is a matter for local legislation. And there seems no good reason why the traditional attitude of the bishops in the United States should not be maintained, permitting the secular laws of descent to rule in the absence of a will.

Article 3

The History of the Cleric's Testament

274. The imperial legislation of the empire, influenced by the anxiety of the canons to prevent the alienation of ecclesiastical property to the loss of the Church, exercised a degree of vigilance which was probably helpful.

275. Justinian forbade the Archbishop of Contantinople and the administrators of the various charitable institutions of that city to transfer or sell any property acquired by them in any way after they had been installed in office.[67] This touched the gifts made to them personally, and interfered with the testamentary disposition of them. But in the Novels he permitted bishops to dispose of such gifts but only for the relief of the distressed or the greater advantage of the Church.[68]

276. There was a strong sentiment in the Church against the bishop's bequeathing even his own property to strangers. This

[66] Canon 6, n. 6. "Si qua ex ceteris disciplinaribus legibus, quae usque adhuc viguerunt, nec explicite nec implicite in Codice contineatur, ea vim omnem amisisse dicenda est, nisi in probatis liturgicis libris reperiatur, aut lex sit iuris divini sive positivi sive naturalis."

[67] C. 1, 3, 41, 3 and 5; C. 1, 3, 41, 11. He had also forbidden them to convey the realty of the Church or of a charitable institution; C. 1, 2, 14.

[68] *Nov.* 131, 13.

feeling manifests itself in the legislation of Theodosius the Younger regarding the estate of intestate clerics. If they left no heirs, their property must be given to the church to which they were attached or to their monastery.[69] On the other hand, what purports to be a constitution of Leo and Anthemius (472) regards what the cleric acquires as an individual as a *peculium* of his own, free from the *patria potestas* of his natural father, capable of being transmitted to whomever the cleric shall choose.[70] But the beneficiaries were restricted in the Novels to charitable and religious works.[71] With this restriction, Justinian affirmed the privilege and relieved the cleric's will of the action *querela inofficiosi,* that is, as has been noted,[72] a suit instituted by parents, brothers, or sisters or children, on the ground that they had not been remembered in the will to the extent of their legitimate share of one-fourth the estate.[73] But in the Novels, he modified the privilege and permitted children and parents to enter such a suit for their share.[74]

277. The right of the cleric to make a will, prescinding from the question of beneficiary, was always strenuously defended by the canons, though by particular rather than by general legislation.[75] At

[69] *Codex Theod.*, 5, 3, 1; C. 1, 3, 20; *Nov.*, 131, 13; De Héricourt, *op. cit.*, H 181; see also the Council of Carthage (525)—Mansi, VIII, 644 B; and the Letter of Salvianus to Salonius—*MPL,* LIII, 171.

[70] C. 1, 3, 33; *cf.* also Schmalzgrueber, *op. cit.*, I, III, 18, 5.

[71] *Nov.*, 123, 37.

[72] *Cf.* § 109, this treatise.

[73] C. 1, 3, 49 (531); I. 2, 18, 6, 7; I, 3, 1, 14; D. 5, 2, 8, 6; *Nov.*, 18, 1.

[74] *Nov.*, 123, 19 (546).

Parents, moreover, were not permitted to disinherit their children for the reason that the latter had entered a monastery or had become clerics; C. 1, 3, 54, 5; *Nov.*, 123, 41.

And they who were legatees on condition that they marry or have children were entitled to claim and dispose of the legacy during life or by will if they embraced the religious life—C. 1, 3, 52, 13; Thomassin, *op. cit.*, III, 1, 23, 8.

[75] Council of Lyons (567), c. 2—Harduin, III, 354; Mansi, IX, 787 C; Fifth Council of Paris (615), c. 10—Mansi, X, 541 D; Letter of Gregory the Great *ad Mariamnum, Episcopum Ravennae*—Mansi, X, 1 A; (*MPL,* LXXVII, 793); Council of Walter, Bishop of Rouen (1189), c. 15—Mansi, XXII, 584 B; Addition to the Council of Oxford (1222)—Mansi, XXII, 1179 D; Council of Cologne (1266), c. 7—Mansi, XXIII, 1138 B; Council of London (1342), c. 8—Harduin, VII, 1662.

Carthage in 525 the Fathers of the Council were shocked at the thought of a bishop's dying intestate.[76]

But a cleric was not permitted to bequeath anything to non-Christians, even if they were his relatives.[77] And well into the Middle Ages there appears a background of feeling against the bishop's giving by will the property he had acquired for himself as bishop, except for the benefit of the Church.[78] In one instance, a bishop who bequeathed his personal estate to strangers was regarded as unworthy of his office.[79]

278. **By the time of Gregory IX, however,[80] it was conceded that clerics might dispose by will not only of their patrimony but also of gifts made to them as clerics, and with no restriction as to beneficiary.**[81]

279. But Schmalzgrueber contends that this right of clerics does not derive from the provisions of the general law.[82] This would seem the case at present also, except as to Cardinals. However, all bene-

[76] Mansi, VIII, 644 B. This anxiety was probably inspired by the desire to preserve the property of the see intact and to benefit charity by the dispositions which the bishop would leave behind for the guidance of his administrator or successor. And the Council of London (1257) warned the king not to interfere with the administration of a bishop's will; Mansi, XXIII, 950 E.

[77] Council of Hippo (393), c. 14—Mansi, III, 921 D; Council of Carthage (419), c. 27—Mansi, IV, 429 D; Council of Carthage (525)—Mansi, VIII, 643 D and 644 B; Breviary of Fulgentius Ferrandus, c. 32—Mansi, VI, 469 D; *Capitula* of Hadrian, c. 47—Mansi, XII, 878 E.

[78] Council of Agde (506), c. 6—Mansi, VII, 326 B; c. 3, C. XII, q. 3; Letter of Gregory the Great *ad Maximianum—MPL,* LXXVII, 711; *idem ad Scholasticum Defensorem—MPL,* LXXVII, 1133; Wernz, *op. cit.*, III, 274.

[79] Council of Carthage (525)—Mansi, VII, 644 B.

As late as 1859, the Council of Bordeaux counseled that the bishop bequeath his personal estate to his church; tit. 3, c. 1, n. 5—*Coll. Lacensis,* IV, 756 b.

[80] De Héricourt, *op. cit.*, D. III, 126.

[81] Appendix of the Third General Council of the Lateran (1179), pars 29, c. 5 (citing the rescript of Alexander III to the Bishop of Palermo)—Mansi, XXII, 380 E; c. 9, X, *de testamentis et ultimis voluntatibus,* III, 26; cf. also for similar legislation the Council of Prague (1346)—Mansi, XXVI, 87 A; Council of Prague (1355)—Mansi, XXVI, 393 D; Council of Prague (1860), tit. 8, c. 4—*Coll. Lacensis* V, 593 c; Greco-Melchite Council (1812), c. 19—*Coll. Lacensis,* II, 588 c.

[82] *Op. cit.*, III, III, 25, 4.

ficed clerics are bound to make a will, and every cleric may distribute his personal estate to pious causes under Canon 1513, § 1. The will required of beneficed clerics will be the subject of a later investigation.

280. On the other hand, restraints were sometimes placed on clerics as to the disposition of even their personal estate. A partial incapacity of this kind was imposed in the fifteenth and sixteenth centuries, when they were forbidden to make bequests to women who had been an occasion of sin to them or to children who had been born as the result of sin.[83] A similar incapacity was imposed touching property which the cleric had acquired as the profits of trade.[84] Total incapacity was inflicted as a penalty for the alienation of property belonging to the benefice,[85] and for the failure of the cleric to reside within the territory of his benefice.[86]

281. The Income of the Benefice. The earliest incapacity grew out of the nature of the property in the cleric's possession. The property affected by this incapacity was the income of the benefice and the fund accumulated from it. Of this the cleric could not dispose by will. It descended to the benefice, or rather remained a part of the benefice.[87] If a cleric attempted to make a bequest of property

[83] St. Pius V, const. *Quae ordini*, 27 January, 1571—*Bullarium Romanum*, VII, 770; St. Pius V, const., *Ad Romanum spectat*, 5 March, 1572—*Bullarium Romanum*, VII, 883; Paul V, const., *In eminenti*, 8 April, 1606—*Bullarium Romanum*, XI, 299.

The first two of these constitutions forbade the cleric to bequeath even his patrimony to any illegitimate child, even though legitimated, except to an orphan asylum or a foundling asylum.

[84] Pius IV, const., *Decens*, 5 November, 1560—*Bullarium Romanum*, VII, 78.

[85] Paul III, const., *Romani Pontifices*, 3 January, 1542—*Bullarium Romanum*, VI, 317; Pius IV, const., *Grave nobis et molestum*, 26 May, 1560 (even though the whole estate were given to pious causes)—*Bullarium Romanum*, VII, 27.

[86] Pius IV, const., *In suprema*, 25 November, 1564—*Bullarium Romanum*, VII, 332; Urban VIII, const., *Sancta Synodus Tridentina*, 12 December, 1634—*Bullarium Romanum*, XIV, 457; *Fontes*, 215.

The goods of a monk acquired by him while he was living outside the cloister were confiscated to the Apostolic Camera by Gregory XIII, const., *Officii nostri partes*, 21 January, 1577—*Bullarium Romanum*, VIII, 162.

[87] Cc. 1, 5, X, *de peculio clericorum*, III, 25; c. 12, X, *de testamentis et ultimis voluntatibus*, III, 26; cc. 1, 2, X, *de successionibus ab intestato*, III, 27.

thus acquired for the church or from the church, it could be reclaimed.[88]

282. In the eighth and ninth centuries, however, there sprang up the custom of bequeathing this property (that is, the income of the benefice). But it was vigorously condemned by the Third General Council of the Lateran and by Alexander III,[89] though the Pope permitted the custom of making moderate bequests to the poor, to domestics, to charitable institutions, and to benefactors.[90] The same permission was then granted in many particular councils.[91] But

[88] Third General Council of the Lateran (1179), c. 15—Mansi, XXII, 226 D (c. 7, *de testamentis et ultimis voluntatibus,* III, 26); Appendix of the Third General Council of the Lateran (1179), pars 29, c. 8 (citing the rescript of Alexander III to the Bishop of Le Mans)—Mansi, XXII, 381 C (c. 8, *de testamentis et ultimis voluntatibus,* III, 26); Council of Nîmes (1284)—Mansi, XXIV, 543 E.

The cleric who attempts to dispose of such property is excommunicated; Statutes of Liége, c. 34—Mansi, XXIV, 938 B. And the property of which he attempts to dispose is to be given to the poor; Council of Tarragona (1339)—Mansi, XXV, 877 A.

To his successor in the benefice he was required to transmit the *utensilia,* the house, the furniture, the live stock, and the grain; Statutes of Le Mans (1247)—Mansi, XXIII, 758 D; Council of Bayeux (1300), c. 58—Harduin, VII, 1234; Council of Würzburg (1289), c. 12—Mansi, XXIV, 1192 C; Council of Treves (1310), c. 78—Mansi, XXV, 268 B.

[89] Cc. 7-9, X, *de testamentis et ultimis voluntatibus,* III, 26; Wernz, *op. cit.,* III, 274.

[90] C. 12, X, *de testamentis et ultimis voluntatibus,* III, 26; Wernz, *op. cit.,* III, 274; *ASS,* III (1867), 277.

[91] De Héricourt, *op. cit.,* D. III, 126; Synodical Constitutions of Odo, Bishop of Paris (*circa* 1200)—Mansi, XXII, 683 A; Ancient Precepts of Rouen (1235), c. 54—Mansi, XXIII, 381 A; Council of Clermont (1268), c. 4—Mansi, XXIII, 1206 D; Council of Nîmes (1284)—Mansi, XXIV, 543 E; Council of Würzburg (1289), c. 12—Mansi, XXIV, 1192 C; Council of Cahors (1289)—Mansi, XXIV, 1023 D; Statutes of Liége, c. 34—Mansi, XXIV, 1938 B; Synod of Cologne (1300), c. 5—Harduin, VII, 1217; Council of Bayeux (1300), c. 58—Harduin, VII, 1234; Council of Petrokow (1577)—Mansi, XXXVI B; 719 B.

Curious problems arose as to just what portion of the income was thus at the cleric's disposal. One council determines that if the cleric dies after Easter, he is entitled to distribute the autumn crops of that year; Council of Walter, Bishop of Rouen, c. 16—Mansi, XXII, 584 C. Under the same circumstances, he could dispose of the income up to Michaelmas (September 29); Synod of Norwich (1255)—Mansi, XXIII, 913 A. If the decedent was alive on March twenty-fifth,

the beneficiary in any event could not be a woman who had been an occasion of sin to the cleric, nor a child born of such a sin, even if they were poor.[92] Property illegally bequeathed to such a woman was confiscated for the poor,[93] or escheated to the cleric's church.[94]

283. **The special privilege of making unrestricted disposition of this property was granted on occasion to the clergy living at Rome.** This privilege seems to have been first granted under the constitution, *Etsi universis,* of Sixtus IV (1474), which enabled these clerics to dispose also of any estate they owned within ten miles of the city. But if they died intestate, their heirs could not claim the fund accumulated from the income of the benefice.[95] The restriction as to heirs by intestate succession was removed, however, by Julius III (1550).[96] Pius IV (1560), in ordaining that the estate of a cleric derived from the profits of trade was forfeit to the Apostolic Camera, made an exception in favor of those mentioned in the two

the tithes and the income of the whole year were available for distribution by the decree of the Council of Worcester (1240), c. 51—Mansi, XXIII, 541 E.

If this fund was not adequate to discharge the decedent's debts, he was allowed the income of an extra year; Council of Mayence (1310)—Mansi, XXV, 321 B; Council of Prague (1346)—Mansi, XXVI, 87 A; Council of Prague (1355)—Mansi, XXVI, 393 D. Two centuries earlier, the Constitution of the Bishop of York had set aside this amount of extra income for the repose of the soul and the payment of debts of decedent canons; Mansi, XXI, 495 B.

Moreover, if the property of the benefice was permitted to deteriorate, the cost of repairs was a charge against the cleric's personal estate, at least against the gifts that had come to him by reason of his office; Constitutions of the Bishop of Salisbury, c. 42—Harduin, VII, 101; Mansi, XXII, 1121 C; Council of Scotland (1225), c. 63—Mansi, XXII, 1241 C; Provincial Constitutions of St. Edward, Archbishop of Canterbury, c. 26—Mansi, XXIII, 423 C.

[92] Council of Mayence (1225), c. 5—Hefele, V, 1449; Council of Tours (1239), c. 7—Mansi, XXIII, 499 C; Council of Saumur (1253), c. 30—Mansi, XXIII, 818 B; Council of Mayence (1261), c. 27—Mansi, XXIII, 1090 E; Council of Treves (1310), c. 78—Mansi, XXV, 268 B.

[93] Synod of Chichester (1289), c. 23—Mansi, XXIV, 1060 C; Constitutions of York (1518), c. 6—Mansi, XXXV A, 193 C.

[94] Council of Cologne (1310), c. 15—Mansi, XXV, 241 A; Council of Mayence (1310)—Mansi, XXV, 320 E; Statutes of Autun (1468), c. 29—Mansi, XXXII, 343 E; Provincial Council of England (1509)—Mansi, XXXI A, 400 A; Council of Petrokow (1577)—Mansi, XXXI B, 719 B.

[95] 1 January, 1474—*Bullarium Romanum,* V, 211.

[96] Const., *Cupientes,* 10 March, 1550—*Bullarium Romanum,* VI, 412.

former constitutions.[97] In 1565, he extended the privilege to all the property wherever situated of clerics who would build in a certain section of the city which he was developing.[98]

284. Bequests of Ecclesiastical Income in Recent Times. At the end of the seventeenth century the cleric is regarded by the universal custom of France and Spain as having a right to dispose by will of the income of his benefice,[99] while in 1858 the Council of Vienna notes that though originally the *beneficiarius* could not legally dispose by will of the income of his benefice, nevertheless the right was later granted him of disposing of this fund for pious causes; and that even later in many regions a custom grew up whereby a general disposition of such funds by will was permitted on account of the difficulty of separating them from the rest of the cleric's estate. Such a custom, it says, is immemorial in Austria. But it reminds clerics that in death the same obligation of charity rests on them as in life.[100]

But other councils of the nineteenth century are more conservative. The Council of Prague (1860), for instance, cites the Council of Trent,[101] and states that it is the mind of the Church that the funds received as income from a benefice should be distributed to the poor. The Council, however, permits them to be bequeathed to poor relatives and to benefactors.[102]

[97] Const., *Romanus Pontifex,* 5 November, 1560—*Bullarium Romanum,* VII, 789.

[98] Const., *Romanum,* 23 August, 1565—*Bullarium Romanum,* VII, 381.

[99] Council of Bahia (1707), lib. 4, tit. 38—*Coll. Lacensis,* I, 858 A. And De Héricourt says that parents succeed to all the estate of the cleric except what actually belongs to the principal of the benefice; *Op. cit.* D III, 126.

[100] Tit. 7, c. 4—Mansi, XLVII, 838. This Council also provided that the archpriest should be the administrator of the will of the deceased cleric; *l. c.*
At about the same time, by a Concordat between Pope Pius IX and the Emperor Franz Joseph, it was provided that bishops and priests were to be permitted to make wills according to the canons, but that they were not to be permitted to bequeath the ornaments of the diocese, pontifical vestments or their books; Art. 21—*Coll. Lacensis,* V, 1224 b.

[101] Sess. XXV, *de ref.,* c. 1, where it is provided that the bishop may give out of the income of his benefice assistance to his parents only when they are poor.

[102] Tit. 8, c. 4—*Coll. Lacensis,* V, 593 c. *Cf.* also the Convention of the Bishops of Austria (1856), c. 42—*Coll. Lacensis,* V, 1254 a; Greco-Melchite

285. Succession in the benefice itself by will or *ab intestato* was never tolerated; nor were pacts by which the incumbent agreed to transmit to another his benefice. On the other hand, the right to nominate the incumbent does pass to the heirs of the person who enjoyed it.[103]

286. The Cleric's Duty to Make a Will. To protect the property of the Church, the canons of the nineteenth century were insistent that bishops and priests regard it as a sacred duty to make their wills.[104] But proper distribution of their personal estate was also in the mind of the legislator, for they are told to remember the poor.[105]

287. In the United States, the Fourth Provincial Council of Baltimore (1840) ordained that all bishops should hold the property of their dioceses in such a way that it would pass validly under the secular law to their successors, have a proper inventory of church property made, and make a will.[106]

The Sacred Congregation for the Propagation of the Faith, in approving this decree (December 15, 1840), prescribed that the bishop should make one of the bishops of the United States his heir; preferably his co-adjutor, if he has one. He is counseled to keep one copy and send a copy to the Archbishop of Baltimore. The latter was to send his to the senior bishop of the United States.[107]

Because of the variation in the laws of the States, it seemed necessary to modify this plan. Instead of the Archbishop of Baltimore as the custodian of the wills of the bishops of the country, it seemed bet-

Council (1812), c. 19—*Coll. Lacensis,* II, 588 c; Council of Gran (1858), tit. 6, n. 4 (citing c. 12, X, *de testamentis et ultimis voluntatibus,* III, 26 and c. 19, C. XII, q. 1)—*Coll Lacensis,* V, 59 a; Council of Venice (1859), part 2, c. 17, n. 2—*Coll. Lacensis,* VI, 316 b; Council of Colocza (Hungary), (1863), tit. 4, c. 5—*Coll. Lacensis,* V, 670 d; Council of Utrecht (1865), tit. 10, c. 4—*Coll. Lacensis,* V, 928 d.

[103] Schmalzgrueber, *op. cit.,* III, I, 5, 72, 73.

[104] Council of Rheims (1849), tit. 12, c. 1—*Coll. Lacensis,* IV, 128 c; Council of Ireland (1850), decree 22, n. 6—*Coll. Lacensis,* III, 794 c; Council of Sens (1850), tit. 4, c. 4—*Coll. Lacensis,* IV, 905 a; Council of Colocza (1863), tit. 4, c. 5—*Coll. Lacensis,* V, 670 d; Second Council of Australia (1869), decree 5—*Coll. Lacensis,* III, 1079 a.

[105] Council of Bordeaux (1850), tit. 4, c. 11—*Coll. Lacensis,* IV, 590 a.

[106] C. 8—*Coll. Lacensis,* III, 71 c.

[107] *Coll. Lacensis,* III, 81 a; *Coll. S. C. P. F.,* 916.

ter that each archbishop should care for the wills of the bishops of his province. He, in turn, filed his with the senior bishop of his province. To provide for central control, it was provided that the Sacred Congregation for the Propagation of the Faith should be given a copy; and to make that possible, the bishop was required to file two copies with his metropolitan.

The Fifth Provincial Council of Baltimore suggested this plan to the Sacred Congregation, and it was approved September 30, 1843.[108] The Council also provided that the archbishop is to be given the copies within three months of the consecration of the bishop, and that the latter must be given due warning if he has not complied with this regulation within the proper time.

There were other regulations in the original decree of the Sacred Congregation which were left in full force. The bishop was to notify the prelate whom he appointed his heir that he had done so and to explain that the property mentioned in the will consists of the property of the diocese. The notification was then to be burnt. When the bishop died, the prelate named the heir was to appoint a procurator to administer the property until the appointment of a successor to the deceased. An account of the administration was to be rendered to the successor on his installation. And the bishops were urged to provide that religious communities should follow a similar plan, where it was necessary to safeguard the succession, and that one copy of the will of the superior should be preserved in the archives of the community and another in the files of the bishop.[109]

288. The Second Plenary Council of Baltimore (1866) cites the decree of the Sacred Congregation for the Propagation of the Faith of 1840, and the modifications introduced in it at the suggestion of the Fifth Provincial Council. It re-affirms the law as it stood after the modification.[110] It requires bishops to have a due inventory

[108] C. 1—*Coll. Lacensis,* III, 89 b.

[109] The Provincial Council of Cincinnati (1855) decreed that the bishops of the province were to hold the property of their dioceses in fee simple and no longer as a corporation sole; and that they were to make a will naming as beneficiary a bishop in another State in order that thus the will might be made subject to the Federal court; sess. 2, *Congregatio quarta privata—Coll. Lacensis,* III, 192 a.

[110] Tit. 4, c. *un.*, n. 204—*Coll. Lacensis,* III, 455 c.

of the property of the diocese.[111] Priests are to provide a similar inventory of the property of the parish. They are forbidden to mingle their own property with that of the parish or to lend money to the parish without the permission of the bishop and proper attestation by worthy witnesses.[112]

289. The Third Plenary Council of Baltimore (1884) approves the plan of the decree of the Sacred Congregation for the Propagation of the Faith as modified.[113]

It repeats the precept forbidding rectors and administrators to mingle their own property with the goods of the church or the institution, ordaining that one copy of an inventory is to be kept in the files of the church or institution, and the other sent to the diocesan archives. The inventory is to be made annually and sent to the chancery with due modifications from year to year. It is to be handed to the successor in office upon his installation, either by his predecessor or by the vicar forane. In case of doubt whether gifts were made to the church or to the priest personally, if they serve the uses of the church, they are presumed given to the church; consequently, they are not to be claimed by the heirs of the priest in charge.

Article 4

The Cleric's Present Testamentary Capacity

290. Three main problems rather obviously present themselves in a discussion of the present law touching the testaments of clerics. The first is whether the cleric is free to make a will; the second, whether there are restrictions placed upon his making a will; and the third, whether there is an obligation resting on him to make a will. The first two problems will be considered in this article, the third being reserved for the article following.

291. The answer to the first problem is almost at hand without investigation. Though the cleric was never given explicity the right to make a will under the general canons, still that right was always recognized even by those earlier Fathers, who, influenced by the

[111] *L. c.*, n. 188.
[112] *L. c.*, n. 193.
[113] N. 269.

notion that the Christian community should hold its property in common, thought that the cleric's personal property should become the property of the community upon his ordination. Never was it stated in a general or a particular law that admission to the clerical state, or even consecration as a bishop, deprived the persons thus privileged of the right to own their personal estate or to dispose of it *inter vivos* or *mortis causa.*

On the other hand, by particular legislation, the canons aimed at protecting the interests of bishops and priests even against their superiors in order that the disposition of their property after their decease might proceed in an orderly fashion and according to the wishes they had expressed in their wills. Indeed, the right of a cleric to make a will, so far from being denied by the canons, has been more than once vigorously upheld.

The theories on which the *ius spolii* were founded offer no argument for the position that a cleric's property belongs to his church, to his diocese, or even to the Holy See; or for the contention that it must automatically descend at his death to these heirs. For the law of descent based on intestacy, so far from denying a man's right to make a will, is really an interpretation of his will, a conclusion as to what he would wish to do, had he had the opportunity to make a will.

Consequently, the response to the question as to whether the cleric is competent under the canons to make a will is affirmative.

292. **The restrictions** that were at one time or another placed upon a cleric's capacity to make a will concerned either the objects of his generosity or the various kinds of property that he possessed. In certain kinds of property he was considered at various times to have only a temporary estate and to be consequently incapable of disposing of it by will.

293. As to the objects of their generosity, clerics were forbidden in the earlier legislation of the councils to make bequests even from their personal estate to non-Christians, even though the latter were their relatives. Speaking only in the juridical sense, that prohibition was never part of the general discipline of the canons, and had ceased to leave any vestiges even in particular legislation long before the Middle Ages.

294. It was regarded as unseemly that a bishop should leave his personal estate to strangers. This was based on the notion, no doubt, that a man who was so callous to the needs of the people of his diocese as to forget them and bequeath his property to utter strangers was hardly animated by the spirit of charity that should be expected in a bishop. But it is difficult to find any canon that invalidates such a bequest, unless it be that of the Council of Carthage which regards such a bishop as unworthy of his position.[114] Regarding the matter again only juridically, while this prohibition is more than probably in accord with the spirit of the present law, whatever canonical obligatory force it may have had is now altogether nugatory.

295. **The goods to the use of which he was entitled, but of which the cleric was forbidden to dispose by** will included: first, the actual capital property of the church or the pious foundation, including vestments and furnishings; second, the income derived from the capital, chiefly as crops and fruits; and third, gifts made to him after he became a cleric.

296. As to the third class of property, it was admitted quite early in the history of the canons that where these gifts were clearly and indubitably meant for him personally, they belonged to him. Indeed, the real reason for the original prohibition was based on the theory that these gifts were not meant for the cleric at all, but for the church. This interpretation of the donor's intention was made a presumption of law (*iuris et de iure*) and became crystallized in a prohibition against the cleric's claiming the gift as his own.[115] Though canonized by imperial constitutions as to bishops and administrators of charitable institutions, this presumption soon became obsolete as to priests, and eventually also as to bishops, though it continued well into the Middle Ages as a restriction on the latter. By the time of Gregory IX, however, the restriction had disappeared entirely.[116]

297. As to the first class of property, *i. e.*, the capital property of the church, it was just as certainly forbidden always and everywhere,

[114] Council of Carthage (525)—Mansi, VIII, 644 B.

[115] C. 1, 3, 41, 3 and 5; C. 1, 3, 41, 11.

[116] De Héricourt, *op. cit.*, D. III, 126; c. 9, X, *de testamentis et ultimis voluntatibus*, III, 26; Wernz, *op. cit.*, III, 274.

by particular as well as by general legislation, to dispose of it as one's own *inter vivos, mortis causa,* or by will.[117] It will be proper to discuss what measures the general legislation provides to guarantee the security of this property on the death of the incumbent. The appropriate place for that discussion will be where the obligation of the cleric to make a will is considered.

298. The second class of property is a class of which even today the cleric may be said, as a general principle, not to have free disposition. At first, as has already been indicated,[118] the income of the benefice was added, under the regulations of particular councils, to the capital of the benefice. Then an attempt to dispose of it freely was thwarted by Alexander III and the Third General Council of the Lateran, though the custom was so far recognized as to allow clerics to dispose of the property to the poor, to domestics, to relatives who were poor, to charitable institutions, and to benefactors.

299. Again, as a general principle, it may be stated that this is the law today.[119] The reason is that under the most recent legislation

[117] Indeed, the alienation even for the advantage of the Church of ecclesiastical property is severely supervised by the canons. Witness Canon 1530, § 1. "Salvo praescripto, can. 1281, § 1, ad alienandas res ecclesiasticas immobiles aut mobiles, quae servando servari possunt, requiritur: 1°. Aestimatio rei a probis peritis scripto facta; 2°. Iusta causa, idest urgens necessitas, vel evidens utilitas Ecclesiae, vel pietas; 3°. Licentia legitimi Superioris, sine qua alienatio invalida est."

Canon 1532, § 1. "Legitimus Superior de quo in can. 1530, § 1, n. 3, est Sedes Apostolica, si agatur: 1°. De rebus pretiosis; 2°. De rebus quae valorem excedunt triginta millium libellarum seu francorum."

§ 2. "Si vero agatur de rebus quae valorem non excedunt mille libellarum seu francorum, est loci Ordinarius, audito administrationis Consilio, nisi res minimi momenti sit, et cum eorum consensu quorum interest."

§ 3. "Si denique de rebus quarum pretium continetur intra mille libellas et triginta millia libellarum seu francorum, est loci Ordinarius, dummodo accesserit consensus tum Capituli cathedralis, tum Consilii administrationis, tum eorum quorum interest."

[118] *Cf.* §§ 281, 282, this treatise.

[119] Canon 1473. "Etsi beneficiarius alia bona beneficialia habeat, libere uti frui potest fructibus beneficialibus qui ad eius honestam sustentationem sint necessarii; obligatione autem tenetur impendendi superfluos pro pauperibus aut piis causis, salvo praescripto can. 239, § 1, n. 19."

the benefice and its funds hold the same position in regard to the incumbent that they held heretofore.

300. But Canon 239, § 1, n. 19, expressly confers on Cardinals as a privilege the right of disposing of the income of their benefices.[120]

301. The Nature of a Benefice. To understand the rights of testamentary disposition that a cleric has in the income of his benefice, a clear notion must be obtained of what a benefice is. A benefice is defined as a juridical entity or a non-collegiate moral person (*i. e.*, a corporation not composed of persons, but rather an institution regarded as a corporation).[121] It is composed of two constitutive parts: first, a sacred office; and second, the right of its incumbent to a temporal income.

The sacred office is first, a duty imposed by divine institution (as in the case of the Holy See itself) or established by ecclesiastical charter (as in the case of a parish); second, it is permanent in its nature; third, it is governed by the canons as to its incumbent; and fourth, it is endowed with at least some participation of ecclesiastical power either of orders or of jurisdiction.[122]

It suffices that the office annexed to the benefice should imply the power of orders in the incumbent, *v. gr.*, the duty of reciting the divine office, or of saying Mass. Even the power of sacred administration suffices, it would seem, so that the office of sacristan could be attached to a benefice. But the position of sexton or of organist

[120] Canon 239, § 1, n. 19. "Praeter alia privilegia quae in hoc Codice suis in titulis enumerantur, Cardinales omnes a sua promotione in Consistorio facultate gaudent: De reditibus beneficiariis libere disponendi etiam per testamentum, salvo praescripto can. 1298 [the prescription of the latter Canon will be discussed when the obligation of making a will is considered]."

[121] Canon 99. "In Ecclesia, praeter personas physicas, sunt etiam personae morales, publica auctoritate constitutae, quae distinguuntur in personas morales collegiales et non collegiales, ut ecclesiae, Seminaria, beneficia, etc."

[122] Canon 145, § 1. "Officium ecclesiasticum lato sensu est quodlibet munus quod in spiritualem finem legitime exercetur; stricto autem sensu est munus ordinatione sive divina sive ecclesiastica stabiliter constitutum, ad normas sacrorum canonum conferendum, aliquam saltem secumferens participationem ecclesiasticae potestatis sive ordinis sive jurisdictionis."

Canon 1409. "Beneficium ecclesiasticum est ens iuridicum a competente ecclesiastica auctoritate in perpetuum constitutum seu erectum, constans officio sacro et iure percipiendi reditus ex dote officio adnexo."

seems to be too remote from the power of orders to be regarded as sacred in the sense required to attach it to a benefice.[123]

There are two essential conditions on which a benefice depends for the validity of its establishment: first, it must be constituted by competent ecclesiastical authority, at least the union of the endowment and the sacred office must be made thus; second, the duty itself must be objectively perpetual, though not demanding continual exercise. It need not be subjectively perpetual, that is, it need not be granted to the beneficiary for the term of his life.[124]

302. The question now arises as to what precisely is the income of the benefice of which the cleric may not dispose as he wishes. It has been maintained in the past that the cleric is restricted as to all income derived from an office for which ecclesiastical appointment (*missio canonica*) is necessary, even though it be not a benefice and even though the endowment had never become ecclesiastical property. This is undoubtedly an extreme opinion, and Wernz regarded it as unfounded in the law.[125]

[123] Vermeersch-Creusen, *op. cit.*, II, 742; Vromant, *op. cit.*, 213.

[124] Vromant, *l. c.* In Belgium, says Vromant, though a pension is paid by the government to the *vicar cooperator*, the office has not been established as a benefice by ecclesiastical authority. In France the same is true; Vromant, *op. cit.*, 214.

Pensions are not benefices even though they are paid out of the income of a benefice, unless they are government pensions establishd by concordat in lieu of restitution of confiscated benefices; Ferreres, *Theol. Mor.*, I, 695, 697.

[125] Wernz, *op. cit.*, III, 186 (the opinion is Hollweck's, p. 35; cited by Wernz).

As to the income of the benefice as such there is diversity of opinion among the authorities as to the *nature* of the obligation binding the cleric to use the superfluous amount for the poor. Wernz maintains that the practice of many centuries shows that the title to the income belongs to the *pastor*. *Cf.* Sebastianelli, *De Rebus*, 272. As a consequence of this opinion, the obligation to make distribution to the poor would be a personal obligation *ex oboedientia*, not *ex iustitia*, and would not descend to the heirs; *cf.* Wernz, *l. c.*, Vermeersch-Creusen state that this opinion was probable prior to the New Code, and contend for the same opinion as being valid after the Code; *op. cit.*, II, 798; *cf.* also for the same opinion, Vromant, *op. cit.*, 216; De Meester, 1424; Ferreres, *Insts. Can.*, II, 456; *idem, Theol. Mor.*, I, 691-698.

Another opinion holds that the incumbent has only the use and the usufruct of the income, *salva substantia*. Pistocchi holds this view and contends that

303. Next in rigor is the opinion of the learned Zallinger who believes that the cleric is restricted as to the distribution of the so-called *parsimonialia* and the *quasi-patrimonialia.* The *parsimonialia* are composed of that portion of the income which an ordinary incumbent would have spent for living expenses but which the present incumbent has saved by living frugally. Canonists and moral theologians quite generally concede that he may dispose of such property as he likes. The *quasi-patrimonialia* in general are the funds that have come to the cleric by reason of his own industry. It is clear that most of these funds will be derived indirectly at least from the office which he holds, though not from the endowment itself. The cleric is generally conceded the right to make whatever disposition he likes of these funds also.[126]

304. There is a further difference of opinion as to what income constitutes the *quasi-patrimonialia.* First, there seems to be unanimity in the following conclusions. As funds of the benefice are to be classified salaries paid by the government in lieu of confiscated ecclesiastical property; the contributions of the faithful imposed by a fixed tax; and stipends paid to the holder of the benefice for founded Masses, that is, for Masses to be said at regular intervals for which

there is no longer, since the Code, any question as to whether the obligation of the cleric to dispose of these goods to the poor proceeds from justice or from charity. Consequently, he asserts that should a cleric appropriate the superfluous funds of the income to himself, he takes ecclesiastical property and is burdened with the obligation of restitution, which descends to his heirs. Furthermore he incurs, under this opinion, the censures decreed against those who misappropriate church property; *De Re Beneficiali,* pp. 415-417; *cf.* § 728-736, this treatise.

However, the milder opinion is sufficiently probable to be followed. When there is no question as to the kind of property in question, that is, when it is certainly not the capital property of the benefice, it is not necessary to hold that the obligation proceeds *ex iustitia.* On the other hand, when it is certain that the property is really income from the benefice, the cleric himself rests under a grave obligation of distributing the superfluous amount to the poor, to relatives who are poor, to other pious or religious purposes, or to leave it in the funds of the benefice. In order to constitute a grave sin, however, Ferreres contends that a quantity is required much greater than that sufficient in ordinary theft; *Theol. Mor.,* I, 691-698.

126 Zallinger, *op. cit.,* III, 26, 264; *contra:* Wernz, *l. c.;* Pistocchi, *op. cit.,* p. 414.

the stipends are paid out of the income of the endowment to which the office is attached.

On the other hand, the following funds should be regarded as *quasi-patrimonialia:* voluntary offerings of the faithful, even though the monthly amount is relatively certain; or though it come as an offering from a certain person or corporation which holds itself responsible to give the priest a living; the daily allowance distributed to canons; and the stipends for founded Masses when the office held by the celebrant is not attached to the endowment out of which the stipends are taken. Only when it is expressly stated in the foundation that these stipends are to be regarded as income of the benefice can they be considered as such. Stipends of this kind would be those derived from a fund given to a parish church for annual Masses to be celebrated there. The pastor's office is not attached to the fund, and the stipends he would take from it would not be income of the benefice, unless it were so stated in the articles of foundation.

It is about the *iura stolae* that the controversy principally turns. These are the offerings made to the minister of the Sacraments by those who receive them and include the donations made for funerals, weddings, and baptisms. Prümmer holds that such donations as belong to the office as by right are part of the income of the benefice. Thus the offerings to which a pastor is entitled under the law would be part of that income. On the other hand, donations that commonly come to assistants and chaplains, would not be income of the benefice. If the endowment was founded primarily for the relief of the poor, Prümmer and Cappello would hold that all stole fees obtained by reason of the office attached to it belong to the income of the benefice, and therefore are not available to the cleric for free disposition. Prümmer holds the same view with regard to the Christmas and Easter collections, where these belong to the pastor.[127]

But that even stole fees belong to the cleric so that he may freely dispose of them was said by Reiffenstuel to be the common opinion, and De Meester, Pistocchi, and Vromant agree that this is a valid opinion today. De Meester seems assured that it is probable in

[127] Prümmer, *op. cit.*, II, 36, 37; Cappello, *De Censuris*, 334, n. 6; Chelodi would hold that *iura stolae* and similar taxes are not ecclesiastical property; *Ius Poenale*, 78, n. 4.

practice.[128] And he arrives at this conclusion because the Pontifical Commission for the Authentic Interpretation of the Canons of the Code referred the problem to the Sacred Congregation of the Council, which was unwilling to give a decision.[129] And as to the *quasi-patrimonialia* that are not stole fees, even Prümmer concedes that the common opinion places them at the free disposal of the cleric.[130]

305. **But suppose that the *quasi-patrimonialia* should be used by the bishop as a fund or endowment to which he would attach an office.** This he may do, even when these funds are indefinite and uncertain.[131] Do these funds then become income of the benefice so as to be withdrawn from the free disposal of the incumbent? Pistocchi says they do, because otherwise the clear intention of the legislator would be defeated. The legislator demands a *certain* dos (endowment). If the funds were left to the free disposal of the cleric they would not have the character necessary to make them the endowment of the benefice.[132] But such mathematically exact argumentation ascribes to the law a rigidity that is not evident in Canon 1415, § 3. Consequently, Vromant more correctly holds for the opposite view, and calls it probable in practice. He argues that under Canon 1473,[133] the mind of the legislator seems to be restricted to the funds which prior to the Code were affected by this reservation.[134]

[128] Reiffenstuel, *op. cit.*, III, 25, 4-7; De Meester, *op. cit.*, 1424; Vromant, *op. cit.*, 216; Pistocchi, *op. cit.*, p. 414.

[129] S. C. C. in Causa Utinen., 14 June, 1922—*AAS,* XIV (1922), 229.

[130] *Op. cit.*, II, 36; Vromant, *op. cit.*, 216.

[131] Canon 1415, § 1. "Beneficia ne erigantur, nisi constet ea stabilem et congruam dotem habere, ex qua reditus perpetuo percipiantur ad normam can. 1410."

§ 2. "Si dos in numerata pecunia constituatur, Ordinarius, audito dioecesano administrationis Concilio de quo in can. 1520, curare debet ut quamprimum collocetur in tutis et frugiferis fundis vel nominibus."

§ 3. "Non prohibetur tamen, ubi congrua dos constitui nequeat, paroecias aut quasi-paroecias erigere, si prudenter praevideat ea quae necessaria sunt aliunde non defutura."

[132] Pistocchi, *op. cit.*, pp. 415-417.

[133] Canon 1473. *Cf.* footnote 119, this chapter, for the text of this canon.

[134] Canon 18. "Leges ecclesiasticae intelligendae sunt secundum propriam verborum significationem in textu et contextu consideratam; quae si dubia et

Now in doubt, he continues, the scope of the old law is not to be enlarged.[135] It is not to be presumed that the legislator wished to correct the prior law, for correction is an odious matter, or to impose a new burden without clear and definite words. The new disposition of the law, so far from imposing a new obligation, or changing the relation of the cleric to the *quasi-patrimonialia,* seems merely to aim at making it easier for bishops to erect parishes for the good of souls.[136]

306. Finally, there remains the problem of the income of priests in the United States from offices which they hold. If parishes in the United States are not benefices, that is, if they are not parishes in the canonical sense, then the question is solved at once. If there is no benefice, there is no income from the benefice, and whatever the cleric obtains as income is at his free disposal. But even under this hypothesis, the bishop's office is a benefice, and the income he derives from it is subject to the restrictions of Canon 1473.

307. But it seems fairly clear that all parishes in the United States are parishes in the canonical sense and therefore benefices. This conclusion is based on three arguments.

308. The first argument is the decree of the Sacred Consistorial Congregation declaring that when regions, once under the authority of the Sacred Congregation for the Propagation of the Faith, are placed under the discipline of the common law, quasi-parishes become by that very fact parishes and are to be known as such.[137]

obscura manserit, ad locos Codicis parallelos, si qui sint, ad legis finem ac circumstantias et ad mentem legislatoris est recurrendum."

[135] Canon 6, 2°. "Canones qui ius vetus ex integro referunt, ex veteris iuris auctoritate, atque ideo ex receptis apud probatos auctores interpretationibus sunt aestimandi.

"3°. Canones qui ex parte tantum cum veteri iure congruunt, qua congruunt, ex iure antiquo aestimandi sunt; qua discrepant, sunt ex sua ipsorum sententia diiudicandi."

Canon 23. "In dubio revocatio legis praeexistentis non praesumitur, sed leges posteriores ad priores trahendae sunt et his, quantum fieri possit, conciliandae."

[136] Vromant, *l. c.; ita:* Vermeersch-Creusen, *op. cit.*, II, 798; and Claeys-Bouuaert-Simenon, *Man. Iur. Can.*, III, 233.

[137] S. C. Consist., 1 August, 1919—*AAS,* XI (1919), 346, 347; *cf. AER,* LXI (1919), 551, 552; LXXXIX, 628-630.

Thus when the dioceses of the United States passed under the discipline of the common law, their quasi-parishes became real parishes in the canonical sense of the term.

309. **The second argument** derives from the letter of the Apostolic Delegate, of the tenth of November, 1922, embodying replies of the Pontifical Commission for the Authentic Interpretation of the Canons of the Code issued 26 September, 1921, in which it is ordained that parishes established before the promulgation of the Code became *ipso facto* canonical parishes, and that no decree of erection is necessary, but only the fixing of territorial limits and the appointment of a pastor to take charge of the district.[138]

310. **The third argument** is offered by the decree of the Sacred Congregation of the Council under the date of the fifth of March, 1932, which was issued in answer to two questions raised by the Bishop of Prince Albert and Saskatoon concerning the *Missa pro populo*.[139] This decree is, of course, a private rescript and is of obligation only on the persons for whom it was intended.[140] Nevertheless it answers the arguments usually advanced to contradict the contention that parishes in the United States are canonical parishes. The Bishop in the present case had advanced two arguments as reasons why his pastors were probably not obliged to offer the *Missa pro populo*.

311. **The arguments were: first, that no formal decree of canonical erection of the parishes had been issued; and second, that the boundaries had not been determined by decree.**

The observations prefixed to the answers given by the Sacred Congregation in this instance affirm that while a formal decree is prescribed for the erection of a parish it is not required for the validity of the act. And as to the establishing of boundaries by decree, the answer asserts that they may be established not only by decree, but by actual observance as well.

312. **Where it is provided that the Christmas and Easter col-**

[138] Woywod, *Canonical Decisions*, p. 14; *cf. AER, l. c.*

[139] *AAS*, XXV (1933), 436-438; *cf. AER, l. c.*

[140] Canon 17, § 3. "Data autem per modum sententiae iudicialis aut rescripti in re peculiari, vim legis non habet et ligat tantum personas atque afficit res pro quibus data est."

lections belong to the pastor, it seems that Prümmer is correct in regarding these as income of the benefice, whatever one may think of his attitude towards stole fees. There appears no reason to doubt that they are meant in lieu of salary or in addition to it.[141]

313. The salary determined by diocesan statutes must also be regarded as income from the benefice. But the salary of an assistant is a pension and not be regarded as the income from a benefice.[142]

However, where the salary is determined in amount by the statutes, it would seem that the incumbent has that amount at his free disposal. The same can not be said of Christmas and Easter collections, the amount of which is necessarily uncertain, just as the crops that are the yield of a farm that is part of a benefice. When the salary is definite, it is fair to conclude that the amount fixed is regarded as reasonably necessary for the priest to enable him to live as befits his dignity. Whatever he may save out of that salary should probably be regarded as *parsimonialia,* that is, a fund which he had a right to spend and would have spent had he lived in the manner in which a priest is entitled to live. Of course, the common opinion entitles him to dispose of the *parsimonialia* as he sees fit.

314. Even as to Christmas and Easter collections, it has been indicated already that an opinion probable in practice holds that where such voluntary offerings are constituted the endowment of a benefice, they need not be regarded as subject to the restrictions of Canon 1473.[143]

It is sufficiently probable also that stole fees are *quasi-patrimonialia,* and therefore subject to the free disposal of the recipient.[144]

315. The Free Disposal of Salary and Income in the United States. Thus there seems no doubt that a priest holding a benefice in the United States is not restricted as to the disposal of his salary, by will or otherwise; and that he is probably free also as to the rest of the income that he derives from his parochial office.

316. As to the *mensa episcopalis,* or the income from the bishop's benefice serving for his support, since in the United States it is

141 Prümmer, *op. cit.,* II, 36.

142 Ferreres, *Theol. Mor.,* I, 695.

143 Vromant, *l. c.;* Vermeersch-Creusen, *l. c.*

144 Vromant, *l. c.;* De Meester, *l. c.;* Vermeersch-Creusen, *l. c.*

also usually derived from collections, it would seem to stand in the position of the Christmas and Easter collections of pastors. Therefore, by an opinion probable in practice, the bishop could dispose of it by will or by gift.[145] *A fortiori,* if the *mensa episcopalis* should be determined by a provincial council and fixed at a definite sum, it would be completely at the bishop's disposal, for in that case it would be like the salary of a pastor.

Article 5

The Cleric's Obligation of Making a Will

317. The third probem under modern canon law remains to be discussed here, the obligation, namely, resting on clerics to make a will. By the general law, Cardinals, residential bishops, and other clerics possessing a benefice are obliged to make a will, or to execute some other adequate instrument by which certain property of the Church will be guaranteed to be preserved to it according to the regulations of Canons 1298-1300. These persons are also commanded to appoint as soon as possible some worthy persons who will take charge of all the furnishings, the books, and the documents belonging to the church, in order that in due time they may be handed to the proper person, usually the successor of the decedent.[146]

[145] Vromant, *l. c.;* Vermeersch-Creusen, *l. c.*

[146] Canon 1301, § 1. "S. R. E. Cardinalis, Episcopus residentialis aliique clerici beneficiarii obligatione tenentur curandi testamento vel alio instrumento forma iuris civilis valido ut canonica praescripta, de quibus in can. 1298-1300, debitum effectum etiam in foro civili sortiantur."

§ 2. "Quamobrem tempestive ac forma iure civili valida personam integrae famae designent ad normam can. 380, quae, adveniente ipsorum morte, non solum sacram supellectilem, sed etiam libros, documenta aliaque quae ad ecclesiam pertinent et in eorum domo reperiuntur, occupet et cui debentur, remittat."

Canon 380. "Statim a capta possessione, Episcopus sacerdotem designet, qui, sede vacante aut impedita, clavem secreti tabularii seu armarii quae apud Episcopum erat, assumat."

Canon 1298, § 1. "Defuncti S. R. E. Cardinalis, qui in Urbe domicilium habebat, quamvis Episcopus suburbicarius aut Abbas *nullius* esset, quaelibet sacra supellex, exceptis annulis et crucibus pectoralibus etiam cum sacris reliquiis,

318. **The subject matter of these canons** is the sacred vessels and equipment destined for divine worship, which belong to the cleric. Some of these objects might have a profane, as well as a sacred use, but when they have been permanently dedicated to sacred functions, v. gr., a sacred throne, they are governed by the provisions here set forth..[147] The list of the objects due the cathedral church of a resi-

aliaeque res omnes stabiliter divino cultui destinatae, nulla habita ratione qualitatis et naturae redituum quibus comparatae sint, cedunt pontificio sacrario, nisi Cardinalis eas donaverit aut testamento reliquerit alicui ecclesiae vel oratorio publico vel loco pio vel alicui personae ecclesiasticae seu religiosae."

§ 2. "Optandum ut Cardinalis, qui huiusmodi facultate uti velit, saltem ex parte praeferat illas ecclesias, quas in titulum administrationem seu commendam obtinuerit."

Canon 1299, § 1. "Defuncti Episcopi residentialis, etiamsi cardinalitia dignitate fulserit, sacra supellex cedit ecclesiae cathedrali, exceptis annulis et crucibus pectoralibus etiam cum sacris reliquiis, salvo, praescripto can. 1288, et iis omnibus utensilibus cuiusvis generis quae legitime probetur ab Episcopo defuncto comparata fuisse bonis ad ipsam ecclesiam non pertinentibus neque constet in ecclesiae proprietatem transiisse."

§ 2. "Si quando Episcopus duas vel plures dioceses successive rexerit aut simul praefuerit duabus vel pluribus diocesibus unitis aut in perpetuam administrationem concessis, cathedralem ecclesiam habentibus propriam et distinctam, quae sacra utensilia constiterit reditibus unius tantum dioecesis fuisse comparata, ea eiusdem cathedrali ecclesiae cedunt; secus dividi debent, aequis partibus, inter singulas ecclesias cathedrales, dummodo diocesium reditus ne sint divisi, sed unam episcopalem mensam perpetuo constituant; si vero reditus divisi sint ac separati, divisio fiat inter singulas ecclesias cathedrales pro ratione fructuum quos in singulis dioecesibus Episcopus perceperit ac temporis quo eisdem praefuerit."

§ 3. "Episcopus obligatione tenetur inventarii sacrorum utensilium authentica forma conficiendi, in quo pro rei veritate quando acquisita sint, exprimat, distincteque describat si qua non ex ecclesiae reditibus ac proventibus, sed ex propriis bonis vel ex donatione sibi facta comparaverit; secus omnia reditibus ecclesiae comparata praesumuntur."

Canon 1300. "Quae in can. 1299 praescripta sunt, applicantur quoque clerico qui in aliqua ecclesia beneficium saeculare vel religiosum obtinuerit."

Canon 1288. "Sanctissimae Crucis reliquiae, quas in cruce pectorali Episcopus forte defert, ecclesiae cathedrali, ipso defuncto, cedunt, Episcopo successori transmittendae; et si defunctus pluribus praefuerit dioecesibus, ecclesiae cathedrali dioecesis, in cuius territorio supremum diem obiit aut, si extra dioecesim mortuus est, ex qua ultimo discessit."

[147] Vermeersch-Creusen, *op. cit.*, II, 626.

dential bishop is given by Pope Pius IX in the *Quum illud,* and derives from the Constitution of Pope St. Pius V, *Romani Pontifices.*[148] The list includes mitres, chasubles, pluvials, tunics, dalmatics, gloves, albs, cinctures, linen amices and the like; missals, graduales, chant and hymn books, pontificales and canons; chalices, patens, pyxes, ostensoria, thuribles, the holy water vessel with aspersorium, the pitcher and the basin, holy oil vessels, cruets and basin, the bell, the archbishop's cross, the candelabra and the cross, croziers, and the faldstool.

319. The Wills of Cardinals. By the Constitution of Urban VIII, *Aequum est,* this property of a deceased Cardinal escheated to the Apostolic Camera, though it became customary to give the Cardinals individual briefs permitting them to dispose of the income of their benefices [149] and to bestow their sacred furniture on a church, a chapel, or a pious institution.[150]

Should the Cardinal fail to make a bequest as provided in the first paragraph of Canon 1298, the goods specified there escheat to the pontifical treasury. All the property escheats, without reference to the quality (that is, to the richness of it), or the sources of the income with which the property was purchased. The only property excepted is rings and pectoral crosses, including relics of the Holy Cross. As to the last item, the Cardinal enjoys a greater privilege than bishops, for the relics of the Holy Cross belonging to the residential bishop escheat to his cathedral church. Canon 1299, § 1, and Canon 1288.

The beneficiaries of the Cardinal's generosity may be any ecclesiastical person, physical or moral; that is, a priest, a professed religious, a religious community, an institute of religious without vows,

[148] *Litt. Apost., Quum illud,* 1 June, 1847, n. 3—*Fontes,* n. 505; *ASS,* III (1867), 278, 279; const., *Romani Pontifices,* 30 August, 1567—*Fontes,* n. 123; *Bullarium Romanum,* VII, 609; *ASS,* III (1867), 238 and 278.

[149] As is done now by general law in Canon 239, § 1, n. 19. *Cf.* Hilling, *Das Personensrecht,* p. 128.

[150] This is stated in the *Quum illud,* n. 2; and also in the Constitution of Benedict XIV, *Inter arduas,* 22 April, 1749—*Fontes,* n. 396. But Benedict XIV indicates that if it is bequeathed to a private chapel when that is not specially conceded in the indult, the property escheats to the Camera.

and ecclesiastical corporations duly established by ecclesiastical authority. But he is recommended in the second paragraph of Canon 1298 to show preference for those churches or persons with whom he was in any way connected.[151]

320. Residential bishops must provide by a will or other instrument, valid in the secular forum, that this property of theirs will pass to their cathedral churches. This binds all residential bishops, whether they be Cardinals or not, except the suburbicarian bishops, and even they are obliged to transmit to their successors the relics of the Holy Cross as provided by Canon 1288.[152]

Goods of the kind specified, if acquired with funds not belonging to the church, are excepted from the general provision, unless they have been given to the church. So also are all rings and pectoral crosses (but not relics of the Holy Cross). The presumption is, however, that they were bought with the income of the church or the benefice. The presumption will, of course, yield to contrary proof.

Proof, however, is difficult to offer unless there is an inventory, and the bishop is consequently admonished to make an inventory in authentic form, showing all the property described by Canon 1299. In the inventory he is to indicate when it was acquired and whether purchased with funds of the church or his own personal funds, signifying whether or not it was a gift to himself personally or to the church. As has been already suggested, the property of the *mensa episcopalis* in the United States, under an opinion probable in practice, may be regarded as the property of the bishop; and this is al-

[151] The *Quum illud* and the Constitution, *Inter arduas,* both recommend this preference.

Discussion of Canon 1298 may be found in: Vermeersch-Creusen, *op cit.*, II, 626; Cocchi, *op, cit.*, III, 126; Prümmer, *Man. Iur Can.*, 397; De Meester, *op. cit.*, 1277; Blat, *op. cit.*, 169; Cance, *op. cit.*, III, 74.

[152] The *Quum illud,* n. 3, explained that the Constitution, *Romani Pontifices,* included Cardinals who were residential bishops except the suburbicarian bishops. And under Canon 6, n. 2, this provision of the law prior to the Code must be accepted in view of the fact that the law itself is repeated in Canon 1299, § 1.

Cf. Canon 6, n. 2. "Canones qui ius vetus ex integro referunt, ex veteris iuris auctoritate, atque ideo ex receptis apud probatos auctores interpretationibus, sunt aestimandi."

most certainly true if the *mensa episcopalis* is a determined annual salary.[153]

321. In the event that the bishop ruled two or more dioceses either successively or simultaneously (that is, in the latter case, because the dioceses were united *in perpetuum* or for the life of the incumbent), the sacred equipment must be transmitted to the church with the funds of which it was bought. The bishop's will is almost indispensable in this situation. If the bishop leaves no will, the canons attempt to make equitable distribution. Rules for such distribution are set forth in paragraph 2 of Canon 1299.

Rules for distribution when the deceased bishop has ruled two dioceses and died without a will aim at giving each cathedral church what is its due. If it can not be established with what income the goods were bought, either of two situations is possible: the property is either divisible or indivisible. It is divisible when the incumbency was successive. It is indivisible when the incumbency was simultaneous and the income from both dioceses constitutes one *mensa episcopalis*. Simply because the goods bought with the various funds are not kept separate does not make the property indivisible. The solution of this problem is reached by consulting the documents, invoices, and memoranda that are available.

The property is really indivisible, however, where the *mensa episcopalis* was administered as a single unit. In that case, the goods are

[153] *Cf.* § 316, this treatise. For a discussion of the obligations under Canon 1299, *cf.* Vermeersch-Creusen, *op cit.*, III, 627; Blat, *op. cit.*, 170; Cocchi, *op cit.*, III, 127; Cance, *op. cit.*, III, 74; Prümmer, *op. cit.*, 397; De Meester, *op. cit.*, 1277. *Cf.* also S. C. EE. RR., *in Causa Feretrana*, 4 April, 1851—Bizzarri, p. 593.

Cf. a decision in favor of the bishop's heirs, giving them his cappa and his rochet; S. C. EE. RR., *in Causa Balneoregien.*, 6 April, 1622—*Fontes*, n. 1712.

The *paramenta, utensilia and supellectilia* of the bishop's chapel were awarded the cathedral in the decree of the Sacred Congregation of the Council, *in Causa Massen.*, 24 April, 1858—*Fontes*, n. 4163.

Where a chapter to which the bishop had formerly belonged claimed a vestment on the ground that it was bought by him out of funds belonging to the chapter, it was awarded to the cathedral in spite of the fact that the chapter produced one witness to show that the bishop had intended to bequeath it to them; S. C. C. *in Causa Fulginaten.*, 27 March, 1858—*Fontes*, n. 4161.

to be divided among the dioceses over which the bishop ruled. The basis of the division is derived from the length of time the bishop governed each diocese and from the ratio of the income derived from one to the income obtained from the other.[154]

322. **As to beneficed clerics** who are not residential bishops, including therefore abbots *nullius* and prelates *nullius,* as well as canons and pastors, the general principle is that the sacred vessels and equipment of their benefices are not to be disposed of by will, but left to their churches, unless they were bought with funds that were not ecclesiastical or were gifts made personally to the priest. Of course, under Canon 1301, § 1, beneficed clerics are to make a will, or execute some substitute instrument, valid in the secular law, guaranteeing the rights of their church in that property. The presumption is that it was bought with funds of the church. But this presumption can be overthrown by proof to the contrary. The cleric, as well as the bishop, is commanded to provide an inventory of these various items, indicating the source of their origin, the date when they were ac-

[154] Various decisions illustrate the *praxis curiae.*

Where a bishop had ruled one diocese eleven years and another, two years, only the vestments were given to the cathedral church of the latter—S. C. C. *in Causa Suessana seu Catacen.,* 28 September, 1709—*Fontes,* n. 3081; the same case, 25 January, 1710—*Fontes,* n. 3084.

Where a bishop was a few months in one diocese and seventeen years in another, even the vestments were awarded the cathedral church of the latter because it was established that they had belonged to his predecessor in that see and had been lent to the decedent—S. C. C. *in Causa Trivicana seu Tricaricen.,* 8 June and 6 July, 1726—*Fontes,* n. 3320.

A custom of awarding one-third of this property was overruled and one-fourth granted as being the real proportion of the income from the plaintiff see in relation to the bishop's total income—S. C. C., 24 August, 1867—*ASS,* III (1867), 238.

Where an archbishop was only administrator of another diocese, the latter was still held entitled to its proportionate share of this property—S. C. C. *in Trecen.,* 30 August, 1845—*Fontes,* n. 4090.

Where a bishop had made an inventory of the portion of this property purchased while he was an incumbent of a former see, all the goods in the inventory were awarded to it. It was, however, otherwise evident that he had not purchased it from his patrimony, for he had been a monk prior to his elevation to the episcopacy—S. C. C. *in Causa Acerrarum seu Matheranen. et Acheruntina,* 18 December, 1734, and 15 January, 1735—*Fontes,* n. 3437.

quired, and whether they are church property or part of the cleric's personal estate.[155]

323. The prescriptions of the Third Plenary Council of Baltimore (1884) also bind priests and bishops in the United States. Because of their significance, it is appropriate that the full text of the laws be given here.

> N. 268. Ne unquam bona cultui divino piisque operibus dicata ad alios usus divertantur, statuimus ac omnibus istarum provinciarum Episcopis in Domino praecipimus, ut duplex rerum inventarium rite confectum habeant; unum in quo res omnes ecclesiasticae, quas sive nomine proprio (*in fee simple*), vel suae fidei commissas nomine aliorum (in trust), vel soli ut corpus morale (corporation sole) possident, accurate describantur; alterum in quo res suae propriae (personal property) aeque fideliter notentur. Hac enim ratione optime de bonis suis tam Ecclesiae quam contentionis aut sacrilegae alienationis periculo provisum erit. "Et iustum est hoc apud Deum et homines, ut nec Ecclesia detrimentum patiatur ignoratione rerum Episcopi, nec Episcopus vel eius propinqui sub obtentu Ecclesiae proscribantur." [156]
>
> N. 269. Summorum Pontificum ac Predecessorum nostrorum cura de bonis externis Ecclesiae hac in regione secure firmiterque servandis quanta fuerit, ex actis et decretis conciliorum nostrorum tam provincialium quam plenariorum apertum est. Nec minori Nos sollicitudine bonorum illorum securitati providere intenti, Episcopos iterum iterumque monemus, oneratam esse suam conscientiam, ut testamento vel alio legali documento, prout spectatis locorum adiunctis vel legum in suo Statu vigentium indole melius videtur, se-

[155] Vermeersch-Creusen, II, 628; Cance, *l. c.;* Prümmer, *l. c.;* Blat, *op. cit.*, 171; Cocchi, *op. cit.*, III, 128; Bargilliat, *op. cit.*, 1446; Benedict XIV, const., *Ad honorandam*, 27 March, 1752, § 27 (referring especially to the chaplains of the Vatican Basilica but the general principle is affirmed)—*Fontes*, n. 420.

[156] Canons of the Apostles, c. 40—Harduin, I, 18, 19, 37.

This inventory should make special mention of the sacred vessels and equipment, the date they were acquired, and the funds from which they were bought, in accordance with Canon 1299, § 3, and contain a complete account of all the property of the church held by the bishop in fee, in trust, or as a corporation sole. There should be a separate inventory for his personal property.

> curae bonorum ecclesiasticorum quae penes se sunt ad successores transmissioni consulant. Huius porro instrumenti duo exemplaria conficiant, quorum uno apud se in archivo diocesano retento, alterum apud Archiepiscopum deponant; Archiepiscopus autem apud seniorem suffraganeum. Haec testamentorum depositio intra tres menses a sua cuiusque consecratione omnino fiat. Neque omittant de bonis suis propriis testamento accurate et solerter confecto tempestive providere quo nulla, ipsis vita decedentibus, de privata proprietate difficultas oriatur.

324. The Council refers to Nos. 191 and 204 of the Second Plenary Council of Baltimore.[157] Because of this reference it seems that the Third Plenary Council not only imposes on the newly appointed bishop the obligation of forwarding a copy of his will to the metropolitan, but also requires that the metropolitan admonish the bishop after a delay of three months.

The Second Plenary Council required that the metropolitan exercise his duty of supervision in this matter with fairly intimate responsibility to the Sacred Congregation for the Propagation of the Faith. Two copies of the will were required to be filed with the metropolitan that he might forward one to the Sacred Congregation. Moreover, if the bishop failed to heed his admonitions, he was to take the matter up with the Sacred Congregation. While it seems probable that the Third Plenary Council endorsed these measures, even though it speaks of sending but one copy to the metropolitan, the question nevertheless arises whether at the present time the copy of the will must be filed with the Sacred Congregation and notification sent to it when the bishop proves inattentive to the metropolitan's exhortations. The answer seems to be negative. For the dioceses of this country are no longer under the Sacred Congregation for the Propagation of the Faith. And the obligation of substituting the Sacred Consistorial Congregation is not to be raised without definite legislation imposing it.

325. The Relative Importance of a Will and an Inventory. The necessity for the making of a will to guarantee the possession of church property is important in the United States today only as a measure of added precaution. Actually, the inventory is more im-

[157] *Cf.* §§ 287, 288, this treatise.

portant, and that in turn only for property which the bishop holds as an individual whether in title or in possession.

Where the bishop is a corporation sole, all the property belonging to him as a corporation sole passes automatically to his successor without a will. Where the diocese is incorporated, the corporation does not die with the bishop. Where the parishes are incorporated, they retain their property as corporations, even when the bishop dies. Where the bishop is trustee, the legal title is in him, but the equitable title is in the parishes for which he is trustee, and to such an extent that even under the secular law the property of one parish can not be diverted to another. When the bishop dies, the court is simply petitioned to appoint his successor as trustee in his place. It would seem, then, that the most important measure of precaution as to diocesan property in the United States, is to provide that the property is vested in the bishop not as a private individual, but in one of the forms just indicated.

326. It would be advantageous, too, if the various funds of the diocese were incorporated, such as the seminary fund and the missionary fund. In case these funds were incorporated, the death of the bishop would make no difference to the corporation which would simply continue its existence.

However, where these funds are held in the bishop's name in fee simple, an inventory and a will become most practicable. The same must be said of the vestments and the equipment which as a matter of course he holds in his own name. But even as to the latter, the court will raise a constructive trust, if it can be shown that the bishop really did not own the property. It is almost impossible to prove this without an inventory signed by the bishop himself.

327. Summarizing the obligations of the bishop in this matter, observe that he is bound by the general law to make an inventory of his sacred equipment (including vestments and the rest) and leave this property by will to the cathedral, bequeathing the relics of the Holy Cross to his successor. But a formal declaration, signed by the bishop, with his seal attached, that this property belongs to the cathedral would suffice, even under general canon law.[158]

[158] *Cf.* § 320, this treatise.

By the particular law of the Third Plenary Council of Baltimore, he need make only a similar formal statement, specifying in addition that all funds under certain accounts in his books belong to the diocese. This would meet the requirements of the Council and would be valid in the secular courts.

Of course, by varying the statement somewhat he can make it a will, bequeathing those funds to the diocese. But a will might seem less advisable for three reasons. First, it would be subject to all the restrictions which the secular law imposes upon wills: for instance, the formalities of witnesses; invalidation for execution too near the date of death; and the prohibition on excessive gifts to charity and religion. True, the funds may be bequeathed to his successor, and that would seem to be definite enough as to beneficiary. He could even bequeath them to a trustee for his successor. But the court can always look behind the obvious instrument and judge the matter on the real state of affairs so far as it can be established. The second objection is that a will usually implies an assumption of ownership. Consequently, where there is no ownership, a will might be regarded as objectionable, when other legal means are adequate. The third reason is that the secular law does not favor subterfuges, and that would seem to be the character of a will made concerning property one does not own. The secular law regards itself as competent to protect the rights of owners and of claimants of property held by a decedent but not owned by him. Of course, that it may do so, the real owners must be able to demonstrate their title to the court.

But whether it be a will or a formal statement of the rights of the cathedral and of the diocesan funds, it must be forwarded to the metropolitan within three months of the newly appointed bishop's consecration. The declaration will satisfy Canon 1301, § 1, as to the *utensilia,* and No. 269 of the Third Plenary Council of Baltimore, as to other diocesan funds.

It is a matter of obligation, too, for the bishop to make a will disposing of his own property, but of that will it is not necessary to send a copy to the metropolitan or even to preserve a copy in the diocesan archives. It may be kept in a safety vault, or with the executor. It would seem more prudent, however, that it be available to the diocesan consultors immediately on the death of the bishop.

For that reason, the practical arrangement would seem that a copy of it should be kept in the bishop's personal files in the chancery.

328. **The discipline of the general law provides that pastors and beneficed clergy shall make an inventory** of the furnishings and equipment of the church and rectory, indicating such as belong to the church, and specifying when they were purchased, from what funds, and whether they were gifts to the church or to the pastor personally. Either by will or formal declaration, they are to make certain that the church or benefice shall come into possession of its property at their decease. If there is no inventory, the property is presumed to belong to the church. Again, it may be observed that the declaration seems preferable to the will.

329. **As to the other property of the benefice,** the provisions of the Third Plenary Council govern. They are given herewith in full.

> N. 276. Praeterea, ne rectores et piorum locorum curatores proprias suas res rebus Ecclesiae immisceant cum famae suae discrimine, fidelium offensione, vel iniuria Ecclesiae, duplex conficiant rerum inventarium. In utroque hoc inventario diligenter bona tam mobilia quam immobilia, quae ad missionem vel locum spectant, notentur; in eo vasa sacra sacramque omnem supellectilem describant; omnia recenseantur quaecumque pertinent ad domum presbyteralem, scholas et coemeterium, neque omittant indicare reditus permanentes, si qui sint, et onera quibus ecclesia vel locus subiicitur. Inventarii unum exemplar a rectore vel curatore et aedituis vel consiliariis (church committeemen) subscriptum ad cancellarium mittatur ut in archivo diocesano servetur, alterum in archivo missionis vel loci asservabitur. Inventarium singulis annis a rectore et aedituis vel consiliariis recognoscatur, bona intra annum acquisita vel onera suscepta addantur, quorum item catalogus rite signatus cancellario transmittatur. Ne contentioni inter successorem et decessorem locus relinquatur, decernimus ut quoties sacerdos missionis cui praesit possessionem assumit, inventarium huius missionis ad illud usque tempus rite descriptum, eidem a praedecessore vel a vicario foraneo exhibeatur. Quia de quibusdam muneribus, ut quidam ex Nobis alia occasione prudenter notarunt, maxime rerum mobilium, ut supellectilis, ornamentorum sacerdotalium, vasorum aureorum argenteorumque, sive ab individuis fideli-

bus sive a sodalitatibus sponte ecclesiae rectori oblatis dubium sat frequenter oritur, utrum ad hunc pertineant an ad missionem vel ecclesiam: decernimus, nisi contrarium explicite fuerit a donatoribus declaratum, res istas esse ecclesiae proprietatem, atque ideo neque rectorem in discessu a missione, neque eius haeredes post ipsius obitum, ius habere ad eas removendas vel vendendas. Servetur itaque regula statuta, ea scilicet quae ecclesiasticis usibus apta rectori missionario donantur, esse missioni donata, nisi contrarium clare et indubitanter pateat.

N. 277. Etiamsi nulla iustitiae lex id hic iniungat, spiritus tamen Evangelii et Christiana caritas postulant, ut ad pias causas promovendas contribuant sacerdotes ex superfluis suis,[159] atque ut morientes in eundem finem disponant de parte saltem substantiae quam ipsos possidere contigerit. Haud raro tamen ex oblivione vel neglectu neque Ecclesiae neque pauperum recordantur decedentes presbyteri; quin et accidit, ut cum suis bona ecclesiae vel piarum causarum permixta relinquant, et ita cum scandalo fidelium atque religionis tum spirituali tum temporali damno haeredes suos ditescere sinant, aut gravibus litibus praebeant occasionem. Omnes ideo hortabatur Conc. Prov. Neo-Eboracense III, decr. VI, ut de bonis suis, si ulla essent ipsis, testamentum ad normam legum tempestive conscriberent; quod hortamentum, quia saepe hactenus neglectum, vehementer denuo inculcamus, simul monentes, ne usque ad extremum differatur ultimae voluntatis instrumenti confectio, hac praeter alias de causa, quod leges civiles non agnoscant dispositiones in pias causas per testamentum, nisi hoc duobus saltem mensibus ante mortem fuerit conscriptum.[160] Ad prudentiam autem confessarii pertinebit cum aegrotante sacerdote hac de re agere, antequam sacramentalem eius confessionem excipiat. Maxime porro optandum, ut unus saltem sacerdos pietate ac prudentia commendabilis, uti executor testamenti constituatur.

[159] This was stated while the country was still under the Sacred Congregation for the Propagation of the Faith, and before the parishes were real benefices. For the present situation and the obligation arising under it *cf.* §§ 306-316, this treatise.

[160] Few States have this provision, and it varies from State to State. Indeed, so far as investigation reveals, it is no longer part of the New York provisions. *Cf.* § 552, this treatise.

330. The obligation of making a will contained in this law of the Third Plenary Council is imposed on all priests who own any property. The purpose of the law is to assure generosity to the Church and the poor. Some diocesan statutes provide that pastors must make a will and deposit it with the chancellor. Of course, this provision binds in the dioceses where it is found. But all priests in the United States are expected to make a will, if they own property, though they need not deposit it with the chancellor except in those dioceses where the obligation is imposed. As to priests who are not pastors, while they seldom have sufficient property to demand their compliance with this provision; nevertheless when they do have it, they must make a will.

While a sufficient period of time has elapsed since the Third Plenary Council of Baltimore to install a contrary custom, still it is not evident that the provision has been disregarded constantly by those priests who, though not pastors, have had property of which they might dispose. The Council itself exempted those who have no property, and it is these principally who have not made wills. Therefore, the precept of the Council seems to bind all priests even today, if they are possessed of property.

331. The Council also provides for the inventory, as required by Canon 1300, but includes all the property of the benefice, the church, the school, and the cemetery, as well as rents, dividends, and interest payable to the church and all obligations, financial or otherwise, which the benefice must discharge whether periodically or by a single performance. This inventory is to be signed by the pastor, with his committeemen. One copy is to be filed with the chancellor. It is to be re-executed each year in the same manner and to enumerate the additions made to the assets or liabilities of the church within the preceding year. The will of the pastor need not contain any reference to this property if he has made an adequate inventory. When he files the inventory as required by the Third Plentary Council he satisfies the obligation of Canon 1301, § 1.

332. The Council adds a presumption as to gifts, stating that if they are such as serve the purposes of the church, even the pastor must regard them as belonging to it, and not to himself, unless the donors expressly mentioned that they are personal gifts to the pastor. *A*

fortiori, after the decease of the pastor, they are to be regarded as belonging to the church by the executor.

333. There is to be an executor. The Third Plenary Council advises the opportune appointment of an agent of this kind. The general law (Canon 1301, § 2) requires it in the case of all beneficed clerics, residential bishops, and Cardinals. Under the general law, his duty is to take into custody all the property of the church whose pastor is dead. Thus, he is rather the representative of the church, appointed to assert its claims against the estate of the decedent. On the other hand, under the Third Plenary Council he is the real executor of the priest's will, and should be a priest. The one priest might discharge the obligations of the general law and of the Third General Council. The general law imposes a strict obligation on the persons whom it binds to make this appointment, while the Third General Council strenuously recommends it.

334. Scholion. The personal estate of a cleric, though in a sense purely temporal in character, is entitled to the *privilegium fori*, just as the cleric himself is entitled to it. For by every fiction under which a decedent's estate is distributed, his personality is regarded as continuing in existence directing the distribution by the force of his will. For that reason, his estate takes on the character of his personality. But by the accepted usage, a cleric's estate is distributed under the secular authority, except as to bequests to charitable causes. Of course, even as to these there is formal distribution through the secular courts, but a Catholic's conscience is bound by the decisions of the canonical executor, whose right it is under the canons to judge in all matters concerning gifts to charity and religion.[161]

Article 6

The Wills of Religious

335. Though religious have sometimes been regarded as civilly dead, they have usually been considered in the secular law as capable of inheriting and transmitting an inheritance. But because of their peculiar situation under the vow of poverty,

[161] *Cf.* Wernz, *op. cit.*, III, 274.

special legislation has generally been necessary to provide for the problems arising out of their estates. Probably the earliest special provision of this kind is an imperial decree, said to have been enacted by Theodosius in 434, who provided that the patrimony of monks and religious who should die intestate without heirs in the direct line, was to be given to the monastery where they were consecrated to the Lord.[162]

When they were the beneficiaries of bequests made on condition that they marry or have childhen, the law permitted them, in Justinian's time, to claim and dispose of the property either by gift or bequest.[163] The only exception to this permission was made when the remainderman was the poor or captives, that is, when the testator provided that if the beneficiary did not marry, the inheritance was to be taken by the poor or by captives.[164]

Under the later imperial law, any one who gave up the religious life, left with the monastery whatever he possessed when he entered.[165] The same provision is incorporated in the canons of the Decree of Gratian.[166] The share of his patrimony which he inherited after his entrance into religion he was also required to leave in the hands of the monastery, should be fail to persevere.[167] And parents were forbidden to disinherit children who had embraced the religious life.[168]

336. By the Rule of St. Benedict, candidates before profession were to leave all their property to the poor or to the monastery. Wealthy persons who gave their children to religion were required to take an oath that they would give nothing more to these children personally, but only to the monastery, retaining if they wished the

[162] *Codex Theod.*, 5, 3, 1; C. 1, 3, 20; *Nov.*, 131, 13; Thomassin, *op cit.*, III, 1, 17, 1; De Héricourt, *op. cit.*, H 181.

[163] C. 1, 3, 52, 13.

[164] *Nov.*, 123, 37; Thomassin, *op. cit.*, III, 1, 23, 8.

[165] *Nov.*, 5, 4.

This precept was not effective in France, as Migne observes in commenting on a letter of Pope Gregory the Great written to sustain an ex-nun's bequest to the poor, where she reserved the legitimate share for her children—*MPL*, LXXVII, 114.

[166] C. 1, C. XVII, q. 4.

[167] C. 1, 3, 54, 7.

[168] C. 1, 3, 54, 5; *Nov.*, 123, 41.

usufruct of such property. But it permitted the religious to dispose of his property after his profession, if only then he came into his inheritance.[169]

337. The general canonical position is that a monk can not make a will because he owns nothing.[170]

338. It seems that the communities founded after the tenth century adopted at first a more rigid attitude towards the monastery's succession to the inheritance of its monks. This is implied in the indults granted by the Holy See to abbots, permitting them to take such inheritances. An indult of this kind was granted in 1246 to the abbots of the Cistercians.[171] Later the Canons Regular and the Dionysian monks were granted the same favor.[172] In 1265, the Dominicans and Franciscans received it.[173] But Clement V for-

[169] Thomassin, *op. cit.*, III, 1, 21, 7-9; De Héricourt, *op. cit.*, H 181.

[170] Synodal Constitution of Constantinople (869), c. 6—Mansi, XVI, 539 D; Council of Oxford (1222), c. 47—Mansi, XXII, 1166 D; Provincial Council of England (1509)—Mansi, XXXI A, 400 B; Greco-Melchite Council (1835), c. 19—*Coll. Lacensis*, II, 588 d.

Two interesting cases appear in the Letters of Pope Gregory the Great. In one instance, an abbess claimed the right to make a will because she had not adopted the habit of her community. The Pope denied the right; *Ad Januarium —MPL*, LXXVII, 945 (c. 7, C. XIX, q. 3; c. 2, X, *de testamentis et ultimis voluntatibus*, III, 26; Decrees of Gregory IX, 124—Mansi, XXIII, 144 D). In the other letter he gave an abbot permission to make a will. The latter had previously been a hermit and had entered religion without adverting to the necessity of making a will in favor of his son; *Ad Probum Abbatem*—Mansi, X, 262, C; *MPL*, LXXVII, 1344.

[171] Innocent IV, const., *Devotionis vestrae*, 22 October, 1246—*Bullarium Romanum*, III, 522.

In 1570 Burgundy extinguished the right of the Cistercians to inherit, a right they had enjoyed from the days of Innocent IV till that time. Later the Dionysian monks were similarly incapacitated; and finally in 1582, the Knights of Jerusalem, though the latter were permitted to take inheritances as to usufruct. When Henry IV recalled the Jesuits to France, he deprived the religious of the right to inherit, unless they returned to the world after their first vows; Thomassin, *op. cit.*, III, 1, 25, 8, 9. These provisions are probably a counterpart of the mortmain statutes in England.

[172] Thomassin, *op. cit.*, III, 1, 25, 2, 3.

[173] Clement IV, const., *Virtute conspicuos*, 21 July, 1265—*Bullarium Romanum*, III, 741; Thomassin, *l. c.*

bade the Friars Minor to receive inheritances or legacies.[174] The indults were really declarations that the abbots were not prohibited under the rule of the institute from accepting such inheritances. As late as 1436, Pope Eugene IV was called upon to invalidate the laws and customs of an Italian community by which it was incapacitated to take by inheritance.[175]

339. The Benedictine was not forbidden to claim his inheritance. An account by Blessed Odo, an abbot of Clugny, tells of two Benedictine nuns who were permitted to leave the enclosure for this purpose. That this custom was universal in Germany in 1523 is suggested by an appeal to the Holy See from the princes of that country petitioning that religious be deprived of the right to inherit, and that a pact be substituted between the monastery and the parents of the religious. In 1527, Sigmund, King of Poland, ordained that a nun's inheritance should remain a trust with her nearest relative, one-half of the income to be paid her and one-half to the State, the capital to be paid to her kindred at her death. Such a pact as that suggested in Germany seems to have been made at times in Spain, for if the pact had been made against his will, the religious there could renounce the amount agreed on, and claim the inheritance.[176]

340. The Will of the Novice under the Present Law. Under the present law a novice can make no disposition of his goods and an attempt to do so is not only illegal but also invalid.[177] Before temporary vows are taken in a religious congregation, however, the novice must make a will.[178] Should the novice die before making the will, his estate belongs to his kin and not to the community.[179]

The law commanding that the novice make a will obliges novices

[174] C. 1, *de verborum significatione*, V, 11 in Clem.

[175] Eugene IV, const., *Regularem vitam*, 30 June, 1436—*Bullarium Romanum*, V, 25.

[176] Thomassin, *op. cit.*, III, 1, 25, 2, 9.

[177] Canon 568. "In novitiatus decursu, si suis beneficiis vel bonis quovis modo novitius renuntiaverit eadenve obligaverit, renuntiatio vel obligatio non solum illicita, sed ipso iure irrita est."

[178] Canon 569, § 3. "Novitius in Congregatione religiosa ante professionem votorum temporariorum testamentum de bonis praesentibus vel forte obventuris libere condat."

[179] Schäfer, *De Religiosis*, 270.

in all congregations but not in communities without vows,[180] or in communities of *moniales* who *de iure* should have solemn vows, though *de facto* their vows are simple vows because of special circumstances. But it is binding in even diocesan congregations, and in houses *sui iuris* where simple vows are provided for in the constitutions, for these two types of community are included under the name of congregation in Canon 488, n. 2.[181]

341. The obligation of this law is strict even if the novice possesses no property at the time. The novice is not free to make a will or not, in spite of the phraseology, *libere condat.* The word *libere* indicates that the novice is not to be coerced as to the manner of disposition. The act of making the will, however, is commanded by the law. They who deny that the obligation is binding when the novice is not possessed of property are influenced by the provisions of secular law forbidding pacts and donations of future goods. A will, however, is not a pact or a donation.[182] The obligation is not satisfied by any sort of disposition other than a will, not even by a *donatio mortis causa* in the wide sense. In the strict sense [183] it would not be valid. It would be forbidden as an actual gift. The will, however, may be revoked, should the novice leave the community.

342. Schäfer, Fanfani, Vermeersch-Creusen, and De Meester maintain that the obligation binds minors as well as others, for the legislator knew that most of the novices would be minors. The contrary opinion, however, has been asserted. The reason advanced for the latter view is derived from a contrast between the law prior to the Code and the law under it. Previously the professed religious who had not made a will, could not make one following profession without the permission of the Holy See. Now that permission is not necessary. Consequently, the argument maintains, the chief reason

180 Schäfer, *op. cit.,* 256.

181 Vermeersch-Creusen, *op. cit.,* I, 667; Prümmer, *Man. Iur. Can.,* 212; Schäfer, *l. c.;* Turner thinks all these should be bound because of the analogy between their situation and that of religious in congregations; *Vow of Poverty,* p. 165.

182 Schäfer, *l. c.;* Vermeersch-Creusen, *l. c.*

183 As defined in Art. 2 of Chapter II.

for insisting that a novice, though a minor, should make a will has ceased to exist.

The former opinion seems better for three reasons. First, it would seem that the legislator would prefer the matter settled before the novice takes vows. The will can be ratified when legal age has been attained by a mere sentence, executed with due formalities. Such a ratification would not be a source of much anxiety to the religious, whereas the act of original disposition would be. Even if the whole will would need to be re-written to comply with the demands of the secular law, it can not be said that the act of copying is fraught with the same concern as even a mental choice of beneficiaries.

Second, even though the novice would not be bound by the secular law to observe the provisions of his will, he would be bound in conscience to observe them. Since a real obligation arises out of his act, it can not be said to be futile. Since it has its effect, there seems no good reason for denying that the canons wish it to be performed even when its legal validity can not be sustained.

Third, Vromant calls it the *praxis* of the Sacred Congregation of Religious to require that even minors should comply with this requirement, quoting a reply of the Pontifical Commission for the Authentic Interpretation of the Canons of the Code to the Superior General of the Redemptorists. It reads as follows:

> Testamentum, de quo Codex in can. 569, § 3, conficiendum est, etiamsi ex lege civili invalidum sit, et tum quoque si novicius non habeat bona praesentia, sed tantum forte obventura . . . Sed curandum est, ut cum primum fieri poterit, testamentum ex lege civili vim habeat, nulla tamen in eo mutata dispositione nisi secundum can. 583, § 2.[184]

343. The time at which the novice is to make the will is not defined, but there is sufficient indication that it should be some time within the last week or two prior to profession, but not until the Superiors have decided to admit him to profession. In case an addi-

[184] Vermeersch-Creusen, *l. c.;* Schäfer, *l. c.;* Fanfani, *De Iure Religiosorum,* 200; Creusen, *Religieux et Religieuses,* 176; De Meester, *op. cit.,* 1001; Vromant, *op. cit.,* 277; Turner, *op. cit.,* pp. 167-170.

tional period of six months is required for further trial (Canon 571, § 2), the making of the will is likewise postponed.

344. If the religious transfers to another congregation, there is no obligation of executing a new will.[185]

345. **Contrary constitutions forbidding the novice to make a will are abrogated,** Schäfer says, but not if they merely touch the liberty of the novice in the actual making of the will. But such constitutions would nevertheless seem to be opposed to the prescriptions of the canons which provide that the novice may make his will *freely*, without duress or coercion.[186]

346. They who made temporary profession prior to the New Code have a *ius quaesitum* (a vested right) to make their will according to the constitutions as they were at the time when they made temporary profession, and of changing it according to the provisions of the same constitutions. Indeed, they need make no will at all, if the constitutions did not require it.[187]

347. **The will, duly made prior to temporary profession, may not be changed without the permission of the Holy See,** except in an emergency when there is not sufficient time to obtain that permission. The permission of at least the local superior is required, if there is not time to approach the major superior.[188]

A *donatio mortis causa* or a codicil made at variance with the provisions of the original will is a sufficient modification to require the permission of the Holy See. But an explanatory codicil, or a

[185] Schäfer, *l. c.*

[186] *Cf.* Schäfer, *l. c.*

[187] Canon 4. "Iura aliis quaesita, itemque privilegia atque indulta quae, ab Apostolica Sede ad haec usque tempora personis sive physicis sive moralibus concessam in usu adhuc sunt nec revocata, integra manent, nisi huius Codicis canonibus expresse revocentur."

Canon 10. "Leges respiciunt futura, non praeterita, nisi in eis de praeteritis caveatur."

Vermeersch-Creusen, *l. c.;* Vromant, *l. c.;* Schäfer, *l. c.;* Turner, *l. c.*

[188] Canon 583, § 2. "Professis a votis simplicibus in Congregationibus religiosis non licet: . . . Testamentum conditum ad norman can. 569, § 3, mutare sine licentia Sanctae Sedis, vel, si res urgeat nec tempus suppetat ad eam recurrendi, sine licentia Superioris maioris aut, si nec ille adiri possit, localis.

A petition for such permission should be addressed to the "Congregatio Negotiis Religiosorum Praeposita."

re-execution of a will that was invalid for lack of the form required by secular law does not require such permission. The same seems to be the proper conclusion when the only beneficiary named in the prior will dies before the religious.[189]

As a matter of prudence merely, Sisters could profitably approach the bishop when it is impossible to apply to the Holy See. But the failure to obtain the bishop's permission, except in the case of diocesan congregations, could not be construed as a violation of the canons.[190]

348. A will can be made without permission even after profession by one who failed to make it previously. This seems to be the correct view for two reasons. First, the obligation would seem to rest on him until he had complied with it; the date of profession is stated not *ad finiendam* but *ad urgendam obligationem*. Second, the prohibition in Canon 583, § 2, supposes the will made and forbids not the original execution, but a change. Cocchi, however, thinks the permission of the Holy See is required for even the original drafting of the will after profession.[191]

Since it is a will that the canons forbid to be changed, it follows that a *donatio mortis causa,* granted that such a gift was made prior to profession, could be revoked by a subsequent will.

After profession it would seem that a *donatio mortis causa* could not be made in any event, whether to supply for the omission of the act of making a will, or to revoke a prior *donatio mortis causa*. It would not be forbidden, it is true, by the canon that forbids the modification of a testament, for there is no testament involved. But one can hardly make a *donatio mortis causa* when he is obliged to make a will. And the obligation to make a will endures after profession, as has been indicated. It certainly would not be lawful to modify by a *donatio mortis causa* the will made prior to profession.

349. As to novices in Orders, that is, where solemn vows are professed, they are permitted to make a will to endure for the period of the novitiate and of temporary profession. Since the canons of

[189] Schäfer, *op. cit.,* 271; Turner, *op. cit.,* p. 174 ff.

[190] Cocchi, *op. cit.,* II, 74; Ferreres, *Insts. Can.,* I, 871.

[191] Cocchi, *l. c.;* for the former opinion see Vermeersch-Creusen, *l. c.;* Schäfer, *l. c.;* Turner, *op. cit.,* p. 166.

the general law make no provision in the matter, they are governed by their own constitutions. The same capacity would seem to reside in any members of an Order who are exempt from solemn vows and in *moniales,* that is women who belong to an Order whose rules prescribe solemn vows but who are exempt from solemn vows because of circumstances.[192]

But within sixty days of solemn profession, the religious must dispose of all the goods he owns. This disposition is made conditionally, that is, provided solemn profession takes place. When profession occurs, any will made prior to that time becomes invalid.[193]

350. Prümmer argues that this disposition can be called a will in a wide sense, because the religious can thus dispose of property which he possesses only *in spe,* such as his patrimonial inheritance.

But as to such inheritances a distinction was wont to be made between communities that could succeed in place of the religious and those that could not. In the case of the latter, when an inheritance fell to one of its members, it was divided as if he were dead.

In the others, he was permitted in the disposition he made sixty days prior to solemn profession to name as future beneficiaries his family, the monastery, charity, or Masses for his soul.

Vermeersch-Creusen agree with Prümmer in supporting the right of the religious to make such a disposition under the present legislation. For they maintain that it would seem to be a hardship to the families of religious and full of peril to the Orders themselves, if a change were to be introduced by reason of a rigorous interpretation

[192] Vermeersch-Creusen, *l. c.;* Schäfer, *l. c.,* and 256; Larraona *Comm. pro Rel.,* I (1920), 72, n. 2.

[193] Canon 581, § 1. "Professus a votis simplicibus antea nequit valide, sed intra sexaginta dies ante professionem sollemnem, salvis peculiaribus indultis a Sancta Sede concessis, debet omnibus bonis quae actu habet, cui maluerit, sub conditione secuturae professionis, renuntiare."

§ 2. "Secuta professione, ea omnia statim fiant, quae necessaria sunt ut renuntiatio etiam iure civili effectum consequatur."

Cf. Schäfer, *op. cit.,* 256; Turner, *op. cit.,* p. 181 ff. The period of sixty days derives from the provisions of the Council of Trent, Sess. XXV, *de reg.,* c. 16. The permission of the bishop is no longer needed for this renunciation; Prümmer, *op. cit.,* 217.

of Canon 582.[194] They argue that Canon 581, § 1, though prescribing disposition of the property which is actually in the hands of the religious, does not forbid him to make provisions for property that may come to him in the future, especially if he has a right to it and the customs of the Order permit. Larraona supports this view, and maintains that the property to which a religious is heir is actually possessed by him, though he would not defend this in States where a disposition of an expectancy is invalid. In such States, the disposition of the expectancy could not be made effective immediately after profession.[195]

Such a disposition of an expectancy is valid in the United States. Consequently, it would seem that a religious could make unqualified disposition of the inheritance to which he is entitled, if the customs of the Order permit, prior to his taking solemn vows. There is no need in this country to ratify such a disposition after solemn profession, because it can be made validly in the first instance. If the religious does not make solemn profession, he can revoke the will. The disposition, however, could not be made effective except at his death, where realty is concerned. To be effective prior to death, a deed would need to be executed after the inheritance had vested in the religious. This he would be unable to execute under solemn vows.

351. If the disposition is not made in due time, the property passes to the Order.[196] The religious can not make a valid will.[197] Whatever he acquires by donation or legacy he acquires for the Order, except in the case of the Friars Minor and the Capuchins, in which Orders he acquires the title for the Holy See, the use and the usufruct (the income) for the community.[198] This provision holds

[194] Canon 582. "Post sollemnem professionem, salvis pariter peculiaribus Apostolicae Sedis indultis, omnia bona quae quovis modo obveniunt regulari: 1°. In Ordine capaci possidendi, cedunt Ordini vel provinciae vel domui secundum constitutiones; 2°. In Ordine incapaci, acquiruntur Sanctae Sedi in proprietatem."

[195] Larraona, *Comm. pro Rel.*, I (1920), 79 and 182; Vermeersch-Creusen, *op. cit.*, I, 685; Schäfer agrees with this view; *op. cit.*, 274, *Cfr.* Cocchi, *op. cit.*, II, 82; Turner, *op. cit.*, pp. 185, 186.

[196] Prümmer, *op. cit.*, 217.

[197] Vermeersch-Creusen, *op. cit.*, I, 667.

[198] Vermeersch-Creusen, *op. cit.*, I, 685. Father Ilg, in commenting on the

good even when he becomes a titular bishop. If he becomes a residential bishop, he acquires the property for the diocese, the vicariate, or the prefecture.[199]

Constitutions of the Friars Minor, §§ 306-311, notes that Clement V has forbidden them to be appointed testamentary heirs or heirs by intestacy, but maintains that this prohibition does not extend to legacies. A legacy may be accepted by the Friars as an alms, he says, if it is bequeathed in a lawful manner, without prejudice to the rightful heirs, and in one payment. He cites Pope Nicholas III as having declared as much. But he warns that the Friars can not accept it as by right or as imposing an obligation, and says that this must be made clear to the executor of the will by a protestation made in writing. However, while the legacy is not regarded due the Friars by any civil right, they are permitted to approach the executor and suggest that he examine his conscience to see whether he is acting properly. *Cf.* Ilg. *Explanation of the Rule of the Friars Minor,* pp. 107, 108.

[199] Vromant, *op. cit.,* 241.

But if he had simple vows, on promotion to a dignity, he recovers his property for use, usufruct, and administration, and acquires new property in full personal right—Vromant, *l. c.*

CHAPTER IV

TESTAMENTARY FORMALITIES

352. Canon 1513, § *2.* **In ultimis voluntatibus in bonum Ecclesiae serventur, si fieri possit, sollemnitates iuris civilis; hae si omissae fuerint, heredes moneantur ut testatoris voluntatem adimpleant.**

353. **Why Formalities Are Required.** Formalities required to make a legal act valid spring from one of two sources: traditional survival and present necessity. Forms often outlive their usefulness, and in that degree are purely traditional. On the other hand, they usually possess juridical utility, that is, they speed the administration of justice in the hands of men. Men, for instance, do not know intuitively when fraud has entered into a transaction. The adoption of certain formalities supplies the law with a presumption that there is no fraud. On the other hand, however, it may be just as probable that fraud has not been practiced even where the formalities have not been observed. But in the face of the law, the absence of its formalities is conclusive on the point, and the legal act that lacks the juridical formalities is also devoid of juridical validity.

In the matter of testaments, there is great divergence in the various legal systems touching the formalities required. Above all, where the question of bequests to pious causes is concerned, the canonical system stands at variance with nearly every other. That this variance may be the better understood, a brief survey of canonical procedure in history is indispensable. That survey will be instituted in the first article of the succeeding chapter. The present chapter deals with secular formalities, and consists of three articles: the first, dealing with the formalities of the nuncupative will; the second, with the formalities of the written will; and the third, with the formalities of revocation.

Article 1

The Formalities of the Nuncupative Will

354. **The provisions of Roman law touching the execution of** wills gained the ascendency on the Continent, as the jurisdiction of

the secular courts over testaments became more general.[1] On the contrary, the English will, remaining under the exclusive jurisdiction of the ecclesiastical courts, retained the simplicity that had been customary before the revival of Roman law. Consequently, the Continental will became largely the Roman will, while the English will was practically the canonical will.

355. No solemnity seems to have been required by the early English law to make any will. It was necessary only to establish testamentary intention, which the testator could communicate as he would any other wish he might have.[2] Wills, therefore, could be made and proved by word of mouth only. This statement, of course, is not contradicted by the canonical requirements which governed the ecclesiastical courts in England; for the will might be oral, even though the presence of the pastor and two witnesses was required for its validity.[3]

356. The same informality seems to have prevailed also when land was devised by being conveyed to uses.[4] The declaration of the uses to which the land was to be put could be oral as well as written. Wherever lands were not affected by the prohibition against devises, as in the boroughs, it seems that land could be devised without a written will.

357. Writing Introduced as a Requisite. Under the Statute of Wills, 32 Henry VIII, c. 1, it was ordained that lands might be devised, but it was required that the devise be made in writing. The Statute, however, left the rules for bequeathing personalty untouched. Indeed, even a devise under this act was valid though it was contained in an unsigned codicil, written by a person not the testator, in which the latter's name did not appear, and bearing every evidence of not being a final disposition. Notes dictated to his secretary by the testator were regarded as containing a valid devise. The writing was all that was required.

[1] *Cf.* § 43 supra.

[2] *Cf.* Swinburne, *Wills,* Part 1, § 11 (cited by Rood, *op. cit.,* 216).

[3] The canonical requirements are expressed in the Constitutions of the Bishop of Salisbury, c. 70—Harduin, VII, 107; the Synod of Oxford (1287), c. 50—Harduin, VII, 1114; the *Monitio* of the Archbishop of Canterbury (1455)—Mansi, XXXII, 161 B.

[4] *Cf.* § 42, supra.

358. The courts recognized that an opportunity for conspiracy and perjury was offered by this rather lax procedure, but they were helpless until a rather shocking case presented itself in 1676. A young woman, who had married a rich old man and had been guilty of infidelity, contested a written will in which a great sum was bequeathed to charity. She produced nine witnesses to swear that the testator had later made an oral will leaving his estate to her. But close scrutiny revealed conspiracy. She was found guilty of subornation of perjury (inducing others to commit perjury), and her witnesses were found guilty of perjury itself.

359. The next year the Statute of Frauds was passed, 29 Charles II, c. 3. This Statute made provisions for both oral and written wills. The regulations for oral (nuncupative) wills may well be scrutinized first. They are found in §§ 18, 19, 22 of the act and read as follows:

> § 18 (always cited as § 19). And for the prevention of fraudulent practices in setting up nuncupative wills, which have been occasion of much perjury; be it enacted by the authority aforesaid, that from and after the aforesaid four and twentieth day of June, no nuncupative will shall be good where the estate thereby bequeathed shall exceed the value of thirty pounds that is not proved by the oaths of three witnesses (at the least) that were present at the making thereof; nor unless it be proved that the testator, at the time of pronouncing the same, did bid the persons present or some of them to bear witness that such was his will, or to that effect; nor unless such nuncupative will were made at the time of the last sickness of the deceased and in the house of his or her habitation or dwelling, or where he or she hath been resident for the space of ten days or more next before the making of such will, except where such person was surprised or taken sick being from his own home, and died before he returned to the place of his or her dwelling.
>
> § 19 (always cited as § 20). And be it further enacted that after six months passed after the speaking of the pretended testamentary words, no testimony shall be received to prove any will nuncupative, except the said testimony or the substance thereof were committed to writing within six days after the making of the said will.
>
> § 22 (always cited as § 23). Provided always, that notwithstanding this act, any soldier being in actual military

service, or any mariner or seaman being at sea, may dispose of his movables, wages, and personal estate as he or they might have done before the making of this act.[5]

360. These provisions are repeated in most of the States of the Union with certain variations.[6] Colorado, Connecticut, Louisiana, New Mexico, and Wyoming seem to be the only States that do not permit an oral will under any circumstances. In the other States there are restrictions based on eight elements: viz., the quality of the testator, the amount bequeathed, the quality of the witnesses, the time of making the will, the place where the will is made, the consignment of the provisions to writing, the time of probation, and the protection of the testator's kin.

361. The privilege is allowed in some States with no formalities

[5] Compare this with the Roman law exemption of soldiers and sailors; D. 29, 1, 1 pr., *Cf.* footnote n. 65; Chapter II.

[6] At this point the sections of the State statutes dealing with nuncupative wills is given. As the variations are noted later, merely the name of the State will be given to indicate that the variation is adopted there. For method of citing statutes, *cf.* bibliography.

Alabama (§§ 10602-10606); Arizona (§§ 3639, 3640); Arkansas (§§ 10497-10500); California (§§ 54, 55, 325); Delaware (§ 3245); District of Columbia (tit. 29, § 22); Florida (§§ 5464-5466); Georgia (§§ 3925, 3926, 3928); Idaho (§§ 15-234, 15-235); Illinois (c. 148, § 17); Indiana (§ 3453); Iowa (§§ 11850, 11851); Kansas (§§ 22-273, 22-274); Kentucky (§§ 4830, 4831); Maine (C. 88, §§ 18-20); Maryland (Art. 93, § 343); Massachusetts (c. 191, §§ 5-7); Michigan (§ 13483); Minnesota (§§ 8737, 8767); Mississippi (§§ 3556-3559); Missouri (§§ 529-532); Montana (§§ 6992-6994); Nebraska (§§ 30-206, 30-207); Nevada (§§ 9909-9911); New Hampshire (c. 297, § 16); New Jersey (pp. 5864, 5865, 5871); New York (§ 16); North Carolina (§ 4144); North Dakota (§ 5645); Ohio (§§ 10601, 10602); Oklahoma (§ 1541); Oregon (§§ 10-512, 10-514); Pennsylvania (§ 8310); Rhode Island (§§ 4303, 4310, 4326); South Carolina (§§ 8937-8943); South Dakota (§§ 609, 3217) Tennessee (§§ 8094-8097); Texas (Arts. 8287-8290); Utah (§§ 101-1-17, 101-1-18); Washington (§ 1395); Virginia (§ 5231); Vermont (§§ 2752, 2753); West Virginia (§ 4043); Wisconsin (§§ 238.16, 238.17); Wyoming (§ 88-104).

Louisiana recognizes what it calls a nuncupative will, but which is really the nuncupative will of Roman law, not that which is recognized by the other States, that is, it is a will dictated to a notary in the presence of witnesses or to one of the witnesses. It may be also the publication of a will, that is, a declaration to a witness that a will already written is the testator's; Arts. 1576-1581.

but only to soldiers in active service and to mariners at sea.[7] Other States restrict the privilege to soldiers and sailors and require even these to comply with the formalities of witnesses.[8] A few recognize such wills when made even by soldiers and sailors only when the latter were in peril of death at the time the will was made.[9] Two States concede the privilege to all who are in peril of death from an injury received the same day.[10] But most of the States have no restriction as to the quality of the persons who may avail themselves of this privilege.

362. **There is a restriction on the kind and amount of property that may be given by a nuncupative will.** Georgia is the only State permitting a devise of realty by this device. The other States require a devise of land to be in writing.

On the other hand, wherever soldiers and sailors are authorized to make a nuncupative will, they are permitted to dispose of all their personal property in this fashion, except in States fixing the limit in every case at one thousand dollars.[11]

The restriction as to the amount takes various forms. The formalities of a nuncupative will resolve themselves about two elements: first, its oral nature; and second, precautions taken against fraud. The English Statute of Frauds permitted a nuncupative will to dispose of property in amount less than thirty pounds without the formalities prescribed in the Statute; and of property in amount greater than thirty pounds with no limitation, if the precautions against fraud were observed. Some States follow this plan, setting the limit beyond which it is necessary to observe the requirements of the Statute, the figures varying from thirty to two hundred dollars.[12]

[7] Maryland, Massachusetts, Minnesota, New York, Rhode Island, Virginia, and West Virginia.

[8] District of Columbia, Indiana, Iowa, Kentucky, New Hampshire, and Oregon.

[9] Montana, North Dakota, Oklahoma, and South Dakota.

[10] California, Utah.

[11] California, Montana, Nevada, North Dakota, Oklahoma, South Dakota, and Utah.

[12] $30.00 in Texas; $50.00 in Arizona and South Carolina; $80.00 in New Jersey; $100.00 in Maine, New Hampshire, and Pennsylvania; $150.00 in Nebraska and Wisconsin; and $200.00 in Washington.

Other States, on the contrary, exempt no amount, but recognize a nuncupative will in any amount only if it is fortified with the formalities required.[13] Finally, other States not only require the formalities for every amount, but refuse to recognize a bequest under a nuncupative will even when fortified with due formalities, if it exceed a specific sum, varying from fifty to five hundred dollars. Soldiers and sailors are exempt on the usual conditions, that is, they may dispose of their whole personal estate.[14]

363. The Witnesses to a Nuncupative Will. Three witnesses at the least were required under the English Statute of Frauds to sustain an oral bequest where the amount exceeded thirty pounds. The number of witnesses constitutes one of the formalities also in the United States. Three witnesses are still required in some States;[15] two in others;[16] while some States are silent as to the number required.[17] The witnesses must all be present at the same time and hear the identical declaration, and they must be competent at the time the will is made as well as at the date of the proving of the will. If they are beneficiaries under the will, they are incompetent as witnesses, and they can not render themselves competent by renouncing the bequest.

364. Invitation by the testator is required that the witnesses may understand that he is uttering a testamentary disposition. Most of the States require, therefore, that the testator ask some one to act as witness to his last will as he uttered it.[18] But implicit invita-

[13] Florida, Georgia, Idaho, Illinois, Kansas, North Carolina, and Ohio.

[14] $100.00 in Indiana and Mississippi; $200.00 in Delaware, Missouri, and Vermont; $300.00 in Michigan and Iowa; $500.00 in Alabama and Arkansas.

[15] Arizona, Florida, Georgia, Maine, Nebraska, New Jersey, New Hampshire, South Carolina, Texas, Wisconsin.

[16] Arkansas, Delaware, Illinois, Iowa, Kansas, Kentucky, Michigan, Mississippi, Missouri, Montana, Nevada, North Carolina, North Dakota, Ohio, Oklahoma, Pennsylvania, South Dakota, Tennessee, Utah, Washington.

[17] Alabama, Idaho, Indiana, Maryland, Massachusetts, Minnesota, New York, Oregon, Rhode Island, Vermont, Virginia, and West Virginia.

[18] Alabama, Arizona, Arkansas, California, Delaware, District of Columbia, Florida, Georgia, Kansas, Kentucky, Maine, Mississippi, Missouri, Montana, Nebraska, Nevada, New Hampshire, North Carolina, North Dakota, Ohio, Oklahoma, Pennsylvania, South Carolina, South Dakota, Tennessee, Texas, Utah, Washington, and Wisconsin.

tion suffices, and the witness need not be called by name. However, though only one need be invited, the required number must testify that at least one was invited.

365. **A further restriction regards the time of the making of the will.** Except in the case of soldiers and sailors, the nuncupative will is valid only if made during the last illness. But the mere failure of the testator to make a written will until the crisis of his illness does not prevent him from making a nuncupative will. The last illness is understood to mean the last few hours of illness when the danger of death is imminent.

366. **Add to the restriction of time, that of place.** Except soldiers and sailors, persons privileged to make nuncupative wills must make them, in certain of the States, at their home, where they were resident for the ten days prior to the act, unless they were taken ill by surprise on a journey.[19]

367. **The nuncupative provisions must be consigned to writing within a definite time.** This requirement is found in the English Statute of Frauds and has been adopted by the various States, the time limit varying from three to sixty days.[20] However, under the English Statute of Frauds, consignment to writing was not necessary if the will was probated within six months of the time when it was made. Some States agree with this;[21] others simply require probate within six months without making any exemption as to consignment

[19] Alabama, Arkansas, Georgia, Maine, Mississippi, Missouri, Nebraska, New Jersey, New Hampshire, North Carolina, Pennsylvania, Tennessee, Texas, Washington, and Wisconsin.

[20] Within three days in Delaware; within six days in Alabama, Arizona, Florida (they must be sworn to within the same time before a notary), Maine, Mississippi, Nebraska, New Hampshire, New Jersey, Pennsylvania, South Carolina, Texas, Vermont, and Wisconsin; within ten days in Kansas, North Carolina, Ohio, and Tennessee; within fifteen days in Arkansas and Indiana; within twenty days in Illinois (or within ten days of death); within thirty days in California, Idaho, Missouri, Minnesota, Montana, Oregon, South Dakota, and Utah; within sixty days in Kentucky.

[21] Alabama, Arizona, Arkansas, Florida, Maine, Mississippi, Missouri, Nebraska, New Jersey, North Carolina, Pennsylvania, South Carolina (but probate in no case allowed after one year), Tennessee, Texas, Vermont, and Wisconsin.

to writing;[22] others require only the consignment to writing within a definite time and leave the question of probate as in the usual written will;[23] others require both the consignment within a definite period and the probate within six months;[24] while a final group require both procedures and the probate of the writing as well.[25]

368. For the protection of the kindred of the deceased, it is forbidden in some jurisdictions that the will be probated within fourteen days of the death of the testator, and until the widow and the next of kin have been cited to appear.[26]

369. All restrictions were waived for soldiers and sailors by the English Statute of Frauds. In many of the States there is no restriction on them either as to formalities or the amount to be bequeathed, provided it be personalty.[27]

A soldier is privileged only when on an actual military expedition, whether in battle, on the march, in camp, or in the hospital. Every person in military service before the enemy is a soldier within the meaning of the statutes. A seaman is at sea when he boards the boat for a voyage, even while it lies at anchor in a foreign port, as long as he is continuing the voyage. Every person engaged as a member of the crew is a seaman within the meaning of the laws.[28]

[22] Georgia, North Dakota, Ohio; Nevada in the same fashion requires probate within three months.

[23] Delaware, District of Columbia, Illinois, and Kentucky.

[24] California, Indiana, Kansas, Montana, New Hampshire, Oregon, and Washington.

[25] Idaho, South Dakota, and Utah.

[26] Alabama, Arizona, Arkansas (as to citation of kin), California (as to fourteen days), Florida (not within sixty days), Illinois (not within sixty days), Indiana (as to citation of kin), Maine, Mississippi, Montana, Nebraska, Nevada, New Jersey, North Carolina (as to citation of kin), Oregon, Pennsylvania, South Carolina, Tennessee, Texas, Utah (not within ten days), Washington (as to citation of kin), and Wisconsin.

[27] Alabama, Arizona, Arkansas, Michigan, Mississippi, Missouri, Nebraska, New Jersey, Pennsylvania, South Carolina, Texas, Washington, and Wisconsin.

[28] Rood, *op. cit.*, 238, 239.

ARTICLE 2

THE FORMALITIES OF WRITTEN WILLS

370. The usual form of will required in the United States is the written will. This provision derives from the English Statute of Frauds, § 5, which reads as follows:

> And be it further enacted by the authority aforesaid, that from and after the said four and twentieth day of June all devises and bequests of any lands and tenements, devisable either by force of the Statute of Wills or by this statute or by force of the custom of Kent or the custom of any borough or any other particular custom, shall be in writing and signed by the party so devising the same or by some other person in his presence and by his express directions, and shall be attested and subscribed, in the presence of the said devisor, by three or four credible witnesses or else they shall be utterly void and of none effect.[29]

371. Observe that the English Statute of Frauds required the presence of witnesses only for devises of land. Consequently, per-

[29] The Statutes of the various States touching this matter are found in the sections noted below. Where the matter is explained in the subsequent sections, reference will be made merely to the State, without noting the source in the laws of the State.

Alabama (§§ 10598, 10599); Arizona (§ 3637); Arkansas (§§ 10494, 10495); California (§§ 50-53); Colorado (§ 5187); Connecticut (§§ 4876, 4877); Delaware (§ 3241); District of Columbia (tit. 29, § 23); Florida (§§ 5460, 5462); Georgia (§§ 3838, 3846-3849); Idaho (§§ 14-303, 14-304); Illinois (c. 148, § 2); Indiana (§ 3452); Iowa (§ 11852); Kansas (§§ 22-202); Kentucky (§ 4828); Louisiana (Arts. 1575-1581); Maine (c. 88, § 1); Maryland (Art. 93, § 332); Massachusetts (c. 191, §§ 1-3); Michigan (§ 13482); Minnesota (§ 8735); Mississippi (§ 3550); Missouri (§ 507); Montana (§§ 6980-6982); Nebraska (§ 30-205); Nevada (§ 9907); New Hampshire (c. 297, § 2); New Jersey (p. 5867, § 24); New York (§ 22); New Mexico (§§ 154-105, 154-108); North Carolina (§ 4131); North Dakota (§§ 5648, 5649); Ohio (§ 10505); Oklahoma (§§ 1545-1547); Oregon (§§ 10-503, 10-504); Pennsylvania (§§ 8308, 8309, 8312); Rhode Island (§ 4303); South Carolina (§ 8916); South Dakota (§§ 612-615); Tennessee (§§ 8089, 8090); Texas (Art. 8283); Utah (§§ 101-1-5 to 101-1-9); Washington (§§ 1395-1397); Virginia (§ 5229); Vermont (§§ 2751, 2755); West Virginia (§ 4041); Wisconsin (§ 238.06); Wyoming (§ 88-104); Alaska (§ 564).

sonalty could be bequeathed by an informal written will, and in any amount. In the United States, no witnesses are required for a written will disposing of personalty in Florida and Tennessee.[30] Pennsylvania requires no subscribing witnesses for any written will, even when it devises realty, unless the will contains a bequest to charity or religion. In the remaining States, however, no distinction is made as to written testamentary disposition between personalty and realty. The formalities required by them for a written will devising realty, they demand also in a will disposing of personalty.[31]

372. Elements of the Formalities for Written Wills. In the formalities required by the English Statute of Frauds, observe the following elements. First, the will shall be in writing; second, it shall be signed by the testator or by some other person in his presence and by his express direction; and third, it shall be witnessed. The complications of law that may arise out of these three elements require careful analysis. The first to challenge scrutiny is the writing.

373. An analysis of the act of writing a will discloses four points worthy of examination: the language used; the method of making the inscription; the materials on which it may be made; and the unity and coherence in the document, if it be written on separate sheets.

The will may be written in any language, though it is probated in the language of the court. It may be written even in a language which the testator did not understand, provided that he understands the meaning of the document and its contents. The presumption in some jurisdictions is that when the testator affixed his signature to a will, he understood its contents, even though they are expressed in a language which he did not understand.

The writing may be done by printing, by typewriting, with pen and ink, or with a lead pencil.[32]

[30] Tennessee (§ 8089). Florida requires no subscribing witnesses; Georgia permits devises of land by oral will, in cases where a nuncupative will is recognized (§§ 3925, 3928). *Cf.* Brown v. Avery (1912), 63 Fla. 376, 58 So. 34.

[31] It is impossible to convert realty into personalty after the death of the testator. The fund realized from the sale of the land is regarded by the courts as realty; Rood, *op. cit.*, 243.

[32] But wills signed in pencil are in peril of being regarded as merely deliberative; Rood, *op. cit.*, 246 (footnote).

The material on which it is written may be any kind that is capable of retaining the impression, though a will has been denied probate because it was written on a slate.

As to unity and coherence, the will may be valid even though written on several sheets, and signed only on the last.[33] All the sheets are presumed to have been present when the will was signed, but the presumption yields to proof.

A pre-existing document may be incorporated in a will by reference, even though it is not in the hands of the testator when he makes the will, and can be given the effect requested by the testator in the will.[34]

To establish such incorporation three requisites must appear on the face of the will, and two other corroborating incidents must be available by extrinsic proof. On the face of the will there must appear, first, adequate identification of the document; second, explicit reference to it as already in existence; and third, the unequivocal desire of the testator that it be incorporated. By extrinsic evidence it must be shown: first, that the writing offered is the one named in the will; and second, that it was in fact in existence at the time the will was made.[35]

374. The signature of the testator or of some one for him is the second element discernible in the formalities specified by the English Statute of Frauds. It is required in all the States of the

[33] This would be reckless procedure. It is better to have the will on one sheet. If there are several sheets, they should be bound together to prevent removal of any one of them. Where only the first sheet of a will was signed, the court presumed that the remaining sheets were executed later; Maginn's Estate (1923), 278 Pa. 89, 122 Atl. 264. Numerous charitable bequests were defeated under this decision.

[34] New York and Connecticut admit this only in the case of a codicil ratifying a pre-existent invalid will; Rood, *op. cit.*, 249. *Cf.* Booth *et al.* v. Baptist Church *et al.* (1891), 126 N. Y. 215, 28 N. E. 238; Phelps v. Robbins (1873), 40 Conn. 250, at pp. 271, 272; Appeal of Bryan *et al.* (1904), 77 Conn. 240; 58 Atl. 748; Bryan v. Bigelow *et al.* (1905), 77 Conn. 604, 60 Atl. 266; Hatheway *et al.* v. Smith (1907), 79 Conn. 506, 65 Atl. 1058.

[35] The document may be a deed, a note, or a mere memorandum. It need not be signed or executed by the testator. It is of no importance that it is invalid of its nature, for even then it serves as a memorandum. But oral statements can not be incorporated in this way.

Union that written wills be signed. But Pennsylvania waives the signature if the testator is prevented from signing by the extremity of his last illness.[36]

375. The circumstances attending the act of signature are reducible to the following: the designation of the place of signature on the face of the will; the dating of the will; the time of signature; the physical act of the testator; his intention to sign, and the part of the will on which the signature is placed.

376. It is not essential to designate on the face of the will the place where the signature was made or the time when it was affixed. Both may be established by parol evidence.

377. The time at which the testator should sign the will may be stated generally to be after the will has been written and before the witnesses have affixed their signatures. But in those States where it is not required that the testator should sign at the end of the will, he may sign before the will is written, even before he has completed it in his mind, and even though originally he did not intend it to be a testamentary signature, provided that he later adopted it as such when the will was completed. This conclusion is useful principally *post factum* to vindicate the validity of a will; and is not to be used as a practical measure in drafting a will.

The validity of a signature affixed after the witnesses have subscribed is a controversial point. No State denies its validity by statute. In a few States, however, and in England, it is regarded as invalid.[37]

378. The physical act of signing may be almost any sort of impression that can pass as a mark made by the testator. The use of an uncommon form of signature may raise a presumption that the testator did not wish it to be a testamentary signature. But that presumption will, of course, yield to proof. But even a misspelled name or a wrong name, if the latter is appended by a secretary in explanation of a mark, will not invalidate the signature.

379. The intention of the testator to accept the physical sign

[36] Showers v. Showers (1856), 27 Pa. St. 485; 67 Am. Dec. 487. But not if it is the hysteria of the family that prevents the signature; Butler's Estate (1909), 223 Pa. 252, 72 Atl. 508.

[37] Rood, *op. cit.*, 292.

as his signature is the all important and governing factor. Even the correct name in full is no testamentary signature if it is not intended to be such. Even the affixing of a seal, though it could possibly be regarded as a signature, is not generally so accepted today. Therefore it is not a sufficient signature. It is not intended as such by the testator.[38]

380. The part of the will at which the signature should be placed was not stated by the English Statute of Frauds. Such is the condition in many of the States, where the intention of the testator to make testamentary signature must be gathered from the circumstances. But for two reasons other States demand that the will be signed at the end. Those reasons are: first to prevent fraud, that is, to make more certain that the document offered for probate is the one actually executed by the testator without any additions at the end; the second reason is, to render more certain the testamentary character of the document, that is, to aid the court in determining that the document is not a mere memorandum or rough draft of a future will. Signing at the end seems so natural that there appears to be no good reason for eccentric performance. Wisdom counsels signature at the end.[39]

A controversy arises immediately regarding the actual manner in which the requirement of signing at the end can be met. Must the signature be placed immediately after the last word in the last sentence of the will? A few jurisdictions would demand almost that. Yet it seems within the fair significance of the statutes that the

[38] New Hampshire, New Jersey, and Rhode Island expressly excuse the testator from using a seal, though New Jersey says that a seal is customary. The remaining States are silent. Where a seal is not required by express statute, it is not necessary. It matters not that the clause asserting the attestation by the witnesses states that the will was sealed. On the other hand, the affixing of a seal does not invalidate a will.

[39] Signature at the end is required by statute in Arkansas, California, Idaho, Kansas, Minnesota, Montana, New York, North Dakota, Ohio, Oklahoma, Pennsylvania, South Dakota, and Utah.

The will must be *subscribed* by the testator in Connecticut and Kentucky. In New Jersey the courts hold that everything in the will must precede the subscription.

testator should place it just so close to the matter of the will as to prevent fraudulent insertions.

381. Dispositions following the signature are *ipso facto* incorporated into the will, if the testator makes reference to them in the body of the instrument.[40] But if no reference is made to these dispositions, the whole will usually fails, except in England, where the provisions that precede the signature are sustained. The rule, as it exists in the States, supposes that the testator wrote the whole will first, and then placed his signature in the middle. If the whole of the will preceding the signature was the only will at the time the signature was affixed, it is valid. The addition of subsequent dispositions after the signature does not operate as a revocation.

382. Signature may be made for the testator, except in Connecticut, New Jersey, and Utah. In the remaining States, the testator may sign by another who executes this task at his direction,[41] or at his *express* direction.[42]

The person who signs the will for the testator is required in some jurisdictions to sign his own name as a witness;[43] but in most of the States that require this, the omission of it does not invalidate the will.[44]

The mere knowledge of the testator that another is signing his will, even though it be accompanied by his acquiescence, does not suffice. But even a gesture can be a straightforward direction and consequently adequate.[45]

[40] This is not true in New York; Rood, *op. cit.*, 259. *Cf.* footnote n. 34, this Chapter.

[41] Alabama, Arizona, Arkansas, California, Colorado, Idaho, Indiana, Illinois, Kentucky, Maine, Mississippi, Missouri, Montana, New Mexico, New York, North Carolina, North Dakota, Oklahoma, Oregon, South Dakota, Texas, Virginia, Washington, and West Virginia.

[42] Delaware, District of Columbia, Florida, Georgia, Iowa, Kansas, Maryland, Massachusetts, Michigan, Minnesota, Nebraska, Nevada, New Hampshire, Ohio, Pennsylvana, Rhode Island, South Carolina, Tennessee, Vermont.

[43] Arkansas, California, Idaho, Montana, New York, North Dakota, Oklahoma, Oregon, South Dakota, and Washington (in the last unless the testator has made his mark).

[44] California, Idaho, Montana, New York, North Dakota, Oklahoma, and South Dakota.

[45] Rood, *op. cit.*, 267.

383. The presence and the subscription of witnesses constitutes the third and final element of the formalities prescribed by the English Statute of Frauds for written wills. At the outset, observe that many States recognize as valid, wills wholly written, dated, and signed in the testator's own handwriting, that is, holographic wills, though not attested or subscribed by witnesses.

384. Of the States that recognize holographic wills, Wyoming requires that they be proved as any other document; Texas and Virginia, that they be proved by two witnesses; Arkansas requires three witnesses for proof, and will not suffer a holographic will to bar a written will, even though the latter precede the former. Three witnesses are required also by North Carolina and Tennessee, which States demand in addition that the will be found among the valuable papers of the decedent or in the custody of some one to whom the testator entrusted it. Connecticut recognizes a holographic will that is valid in the jurisdiction where it was made. Florida and Pennsylvania are silent on the point of holographic wills, but it would seem that Florida permits a holographic will of personalty, since it requires no subscribing witnesses for such a will. Pennsylvania requires witnesses only to prove a will, even of realty, and not to subscribe it. But the witnesses are something more than witnesses to the handwriting of the decedent; they are witnesses to the will as well, even though they do not subscribe it.

It is the most populous of the States that do not regard the holographic will as valid, viz., New York, Pennsylvania, Massachusetts, New Jersey, Ohio, etc.[46]

385. Holographic wills, where valid, may be written with any sort of instrument except a typewriter, and on any sort of material. Printed forms are excluded. Any interlineations by the hand of another, if they constitute a part of the will, invalidate it. Since no

[46] *Cf.* § 371, supra. Holographic wills are recognized in the following jurisdictions: Arizona (§ 2637); Arkansas (§ 10494); Californa (§ 53); Idaho (§ 14-304); Kentucky (§ 4828; Rutledge v. Wiggington 1915, 166 Ky. 421, 179 S. W. 389); Louisiana (Art. 1588); Mississippi (§ 3550); Montana (§ 6981); Nevada (§ 9928); North Carolina (§ 4131); North Dakota (§ 5648); Oklahoma (§ 1545); South Dakota (§ 612); Tennessee (§ 8090); Texas (Arts. 8284, 3344); Utah (§ 101-1-6); Virginia (§ 5229); West Virginia (§ 4041); Wyoming (§ 88-502).

witnesses are required, the use of incompetent witnesses does not harm the will.

386. The Requisite of Subscribing Witnesses. Where the holographic will is not recognized as valid, or where the will is not wholly written by the testator, subscribing witnesses are required in all the States except Pennsylvania.[47] The aspect of the legislation in the various States touching witnesses presents a confusion that is bewildering. This is due chiefly to the variations in the terms of the various statutes that have been modeled after the English Statute of Frauds. The Statute of the State of Utah is perhaps the most exact and the most exacting in this matter. It probably expresses what the legislators in the other States intended. Nevertheless, as statutes are to be interpreted strictly, what the legislators failed to express can not be used to defeat a will.[48]

387. That some clear notion of the state of the law in the United States may be obtained, let the attesting by witnesses be viewed from four points, viz., the acts of the testator, the acts of the witnesses, the number of witnesses, and the quality of the witnesses.

388. As to the acts of the testator, the requirements of most of the States would be met if the testator implicitly acknowledged the

[47] *Cf.* §§ 371, 384, this treatise.

[48] The Statute in Utah (§ 101-1-5) requires that every will other than a nuncupative will must be in writing, and every will other than a holographic or nuncupative will must be executed and attested as follows: (1) it must be subscribed at the end thereof by the testator himself; (2) the subscription must be made in the presence of the attesting witnesses; (3) the testator must, at the time of subscribing the same, declare to the attesting witnesses that the instrument is his will; (4) there must be two attesting witnesses, each of whom must sign his name as a witness at the end of the will at the testator's request, in his presence, and in the presence of each other. A witness to a will must write with his name the place of his residence.

The Statute in New York approaches this in clarity, but does not require that the testator sign himself or in the actual presence of the witnesses. The Statutes in North Dakota, Oklahoma, and South Dakota are very similar to that of New York.

Contrast with the thoroughness of these statutes the provisions of Wyoming which simply require that all wills, except holographic wills, to be valid, must be in writing, witnessed by two competent witnesses and signed by the testator or by some person in his presence and by his express direction.

instrument to be his own to each of the witnesses separately, without indicating to them that it is a will and without even showing them his signature.

Therefore, it is not essential that the witnesses should have known the testator prior to the acknowledgment. They need not see the signature made; they need not be present together when the acknowledgment is made, that is, a dual acknowledgment suffices; they need not know the contents of the will; they need not be aware that the testator knows the contents of the will (for instance, if he were blind, they need not know that the will had been read to him); they need not notice the presence of the testator; they need not see the whole will (it suffices that the whole will was present); they need not know it is a will; they need not see the signature.

The requirements are more strict in some of the States, particularly as to the acknowledgment of the instrument precisely as a will and as to the exhibition of the signature of the testator. But here the most liberal rule has been presented. By contrast, the modifications can be observed in the process of the discussion.

389. **The signature must be shown to the witnesses in some of the States,**[49] and actually made in the presence of the witnesses in Georgia, Kansas, and Utah.

390. **The will must be declared in the presence of the witnesses present simultaneously** in Louisiana, New Jersey, Virginia, West Virginia, and Rhode Island, though it seems sufficient that it be declared merely his own instrument, and not necessarily his will. A quarter of the States, however, require that the testator definitely state the instrument to be his will, and among them are Louisiana and New Jersey just noted.[50]

391. There is sufficient implied acknowledgment, where no more is required, if the testator asks the witnesses to attest or subscribe his

[49] Arkansas, California, Idaho, Montana, New Jersey, New York, North Dakota, Ohio, Oklahoma, Rhode Island, South Dakota.

[50] So also Alabama, Arkansas, California, Colorado, Idaho, Kansas, New York, North Dakota, Ohio, Oklahoma, South Dakota, and Utah.

In some other States this requirement has been assumed, but it has not been definitely decided that it is necessary in the absence of express statute.

will. But such a request need not be made or proved except in the States where such a request is required by the statute.[51]

Sufficient implied acknowledgment also occurs when the testator admits the instrument to be his in answer to a question, though his answer be a syllable only; or when after calling the witnesses for the purpose of witnessing his will, he sits mute while the will is handed about to be signed; or tacitly allows the attorney to ask the witnesses to subscribe the document for the testator.

392. **Where the testator is obliged to specify that the document is his will,** it is not sufficient compliance with the statute if the witnesses learnt the nature of the instrument from a third person. But if the testator uses the word *will* when he asks them to be witnesses, it suffices; or if they hear the document read, for then they know it is a will.

393. **The acts of the witnesses are chiefly two, to attest and to sign the will in the presence of the testator,** and that is all that is required of them in most States.[52] Attestation indicates that the witnesses examine the instrument sufficiently to be able to identify it.[53] Attestation and subscription must be done by the same set of witnesses. The functions may not be divided. An attesting witness can not delegate another person to sign his name. Ordinarily, however, it is not necessary that they should sign in the presence of each other, though this is required in about one-quarter of the States.[54]

[51] It is required in Alabama, Arkansas, California, Idaho, Indiana, Kansas, Montana, New Mexico, New York, North Dakota, Oklahoma, South Carolina, South Dakota, Tennessee, Utah, Vermont, and Washington.

[52] Though Iowa, Michigan, and Wyoming simply require that they witness the will, the language is held to include signing; and the same interpretation is attached to the word *attest* in the Statutes of Colorado, Illinois, Mississippi, New Mexico, and Washington.

[53] So they must see the interlineations, if there are any; otherwise, they would be unable to testify concerning them.

[54] Arizona, California, Colorado, Louisiana, Missouri, Montana, New Mexico, Rhode Island, South Carolina, Utah, Vermont, West Virginia, and Wisconsin. But even in these jurisdictions, the witnesses need not notice each other sign. Simultaneous presence is sufficient. Signing after the death of the testator is futile. But signing after the testator has signed is upheld by the decisions except in England, Georgia, Kentucky, Massachusetts, New York, and Wisconsin; Rood, *op. cit.*, 291, 292.

The witnesses must intend their signatures to be testamentary, that is, made in compliance with the statutes providing for the execution of testaments. Signatures will be presumed to have been so made unless they appear in an unusual place.[55] But they may be placed anywhere unless they are expressly required to be at the end of the will. In Kentucky, it is held that because the witnesses are obliged to *subscribe* the will, the signatures must be at the end of it.[56] But the interpretation of the word *subscribe* is more liberal in other jurisdictions where it is used in connection with the signatures of witnesses. The signatures of the witnesses must be attached to the will in any case. It does not suffice that one witness should sign the will and another the codicil; or that the testator should sign the original will, and the witnesses a duplicate. If any given portion of the will, complete in itself, is signed by the testator, it must be signed also by the witnesses.

The material form of the signature of a witness is not very important. Even in those jurisdictions where it is required that the witness sign his *name*, it is held sufficient signature if he makes his mark.[57] Another person may even guide the hand of the witness while he writes his signature. But the signature should not be made entirely by a third person. Some courts hold that this would be an invalid signature.[58] The addresses of the witnesses are required to be written on the will in a few States, but not under penalty of the invalidity of the will.[59]

The presence of the testator has already been indicated as being necessary to the validity of the signature of the witnesses.

Alterations can not be attested by the mere approval on the part of the original witnesses, though one opinion held that they could; Rood, *op. cit.*, 293.

[55] Where a witness merely crossed an "F" in his name written on another occasion, it was no signature as required by the statutes; Rood, *op. cit.*, 294.

[56] The following States require the witnesses to sign at the end of the will: Arkansas, California, Idaho, Montana, New York, North Dakota, Oklahoma, South Dakota, and Utah.

[57] The following States require the signature by *name:* Alabama, Arkansas, Kentucky, Missouri, Montana, Nevada, New Jersey, New York, North Dakota, Oklahoma, Oregon, South Dakota, Texas, and Utah.

[58] Rood, *op. cit.*, 300.

[59] Idaho, Montana, New York, Oklahoma, South Dakota, and Utah.

Indeed the statutes of all the States require this, except Arkansas, Iowa, New York, and Wyoming. The reason for this provision is that the testator may prevent the substitution of a foreign document in the place of his will. But even if the testator be present, the signature of a witness is invalid, if he should sign secretly. On the other hand, if the testator is some distance away but nevertheless is able to see what is being done, he is conceived to be present. Some decisions, however, maintain that the testator must be able to see the will and the act of signing. A blind man is generally held sufficiently present at the signing done by the witnesses, if he *knows* what is being done, even though he can not *see* what is being done. The presumption is that the testator was present if the will was signed in the same room with him; if not in the same room, the presumption is the other way. Both presumptions yield to proof.

394. The number of witnesses is usually two in the United States.[60]

395. The quality of a witness means in this place his competence. Competence rests on credibility and disinterestedness. The latter quality seems wanting in one who is beneficiary under the will. This was recognized soon after the passage of the English Statute of

[60] Three are required in Connecticut, Georgia, Maine, Massachusetts, New Hampshire, South Carolina, and Vermont.

Louisiana requires three resident witnesses, or five non-resident witnesses, in the case of a will dictated to a notary, who reads it to all the witnesses (a public will); all the witnesses sign, and one at least must sign his name. In the case of a private will five resident or seven non-resident witnesses are required. A private will is one that is either written by the testator in the presence of the witnesses or by one of the witnesses in the presence of the testator and of the remaining witnesses. It may also be declared by the testator to the witnesses to be his last will and testament. It must be read to the witnesses either by the testator or by one of the witnesses in the presence of the testator. At least two of the witnesses must sign their names; the others, as well as the testator, may make their mark.

The mystic testament is much like the usual testament in the remainder of the United States. The will is enclosed in an envelope, upon which the notary draws an act of superscription asserting that the testator declared in his presence and the presence of three witnesses that the will was his. All sign the act of superscription and the envelope is sealed. Only one who can sign his name may make this kind of testament.

Frauds. At first, witnesses were made competent upon their releasing their interest. Then the courts swung about and inclined to the doctrine that if an interested person were necessary to prove a will, the will must fail. To remedy this situation, a statute was passed in 1752, 25 George II, c. 6, affecting England and the American colonies, sustaining wills where a witness was a beneficiary by invalidating the devise or bequest to all subscribing witnesses or to any persons claiming under them, except charges on land for the payment of debts. However, this statute did not invalidate bequests or devises to the wife of a witness. The consequence was that the courts held such a devise or gift to invalidate the will. On the other hand, they rather contradicted the statute by holding that as bequests of personalty did not require witnesses, they were not affected by the statute, and witnesses were not deprived of them.

But the Statute of Wills, 1. Victoria, c. 26, invalidated bequests to spouses of subscribing witnesses, made the witnesses competent, and thus saved the will even under these circumstances. Moreover, the statute required all wills to be in writing, and thus overruled the courts on the matter of bequests of personalty to subscribing witnesses. Henceforth, these bequests were to be invalid.

396. The present law in the United States runs with the spirit of the Statute, 25 George II, c. 6. But most of the States have legislation that reverts to the original position of the English courts, and witnesses are made competent upon their releasing their interest. And the bequest or devise to the witness is rendered void only when it is necessary to make the witness competent to prove the will. Consequently when there is a sufficient number of witnesses without the interested witness, he does not lose his gift.[61] The bequest to a

[61] It is so in Arizona (§ 3645); Arkansas (§§ 10529-10531); California (§ 51); Colorado (§ 5190); Connecticut (§ 4877); Iowa (§ 11854); Kansas (§ 22-212); Kentucky (§ 4836); Massachusetts (c. 191, § 2); Michigan (§ 13484); Minnesota (§ 8739); Mississippi (§ 3554); Missouri (§ 542); Montana (§§ 6986, 6987); Nebraska (§ 30-208); Nevada (§ 9908); New York (§ 27); North Dakota (§ 5680); Ohio (§ 10515); Oklahoma (§ 1575); Oregon (§ 10-520); South Carolina (§ 8919); South Dakota (§ 638); Texas (Art. 8297); Washington (§ 1408); Vermont (§ 2755); West Virginia (§ 4049)· Wisconsin (§ 238.09); Wyoming (§ 88-104).

spouse of a witness is voided in some jurisdictions when it is necessary that the latter should testify to a will.[62]

If the witness is entitled to succeed to some portion of the decedent's estate even outside the right he has under the will, some statutes allow him to take the amount due by the extrinsic claim even when his testimony is necessary to prove the will. But he is in no case permitted to take more than was given him in the will.[63]

Creditors are permitted in some States by specific statute to be witnesses of the will without loss of their claim against the testator's estate.[64] Valid charges on the land of the decedent, in the language of the Statute, 25 George II, c. 6, are upheld by certain statutes when they are held by witnesses to the will.[65]

Immunity is expressly granted in a few States to the executors of the will, who are thus allowed to be witnesses;[66] but Illinois lists among those interested and therefore incapable of taking a bequest under the will, executors, testamentary trustees, and the stockholders of corporate executors or trustees.[67] In Connecticut and Utah[68] heirs may be witnesses without detriment to their interests; Georgia permits a husband to be a witness even if his wife be a legatee;[69]

[62] Kentucky (§ 4836); Massachusetts (c. 191, § 2); South Carolina (§ 8919); Vermont (§ 2755); West Virginia (§ 4049); Wisconsin (§ 238.08).

[63] This provision obtains in Arizona (§ 3645); Arkansas (§§ 10529-10531); Colorado (§ 5190) Iowa (§ 11854); Kansas (§§ 22-212); Michigan (§ 13485); Minnesota (§ 8739); Mississippi (§ 3554); Nebraska (§§ 30-208); New York (§ 27); North Dakota (§ 5681); Ohio (§ 10515); Oklahoma (§ 1576); Oregon (§ 10-519); South Carolina (§ 8919); South Dakota (§ 639); Texas (Art. 8296); Washington (§ 1408); West Virginia (§ 4049); Wisconsin (§ 238.09); Wyoming (§ 88-104).

[64] In California (§ 51); Colorado (§ 5191); Delaware (§ 3242); Kentucky (§ 4837); Mississippi (§ 3555); Nevada (§ 9908); New Hampshire (c. 297, § 3); Oregon (§ 10-521); Vermont (§ 2755); West Virginia (§ 4051).

[65] Nebraska (§ 30-209); New Jersey (p. 5862); North Dakota (§ 5680); Oklahoma (§ 1575); Oregon (§ 10-518); Rhode Island (§ 4323); Utah (§ 101-1-12); Washington (§ 1408).

[66] In Kentucky (§ 4838); North Carolina (§ 4138); Rhode Island (§ 4325); West Virginia (§ 4051).

[67] C. 148, § 8.

[68] Connecticut (§ 4877); Utah (§ 101-1-13).

[69] § 3849.

Virginia does not regard a witness incompetent who receives a gift under the will;[70] and it has been held in Alabama that the statutes in this field are superseded by another statute providing that interested persons are competent witnesses generally, though the contrary has been held elsewhere under a similar statute.[71]

397. On the other and more rigorous side appear a few of the States. New Hampshire, for instance, simply declares that a witness is incompetent who is a legatee or a devisee under the will, or whose spouse is a legatee or a devisee;[72] Louisiana incapacitates heirs and legatees for the office of witness except in the case of mystic testaments;[73] but other States specifically invalidate the bequest and thus render the witness competent, without any provision for other witnesses to take his place or validation of the gift if other competent witnesses are capable of proving the will.[74] Persons claiming through a witness are incapacitated to take gifts granted in the will in New Jersey and North Carolina.[75]

398. Competent witnesses are not required by express statute in certain States;[76] but most of the States have some modifying adjective to describe the kind of witness required. A qualified witness is also understood to be required in those States where it is not expressly so stated. In general, he must be capable of being sworn as a witness, and free from the disqualifications of mental unsoundness, interest in the estate, and extreme infancy. Minors capable of understanding what is being done when the will is acknowledged can be competent witnesses. Persons above the age of fourteen years are presumed competent; persons under that age are presumed incompetent. But in Arizona and Texas the witness must be above the age of fourteen years; and in Louisiana women and minors under the age of sixteen are incapacitated.

[70] §§ 6208, 5229.

[71] Rood, *op. cit.*, 308 h.

[72] C. 297, § 3.

[73] Arts. 5192, 5193.

[74] Georgia (§ 3849); Illinois (c. 148, § 8); Indiana (§ 3472); New Mexico (§ 154-107); Rhode Island (§ 4322); Utah (§ 101-1-12).

[75] New Jersey (p. 5862); North Carolina (§ 4138).

[76] Alabama, Arkansas, Connecticut, Florida, Idaho, Montana, New Jersey, New York, North Dakota, Oklahoma, Rhode Island, Utah.

The spouse of the decedent is not a competent witness to his will even in States where other parties in interest are competent. But confidential advisers are competent, because the testator waives secrecy by accepting them as witnesses, but only to the extent of sustaining the will.[77]

399. **A witness incompetent when the will was made could not become competent to prove the will,** even though the impediment had ceased meanwhile. The converse is also true, unless the statutes rule otherwise, as they do in some States.[78]

400. **Scholion I. Certain States have statutes requiring that wills containing bequests to charity shall be executed several weeks in advance of death,** and invalidating the gifts to charity if the requirement is not fulfilled. The period is set at thirty days in California, Idaho, Montana, and Pennsylvania; at ninety days, in Georgia; and at one year in Ohio, if the testator leaves issue, or an adopted child, or the legal representative of either. These bequests, as well as bequests to a minister of religion, are invalid in Louisiana, if made *in articulo mortis*. (*Cf.* § 552, this treatise.)

401. **Scholion II. In general the same formalities are required for the re-execution and re-publication of a will,** as for the original draft.[79]

Re-publication becomes important where a minor wishes to ratify a will previously made. This act may be done directly, *i. e.*, on the will itself; or indirectly, *i. e.*, by a codicil. The codicil revives the will by incorporation. Consequently there must be adequate reference to the prior will, though the will be not present; but a formal intention to incorporate it in the codicil is not requisite, for a presumption of intention is raised by the mere reference to the former

[77] Rood, *op. cit.*, 317, 318.

[78] V. gr., in Alabama, Massachusetts, and Wisconsin.

[79] The new document must be complete in itself. It is not sufficient to supply the defects in the original instrument.

But in Pennsylvania, where the witnesses are not required to subscribe the will, it would seem that oral re-publication would suffice, for the testator originally could have acknowledged the instrument as his will in that fashion. There seems no reason why he should not be able to do so a second time. *Cf.* §§ 371, 384, this chapter.

will.[80] The presumption can be contradicted only by a contrary intent appearing on the face of the will itself.[81]

402. The effects of re-publication are chiefly three: first, it makes the re-executed will valid and effective, even though it was invalid previously due either to some informality, or to a lack of capacity in the testator; second, it embraces and validates any corrections or interlineations made in a prior will (though it does not touch separate codicils written on separate documents to which it does not refer); and third, it makes a will speak as of the day of re-execution. Any conditions expressed in the original will that have already failed of fulfillment cease to be conditions under the re-execution.[82]

403. Scholion III. Conflict of laws may arise as to wills in three ways: by the enactment of new legislation; by the change of domicile on the part of the testator; and by the granting of property in jurisdictions distinct from that in which the testator has his domicile.

404. New legislation may be enacted after the drafting of the will, either before or after the death of the testator. If enacted after the testator's death, it can not affect vested rights. But it does affect rights held in abeyance under the terms of the will; and it regulates also the formalities of procedure that are juridically subsequent to death.

Prior to the death of the testator, the legislator may affect his will in any way he chooses. Four kinds of new legislation should be considered in this regard: first, that which interprets definitively the intention of the testator; second, that which inaugurates a new public policy; third, that which changes the formalities or the requirements

[80] *Cf.* § 373, this treatise.

[81] A letter announcing the testator's marriage and directing an attorney to make a change in the will by preparing a codicil to provide for the testator's wife, was held to be a sufficient re-publication of the will revoked by the marriage; Barney v. Hayes (1892), 11 Mont. 571, 29 Pac. 282.

[82] But a gift to a charitable use declared void if made within thirty days of the death of the testator was valid even though reaffirmed in a codicil made within thirty days of death; *In re* McCauley's Estate (1903), 138 Cal. 432, 71 Pac. 512; Morrow's Estate (1903), 204 Pa. St. 479, 54 Atl. 313, in which case even the terms of the bequest to the charity had been changed in the codicil.

Rood, *op. cit.*, 392-397.

for capacity; and fourth, that which changes the law on the revocation of wills.

405. **Enactments that aim at supplying the omissions** left by the testator offer little difficulty. They rather supplement his will or interpret it juridically. Consequently, this sort of legislation is applicable even to wills made before the legislation was passed. If it supplies a good rule for wills made after the enactment, it offers a good rule for those wills made prior to that time.

406. **There seems to be a tendency to believe that enactments inaugurating a new public policy, such as rules regulating bequests to charity,** should not affect prior wills, even though the testator does not die until after the date of the enactment. Thus in England and in a few of the States here, a gift to charity in a will valid at the time the will was made, is conceived to be valid even though invalidating legislation had subsequently been passed prior to the death of the testator.[83]

407. **Legislation touching the capacity of the testator or the formalities of execution,** Alabama holds, affects wills only to the extent of validating such as comply with its provisions. As to other wills, they are valid if they comply with the law as it stood when they were made. The opinion in other States is not uniform.[84]

408. **Statutes that provide for revocation of a will on the marriage of a testator or the birth of a child to him** are uniformly regarded as not revoking wills when the marriage or birth preceded the legislation; but if either was subsequent to the legislation, then the will is revoked.

409. **Change of domicile** is regarded as placing the will under the requirements of the jurisdiction where the new domicile is obtained, at least as to the capacity of the testator and the formalities of the instrument.

410. **Where the property given in a will lies in a jurisdiction**

[83] Thus Pensylvania Courts upheld a gift to a church made with one witness, though the statute requiring two witnesses had been passed subsequent to the execution of the will and prior to the death of the testator; Taylor v. Mitchell (1868), 57 Pa. St. 209.

[84] One opinion would deny the validating effect to the new legislation, while the other would sustain it.

diverse from that of the testator's domicile, the provisions touching realty are governed by the law of the place where the realty lies. But the law of the testator's domicile governs the bequest of personalty, even when it lies in a diverse jurisdiction; and the will can not be probated in the latter jurisdiction even though it complies with the laws there and not with the laws of the domicile.[85]

411. The wills of foreigners proved and allowed in any foreign State or country where the testator had his domicile, may be admitted to probate in most of the States.[86] Certain States require that such wills be written and signed by the testator,[87] while Indiana and Massachusetts simply require that it be a written will.[88] To pass real estate lying within its jurisdiction a State may demand that a will made outside its jurisdiction conforms to its laws.[89] Montana seems to require this of all wills, whether of personalty or realty.[90]

[85] Rood, *op cit.*, 399-409.

[86] Alabama (§ 10620); Arizona (§ 3902); Arkansas (§ 10516); California (§ 40); Colorado (§ 5210); Connecticut (§ 4889); Delaware (§§ 3246, 3247); District of Columbia (tit. 29, § 88); Florida (§ 5475); Georgia (§§ 3875, 3876); Illinois (c. 148, §§ 9, 10); Indiana (§ 3477); Kansas (§ 22-227); Kentucky (§ 4831); Maine (c. 76, §§ 14, 15); Maryland (Art. 93, §§ 344, 361); Massachusetts (c. 192, § 9); Michigan (§ 15535); Minnesota (§§ 8738, 8759); Mississippi (§ 1614); Missouri (§ 540); Montana (§ 10040); Nebraska (§§ 30-222, 30-225); Nevada (§ 9621); New Hampshire (c. 297, § 5); New Jersey (§ 2605); New York (§§ 22a, 23, 24); New Mexico (§ 154-102); North Dakota (§§ 5653, 5655, 8634); Ohio (§§ 10535-10539); Oklahoma (§§ 1107-1109; 1549-1551); Oregon (§§ 10-515, 10-516); Pennsylvania (§ 18923); Rhode Island (§ 4326); South Carolina (§§ 8936, 8948); South Dakota (§§ 617-619; 3220-3222); Tennessee (§§ 8114-8116); Texas (Art. 8301); Utah (§ 101-1-14); Washington (§ 1395); Vermont (§ 2769); Wisconsin (§ 238.07); Virginia (§ 5251); West Virginia (§§ 4043, 4073); Wyoming (§ 88-302).

[87] Iowa (§ 11877); Maryland (Art. 93, § 344); Michigan (§ 15535); Minnesota (§ 8738); New York (§§ 22a, 24); Rhode Island (§ 4326); Washington (§ 1395); Vermont (§ 2769); Wisconsin (§ 238.07).

[88] Indiana (§ 3477); Massachusetts (c. 191, § 5).

[89] It is so in Arkansas (§ 10516); California (§ 40); Connecticut (§ 4889), subjecting the will to all the State laws on inheritance, succession, and taxation; Florida (§ 5475); Georgia (§ 3876); Kentucky (§ 4854); New Jersey (pp. 2604, 2605); Oregon (§§ 10-515, 10-516); Pennsylvania (§ 18923); Virginia (§ 5251); West Virginia (§§ 4043, 4073).

[90] § 10039.

More liberal attitudes are found in those States that regard as valid in their own jurisdictions wills valid by the law either of the domicile of the testator at the time the will was made or of the place where the will was executed.[91] Texas recognizes the formalities of the testator's domicile; and a few other States, the law of the place where the will was executed.[92]

412. Scholion IV. Prudence dictates that the witnesses to a will should read and subscribe a full and explicit attestation clause. Witnesses may become dishonest or hostile, or they may forget what was done. A suitable form of attestation would probably be the following recommended by Rood.

> The above instrument, composed of [ten] sheets, all marked with our initials, and fastened together with [brass eyelets], was, this [tenth] day of [December], A. D. [1903], signed, sealed, and published by [John Smith], as his last will and testament, in the joint presence of the undersigned, the said [John Smith] then being of sound and vigorous mind and free from any constraint or compulsion; whereupon we (being without any interest in the matter other than friendship, and being well acquainted with him, but not members of his family), immediately subscribed our names hereto in the presence of each other and of the said testator, for the purpose of attesting the said will, as he requested us to do.
>
> John Doe, Physician, 520 State Street, Coverdale.
> Richard Rose, 1011 McKenzie Place, Coverdale.
> Carmela Sinclair, Nurse, 423 Sobol Avenue, Coverdale.

413. Scholion V. Formalities in England and Canada. As the formalities observed in the various States of the Union derive

[91] North Dakota (§§ 5653-5655); Oklahoma (§§ 1549-1551); South Dakota (§§ 617-619).

[92] Kansas (§ 22-227); New Hampshire (c. 297, § 5) New Mexico (§ 154-102); Utah (§ 101-1-14).

Ferreres says that almost all codes recognize the validity of wills made by their subjects in foreign nations according to the law of the foreign nation and cites Spain (Art. 732); France (Art. 999); Ecuador (Art. 1077); Argentina (Arts. 3635, 3669); Chile (Art. 1027); Mexico (Art. 3565); Peru (Art. 670); Ferreres, *Insts. Can.*, II, 560. But the general rule seems to be otherwise in the United States as to persons domiciled within the State.

from the English Statute of Frauds, so do the formalities in the other English-speaking lands, including the provinces of Canada. A summary of the digests of the laws in these provinces, derived from the Law Directory of Martindale and Hubbell, indicates that the provisions there may be stated as follows: The will must be in writing and signed at the foot by the testator;[93] or by some person in his presence and at his direction;[94] and such signature shall be made or acknowledged in the presence of two or more witnesses;[95] with the witnesses present at the same time;[96] who shall attest and subscribe the will in the presence of the testator,[97] at the request of the testator,[98] and in the presence of each other.[99] The testator must sign in the presence of the witnesses in British Columbia and Newfoundland, but the former requires no declaration of the will as such, that is, no revelation of the nature of the instrument.

It is expressly provided that executors may be witnesses in Alberta, New Brunswick, Nova Scotia, and Ontario; and the latter two permit the creditor also to act in that capacity by express authorization in the statute. British Columbia makes a gift in the will to a witness void; New Brunswick, Prince Edward Island, and Sas-

93 Thus it is provided in the statutes of England, the Philippine Islands, the provinces of Alberta, Manitoba, New Brunswick, Nova Scotia, Ontario, Prince Edward Island, Saskatchewan.

The statutes of Manitoba provide that the signature shall be near the foot.

The statutes of Alaska, Hawaii, British Columbia, and Newfoundland simply require that the will be signed by the testator, without stating at what part of the will.

94 England so provides, and the other political units noted in the last footnote, except Hawaii and Manitoba; the Philippine Islands provide that this be done at the *express* direction of the testator.

95 England so provides and all the political units noted in the first footnote, except that the Philippine Islands require three witnesses.

96 This further provision is made by England, Alberta, British Columbia, New Brunswick, Nova Scotia, and Saskatchewan.

97 England so provides and the political units noted in the first footnote, except that the witnesses are required to *sign* rather than subscribe in the Philippine Islands, Manitoba, and Newfoundland.

98 Thus it is provided in Alaska, the Philippine Islands, and Manitoba.

99 Thus the provision runs in England, the Philippine Islands, Manitoba, and New Brunswick.

katchewan also invalidate a gift of this kind, adding that it is invalid even when given to a spouse of the witness; Alberta and Nova Scotia allow the gift to stand if there are enough witnesses to prove the will without the testimony of the legatee; while Ontario regards as valid a gift made to a witness, but not one made to his spouse.

A holographic will is valid in Alberta, Manitoba, Newfoundland, and Quebec;[100] and the nuncupative will, in Newfoundland, Prince Edward Island, and Ontario; in the latter two provinces for the wills of soldiers and sailors only.

Scotland recognizes holographic wills and nuncupative wills disposing of an amount not more than one hundred pounds Scots.

414. Scholion VI. Beyond the sphere of the English influence, the effect of the Roman law is notable in the laws of most nations probably more in the matter of testamentary formalities than in other departments of the law. To illustrate the assertion, it is desirable to review at this point the legislation of these nations on the subject, and the digests of the Law Directory of Martindale and Hubbell enable the canonist to make a valuable summary of it.

The holographic will is recognized by the statutes of nearly all the nations.[101]

Nuncupative wills are known only in Switzerland and Sweden. Chile allows oral wills in the presence of three witnesses when the testator is in imminent danger of death. Such a will is not valid for more than thirty days unless it is reduced to writing in the presence

[100] In Quebec the authentic form for wills requires that they be made in the presence of two notaries, or before one notary and two witnesses. The English form is also permissible, executed in the presence of two witnesses who sign the will in the presence of the testator and of each other.

[101] France (Arts. 969, 970); Belgium (Arts. 969, 970); Italy, Switzerland, Germany, Czecho-Slovakia, Bulgaria, Rumania, Japan, Argentina, Panama. Spain and Cuba require that such wills be probated before a judge within five years. Sweden permits this form in an emergency only, to be valid for three months unless the testator had no opportunity within that time to make the will in the required form; and recognizes nuncupative wills with the same proviso. Hungary's regulations as to nuncupative wills are the same, except that in any case Hungary requires two witnesses for even this form of will. Netherlands has a form of will called holographic, but it is really the secret will with two witnesses, instead of four, which are required in that country for the secret will.

of a judge of the first instance. Mexico has the same provision as Chile, but regards the will as invalid unless death follows within one month; and in any event the will must be solemnized before a judge by the witnesses who have heard the will made.

415. A will made in the presence of only two witnesses is permitted in the Scandinavian countries;[102] and Hungary recognizes a will called holographic that is practically the English will, in which the testator is required to subscribe the instrument in the presence of two witnesses, to publish it to them as his will, and the witnesses to attest on the face of the will the fact of publication, that is, that the testator actually declared the instrument to be his will. Hungary has another form called the *allographic,* which is in the same form as the previous sort of will, except that four, instead of two, witnesses are required to attest.

416. Private wills are recognized in Spain, Mexico, and Brazil, as well as in Louisiana. Brazil requires the testator to write it, and read it to five witnesses, all of whom sign it, and three of whom probate it. Spain permits it only in the case of an epidemic, and it differs in this jurisdiction from the public will only in the number of witnesses, three instead of five being required. In Spain the will is valid for only two months after the epidemic has come to an end or three months after the death of the testator.

In Mexico, the private will is allowed only in the case of an emergency, but soldiers and civil employes of the army are permitted to use this form on entering a campaign. Five witnesses are required, one of whom writes the will. It is signed by the testator and the witnesses with a notation on the face, of the place, the hour, and the date. It is valid for only one month, unless the testator died from the peril which threatened; and must be probated by the witnesses who signed it.

417. Brazil also permits a codicil, that is, an informal will, to make small bequests to charity and to appoint an executor.

418. Military and maritime wills are provided for in some of the nations that derive from Spain, and soldiers and sailors are per-

[102] Sweden, Norway, and Denmark (the last requires that it be signed in their presence).

mitted to make their wills in the presence of the captain of the regiment or of the commander of the vessel and two witnesses.[103]

419. Many nations recognize the mystic or secret testament. The requirements for this will under the various statutes are somewhat diverse. A rather exact statement of them will be made in the text, with an indication in the footnote giving reference to the nations that have adopted the respective formality.

In general, the mystic testament is written by the testator [104] or by a third party for him.[105] It is signed by the testator,[106] sealed up by him,[107] and handed to a notary [108] in the presence of witnesses, either six,[109] or five,[110] or four,[111] or three.[112] The notary encloses this document in an envelope and seals it,[113] the testator declaring that the document contains his will,[114] stating whether he wrote it himself or whether a third person wrote it for him,[115] and adding that he signed it.[116] The notary draws up a protocol of this

[103] Spain, Chile, Cuba, Panama and Venezuela. The last three require no witnesses for military wills, while Chile requires none for either military or maritime wills. Argentina exempts military wills from the usual formalities for a period of ninety days after the making of the will.

[104] France (Arts. 976-980); Belgium (Arts. 976-980); Spain, Italy (Art. 782); Bulgaria, Mexico, Chile, Brazil, Venezuela, Cuba, Panama, Louisiana (Arts. 1584-1586).

[105] France, Belgium, Spain, Italy, Bulgaria, Mexico, Chile, Brazil, Venezuela, Cuba, Louisiana.

[106] France, Belgium, Spain Italy, Chile, Mexico, Argentina, Louisiana.

[107] France, Belgium, Spain, Netherlands, Mexico, Argentina, Cuba, Panama, Germany (according to Lehmkuhl, *op. cit.*, I, 1162).

[108] France, Belgium, Spain, Italy (filed with the notary), Netherlands, Mexico, Argentina, Brazil, Cuba, Germany.

[109] France, Belgium.

[110] Spain, Argentina, Brazil, Cuba, Venezuela.

[111] Italy, Netherlands.

[112] Mexico, Chile, Panama.

[113] France, Belgium, Venezuela, Louisiana.

[114] France, Belgium, Spain, Mexico, Chile, Argentina, Cuba, Panama, Venezuela, Louisiana, Germany.

[115] France, Spain, Cuba, Venezuela, Louisiana.

[116] France, Venezuela, Louisiana.

declaration on the outer cover;[117] and the protocol is signed by the notary, the testator, and the witnesses.[118] The notary places the necessary stamps on this protocol and affixes his seal,[119] noting the hour, the place, and the date, and certifying to the testamentary capacity of the testator,[120] setting down also the names and addresses of the testator and the witnesses.[121] Another person may sign for the testator if he can not sign the will [122] or the protocol.[123] But the one who signed the will should appear before the notary; the testator should declare that this person signed for him; and the third party should sign the protocol.[124] If the testator has written the whole will himself, he places a scroll at the foot of each page, but signs the last;[125] but if another has written the will for him, he must sign every page.[126] The document is to be stitched before it is given to the testator by the notary in Brazil. All the acts are required to be done at one and the same time without interruption.[127] The blind can not make a mystic will,[128] nor one who can not read,[129] whereas it is the only kind of will that the deaf and dumb are permitted to make.[130]

420. **The ordinary will in these countries is, however, the open or notarial will.** Rumania and Russia simply ordain that the will be deposited with the notary, while Russia adds that the testator may have the will written for him by a writing witness. Germany

[117] France, Netherlands, Mexico, Chile, Argentina, Cuba, Venezuela, Panama, and Louisiana.

[118] France, Spain, Netherlands, Mexico, Chile, Argentina (three out of the five witnesses must sign), Brazil, Venezuela, Panama, Louisiana, Germany.

[119] Mexico.

[120] Spain, Argentina, Cuba.

[121] Argentina.

[122] Brazil, Bulgaria, Cuba, Mexico.

[123] Argentina, Louisiana.

[124] Mexico.

[125] Spain, Mexico, Cuba.

[126] Spain, Italy, Bulgaria, Cuba.

[127] France, Argentina, Louisiana expressly require it.

[128] So stated in Chile.

[129] Argentina and Brazil.

[130] Thus provided in Chile. Argentina ordains that the deaf, the dumb, or the deaf-mute cannot make an open will, implicitly indicating that they must make a mystic will.

ordains that the will be dictated to the judge or notary and deposited with him. Japan, Norway, and Denmark recognize the will made in the presence of a notary, and Denmark recommends it in preference to the will made in the presence of two witnesses.

Once more, it is to be observed that the regulations in the various nations touching the formalities attached to the form of testament under discussion are diverse. Again, it seems to be the most exact method to state a general rule, and to note in a special reference the names of the nations that have adopted the various provisions contained in it. The source of the summarized rule is the Law Directory previously acknowledged.

Two notaries and two witnesses or four witnesses and one notary are required in France, Belgium, Germany, and Austria.[131] The second provision obtains in Italy (Art. 777) and Bulgaria. Elsewhere three witnesses with the notary suffice;[132] while two witnesses suffice in Switzerland and Netherlands. Stamped paper must be used by the notary in Mexico, where it is also required that the notary and the witnesses must be acquainted with the testator.

The testator describes to the notary in the presence of the witnesses the dispositions he wishes to make,[133] or dictates the will to him,[134] or hands it to him already written.[135]

The notary writes what he is told to write,[136] and after he has written it, he reads it to the testator in the presence of the witnesses.[137] Then the document is signed by the testator, the notary, and the witnesses.[138] If the testator can not sign, a fourth witness

[131] France and Belgium (Arts. 971-975); Germany and Austria (Lehmkuhl, *l. c.*).

[132] Spain, Mexico, Chile, Argentina, Cuba, Panama, and Venezuela.

[133] France, Brazil (in Portuguese), Cuba.

[134] Mexico, Argentina, Brazil (in Portguese). Argentina ordains that if the testator does not know Spanish, two interpreters must be employed to reduce the will to Spanish for him, the will must be written in both languages, and the witnesses must understand both.

[135] Argentina.

[136] France, Bulgaria, Mexico, Argentina, Brazil, Cuba, Louisiana.

[137] Mexico, Chile, Argentina, Brazil, Cuba, Panama, Venezuela, Louisiana.

[138] France, Switzerland, Mexico, Argentina, Brazil, Chile, Venezuela, Cuba.

is required to sign for him,[139] and the reasons why he did not sign are to be noted on the face of the will.[140] When the testator can not sign, two witnesses must be able to write;[141] otherwise, one.[142] If one witness signs for the others, the notary must certify that fact.[143] The notary sets down on the face of the will the hour, the place, and the date;[144] the names and the addresses of the witnesses; states whether he has received the will already written or has written it himself;[145] and certifies that the whole will was made as one act without interruption.[146]

ARTICLE 3

THE FORMALITIES OF REVOCATION

421. **Intimately associated with the formalities of making wills are the formalities of revocation.** These are nothing more than the requirements stated by the law for the recall of previous testamentary dispositions.

422. The interest of the canonist in the latter formalities is really the converse of his concern with the formalities required to be observed in the drafting of a will. Here he is concerned chiefly with the nullification of bequests already made. This is all the more important in view of the provision of Canon 1513, § 2, which touches only the making of wills, and therefore seems to leave the legislation for revocation to the secular law.[147] Thus, if a bequest to pious causes were revoked by an act valid in secular law, it would be valid also in canon law.

423. Indeed, the Sacred Congregation of the Council recognizes the testator's right to revoke such bequests,[148] even though the revoca-

139 Mexico, Argentina (permits a witness to sign for him).
140 Mexico, Louisiana.
141 Argentina.
142 Argentina, Chile, Louisiana.
143 Argentina.
144 Mexico, Switzerland.
145 Argentina.
146 Mexico.
147 For Canon 1513, § 2, *cf.* § 352, this treatise.
148 *In Causa Ianuen.*, 28 September, 1737, § *Momenta*—Pallottini, XI, 560.

tion be contained in a will made in a form less solemn than that in which the bequest was made.[149] The canon law rule is probably extensive enough to regard a revocation valid, even if not made according to the formalities of secular law, if the revocation can be adequately proved. But since the formalities of secular law aim at providing adequate proof, which presumably would not be forthcoming in their absence, it may be considered a safe principle to hold that a revocation that lacks the formalities of the secular law will generally be invalid also in canon law. As an illustration of this principle, consider the case where an act that was probably a valid revocation in secular law was not permitted to stand as such under the canons. The testator had deposited his will, written and signed by him, with a notary. The will contained marginal arrangements for the celebration of Masses. Later, the testator took the will away from the notary, and made no other. The Sacred Congregation sustained the bequests for Masses contained in it.[150]

424. **A testator can not incapacitate himself for revocation by any declaration made in a will, or attached to a bequest, that he will permit it always to remain just as he made it.** The declaration can not be regarded as a promise because it has been made to no one and accepted by no one. Therefore, such a will or bequest may be altered, revoked, or superseded at any time.

425. **A testator may revoke a prior will in one of two ways. First, he may destroy it; second, he may revoke it by a later document.** Further, the later document may be one of three kinds. First, it may be a will or codicil by which further, different, and inconsistent provisions are added to the preceding will, extending, modifying, or revoking it in part, but affirming it also as to other portions. Second, it may be a later will superseding the first entirely. Third, it may be a revoking document, having no testamentary character and not intended to produce any testamentary effect.

426. **Parol Revocation.** That revocations also must be made in writing was the immediate conclusion resulting from the requirements of the Statutes, 32 and 34 Henry VIII (1540 and 1542), authorizing

[149] *In Causa Anconitana,* 28 September, 1771—Pallottini, XI, 559.

[150] *In Causa Ianuen., l. c.*

devises of land but requiring them to be in writing. But the courts decided that as the statutes did not speak of revocations, parol revocations were adequate. But the Statute of Frauds required that revocations of devises of realty must be in writing, unless the prior will be actually destroyed. Thus it invalidated all parol revocations of devises of land.

427. Written Revocation. Section six of the English Statute of Frauds, the provision to which reference has just been made, is the foundation of the statutes touching revocation in the United States. Consequently, it is desirable to quote it in full. It reads:

> And moreover no devise in writing, of any lands, tenements, or hereditaments, nor any clause thereof, shall at any time after the said four and twentieth day of June, be revocable otherwise than by some other will or codicil in writing, or other writing declaring the same, or by burning, cancelling, tearing, or obliterating the same, by the testator himself, or in his presence and by his directions and consent, but all devises and bequests of lands and tenements shall remain and continue in force until the same shall be burned, cancelled, torn, or obliterated, by the testator or by his directions, in manner aforesaid, or until the same be altered by some other will or codicil in writing, or other writing of the devisor signed in the presence of three or four witnesses declaring the same, any former law or usage to the contrary notwithstanding.[151]

[151] The statutes of the States in this country modeled after this section will be found in the various statute books as follows: Alabama (§ 10600); Arizona (§ 3638); Arkansas (§§ 10494, 10501); California (§§ 72, 74); Colorado (§ 5188); Connecticut (§ 4880); Delaware (§ 3250); District of Columbia (tit. 29, § 23); Florida (§ 5461); Georgia (§§ 3830, 3916-3921); Idaho (§§ 14-307, 14-308); Illinois (c. 148, § 19); Indiana (§ 3455); Iowa (§ 11855); Kansas (§ 22-241); Kentucky (§ 4833); Louisiana (Art. 1691); Maine (c. 88, § 3); Maryland (Art. 93, §§ 333, 334); Massachusetts (c. 191, § 8); Michigan (§ 13486); Minnesota (§ 8741); Mississippi (§ 3551); Missouri (§ 520); Montana (§§ 6995, 6996, 6998); Nebraska (§ 30-210); Nevada (§ 9912); New Hamsphire (c. 297, § 13); New Jersey (pp. 5861, 5870); New York (§ 34); New Mexico (§ 154-109); North Carolina (§ 4133); North Dakota (§§ 5660, 5661, 5664); Ohio (§ 10555); Oklahoma (§§ 1556, 1557); Oregon (§ 9-904); Pennsylvania (§ 8331); Rhode Island (§ 4307); South Carolina (§ 8921); South Dakota (§§ 623, 624, 627); Tennessee (§§ 8096-8098); Texas (Art. 8285);

428. The revocation of one will by another may be express or implied, partial or total. Express revocation obtains when the later will declares the former will, or all former wills, revoked; implicit, when the later will contains provisions inconsistent with those in prior wills. The revoking will may be a former will, once revoked, but now duly re-executed, with sufficient witnesses attesting the second execution. But even though the rest of the revoking will is inoperative, the revoking clause is effective and the will revoked by it can not be probated.[152]

429. Reasons assigned on the face of the will for the revoca-tion of a former will, when they lack foundation and are evidently the real motive for the act, render the revocation ineffective. But if the testator, in spite of his assignment of reasons, should have known the

Utah (§§ 101-1-19, 101-1-22); Virginia (§ 5233); Vermont (§ 2756); Washington (§ 1398); West Virginia (§ 4045); Wisconsin (§ 238.14); Wyoming (§ 88-105).

Though the language of the English Statute of Frauds seems restricted to devises *in writing*, it does not mean that oral wills can not be revoked. Indeed, Rood quotes Swinburne as saying that such wills can be revoked by any expression of the testator demonstrating his wish to die intestate; Rood, *op cit.*, 324 (citing Swinburne, *op. cit.*, part 7, § 15, 531).

A written will of personalty can be revoked only by observing the formality for all written wills, except that Florida, Pennsylvania and Tennessee allow a written will to be altered and revoked by word of mouth under circumstances in which a nuncupative will is allowed, the whole transaction to be proved by witnesses. Florida (§ 5463) requires three witnesses; Tennessee (§ 8097); Pennsylvania (§ 8332).

The statutes patterned on the English Statute of Frauds govern all revocations of written wills within the jurisdictions for which they were enacted, and must be complied with strictly. Even if the observance of the due formalities was prevented by fraud on the part of the beneficiary, the revocation can not be given effect, unless it meets the statutory demands.

[152] The courts will not try to determine whether the revocation was based on a condition that the whole revoking will should be operative. So, wills revoked have been refused probate when the other provisions of a revoking will could not be determined because the will was not at hand, or when the greater part of the devises or bequests in the revoking will were invalid, v. gr., because they were gifts to charity made within the thirty days just preceding the death of the testator, and this even though the revoked will contained the exact charitable provisions contained in the latter will. *Cf.* Price *et al.* v. Maxwell *et al.* (1857), 28 Pa. 23; Lutheran Congregation App. (1886), 113 Pa. 32, 5 Atl. 752.

truth, the revocation is absolute. This would be the case if the testator alleged that he revoked because meanwhile he had made a gift to the beneficiary, when as a matter of fact, he had done no such thing. But where false reasons do not appear on the face of the instrument, parol evidence can not be admitted to prove a false assumption of law or of fact on the testator's part as the motive for revocation.

430. **The revocation must be a present act,** as distinguished from an intention to act, even though the latter be formally executed. The revocation, however, may be conditioned on the occurrence of a future event, and becomes, in that case, effective only when the condition is fulfilled.

431. **A revocation of all wills revokes all codicils,** and it is not permitted to show in the face of such a general revocation that any former will or codicil is not inconsistent with the revoking will. Parol evidence will not be admitted to show that the testator wished to exempt any particular will from the operation of the revocation.[153]

432. **If a later will be lost, it will not be presumed to have revoked a former will,** or to have contained provisions inconsistent with those of the former. Even if general inconsistency be proved, the prior will is sustained unless it can be shown in what the inconsistency precisely was to be found. But if the later will is withheld or destroyed by the proponents of the former will, a presumption of revocation is raised.

433. **When two or more inconsistent wills are presented for probate,** parol evidence will be accepted to prove which preceded the other, if this fact can not otherwise be determined from the face of the will. If the precedence of none can be established, all fail for uncertainty.[154]

[153] But if a will is revoked by description, a codicil to the same will, not included in the description, is not revoked.

[154] Of course, if there are no inconsistent provisions, and no revocation in any of the wills, both may stand, and the court will read them as one instrument.

Inconsistency means that the later will or codicil disposes of the same property either in the same way as the prior will or in a different way, or disposes of the whole estate, or shows itself to be intended as a substitute for the prior will.

434. Where holographic wills are valid, they are capable of revoking a will subscribed by witnesses.[155]

435. If the testator intended to make a will, he did not intend to execute some *other writing*. Hence if the document which he intended to be a will is invalid because it lacks the requisite formalities, it can not be sustained as a writing which does not require those formalities. Consequently, its power to revoke fails, for if it is not a will, it is nothing, inasmuch as the testator intended it to be nothing else.[156] But this question is of importance only in those States that permit a will to be revoked by this *other writing* that is not a will and to which the witnesses need not affix their signatures.[157]

436. Revocation by destruction is allowed by section six of the English Statute of Frauds. All the States permit this form of revocation, too. The words used by the English Statute are, *burning, can-*

But when the later document purports to be a codicil, its provisions insofar as they are in conflict with the prior document are strictly interpreted. Parol evidence may be admitted to show that it was intended as a codicil.

[155] For, though the sixth section of the English Statute of Frauds refers to the signing of the revoking instrument by three or four witnesses, it is held in the United States that this provision refers exclusively to the *other writing*, and that this *other writing* is not conceived by the Statute of Frauds as testamentary in character.

In Arkansas, however, a holographic will can not be pleaded in bar of a duly attested will; § 10494.

In Tennessee, no written will is revoked by a nuncupative will unless the latter be reduced to writing during the life of the testator, read to him, and approved by him; and these facts are to be proved by two witnesses; § 8097.

[156] But if the revoking will is properly executed, it matters not that some of its provisions are invalid. If, however, the whole will is adjudged invalid because of *undue influence,* the revoking clause is also invalid.

[157] It is recognized, *e. g.*, in the District of Columbia, Florida, Mississippi.

Most of the States require that this *other writing* be executed with the same formality as wills. And a few of the States exclude the *other writing* altogether and require that the only kind of document that can act as a revocation is a will or a codicil. It is thus in Colorado, Connecticut, Idaho (only by subsequent will), Illinois, Iowa (only by subsequent will), Maryland (except as to wills made prior to August 1, 1884), Missouri, Nevada, South Carolina, Washington, and Wisconsin.

celling, tearing, or obliterating, and these words are in general repeated in the legislation of the States.[158]

437. Destruction of a will, to be effective as revocation, must be composed of the physical and mental act of the testator. He must destroy the will, and he must intend both the destruction and the revocation.[159] But the duplicate is revoked when the original is destroyed, provided that this was the testator's wish. But one will can not be destroyed as a symbol of other wills; nor a codicil for a will, or *vice versa;* except that in some States, the revocation of a will operates as a revocation of its codicils.[160]

158 Louisiana uses none of these words, or Indiana. Louisiana simply recognizes an act which by its nature supposed that the testator changed his will, that is, an act of explicit or implicit revocation.

New Mexico and Tennessee do not recognize destruction as revocation; New Mexico (§ 154-109); Tennessee (§ 8089).

It seems, however, that any act of destruction would be valid in the other States, though Delaware provides only for cancellation. On the other hand, cancellation is not included as a means of revocation by Colorado, Georgia, Rhode Island, and South Carolina.

159 A will found among waste paper must be admitted to probate even though the testator thought that he had sufficiently destroyed the will by casting it in the waste, and even though he believed that he had actually destroyed it.

Similarly, if the testator destroyed another document, believing it to be his will, even though the wrong document were given him by a scheming beneficiary, the will would not be revoked; nor if the beneficiary stole the will from the fire before the flames touched it, or threw the wrong document on the fire when he was commanded by the testator to throw the will there.

These interpretations represent the strictly legal view. Fraud has been held not to interfere with a revocation where the testator has been deceived into omitting one or other of the formalities required for the validity of his act. But these decisions were rendered under statutes that did not provide definite requisites for the valid revocation of wills.

Moreover, it is possible that a court of equity would decree that the beneficiary, though taking under the unrevoked will by the strictly legal interpretation of the statute, would nevertheless hold the bequest as a constructive trust for the persons otherwise entitled to it. And this would be true if the testator refrained from revoking the will, relying on promises made in bad faith by the beneficiary.

160 It is thus enacted in California, Idaho, Montana, North Dakota, Oklahoma, South Dakota, and Utah; *cf.* Rood, 346 (footnote).

Piecing together a destroyed will does not prevent the operation of the revocation, or snatching it from the fire, if the fire had begun to burn it even in a slight degree. Consequently, if the will bears any signs of destruction, the revocation is operative; if, for instance, the paper is torn, or the seal is torn off. The destructive act would need to be coupled, of course, with the intention of the testator to revoke. But to tear off the seal seems to indicate in itself such an intention.[161]

438. Intention is the mental act necessary for valid revocation. Consequently, the accidental destruction of a will does not revoke it; nor destruction by the testator while he is under duress or while he is mentally incompetent. Destruction under the directions of the testator by a third person is also unavailing unless the testator not only intends the destruction, but also gives the direction to the person performing the act for him. Though the will may have been destroyed, it still exists in the contemplation of the law, and may be proved by parol evidence.

If the destructive intention is revoked prior to complete destruction, or rather, before the testator has proceeded as far in the act of destruction as he had originally intended, the will remains in full force, even if he had begun to tear the document on which it is written.

439. If a will can not be found, there is a presumption that it has been revoked, rather than that it has been merely lost or destroyed by another. The same presumption obtains if the will is found mutilated; or if one of the copies is missing or found mutilated. The presumption exists only in the absence of the proof to the contrary. It may be disproved by the aggregate of the circumstances, even though any single circumstance could not overthrow it. Declarations of the testator are usually admitted either to sustain or to

161 Adequate destruction is also found in the act of cutting off the signature, or scraping it off with an eraser. To draw a line through the signature would be a cancellation; and so would the act of drawing straight lines across the text, even with a lead pencil.

But the mere verbal statement by the testator that he cancels his will leaves the courts undecided as to its effect. The weight of opinion seems to be that this is not cancellation. That view seems reasonable, for the statutes provide not for a statement of cancellation, but for actual cancellation.

overthrow the presumption, though there is an objection to them, unless they are a part of the *res gestae* (*i. e.*, an intimate part of the transaction itself), on the ground that they would be thus admitted to prove in effect the execution of a will, and this is not allowed.[162]

440. Destruction of a part of the will, the remainder to continue in force, seems not to be within the contemplation of the statutes, nor settled by decision in most of the States.[163]

441. Revocation by mistake is inoperative. So, too, revocation on condition when the condition fails of fulfillment.

If the testator destroyed his will because he intended to proceed immediately to the making of a new will, the revocation is ineffectual if as a matter of fact he did not proceed at once to do so. But if his intention to make a new will was a mere general intention, the revocation is effectual. But it would lack all effect, if the testator thought it was ineffective when he made it, although as a matter of fact it completely satisfied all the conditions requisite for validity.

442. The revival of a prior will made even before the revoked will is a question intimately concerned with revocation itself. If the earlier will was destroyed, of course there is no problem. What has ceased to exist, can not revive.

But suppose that another will is found, and it is shown to have been executed prior to the time of the will that is now revoked. Is the earlier will valid? Three judicial opinions have grown up touching the problem. First, it was held valid in the common law courts of England and in a few courts in the United States on two grounds: first, that revocation by the intervening will can not be proved, when that intervening will is now revoked and not entitled to probate; second, the intention contained in the intervening will to revoke the

[162] The presumption could be effectively rebutted by showing that the testator did not have an opportunity of access to the will after it was last known to have been in existence.

[163] It seems well settled, however, that the cancellation of any portion can not have the effect of a new devise, as would be the case if a certain restricting clause were stricken out in order to increase the amount of the gift. As the change is ineffectual, the whole will is allowed probate. A few States regard a partial obliteration of any kind as of no effect; others give effect to it, and the latter is the rule in England.

will preceding it is now in turn revoked by a third act; consequently the intention to revoke the first will is withdrawn and it should be permitted to exist in full effect.

The second opinion is that the first will is revoked at the very moment when the revoking clause is inserted in the intervening will. Where it is thus revoked by an explicit clause it is not in the same case as if it were revoked by merely inconsistent dispositions in the intervening will. In the latter case, of course, when the intervening will can not be probated, its dispositions can not come before the court; the court can not see that they are inconsistent with the first will; and consequently the court can not regard them as revoking the first will.

The third opinion looks for the intention of the testator, and makes that the governing factor. As might be expected, it was developed in the ecclesiastical courts of England having jurisdiction over testamentary dispositions of personalty. Parol evidence is admitted under this view to establish the testator's intention. If the testator intended to revive the prior will, it was revived; if he intended otherwise, it did not revive. The intention may be established by the circumstances, the declarations of the testator in the very act of revoking the second will (the *res gestae*), or the testimony of one witness.

The three opinions have been accepted in this country.

443. Some of the States have legislated in this matter by statute. Over one-half of the States have statutes declaring that the revocation of the later will does not revive the earlier, unless it appears from the terms of the revocation itself that it was the intention of the testator to revive it.[164] But a few States require re-execution of the first will, in writing, or by the execution of a will or codicil re-publishing the earlier will.[165]

[164] Alabama (§ 10601); Arkansas (§ 10510); California (§ 75); Idaho (§ 14-310); Indiana (§ 3455); Kansas (§ 22-242); Missouri (§ 524); Montana (§ 6999); Nevada (§ 9913); New York (§ 41); New Mexico (§ 154-110); North Dakota (§ 5665); Ohio (§ 10562); Oklahoma (§ 1561); Oregon (§ 10-511); South Dakota (§ 628); Utah (§ 101-1-23); Washington (§ 1405).

[165] Kentucky (§ 4834); Virginia (§ 5234); West Virginia (§ 4046).

444. Where the destruction of the will is done by another, it must be done in the presence of the testator, not merely at his request, and on this all the statutes agree. Several of the jurisdictions require two witnesses to prove that the one who performed the act of destruction had due authority from the testator and that he actually carried out his commission.[166]

445. The Rights of Pious Causes Under a Revoked Will. A prior will may thus be sustained in spite of an apparent revocation, and a charitable or religious institution, beneficiary under the revoked will, would be justified in urging upon the secular court every consideration that would make the revocation invalid. Such action should be taken even though the institution may believe that the testator actually did intend to revoke the bequest he made. For it is not entitled to take the worst view of a situation. As for having certainty that the testator wished to revoke the gift, that is difficult to possess. If such certainty is really possessed of the testator's intention to revoke the bequest, it would seem that the institution must acquiesce in his wish in spite of the fact that the revocation is invalid in the secular law. But where there is no such certainty, the secular court may be allowed to decide the matter. And that will usually be the case.

The claim must be urged in the secular court rather than in the ecclesiastical for three reasons. First, it is not the bequest that is directly in issue, but the act revoking it; second, the grounds for the action are not directly the intention of the testator but the formalities which he failed to observe; and third, the plaintiff is seeking the benefit of the secular law, not appealing from its formalities. The secular court aims at arriving at the testator's intention indirectly, but its decision as to his intention is based on the rules which the secular statutes have imposed on him for manifesting it.

446. Where there is question of the revival of a will earlier than the revoked will, and the charitable institution is beneficiary under the earlier will, the proper court is the ecclesiastical. Here

[166] Alabama, Arkansas, California, Idaho, Montana, New York, North Dakota, Oklahoma, Oregon, South Dakota, and Utah.

In Iowa, cancellation by the testator himself must be witnessed in the same way as the actual execution of the will.

the testator's intention is directly in issue. If he intended that the provisions of the earliest will should revive, they must not be allowed to fail for want of any compliance with the secular formalities.

447. Where a revoking will made within thirty days of the death of the testator contains a bequest to charity exactly like that in the revoked will, the charitable institution might have an action against the revoking will in the secular as well as in the ecclesiastical court. If it has, it should prosecute that action, for some heirs will respect the decrees of the secular court when they might turn a deaf ear to the ecclesiastical. But even if there is no action in the secular court, the bequest to charity must be sustained by the ecclesiastical judge.

CHAPTER VII

THE CANONICAL ATTITUDE TOWARDS FORMALITIES

ARTICLE 1

THE FORMALITIES OF CANON LAW

448. The point of departure in a survey of the formalities of canon law must be the formalities of Roman law. To these the canonist fell heir, as he was influenced by Roman law in general in no insignificant degree.

449. The fully developed form of the Roman will was the *testamentum tripartitum* of Justinian.[1] The formalities of this form of will required the presence of seven witnesses who would sign and seal the will in the presence of the testator, who was required to sign it also in their presence.[2]

[1] *Cf.* § 31, this treatise; I. 2, 10, 3. It was called *tripartitum* because it was made of elements from the *ius civile*, the *ius praetorium*, and the imperial statutes. From the *ius civile* it retained the unity of time for the acts of the transaction; from the *ius praetorium*, the seals of the seven witnesses; and from the imperial statutes, the signature of the testator and the witnesses at the foot of the will.

[2] *Cf.* § 30, this treatise; C. 6, 23, 21; Moyle, *op. cit.*, I, 250; Lehmkuhl, *Theol. Mor.*, I, 1161. If it was stated on the face of the will that it was holographic, the testator's signature was not required; C. 6, 23, 28, 6. Imperial law also demanded at one time that the name of the heir be written by the hand of the testator or the witnesses; I. 2, 10, 14; C. 6, 23, 29. But this provision was repealed by Justinian. There were forms of Roman wills, permitted under the law, which lacked some of these formalities, or were valid even though certain other formalities were used. But the law also specified that the use of these forms was limited, indicating very definitely by whom or under what circumstances they might be employed. Chief among these were the nuncupative will; *cf.* § 33, this treatise; I. 2, 10, 14; C. 6, 23, 21, 2; C. 6, 23, 19; the will of a blind man; *cf.* C. 6, 22, 8; footnote n. 65, Chapter II, this treatise; the codicil; *cf.* §§ 49, 86, 87, this treatise; I. 2, 25, pr. and 1; C. 6, 36, 8, 3; the wills of rustics; *cf.* C. 6, 31, 2-4; the will of soldiers and sailors in the active employ of the State; *cf.* D. 29, 1, 1 pr., and the wills of parents as to their heirs; *cf.* Nov. 107, 1; C. 3, 36, 16.

450. Unless the witnesses were all properly qualified, it was as if they had not been present. Legal capacity to witness a will depended on the capacity to make a will.[3] Heineccius bases capacity of witnesses on their right to be present at the sessions of the *comitia*.[4] In any event, the following were disqualified: women, slaves, persons of unsound mind, the deaf, the dumb, children under the age of puberty,[5] libellers and lampooners,[6] heretics,[7] apostates,[8] adulterers,[9] the blind, and the infamous.[10] The *paterfamilias* and the *filius familias* could validly act as witnesses of the same will, as could two brothers who were under the same *patria potestas.* However, one who was subject to the *patria potestas* of the testator could not validly witness his will. On the same principle, the *paterfamilias* could not validly witness the will of his *filius familias,* nor could any one subject to the same *patria potestas,* unless the son had been emancipated.[11] By a rescript of Hadrian, the use of a slave as a witness, if he was thought free in good faith, does not invalidate the will.[12] The heir can not be a valid witness, nor any persons subject to his *patria potestas,* nor his brother, unless the latter is emancipated.[13] But legatees and beneficiaries of trust bequests can be valid witnesses.[14]

451. The Disregard of Roman Formalities. Even before the end of the century of Justinian, numerous Church councils in the regions conquered by the Franks were ordaining that wills are valid even though they fail in some of the requirements of the secular law.[15] The language of these Councils is general, but the aim is

[3] Moyle, *op. cit.,* I. 250.

[4] *Elem. Iur. Civ.,* V, 2, 10, 495.

[5] I. 2, 10, 6; Sherman, *op. cit.,* II, 681.

[6] D. 28, 1, 18, 1.

[7] C. 1, 5, 4, 5.

[8] C. 1, 7, 4.

[9] D. 22, 5, 14.

[10] Heineccius, *op. cit.,* V, 2, 10, 495; Lehmkuhl, *op. cit.,* I, 1161.

[11] I. 2, 10, 8, 9; Gaius, 2, 105, 106.

[12] I. 2, 10, 7; C. 6, 23, 1.

[13] I. 2, 10, 10; D. 28, 1, 20.

[14] I. 2, 10, 10; Gaius, 2, 108.

[15] Fourth Council of Orléans (541), c. 19—Harduin, II, 1438; Third Council of Paris (557), c. 1 (in approving this Council, Clothaire I permitted the ancient

undoubtedly to protect bequests in which the Church is bound to have a special interest. The rigidity of the Roman formalities appears notably tempered also in the Bavarian Council (772), which recognizes legacies written merely on a card, or if they are oral, pronounced in the presence of two or three witnesses.[16]

452. Thus from the fifth century onward, the nations of the West commenced receding from the Roman rules as to testamentary formalities.[17] Indeed, from the time of the Fourth Council of Orléans (541), formalities were no longer permitted to invalidate wills of themselves. Henceforth, it sufficed that the intention of the testator was clear. And this test came to be accepted even by the secular authorities.[18] Consequently, a will was valid before the secular law whether made according to its requirements or according to the principls of canon law.[19] Indeed, canon law seems in this matter to have derogated both Roman and Gallic law in France, though during that period of adjustment both laws were tolerated by the invading Franks.[20] On the other hand, the laws of the Franks, as of the other German invaders, contained no provisions for testamentary succession.[21] This, it would seem, facilitated their adoption of the regulations of canon law when they came to accept testamentary disposition. This conclusion seems the more probable since the leaders in the Church were at that very time evolving the law which in the course of time was to become the written law of the universal monarchic Church. This law became more and more lawyerly in form,

inhabitants and their posterity to be governed by Roman law, but in this present matter of the formalities required in wills, he derogated even the provisions of the Roman law)—Harduin, III, 337 and 343; Mansi, IX, 743 D and 761 A; Thomassin, *op. cit.*, III, 1, 21, 4; Council of Lyons (567), c. 2—Harduin, III, 354; Mansi, IX, 787 C; Hefele, III, 184; Second Council of Tours (567), c. 25—Mansi, IX, 804 D; Council of Macon (581), c. 4—Mansi, IX, 932 D; Fifth Council of Paris (615), cc. 6 and 10—Harduin, III, 552, 553; Phillips, *l. c.*

[16] C. 2—Mansi, XII, 851 B.

[17] Phillips, *op. cit.*, 406.

[18] *Dict. Encyclopéd.*, VI, 397.

[19] Thomassin, *op. cit.*, III, 1, 24, 4.

[20] Thomassin, *op. cit.*, III, 1, 24, 2; Pollock-Maitland, *op. cit.*, I, 13, 14.

[21] *Cf.* Chapter I, Art. 4.

and welded into a practical legal system elements from both the Roman and the Germanic laws.[22]

453. The Roman law which the new nations knew was derived, outside of Italy, from the Visigothic Code; in Italy, from the Institutes and the Code of Justinian. It seems that it was a traditional, customary law, which paid little heed to texts. Many of the rules and the juridical ideas which were generally prevalent in the West had their origin in this low form of Roman law.[23]

As for the Digest, during many centuries Pope Gregory the Great is one of the very few jurists of the West whose use of it can be proved.[24] As a matter of fact, the Digest was lost for four hundred years, and was recovered only at the beginning of the twelfth century. As a result of that discovery, say Pollock and Maitland:

> the monarchy of theology over the intellectual world was disputed. A lay science claimed its rights. . . . It was a science of civil life to be found in the human, heathen Digest. . . . The challenged Church answered with Gratian's *Decretum* and the Decretals of Gregory IX. The canonist emulated the civilian and for a long time maintained in the field of jurisprudence what semed to be an unequal combat. Unequal it was in truth. The *Decretum* is sad stuff when set beside the Digest.[25]

454. Early Customary Canon Law on Formalities. This statement of the case is a possible explanation of the development of written canon law. But it is more important as providing an answer to those canonists who would suppose that Pope Alexander III, in writing to the Bishop of Ostia and to the judges of Velletri, derogating the requirements of Roman law as to testamentary formalities, was, on the one hand, introducing new legislation; or, on the other hand, legislating only for his own temporal domain and not for the universal Church.[26] It is far more probable that the Supreme Pontiff was only defining what was already the universal customary law of

22 Pollock-Maitland, *op. cit.*, I, 18.
23 Pollock-Maitland, *op. cit.*, I, 15.
24 Pollock-Maitland, *op. cit.*, I, 11.
25 *Op. cit.*, I, 23, 24.
26 *Ita Rom, op. cit.*, II, 339.

the Church, which had been developed through the centuries following the barbarian invasions and accepted by the barbarians in lieu of provisions which they could not find in their own laws.[27] Alexander III, so far from attempting to launch an innovation on the Christian world, was rather struggling against innovation. He was fighting what might seem almost a superstitious desire (unless the words of Pollock and Maitland are misleading), to extend the influence of the recently revived Roman law everywhere and in every field at the expense of solidly entrenched customary law.[28]

It is hardly correct, then, to suppose with D'Annibale that the provisions of Alexander III became universal law only when and because they were later incorporated into the Decretals of Gregory IX, or even because Alexander's own influence won them universal recognition. They were universal before Alexander. It was Roman law that was seeking to dislodge them, and it was Alexander who stood for the old against the new.

455. What, then, were those regulations of Alexander III? They are contained in two canons of the Decretals of Gregory IX. One is for profane legacies and the other, for pious legacies.

456. The first regulates the formalities touching profane legacies and reads (in free translation):

> Alexander III to the Bishop of Ostia. When, my brother bishop, you visited me, you explained that there is a custom obtaining in your diocese by which those constituted in authority rescind wills made without the subscription of seven or five witnesses as the human laws (*i. e.*, Roman law) decree. But since that is more rigorous than the requirements of the divine law, of the precepts of the Fathers, and of the general customary law of the Church, since it is written, "In the mouth of two or three witnesses every word may stand," [29] we condemn the new custom, and we decree as permanently valid the wills which your subjects may make in the presence of their priest and of three or two other suitable persons, and we forbid that such wills be henceforth rescinded under penalty of excommunication.[30]

27 Thomassin, *op. cit.*, III, 1, 24, 6; Wernz, *op. cit.*, III, 274.

28 Wernz, *l. c.;* Thomassin, *op. cit.*, III, 1, 24, 4.

29 Matt. XVIII, 16.

30 The foregoing is found in c. 10, X, *de testamentis et ultimis voluntatibus,*

457. The second provides for legacies to charity and religion, and reads (in free translation):

> It has come to our knowledge that when it becomes your duty (*i. e.*, of the secular judges) to scrutinize bequests to the Church, it is your wish to proceed according to human law and not according to the divine, and that unless the will has been witnessed by seven or five witnesses you dismiss it without judgment. Now since these cases pertaining to the jurisdiction of the Church should be adjudicated not according to secular law but according to the canons, and under these, by the authority of Holy Scripture, two or three witnesses suffice, we command that when any such case is brought to your tribunal you shall judge it not according to secular law but according to the statutes of ecclesiastical decrees, requiring no more than three or two lawful witnesses, because it is written, "In the mouth of two or three witnesses every word may stand." [31]

III, 26, and reads as follows in the source: Quum esses, frater episcope, in nostra praesentia constitutus, diligenti nobis narratione proposuisti, talem in tuo episcopatu consuetudinem obtinere, quod testamenta, quae fiunt in ultima voluntate ab iis, qui potestatem habent super alios, penitus rescinduntur, nisi cum subscriptione septem vel quinque testium fiant, secundum quod leges humanae decernunt. Quia vero a divina lege et sanctorum Patrum institutis, et a generali ecclesiae consuetudine id noscitur alienum; quum scriptum sit: "In ore duorum vel trium testium stet omne verbum," praescriptam consuetudinem penitus improbamus, et testamenta, quae parochiani vestri coram presbytero suo et tribus vel duabus aliis personis idoneis in extrema de cetero fecerint voluntate, firma decernimus permanere et robur obtinere perpetuae firmitatis, sub interminatione anathematis prohibentes ne quis praesumptione qualibet huiusmodi rescindere audeat testamenta.

[31] This decree was sent to the judges of Velletri. It is found in c. 11, X, *de testamentis et ultimis voluntatibus*, III, 26, and reads in the source: Relatum est auribus nostris, quod, quum ad vestrum examen aliqua super testamentis relictis ecclesiae causa deducitur, vos secundum humanam, et non divinam legem in ea vultis procedere, et, nisi septem vel quinque idonei testes intervenerint, omnino deinde postponitis iudicare. *Unde quia huiusmodi causae de iudiciis ecclesiae, non secundum leges, sed secundum canones debent tractari, et his, divina scriptura testante, duo aut tres idonei testes sufficiunt, discretioni vestrae per apostolica scripta.* Mandamus, quatenus, quum aliqua causa talis ad vestrum fuerit examen deducta, eam non secundum leges, sed secundum decretorum statuta tractetis, et tribus aut duobus legitimis testibus requisitis quoniam scriptum est: "In ore duorum vel trium testium stat omne verbum."

458. The presence of the priest is set down in Alexander's decree in such a way as to leave it uncertain whether this formality was part of the customary law of the time. However, the benign intervention of the priest was known at an early date, as is witnessed by the *Responsiones* of Egbert, Archbishop of York (748), in which the priest is ordered to take "the last words" of the dying man in the presence of two or three witnesses to forestall the avarice of relatives.[32] The Synod of Gran, Hungary (1114), while expressing its opposition to the holding of public office by clerics, permitted nevertheless that they should witness the wills of the dying.[33] Especially after the Third General Council of the Lateran, which reenacted the two decrees of Alexander III, there began a great series of enactments by particular councils, establishing the legislation there enacted for their own territory.

459. In 1204, William, Archbishop of Paris, commanded his priests to warn their penitents to make due restitution before they disposed of their property by will.[34] A few years later, the Bishop of Salisbury ordered the presence of the priest at the making of

It should be noted here that the Pope does not require the presence of the priest as a witness in the case of wills making gifts to pious causes. The priest's presence was required, however, in the decree sent to the Bishop of Ostia touching profane legacies. From the general tenor of the admonition as to bequests to charity, it seems clear that he requires the witnesses only for the purpose of proving that they were made, not as a *conditio sine qua non;* so that they should be regarded as valid, even if the requisite number of witnesses was not present, provided they can be proved in some other way; Fagnanus, *In libros Decretalium,* III, 26, 10; Pirhing, *op. cit.,* III, 26, 19; Reiffenstuel, *op. cit.,* III, 26, 143.

These provisions were enacted as a general law for the universal Church, if they were not such even previously, in the Third General Council of the Lateran (1179), pars. 50, cc. 8 and 20—Mansi, XXII, 429 C. and 434 C. Later they were then incorporated in the Decretals of Gregory IX.

Note the similarity between this informal will and the Roman codicil of earlier imperial times; *cf.* Chapter I, Art. 4; Chapter II, Art. 1. Observe that as the codicil was employed chiefly to institute a trust bequest, so most of the bequests made in the period following the German invasions were through the trustee, or *salman.*

[32] C. 2—Mansi, XII, 482 E.

[33] C. 60—Mansi, XXI, 111 A.

[34] Constitutions, c. 10—Mansi, XXII, 767 D.

wills for their validity, requiring the priest to urge the testator to make bequests to charity.[35] Observe that he speaks of the *priest* as witness, as does the decree of Alexander. Neither speak of the pastor as such. But from the organization of the Church at the time, it would seem that the pastor was meant in both instances. Indeed, the decree of Alexander III would scarcely admit of any other interpretation. Besides, it was the pastor who was responsible for his parishioners at the moment of death.

460. Many of the Councils speak thus, of the *priest*, not of the pastor, as the official witness.[36] Many more mention the pastor specifically.[37] The Constitution of the Archbishop of Canterbury (1455) declares that the will is invalid if the pastor was not present as a witness.[38]

461. Some later councils dispense with the pastor in the case of an emergency and allow any other priest to be a witness.[39] Some dispensed with the necessity of any priest when there was an emergency.[40] And some simply require in any case the presence of the pastor or some other cleric.[41] The Council of Toulouse (1229) required no

[35] C. 70—Harduin, VII, 107.

[36] Synod of Paris (1197), c. 8, n. 6—Mansi, XXII, 680 C; Council of Narbonne (1237), c. 5—Harduin, VII, 146; Council of Le Mans (1247)—Mansi, XXIII, 758 D; Council of Bourges (1286), c. 30—Harduin, VII, 960.

[37] Council of Arles (1234), c. 21—Harduin, VII, 239; Council of L'isle (1251), c. 6—Harduin, VII, 434; Council of Ruffec (1258), c. 7—Harduin, VII, 503; Council of Avignon (1282), c. 10—Harduin, VII, 882; Council of Liége (1287), c. 34—Mansi, XXIV, 938 B; Synod of Oxford (1287), c. 50—Harduin, VII, 1114; Council of Constance (1300), c. 62—Mansi, XXV, 52; Council of Treves (1310), c. 75—Mansi, XXV, 267 B; *Monitio* of the Archbishop of Canterbury (1455)—Mansi, XXXII, 161 B.

[38] *L. c.*

[39] Council of Avignon (1282), c. 10—Harduin, VII, 882; Council of Reggio (1285), c. 16—Mansi, XXIV, 582 D; Synod of Cologne (1300), c. 6—Harduin, VII, 1217; Council of Bayeux (1300)—Harduin, VII, 1234; Council of Avignon (1326), c. 20—Harduin, VII, 1503; Council of Avignon (1337), c. 24—Mansi, XXV, 1094 C; Council of Lavaur (1368), c. 62—Harduin, VII, 1830.

[40] Council of Rouen (1231), c. 21—Mansi, XXIII, 216 C; Council of Bayeux (1300), c. 56—Harduin, VII, 1234.

[41] Council of Beziers (1246), c. 44—Mansi, XXIII, 702 D; Council of Albi (1254), cc. 37, 38—Harduin, VII, 463, 464; Council of Arles (1275), c. 8—

more, but it demanded the presence of the cleric and the other witnesses under the *express* penalty of the invalidity of the will.[42]

462. **Certain Councils are not precise in their language as to the number of witnesses.** Their decrees are perhaps significant, implying that the mind of the Church is so well known as to permit inexactness. Consequently, they merely require that worthy witnesses attest the will along with the pastor. The emphasis seems to be laid upon the worthiness, as if the other qualifications, including the number were well known.[43] This demand for worthiness is made more explicit in certain legislation which expressly requires that the witnesses be Catholics.[44]

463. The Council of Avignon (1282) forbade the faithful to act as witnesses unless the pastor were present.[45] Many councils enacted similar legislation, adding penalties for those disobeying the command. The testator who acts in disobedience to this precept is deprived of Christian burial, and the notary who cooperates in drafting the will is excommunicated or interdicted from the right to enter a church.[46]

.464. **Several of these councils assign reasons for requiring the presence of the priest:** for instance, he is able thus to prove authentically both the will and the faith of the decedent (for the will of a heretic was invalid);[47] to persuade the testator to make resti-

Harduin, VII, 728; Council of Nîmes (1284)—Mansi, XXIV, 543 C; Council of Cahors (1289)—Mansi, XXIV, 1024 B.

[42] C. 10—Harduin, VII, 179.

[43] Council of Ruffec (1258), c. 7—Harduin, VII, 503; Synod of Oxford (1287), c. 50—Harduin, VII, 1114; *Monitio* of the Archbishop of Canterbury (1455)—Mansi, XXXII, 161 B.

[44] Council of Beziers (1246), c. 44—Mansi, XXIII, 702 D; Council of Albi (1254), cc. 37, 38—Harduin, VII, 463, 464; Council of Arles (1275), c. 8—Harduin, VII, 728.

[45] C. 10—Harduin, VII, 882.

[46] Council of Arles (1234), c. 21—Harduin, VII, 239; Council of Narbonne (1237), c. 5—Harduin, VII, 146; Council of Beziers (1246), c. 44—Mansi, XXIII, 702 D; Council of L'isle (1251), c. 6—Harduin, VII, 434; Council of Albi (1254), cc. 37, 38—Harduin, VII, 463, 464; Council of Nîmes (1284)—Mansi, XXIV, 543 C; Council of Arles (1275), c. 8—Harduin, VII, 728.

[47] Council of Narbonne (1237), c. 5—Harduin, VII, 146; Council of Beziers (1246), c. 44—Mansi, XXIII, 702 D; Council of Albi (1254), cc. 37, 38—

tution where it is due;[48] and to prevent legacies from being given to heretics.[49]

465. From the foregoing decrees of particular councils it is apparent that the legislation of Alexander III was regarded generally as prescribing that a priest should witness wills if that were possible. As to the rest, there was evidently disagreement among the doctors. The effect of the legislation was widespread, for the councils which re-enact these provisions represent the Church in England, France, Italy, and Germany.

466. After the Protestant revolt, a conciliatory tone appears in the canons touching the priest's presence at the drafting of wills. Nevertheless, throughout it all there seems to be evident the conviction that the old position has not been relinquished, and that the Church still regards herself as the ultimate moderator in the matter of wills. Pastors are still commanded at this period to provide that their parishioners shall make due disposition of their temporal affairs in good season, so that injuries may be redressed and the works of charity promoted.

As late as 1579 the pastor was still held to be the official witness in some parts of France.[50] The Council of Benevento (1693) still maintained that the pastor or confessor may take bequests to charity in the presence of two witnesses, requiring that a document proving the compliance with this formality should be preserved in the archives of the bishop.[51] However, the act for which the Council here provides would seem to be rather a *donatio mortis causa* or gift *inter vivos* than a testament. But in 1725, the Council of Avignon had real legacies in mind when it asserted the right of the pastor to be employed according to the canons as a legal and official witness of all wills and legacies.[52]

Harduin, VII, 463, 464; Council of Arles (1275), c. 8—Harduin, VII, 728; Council of Bourges (1286), c. 30—Harduin, VII, 960.

[48] Council of Avignon (1282), c. 10—Harduin, VII, 882; Council of Bourges (1286), c. 30—Harduin, VII, 960.

[49] Council of Arles (1234), c. 21—Harduin, VII, 239.

[50] Thomassin, *op. cit.*, III, 1, 24, 13.

[51] Tit. 27, c. 1—Mansi, XXXVI B, 572 D; *Coll. Lacensis*, I, 54 b.

[52] Tit. 47—*Coll. Lacensis*, I, 581 a.

On the other hand, the Council of Avignon (1540) and the Council of Naples (1576) warned against pious fraud.[53] This is the burden of much of the testamentary legislation in the councils of the nineteenth century, which warn against the slightest semblance of avarice or importunity. While advising pastors to admonish their parishioners to make reparation of injuries and to provide for the payment of their debts and the relief of the poor, they forbid, generally speaking, intervention with the drafting of wills or with their administration.[54] But a priest was permitted to draw up the will in the case of an emergency under one set of statutes;[55] while under another, it was ordered that when the priest admonished the testator to make reparation for injuries, he should do it in the presence of witnesses who could prove his disinterestedness.[56]

467. The original provisions of the decree of Alexander III were re-enacted by the Council of Rome (1725),[57] Benedict XIV re-issued them for papal territory and Bologna,[58] and Gregory XVI (1834), in his civil code, retained them with some modifications.[59]

[53] Council of Avignon, c. 56—Harduin, X, 1868; Council of Naples, c. 45—Mansi, XXXV B, 850.

[54] Synod of Mount Lebanon (1736), pars, 2, c. 9, n. 3—*Coll. Lacensis,* II, 155 a; Greco-Melchite Council (1835), c. 5—*Coll. Lacensis,* II, 583 a; Council of Avignon (1849), tit. 6, c. 5, n. 17—*Coll. Lacensis,* IV, 348 c; Council of Westminster (1852), tit. 25, c. 8—*Coll. Lacensis,* III, 942; Council of Cashel (1852)—*Coll. Lacensis,* III, 838; Council of Halifax (1857), tit. 15, c. 4—*Coll. Lacensis,* III, 746; Council of Australia (1869), decr. 6—*Coll. Lacensis,* III, 1079 b.

[55] Council of Halifax, tit. 15, c. 4—*Coll. Lacensis,* III, 746.

[56] Council of Cashel—*Coll. Lacensis,* III, 838.

[57] Tit. 20, c. 1—*Coll. Lacensis,* I, 381 a.

[58] *Insts.,* III, 5, 5; Gasparro, *op. cit.,* II, 4, 64; Mansi, *Epitome,* 276.

[59] *Codex,* nn. 36, 37; Wernz, *op. cit.,* III, 274.

Pope Benedict's regulations were that eight days after the signing of the will, the pastor and the witnesses should go before a notary, where the pastor would declare that he wrote the will, and state its contents, unless the will was signed by the testator. After the explanation by the pastor, the witnesses would then acknowledge that the signatures on the will were theirs. They would also, in the case where the testator had not signed the will, give their version of the transaction. If he had signed, they would merely acknowledge their signatures, and testify that the testator acted in accordance with the statements on the face of the will. Then the will was given to a judge for authentic ratification, unless custom provided merely for public filing. Before the judge

468. D'Annibale thought that both decrees of Alexander III were meant for the States of the Church only. Schmalzgrueber seems to admit this conclusion for the decree touching profane legacies, saying that the Holy Father can not modify secular laws respecting merely profane matters beyond the boundaries of his own temporal domain. Reiffenstuel held that even in the Roman Empire the ecclesiastical

ratified the document, he was to cite all parties concerned. Benedict XIV, *op. cit.*, III, 5, 16; Mansi, *op. cit.*, 276; Ferraris, *op. cit.*, VII, *s.v.* "*Testamentum,*" I, 61; Schmalzgrueber, *op. cit.*, III, III, 26, 33. Pope Benedict also permitted a man who resided in the city to make his will in the presence of the pastor of his country residence; Benedict XIV, *op. cit.*, III, 5, 7.

A great deal of jurisprudence was developed in the course of the centuries touching the decree. The common opinion held that the pastor was required to be present with two witnesses; Barbosa, *op. cit.*, III, 26, 10, 2 and 7; Benedict XIV, *op. cit.*, III, 5, 8. The presence of the chaplain did not suffice; Ferraris, *l. c.*, n. 59; Phillips, *op. cit.*, 407; Mansi, *l. c.* Mansi would not permit the confessor to act in this capacity under pain of invalidity. But the Sacred Roman Rota took a different view of the matter; S. R. R., 13 November, 1645—Rubei, *Resolutiones,* XXXV, 157; Mansi, *l. c.*, Benedict XIV, *l. c.*

The pastor was obliged to write the will in the presence of the witnesses, and the will was to be signed by all, the pastor, the testator and the witnesses. A sign of the cross sufficed, if the persons could not write, except that the pastor must always sign his name; Ferraris, *l. c.*, n. 60; Mansi, *l. c.* Two extra witnesses could supply the absence of the pastor; Mansi, *l. c.* And in profane causes, two witnesses without the pastor did not establish a will, for they need not be believed; Fagnanus, *op. cit.*, III, 10, 56.

Women could not be admitted as witnesses, under the more common opinion which held that Alexander III had corrected the Roman law only as to the number of witnesses; Barbosa, *l. c.;* Fagnanus, *op. cit.*, III, 26, 10, 36; Benedict XIV, *l. c.*, n. 10; Mansi, *l. c.;* Ferraris, *l. c.*, n. 59; S. R. R., 7 February, 1583—Rubei, *op. cit.*, XXXV, 91, 109. Others contended that women could be valid witnesses—Abbas Panorm., *Decretalium,* VI, 10, 7; Pirhing, *op. cit.*, III, 26, 12.

The witnesses were to be invited especially to witness the will. This was the doctrine taught by one school; Fagnanus, *l. c.*, n. 20; Reiffenstuel, *op. cit.*, III, 26, 133; Schmalzgrueber, *op. cit.*, III, III, 26, 31; Barbosa, *l. c.;* S. R. R., 7 February, 1583—Rubei, *op. cit.*, XXXV, 91. But the opposite was also held by learned canonists—Abbas Panorm., *l. c.;* Pirhing, *l. c.* Pirhing even maintained that witnesses need not subscribe the will.

Alexander III punished those who violated the decree with excommunication. From this penalty, canonists reached the conclusion that a violation was a grave sin; Abbas Panorm., *l. c.;* Barbosa, *l. c.*

courts were obliged to follow the requirements of the secular law in dealing with purely temporal affairs.[60] However, D'Annibale admits that for a time during the Middle Ages, the decree touching profane legacies was valid everywhere, just as the other decree for pious legacies. Barbosa also insists upon the correctness of this conclusion.

Allowing that the Holy Father can not make purely secular law for domains that he does not govern as a secular prince, it seems fairly evident that Alexander III was merely re-iterating the customary secular law as it had stood for centuries. He was attempting to forestall modifications of it by men under the influence of the newly revived Roman law. It is not surprising, if this conclusion be correct, that his decree did hold everywhere for a time during the Middle Ages, especially as clerics were administering the secular law touching wills, as well as the canon law. The councils in the various provinces followed the leadership of the Supreme Pontiff, supplying secular law for the administration of wills on the basis of his admonition; struggling to retain the old customary law wherever it had been developed. The excommunication imposed by the Pope can be readily understood. The matter of wills was intimately related with the moral and social distribution of wealth, and a change in the law would have affected the social structure profoundly. It was because the question was so intimately bound up with morals that the Holy Father could forbid the secular authority to introduce revolutionary measures. The letter containing the decree touching profane legacies was sent to the Bishop of Ostia, but the decree itself was later adopted by the Third General Council of the Lateran. It is hardly probable that a General Council would have adopted it, if it were meant to be purely local in its effect.

Article 2

Secular Formalities and Pious Legacies

469. Secular Formalities to Be Observed. At the outset observe that there is now a strict obligation on the part of testators to observe the formalities required under the secular law for the validity

[60] Reiffenstuel, *op. cit.*, III, 5, 7; Schmalzgrueber, *op. cit.*, III, III, 26, 33; D'Annibale, *l. c.*

of wills when they make bequests to charity and religion.[61] Two distinct obligations are involved in Canon 1513, § 2. One rests on the testator, the other on the heir. The fact that the heir will be obliged to fulfill the will in any case does not excuse the testator from obeying the law as expressed here.[62]

470. But if the formalities have been omitted, a bequest for the benefit of the Church does not fail. Before the full significance of this provision is analyzed, observe that the plan on which the discussion will proceed will present the following questions. First, what beneficiaries does the present law embrace? Second, what was the doctrinal interpretation prior to the Code of the decree of Alexander III touching pious legacies? Third, what is the doctrine under the present law?

471. As for legacies to causes that are pious, even clerics seem to be bound to observe the secular formalities under pain of invalidity. Schmalzgrueber holds that wills made without due formality, unless a pious cause is the beneficiary, are invalid in conscience, even though made by a cleric.[63]

Lehmkuhl notices the opinion of authors preceding him who regarded the formalities of secular law as not binding in conscience at all, but merely necessary as the foundation of an action in the courts. But he disagrees with that view, maintaining that under the secular laws of his day gifts which deprive the necessary heirs of

[61] Canon 1513, § 2. *Cf.* § 352, supra.

[62] If there is an obligation to observe the formalities, there is a corresponding obligation to know them. Of course, if one draws up his will through an attorney, it would seem that he has fulfilled the obligation imposed by the canon. But since many persons for one reason and another are unwilling to consult an attorney, it would seem well within the pastor's duty to inform his parishioners of the formalities required. This could easily be done on the announcement sheet, or in the parish bulletin. Where holographic wills are recognized, since they are the simplest in formality, the pastor might explain that if the testator writes out the whole will, noting the date in his own handwriting and signing, the will is valid. But two witnesses must subscribe in Pennsylvania.

[63] *Op. cit.*, III, III, 26, 34, 39. The opinions of theologians cited in this section will be found in their works as follows: Lehmkuhl, *op. cit.*, I, 1146; Ferreres, *Insts. Can.*, II, 486; *Theol. Mor.*, I, 646, 648, 962; Cocchi, *op. cit.*, VI, 191; Vermeersch, *Theol.. Mor.*, II, 348; Genicot, *op. cit.*, I, 610, 673, 674; Noldin, *op. cit.*, II, 561.

their legitimate portion of the estate (see Chapter III, Arts. 2 and 5), are invalid in conscience. Dispositions that are not prejudicial to the heirs are to be held invalid in conscience, he thinks, but only after the judge has declared them invalid. He thinks that the law contemplates this procedure in Netherlands, France, and Germany. In England, he continues, the formalities are so few that a will evidently invalid for want of them is invalid also in conscience. This view would apply, because of the derivation of statute, to the formalities also of the United States and of the provinces of Canada. However, Lehmkuhl admits that even in England if the will is only dubiously invalid, it need be held invalid definitely and in conscience only after the decree of the judge.

Ferreres says that the formalities oblige in conscience *at least* after the decree of the judge. Cocchi agrees that they oblige in conscience after the decree, but says that the more probable opinion is that they do not bind thus prior to that decree.

Vermeersch says that he stands for the least possible obligation in conscience deriving from the provisions of the secular law. Catholics, he thinks, should not be burdened more grievously than unbelievers. The profession of religious indifference on the part of legislators, he contends, demonstrates that they expect to enforce their laws not by an appeal to conscience, but by external vigilance. However, he admits that in the matter of justice the secular laws bind in conscience when obedience to them is necessary for the preservation of public peace and order. Judicial decrees are thus binding. Even before such a decree is passed, laws are binding in conscience when they are complementary of the natural law.

Genicot is in agreement with the milder opinion, even as to laws touching the capacity of the testator. But he admits that both opinions are probable. Cocchi also extends his opinion to laws incapacitating the testator, and to those imposing disabilities on the beneficiaries, or affecting the subject matter of the testamentary act, maintaining that none bind in conscience until after the decree of the court.

Noldin asserts that the Austrian and German Codes certainly invalidate, even before the decree of the court, bequests that are not fortified with the due formalities. If it is not certain whether other civil codes do this, he continues, the legatee may take under the will without notifying the heir *ab intestato;* but he can not add the testator's signature or impede the due course of law in any unjust fashion. In case of an impending suit, he should waive his claim, when he is certain that the necessary formalities are lacking, so as not to put the real heir to unnecessary expense. This is an obligation in charity and *per se gravis.*

472. How do the eminent authors arrive at the conclusion that the formalities are binding in conscience only after the court declares the will invalid? Possibly from the care taken by secular law that the will be under the supervision of public officials from the very first moment of its existence. By reason of this scrupulous supervision it might seem that the secular law held itself responsible for proper distribution of the estates of decedents. Consequently, if such close surveillance were evaded, it might seem that the beneficiaries could hold themselves exempt from the obligations of the laws. This is to argue that because a legislator takes precautions to enforce his law, he gives a free hand to those not affected by his precautions. It seems to impute a contrary significance to an act that has a very obvious meaning.

Vermeersch's reason, of course, is something very similar to that just advanced. He adds another argument which is substantially this: Catholics would be unequally burdened if they were obliged to observe in conscience the laws that other persons obey only when they are under the vigilance of the police power. This reason seems fallacious. The argument is substantially this: no one is bound in conscience by the secular law because Catholics would be obliged to obey them while others disobey them. That seems to be invalid argumentation. Moreover, the chief argument of the proponents of this opinion seems to be founded in the intention of the legislator. In the United States, at least, their contention seems not to be verified. Though legislators in this country do regard all religions as of equal importance; they seem not to regard religion as of no importance or to have forsworn conscience.

As to the formalities of wills, especially, since no one is entitled to the property of another after the death of the latter except by the grace of the positive law, whether secular or canonical, it would seem that if the positive law sets conditions on which that property may pass to another, the failure of the conditions simply prevent the passing of the property.

Therefore, Schmalzgrueber seems to argue more correctly on this point, when he holds all gifts invalid in conscience when they are made under a will lacking the secular formalities. Those made to pious causes, of course, are excepted, but only because positive canon law supersedes positive secular law. Of course, if there is doubt whether the formalities have actually been observed, it requires the decree of the judge to bind either party in conscience.

In practice, however, in the United States, distribution is made under the decree of the judge, so that there is usually no doubt about the obligation of respecting it in conscience.

473. The first point to be discussed in the matter of bequests to pious legacies, is what beneficiaries are included under the exemption expressed in Canon 1513, § 2? What is meant by the words, *"in bonum Ecclesiae?"* This phrase includes all religious and charitable beneciaries, as is proved by two arguments: one from tradition, and the other from the context. The latter will be presented later in the study. The argument from tradition is presented immediately.

Alexander III spoke only of *bequests to the Church* in his decree. The common interpretation of the doctors held that he meant all charitable bequests because of the identity of purpose found in them all.[64] Now Canon 1513, § 2, incorporates the ancient law in this matter, and is consequently to be interpreted according to the doctrine of approved authors who preceded the Code. Thus, when this canon speaks of gifts *"in bonum Ecclesiae,"* it immediately suggests the *"testamenta relicta ecclesiae"* of the decree of Alexander, and with that suggestion comes the interpretation that followed the decree of that Pope.[65]

474. Vromant restricts the significance of the canon to legacies made to an ecclesiastical moral person, that is, to one duly established by ecclesiastical authority. This is the view of Cance and Gil-

[64] Abbas Panorm., *op. cit.*, VI, 11, 7.

[65] Canon 6, n. 2. "Canones qui ius vetus ex integro referunt, ex veteris iuris auctoritate, atque ideo ex receptis apud probatos auctores interpretationibus, sunt aestimandi."

let. Cance maintains as a consequence that a bequest for Masses left to a priest is governed by the formalities of the secular law.[66] Noldin is cited as having held this restricted view at one time,[67] but if he once maintained it, he has abandoned it. He holds that all charitable bequests are privileged.[68]

The authors who hold the restricted view seem not to recognize the great similarity between the language of the present canon and that of Alexander III. Consequently, Vermeersch-Creusen seem to reason more correctly that the present exemption embraces all bequests to charitable and religious purposes.[69]

475. The argument from the context refers to both Canon 1513, § 1, and to Canon 1514.

In Canon 1513, § 1, pious causes in general are named as being entitled to receive gifts made to them by persons not incapacitated by the natural or the ecclesiastical law. It is almost inconceivable that the legislator, being aware that he had so recently referred to pious causes in general, would have unobtrusively made a restriction in the very next paragraph of the same canon without a more explicit indication of his wish.

In Canon 1514 the legislator immediately speaks of pious causes in general, as if this had been the subject matter of the intervening legislation.[70]

476. The Doctrinal Attitude Towards Formalities Before the Code. Exemption from all formalities, not only from those of the secular law, has always been regarded as the distinction of bequests to pious causes. In this, they were looked upon as favored in

66 Vromant, *op. cit.*, 156; Cance, *op. cit.*, III, 146; Gillet, *in Collectanea Mechlinensia* (1927), 84 (cited by Cance).

67 Cited by Vermeersch-Creusen, *op. cit.*, II, 835 (footnote).

68 *Theol. Mor.*, II, 556.

69 *Cf.* § 95, this treatise.

70 Canon 1514. "Voluntates fidelium facultates suas in pias causas donantium vel relinquentium, sive per actum inter vivos, sive per actum mortis causa, diligentissime impleantur etiam circam modum administrationis et erogationis bonorum, salvo praescripto can. 1515, § 3."

See Vermeersch's discussion in *Periodica,* "De testamento ad causas pias et canone 1513, § 2," XIX (1930), 49*-63*. *Cf.* Cappello, "Vis ac ratio monitonis de qua in canone 1513, § 3 [2]," *op. cit.*, 40*-42*; *AER,* LXXXIX (1933), 528.

the same way as the wills of soldiers and sailors under the Roman law; and as the wills of parents making bequests to their heirs needed no more formality that the wills of soldiers and sailors, canonists were accustomed to rank the bequest to pious causes with the two types just named.

477. Indeed the Sacred Congregation of the Council has remarked that this exemption is not a privilege but a rational exemption inasmuch as the danger of fraud and machination is not to be feared where charitable or religious beneficiaries are concerned.[71]

478. Alexander III had required two or three witnesses even for bequests to pious causes.[72] But he did not require the presence of the pastor,[73] and there was no restriction placed on the kind of witness that could be employed. It was admitted unanimously by the doctors that women could be witnesses of these bequests,[74] and that the witnesses need not be specially invited by the testator to act as such.[75] But canonists were also unanimously agreed that Alexander required these witnesses only for the purpose of probate, that is, to sustain the bequest against those who might challenge it, and that he regarded the bequests in themselves valid even though no witnesses were

[71] *In Causa Ariminen.*, 24 July, 1858, § *Quin*—Pallottini, XI, 563.

[72] He referred to the Gospel of St. Matthew, and quoted the words of our Lord that every word should stand by the testimony of two or three witnesses. He did not mean to insinuate that to require more witnesses was to violate the divine law, but merely to say that it was customary to require no more and that this custom was fully warranted by the divine law and by the Fathers. He was really defending the custom of the time, rather than attacking the Roman law system as such.

[73] Barbosa, *op. cit.*, III, 26, 11, 2; Soglia, *op. cit.*, II, 4, 122.

[74] Fagnanus, *op. cit.*, III, 26, 10, 35; *idem*, III, 26, 11, 14; Gasparro, *op. cit.*, II, 4, 60; Reiffenstuel, *op. cit.*, III, 26, 155; Santi, *op. cit.*, III, 26, 23; Soglia, *l. c.;* Schmalzgrueber, *op. cit.*, III, III, 26, 46.

[75] Barbosa, *l. c.*, n. 5; Fagnanus, *op. cit.*, III, 26, 10, 15; *idem*, III, 26, 11, 14; Gasparro, *l. c.*, Reiffenstuel, *l. c.*, n. 154; Schmalzgrueber, *l. c.*

Fagnanus and Soglia did demand certain qualifications in the persons who were to act as witnesses of even pious bequests. Fagnanus disqualified not only the insane, but also children under the age of puberty; *op. cit.*, III, 26, 10, 15; the enemies also of the testator and the members of his immediate family; *op. cit.*, III, 26, 10, 34. Soglia disqualified spendthrifts and children under the age of puberty; *l. c.*

present when the will was made. De Luca says this opinion is the one constantly followed in practice by the Sacred Roman Rota.[76] Consequently, under this practically universal opinion, if the testator is capable in the sense that by the natural law he is able to dispose reasonably of his property, and if the actual making of the will can be proved, the absence of witnesses can not impair the validity of the bequest.[77]

479. How can it be proved that a testator had made a will without witnesses? Even under the secular law of many modern nations, a holographic will is valid without witnesses. Thus, under secular systems a document entirely written by the testator needs no witnesses. But the canonists held that a document merely signed by the testator would suffice.[78] And under a decision of the Sacred Congregation of the Council (1806) a private document showing a legacy for Masses, which did not appear in any codicil or will (because the will had been lost), was held adequate to prove the gift.[79] Whatever document is necessary for proof can be demanded by the proper judge under proper sanctions.[80]

480. Indeed, the canonists regarded a mere nod sufficient, if it could be proved,[81] and *a fortiori* words orally uttered were considered adequate.[82]

[76] De Luca, *op. cit.*, XIV, 7; Pirhing, *op. cit.*, III, 26, 12; Reiffenstuel, *l. c.*, n. 143; Soglia, *l. c.;* Zallinger, *op. cit.*, III, 26, 292; Phillips, *op. cit.*, 407; Schmalzgrueber, *l. c.*, Lehmkuhl, *op. cit.*, I, 1162; Wernz, *op. cit.*, III, 274 and 279; Cocchi, *op. cit.*, VI, 192.

[77] Fagnanus, *op. cit.*, III, 26, 10, 15.

[78] De Luca, *l. c.;* Barbosa, *l. c.*, n. 4; Gasparro, *l. c.*, n. 62; Reiffenstuel, *l. c.*, n. 147; Soglia, *l. c.;* Schmalzgrueber, III, III, 26, 46; Lehmkuhl, *op. cit.*, I 1162; Cocchi, *l. c.;* Vromant, *l. c.;* De Meester, *op. cit.*, 1466.

[79] *In Causa Thelesina,* 25 January, 1806—Pallottini, XI, 562.

[80] Schmalzgrueber, *op. cit.*, II, III, 19, 46.

[81] Barbosa, *l. c.;* De Luca, *l. c.;* Gasparro, *l. c.*, n. 61; Reiffenstuel, *l. c.;* Schmalzgrueber, *l. c.;* Cocchi, *l. c.*

[82] Schmalzgrueber, *l. c.;* Pirhing, *l. c.;* Soglia, *l. c.*, n. 123; Cocchi, *l. c.* They referred to the decision of Gregory IX contained in the Decretals (c. 4, X, *de testamentis et ultimis voluntatibus,* III, 26): "Indicante (*et infra*): Cognovimus autem R referente, quod moriens uxor Redempti unam concham argenteam nudis verbis iussit venundari, et suis dari libertis, et scutellam argenteam cuidam monasterio reliquisse; in quibus utrisque voluntatem eius per omnia volumus adimpleri."

481. If the heir is the only person who heard the words spoken he is bound to reveal them to the Ordinary, and he can be put on his oath to testify to whether he knows anything of such a bequest. His acknowledgment of the bequest is adequate proof.[83] However, if the heir does not know of it, he need not believe the testimony of only one witness, even though the witness be the pastor or the confessor of the testator,[84] unless there is adminicular proof to corroborate the testimony of the single witness.[85]

482. Because of its privileged character, a bequest to charity contained in a will that is invalid as to other bequests must still be sustained, if the charitable bequest can be proved.[86]

483. The geographical extent of the decree of Alexander III touching pious legacies is a matter of no small concern. Henry Canisius thought the decree was not meant to apply to the whole world, but only to the temporal domain of the Holy See.[87] D'An-

[83] Lehmkuhl, *l. c.*

[84] Lehmkuhl, *l. c.;* Reiffenstuel, *l. c.*, nn. 152, 153; Noldin, *l. c.;* Ferreres, *Theol. Mor.*, I, 962; Vermeersch, *Theol. Mor.*, II, 564.

[85] S. C. C. *in Causa Ariminen.*, 27 February, 1858, § *Nec*—Pallottini, XI, 563. If the proofs are equal on both sides, the pious cause is entitled to the decision; Schmalzgrueber, *op. cit.*, II, III, 27, 30.

[86] This was the common opinion; Pirhing, *op. cit.*, III, 26, 88; Reiffenstuel, *l. c.*, n. 161; Santi, *l. c.*, Soglia, *l. c.*, n. 123; Phillips, *l. c.;* Zallinger, *l. c.* It was also the burden of a decree of the Sacred Congregation of the Council, *in Causa Anconitana*, 28 September, 1771, § *Quae*—Pallottini, XI, 561.

Indeed, where the principal portion of an invalid will disposes of a gift to a pious institution, the gifts to secular beneficiaries are also sustained on the principle that the accessory is ruled by the law applying to the principal—Reiffenstuel, *l. c.;* Santi, *l. c;* Zallinger, *l. c.*

As was noted when the Roman law of inheritance was considered, legacies could not be paid unless the heir entered into his inheritance (*cf.* Chapter III, Art. 1). At that point it was noted that various devices of the law were adopted to make it worth while for the heir to accept the inheritance, and to protect him against the danger of being burdened with obligations rather than assets. Canonists, however, were of the opinion that pious legacies, being privileged were valid even prior to the acceptance by the heir; indeed, even if the heir should refuse to accept the inheritance; Soglia, *l. c.* In the Anglo-American law, all legacies are valid, whether the beneficiary is secular or charitable, without acceptance by the heir.

[87] Cited by Pirhing, *op. cit.*, III, 26, 20.

nibale is of the same opinion. If the decrees were originally meant for the temporal jurisdiction only, they became general law by adoption in the Third General Council of the Lateran and by incorporation the Decretals. The force of this incorporation is not overlooked by D'Annibale. But he employs the connection existing between two decrees to advance his own view. Canonists all admit that the decree touching secular bequests has fallen into desuetude. From this fact D'Annibale argues that just as the Church has surrendered her right outside the Papal States to insist upon the observance of this decree, so she has similarly relinquished her right to enforce the payment of pious legacies lacking the secular formalities. Consequently, he regards as dubious the obligation resting on the heirs to pay pious legacies that fail in the secular forum.[88]

484. Mere silence on the part of the Holy See can not be construed as consent to derogation. Santi observes well that silence may be interpreted as consent only on three conditions, viz., first, that the person who is silent understands that what is being done is adverse to his interests; second, that he is bound to interfere; and third, that he is able to interfere efficaciously. Let it be true that legacies to charity are not privileged in France, Austria, Germany, and Italy;[89] and that, as De Héricourt remarks, in France the sovereign courts require the solemnities of the secular forum to be observed,[90] there is in all this nothing more than a *status quo*. For it is certain that at least the last condition outlined by Santi has not been fulfilled in the apparent surrender by the Church of this right over pious bequests. While the secular courts were imposing their decisions on legacies to religion and charity, the Church was helpless to protest efficaciously against it.[91]

485. The Constant Binding Force of the Decree Everywhere.

[88] Prümmer, *Theol. Mor.*, II, 277, cites as holding the same opinion: Daelman (*De iust.*, p. 2, q. 2, obs. 8); Haine (*De contract.*, q. 53); Retzbach (Die Verbindlichkeit formloser letztwilliger Verfügungen zu frommen Zwecken, Freiburg, 1917, 47 sq.). It was thought by some that thus a probable opinion had been established.

[89] Wernz, *op. cit.*, III, 274, 279.

[90] *Op. cit.*, D. III, 126.

[91] Santi, *op. cit.*, III, 26, 24.

Consequently, though D'Annibale held that until the Holy See settled the question definitively, he would not, outside the Papal States, disturb a penitent who refused to pay a pious legacy invalid in the secular forum, nevertheless the common opinion of canonists was that the decree of Alexander III on pious legacies always bound and had never ceased to bind the whole world, obligatory in both the ecclesiastical and secular forum. Thus secular judges could not legally invalidate such bequests.[92]

486. It seemed that the Holy See had definitely settled the point even when D'Annibale was writing. And it seemed that it had confirmed the common opinion. It was in virtue of a decision in the following case. A certain Eudorius had instituted one Boniface his sole beneficiary. But in a private document a secret trust was established. This was not recognized by the secular courts. Under the trust, Boniface was required to pay certain bequests to charity. He neglected to make the payments. The Sacred Penitentiary, rendering a decision as to the obligation resting on Boniface, decreed that he was obliged to fulfill the wishes of Eudorius so far as they were known to him.[93] This decision was accepted by almost all canonists as putting the question beyond doubt. But a minority, whose views were those of D'Annibale argued that it was not decisive, as it touched only the particular case. Moreover, they contended that the obligation in that case arose not from the will of Eudorius, but from the *contractus innominatus,* the secret trust, by which he had obliged himself to make payment.

487. But in 1901, another decision was rendered by the Sacred Penitentiary, consistent with the first. It was issued in reply to a query which explicitly mentioned the adverse opinion and asked if it might be followed. The reply was that "the practice of this Sacred Tribunal is that, as a rule, pious bequests are to be regarded as valid and binding in conscience." But at the same time, the Sacred Peni-

[92] Soglia, *l. c.;* Bargilliat, *op. cit.*, 1481; Pirhing, *op. cit.*, III, 26, 19; Schmalzgrueber, III, III, 26, 44 and 49; Mansi, *l. c.;* Benedict XIV, *op. cit.*, III, 5, 4.

Kenrick admitted that canon law demanded payment of these gifts, but says that he would hesitate to refuse the Sacraments for non-compliance; cited and approved by Tanquerey, *Theol. Mor.*, II, 699 (Kenrick, *Theol. Mor.*, II, 37).

[93] 23 June, 1844—*ASS,* II (1866), 369.

tentiary expressed itself as ready to permit a compromise between the heirs and the charity affected.[94]

488. Even after that decision some small degree of recognition continued to be given to the view of D'Annibale, but the majority of canonists regarded it as devoid of probability.[95]

489. Canon 1513, § 2, did not remove all doubt, though Cocchi believes that it did.[96] In his Moral Theology Prümmer continues to look upon the adverse opinion as probable, and concludes that the words of the present canon do not appear to impose a strict obligation in justice. Blat maintains that there is no obligation to pay at least *in foro externo,* though he insists that the admonition must be given. Noldin's opinion coincides with Prümmer's. In his Manual of Canon Law, Prümmer pays due notice to the more common opinion prior to the Code, but says that since the present canon requires only that the heirs be admonished to fulfill such a legacy, the confessor can sometimes absolve a penitent who will not comply.[97]

490. Moreover, the obligation imposed by the present canons is regarded as resting on the Ordinary. The latter passes juridical sentence on the heirs. After that, it is maintained, they decide their obligation with their conscience and their confessor. This view practically coincides with Blat's argument that there is no obligation *in foro externo.* The requirements of the external forum seem to be satisfied when the admonition is given. And this admonition, it is said, should not be too precise, or condemn the heir to a sum too definite, since the canons require that the admonition should order merely compliance with the testator's last will.[98]

[94] *S. C. P. F. Coll.* 2099; Tanquerey, *op. cit.*, II, 700; Augustine, *Canon Law,* VI, 571. The readiness of the Holy See to permit a compromise was reaffirmed in a reply of the Sacred Penitentiary, 23 April, 1927; Vermeersch, in *Periodica, l. c.*

[95] Lehmkuhl so regarded it; *AER,* XX (1899), 57.

[96] "Hinc finita est antiqua controversia," he says, "circa valorem testamenti et legati ad causas pias quod informe sit; Codex autem amplexus est sententiam longe communiorem quae docebat testamenta informia ad causas pias valere et ideo in foro conscientiae obligationem inducere; quae sententia confirmata erat ex clara definitione Alexandri III, ex praxi Curiae Romanae"; *op. cit.*, VI, 192.

[97] Prümmer, *Theol. Mor.*, II, 277; *Man. Iur. Can.*, 448, n. 1; Blat, *op. cit.*, 425; Noldin, *op. cit.*, II, 556.

[98] *Le Canoniste Contemporain,* XLVIII (1926), 363.

491. The most complete argument for the improbable view is advanced by Nasoni. As a preliminary position, he holds that if the will is not juridically declared invalid, the pious legacies must stand. He is of the opinion, therefore, that the formalities bind in conscience only after the decree of the court. Wherever the court upholds the will, moreover, it can not nullify bequests to charity. Therefore, it can not invalidate them because they were made within a month of the death of the testator. This much Nasoni grants.

But if the whole will is juridically declared to be invalid, what then are the consequences for charity and religion? He concedes that even then the Ordinary and the pastor are obliged to urge payment of the legacies. He grants that there is even an obligation of some kind resting on the heirs, otherwise the pastor and the Ordinary would not be obliged by the canons to make the admonition.

492. But is the obligation of the heirs an obligation of justice? He glances at an argument in favor of the view that it is. It derives from the first paragraph of Canon 1513. This paragraph confers on all men the right to make a bequest to charity even though they be incapacitated under the secular law. *A pari*, it is argued, the second paragraph makes all wills to charitable causes valid even though they lack the secular formalities.

Nasoni regards this as specious argumentation. He even concedes that if this kind of argument is to be admitted, one could really advance from the first to the second paragraph of Canon 1513, not *a pari* but *a fortiori*. A legislator who gave capacity to all men would certainly be able, if he wished, to prescribe conditions for one who has capacity. And in this instance, the conditions, when fulfilled, would establish a right in the legatee. On the contrary, the first paragraph of Canon 1513 is not concerned directly with the testator but with the passive subject of the gift, that is, with the charitable institution. It confers capacity not on the testator to give but on the institution to receive. It touches the making of the will only indirectly. Consequently, it may not be employed to interpret the second paragraph, which deals directly with the will. The significance of the second must be determined on other grounds.[99]

493. Nasoni argues that the obligation is not one of justice.

[99] *Cf.* § 174, this treatise.

His arguments are derived, one from the text and the other from the sources whence it derives. From the text, he argues from what the canon positively enacts, and from what it omits.

The positive enactment requires exhortation by the Ordinary, not an admonition. The latter would imply an obligation; whereas the value of an exhortation is based on the validity of the arguments that accompany it. He thinks this position is confirmed by the fact that in the second clause, the second paragraph of Canon 1513 commands the Ordinary to exhort the heirs to fulfill, not the testament of the decedent nor the provisions of the testament, but the testator's *last will.* He assumes that stress is laid on the attitude of mind of the testator rather than on the document in which it is contained. For, the singular is used, *"voluntatem,"* while in the first clause of the same paragraph, the plural is used, *"in ultimis voluntatibus,"* to indicate the document. The argument from the omission in the text is simply this: the legislator was aware of the controversy, could have settled it by placing the obligation directly on the heirs, and did not do so.

In arguing from the sources whence the present law derives, he analyzes chiefly the decree of 1901 of the Sacred Penitentiary. In that decree, the Sacred Tribunal stated that *in practice,* it regarded these bequests as valid, but that it was prepared to admit the heirs to a compromise. Therefore, implicitly the Sacred Tribunal conceded that there was a possibility of theoretical doubt in the matter. The present law does not settle the theoretical doubt; while, so far as practice is concerned, it seems to have introduced greater leniency than was tolerated prior to the Code. With four additional arguments contrasting the previous discipline with the present, he attempts to prove that the contrast is all in favor of the minority view. First, the present law prescribes the observance of secular formalities, which was not required in the former discipline; second, it does not now state that it regards these bequests as generally valid, as the Sacred Penitentiary did in the decree of 1901; third, the present law imposes no obligation directly and expressly on the heir; and fourth, it mentions nothing of the necessity of approaching the Sacred Penitentiary for a compromise.

494. He draws two conclusions from his arguments: first, it is not necessary to approach the Sacred Penitentiary for a compromise; second, if the penitent refuse to compromise, he can not be refused absolution.[100]

495. But the obligation *in foro interno* is granted by even those canonists who feel that the heirs can not be compelled *in foro externo* to comply. For, granted that it is only the Ordinary who is bound by the present law *in foro externo,* his public obligation implies a private obligation in the person he must admonish. Consequently, it is generally conceded that a confessor should refuse absolution to a penitent who was recalcitrant.[101] However, Prümmer and Noldin, on the theory that the opinion holding for freedom in the internal forum is probable,[102] would regard the penitent as entitled to the benefit of the probable opinion.[103]

496. In the midst of the controversy a declaration was issued by the Pontifical Commission for the Authentic Interpretation of the Canons of the Code, 17 February, 1930. It was as follows:

D. Utrum verbum *moneantur,* de quo in canone 1513, § 2, sit praeceptivum, an tantum exhortativum.

R. *Affirmative* ad primam partem, *negative* ad secundam.[104]

497. It is thought in some quarters that this response settles

[100] Nasoni, in *Perfice Munus,* III (1928), 848 ff.

[101] Genicot, *op. cit.,* I, 675; Tanquerey, *op. cit.,* II, 700; De Meester, *op. cit.,* 1466; Vromant, *l. c.;* Vermeersch-Creusen, II, 835; Claeys-Bouuaert-Simenon, *op. cit.,* III, 265; Cocchi, *op. cit.,* VI, 192; Vermeersch, *Theol. Mor.,* II, 564.

[102] Prümmer, *Theol. Mor.,* II, 277; Noldin, *l. c.*

[103] Prümmer considers Canon 2348 as inapplicable here. That canon reads. "Qui legatum vel donationem ad causas pias sive actu inter vivos sive testamento, etiam per fiduciam, obtinuerit et implere negligat, ab Ordinario, etiam per censuram, ad id cogatur."

Prümmer contends that this canon seems to affect only legacies that are valid in the secular law; or at most, legacies not yet declared invalid by the decree of the secular judge. It seems that this canon may not be used as proof for either opinion, for it is capable of being reconciled with either. It is clearly accessory to the law as contained in the Third Book. And no matter which opinion is held, Prümmer seems correct in his view of Canon 2348. One can not easily reconcile the *"moneantur"* of Canon 1513 with the *"cogatur"* of Canon 2348 unless the subject matter of each canon is different.

[104] *AAS,* XXII (1930), 196; *AER,* LXXXIX (1933), 528; *Ius Pontificium,* X (1930), 144.

the matter definitely. They who think so explain why the legislator employed the form *moneantur* rather than some other language to indicate the nature of the obligation.

The *Ecclesiastical Review* explains:

> "While the Church maintains her right to recognize as valid even an informal will *ad causas pias,* she nevertheless realizes that it may not always be possible to enforce her laws. Modern civil laws do not recognize her claims in this regard; and even the faithful may be so impressed with the force of civil law as not to discern the rights of the Church, so that with more or less good faith they do not consider themselves bound by an informal will for pious causes. Therefore, lest greater difficulties arise with the State or the possibly good faith of Catholics be disturbed to no good effect, the Code does not want ecclesiastical authorities to fulfill informal wills. They should rather advise them and urge them to execute these bequests, using such arguments as prudence dictates in the various circumstances."

498. But what was the state of the question when the declaration of the Pontifical Commission was issued in 1930? Prior to the proclamation of the Code, the opinion of the minority was regarded as probable even by the authors who held the opposite view, though it seemed to lack intrinsic worth inasmuch as it argued from the obsolescence of the law outside the Papal States.

Then came the Code, which was hailed as settling the controversy. But authors arose who saw probability still in the old minority opinion on account of the obscure language of Canon 1513, § 2. Nasoni's whole argument aims practically at demonstrating that so far from destroying the probability of the minority view, the Code actually increased it.

Then appeared the declaration of the Pontifical Commission. It says that the word *moneantur* is a command, not an exhortation. But on whom is it a command? Clearly it is a command on the Ordinary. It requires a wide interpretation to conclude that because the duty of the Ordinary, already fairly clear in the Code, is now declared to be in virtue of a command and not a counsel, therefore the act by which the Ordinary approaches the heir is to be a command. It seems, therefore, that this latest declaration states that the Ordinary is not free to give the admonition or not, as he chooses, but that he must give it, subject, of course, to the dictates of prudence which excuse from the observance of merely positive law.[105]

499. The matter, so far as the heir is concerned, remains in the same case as it was prior to the declaration, except that perhaps the majority opinion gains moral support from the fact that the declaration of a stricter obligation for the Ordinary raises a presumption of stricter obligation for the person who is to be admonished.

500. What position does this treatise sustain? There seems to be no doubt that the heir is bound in conscience. This view is supported by a radical disregard of a controversy that seems to lack the foundation of reality. It is a war over a negative conclusion. Nasoni can not stand without D'Annibale, for he merely attempts to show that D'Annibale was not discredited by the Code. But D'Annibale's opinion itself was never probable. It was based on a fictitious obsolescence which the canons never recognized, and which they do not recognize to this day. The law is worded more cautiously perhaps in the Code, but the fundamental right which it asserts is the one asserted by Alexander III. It is the right of canon law to govern bequests to charity and religion.

501. It is too much to expect the canons to outline the degree in which canon law binds in conscience. That is the task of moral theology. That the canons do impose an obligation of paying such bequests is only too clear from Canon 1513, § 2. Otherwise, the words of this paragraph would have been, "In ultimis voluntatibus in bonum Ecclesiae serventur, si fieri possit, sollemnitates iuris civilis," and no more. To say one word beyond that is to impose an obligation even where the formalities have not been observed. It is the function of moral theology to say what that obligation is *in foro interno*. But it may be noted here that it seems inconceivable that it should not be *per se gravis* or that it differs from the obligation of other positive laws establishing economic relations between persons sub-

[105] They who think that the declaration means that the Ordinary is to give a command evidently think that the question addressed to the Pontifical Commission was, *e. g.*, "Utrum *monitio* de qua in canone 1513, § 2, sit praeceptiva, an tantum exhortativa."

ject to it. Such legal relations carry with them an obligation in commutative justice. So, too, does this positive law establishing the relations between the pious cause and the person into whose hands the estate of the decedent has passed.

502. If the confessor becomes aware that admonition will be of no avail, but that his penitent would consent to a compromise, he should write directly to the Sacred Penitentiary explaining to what extent the penitent is willing to comply with the obligation. A reasonable compromise will be readily accepted under the circumstances.[106] If the case is known *in foro externo,* it should be called to the attention of the Ordinary, whose duty it is to prevent a contest in the secular forum, either by persuading the heirs to pay the bequest, or if he makes no progress in that direction, by obtaining a compromise from the Sacred Congregation of the Council.[107]

503. If there was ever a problem urgent enough to justify action by the Ordinary without recourse to the Holy See, it is conceivably this one. Canon 81 permits the Ordinary to dispense from the general laws of the Church if three conditions are verified: first, if recourse to the Holy See is attended with difficulties; second, if there is grave risk in delay; and third, if the subject is one in which the Holy See is accustomed to grant a dispensation.[108] A compromise in this matter is a partial dispensation. It is a relaxation of Canon 1513, § 2, in a particular case to the extent of the amount waived.[109] There is adequate reason for the dispensation, namely,

[106] Santi, *l. c.,* n. 26; De Meester, *op. cit.,* 1466.

[107] The reason for avoiding the contest is the probability that nothing can be salvaged after an adverse decision has been rendered. Even where there is a probability that the charitable bequest will be sustained, the degree of doubt attaching to the outcome is sufficient ground for compromise. Only where the attack is evidently puerile and incapable of being sustained would it seem safe to defend the bequest in the secular tribunal.

[108] Canon 81. "A generalibus Ecclesiae legibus Ordinarii infra Romanum Pontificem dispensare nequeunt, ne in casu quidem particulari, nisi haec potestas eidem fuerit explicite vel implicite concessa, aut nisi difficilis sit recursus ad Sanctam Sedem et simul in mora sit periculum gravis damni, et de dispensatione agatur quae a Sede Apostolica concedi solet."

[109] Canon 80. "Dispensatio, seu legis in speciali casu relaxatio, concedi potest a conditore legis, ab eius successore vel superiore, nec non ab illo cui iidem facultatem dispensandi concesserint."

the good of the souls of the heirs and the promotion of the interests of the charitable institute. And the law from which the dispensation is granted is an ecclesiastical law, for though the right to hold and acquire property belongs to the Church by divine law, the Church can not take property to which she is not entitled. And the Church is not entitled to the property of another under a bequest unless the bequest is valid. As has been indicated already, a bequest is valid by the provisions of positive law; in the case of pious bequests, by canon law authorizing charitable and religious institutions to take property bequeathed to them. *Cf.* §§ 6-10; 173, 174, this treatise.

The three conditions required for independent action are verified in practically every case of this kind in the United States. First, the dispensation is one which the Holy See is accustomed to grant, as is evident from the decree of the Sacred Penitentiary of 1901. Second, access to the Holy See is difficult, considering the distance beyond the seas and the length of time required for the exchange of letters. Third, there is usually the probability, nay even the certainty, of the loss of the whole bequest if prompt action is not taken to avert litigation.

Wherefore it seems to accord logically and juridically with the precise intention of Canon 81 that the Ordinary, aware that a bequest to charity is likely to fail if contested in the secular courts, should call in the heirs even before they signify their intention of making the contest. Psychologically, this is the better plan if a compromise, or even a relatively small payment, is sought. Once the heirs have set their minds upon a contest, there arises a certain fixedness of purpose from which it is difficult to divert them. Then in the conference with the heirs, *uno tractu,* the Ordinary should bargain with them and obtain as much of the bequest as he can in the interests of charity, making due concessions to the rights of the heirs.[110] He must give his word that he will attempt to collect no more than the amount agreed on in the conference, and perhaps he might sign an instrument of release. Otherwise the conference would be something of a farce, and no great credit to the episcopal dignity. That is why he must seize the propitious moment and make a final commitment without recourse to the Holy See, and that is

[110] *Cf.* Chapter III, Art. 5.

why he may do so with a safe conscience under the warrant given him in Canon 81, constructed, it would seem, almost to meet the exact requirements of this case.

504. Scholion I. As to gifts *inter vivos*, there is a divergence of opinion as to the validity of charitable bequests that lack the formalities required by the secular law. Canon 1513, § 2, speaks only of bequests contained in testamentary dispositions. It is these that the heirs must be warned to pay. § 1 of the same canon, while it mentions gifts *inter vivos,* contends only for the freedom of the individual to make such gifts.

Vermeersch, Cocchi, and Noldin hold that even these gifts for charitable purposes are valid if they lack the formalities of secular law. Vermeersch thinks, however, that persons who refuse to pay gifts thus invalid under the secular law should not be disturbed. This is undoubtedly correct, for the opposite view has at least extrinsic probability, as Cocchi admits, supported as it is by such names as Blat, De Meester, Vromant, Cance, Claeys-Bouuaert-Simenon, Gillet, and Kiselstein.[111]

505. The opinion that holds gifts invalid seems the more correct for two reasons. First, the opposite view seems to require an unwarranted extension of the terms of Canon 1513, § 2. Second, the historical position of the canons in this matter has been concerned only with testamentary bequests. Under Canon 6, n. 2, when the provisions of a prior law are incorporated in the Code, they are to be interpreted in the light of the prior law, unless there is an explicit derogation or extension in the Code.

111 Vermeersch-Creusen, *op. cit.,* II, 850; Vermeersch, *Theol. Mor.,* II, 447; Cocchi, *op. cit.,* VI, 192; Noldin, *op. cit.,* II, 555; Blat, *op. cit.,* 426; De Meester, *op. cit.,* 1466; Vromant, *op. cit.,* 155-157; Claeys-Bouuaert-Simenon, *op. cit.,* III, 265; Cance, *op. cit.,* III, 145; Gillet, *Collectanea Mechlinensia* (1927), 82 (cited by Cance); Kiselstein, *Rev. eccl. de Liège* (1919-1920), 94, 95, (cited by Cance). Gifts of chattels are generally perfected by delivery of the object. But gifts of lands, tenements, and hereditaments require written formalities. Even incorporeal chattels require definite formalities in France and Belgium; Cance, *op. cit.,* III, Appendix, xxxi. De Meester's argument for regarding these gifts invalid is based on the ground that the donor is still alive and can comply with the necessary requirements.

CHAPTER VIII

THE TESTAMENTARY BENEFICIARY

506. The interests of testamentary beneficiaries are often defeated under requirements of the secular law which operate directly or indirectly on the beneficiaries. The indirect operation of such impediments will be discussed in Chapter IX. Here direct operation is the subject of study.

Bequests may be defeated by direct operation of the law on the beneficiary in one of three ways: first, because they are contrary to public policy; second, because the testator may have sought to control the beneficiaries *in perpetuum;* and third, the beneficiaries may be too indefinite to be recognized. The disabilities arising both from public policy and from the statute against perpetuities (*i. e.*, against perpetual control of beneficiaries) affect physical persons and moral persons (*i. e.*, corporations); those arising from indefiniteness of beneficiary spring usually from the naming of an uncertain group the members of which can not be determined.

507. The problem, however, turns chiefly about moral persons. It will be pertinent, then, to focus the light of this discussion on the capacity of moral persons to take under wills, and then touch incidentally as the discussion progresses on the incapacities of physical persons, so far as they are related or similar to the former.

508. Moral persons may be recognized and constituted by both ecclesiastical authority and secular authority. But unless a moral person is recognized by a system of law, it can not be a subject of rights under that system. This is true of canon law and secular law. Consequently, a moral person established by the canonical system would not, as such, be a subject of rights under the secular system, unless it were established also under the authority of the latter. A correct understanding of the capacity of a moral person to take under a will demands a knowledge of its relation to the canonical and secular systems. To discuss this relation will be the function of the first Article of this Chapter. The second will discuss the direct disabilities under which moral persons labor in the matter of accepting legacies, with incidental references to disabilities affecting physical persons. Indirect disabilities that result from indefiniteness in the language of a bequest and from perpetuity in the appointment will be considered in a later Chapter. It will indicate how the formation of a corporation recognized by both the secular and the canonical system obviates the difficulty that arises from these impediments. A further chapter will concern itself with bequests for Masses, which are regarded as defective sometimes through indefiniteness of beneficiary; sometimes, because of perpetuity in the appointment.

Article 1

The Relation of Corporations to the Law

509. Canon 99. "In Ecclesia, praeter personas physicas, sunt etiam personae morales, publica auctoritate constitutae, quae distinguuntur in personas morales collegiales et non collegiales, ut ecclesiae, Seminaria, beneficia, etc."

Canon 100, § 1. "Catholica Ecclesia et Apostolica Sedes moralis personae rationem habent ex ipsa ordinatione divina; ceterae inferiores personae morales in Ecclesia eam sortiuntur sive ex ipso iuris praescripto sive ex speciali competentis Superioris ecclesiastici concessione data per formale decretum ad finem religiosum vel caritativum."

Canon 1495, § 1. "Ecclesia catholica et Apostolica Sedes nativum ius habent libere et independenter a civili potestate acquirendi, retinendi et administrandi bona temporalia ad fines sibi proprios prosequendos."

§ 2. "Etiam ecclesiis singularibus aliisque personis moralibus quae ab ecclesiastica auctoritate in iuridicam personam erectae sint, ius est, ad normam sacrorum canonum, bona temporalia acquirendi, retinendi et adminisstrandi."

Canon 1499, § 1. "Ecclesiae acquirere bona temporalia potest omnibus iustis modis iuris sive naturalis sive positivi, quibus id aliis licet."

§ 2. "Dominium bonorum, sub suprema auctoritate Sedis Apostolicae, ad eam pertinet moralem personam, quae eadem bona legitime acquisiverit."

510. Canon 100, § 1, declares an ordinance of divine positive law when it points to the juristic personality of the Church. It reveals to us the chief and supreme corporation with which the canons are concerned, viz., the Church catholic and universal. Intimately connected with this juristic personality is the right of the Church as a corporate entity to acquire, hold, and administer the temporalities necessary or useful to the prosecution of the purposes for which it was instituted, as Canon 1495, § 1, clearly declares.[1]

511. From the earliest days the Church has been endowed with the temporalities required for her mission.[2] Moreover, it

[1] *Cf.* the Allocution of Pope Pius IX, *Quibus luctuosissimis,* referring to the conclusion of the Concordat with Spain, 5 September, 1851: "Omni studio et contentione vindicandum et tuendum curamus ius, quo Ecclesia pollet; acquirendi sc. et possidendi quaecunque bona stabilia et frugifera, veluti innumera prope conciliorum acta et SS. Patrum sententiae et exempla, Praedecessorum Nostrorum constitutiones apertissime loquuntur, sapientissime docent et demonstrant"—*Fontes,* n. 512.

Cf. Propositions 26 and 27 condemned in the Syllabus of Pope Pius IX, 8 December, 1864—Denzinger, *Enchiridion,* nn. 1726, 1727; *Fontes,* n. 543. Proposition 26: "Ecclesia non habet nativum ac legitimum ius acquirendi et possidendi." Proposition 27: "Sacri Ecclesiae ministri Romanusque Pontifex ab omni rerum temporalium cura et dominio sunt omnino excludendi." *Cf.* the Encyclical, *Quanta cura,* of Pope Pius IX, 8 December, 1864—*Fontes,* n. 542.

The Church has maintained this position constantly against many opponents, v. gr., Arnold of Brescia (died 1155); the Waldenses (at the beginning of the thirteenth century); Marsilius of Padua (died 1327); Wycliff (died 1387); and the Gallicans. *Cf.* the Bulla, *Inter Cunctas,* of Martin V, where the propositions of Wycliff are condemned, 22 February, 1418—Harduin, VIII, 9110; Vermeersch-Creusen, *op. cit.,* II, 817; Cocchi, *op. cit.,* VI, 165; Cance, *op. cit.,* III, 125; Bargilliat, *op. cit.,* 1477; Prümmer, *Man. Iur. Can.,* 442.

[2] In the first centuries, the Church did not possess lands, but the offerings of the faithful were sufficient to support her ministers and to enable them to care for the needy and the sick. Moreover, great numbers of men belonging to the first rank of society, on the occasion of their baptism, or ordination, or religious profession, surrendered their patrimony to the poor and entrusted it to the Church for distribution; Thomassin, *op. cit.,* III, 1, 16, 5. This tradition derives from the days of the Apostles when Christians sold their goods and brought the price of them to the Church. It was with the Apostles, too, that the custom of taking up collections arose as a source of revenue to meet the expenses of ecclesiastical government and to alleviate the distress of the poor; De Héricourt, *op. cit.,* H 179.

seems clear that throughout the third century the Church held property as an association.[3]

But by what title did the Church hold property in the empire in which she was proscribed? De Rossi thinks that the Christians of this century held their property as burial societies,[4] and that the customs of these societies accord in a striking degree with the manners of the Christians of the third century. Indeed, Marucchi tells us that this is the common opinion held by the greater number of historians and archeologists. But Duchesne thinks otherwise.[5] He holds it

[3] Endowments of land were conferred on the Church even under the pagan emperors. Under Alexander Severus (222) a dispute arose between certain tavern keepers and a Christian community of Rome over the ownership of some land that had formerly been State property. The matter was brought before the prince, who decided in favor of the Christians. The churches which, according to Origen, were destroyed in 235 by the order of the Emperor Maximin, appear to have belonged to Christian communities. There seems no doubt either that the cemetery given into the charge of Callistus by Pope Zephyrinus (198) belonged to the community; Duchesne, *Christian Church,* p. 278. At Antioch there was a house belonging to the church there from which Paul of Samosata did not wish to depart when he was condemned. Moreover, there was certain property of the Church that had fallen into the hands of the Emperor Aurelian, who actually agreed to hand it over to whomsoever the Bishop of Rome would designate; De Héricourt, *op. cit.,* H 179.

At length, even a more propitious day came when Constantine and Licinius decreed at Milan (313) that the confiscated property of the Christians should be returned to them, not only that which they had held as individuals, but also that which they had held as associations; Eusebius, *Hist. Eccl.,* X, 5—*MPG,* XX, 883; Phillips, *op. cit.,* 406.

[4] Marucchi, *Archeol. Chret.,* I, 117; Pollock-Maitland, *op. cit.,* I, 2.

What was a funeral society in those days? Funeral societies were first permitted during the Republic. In them artisans might be enrolled for the purpose of providing for their funerals and for the care of their graves. In the time of Hadrian, there existed funeral societies that had a religious aspect. Until the end of the second century they were permitted to exist only outside the city, lest they serve as hotbeds of political conspiracy. Septimius Severus revoked this restriction. Some of these associations bore the name of a god; others, the name of a founder.

[5] He attempts to prove that the Christians were unalterably opposed to these societies. He urges further that the Church in large towns like Rome, Carthage, or Alexandria, might easily number at this period from thirty to forty thousand souls. He regards it as inconceivable that such a multitude could pass for a funeral club in the eyes of the civil authorities.

more probable that, if the Christian communities enjoyed long intervals of peace after the death of Marcus Aurelius, holding valuable property during such intervals, they were frankly tolerated as religious organizations. Tolerating the Christians, he suggests, was tolerating the Church. The places of meeting, the location of the cemeteries, and the names and the addresses of the leaders were known to the authorities. The bishop was always at the disposal of the magistrate even when an edict of persecution was issued. He was arrested, and the property of the Church confiscated. When the edict was revoked, the property was returned.

512. Restitution of this kind occurred when Licinius and Constantine in 313 ordered the property of the Christians to be returned to them.[6] Even the property of the martyrs was returned to the Church under their decree, if the deceased had no heirs.[7] Soon, in the course of history, Constantine became sole emperor and openly assumed the role of protector of the Church, enabling her by legal enactment to receive donations and legacies, and bestowing munificent gifts upon Christian communities.[8]

[6] Eusebius, *l. c.; idem, De Vita Constantini,* II, 35, 36, 39, 40—*MPG,* XX, 1011, 1015.

[7] It was, in a sense, an act of making a will for them, for Constantine says he believes that would be their wish.

[8] *Codex Theod.,* 16, 2, 4; C. 1, 2, 1; Phillips, *l. c.;* Thomassin, *l. c.,* n. 1; De Héricourt, *op. cit.,* H 180; Weber, *Christian Era,* 1, 20, 21. This was a signal for the manifestation of a bounty to the Church that firmly entrenched the custom of meeting the necessities of religion by generous donations. Pulcheria, who had been declared Augusta by her brother, Theodosius the Younger (414), and who, after the death of this prince (450), had reigned at first alone and then with her husband, Marcian, left by will all her money and lands to the Church; De Héricourt, *l. c.*

When St. Ambrose became Archbishop of Milan, he gave to the Church the proprietorship of his land, reserving the usufruct to his sister, a precedent that was eventually enshrined in the Decretals of Gregory IX; c. 3, X, *de successionibus ab intestato,* III, 27; De Héricourt, *l. c.;* Thomassin, *l. c.,* n. 5. St. Gregory Nazianzen left his estate to the poor of the church at Nazianzen and St. Paulinus gave all his property to the poor; Thomassin, *l. c.* St. Cyril of Alexandria left the larger portion of his estate to his successor in office, as the former's nephew testified in the Council of Chalcedon (451)—Harduin II, 331.

Preachers and spiritual writers aided the movement by their exhortations. Salvian condemns all, and especially bishops, who make bequests to strangers,

513. The manner in which the Church was instituted heir in the days immediately following the decrees of Constantine was not uniform. Most frequently, it approximated the custom that had grown up prior to Constantine. This custom, probably influenced by the Roman practice of making deities the heir, was to institute as heir either our Lord or the angels and the saints.[9] When a pagan deity was instituted heir, it is not clear who was regarded as the actual owner of the property. Probably it was the State, for even the administration of such property was in the hands of the civil magistrates, and not of the pagan priests.[10]

On the other hand, the Christian Church was independent of the State,[11] and the proprietor of the goods bequeathed to it was now the patrimony of the Church, now Jesus Christ, now the Christian Church in general, now the Pope. But when this property was regarded as belonging to the Church as a whole, it was by a sort of eminent domain, and it is fairly evident that in each community the

forgetting the poor and ignoring the penitential value of alms. He contends that even were it not necessary to give alms to atone for personal sin, there would still be an obligation resting on every one to render gratitude to God for His bounty; *Ep. ad Salonium—MPL*, LIII, 171; *Adversus Avaritiam—MPL*, LIII, 175; 189, 190. St. Jerome, writing to a certain Julian, whose wife and two daughters were dead, urged him to give his daughters their spiritual dowry by surrendering his wealth to the poor and entering religion; *Ad Julianum*, Ep. CXVIII, n. 4—*Corpus Script. Eccl.*, LV, 440.

The Church also benefited by the decease of one who died in captivity if his children or heirs had failed to ransom him, the estate to be used by the Church for ransoming other captives; *Nov.*, 115, 3, 13. And the property of the college of the *curiales*, if it came into the possession of the Church, could be retained, because of the similarity of function between the two colleges; *Nov.*, 131, 5.

Monasteries and churches were entitled to whatever the monks or clerics owned on entering the service of either or whatever was obtained by these persons by bequest or inheritance; *Nov.*, 5, 4; C. 1, 3, 54, 15; *Nov.*, 123, 37. If the cleric persevered, he was to spend these sums on charitable works during life or by bequests in his will; *Nov.*, 123, 37.

[9] Ulpian, *Reg.*, 22, 6; Buckland, *op. cit.*, p. 170; Savigny, *Diritto Romano*, II, 266, 268; Phillips, *op. cit.*, 406.

[10] Buckland, *l. c.;* Savigny, *l. c.*, n. 267.

[11] Acts XXV, 10; cc. 1-5, D. X; c. 1, D. XCVI; c. 7, X, *de testamentis et ultimis voluntatibus*, I, 2; c. 12, X, *de rebus eccl. alienandis*, IV, 13; Savigny, *l. c.*

property of the Church belonged to the church of the place by a subsidiary title.[12]

514. At any rate, the will of the *ecclesia particularis*, the diocesan or the parochial church, did not reside wholly within itself. Its life was that of a member. When the legists, after the recovery of the Digest, discovered the *universitas* (corporation) of Roman law, and understood in what way it differed from partnership and mere aggregation, the canonists seized the idea as fitting the plan of organization of the Church. There was always a collegiateness apparent in the whole organization of the Church, from the Supreme Pontiff down to the smallest ecclesiastical unit. They saw the Church as a *universitas;* and they knew that a *universitas* is a *persona.* Pope Innocent IV went on to say that it is a *persona ficta,* that is, the organized group was distinct from the Church, which had an existence of its own. The will of the group might even differ from that of the Church. The Church is the substratum of rights and duties, just as a *persona physica.* The Church is, as the mystics say, the Bride of Christ. The organized group of the Church, at any given time, only represents the Church, or misrepresents it if it happens to be corrupt. The *persona* is therefore rather a personified institution than a group of men. Indeed, it could be represented, on the human side, by only one man, being in effect, if not called by the name, a corporation sole.[13]

Thus in Canon 100, § 1, both the Church and the Holy See are declared to be moral persons, the Church being the juristic person, and the Holy See being the corporation sole, the latter a member in the larger *universitas,* the supreme member, standing at the head of all the others, being what in secular affairs is called the government.[14]

515. As to the property held by moral persons composing the Church, writers like Savigny find it difficult to reconcile the idea of the separate administration by parishes with the broader right of dominion residing in the Church as a whole.[15] But they are right in

[12] Buckland, *l. c.;* Savigny, *l. c.,* 268, 270.

[13] Pollock-Maitland, *op. cit.,* I, 501-503.

[14] Vermeersch-Creusen, *op. cit.,* II, 817.

[15] *Cf.* C. 1, 3, 26.

concluding that ownership was in the particular church and that the subject of succession was the individual church in the local community.[16]

Ownership by the particular church is now enshrined in the provisions of Canon 1499, § 2,[17] and this puts an end to the old controversy. For, even canonists were not always agreed on the exact juridical relation of the individual moral person to the property which it had acquired. There were six divergent views. Some said that the property belonged to God. Others, that it belonged to our Lord or St. Peter.[18] Some thought that the universal Church as a corporation was the proprietor of even the property of the individual churches. Others held that the dioceses or the bishops owned all the property in their jurisdiction. Others, that ownership resided in the members of the parish or of the religious order. Finally, some believed that ownership was in the poor.[19]

516. St. Thomas, however, contended that all the property of the Church belonged to the Supreme Pontiff as the principal dispenser, but not as owner or possessor.[20] And that is practically the view endorsed in Canon 1499, § 2.[21] The ownership of all the property of the Church is thus placed under the supreme authority of the

[16] Buckland, *l. c.;* Savigny, *l. c.*, pp. 269, 270, 274.

[17] *Cf.* § 510, this treatise, for the text of this canon.

[18] Schmalzgrueber alleges as proponents of this opinion Innocent IV, Navarrus, and Donatus; *op. cit.*, III, III, 25, 3. And Reiffenstuel seems to favor it; *op cit.*, III, 25, 47. But it is offered as an objection to that view that neither our Lord nor St. Peter could be held for the debts of the moral person; Prümmer, *Man. Iur. Can.*, 443; Vromant, *op. cit.*, 48, 50.

God, indeed, has supreme dominion over all goods on earth but under His Providence the secondary and useful ownership has been given to men. And if in a foundation property is given to God or to our Lord or to a saint, it is to be understood that the gift has been actuated by love of these persons and of God. If it is given to St. Peter, it should be understood that the Holy See is meant, or a church dedicated to St. Peter, as the context will indicate one or the other; Vromant, *op. cit.*, 48, 50; Wernz, *op. cit.*, III, 139, ad 3um.

[19] The poor are rather one of the purposes for which the Church owns property, not the subject of the ownership of that property; Vromant, *l. c.*, Wernz, *l. c.*, ad 4um.

[20] *Summa Theologica*, 2, 2, q. 100, a. 1, ad 7um.

[21] A. Couly, in *Le Canoniste Contemporain*, XLIV (1921), 16, 17.

Holy See. Consequently, the Supreme Pontiff has the right to govern ecclesiastical property, to supervise the administration of it, to determine the rights of the administrators, to control their operations, and exceptionally to dispose of the whole or of part of the estate.[22] Ecclesiastical moral persons agree to this when they are established, insofar as it is morally necessary for the common good.[23]

517. However, the Supreme Pontiff must have a grave reason to dispose of the property of subject moral persons, and he must be guided by equity. Granted these two requirements, he can condone usurpations, or give the community property of one religious family to another. His power in this regard is comparable to the eminent domain of the State.

518. Outside of the exceptional case, juridical acts concerning the property of subject moral persons must be performed in their name. The patrimony of each group is distinct from that of every other, even if there be but one administrator for several. The property of one may not be used to pay the debts of another. This is verified also in the case of the bishop's power over the moral persons subject to him; and of a major superior's, over the houses subject to him, unless particular statutes provide otherwise.[24]

519. The moral persons subject to these rights may be, as Canon 99 indicates, collegiate or non-collegiate. But they must be ecclesiastical. A general term by which they may be indicated is the word, "institution." [25] If the purpose of the institution is merely secular, even though it be altruistic or philanthropic, it can not be established as an ecclesiastical institution.[26]

[22] S. C. C. *in Causa Forosempronien,* 25 January, 1817, § *Cum-Pallottini,* XI. 570.

[23] Vromant, *op. cit.,* 49.

[24] Vromant, *op. cit.,* 49; Prümmer, *l. c.,* Cance, *op. cit.,* III, 128; Bargilliat, *op. cit.,* 1484; Wernz, *l. c.,* ad 5um and 6um.

[25] The word is to be understood in its concrete significance, as an object created, built, or erected for a certain end, not as the means to an end in the abstract; Vermeersch-Creusen, *op. cit.,* II, 812; Cocchi, *op. cit.,* VI, 159; Cance, *op. cit.,* III, 121; De Meester, *op. cit.,* 1431.

[26] Vermeersch-Creusen, *l. c.;* Cocchi, *l. c.;* Blat says that the *montes pietatis* (loan shops conducted as a charitable enterprise) in Belgium are purely secular; *op. cit.,* 398.

520. Lay Institutions. Even though the purpose of the institution be the promotion of religion, of Christian virtue, of the corporal and spiritual works of mercy to serve God, the institution may still be only a lay institution. A lay institution is one which has not been formally established by ecclesiastical authority. It makes no difference whether it was founded by laymen or by clerics, or whether it has been granted incorporation by the secular authority.

521. Concerning the nature of the property of lay institutions devoted to the exercise of Christian piety, there are two opinions. The first holds that the property is ecclesiastical; the other denies it. Cocchi adheres to the former opinion and bases his view on the ground that such institutions are ecclesiastical *per destinationem* (that is, they take on the nature of the end which they serve). De Meester would not go so far, but agrees substantially with the view, provided the institution is formally approved, even though not established, by ecclesiastical authority. But the mere affiliation of an institute with an ecclesiastical person does not make it ecclesiastical, he says. In this he contradicts Vermeersch-Creusen. But though De Meester would not permit an institution merely affiliated to another to be called an ecclesiastical institution, he regards its property as ecclesiastical on the ground that the accessory puts on the nature of the principal. Consequently, as to the nature of the property, he is in agreement with Vermeersch.

On the other hand, Vermeersch holds with Vromant, Maroto, Cappello, and Wernz, that even approved lay institutes are exempt as to their property from the canons governing ecclesiastical property. They are supported in some measure by a decree of the Sacred Congregation of the Council in regard to the St. Vincent de Paul Society (which is commended by ecclesiastical authority but not formally approved), declaring that the property of the Society belongs to the members, except what has been given them in trust for distribution to the poor. As to these gifts, they are governed by Canons 1515 and 1516, which will be discussed in due course, involving responsibility to the Ordinary for the faithful discharge of the trust.[27]

[27] The decree is that of the S. C. C. *in Causa Corrienten.*, 13 November, 1920—*AAS,* XIII (1921), 135; *Periodica,* X (1921), 293; *NRT,* XLVIII (1921), 317.

522. Therefore an institution is not ecclesiastical unless it is founded by ecclesiastical authority, or has been incorporated into or annexed to an ecclesiastical institution.[28] Establishment by ecclesiastical authority may take place under the general law, that is, under general legislation providing that certain kinds of institutions shall be ecclesiastical;[29] or by a formal decree of establishment issued by the superior competent in the premises.[30]

523. Further, an ecclesiastical institution is either collegiate

For the opinions, see Vermeersch-Creusen, *op. cit.*, II, 812, 865; Vromant, *De Fidelium Assoc.*, 37; Maroto, *op. cit.*, I, 475; Cappello, *Summa*, n. 55; Wernz, *op. cit.*, III, 196; Cocchi, *op. cit.*, VI, 161; De Meester, *op. cit.*, 1431.

Maroto observes that the property held by these lay institutions is to be considered as belonging to the donors until it has been used in the way prescribed in the donation. Meanwhile, he continues, the association administers the property in the name of the donor. On dissolution of the association, it is to be restored to the donor, or if this is impossible, to the Ordinary for the use intended. But this seems not to square with the intention as it usually exists in the mind of the donor and of the association. The donor can not be conceived, it would seem, as expecting to receive the gift back. Surely, if the Ordinary is the executor of all such gifts, he is competent to see that proper distribution is made, even should the association be dissolved; *cf.* Canon 1515, § 1.

De Meester remarks that a bequest to such a society can not be called a foundation, but only a charitable legacy, and the full significance of the remark will appear later when foundations come up for discussion; *op. cit.*, 1499.

[28] The sufficiency of this incorporation with an existing institution is denied by De Meester, as has already been indicated, though he concedes that the older opinion admitted that it sufficed; *cf.* § 521. He admits, moreover, that the property of the affiliated institution is ecclesiastical; *op. cit.*, 1431.

[29] V. gr., Canon 531. "Non modo religio, sed etiam provincia et domus sunt capaces acquirendi et possidendi bona temporalia cum reditibus stabilibus seu fundatis, nisi earum capacitas in regulis et constitutionibus excludatur aut coractetur."

[30] Canon 686, § 2. "Associationes erigere vel approbare pertinet, praeter Romanum Pontificem, ad loci Ordinarium, exceptis illis quarum instituendarum ius, apostolico ex privilegio, aliis reservatum est."

Canon 1414, § 1. "Beneficia consistorialia una Sedes Apostolica erigit."

§ 2. "Praeter Romanum Pontificem, Ordinarii in suo quisque territorio beneficia non consistorialia erigere possunt, salvo praescripto can. 394, § 2."

§ 3. "Attamen Vicarii Generales nequeunt beneficia erigere nisi ex peculiari mandato."

§ 4. "Etiam Cardinalis in proprio titulo vel diaconia potest beneficia non curata erigere, nisi ecclesia sit religionis clericalis exemptae."

or non-collegiate. In the collegiate institutions, it is the physical persons who are incorporated; a non-collegiate institution is an incorporated enterprise, the work itself being incorporated. Thus, a collegiate institute is a society of persons which is effectively directed by ecclesiastical incorporation to its common purpose and aim; or, more strictly, a moral body established by ecclesiastical authority acting collectively through the votes of its members. The Church itself is a collegiate institution; so also a religious order, and a pious association of laymen.[31]

524. A non-collegiate ecclesiastical institute is a fund, assigned by ecclesiastical authority to a definite purpose, and regarded by disposition of positive law as beyond the dominion of any physical person or society, an entity formally separate and distinct from all other estates and self-existent. Examples of this kind of ecclesiastical institute are schools, seminaries, hospitals, hospices, orphan and foundling asylums, and homes for the aged.[32]

Non-collegiate institutions can be established by the bishop of the diocese, or recognized after their establishment by his decree.[33]

A non-collegiate institution may be established within a collegiate institution, as a seminary within a religious order. It may also merely exist within the collegiate institution without formal establishment. De Meester says that in the latter case it is not an ecclesiastical person, though its property is ecclesiastical.[34] If it is not

[31] Vermeersch-Creusen, *op. cit.*, II, 812; Cocchi, *op. cit.*, VI, 159; Cance, *op. cit.*, III, 121; De Meester, *op. cit.*, 1431.

[32] Vermeersch-Creusen, *l. c.;* Cocchi, *l. c.;* Cance, *l. c.;* De Meester, *l. c.*

These institutions are ecclesiastical only when they are established out of love of God and by the authority of the Church; not when they are merely philanthropic, or established by the State, or by lay persons; *cf.* § 95, this treatise.

[33] Blat, *op. cit.*, 398.

Besides the bishops, the following persons are competent: the Vicar General, the Administrator, the Vicar Capitular, Vicars and Prefects Apostolic and Abbots and prelates *nullius.*

Canon 1489, § 1. "Hospitalia, orphanotrophia aliaque similia instituta, ad opera religionis vel caritatis sive spiritualis sive temporalis destinata, possunt ab Ordinario loci erigi et per eius decretum persona iuridica in Ecclesia constitui."

Cf. Canon 198, § 2, to see that the *Ordinarius loci* includes those persons named in the note.

[34] Vermeersch-Creusen, *l. c.;* De Meester, *l. c.*

properly established, or at least annexed to an ecclesiastical collegiate person, it has no recognition in the canons.

525. Do these ecclesiastically established institutions have any rights under the secular laws? They have none in virtue of their canonical establishment. They may exercise property rights through trustees or through their members. If they seek and obtain recognition as a corporation by the State, they may enjoy these rights also as a corporate body.

526. However, the Church and the Holy See are not recognized as juristic personalities in the United States. Consequently, the Church is not regarded as possessing the right to establish corporations, except in those territories which once belonged to Spain, viz., Cuba, Porto Rico, and the Philippine Islands. There the juristic personality of the Church is recognized under Article 800 of the Treaty of Paris, December 10, 1898.[35] The juristic personality of the Church is not recognized in France[36] and probably not in Mexico, Russia, and Spain.[37] Cappello says that the English and Austrian laws recognize the Church as a juristic person.[38] This is so in Italy since the recent Concordat,[39] and in most of the Spanish-

[35] Brown, *Juristic Personality*, p. 115; Dignan, *Legal Incorporation*, p. 237.

[36] Pistocchi, *op. cit.*, pp. 15, 16.

[37] Prior to the present regime in Spain, the juristic personality was recognized under Articles 40 and 41 of the Concordat of 1851; Article 3 of the Concordat of April 4, 1864; and Articles 38 and 746 of the Civil Code; cited by Ferreres, *Inst. Iur. Can.*, II, 469.

[38] *Summa.*, p. 108. Austria admits that the Church in the State is composed of a group of corporations, *"complexus corporationum"*; Pistocchi, *l. c. Cf. Conventio*, 25 September 1855, Arts. 1, 29-32—*Coll. Lacensis*, V, 1221.

[39] *Cf.* Arts. 2 and 23—*AAS*, XXI (1929), 210, 220. Prior to the Concordat, the Italian law was just the contrary; but it did recognize ecclesiastical institutions (Art. 2, Civil Code), though it reserved the right to refuse them recognition. In Bavaria, under the Concordat of 24 January, 1925, the Church's personality is recognized in Art. 1 and in Art. 10, § 1, a, the State provides for the support of bishops, cathedral canons, and pastors from the income of Church property. In Poland, under the Concordat of 10 February, 1925, Art. 10, the Church is recognized as competent to erect benefices; and under Art. 14 ff. these are supported by the State. Citations noted above are from Pistocchi, *l. c.*; *cf.* also Ottaviani, *op. cit.*, Appendix ii. The Concordat with Germany, 20 July, 1933, recognizes the Church's personality in Art. 2; *cf. AAS*, XXV (1933), 390. The Concordat also provides that the Concordats with Bavaria, Prussia,

American countries.[40]

527. As to the subordinate corporations, France now recognizes diocesan corporations, capable of acquiring property necessary for the conduct of religious services.[41] But even prior to this concession, France recognized cultural associations and their right to receive foundations.[42] But before such recognition was extended to the cultural associations, all gifts and legacies to parishes were

and Baden shall remain in effect. The Concordat, with Prussia (1929) recognizes the Church in Arts. 1 and 3; *cf. AAS,* XXI (1929), 522, 525. This is true of the Concordat with Lithuania, 27 September, 1927, Art. 1; *cf. AAS,* XIX (1927), 426; the Concordat with Rumania, Art. 9; *cf. AAS,* XXI (1929), 445; and the Concordat with Lettonia, 30 May, 1922; Art. 1; *cf.* Ottaviani, *l. c.*

[40] Under the Concordats with Ecuador (Art. 19); Colombia (Arts. 5, 6); Costa Rica (Art. 17); Guatemala (Art. 18); Nicaragua (Art. 17); Venezuela (Art. 22); and San Salvador (Arts. 17, 18); and under the Civil Codes of Argentina (Arts. 33 and 41); Chile (Art. 547); Ecuador (Art. 536); San Salvador (Art. 620); Venezuela (Art. 13); Colombia (Arts. 24 and 27).

V. gr., Art. 17 of the Concordat with San Salvador agrees that as to ancient and new ecclesiastical foundations, no suppression or union can be made without the authority of the Holy See, or the authority conferred on bishops by the Council of Trent. This provision is not revoked by the Code, for under Canon 4, Concordats are unaffected by the Code.

All the references in this noted are cited from Ferreres, *Insts. Can.,* II, 468, 469.

[41] This form of corporation was accepted for France by Pope Pius XI, 18 January, 1924, as restoring legal existence to the Church in France; at the same time, he protested that these associations differ widely from those condemned by Pope Pius X, and that he is not reversing the former policy. The new associations are said to conform to the canons and to offer an outlet to the Holy See in the more critical problems that might arise in the administration of the Church; Encyclical, *Maximam gravissimamque,* 18 January, 1924—*AAS,* XVI (1924), 5; *Periodica,* XIII (1924), 20.

Mothon says that a certain number of dioceses in France have taken over the property of ecclesiastical moral persons (*i.e.,* parishes, seminaries, religious houses, scholastic and charitable institutions). Foundations must be made in the name of the diocese, to be administered by the diocese for the parish or the institution. The consent of the founder and the beneficiary are both required—*Insts.,* 2605. But Cance seems explicit enough in saying that diocesan associations are to take over property only for divine worship; *op. cit.,* III, *Appendix* xxxi.

[42] By the law of December 9, 1905, Art. 5—Bargilliat, *op. cit.,* 1513.

null and void. The testator, however, could impose on his heirs the obligation of having Masses said in perpetuity.[43]

528. **In the United States, in general any ecclesiastical corporation can become a legal corporation** by complying with the formalities set forth in the statutes of the various States. Variations are sometimes found within the same State between ordinary corporations and ecclesiastical corporations as to the requirements of the statutes, for instance, as to the number of incorporators.

529. **Pennsylvania does not recognize a corporation if the majority of incorporators are clergymen,** though it will incorporate Brothers and Sisters.[44] No conveyance is valid unless the association is incorporated in Delaware and Vermont;[45] but a conveyance to a church group is valid in the District of Columbia even if it is not incorporated and has not appointed trustees.[46] Virginia and West Virginia forbid the incorporation of religious societies, but permit subordinate church organizations to incorporate.[47] Thus Church lyceums and dramatic societies can incorporate and transact business for the parish.

530. **A review of the method in which parochial property may be held in the various States** will illustrate the tenor of the laws touching the incorporation of ecclesiastical corporations in general, though the establishing of a certain method for parochial incorporation would not necessarily exclude the existence of a diverse plan for charitable institutions.

531. **Tenures in Fee Simple Disapproved.** The Sacred Congregation of the Council has expressed itself as abolishing the method of holding diocesan property in the name of the bishop in fee simple, stating that the parish corporation is to take its place, and if that can

[43] Cour d'appel de Rennes, 18 December, 1911—cited in Bargilliat, *l. c.*

[44] All funds outside the plate, Easter and Christmas collections or annual voluntary contributions of some other sort, are to be in lay control (§ 2611; Act of June 2, 1887).

[45] Delaware, §§ 2181, 2182; Vermont, §§ 2627, 2628.

[46] Tit. 5, § 323.

[47] Virginia (const., § 59); *cf.* Trustees of the General Assembly of the Presbyterian Church in the United States *et al.* v. Guthrie *et al.*, 86 Va. 125, 10 S. E. 318; West Virginia (const., Art. 6, § 47). Brown, *op. cit.*, p. 119.

not be done, the property is to be held by the bishop as a corporation sole.[48]

532. The form of parish corporation approved by the Sacred Congregation is that in which of the five members of the corporation three are the following, the bishop, the vicar general, and the pastor. Where this form of corporation can not be established under the statutes of the State, then the corporation sole seems preferable, that is, the bishop as chief officer of the diocese is incorporated, and his successors in office succeed without any dissolution of the corporation. The parish corporation as herewith described can be established in a number of the States.[49]

[48] 29 July, 1911—*AER,* XLV (1911), 585, 586; *cf.* Dignan, *op. cit.*, pp. 239, 240; Brown, *op. cit.*, p. 137; Bartlett, *Church Property,* p. 90.

[49] Connecticut (two lay members appointed annually by the three incorporators already indicated; in case of the death or disability of the bishop, the administrator and the chancellor take the place of the bishop and the vicar general; §§ 3574, 3576); Delaware (the bishop and the pastor are *ex officio* members of the corporation; they select one other member annually; the other two members are elected annually by the congregation; the pastor is *ex officio* president; § 2176); Maryland (organization is the same as Delaware's, except that the Ordinary may appoint more than one person annually; Art. 23, § 286); Massachusetts (the bishop, vicar general, and pastor, with their successors are *ex officio* members of the corporation, and they associate two laymen with them annually; c. 67, § 44); Minnesota (the same plan obtains as in Massachusetts with a two-year term for the laymen and specific mention that the administrator succeeds in the place of the bishop; a diocesan corporation can be organized with the chancellor in the place of the pastor for charitable, religious, and educational work: §§ 7975, 7976); Montana (the same plan obtains as in Minnesota for both parish and diocesan corporations, except that there is no specified term for the laymen; Montana also admits the corporation sole; §§ 6459, 6462); Nebraska (outlines in more general terms the same plan; § 24-802); New Jersey (same plan obtains as in Minnesota for both diocesan and parish corporation, except that in the diocesan corporation two priests instead of two laymen make up the number of incorporators with the officials of the diocese, and no term of office is specified for either the laymen or priests who thus serve; pp. 4327, 4329); New York (plan includes only the parish corporation; c. 52, § 91); Oregon (the same plan obtains as in Minnesota for both types of corporation; § 25-927); Rhode Island (at the January session, 1869, a special act of the legislature authorized the present plan for the Diocese of Hartford; now § 3536; but in 1900 the Bishop of Providence was empowered to become a corporation sole; Acts, January, 1900, pp. 133, 134); Wisconsin

533. The incorporation of the bishop as a corporation sole is possible in a number of States, almost entirely in the far West, except a few dioceses thus incorporated by special act: viz., Baltimore, Boston, Chicago, Manchester, Providence, and Charleston.[50]

Provisions similar to those that enable a bishop to become a corporation sole are found in Michigan and South Dakota, where the bishop and his successors may take the legal title as trustees for the parishes. This arrangement is probably possible in most of the States, except in those that specify exclusively the plan approved by the Holy See or vest the parish property in the vestrymen or parish trustees.[51]

534. The vesting of property in parish trustees is disapproved by the Church. There are possible dangers involved, in that lay control of the parish is thus established. Even where the bishop acts as trustee, the principle of lay control is emphasized, for the bishop merely holds as trustee for the lay group. Since the trust, in the view of the secular law, is what is known as a *dry* trust (that is, a mere formality), the bishop could be compelled by a recalcitrant congregation to turn over the property to the parish.

535. This objection, however, does not seem to apply to the diocesan corporation, which holds all diocesan property, parochial

(the Minnesota plan obtains, but only for parish corporations; § 187.12); Wyoming (the plan seems possible under the general provisions for incorporation in § 28-602).

[50] The corporation sole is permitted in Alabama (§ 7112); Arizona (p. 131); California (Civil Code, § 605g); Idaho (§ 29-1201); Maine (c. 119, § 6); Montana (§ 6463); Nevada (§ 3224); Oklahoma (§ 9937); Utah (§ 931, Compiled Laws, 1917); Washington (§ 3884); Wyoming (§ 28-610); and probably in New Hampshire where a minister and his successors are authorized to hold property (c. 232, § 6).

The special acts were passed as follows: for Chicago (Laws, 1845, p. 322); for Manchester (on March 7, 1901, Laws, 1901, c. 232, p. 723); for Providence (in 1900, Acts, January 1900, pp. 133, 134); for Boston (*cf.* the Constitutions of the Archdiocese, 1919, n. 173); for Charleston (*cf.* Father Hopkins' history of St. Mary's Parish, p. 73); Baltimore was created a corporation sole in 1833; the two last, with their references, are to be found in Dignan, *op. cit.*, pp. 259-263.

Delaware explicitly states that no corporation sole is permitted in that State, §§ 2181, 2182.

[51] Michigan (§ 10845); South Dakota (§ 8871).

and charitable. Ohio seems to provide for such a corporation in permitting the incorporation of the central cathedral church. It allows also the incorporation of any religious endowment. The fact that both these provisions are made seems to indicate that the parish corporation was left unmentioned on the ground that the central corporation would look after parish property.[52]

States that permit diocesan corporations established on the Minnesota plan to hold diocesan property for the promotion of education, charity, and religion are Minnesota, Montana, Nebraska, New Jersey, and Oregon. By special charter the Dioceses of Burlington and Natchez are incorporated.[53]

536. In many of the remaining States a diocesan corporation may probably be formed, and perhaps even on the Minnesota plan. It is even possible that the same plan could be carried out in the organization of parishes. For instance, in Iowa, where this plan is not expressly permitted in the statutes, it is carried out substantially in the Diocese of Des Moines.[54]

537. It does not seem possible, however, to adopt this plan under the statutes of the States retaining the old trustee system, that is, where the parish property is held by trustees, usually automatically incorporated under the State laws.[55]

[52] Ohio (§§ 10022-1; 10011).

[53] In Natchez, the bishop, the vicar general, and four diocesan consultors were incorporated for a period of fifty years; *Constitutiones Diocesis Natchetensis*, 1922, p. 63; in Burlington, the corporation is composed of five members chosen for life with the bishop as president *ex officio;* Articles of Incorporation, 1896; both cited by Dignan, *op. cit.*, p. 261.

[54] Iowa simply provides that religious and charitable corporations may be formed by three or more persons, a majority of whom are residents of the State, to endure for fifty years, §§ 8582, 8583.

The plan seems feasible under the statutes of at least Florida (p. 2087); Georgia (pp. 709, 710); Illinois (p. 760); Kansas (§ 17-701); Kentucky (§ 320); New Mexico (§ 32-506). These States would also probably permit the same plan for the incorporation of charitable institutions (except Illinois). Washington (§ 3863) provides for the incorporation of charitable institutions.

[55] This seems to be the prevailing system in Arkansas (p. 2223); Colorado (§ 2384); District of Columbia (tit. 5, § 312); Indiana (§ 5127); Mississippi (§ 4168); Missouri (const., Art. 2, § 8; Statutes, §§ 4996, 4497); North Carolina (§§ 3568, 3569); North Dakota (§ 4536); South Carolina (§ 8158); South

538. The Defect in the Secular Plan. Even the most acceptable of these plans, that of the corporation aggregate as it is permitted in New York and Minnesota, does not square completely with the Church's notion of the parish as a *persona moralis ecclesiastica non collegialis.* But it is sufficiently approximate to guarantee the administration of parish affairs under the supervision of the hierarchy with the title in the individual corporation.

Article 2

Direct Disabilities Imposed on Beneficiaries

539. Alienation in mortmain in the traditional acceptance of the English common law was a conveyance of lands or tenements to any corporation, sole or aggregate, ecclesiastical or temporal. But as the purchases seem to have been made principally by religious corporations, the term has come to be used almost exclusively of alienations to them, and indeed the legislator seems to have had them chiefly in mind in framing the mortmain statutes.

The feudal theory was the fundamental reason for the enactment of these laws. Under that theory the crown owned all the land of the country in fee. As supreme lord he was entitled to all the fees that feudal practice gave the lord by reason of aids, wardships, marriage dues, and fines for alienation. Even the land itself passed to him on occasion by escheat. When this land passed into the hands of a corporation, the crown lost all these rights. Consequently, it was regarded as legally necessary that the corporation should have the license of the crown before it could, by purchase of land, deprive him of these sources of revenue. This license seems to have been required among the Saxons some sixty years prior to the Norman conquest. It became even more necessary after the Norman kings took over the island as lords in fee simple. On the

Dakota (§ 8870); Tennessee (§ 4408); Texas (Art. 1396). In Missouri a religious corporation can be formed only to hold land (const., Art. 2, § 8); but once formed it can transact other business. Because of the situation in Indiana and Missouri, the Bishop of Indianapolis and the Archbishop of St. Louis hold the property of the diocese in fee simple; *cf.* the Statutes of the Synod of St. Louis, 1929, p. 167 and Dignan, *op. cit.*, p. 263.

same feudal principles, the license of the intermediate lord was required. If these licenses had not been obtained, the respective lords could enter on the land alienated and seize it as forfeited.

540. Tenure in spite of Mortmain Statutes. But in spite of this traditional principle, it seems that the religious corporations were successful in acquiring the property they deemed necessary for their work. This resulted in an enactment under Henry III forbidding these alienations.[56] From the words of the decree, it would seem that the crown was aiming principally at the plan by which donors sought to overcome the prohibition against devising land. The plan was to give the land to the religious house during the donor's life, with a reservation of a life estate. This the crown now forbade. The scope of the decree, therefore, does not seem to extend to all conveyance of land, though that is possible.

541. Consequent upon this decree two other devices seem to have been adopted by the benefactors of religious corporations in their zeal to endow them with property for their work. One was to surrender the land to the corporation to be held by it as the feudal lord, while the donor was the vassal. After that transaction, the corporation could purchase the land from the vassal, for as the corporation was the lord, there was no one to enter in and claim the land. The second device was the lease of the land for a thousand years or more.

542. There followed on the part of the crown the Statute *De Religiosis*, 7 Edward I, which ordained that no person, religious or other whatsoever, should buy, sell, or receive under pretence of a gift or term of years, or any other title whatsoever, nor should by any art or ingenuity appropriate to himself any lands or tenements in mortmain; and if he did, the immediate lord of the fee, or, in case he failed to do so during one year, the lords paramount, and, in case none

[56] Magna Carta, 9 Henry III, c. 36: "Non licet alicui de caetero dare terram suam alicui domui religiosae, ita quod illam resumat tenendam de eadem domo; nec liceat alicui domui religiosae terram alicujus sic accipere, quod tradat illam ei a quo ipsam recepit tenendam: si quis autem de caetero terram suam domui religiosae sic dederit, et super hoc convincatur, donum suum penitus cassetur, ut terra illa domino suo illius feodi in curratur"; cited in Blackstone, *op. cit.*, II, 18, 270.

of them did so, the king, might enter into the land and claim it by forfeiture.

543. The corporations next adopted the following plan. They would enter suit for the land they expected to purchase on the ground that it belonged to them by title prior to that of the person who at the moment seemed to own it. The person who wished to sell, and who was the owner in fact, would fail to appear in court to defend his title, and the land was handed over to the corporation by the adjudication of the court. This kind of suit was known as a *common recovery*. It was later used to defeat entailed estates.

544. The crown moved to curb this practice, and by the Statute of Westminster, 13 Edward I, c. 32, decreed that in such cases a jury shall try the true right of the persons at issue, and if it be found that the corporation has insufficient right to the land, the land is forfeit to the lord of the fee, and finally to the king, if the lords inferior make no claim to it. This right of entry was given the lords even if the tenants should set up crosses on the lands in question (the badges of the crusading orders) to protect them against the claims of the lords.

545. When the same king in his statute *Quia Emptores*, 18 Edward I, authorized the alienation of land to be held by the purchaser of the same lord of whom the prior owner had held it, he expressly ordained that this should not be conceived as authorizing any kind of alienation in mortmain. When the manner of obtaining the crown's permission for such alienation in mortmain was outlined, it was further provided that no such license should be effectual without the consent of the intermediate lords.[57]

546. The next plan of the corporations was the trust or use, by which the land was conveyed to a definite person to be held by him in title, with the actual use of the property in the corporation, which had a right to all the profits derived from the lands.

547. Then the Statute, 15 Richard II, c. 5, ordered that all such uses should be changed into real titles by license from the crown or be sold to private persons; and that for the future, lands sold in trust would be subject to forfeiture just as if the title

[57] 34 Edward I, st. 3.

had vested in the corporation; and the Statute extended even to cemeteries that had been obtained under this device.

548. When the Protestant revolt came, the Statute, 23 Henry VIII, c. 10, enacted that all future grants of lands to be held for superstitutious uses, v. gr., for Masses and the upkeep of shrines, should be void, even if held by the heirs in trust, if it was to endure for a period of more than twenty years. The Chantries Act, 1 Edward VI, c. 14 (1547), completed the work of discrimination by invalidating all such gifts without restriction. But this act did not make the Mass illegal; that was done by the Acts of Uniformity (1549 and 1559).

549. These statutes extended only to superstitious uses, and not to charitable uses, especially as the Statute, 43 Elizabeth, c. 4, recognized the latter sort of gift. Eventually, however, restraint was imposed on these also. It was enacted by the Statute, 9 George II, c. 36, that no lands or tenements, nor money to be laid out thereon, should be given for or exchanged with any charitable uses, unless by deed indented, executed in the presence of two witnesses twelve calendar months before the death of the donor, and enrolled in the court of chancery within six months after its execution, taking effect immediately and without power of revocation. The colleges of Eton, Winchester, and Westminster were exempt.

550. The Roman Catholic Relief Act (1829) contained provisions aimed at abolishing religious orders, but the courts were liberal in their interpretation of the Act.[58]

[58] In 1871, in Cocks v. Manners, a bequest of personalty and semi-realty was given to the Dominican Sisters and upheld; a similar bequest of personalty to the Sisters of Charity was sustained, but the gift of semi-realty failed as a gift to charity; L. R. 12 Eq. 574.

In the case, *In re* Smith, a gift of a residuary estate in trust for "the society or institution known as the Franciscan Friars of Clevedon in the County of Somerset absolutely" was held to be an absolute, immediate gift to the individual Friars, and not to the religious order; consequently it was sustained; 1 Ch. 937 (1914).

In Bourne v. Keane, where Mass stipends were first sustained as a valid bequest, the residuary estate was given to the Jesuits for Masses. The gift was attacked as being made to a monastic order. It was held by the court that sufficient evidence had not been introduced to indicate the nature of the community's constitutions. The gift was handed over to the individual mem-

551. From this survey of the tradition behind the mortmain statutes, it would seem that they had outlived their purpose. Feudalism is no more. Henry VIII had hastened its end by the Statute of Wills, 32 Henry VIII, c. 1 (1540); 34 and 35 Henry VIII, c. 5 (1542, 1543). It was snuffed out at length by the Statute 12 Charles II, c. 24 (1660), which reduced all services arising out of land to mere rent (free and common socage).

552. Mortmain Restrictions in the United States. It was not the motive of preserving the fees arising out of lands that prompted the statute of George II. His was a direct act of discrimination against charity. As the colonies were still subject to England at the time, it has left its mark on the statutes of several of the States. In Pennsylvania, California, Idaho, and Montana, a gift to charity must be made, if in a will, thirty days before death.[59] In Georgia, the period is ninety days.[60] Ohio requires execution a year prior to death where there survives issue, an adopted child, or the legal representatives of either.[61] Prior to 1917, Delaware required land to be recorded for a year prior to the decedent's death if it was to pass to the grantee.[62]

bers with no trust imposed for the benefit of the community; Appeal Cases, L. R. 815 (1919); *cf. AER,* XX (1899), 167; LXII (1920), 646.

[59] Pennsylvania (§ 8312); California (§ 41); Idaho (§ 14-326); Montana (§ 7015).

[60] § 3851.

[61] § 10504.

[62] *Cf.* § 2174; repealed by the Act of April 19, 1917. In the case, Board of Stewards of the Wilmington Conference of the Methodist Episcopal Church v. Williams (1914), 96 Atl. 791; 6 Boyce 52, it was decided that even under this statute though it provided that all gifts to a church corporation of realty or money to be laid out in real estate shall be by deed, duly executed, delivered and acknowledged and recorded at least one year before the death of the donor, to take effect presently for the use of the corporation and without any power of revocation, a bequest of six thousand dollars to the Board of Stewards, plaintiff, for the Conference Claimants' Fund of the Conference was good, since there was no direction in the will that the bequest be laid out in realty.

New York once had a similar provision for charitable organizations organized under the Laws of 1848, c. 319, § 6. The period established was sixty days. Bequests failed because made within the sixty-day period in the case of Porter v. Carolin (1888), 2 N. Y. Supp. 791; though in the same case similar bequests to

553. Mortmain Statutes in Pennsylvania. The same influence is apparent in the discrimination made by the Pennsylvania statutes, requiring two witnesses to subscribe such bequests, while requiring only attesting witnesses as to all others.[63] But the Supreme Court allows gifts to stand even though made within the thirty-day period, if they are made outright to a person who did not know of the trust until after the testator's death.

This decision seems first to have been made in Schultz's Appeal (1876), where it was held that a gift is not to be held charitable merely from the professional character of the beneficiary. There was nothing in the evidence to show that the beneficiary had been present when the bequests were made, or that he had been consulted, or that he had known anything regarding the wishes of the testator. It would be different if the objects of the bequests had been communicated to him before the testator's death. The person who suggests the name of the beneficiary to the testator is not acting as the agent of the beneficiary; consequently, the beneficiary is not privy to his knowledge. In this case, however, the beneficiary had no control over the organizations to which he was to make distribution.

In Hodnett's Estate (1893), the same conclusion was reached in the case of a pastor. The court said the decision would be different if the bequest were made to a religious society and not to a physical person. It remarked that if the statute is practically repealed by this construction, it becomes the function of the legislature to make whatever change may be necessary.

This was also the decision in Flood v. Ryan (1908). In this case the testator had devised land to a church and to an industrial

corporations organized under the Laws of 1852, c. 250, were held valid. Bequests failed for this reason also in the case of Vanderveer v. McKane (1890), 11 N. Y. Supp. 808. The latter case is cited in *AER,* XX (1899), 170; XIX (1898), 542.

[63] Under Act of April 26, 1855. In 1880 it was decided in the Orphans Court of Philadelphia that a bequest for Masses was a private gift, and consequently did not fall under the requirements attaching to bequests to charity; but the Supreme Court declared such a gift a religious use. This was in Rhymer's Appeal, 93 Pa. 142; cited also in *AER,* XIX (1898), 542. A similar decision of invalidity as to Mass bequests was rendered in the case *In re* O'Donnell's Estate (1904), 209 Pa. 63, 58 Atl. 120.

school in Philadelphia, providing that if he died within thirty days, the devise should be given to Archbishop Ryan. The majority of the court held that the devise was valid, citing the two prior cases as precedents. The dissenting opinion held that a secret trust was proved from the alternatives on the face of the will; that parol proof is competent to show a secret trust; that in O'Donnell's Estate, (cited in the preceding paragraph), the mere fact that the priest did not know of the bequest prior to the death of the testator did not prevent the court from regarding a bequest as made to him in his religious capacity (but this was because the bequest was a charitable bequest on the face of it and not a gift to the priest); that a bequest to Archbishop Kenrick had been declared invalid in the Missouri courts on the basis of parol testimony (on the face of the will the gift was made to him in his private capacity, but a previous will had made the same gift to him in his official capacity and he could not take it as an official under the Missouri constitution as it stood at that time); and finally that in the first case in which this decision was reached in Pennsylvania, the beneficiary had no control over the beneficiaries to whom he was to make distribution.

The same decision was reached in the case *In re* Buckley's Estate (1921). There a codicil left a bequest to the Protestant Episcopal Bishop should the testator die within thirty days. While upholding the bequest, the court was critical, and remarked that twenty-five legislatures had met since Schultz's Appeal without amending the statute. The decision was thought to be dangerous for four reasons: first, it was against public policy; second, the court becomes accessory to the evasion of a statute; third, the named beneficiary is tempted to misappropriation, since the gift is made absolute to him; and fourth, attorneys are tempted to corruption.[64]

The courts here also hold that devises for superstitious purposes are forbidden by the law of the State.[65] But this prohibition does not extend to bequests for Masses.

[64] Schultz's Appeal, 80 Pa. 396; Hodnett's Estate, 154 Pa. 485; Flood v. Ryan, 220 Pa. 450, 69 Atl. 908; *In re* Buckley's Estate, 207 Pa. 101, 113, Atl. 68. For the case, Flood v. Ryan, *cf. AER,* LXII (1920), 651.

[65] Methodist Church v. Remington (1832), 26 Am. Dec. 61, 1 Watts 218; Miller v. Porter (1866), 53 Pa. 292.

554. Restrictions on the amount of property a corporation may hold. The mortmain statutes seem to be evident in the prohibition in Virginia and West Virginia against the incorporation of churches, and in the limitations in other States on the amount of property that religious and charitable institutions may hold.

A devise or a bequest to religion is void in Mississippi, as well as a *devise* to charity.[66] In Arkansas, a church may not hold more than forty acres;[67] in the District of Columbia, no more than one acre;[68] in Kentucky, no more than fifty acres;[69] in Tennessee, no more than five acres;[70] and in Virginia, no more than four acres in a town, or seventy-five acres outside a town; West Virginia has the same allowance for a church in a town but permits only sixty acres to a church outside a town.[71] In Massachusetts, a church may not possess more than one hundred thousand dollars, exclusive of buildings, nor have an income in excess of ten thousand dollars annually.[72] In Pennsylvania, the rental value of its property is limited to fifty thousand dollars annually; in New Hampshire, the annual income may not exceed five thousand dollars.[73] In Louisiana, the value of the property may not exceed one million dollars.[74]

555. In Vermont, by the Act of 1856, any grant to the bishop in his official capacity is void.[75] Maryland has a similar provi-

[66] §§ 3564, 3565.

[67] P. 2223.

[68] Tit. 5, s. 311.

[69] § 319.

[70] S. 4407.

[71] Virginia, Const., § 43; West Virginia, § 3495. The allowance in Virginia was only thirty acres outside a town under the Acts of 1841-1842, c. 102, § 60. The Act of April 26, 1867, permitted land to be acquired for a bishop's residence. The quantity allowed was increased to seventy-five acres by the Act of February 28, 1866. *Cf.* Protestant Episcopal Ed. Society v. Churchman's Reps (1885), 80 Va. 718. Iowa once had a restriction of this kind for it is said in the case, Seda *et al.* v. Huble *et al.* (1888), 75 Ia. 429, 39 N. W. 685, that the Catholic Church is incapable of taking or holding any property whatever.

[72] C. 67, § 46; c. 68, § 9.

[73] Pennsylvania, § 5595; New Hampshire, c. 232, § 10.

[74] General Statutes, § 1266.

[75] *Cf.* Dignan, *op. cit.*, p. 262. Now § 2626. But those who came to hold property in spite of the Act of 1856 are deemed to hold it in trust for the purposes for which it was conveyed.

sion in the Declaration of Rights prefixed to the Constitution, allowing two acres to the church, and requiring (after the fashion of the crown's license) an act of the legislature for the validity of any grant, gift, or devise to a clergyman or a religious corporation.[76] The assent of the legislature is thus required for every such gift, to be sought at the first session of the legislature thereafter. But the assent is granted once for all if the charter of a religious corporation authorizes it to take such gifts, devises, and bequests.[77]

Delaware's provisions are practically the same as Maryland's.[78]

[76] Art. 41, Declaration of Rights (1867): "That every gift, sale, or devise of lands, to any minister, public teacher, or preacher of the gospel, as such; or to any religious sect, order, or denomination; or to, or for the support, use, or benefit of, or in trust for, any minister, public teacher, or preacher of the gospel as such, or any religious sect, order, or denomination; and every gift or sale of goods or chattels to go in succession or to take place after the death of the seller or donor, to or for such support, use, or benefit; and also every devise of goods or chattels to or for the support, use, or benefit of any minister, public teacher, or preacher of the gospel as such; or any religious sect, order, or denomination, without the leave of the legislature, shall be void; except always any sale, gift, lease, or devise, of any quantity of land, not exceeding two acres, for a church, meeting, or other house of worship, and for a burying-ground, which shall be improved, enjoyed, or used only for such purpose; or such sale, gift, lease, or devise, shall be void."

[77] In the case, Newton v. Carberry (1840), Federal Cases 10,189 and 10,190, a devise to go to the aid of a new Catholic church then building in Georgetown was held void under this Declaration; so also a bequest of one hundred dollars to the President of Georgetown University to be distributed equally among the priests of the school for the celebration of Masses. But legacies to clergymen were sustained on the ground that they were made to the priests as private individuals, not to them in their official capacity. And a bequest was held valid that was made to the President and the Council of Mt. St. Mary's College; Mt. St. Mary's College v. Williams (1918), 132 Md. 189, 103 Atl. 479.

Bequests to the following have also been sustained: Georgetown College, St. Vincent's and St. Joseph's Orphan Asylum—Speer v. Colbert, 200 U. S. 143.

[78] The case of Monaghan v. Joyce (1918), 12 Del. Ch. 28, 103 Atl. 582, refers to this statute, § 2181. It is held in this case that the statute in question, providing that no grant, conveyance, devise, or lease of personal or real estate for the "benefit of any person and his successors in any ecclesiastical office" shall vest any estate in such person or his successor, does not apply to a devise of real, personal, or mixed property to a bishop by name or to "his successor the Rt. Rev. Bishop of the W. Diocese to be applied to such charitable pur-

But the courts are liberal in interpreting the statute, and have restricted the prohibition to the office, exempting the individual even though his official capacity be designated.

Louisiana makes the same restrictions but only when the attempt to make the bequest occurs *in articulo mortis*.[79]

The Constitution of Missouri of 1865 contained almost the exact words of the Maryland Declaration. But they were omitted in the Constitution of 1875.[80]

The case of Kenrick v. Cole (1876), 61 Mo. 572, was adjudicated while this disabling provision existed. Certain bequests had been left to Archbishop Kenrick in his capacity of archbishop. This was in a will made before the disabling words of the constitution had been adopted. After their adoption, the disposition was changed so as to appear to be given to him as a private individual. The name of the office was omitted in the second disposition, the residuary being given merely to "Peter Richard Kenrick." The court admitted the proof of the former will by parol evidence, against which the plaintiff protested. It was held that the former will disclosed that the gift was made to the Archbishop in his official capacity, and that consequently it must fail.[81]

Another case adjudicated during this period was In the matter of Leopold Schmucker's Estate v. John H. Reel, Executor, Appellant (1876), 61 Mo. 592. An attempt was made here to evade the disability imposed by the creation of a secret trust for Masses. Two bequests were left to the executor for specific charities and one to be used at his discretion, but it was shown that there was a secret memorandum by which the executor was to be governed, acquittal from the Archbishop being required to discharge him of the obligation. The court held that because the trusts were not fully ex-

pose of the Diocese of W. as he may deem fitting"; and the reason is that the devise is not to any person or successor or successors in office, but to a person by the designation of his ecclesiastical office. Moreover, it is held that a gift to a priest or minister in his public office to be used by him for such public, religious and charitable purposes as he sees fit, is charitable.

79 Art. 1489.

80 Const. 1865, Art. 1, § 13.

81 This case is cited also in *AER*, LXII (1920), 653.

pressed on the face of the will, they were too indefinite to be sustained.

556. Scholion I. Perhaps the earliest example of statutes of this kind is found in Roman law in the rescript attributed to the Emperors Valentinian, Valens, and Gratian, sent to Pope Damasus, in which clerics are forbidden to accept donations or legacies from women, any attempted gifts to be forfeit to the State.[82]

The constitution ascribed to Valentinian, Theodosius, and Arcadius, is even more harsh. It forbids a widow to be admitted to the body of deaconesses until she is sixty years of age. The principal of her estate must be given to her children, while she collects the income to do with it what she likes. But the principal she may not bequeath to any church, cleric, or the poor. Such a legacy will not be sustained even to support the claims of other legatees. But the latter may take their share even though the beneficiaries proscribed are excluded.[83]

557. Scholion II. France has the same disqualifications as Louisiana for the priest who assisted the testator in his last illness, and a priest belonging to a religious congregation labors under the presumption that he has used undue influence, even though he did not assist the testator in his last illness.

As heretofore noted, a testator in France can impose on his heirs or legatees the obligation of having Masses celebrated; and it is legal for him to appoint alternative legatees to provide for the case in which the first would fail to fulfill the trust. In France, also, gifts or legacies can be made to associations recognized as of public service, to professional associations, to mutual aid societies, to au-

[82] *Codex Theod.* 16, 2, 20; *cf.* also the Council of Chalons (813), cc. 6, 7—Harduin, IV, 1033; Mansi, XIV, 95 A. But this enactment did not forbid such legacies and donations if they were made to the Church.

[83] *Codex Theod.*, 16, 2, 27; C. 1, 3, 9; Thomassin, *op. cit.*, III, 1, 18, 5. But this decree was repealed two months later; *Codex Theod.*, 16, 2, 28. The Emperor Marcian was not certain whether the latter constitution had repealed both the former decrees. Consequently for the sake of security, he definitely repealed both, and made it legal for any widow, deaconess, virgin, or holy woman to make bequests to the Church, to clerics, to monks, and to the poor; *Nov. Martiani*, 5, 1, *apud Lex Rom. Visigoth.;* C. 1, 2, 13.

thorized religious Congregations, to public institutions, and to diocesan associations.[84]

558. Scholion III. Rights of corporations under a will. The New York statutes contain a proviso that no corporation can take under a will unless it be expressly authorized to do so in its charter. There are statutes in other States limiting the amount of property, real and personal, that corporations can hold. In some of the jurisdictions, these statutes are regarded as invalidating devises that would give the corporation an excess of property. But the more common doctrine is that the heirs of the testator can not attack the devise. This is conceived to be the prerogative of the State in a direct proceeding.

It was once held that for want of a conscience, a corporation could not take property in trust for another, but now under the opinion of Justice Story, a corporation may hold such property in trust if the purpose of it is not repugnant to, or inconsistent with, the proper purpose of the corporation, as expressed in its charter.[85]

559. Scholion IV. The Code's assertion of ecclesiastical property rights. It is against such provisions as the foregoing that

[84] Cance explains the French situation in Appendix xxxi, of Vol. III, *op. cit.* He also gives a list of legacies that would be invalid under the French law, viz., legacies to (1) unauthorized religious Congregations; (2) to self-constituted works or associations before they are recognized as of public service; (3) to a diocesan association for any object other than the support of divine worship; (4) to a diocesan association for the promotion of religion, the training of the clergy, the decoration of buildings, or the aid of the poor; (5) to the bishop of the diocese or to a pastor, if it is apparent that the gift was made to the moral person; (6) a universal legacy to a religious Congregation of women.

As to legacies given to public institutions: (1) pious or cultural charges are regarded as not written; or if the charitable legacy was the moving cause of the whole, the entire legacy is null; (2) non-cultural charges are also void, if they require the intervention of the clergy; (3) a legacy made on condition that the religious services prescribed be performed by the priests of a certain religious Congregation is valid if approved by the Administration, and such approval is required also for all legacies to authorized religious Congregations and to associations recognized as of public service; (4) it is chimerical to impose a perpetual trust on realty.

[85] Vidal v. Girard's Executors (1844), 43 U. S. (2 How.) 127; Rood, *op. cit.*, 199, 202.

the Code felt constrained to repeat the right of the Church, independent of any secular power, to acquire, possess, and administer the temporalities necessary for her mission, as it has done in Canons 1495, 1499, and 1513, § 1. And this right is vindicated not only for the Church as a juristic person and for the Holy See as a corporation sole, but also for the subordinate ecclesiastical corporations as well.

CHAPTER IX

INDIRECT DISABILITIES IMPOSED ON BENEFICIARIES

560. Besides direct disabilities such as those investigated in the preceding chapter, indirect disabilities sometimes deprive charitable institutions of their bequests. Of the direct disabilities, probably only those that proceed from public policy can be called direct in the strictest sense. While the statute against continuing an estate forever (a perpetuity) operates directly against an unincorporated association as having perpetual existence, it has an indirect bearing on other beneficiaries who are not perpetual in themselves but who may constitute a perpetual series. Thus the statute against perpetuities may indirectly incapacitate beneficiaries under a will.

So, too, uncertainty of beneficiary, while it operates directly on an unincorporated association to deprive it of its legacy, it touches only indirectly those beneficiaries who are really uncertain, and who are not definitely designated in the will. In a similar way, uncertainty in the amount of the bequest, or the real purpose of the testator, or the means of carrying out the intention, operates as an indirect invalidation of the gift. Sometimes, the appointment of a trustee to make these elements definite will save it.

561. The Statute, 43 Elizabeth healed all bequests to charity laboring under these indirect disabilities. Wherever that statute is effective, charitable bequests do not fail if they can be shown to be really charitable and public. If they seem to be private trusts, then they are subject to failure on the grounds just indicated, even where the Statute, 43 Elizabeth, c. 4, or its equivalent prevails.

Where such liberal provisions do not obtain, the charitable trust is in a worse way than a private trust if no trustee is named. For, as to a private trust, it is a principle of equity that no trust shall be permitted to fail for want of a trustee. But as to charitable trusts, it is held that no beneficiary can come into court and ask for the appointment of a trustee, for the beneficiary is usually a work of piety or an indefinite class of persons. Of course, where the liberal provisions obtain, an obvious solution of the problem is reached, and the court *ex officio* appoints a trustee.

Moreover, even under the liberal provisions, the court will not exercise to its full extent the power known as *cy pres,* which is the power of commutation. In other words, it will not hold valid a bequest made merely *to charity.* It will not take upon itself the prerogative of making the will for the deceased. And it will not change the purpose of the testator, even if it be fantastic or impossible of fulfillment, unless it can bring the new purpose fairly within the general intention which he expressed.

Article 1

Uncertainty of Beneficiary at Roman Law

562. **The problem arising out of indefiniteness of person was known under imperial Roman law.** The law prior to the imperial constitutions had regarded legacies invalid when they were bequeathed to uncertain persons or institutions.[1] But the Roman emperors inaugurated plans of distribution that would today be regarded as an exercise of the *cy pres* prerogative far beyond that which the courts in the United States would attempt.

563. To Valentinian and Marcian is attributed the constitution that validated bequests to the poor, though no particular poor person were named.[2] In any event, it was confirmed by Justinian.[3] To Leo (468) is credited the constitution that validated bequests left for the ransoming of captives, by which it was ordained that if merely the sum was left without an administrator, the bishop of the testator's origin, or if his origin be unknown, the bishop of the place where he died, should expend the money for the purpose designated, and inform the civil magistrate of the time at which he undertook the task and the amount to be expended. Then each year he was to render an account to the same civil magistrate of the

[1] I. 2, 20, 25; Gaius, 2, 238; Buckland, *op. cit.*, p. 179; Savigny, *op. cit.*, II, 273.

[2] C. 1, 3, 24; Buckland, *l. c.;* Savigny, *l. c.*

[3] C. 1, 3, 48, 1, 2; *Nov.*, 131, 11, 1, 2.

amount spent and of the number of captives ransomed.[4] This provision was also confirmed by Justinian.[5]

564. Justinian ordained that when our Lord is written Heir or Legatee, the church of the place where the testator lived is to be considered the beneficiary and the amount bequeathed is to be distributed to the poor of that place. In the same constitution, the emperor legislated for bequests to the angels and the saints and prescribed that if there was in the place where the testator died a church under the patronage named, the bequest should be given to that church; that failing, to the church in the metropolitan city under that patronage; that failing, by division to all the churches of the place where the testator died. On the other hand, if there were many churches under the same patronage, the bequest should be given to the one for which the testator had special affection; that failing, to the poorest.[6]

In the Novels, Justinian modified this legislation touching the disposition of legacies to an angel or a saint, prescribing that if there was no church under the proper patronage in the place where the testator died, the bequests should be distributed to the church having that patron in the place where he had a domicile.[7]

565. Where the poor are named indefinitely, Justinian ordained that the bequest was to be given to the hospital of the place for the benefit of the sick poor; and to the more needy hospital, if there were more than one hospital in that place. If there is no hospital there, the bequest was to be distributed by the bishop, or his administrator, without any charge, to the mendicants of the place. And the law gave the bishop an action for the collection of such legacies.[8]

566. The pious foundation under Roman imperial law. It would not be too much to assume that the emperors were legalizing a custom that had grown up without recognition from the law. There seems to be no doubt that the custom of making the bishop the

[4] C. 1, 3, 28.
[5] C. 1, 3, 48, 1, 2; *Nov.*, 131, 11, 1, 2.
[6] C. 1, 2, 25, 1, 2; *Nov.*, 131, 11, 1, 2; Savigny, *l. c.;* Phillips, *op. cit.*, 406.
[7] *Nov.*, 131, 9.
[8] C. 1, 3, 48, 2; *Nov.*, 131, 1, 2.

trustee of property bequeathed to the clergy and to charity precedes by many years the conversion of Constantine. Prior to his reign, too, funds bequeathed indefinitely to charity, to our Lord, or to the poor in general, were regarded by Christians as being the property of the Church for the purposes designated. And Savigny admits this as a consequence of the principle that caring for the poor was an essential part of the bishop's competence.[9]

The emperors probably took the custom as they found it, purposing merely to regulate it. Perhaps they were confronted with a problem that was not known in the earliest days of the Church. In those early times all Christians knew their bishop, for they lived in the same city with him. In the days of the imperial legislation, it is quite possible that Christians inhabiting towns at a distance from the episcopal city would not so readily think of the bishop as trustee. To make the custom uniform in the cities and beyond their confines, no more effective agency could be conceived than the constitutions of the emperors.

567. The existence of a custom to hand would explain why the emperors failed to recognize explicitly the juristic personality of pious causes. The faithful saw them in operation, and further commentary would have been confusing rather than helpful. This sin of omission of the emperors is considered carefully by Savigny, who comes to the conclusion that imperial law, though it seems to ignore the juristic personality of foundations, nevertheless implicitly recognized it.[10] Buckland also admits that perhaps the authorization of

[9] Savigny, *l. c.;* Phillips, *l. c.; Nov.* 131, 11, 1, 2; 131, 7; C. 1, 2, 15; 1, 3, 45.

[10] Savigny, *l. c.;* Sohm-Ledlie, *The Institutes,* p. 198.

Ferrini says that the foundation is not a physical or collective person because it is not made up of distinctive persons gathered into a corporation. The institution itself is not a subject of rights, neither as the representation of the purpose of the foundation nor as the physical apparatus for the accomplishment of that purpose. It follows, he says, that a body of rights can exist without a subject; Ferrini, *Pandette,* 114; Sohm-Ledlie, *l. c.*

Until organized, he continues, the foundations are under the bishop to whom such interests belong as part of his office, with the obligation of collecting the amount bequeathed, constructing the building, and naming the administrators. After this, his task is one of supervision, Ferrini, *op. cit.,* 115; Sohm-Ledlie, *l. c.;* C. 1, 2, 15.

gifts to such bodies was in itself an implicit gift of personality or that a gradual extension was made of the recognition granted to other corporations which were essentially under the bishop. However, he feels that the granting of corporate entity to the local church does not explain the corporate entity of homes independent of the church. He admits that it is almost universally held that these homes were incorporated. But supposing the fund with which they were endowed to be incorporated, who owns it? He answers that according to one view it owns itself, while another maintains that the indefinite number of beneficiaries formed the corporation. He seems finally to incline to the opinion that as to permanent asylums, ownership of the fund is in the residents.[11]

568. Under this view, pious foundations under imperial law would seem to depart but little from the provisions of classical Roman law. The latter did not know the foundation as a patrimony immediately destined for a determined and enduring end, administered by a physical person (that is, it did not know the non-collegiate corporation). Every fund had to be assigned to an individual or to a collective subject in existence, the fund made a part of his fund, and he himself obliged to make distribution. When the public corporations, *i. e.*, the cities, were made the distributors of foundations for the distribution of food, a private individual was made the owner, namely, the emperor, or the administrator of the treasury. But even before the end of pagan times there appeared a tendency towards autonomous foundations and a diminution of the importance of the physical person appointed the heir. The latter was gradually placed in the position of a mere administrator.[12]

569. The difficulty that the Romanists find in determining whether these non-collegiate funds were incorporated is exactly that which a modern court sees in enforcing a bequest to persons who are so indefinite that they can not claim it. And without a claimant, who can enforce the proper administration of the fund? The canons now answer, as custom probably answered the emperors, that the non-collegiate corporation is established by the decree of the

[11] Buckland, *l. c.*, pp. 180, 181; Savigny, *l. c.;* Sohm-Ledlie, *l. c.*

[12] Ferrini, *op. cit.*, 107, 112; Savigny, *op. cit.*, II, 272; Sohm-Ledlie, *op. cit.*, 196.

bishop and that thenceforward it is his ward. The courts have answered almost universally in the United States that the fund, though not incorporated, becomes the ward of the court, to be administered by trustees responsible to it.

570. **The trustee may be a physical person, an unincorporated association, or a corporation.** There are four alternatives possible in the attitude of the States towards the necessity of a trustee. First, a State may simply require any sort of trustee; second, it may require that the trustee be a corporation; third, it may require a trustee, and exclude a voluntary association from acting in this capacity; and fourth, it may require no trustee at all. Considering these attitudes in order, the names of the States adhering to each will be set forth immediately.

571. **The Necessity of a Trustee for Charitable Bequests.** Alabama and the District of Columbia seem to require that the *testator* name a trustee in order that a gift to an indefinite class may be sustained. Louisiana, Wisconsin, and Tennessee almost certainly require the intervention of a trustee.

572. In Maryland, only when an indefinite charitable gift is made to a *corporation* for its charitable work can it be sustained.

573. In Virginia, a trustee must intervene and this trustee must be either a physical person or a corporation, a purely voluntary association being incapable of being a trustee. A charitable trust fails, if such an association is named trustee.

574. Explicit statutes enabling the court to appoint trustees where none have been appointed are found in Kentucky, Michigan, New York, North Carolina, Pennsylvania, and West Virginia. This seems to be the law also under the decisions in the remaining States, except Mississippi, which is a sort of eccentric among the States in that for long it has discouraged all charitable and religious bequests, permitting only bequests of personalty, and not even these for the benefit of religion.

575. When one wishes to make a bequest to religion or charity, it would seem that he can name a trustee as easily as not. He should do this for the sake of caution, naming several who might succeed each other in case the one named should die before the testator.

576. **The *cy pres* doctrine nowhere in the United States per-**

mits departure from the general intent of the testator. But there are two degrees in which the means for fulfilling it can be modified. First, it is possible to substitute different objects of charity under the same general intent; and second, the modification may be restricted to a perfection of the means. Many States will substitute new objects, when the ones named are impractical; others will confine themselves to a perfection of the means.

577. The first sort of modification will be made, it seems, in Pennsylvania and California, which seem to be the two most liberal States in this regard; but also in Maine, New Hampshire, Connecticut, Massachusetts, Rhode Island, Illinois, New Jersey, Iowa, Indiana, Georgia, Arkansas, Missouri, and Florida. The States that restrict themselves to the second method are Alabama, Colorado, Delaware, Ohio, South Carolina, Texas, and Washington. The remaining States will not deviate from the rigid interpretation of the will even to this extent.

578. The justification of these conclusions as to the requirements of a trustee and the application of the *cy pres* doctrine will be found in the subsequent discussions of the present chapter.

Article 2

Charitable Bequests in Virginia, West Virginia, and Maryland

579. Practically all the States have liberal provisions on bequests to charity, as has been indicated in the foregoing survey. Certain States, however, were slow in arriving at them. This was due in Virginia, West Virginia, and Maryland to the repeal of the Statute, 43 Elizabeth, c. 4, and to a mistaken notion of the courts that in so doing the court of chancery had been deprived of all jurisdiction over all charitable bequests.

580. New York was in a similar plight, though its courts seemed more deliberate about the mistake, assuming that the legislators in repealing the Statute of Elizabeth had intended to sweep away all the provisions of the common law touching charitable bequests and to provide a new-world system of bequests to corporations organized under the supervision of the State. Three Western States came under the influence of the New York situation, Michigan, Wisconsin, and Minnesota, with similar results for charitable bequests.

581. The reason for the mistaken notion in the southern States was due to a mistaken view taken by the Supreme Court in the case Baptist Association v. Hart's Executors, with Chief Justice Marshall rendering the opinion.[13] The case was decided in 1819. Of the decision, Mr. Justice Gray, of the Supreme Court also, said in Russell v. Allen,[14] that it was decided upon an imperfect survey of the early English authorities, and upon the theory that the English law of charitable uses, which, it was admitted, would maintain the bequest, had its origin in the Statute of Elizabeth, which had been repealed in Virginia (whence the case had come up to the Supreme Court).

Nevertheless, the points distinctly decided in the case were three: first, that the Baptist Association, not being incorporated at the testator's decease, could not take a trust as a society; second, that the bequest could not be taken by the individuals who composed the society at the death of the testator; third, that there were no persons who could take this legacy, were it not a charity, as definite and certain beneficiaries.

582. But in the famous Girard Will Case, decided by the Supreme Court of the United States in 1844,[15] the case of the Baptist Association v. Hart's Executors was reviewed, and the doctrine there laid down was disapproved and overruled. It was held that charitable uses under the common law do not depend for their existence on the Statute of Elizabeth; but that they antedate that Statute, which was intended merely to regulate them. It was asserted that the court of chancery, independently of the Statute, has an original and inherent jurisdiction to enforce them. The Supreme Court was brought to this decision by a re-examination of the authorities, and more particularly from evidence furnished by the publications of the commissioners on the public records in England. Among these records were found many cases where the court of chancery had entertained jurisdiction over charities long before the Statute of Elizabeth. Some

[13] 4 Wheaton 1.

[14] 107 U. S. 163 (1882).

[15] Vidal v. Girard's Executors, 2 How. 127.

fifty of these cases extracted from the printed calendars were laid before the Supreme Court.

The consequence of this decision was that in the States where they are not forbidden by statute, courts of equity are enabled to exercise an original jurisdiction in equity over charities and to apply to them the rules of equity, together with such other rules, applicable to charitable uses, which are proper under the constitutions and statutes of the respective States. The courts do this in virtue of their inherent powers, without reference to the question whether the Statute of Elizabeth has been adopted in their jurisdiction or not.

583. This doctrine has been followed in the Supreme Court of the United States ever since.[16] In one of the subsequent cases, Ould v. Washington Hospital, Mr. Justice Swayne remarked [17] that "upon reading the Statute [of Elizabeth] carefully, one can not but feel surprised that the doubts thus indicated ever existed. The statute is purely remedial and ancillary. . . . The jurisdiction of the chancellor, and the extent to which it was exercised, before and after the Statute were just the same."

584. History of the Charitable Trust in Virginia. But it was not until 1885 that the courts in Virginia recognized the well established doctrine that corporations may take and hold estates as trustees for purposes not foreign to their creation.[18] Until that time, they had adhered rigorously to the doctrine as laid down by the Supreme Court of the United States in the case of the Baptist Association v. Hart's Executors. The tenacious survival of that doctrine is explained in some measure by the history of the law of charity in Virginia till 1885. Virginia had adopted in 1776 the common law of England and the statutes of a general character. The statutes were repealed in 1792. In the case of Gallego's Executors v. Attorney General (1832),[19] the court said that Virginia was well advised in repealing the Statute of Elizabeth, and that in so doing it had repealed

[16] Perin v. Carey (24 How. 465); Ould v. Washington Hospital, (95 U. S. 303); Russell v. Allen (107 U. S. 163).

[17] 95 U. S. 303, pp. 309, 310.

[18] It was in the case of The Protestant Episcopal Ed. Society v. Churchman's Reps. (1889) 80 Va. 718, 10 S. E. 318.

[19] 24 Am. Dec. 650.

every common law principle reduced to words in that Statute, as if the legislature had deliberately intended to forbid charities of an indefinite character.[20]

It was said that charitable bequests are too vague to be claimed by those for whom the beneficial interest is intended, and could not, independent of the Statute of Elizabeth, be sustained by a court of equity even in England. Since that Statute had been repealed in Virginia, such bequests could not be sustained by a court of equity there. The jurisdiction of the Chancellor in England, it was maintained, is a branch of the prerogative of the crown, and not a part of the ordinary powers of the court of chancery in the exercise of its equitable jurisdiction. Moreover, the act establishing the court of equity in Virginia did not transfer to it that branch of the prerogative. The court added that under our system of government, the legislature, and not the judiciary, is the *parens patriae*.

Commenting on the legislative tendency in Virginia, the court said:

> "No man at all acquainted with the course of legislation in Virginia can doubt for a moment the decided hostility of the legislative power to religious incorporations. . . . Jealousy of the possible interference of religious establishments in matters of government, if they were permitted to accumulate large possessions, as the church has been prone to do elsewhere, is doubtless at the bottom of this feeling. . . . Hence the provision in the bill of rights; hence the solemn protest of the act on the subject of religious freedom; hence the repeal of the act incorporating the Episcopal Church, and of that other act which invested the trustees appointed by religious societies with power to manage their property; . . . hence the tenacity with which applications for permission to take property in a corporate character

[20] In the case in question, a bequest of a pecuniary legacy was made to be distributed among needy and respectable widows; a similar bequest was made to the Roman Catholic congregation in Richmond for the building and support of a chapel; and a third devise of land was made to trustees to permit the Roman Catholics to build a church thereon for the use of themselves and of persons of that religion residing in Richmond. All three testamentary provisions were declared invalid for uncertainty.

(even for the necessary grounds for churches and graveyards) have been refused." [21]

585. The courts consistently followed the doctrine laid down in this decision. But the legislature showed itself continuously more friendly towards trusts for religious uses, and at length came to allow trustees to hold land for the churches; and even, at a later date, to acquire and hold books and furniture for the congregation. Later still, the amount of property that could be held in trust for a church was increased for parishes lying outside towns. Land was also permitted to be acquired for the residence of a bishop. A similar relaxation occurred in the matter of educational trusts, where the change of policy was even more far-reaching.[22]

[21] The decisions in Janney v. Latane (1833), 4 Leigh 327, and in the Literary Fund v. Dawsons (1839), 10 Leigh 147, followed the decision just noted. Numerous decisions of the court of appeals were consistent with it in cases, however, that were not affected by the statutes passed by the legislature in the course of the years. The last of these prior to the case in 1885 was that of Stonestreet v. Doyle (1881), 75 Va. 356.

[22] On April 2, 1839 (Acts 1839, c. 12, p. 11), the legislature passed an act authorizing divises and bequests for the establishment or endowment of unincorporated schools, academies, and colleges, for the education of free white persons, prescribing the manner of enforcing the trusts, but providing that no devise or bequest should be valid if made to any theological seminary. On March 10, 1841 (Acts 1840-1841, c. 26, p. 52, § 6), gifts by will as well as *inter vivos* were authorized to be made to the president and the directors of the literary fund, for the use of any county, or to any city or county directly, and it was decreed that the same might be used and held by the officers named, or by the respective courts in the counties, for the purposes named by the donor but in any event only for literary or educational purposes. On March 28, 1873, colored persons were included within the scope of the first statute just noted.

The attorney for the plaintiff in the case that changed the judicial policy in 1885, after referring to the Acts just noted, summarized the extent of the provisions of the legislature as contained at that time in the Code of 1873, c. 77, §§ 2-6, 10. He said that the statutes legalized every transfer of property, real and personal (except transfers for the use of a theological seminary), made since April 2, 1839, by grant, gift, devise, or bequest, for literary purposes or for the education of persons within the State of Virginia, white or colored, without regard to sex, age, rank, or condition in life; mental, moral, and religious education; and it is declared that the conveyance whether made "to a body corporate or unincorporated, or to a natural person, shall be valid as if made to or for the benefit of a certain natural person." Indeed, the trust is valid even if no trustee

The highest court followed the lead of the statutes, and the bequests, whether strictly charitable or religious, that came before the court were sustained in almost every case that came before it after 1839.[23]

586. After the attorney in the decisive case of 1885 [24] had presented a summary of the doctrine of the State, and of the constant trend towards a more liberal attitude in the legislature and the courts, the court decided that there never had been in the State of Virginia any statute forbidding the courts of equity to exercise jurisdiction over charitable trusts. That power, moreover, belonged to the courts of equity inherently. Consequently, he upheld the bequests as being within the statutes of the State. The bequest was to an incorporated educational society for the education of poor young men for the Episcopal ministry, and therefore not to an unincorporated theological seminary. Thus the general doctrine recognized by the Supreme Court of the United States was established in Virginia.

587. The doctrine was followed in the case of Trustees of General Assembly of the Presbyterian Church in the United States *et al.* v. Guthrie *et al.* (1889),[25] but it was criticized in Fifield *et al.* v. Van

has been appointed, and the court is authorized to appoint one on motion by the Attorney for the Commonwealth. The testator has the right to prescribe what shall be taught and who shall teach. The only gift that is not sustained by these statutes is one to an unincorporated theological seminary.

[23] Brooke v. Shacklett, 13 Gratt. 301; Hoskinson v. Pusey, 32 Gratt. 443; Kelly v. Love, 20 Gratt. 124; Kinniard v. Miller, 25 Gratt. 107; Roy's Executor v. Rowzie, 25 Gratt. 599; Missionary Society v. Calvert's Adm., 32 Gratt. 357. Though two adverse decisions were rendered during that period, the court assigned special reasons for its opinion. The case of Seaburn v. Seaburn (1859), 15 Gratt. 423, held that the devise was not within the statute permitting conveyance of land for the use of a religious congregation. And in the case of Stonestreet v. Doyle (1881), 75 Va. 356, the will was made prior to the Act of 1839.

[24] Protestant Episcopal Ed. Society v. Churchman's Reps. (1889), 80 Va. 718, 10 S. E. 318.

[25] In this case a bequest was made to the Secretary of the Board of Foreign Missions of the Presbyterian Church in the United States. The testator had been for many years a member of the Presbyterian Church, which was a part of the corporation known as the Trustees of the General Assembly of the Presbyterian Church in the United States, which had power to acquire property for any branch committees which it should create. It had created "The Executive

Wyck's Executor *et al.* (1897). The court said that there was much in the reasoning in the Churchman case which might seem to support the claim to the bequest before the court. But there was no necessity for that reasoning, so far as the Churchman case was concerned. It made no difference in that case what was the jurisdiction of a court of chancery at common law or under the Statute of Elizabeth. The court now said it was unwilling to hold that a line of decisions running back over fifty years or more was overturned by expressions of opinion in the Churchman and Guthrie cases, when those expressions were not necessary to the issue. They were not necessary because in those cases the bequest was made to a definite corporation in trust for purposes within its corporate powers, the beneficiaries and purposes both being certain.[26]

588. In 1930, in Fitzgerald *et al.* v. Doggett's Executor, it was explained that the whole history of the Virginia cases establishes the fact that the law in Virginia, independent of statute, is that an indefinite charity, educational, religious, or otherwise, made to an individual or to an unincorporated body, is invalid on the ground of indefiniteness and uncertainty, but that an indefinite charitable bequest or devise to an incorporated body having the same corporate powers or functions as the general object of the testator's bequest is

Board of Foreign Missions," commonly known as the Board of Foreign Missions, and its executive officer was known to the rank and file as "secretary." The court held that the incorporation of the General Assembly was not the incorporation of a church so as to render the bequest void. Nor is it void as being a bequest to an indefinite charity for religious purposes; 86 Va. 125, 10 S. E. 318.

[26] In this case, the residuary bequest was given to two clergymen, or the survivor of them or to whomsoever they might select in case of their death, in trust for the New Jerusalem Church. There was a voluntary association known by the name of the New Jerusalem Church and also a corporation called "The General Convention of the New Jerusalem in the United States." The trustees appointed by the testatrix were members of the executive committee of the latter, and the testatrix was acquainted with them had made gifts to them. And it could not be shown that she knew anything of the voluntary association. Nevertheless, the court held that the voluntary association was meant, and that the bequest was invalid because the beneficiaries were uncertain, the purpose undefined, and the discretion of the trustees practically without limit; 94 Va. 557; 27 S. E. 446.

valid. Such was the law when in 1914 the assembly modified the statute touching these bequests.[27] This modification made future *charitable* bequests valid when made to a corporation, an unincorporated body, or a natural person. Yet the courts held in this case that a voluntary association can not be trustee. The Conference Board of Finance of the Methodist Episcopal Church South, an unincorporated association elected by unincorporated members, was held incompetent to receive bequests for superannuated members. But the bequest was saved in virtue of §§ 589, 590, by which the Attorney for the Commonwealth is obliged to have such a will recorded and, where no trustee has been appointed, or where the appointed trustee dies or refuses to act, to make proper motion to the court for the appointment of a trustee.[28]

589. **In conclusion, the law in Virginia must still be regarded as uncertain.** The courts have been loath to depart from the traditional erroneous interpretation. Even the fairly liberal interpretation of the last case may be evaded in some future case. The legislature progressed more rapidly than the courts, which seem constantly to find deficiencies in the statute to enable them to adhere to the old doctrine. A charitable bequest in Virginia is safe only when the bequest

[27] This act is § 587 of the Code of 1924 (Acts 1914, c. 234). It reads: "Every gift, grant, devise, or bequest which, since the second day of April, in the year one thousand eight hundred and thirty-nine, has been, or at any time hereafter shall be, made for literary purposes, or for the education of white persons within this state, and every gift, grant, devise, or bequest, which, since the tenth of April, in the year one thousand eight hundred and sixty-five has been, or at any time hereafter shall be, made for literary purposes, or for the education of colored persons within this state, *and every gift, grant, devise, or bequest hereafter made for charitable purposes, whether in any case to a body corporate or unincorporated, or to a natural person,* shall be as valid as if made to or for the benefit of a certain natural person, except such devises or bequests, if any, as have failed or become void by virtue of the seventh section of the act of the General Assembly passed on the said second of April, eighteen hundred and thirty-nine, entitled, 'An Act concerning devises made to schools, academies, and colleges.' Nothing in this section shall be so construed as to give validity to any devise to or for the use of an unincorporated theological seminary." The *italics* show the amendment.

[28] 155 Va. 112; 155 S. E. 129.

is made to an incorporated body for the purpose for which it was incorporated.[29]

590. The courts of West Virginia followed the precedent of the Virginia courts, and adhered to the doctrine of the Gallego case.[30] But the statutes of Chapter 57 of the Code of 1906 remedied the evil, and in the case, Hays *et al.* v. Harris *et al.* (1913),[31] these statutes were regarded as a restoration of charitable trusts to the extent of the Statute of Elizabeth. And this seems now to be the ruling doctrine.[32]

[29] The citations from the statutes noted in this discussion have been taken from the cases, with the exception of the citations from the Code of 1924, which have been checked.

[30] Carpenter v. Miller (1869), 3. W. Va. 174; 100 Am. Dec. 744; Weaver v. Spurr (1904), 56 W. Va. 95, 48 S. E. 852; Bible Society v. Pendleton, Trustee (1873), 7 W. Va. 79; Carskadon *et al.* v. Torreyson *et al.* (1880), 17 W. Va. 43; Brown v. Caldwell (1883), 23 W. Va. 187; 48 Am. Rep. 376; Wilson v. Perry (1886), 29 W. Va. 169; 1 S. E. 302; Pack v. Shanklin (1897), 43 W. Va. 304; 27 S. E. 389. In Wilson v. Perry, a bequest was made to an incorporated Presbyterian Publication Committee and was valid; but other bequests were invalid in the same will, viz., five hundred dollars to enclose Mt. Pleasant Church; four thousand dollars for a parsonage, etc. In Pack v. Shanklin, the residuary estate was to be given equally to the trustees for the home missions, the foreign missions (of the Southern Presbyterian Church), and the American Bible Society. These bequests were all declared invalid because of the uncertainty of the beneficiary.

In Weaver *et al.* v. Spurr *et al.* it was declared that in the creation of a trust by will or by deed, the beneficiary must be definite, certain, ascertainable persons, natural or corporate; otherwise the trust must fail.

[31] 73 W. Va. 17; 80 S. E. 827.

[32] *Cf.* Mercantile Banking and Trust Company v. Showacre *et al.* (1926), 102 W. Va. 260, 135 S. E. 9. In this case it was said that the essential element of a charitable or benevolent trust is certainty in its object and certainty as to the class of persons to be benefited, but indefiniteness as to the individuals to be benefited. Generally, the rule against perpetuities has no application to these gifts. Hence a gift or a bequest of the proceeds of land to a trustee to support an annual course of lectures under the direction of a designated board of education creates a benevolent or charitable trust not void for uncertainty or indefiniteness as to beneficiaries. Gallaher v. Gallaher (1929), 146 S. E. 623. In this case a bequest for scholarships for young men of poor parents, with provision for preference to descendants of testator's relatives, was held a valid

591. The conclusion as to West Virginia is that the statutes have brought the decisions in that State into harmony with the doctrine maintained in the majority of States to the full extent of the implications of the Statute of Elizabeth.[33]

592. In Maryland, the courts adopted the wrong doctrine as enunciated in the case of the Baptist Association v. Hart's Executors. This was the basis of the decision rendered in 1822 in the case of Dashiell v. Attorney General,[34] and the courts have never repudiated it, although considerable modification has taken place. As late as 1881, in the case of the Church Extension of the Methodist Episcopal Church v. Smith,[35] the Court of Appeals declared its adherence to the original doctrine and said that according to the uniform course of its decisions, a trust can not be sustained unless it be of such a nature that the beneficiary is definite and capable of enforcing its execution by proceedings in a court of chancery. That case related to a bequest of ten thousand dollars to the Church Extension Society of

charitable trust, not invalidated (as a private trust) because of the preference expressed for relatives.

The statutes providing for religious trusts are found in the Code of 1932 at §§ 3492-3495, where it is ordained that a devise and conveyance is valid even when the beneficiaries are uncertain provided there are trustees of the church or when the church can appoint trustees, or even when the object of the will is so uncertain as not to permit of enforcement, so that choice must be made by the trustees. As to charitable and benevolent trusts, the provisions are found in the Code of 1932 at §§ 3501-3504. The substance of these provisions is that any unincorporated benevolent association to which or for the use of which any property, real or personal, is conveyed, dedicated, transferred, given, or bequeathed, may appoint and remove and fill all vacancies of trustees (§ 3503); and any person interested may sue in chancery for the appointment of a trustee, for the designation of beneficiaries, and where the object is so uncertain as to be unenforceable, actual *cy pres* may be employed to give effect to the bequest (§ 3502).

[33] The reference to the Code of 1906 is taken from the case Hays *et al.* v. Harris *et al.* The references to the Code of 1932 have been checked.

[34] 5 Har & J (Md.) 392, 9 Am. Dec. 572; and 6 Har & J (Md.) 1.

[35] 56 Md. 362. See Newton v. Carberry (1840), where an orphan asylum authorized to take by devise lost its gift because the presumption of the acceptance of the charter was rebutted by evidence showing that no proceedings were ever held under it, though seven years had elapsed; Federal Cases, 10, 189; 10, 190.

the Methodist Episcopal Church, a Pennsylvania corporation, to be used as a part of the perpetual loan fund of the Society. It was shown that the corporation was capable under its charter of taking such a bequest for its general purpose. It maintained a loan fund to be lent to necessitous churches of the denomination within the United States.

But the court held that since the legacy was not given to the corporation for its own use, but only to be held as part of the loan fund, the corporation was constituted a trustee, charged with the duty of employing the fund only for the benefit of such churches, and these were the real beneficiaries. The trust was decided to be so indefinite that it could not be enforced. Similarly, in the same case, a bequest of one thousand dollars to the trustees of the Strawbridge Episcopal Church, for the benefit of the Ladies' Mite Society of the church, was declared invalid.

593. This case, however, is not now regarded to be an authoritative statement of the Maryland rule. In later decisions, testamentary gifts of a significance similar to that of the bequest to the loan fund have been sustained; [36] and it seems that if the rule in the later cases had obtained when the case of the Church Extension Society was tried, a different decision would probably have been rendered.

594. The departure from the earlier rule seems first to have been

[36] *Cf.* Eutaw Place Baptist Church v. Shively (1887), 67 Md. 493, 10 Atl. 244; where a bequest was held valid when it was a sum of money to an incorporated church to be applied to its Sunday School. Erhardt v. Monthly Meeting of Friends (1901), 93 Md. 669, 49 Atl. 561, where a bequest was sustained when it was given to a church corporation for the benefit of a school conducted under its auspices. Women's Foreign Missionary Society v. Mitchell (1901), 93 Md. 199, 48 Atl. 737, where a bequest was upheld when it was given to the named Society (the plaintiff) of the Methodist Episcopal Church, a corporation, in trust, to educate Bible readers in India. Baltzell v. Church Home (1909), 110 Md. 244, 73 Atl. 151, where a bequest was valid when it was given to the Church Home and Infirmary, a corporation, the money to be kept as a separate fund, the income to be used in maintaining infirm persons and free beds in the infirmary.

Board of Foreign Missions v. Shoemaker (1919), 133 Md. 594, 105 Atl. 748, where a bequest was valid when it was given to a church council, the unincorporated governing body of an incorporated church, to be put at interest, the interest to be paid annually to the Board of Foreign Missions, a corporation which conducted the foreign mission work of the religious denomination.

suggested in the opinion rendered in the case of Barnum v. Baltimore (1884).[37] In this case, the court had before it a devise of the residue of the Barnum Estate to the City of Baltimore, in trust for the McDonogh Educational Fund and Institute, to be so applied as to give boys in that institute such useful mechanical education as would enable them to gain a livelihood. The City was already possessed of a fund by that name, which it had acquired under the will of John McDonogh. The legislature had authorized the City by an amendment to the City Charter in 1842 to receive property that might be given it by will or by deed in trust for any general corporation purpose; in aid of the indigent or poor; or for educational or charitable purposes of any kind. It was objected in the present case that the Board of Trustees of the McDonogh Fund was not an incorporated body, but merely an agency of the City, established by City ordinance. The court held, however, that this did not constitute an insuperable difficulty to the maintaining of the validity of the trust.[38] The court was probably moved to this decision by the Act of 1842, already noted, which was, in a measure, a legislative recognition of charitable trusts, so far as the City was concerned.[39] This recognition was ex-

[37] 62 Md. 275; 50 Am. Dec. 219.

[38] The court said: "The municipal corporation, taking the fund in trust, takes it for the benefit of its citizens or the public, to be applied according to the terms of the trust. It is therefore, in a certain sense, *cestui que trust*, as well as trustee. The property acquired by it, though in trust, is for a public use; and the corporation is liable for the execution of the trust by and through the agencies it may create for the purpose. It is not the agencies of the municipal corporation so much to which we must look for the execution of the trust, as to the corporation itself. Therefore, if the present bequest instead of being to the City in trust for an educational purpose, had been to the City in trust to establish or maintain a house of correction, a hospital or a pesthouse, there can be no doubt of the validity of such trust, and that the objects would be sufficiently defined, notwithstanding the trustees or managers of such institutions, appointed by the City, had never been incorporated by law. And that being so, there can be no substantial reason assigned why the present bequest is not equally good."

[39] This Act was extended to include the integral portions of the work of other corporations in the cases subsequent. In Eutaw Place Baptist Church v. Shively, the court said: "The Sunday school, as such, is not an incorporated body, it is true; but it is shown to be an integral part of the church organization, and therefore embraced within the . . . corporate functions and work of the

tended subsequently to include bequests to other corporations also for purposes that might be construed as an integral part of their work.

Moreover, the legislature in 1888 had provided that no devise or bequest for charitable uses shall be held void for uncertainty with respect to the donees, if the will making the gift shall direct the formation of a corporation to take the gift and the corporation is formed within the next succeeding twelve months.[40]

595. The Peculiar Doctrine of Trusts in Maryland. But in spite of the firmly entrenched position of this doctrine, in the case of Art Students' League of New York v. Hinkley *et al.* (1929),[41] it was contended by the defendants that there was a clear intention to create a trust. This argument was used in an attempt to override the rule adopted in previous cases, where the court had indicated that if there were an evident and manifest intention to create a trust, the bequest would be invalid, even if the gift were to a corporation for purposes within the scope of the corporation powers.[42]

Two reasons were assigned to show that there was here an explicit attempt to create a trust: viz., first, the residue of the estate was expressly devised and bequeathed in trust to constitute a fund named in memory of the testator's father; and second, the net income was to be applied by the trustee to aid deserving students, and the trustee was to invest and re-invest the fund and to retain the investments made by the testator during his life without liability for shrinkage and without the obligation of giving bond or other security.

church." Finally, in the case of Baltzell v. Church Home, it was declared that to apply the doctrine of Dashiell v. Attorney General, "there must be a trust which is uncertain as to beneficiaries, or which creates a perpetuity, in order to justify the court in striking down a devise or bequest, unless, of course, there be other reason for doing so." But where the bequest or devise is left to a corporation for work within the proper scope of the corporation purposes it is not so bequeathed to uncertain beneficiaries, nor is it in conflict with the rule against perpetuities, unless it be expressly stated that a trust is being created.

[40] Acts 1888, c. 249—Bagby's Code, 1924, Art. 93, § 337.

[41] 31 Fed. (2nd) 469; Zollman, *Charities*, 42-44.

[42] Baltzell v. Church Home (1909), 110 Md. 244, 73 Atl. 151; Snowden v. Crown Cork and Seal Co. (1911), 114 Md. 650-5-6, 80 Atl. 510; Gray v. Orphans' Home (1916), 128 Md. 592 (601-2), 98 Atl. 202; Conner v. Trinity Reformed Church (1916), 129 Md. 360 (363), 99 Atl. 547.

The argument would have been regarded as valid by a Maryland court if the gift had not been made to a corporation for corporation purposes, but to a natural person instead. But in no case in which a devise or a bequest to a corporation had come before the court since 1842 had this sort of reasoning been sustained. It is obvious that with the change in the doctrine of the court, there came also a change in the definition of the word *trust* when it relates to a charitable use or purpose within the scope of the functions of a corporation-trustee. Rather the change of doctrine probably brought about a *re-definition* of the word *trust*.[43] Indeed, the exceptional character of a devise to a corporation is evident from a contrast with a gift for similar purposes in trust to individual trustees.[44] Such trusts are invalid even when the annual income is to be paid to corporate bodies for corporate purposes.

Yet gifts directly to corporate bodies for corporate purposes have several qualities that mark charitable gifts to individual trustees: viz., first, they are made to a corporation indeed, but for the use of others; second, they contemplate a perpetual existence of the fund,

[43] In the Baltzell case the court said, "When a testator designates the use of property left by him to a [religious] corporation . . . and those uses are just such as the corporation would make of it in carrying out the objects and purposes of its incorporation, it is like making a person a trustee for himself. It would be equivalent to saying the corporation took the property in trust for such purposes as its charter authorized. That may be true in the sense indicated above, as all corporations hold their property in trust to use it as its [their] charter and the law requires, but that is not the kind of trust which the applicants would have to establish the existence of in order to sustain their contention." This was cited with approval in the case of Lydzewski v. Grace Church (1924), 145 Md. 531 (536), 125 Atl. 717. In the case Novak v. Orphan's Home (1914), 123 Md. 161, 90 Atl. 997, the court declared a devise of real property to a benevolent corporation in trust for a purpose within the corporate functions to be invalid, but the reason for the declaration was that the trust was coupled with a condition that the property should not be sold (thus offending against the statute against perpetuities). Even in this case the court clearly indicated that the validity of the trust otherwise would depend on whether it were established for corporate purposes.

[44] For instance, in the case of Missionary Society v. Humphries (1900), 91 Md. 131, 46 Atl. 320, a devise of realty to an individual trustee to collect the income and pay it annually to a number of incorporated bodies for charitable purposes was invalid.

that is, they offend against the statute against perpetuities (but there must be no prohibition against the sale of the property); and third, the beneficiaries, although described as belonging to a certain class, are indefinite and unascertainable individuals. The court aptly remarked in the case, Halsey v. Convention of the P. E. Church (1892):[45]

> The Statute of 43 Elizabeth in regard to charities is not, it is true, in force here, but it is well settled that the court of Chancery has jurisdiction, independent altogether of the Statute, to enforce a trust for charitable and religious purposes, provided the devise or bequest be made to a person or body corporate capable of taking and holding the property so devised and bequeathed, and provided, further, the object and character of the trust be definite and certain. When these exist—when the gift is made to one capable of taking it, and when the trust is declared in definite terms—a court of Chancery has the same power to enforce such a trust for a charitable or religious purpose, as it has to enforce a trust for any other purpose.[46]

Consequently, the mere appointment of a corporation to hold property in trust for a purpose within the scope of the corporate powers is a potent circumstance to show that no trust, as that term is construed in the courts of Maryland, has been created. The court, in all the cases where such trusts have been sustained, has not indicated in what manner it would be possible for the testator or the donor to give evidence of an intent to create a trust in connection with the kind of endowment under discussion here.

But it seems that it is impossible to create a *trust* when an endowment is given to a corporation for corporate purposes; that is, the court would not permit such a gift to be called a trust in any event. A somewhat similar attitude was taken by the Court of Appeals of New York, as will be indicated in its proper place, during the period prior to 1893, at the time when charitable trusts were not recognized in that jurisdiction.[47]

[45] 75 Md. 275; 23 Atl. 781 (at p. 782).

[46] *Cf.* also Art. 16, § 114 of Bagby's Code, 1924.

[47] In this case of the Art Students' League, a will had been executed in New Jersey in the exercise of a power of testamentary disposition of a trust created

596. The conclusion to be reached as to the state of the law in Maryland is very similar to that in Virginia. Where the body of persons to be benefited is indefinite as to individuals and the trust is to be perpetual, the only safe course is to make the trustee a corporation empowered by its charter to carry on works of charity such as that for which the trust is created.[48]

597. In the earlier days, the District of Columbia was governed by the Maryland rule.[49] But in a case in 1922,[50] it was noticed that according to the District Code, gifts to charitable uses do not come within the purview of laws against perpetuities,[51] and answer was given to the argument made against the trust that if the home, beneficiary under the will, should refuse to select deserving applicants, there is no power in chancery to deal with the matter. The court said that when the founder of a charitable use describes the general nature of the trust, he may leave the details to be adminis-

by the father of the testator in Maryland. The will made a bequest to the League in New York. The League claimed that the New York rule should govern, and that the bequest is valid. The court said that the Charitable Uses Act of 1893 in New York would make the bequest valid, but even under the Maryland law, it should be regarded as valid. The court said that there was no essential distinction between this case and those in which the Maryland courts had sustained similar gifts. It is clear, the court said, that the Art Students' League is both trustee and *cestui que trust* (that is, the corporation for whose benefit the trust was created).

[48] For a late case see Home for the Incurables of Baltimore City v. Bruff (1931), 153 Atl. 403. The citation as to the statute of 1842 is taken from the case, the Art Students' League.

[49] Barnes v. Barnes (1827), 3 Cranch C. C. 269, Fed. Cas. No. 1,014; Coltman v. Moore (1873), 1 MacArthur (8 App. D. C.) 197. In the latter case, the bequest was to a municipal corporation to establish a house of refuge for destitute females. The court said that there was no means to ascertain where the house was to be built or what district was to be benefited. The purpose was regarded as too vague to be enforced even if the court had jurisdiction, which it was rather reluctantly willing to admit in view of the decision in the Girard Will case. In the case of Dinwiddie v. Metzger, 45 App. D. C. 310, it was conceded by the parties that the charitable trust which the will attempted to create could not be carried into effect.

[50] Washington Loan and Trust Company *et al.* v. Hammond *et al.* 278 Fed. 569, 51 App. D. C. 260.

[51] Then § 1023, now tit. 25, § 112.

tered by the trustees under the superintendence of a court of chancery; and if a trustee refuses to perform his duty, the court of chancery may remove him and substitute another in his place.[52]

598. In conclusion as to the law in the District of Columbia, the obvious observation is that the holding of the court supports the liberal view. The only doubt remaining concerns a gift made in trust without the appointment of a trustee. It would seem, however, that since the court of chancery is conceived to have power to remove a trustee and substitute another, it should feel itself competent to appoint one, where one has not been named in the first instance. Safe practice, however, might indicate that the bequest should be made, as far as possible, to a corporate body for corporate purposes.

Article 3

The New York Doctrine

599. As was indicated the New York error influenced the attitude of Wisconsin, Minnesota, and Michigan on the subject of charitable bequests. This article will consider both the origin of the error and its effect in the Midwest.

600. In New York, the courts began properly to follow the precedent of the Supreme Court of the United States in the Girard Will case. For, though in 1788 the Statute of Elizabeth had been repealed, the court held in 1844 [53] that charitable bequests were bestowed in England and were recognized by law even prior to the Norman Conquest, and that they were subject to the court of chancery long before the Statute of Elizabeth. This was true, the court remarked, whether the gift was made to a corporation or to individuals, whether it was made to trustees by name, or for a definite and specific object without the naming of trustees. Moreover, the court held that the Revised Statutes providing against perpetuities and regulating uses and trusts were aimed at private trusts and accumulations

[52] This was the opinion of the court also in Russell v. Allen (1882), 107 U. S. 167, 2 Sup. Ct. 330; Cavender v. Cavender (1885), 114 U. S. 464, 5 Sup. Ct. 955; May v. May (1897), 167 U. S. 310, 17 Sup. Ct. 824. But the doctrine of *cy pres* is not operative here; Graff v. Wallace (1929), 32 Fed. (2nd) 960.

[53] Shotwell Exec. v. Mott. *et al.*, 3 Sandford 50; Zollman, *op. cit.*, 46-57.

for remote posterity, and not at public trusts and charitable trusts, which were not within the intention of the legislature or the spirit and object of the enactment; just as the English Statute of Uses, 27, Henry VIII, did not apply to public uses or charities.[54] The case of Williams v. Williams (1853) [55] followed this precedent.[56]

601. Then the struggle between the advocates of a liberal policy towards charities and its opponents began to manifest itself in the courts.[57] The precedent was challenged in Levy v. Levy (1865),[58] where the court said that the peculiar system of charitable jurisprudence in England proceeded in disregard of rules deemed elementary and fundamental by sustaining indefinite charitable gifts through the exercise of chancery powers and of the royal prerogative. The court argued, contrary to the decision in the Girard Will case, which it must have had before it, that the chancery court in England in sustaining these bequests was exercising not its ordinary jurisdiction over trusts, but a jurisdiction extended and strengthened by the prerogative of the crown and the Statute of Elizabeth. The court argued further that along with the Statute of Elizabeth, the statute against superstitious uses and the mortmain acts were repealed in New York. At the time of the repeal, it was maintained, it was supposed that the law for the enforcement of charitable trusts had

[54] Consequently, the bequest involved in the case, which was for the benefit of the poor ministers of a specific denomination, was sustained, though trustees of the fund had not been appointed. The court regarded the testator as competent to empower the executors and the trustees of his will to designate the first trustees of such a fund. If it were otherwise, the trust would be sustained nevertheless, and the court of chancery would appoint the trustees. Another bequest in the same will was also valid, made for the relief of such indigent residents of the town of Flushing as the trustee or trustees of the town for the time being should select.

[55] 8 N. Y. 524.

[56] The Court regarded as valid a bequest of six thousand dollars to a group of individual trustees with power to perpetuate their successors, as a perpetual fund for the education of children of the poor who should be educated in the academy in the village of Huntington, with directions that the fund should be accumulated up to a certain point and that afterwards the income should be distributed for the education of children the names of whose parents were not upon the tax list.

[57] Owens v. Missionary Society (1856), 14 N. Y. 380.

[58] 33 N. Y. 97.

its origin in the Statute of Elizabeth only, and that the legislature in sweeping away all the great and distinctive landmarks of the English system, *must* [59] have intended that the effect of the repeal should be to abrogate the entire system of indefinite trusts, which were understood to be supported by that Statute alone. The whole course of legislation indicates, the court assumed, a policy to prevent any system of public charities except through the medium of corporate bodies.

In 1784 the general law for the incorporation of religious societies had been enacted; and prior to and contemporaneous with the repeal of the Statute of Elizabeth and the mortmain acts, specific acts incorporating such societies were passed creating or authorizing corporations for various religious and charitable purposes, in all of which are to be found limitations upon the amount of property which the societies may hold. The court believed that these acts, with their limitations upon the holding of property, indicated a policy to confine within certain limits the accumulation of property perpetually appropriated even to charitable and religious objects. Granted such a policy, the repeal of the Statute of Elizabeth and of the mortmain acts was an inconsistent act, the court maintained, unless it was intended to abrogate the whole law of charitable uses as understood and enforced in England.

In other words, it was argued that a new charitable system had been set up in New York in the form of charters, enabling corporations by legislative enactment to receive, possess and administer charitable gifts of every kind. The statute of uses and trusts, defining what trusts may be created, the court regarded as binding even where charitable trusts were concerned; but it ceased to operate in particular cases as often as the legislature chartered a corporation for a charitable purpose, with power to take and hold property in perpetuity for such purpose.

602. **The discussion continued** in the cases of Bascom v. Albertson [60] and Burrill v. Boardman.[61]

59 Italics are inserted. Can the court be suspected of naïve *ex parte* reasoning?

60 1856, 34 N. Y. 584.

61 1871, 43 N. Y. 254. Prior to the Act of the legislature in 1893, this was

603. In Holmes v. Mead (1873),[62] **it was finally decided that the system of charitable uses, as recognized in England prior to the Revolution, did not exist in New York,** and that such uses are not exempt from the provisions of the statute abolishing all uses and trusts except such as are authorized by that statute.

Efforts in the interest of upholding important charitable bequests were made thereafter to persuade the courts to reopen the subject to a limited extent, without any better result than an approval of the doctrine laid down in Holmes v. Mead, as in Holland v. Alcock (1898),[63] where the court pointed out that charity, as a great interest of civilization and Christianity, had suffered no loss or diminution in the changed plan which had been adopted in New York. The law has been simplified, and that is all. If the will commanded the creation of a corporation to administer the fund, the fund was sustained.

But from the contemplation of the law were excluded original charities, that is, charities by which the testator wished to found an institution to carry on some good work that would bear his name and be a monument to his memory; or by which he sought to benefit a class of unfortunate persons in his own community in whom he had been interested.[64]

604. The legislature in 1893 had its attention sharply drawn to the matter by the decision in Tilden v. Green, the effect of which was to deprive the public of a great charity in which Samuel J. Tilden sought to employ the bulk of his fortune, aggregating millions. His will directed that a corporation be formed, or the amount distributed in charity according to the discretion of the trustee. It

the last case where an attempt to create an original charity survived the test of the courts. In this case the will of James H. Roosevelt was before the court. The court declined to decide the question whether the peculiar system of charitable uses as it existed in England ever had a foothold in New York. But it decided that the trust was valid, and made Roosevelt Hospital a possibility.

[62] 52 N. Y. 332.

[63] 108 N. Y. 312; 16 N. E. 303; *cf.* Dillon, *Bequests for Masses,* p. 49.

Such attempts failed in Prichard v. Thompson (1884), 95 N. Y. 76; Coltman v. Grace (1889), 112 N. Y. 299, 19 N. E. 839; Read v. Williams (1891), 125 N. Y. 560, 26 N. E. 30; Fosdick v. Town of Hempstead (1891), 125 N. Y. 581, 26 N. E. 801; Tilden v. Green (1891), 130 N. Y. 29, 28 N. E. 880; Booth v. Church (1891), 126 N. Y. 215, 28 N. E. 238.

was the power of choice vested in the trustee that defeated the gift.

Consequently, the legislature passed an act providing that a devise to charitable uses "which shall in other respects be valid under the laws of this State, shall not be invalid by reason of the indefiniteness of the persons designated as beneficiaries; and that, if a trustee be named in such instrument, title shall vest in him, and, if none be named, title shall vest in the Supreme Court, which shall have control over all such devises." [65]

605. In the case, Allen v. Stevens (1899),[66] the court held that this statute aims at restoring the law of charitable trusts as declared in the case of Williams v. Williams, and that it not only protects devises to charity when the beneficiaries are uncertain, but also relieves them of the restrictions under the statute against perpetuities.[67] Under the statute as it now stands, as was said by the court in the case, *In re* McDowell's Will (1916),[68] charitable trusts are certainly relieved of the restrictions under the statutes against perpetuities, and the law of charitable trusts is restored to that which was recognized in England prior to the Revolution. And where the trust fund is inadequate, a change in the scheme of the charity is warranted. The Supreme Court in such a case will apply the trust fund to other charities as nearly as possible like that specifically mentioned in the will.

606. But it has been held also that the mere intention to advance the public welfare is not sufficient to give validity to a trust in perpetuity for the benefit of indefinite and unascertained persons, unless such a trust is authorized under the statute. Thus a devise was invalid where it was made to a trustee to be paid to one or more incorporated institutions for research in agricultural chemistry.[69] And a gift for a charitable and religious purpose can not be sustained

[65] Laws of 1893, c. 701; now § 12 of the Personal Property Law and § 113 of the Real Property Law.

[66] 161 N. Y. 122, 55 N. E. 568.

[67] Hence the court held that the bequest in the case, made for the creation of a home for the aged, could be upheld without directing the formation of a corporation to administer the trust.

[68] 217 N. Y. 454, 112 N. E. 177.

[69] *In re* Frasch's Will (1927), 245 N. Y. 174, 156 N. E. 656.

if it is so indefinite as to include purposes not charitable or religious (that is, purposes that are personal, private, or selfish). Its benevolent purpose will not save it. But the court will give effect to the intention to make a gift for a charitable or religious purpose, if it is at all possible, even though an alternative significance in favor of a secular purpose might be discovered. In the case where these principles were laid down, a bequest was held valid when it was made merely for the advancement of Christ's Kingdom on earth.[70]

607. In conclusion, it may be said that the situation in New York is now as liberal as it was in England under the Statute of Elizabeth.

608. Michigan repealed the Statute of Elizabeth in 1810 and the court in the case, Methodist Church v. Clark (1879),[71] held that there is no evidence that any pre-existing law on the subject was ever recognized in Michigan. It went on to show that even if the bequest in the case were regarded as a public trust, that is, a trust free from the operation of the statutes against perpetuities, the court would have no jurisdiction over it. As a consequence of this attitude, charitable bequests failed in many more cases that followed this.[72]

609. In 1907, however, the legislature passed an act giving the court of chancery jurisdiction over these bequests. It was amended in 1911. In 1915 the title of the act was attacked but the

[70] *In re* Durbrow's Estate (1927), 245 N. Y. 469, 157 N. E. 747.

[71] 41 Mich. 730, 3 N. W. 207. This decision followed Holmes v. Mead in New York (1873) and Ruth v. Oberbrunner in Wisconsin (1876).

[72] Wheeler v. American Tract Society (1896), 109 Mich. 141, 66 N. W. 955; Hopkins *et al.* v. Crossley *et al.* (1903), 132 Mich. 612, 96 N. W. 499; Stoepel v. Satterthwaite (1910), 162 Mich 457, 127 N. W. 673; Lounsbury v. Trustees (1910), 170 Mich. 645 (647), 129 N. W. 36. In the last case, one hundred dollars was left to a cemetery society as a perpetual fund for a burial lot. This bequest was declared invalid, even after a liberalizing statute had been passed in 1907. The case, Stoepel v. Satterthwaite was ruled by the law prior to the enactment of the statute because the testator had died before the act had been passed. In Hopkins *et al.* v. Crossley *et al.*, it was attempted by counsel for the bequest to show that it was personalty and the statute of trusts in Michigan referred only to realty, but the court denied that it had any jurisdiction over charitable bequests, even though they might be free from the operation of the statute against perpetuities.

court by an equal division held the act to be constitutional.[73] Then by an act of the legislature in 1915, the title was amended and the language of the act broadened. The act provides that no gift, grant, or devise in trust or otherwise to religious, charitable, educational or benevolent uses is void for indefiniteness of object or beneficiary or because it contravenes the statute or rule against perpetuities. If no trustee is appointed, or a vacancy occurs in the office, the trust vests in the court of chancery to be executed by the trustee appointed by the court. Such bequests are to be interpreted liberally so that the intention of the testator can be carried out wherever possible. The prosecuting attorney of the county is to represent the uncertain beneficiaries and to enforce such trusts.[74]

610. The case, Moore v. O'Leary (1914) [75] was decided adversely, but not because an indefinite beneficiary had been named, but because a definite beneficiary had been named invalidly.[76]

611. **But the statute restores the charitable system that prevailed under the Statute of Elizabeth,** as seems clear from the case, Scudder v. Security Trust (1927),[77] where a trust was valid that was instituted for the promotion of the welfare and comfort of elderly people without means of support. It was even said that the doctrine of *cy pres* is intended by the statute.[78]

612. **The conclusion as to Michigan is that the widest liberty prevails** under the liberalizing statute and the decisions based on it.

613. **The situation in Wisconsin** may be illustrated by the following diagram:

[73] Loomis v. Mack, 183 Mich. 674, 150 N. W. 370.

[74] Now §§ 13512, 13513.

[75] 180 Mich. 261, 146 N. W. 661.

[76] One bequest was made to the trustee who had been directed orally to distribute it as the testator had been wont. Another bequest was made to a church named, without any amount set down in the will, though it had been specified orally by the testator.

[77] 213 N. W. 131

[78] The court referred to the Appeal of Hannan (1924), 227 Mich. 569 (577), 199 N. W. 423, where it was said that the court would resort to *cy pres,* if necessary, because the residue was to be devoted to charitable purposes, and this most effectually cut it off from any distribution as intestate property.

Narrow View		Liberal View	
Ruth v. Oberbrunner 40 Wis. 238	(1876)	Dodge v. Williams 46 Wis. 70, 1. N.W. 92 50 N.W. 1103	(1879)
Heiss v. Murphy 40 Wis. 276	(1876)	Gould v. Taylor Orphan Asylum 46 Wis. 106 50 N.W. 422	(1879)
Estate of Hoffen 70 Wis. 522 36 N.W. 407	(1888)	Webster v. Morris 66 Wis. 366 28 N.W. 353	(1886)
Will of Fuller 75 Wis. 431 44 N.W. 304	(1890)	Sawtelle v. Witham 94 Wis. 412 69 N.W. 72	(1896)
McHugh v. McCole 97 Wis. 166 72 N.W. 631	(1897)		

Harrington v. Pier (1900)
105 Wis. 485, 82 N.W. 345
Follows Dodge v. Williams, distinguishing some of the cases following Ruth. v. Oberbrunner, and overruling Will of Fuller.

Tharp v. Seventh Day Adventist Church 182 Wis. 107 195 N.W. 351	(1923)	*In re* Briggs' Estate 189 Wis. 524 208 N.W. 247	(1926)
		In re Monaghan's Will 226 N.W. 306	(1929)

The Supreme Court in the three latest cases, Tharp v. Seventh Day Adventist Church, *In re* Briggs' and *In re* Monaghan's Will, leaves the state of the law in much the same uncertain position in which it was found prior to the decision in Harrington v. Pier. This case, moreover, is explicitly approved by the two first of the decisions following it, but in support of divergent views. The two latest cases support the liberal view, and would consequently seem to indicate the position of the court.

614. The New York law stood in favor of charitable trusts when Wisconsin was admitted to the Union, under the decision in Shotwell Exec. v. Mott *et al.* (1844). The Wisconsin statute of uses and trusts was adopted, copied in all essential parts from that of New York, except that personal property was omitted from the statute against perpetuities.

615. Distinction between Realty and Personalty. So much by way of introduction. The theory that in Wisconsin the statute of uses and trusts, including the prohibition against perpetuities, applies to charitable uses where realty is granted, but not as to personalty, has been taken for granted by the courts rather than actually decided since the case of Dodge v. Williams. Whether or not this is the settled law, that is, that real estate is subject to all the restrictions of the law even when given to charity, the courts will probably not open the question.

616. But as to personal property, it was decided in Dodge v. Williams that the statute of perpetuities and of uses and trusts had no application to gifts for charitable purposes. The facts in this case did not call upon the court to go further than that. It may be easily inferred from the language of the opinion that there was considerable doubt as to whether the rule should not be extended also to real estate. In any event, the court demonstrated that the English doctrine of perpetuities was not applied to public trusts in the place of its origin, and that if it was to apply in Wisconsin, it must be by force of special statute.

In this case, the arguments against the bequests were chiefly three: first, that the doctrine of charitable uses does not obtain in Wisconsin; second, that a trust not having all the elements of certainty requisite to a private trust can not be sustained without the aid of the *cy pres* doctrine; third, that a court of equity can not exercise any authority over a donation to charitable uses that it can not exercise in the case of a private trust, except in virtue of the prerogative power of the sovereign, the so-called *cy pres* power, and that the courts of the State do not possess this power.

The arguments opposed were chiefly two: viz., that the legislature did not intend to abolish the common law system of trusts for charitable uses, and that they are still lawful and sustainable without the aid of the *cy pres* doctrine, strictly so-called; second, that the legislative intent was to preserve charitable uses and trusts in all their essential and distinctive features, so far as they are sustainable independently of the *cy pres* remedy of the Statute of Elizabeth and of the exercise of the prerogative power of the crown.[79]

[79] The subject of the trust was personal property. The trustees named were

The decision of the court was most liberal, stopping short only at *cy pres* modification of the testator's plan of charity. It decided that bequests of personal property to charitable purposes are good in Wisconsin even under the rules of common law, if not to the extent warranted by the *cy pres* remedy and the Statute of Elizabeth. It went on to say that the *cy pres* remedy does not necessarily signify those liberal rules of judicial construction of charitable trusts by the court of equity, which prior to the Statute of Elizabeth were applied in chancery, and of which that Statute is only confirmatory.

It said that it was sufficient under the laws of the State that there be a trust and a particular charitable purpose, as distinguished from a gift to charity in general. The court may supply the trustee to administer the trust. The trustee may select the beneficiaries from the general class named by the testator and within its stated general limits.

Certainty of *beneficiaries* who can invoke the judicial power to enforce the trust is not necessary but is rather inconsistent with the very nature of a trust for charitable uses, in that the beneficiaries in a general sense are the members of the public at large. A public charity, within the rule outlined, is sufficiently definite as to *purpose* if its general nature be clearly stated, or can be made certain by the trustees, clothed with the power of administering the trust within the limits of the declared purpose. As to *immediate* beneficiaries, a trust is sufficiently definite if power of selection is lodged expressly or implicitly in the trustee appointed by the testator or the court. If the trustee abuse his power, there is a complete remedy in the exercise of the visitatorial power of the State. The conclusion was that the statute of uses and trusts, as to personal property at least, does not apply to trusts for charitable uses. Moreover, the New York

trustees of several colleges. Neither of the trusts could have been enforced if they had been private trusts. There was an entire absence of beneficiaries who could invoke the judicial power to enforce the trust. The broadest discretion was left the trustees to select the immediate beneficiaries from a class having no limitation as to residence or location, and none as to number, kind, or character, except for the indefinite term, "worthy, indigent females," or "worthy indigent young men studying for the ministry." The method of carrying out the declared purpose had no limitation except that of the work done at the schools named.

doctrine and decisions on this question carried no weight in Wisconsin.

This decision departed from the rule in Ruth v. Oberbrunner and Heiss v. Murphy. But rather than overrule those cases, it distinguished the case at hand from the two previous ones.

It distinguished the case from Ruth v. Oberbrunner on two grounds: viz., first, the devise there was of realty, not of personalty; second, the devise was to be held for the benefit of the Order of St. Dominic and St. Catherine's Female Academy, without indicating a charitable purpose, so that the trust seemed to be devoid of any charitable intent, and to be private. As a private trust, it failed because there was no beneficiary to take legal title under the statute.

It distinguished the case from Heiss v. Murphy also on two grounds: viz., first, the trust was realty; and second, it was for the benefit of "the Roman Catholic orphans of the Diocese of La Crosse," a group so indefinite and uncertain as to be unascertainable.

The reasoning of the court in these two earlier cases inconsistent with that of the later case was treated as merely incidental and not obligatory as precedent. Nothing previously decided was actually overruled.

617. With this decision it is possible to reconcile all except one of the following decisions, that is, Gould v. Orphan Asylum, Webster v. Morris, Estate of Hoffen, Sawtelle v. Witham, and McHugh v. McCole. The Will of Fuller is the only case in which the decision, not the reasoning, seems irreconcilable. Adverse decisions, indeed, were rendered in the Estate of Hoffen and in McHugh v. McCole, but the actual decisions can be brought under the doctrine of Dodge v. Williams, the contrary decisions being due to different circumstances in the cases at bar.[80]

[80] In Gould v. Orphan Asylum, the bequest was to trustees for the care of orphan children of Racine County, and such other poor, neglected, and necessitous children as the managers might decide to receive. The formation of a corporation was not made imperative. But the court decided that the fund, without the intervention of a corporation, could be permanently retained and administered by the trustees. In Webster v. Morris, there were two bequests. One was to a church, the income to be used, one-half for the church, and the other half for "the resident poor." The other bequest was to charity in general with a preference expressed for a school for young men, if the funds were adequate. The court accepted the preference as a command, for if the bequest were

618. The case, Harrington v. Pier, investigated carefully the history of all these decisions, explicitly accepting that of Dodge v. Williams.[81] But the dissenting opinion said that any decision overruled prior decisions only to the extent required by the facts. It argued that the facts at bar could not warrant an overruling of Ruth v. Oberbrunner inasmuch as perpetuity did not enter into the case at all under the facts. The whole fund was to be spent within five years. Moreover, the court has sustained bequests made to corporations to be formed only after the decision was rendered. Nevertheless, it thought that the amount to be expended in temperance work was too indefinite to be sustained under the consistent rulings of the court.

619. In Tharp *et al.* v. Smith *et al.*, though the dissenting opinion held that the general purpose of the testator was sufficiently clear and that he intended distribution of Adventist literature by entrusting funds to proper trustees, the decision held that in view of the numerous organizations of the church and of the fact that the decedent had not been a member of any one of them, a bequest for the benefit of the "Seventh Day Adventist Church" was void for uncertainty.

left to charity in general, it would be invalid. The declared particular purpose was regarded as adequate to save it. In the Estate of Hoffen, the bequest was made to the poor of the City of Green Bay. No trust was established. The beneficiaries were regarded as unascertainable, and the bequest was declared invalid. In the Will of Fuller, there was a trust, a trustee, and a particular purpose expressed; and it was conceded that it was a trust for a charitable use. Nevertheless, the bequest was regarded as invalid because the testator failed to define fully his charitable scheme. In Sawtelle v. Witham, there was a trust, but the trustees refused to act. The fund was to be invested and the income devoted to the support, maintenance, education, or aid to that end, of such indigent orphan children under fourteen years of age in Rock County, Wisconsin, as in the judgment of the executors may be the most needy. The bequest was sustained. In McHugh v. McCole, there were gifts to individuals for the Protestant Episcopal Church, for the Roman Catholic Church, and for Masses. These were all held too indefinite and in fact unascertainable.

[81] And consequently upheld a bequest to trustees to spend money for temperance work in the City of Milwaukee, the greater portion to be used for the benefit of the Crystal Spring Lodge and of the Woman's Temperance Union of said City, or for a building for temperance work, if either of those organizations decided to build, the whole to be expended within five years.

620. *In re* Briggs' Estate, however, a bequest even more indefinite, it would seem, was upheld. It was made to the Y. W. C. A. of Wisconsin. Now there was no such organization. Yet the court held that the bequest did not lapse, but that the court was called upon to appoint a trustee to administer it, with the advice of the National Board of the Y. W. C. A. and of the various local organizations affiliated with that Board. The court would have the final word on what agencies would best serve the purpose of accomplishing the testator's manifest intention, even to the extent of creating new units. This, however, the court insists, does not call into play the *cy pres* power in the sense of prerogative. The court distinguishes the case at bar from the previous one, saying that in the latter the various Adventist churches which might have come under the bequest were not identical in their creeds, and that no distribution could be made without creating discord and dissatisfaction.

621. The case, *In re* Monaghan's Will, cites the act of the legislature of 1917,[82] according to which a testamentary trust, such as was presented to the court in this case, was valid where it gave property to a trustee to be distributed to charities within the county which might be deemed needy and worthy, leaving the amounts to be distributed each year to the trustee's discretion, with directions that the funds were to be distributed for the period of one hundred years, and at the end of that time, that the principal was to be divided among worthy charities.

622. The conclusion to be reached in Wisconsin is that a charitable bequest of personalty seems fairly safe, considering the statute just cited, and the attitude of the court in the last two cases. The statute is even general enough to include devises of realty, it would seem, but the courts would probably not sustain that view. The instability manifested in previous decisions, however, counsels prudence. At least a trustee should be named, with very definite beneficiaries. Indeed, it would seem advisable to leave the bequest

[82] Now § 231.11, which provides that "No trust for charitable or public purposes whether in real or personal property, shall be invalid for indefiniteness or uncertainty where the power to designate the peculiar charitable or public purpose or purposes to be promoted thereby is given by the instrument creating the same to the trustees, or to any other person or persons."

to a charitable corporation for the purposes for which the corporation was chartered. This should by all means be the procedure when realty is devised.

623. **In Minnesota,** the statutes of 1851 had forbidden trusts of realty except such as the statutes authorized [83] and the statutes of 1875 included personalty in the prohibition.[84] But in 1905, villages and towns were permitted to take in trust real and personal property for charitable purposes.[85]

Consequently, in a case coming before the Supreme Court in 1862, the court held that only realty was included in the statute forbidding trusts.[86] Then followed a series of decisions invalidating devises of realty in trust for charitable purposes.[87]

624. But in 1903, in the case, Shanahan v. Kelly,[88] the court rendered a decision regarding trusts of personalty, because such trusts were involved in the case before it. It said that up till that time there had been indecision as to whether trusts of personal property would be valid if made for charitable purposes. It agreed that prior to the enactment of 1875, the bench and bar seemed agreed that such a trust would be valid. But it insisted that since the enactment there had been an assumption implicit in the decisions that both personalty and realty fall under the prohibition against trusts contrary to statute, though only trusts in realty had come directly in issue. It concludes that it is obvious that the enactment of 1875

[83] Cc. 43, 44, R. S. 1851; *cf.* note to § 8081—Mason's Statutes, 1927.

[84] C. 53, being subdivision 5 of § 6710, G. S., 1913; *cf.* note to § 8081—Mason's Statutes, 1927.

[85] R. L. 1905, § 3249, G. S. 1913, § 6710; amended 1915, c. 98, § 1; 1925, c. 133. *Cf.* note to § 8081—Mason's Statutes, 1927.

[86] Baker v. Terrell, 8 Minn. 195, Gil. 165.

[87] German Land Assn. v. Scholler (1865), 10 Minn. 260; where realty was devised to an unincorporated association; Little v. Willford (1883), 31 Minn. 173, 17 N. W. 282; in which realty was devised to a church for a charitable use; Atwater v. Russell (1892), 49 Minn. 57, 51 N. W. 629 and 52 N. W. 26; Lane v. Eaton (1897), 69 Minn. 141, 71 N. W. 1031; where it was declared that a devise of realty was invalid if the unit of the Salvation Army which was beneficiary was unincorporated. As late as 1892 the court *In re* Tower's Estate, 49 Minn. 370, 52 N. W. 27, held that as to personal property the common law ruled.

[88] 88 Minn. 202, 52 N. W. 27.

abolished all trusts in personalty as well as in realty, except as provided in the enactment in itself. It conceived that there was no reasonable rule of construction which would exclude personal property from its scope. This decision seems to have been followed until 1920.[89] But in 1920, in the case, *In re* Bull's Will,[90] the court said that where the estate is personalty, and the trustee is to take charge of it and invest it for the benefit of a class, the trust is not invalid, even though it suspend the power of alienation beyond the period fixed by statute. It seems to base its decision on a liberal interpretation of the very statute that gave rise to the adverse decision in Shanahan v. Kelly.

623. **In any event, it would seem that the enactments of 1927 definitely place Minnesota in the ranks of the liberal States,** even where devises of realty are concerned.[91] As is clear from the context

[89] See the cases: Watkins v. Bigelow (1904), 93 Minn. 210; 100 N. W. 1104; Y. M. C. A. v. Horne (1913), 120 Minn. 404, 139 N. W. 805; Walso v. Latterner (1918), 140 Minn. 455, 168 N. W. 353.

[90] 147 Minn. 62, 179 N. W. 650.

[91] The Statutes of 1927 in this matter, contained in Mason's Statutes, 1927, are as follows:

§ 8090-1. Express trusts of real or personal property, or both, may be created to receive by grant, devise, gift, or bequest, and take charge of, invest and administer in accordance with the terms of the trust, upon and for any charitable, benevolent, educational, religious or other public use or trust.

§ 8090-2. No such trust shall be invalid because of indefiniteness or uncertainty of the object of such trust or of the beneficiaries thereof designated in the instrument creating the same nor by reason of the same contravening any statute or rule against perpetuities, but no such trust shall be construed so as to prevent or limit the free alienation of the title to any trust estate by the trustee in the administration of said trust, except as may be permitted under existing or subsequent statutes.

§ 8090-3. Such trust shall be liberally construed by the courts so that the intentions of the donor thereof shall be carried out whenever possible, and no such trust shall fail solely because the donor has imperfectly outlined the purpose and object of such charity or the method of administration. Whenever it shall appear to the District Court of the proper county that the purpose and object of such charity is imperfectly expressed or the method of administration is incomplete or imperfect, or that the circumstances have so changed since the execution of the instrument creating the trust as to render impracticable, inexpedient, or impossible a literal compliance with the terms of such instrument,

of the statutes, they permit the application of the *cy pres* doctrine to administer the trust in any manner which the court judges expedient when the scheme proposed by the testator himself proves impracticable or impossible, provided, however, that the consent of the donor be obtained, if he be living. However, no cases have been adjudicated by the Supreme Court under these recent statutes, and it might seem the better and more prudent plan to be cautious until the Court has had opportunity to pass upon their significance. It is wiser to leave the gift to a corporation for the purposes granted in its charter.

625. The Dubious Situation in Tennessee. Before proceeding to review the provisions of the States that have always been liberal in this matter, this study should note the rather hesitant attitude of the courts in Tennessee.

The courts there recognize the general principle that courts of equity have jurisdiction over bequests to charity but they have been rather rigorous in interpreting the degree of certainty required in such bequests in order that they may be regarded as valid. They recognize no *cy pres* doctrine, and the Statute of Elizabeth is not in force.

In the case, Ewell v. Sneed (1917),[92] the court gave a list of de-

such court may upon the application and with the consent of the trustee, and upon such notice as said court may direct, make an order directing that such trust shall be administered or expended in such manner as in the judgment of said court will, as nearly as can be, accomplish the general purpose of the instrument and the object and intention of the donor without regard to, and free from, any specific restriction, limitation, or direction contained therein, provided, however, that no such order shall be made without the consent of the donor of said trust if he is then living and mentally competent. The attorney general shall represent the beneficiaries under this act, and it shall be his duty to enforce such trusts by proper proceedings in the courts.

§ 8090-4. Nothing in this act contained shall in any manner impair, limit, or abridge the operation and efficacy of the whole or any part of any existing statute authorizing the creation of corporations for charitable purposes or permitting municipal corporations to act as trustee for any public or charitable purpose under any existing statute. Nothing in this act shall apply to any gift, bequest, devise, or trust made, created, or arising by or under the provisions of the will of any person whose decease occurred before this act takes effect.

[92] 136 Tenn. 602, 191 S. W. 131.

cisions in which charitable bequests were regarded as valid because definite in their object and supported by trustees. It gave another list where such bequests were held either not sufficiently definite to enable the beneficiaries to be ascertained or incapable of being enforced by the court. In some of them the invalidity was due to the failure to appoint a trustee. They might be classified as follows:

Narrow View		Liberal View
White v. Hale 42 Tenn. (2 Cold) 77		Dickson v. Montgomery 31 Tenn. (1 Swan) 348
Daniel v. Fain 73 Tenn. (5 Lea) 319		Franklin v. Armfield 34 Tenn. (2 Sneed) 305
Reeves v. Reeves 73 Tenn. (5 Lea) 644		Frierson v. General Assembly 54 Tenn. (7 Heisk) 683
Rhodes v. Rhodes 88 Tenn. 637 13 S. W. 590	(1890)	Cobb v. Denton 65 Tenn. (6 Baxt.) 235 State v. Smith
Johnson v. Johnson 92 Tenn. 559 23 S.W. 114	(1893)	84 Tenn. (16 Lea) 662 Heiskell v. Chickasaw Lodge 87 Tenn. 668
Jones v. Green 36 S.W. 729	(1895)	11 S.W. 825

The first three cases under the narrow view failed for lack of a trustee. And this situation is approved in Ewell v. Sneed, which refers to Green v. Allen.[93] In the latter case the court is reported as saying that the power to decree execution of charitable trusts, so far as it arises out of the inherent jurisdiction of the court of chancery, rests upon the same principles as the jurisdiction in trusts of every other kind. There must be either a *cestui que trust* (beneficiary) having sufficient legal capacity to take the gift as devisee or donee, or at least a trustee charged with a specific legal trust. And the court in Ewell v. Sneed said that the chancellor can not appoint a trustee.

626. In that same year, 1917, the legislature undertook to enact a statute to prevent the failure of charitable bequests. It ordained that the attempt to create a perpetuity or the failure of

[93] 24 Tenn. (5 Humph.) 170.

the donor to appoint a trustee should not defeat the gift.[94] Nevertheless in the case, Milligan v. Greeneville College (1928),[95] counsel still argued against the bequest from cases prior to and including Ewell v. Sneed, and claimed that an unincorporated association was incapable of taking the bequest left to it because no trustee had been appointed. But the court, though it seems to have ignored the statute, decided that the unincorporated association was a branch of a corporation and entitled to take the bequest on that ground.

Similar evasion was practised in the case, Bushong v. Taylor *et al.* (1930),[96] where the court, argued that in the case at bar, there was a trustee duly appointed, a definite beneficiary, and an object not prohibited by statute, and that consequently the bequest was a charitable one in every sense of the word, and therefore not subject to the statute against perpetuities.[97]

627. The conclusion to be reached in the case of Tennessee is that the courts seem to be lagging behind the legislature. The question of validity is too uncertain here to permit a testator to be careless. A bequest to charity should be made at least to a trustee, and the purposes should be outlined in some detail. A bequest to a charitable corporation would undoubtedly be upheld. As to Mass bequests, no decision has been rendered here by the highest court. The decision as to Masses would seem to be dubious at best, even with the appointment of a trustee.

[94] Chapter 137, Acts of 1917.

[95] 156 Tenn. 373; 2 S. W. (2nd) 90.

[96] 161 Tenn. 522, 33 S. W. (2nd) 80.

[97] In the same year in the case, the Bank of Commerce and Trust Co. v. Banks *et al.*, 161 Tenn. 11, 28 S. W. (2nd) 340, and 29 S. W. (2nd) 658, notice was taken of the decision in Ewell v. Sneed, while the court decided that a hospital could act as trustee *ultra vires* to construct a hospital for cancer patients. In Vanderbilt University v. Mitchell (1931), 162 Tenn. 217, 36 S. W. (2nd) 83, it was held that a trust established to assist poor and deserving students of Georgia was definite enough to be sustained. In Davis v. Bullington (1932), 47 S. W. (2nd) 555, a testamentary direction that a memorial be selected by the executor and a designated committee was held to be too indefinite to be upheld.

Article 4

The Liberal Doctrine

628. The remaining States, except Mississippi, have never offered any serious problem as to the validity of charitable bequests.

629. In New Hampshire, it is held that the language in a will creates a charitable trust when it directs trustees to give the residuary estate to, for, in, and among such charitable, fraternal, benevolent and educational uses, purposes, societies, institutions, associations, and corporations, public or private, as they should select.[98] Since the general purpose of the testator can be effectuated by judicial decree, and since his trustees are empowered to select beneficiaries, the gift is not void for uncertainty.[99] For the court has jurisdiction independently of the Statute of Elizabeth.[100] But a gift to trustees to dispose of it as they see fit is too uncertain to be carried out by the court.[101] However, a gift to a religious association is regarded as a trust to be executed by the persons who from time to time might constitute the association, and is not intended to limit their discretion. But if the trustee would be given discretion to apply the gift to a private person or to a private purpose, the gift would be void.[102] If the donor's scheme for administering a trust breaks down, it is the duty of the court by the doctrine of *cy pres* to devise a plan as nearly like that of the donor as possible. But when the donor's purpose can be ascertained, and it is legal, it is the duty of the court to enforce it.[103]

[98] Carter v. Whitcomb (1908), 74 N. H. 482, 69 Atl. 779; Glover v. Baker (1912), 76 N. H. 393, 83 Atl. 916.

[99] Gaffney v. Kenison (1887), 64 N. H. 354, 10 Atl. 706; where the bequest was left to the most destitute of the testator's relatives. Towle v. Nesmith (1898), 69 N. H. 212, 42 Atl. 900; where the bequest was left to a town to care for widows and children; Snow v. Durgin (1900), 70 N. H. 121, 47 Atl. 89; in which the bequest was again for destitute relatives; Haynes v. Carr (1901), 70 N. H. 463, 49 Atl. 638; where the bequest was to the poor of the State and for the educational and charitable purposes of the State; French v. Lawrence (1911), 76 N. H. 234, 81 Atl. 705; where the bequest was to the feeble Congregational churches of the State; Clark v. Campbell (1926), 82 N. H. 281, 133 Atl. 166.

[100] Haynes v. Carr, cited in the last note.

[101] Clark v. Campbell, cited above.

[102] Glover v. Baker, cited in note 98.

[103] Edgerly v. Barker (1891), 66 N. H. 434, 31 Atl. 900; Haynes v. Carr, cited

630. In Vermont, the courts hold that the jurisdiction over charitable bequests is inherent in the courts of equity [104] and that where trustees appointed to hold land for a church fail to execute their trust or decline it, the heirs at law must hold the gift in trust or the court may appoint a new trustee.[105] Moreover, a gift to a religious unincorporated association is valid as a gift to a charitable use;[106] and the same was held of a gift for a home for good Christian women of sixty years of age and over, residents of Vermont, and of American lineage for two generations.[107]

631. Maine also holds for the inherent jurisdiction of the courts of equity over these bequests.[108] The court is conceived to be able to administer the bequest on failure of the appointed trustees, or to appoint a new trustee.[109] The doctrine of *cy pres* is operative, but in order that it may be applied, two prerequisites must be verified: viz., first, the failure of the specific purpose; and second, a general charitable intent expressed by the testator.[110] But where a legacy was a

in note 99; Hayward v. Spaulding (1908), 75 N. H. 92, 71 Atl. 219; City of Keene v. Eastman (1909), 75 N. H. 191, 72 Atl. 213; Adams v. Page (1911), 76 N. H. 96, 79 Atl. 837; Drury v. Sleeper (1929), 146 Atl. 645; Borchers v. Taylor (1929), 145 Atl. 666.

[104] Burr v. Smith (1835), 7 Vt. 241, 29 Am. Dec. 154. Common law is in force by statute; § 1479 (Gen. Laws 1917).

[105] Stone v. Griffin (1831), 3 Vt. 400.

[106] Smith v. Nelson (1846), 18 Vt. 511.

[107] Boyce v. Sumner (1924), 97 Vt. 473, 124 Atl. 853. *Cf.* also Sheldon v. Town of Stockbridge (1895), 67 Vt. 299, 31 Atl. 414; where several bequests were left to a town: one, for a certain cemetery with provisions that the sum should be always kept intact, and which the court held valid because of the town's obligation of caring constantly for the cemetery; another, for the support of common schools, with the obligation of dividing the income among the districts, which was held valid even though there was now only one district; and a third, for the relief of the poor of the town in general. *Cf.* Downer's Estate (1928), 101 Vt. 167, 142 Atl. 78. In Clement v. Hyde (1878), 50 Vt. 716, 28 Am. Rep. 522, a bequest of one thousand dollars to the treasurer of a certain County and his successors in office was valid where the income was to be expended in the education of poor people in that county.

[108] Tappan v. Deblois (1858), 45 Me. 122.

[109] Bates v. Schillinger *et al.* (1929), 145 Atl. 395.

[110] Doyle v. Whalen (1895), 87 Me. 414, 32 Atl. 1022; Brooks v. Belfast (1897), 90 Me. 318, 38 Atl. 222; Hospital Assn. v. McKenzie (1908), 104 Me.

farm for a home for one or more unmarried women employed in the straw industry, the devise failed because the purpose was impracticable and there was no general charitable intent.[111] A testamentary trust was held not to be defeated, however, by the fact that the testatrix authorized the trustees to select charitable associations not named in the will as beneficiaries of the bequest.[112]

632. Delaware also regards the jurisdiction of equity over charitable bequests as inherent. A bequest is regarded as valid even where the power of selection of purpose and beneficiary is placed within the discretion of the trustee.[113] But there is no *cy pres* doctrine in this State; and where the charitable purpose of a testator was expressed as touching a definite institution, if that institution ceases to exist, the legacy lapses.[114]

633. The courts of South Carolina held in 1888 that beneficiaries under a charitable bequest must necessarily be indefinite and sustained a bequest as sufficiently certain even where it was alleged against it: first, that there were no beneficiaries mentioned, and that even though there was a class named, there was no implied

320, 71 Atl. 1032; Allen v. Nasson Institute (1910), 107 Me. 120, 77 Atl. 638; Lynch v. So. Cong. Church (1912), 109 Me. 32, 82 Atl. 432. In the last case one of the three beneficiaries failed and the other two came under the general intent and thus were permitted to divide the extra share between them.

[111] Gilman v. Burnett (1917), 116 Me. 382, 102 Atl. 108. *Cf.* Edwards v. Packard (1930), 129 Me. 74, 149 Atl. 623. In a case where a priest gave the bulk of his estate for the establishment of a monastery of Carmelites to be devoted to the spiritual interests of the French people of a given section, the court regarded the spiritual welfare of the French people as the general charitable intent, and when the establishment of the monastery became impossible, two priests were appointed trustees to care for the fund for that purpose. However, the court said that *cy pres* was not necessary in this case, as the primary motive was the spiritual welfare of the people; Dupont v. Pelletier *et al.* (1921), 120 Me. 114, 113 Atl. 11.

[112] Prime v. Harmon (1921), 120 Me. 299, 113 Atl. 738. The general charitable doctrine is also upheld in Bills v. Pease (1917), 116 Me. 98, 100 Atl. 146.

[113] Monaghan v. Joyce (1918), 12 Del. Ch. 28, 103 Atl. 582.

[114] Murphy v. McBride *et al.* (1925), 130 Atl. 283; where a devise to the Sisters of Charity of St. Peter's and its successors and assigns, to be used for the support of orphan girls under its care, can not be given to a new corporation, which came into existence after the first corporation ceased to exist.

power of selection conferred on the trustee; second, that the court could not confer a power of selection on a trustee of its own appointment; third, that there was no class of territory from which the beneficiaries could be selected; fourth, that the bequest was not made to an association or corporation which could administer it according to its charter or regulations.[115]

But in 1892 where a bequest was made for the purpose of educating boys for the priesthood, the court said that it must fail for want of a trustee, as it was too uncertain as to beneficiaries without a trustee.[116] The accepted doctrine, however, at the present time is that a valid trust having been created, it will not fail for want of a trustee.[117] The *cy pres* doctrine is not recognized; but where a bequest was made to an orphan asylum for the blind in the city, it was given to an asylum for the deaf, dumb, and blind near the city.[118]

634. **North Carolina** holds that the validity of charitable bequests does not depend on the Statute of Elizabeth, and therefore trusts for public charity may be established for an indefinite number of persons, and the details of the administration may be selected by the trustee under the direction of a court of chancery.[119] While the *cy pres* doctrine is not countenanced in North Carolina, nevertheless the validity of a charitable trust does not depend on the adequacy of the fund to meet the full demands of the testator's intention.[120] And the court will appoint a trustee where the testator has not done so.[121]

115 Bates v. Taylor (1888), 28 S. C. 76, 6 S. E. 327.

116 Brennan v. Winkler (1892), 37 S. C. 457, 16 S. E. 190. And this was followed in Dye v. Beaver Creek Church (1897), 48 S. C. 444, 26 S. E. 717.

117 Harter v. Johnson (1922), 122 S. C. 96, 115 S. E. 217.

118 Smith v. Heyward (1920), 115 S. C. 145, 105 S. E. 275.

119 Whitsett *et al.* v. Clapp *et al.* (1931), 200 N. C. 647, 158 S. E. 183. But a residuary clause providing that on the death of the beneficiary the property in the hands of a trustee shall be invested in such worthy objects as he shall determine as being in accord with what "my wishes and tastes in that direction were when living" was held void for uncertainty; Thomas v. Clay (1924), 187 N. C. 778, 122 S. E. 852. *Cf.* also Humphrey v. Board of Trustees of I. O. O. F. Home (1932), 203 N. C. 201, 165 S. E. 547.

120 Wachovia Banking and Trust Co. v. Ogburn (1921), 181 N. C. 324, 107 S. E. 238.

121 § 4035 a.

635. In Texas, the courts claim inherent jurisdiction in chancery to adjudicate cases in which bequests to charity are involved.[122] If the trustee is unable to discharge the trust, equity will take charge and appoint a substitute.[123] The doctrine of *cy pres* has not been explicitly approved but it has been practically established at least in its restricted significance.[124] Though Texas seems most liberal in interpreting charitable bequests, there is just a little hint in the reasoning of the court that trustees must be appointed where the beneficiaries are uncertain or indefinite. True, the court will appoint a trustee, should the designated trustee be unable to act. The consequence should be that the court would appoint a trustee where one has not been appointed. But that conclusion seems to be beyond a strict view of the opinions in the cases. Caution would indicate, then, that the testator should always appoint a trustee in such cases.

636. Ohio also is liberal in its interpretation of the inherent jurisdiction of courts of equity in this matter. If the founder of the trust describes the general nature of a valid charitable trust, and names the class of beneficiaries, he may leave the details of its administration to be settled by the trustees under the guidance of a court of equity.[125] Ohio does not recognize the claim that because of the uncertainty of the object, a court of equity can not enforce it, or that therefore such indefiniteness renders it void. Ohio regards indefiniteness as a necessary characteristic of charitable trusts. If the objects of the trust are sufficiently definite in the instrument, the fault, if any, is cured by the appointment of a trustee with powers to select the objects within the classes named.[126]

[122] Jones' Unknown Heirs *et al.* v. Dorchester *et al.* (1920), 224 S. W. 596.

[123] Lightfoot *et al.* v. Poindexter *et al.* (1917), 199 S. W. 1152. In this case the doctrine was repeated that charitable bequests are not subject to the statutes against perpetuities. Here a bequest was valid for a tabernacle or coliseum, leaving the determination of the plans to named persons, provided, however, that it should minister to the enjoyment of the people; and a bequest was valid for a chapel costing between twenty-five and thirty-five thousand dollars, where the trustee was allowed a latitude of choice within those amounts.

[124] Gidley v. Lovinberg (1904), 35 Tex. Civ. App. 203, 79 S. W. 831; Inglish v. Johnson (1906), 42 Tex. Civ. App. 118, 95 S. W. 558; Jones' Unknown Heirs *et al.* v. Dorchester *et al.*, cited in note 122.

[125] Gearhart v. Richardson (1924), 109 Ohio St. 418, 142 N. E. 890.

[126] Linney v. Cleveland Trust Co. (1928), 165 N. E. 101. But where a gift

637. Iowa regards the Statute of Elizabeth as part of the common law of the State in so far as it does not conflict with any of the institutions of the State.[127] Where the intention of the testator becomes impracticable or impossible according to the terms of the trust, a court of equity may assume jurisdiction and direct the trustees to administer it and apply the *cy pres* doctrine to it.[128]

638. Oregon, too, regards the court of equity as endowed with inherent jurisdiction over charitable bequests, regardless of whether the Statute of Elizabeth was adopted in that State or not. Consequently, it regards such bequests as valid even when the trustees are uncertain.[129]

639. Louisiana provides that it is lawful to make over any kind of property to trustees for educational, charitable, or religious purposes, and that the provisions of the Revised Civil Code are inap-

was left for religious and philanthropic work among young people, the purpose was considered too vague; Dirlam v. Morrow (1921), 102 Ohio St. 279, 131 N. E. 365. The indefiniteness was no obstacle in Palmer v. Oiler (1921), 102 Ohio St. 271, 131 N. E. 362 (for needy and poor women); nor in Becker v. Fisher (1925), 112 Ohio St. 284, 147 N. E. 744.

[127] Hodge *et al.* v. Wellman *et al.* (1920), 191 Ia. 897, 179 N. W. 534. The court quoted a list of previous cases that had evinced this liberal policy towards charitable bequests: viz., Miller v. Chittenden, 4 Ia. 252; Lepage v. McNamara, 5 Ia. 124; Seda *et al.* v. Huble *et al.* (1888), 75 Ia. 429, 39 N. W. 685; Moran v. Moran *et al.* (1897), 104 Ia. 216, 73 N. W. 617 (in this case five hundred dollars to be divided among the Sisters of Charity was too indefinite); Grant v. Saunders (1903), 121 Ia. 80; 95 N. W. 411 (where a bequest was left merely to the poor and sustained—it would probably not be sustained in most States); Klumpert v. Vrieland (1909), 142 Ia. 434, 121 N. W. 34; *In re* Hubbell Trust, 135 Ia. 637, 113 N. W. 512; Wilson v. Bank (1914), 164 Ia. 402, 145 N. W. 948.

[128] Lupton *et al.* v. Leander Clark College *et al.* (1922), 194 Ia. 1088, 187 N. W. 496. *Cf.* Hipp v. Hibbs, 245 N. W. 247 (1932).

[129] Pennoyer v. Wadhams (1891), 20 Or. 274, 25 Pac. 720; Raley v. Umatilla Co. (1887), 15 Or. 172, 13 Pac. 890; Wemme v. First Church of Christ, 110 Or. 179, 219 Pac. 618. In the last case the object was a maternity hospital for wayward girls; the church which was the beneficiary said that it could not erect the hospital because of conscientious objections and relied on precatory words in asking that the object be changed; but the court would not permit it, because the performance of the prescribed work was still possible. But the court did not decide whether modification would be allowed if the performance should become impossible. *Cf.* also *In re* Prickett's Estate (1929), 275 Pac. 605.

plicable to these trusts, even though they forbid so-called fideicommissary substitutions (that is, provisions by which the testator appoints an heir who is to take from an intermediate heir or trustee).[130] And the courts have held that these bequests are valid and not voided by the statute against perpetuities, even though the beneficiaries are to be determined by the trustee.[131]

640. Charitable trusts are valid even though the beneficiaries are indefinite and even though they offend against the statutes of perpetuities in the remaining States, excepting Mississippi. Thus they are valid in Massachusetts, even when no appropriate trustee is available possessing the qualifications specified.[132] The *cy pres* doctrine is also operative.[133] Indefinite, perpetual charitable trusts are good in Connecticut also, which admits the application of *cy pres* modification where there is a general intent and the plan of the testator can not be carried out;[134] and in Rhode Island;[135] New Jersey;[136] Penn-

[130] General Statutes, §§ 1296, 1303.

[131] Pires v. Youree (1930), 170 La. 986, 129 So. 552.

[132] Attorney General v. Armstrong (1918), 231 Mass. 196, 120 N. E. 678. *Cf.* Coffin v. Attorney General (1919), 231 Mass. 579, 121 N. E. 397; McNeilly v. First Presbyterian Church (1923), 243 Mass. 331, 137 N. E. 691 (where a gift to a church was regarded as made to a public charity and where the church was held to include both the incorporated religious society and the body of communicants associated together). *Cf.* Trustees of Andover Seminary v. Visitors (1925), 253 Mass. 256, 148 N. E. 900 (where a gift for the training of ministers was sustained as a charity). Keown v. Attorney General (1931), 175 N. E. (where a fund was a valid charity when it was left to executors for charitable purposes which would meet their approval). Massachusetts has adopted the English statutes that had been enacted prior to 1606; Zollman, *op. cit.*, 91-94.

[133] Andover Seminary v. Visitors (1925), 253 Mass. 256, 148 N. E. 900.

[134] Newton v. Healy (1923), 100 Conn. 5, 122 Atl. 654; City National Bank v. City of Bridgeport (1929), 109 Conn. 529, 147 Atl. 181; Lyme High School Assn. v. Alling (1931), 154 Atl. 439 (where a charitable gift was valid though made to a school incorporated solely for educational purposes); Cheshire Bank and Trust Co. v. Doolittle (1931), 113 Conn. 231, 155 Atl. 82 (where property to a named trustee was valid as a charitable bequest though it was to be used by her for Home and Foreign Missions indefinitely). The Statutes expressly provide that no designation of purpose need be made by one making a charitable bequest, provided that the power of selection is placed in the trustee or some other person; § 4825.

sylvania;[137] Illinois;[138] Missouri;[139] California;[140] Washington;[141]

[135] Buchanan v. McLyman (1931), 153 Atl. 304 (where a trust creating a place of worship for the benefit of a definite number of persons was held valid); McLyman v. Art Assn. of Newport (1931), 154 Atl. 117 (where a testamentary gift of an estate and one hundred thousand dollars for its maintenance was regarded as valid); Slattery v. Ward (1923), 45 R. I. 54, 119 Atl. 755 (where the trust failed because the trustee was given discretion to make distribution to either a charitable cause or to a private purpose). The *cy pres* doctrine is employed where necessary: R. I. Hospital Trust Co. v. Williams (1929), 50 R. I. 385, 148 Atl. 189; R. I. Hospital Trust Co. v. American National Red Cross (1929), 50 R. I. 461, 149 Atl. 581; City of Newport v. Sisson (1931), 155 Atl. 576 (where a school had been used until 1923 conformably to the testator's wishes, and then closed, the *cy pres* doctrine was called on to make use of the trust fund); Smith v. Ahearn (1932), 161 Atl. 117 (the will simply said that the residue was to be divided; *cy pres* could not be applied because there was no general intent manifest).

[136] Noice v. Schnell (1926), 134 Atl. 81; Trustees of the First Presbyterian Church v. Wheeler (1930), 106 N. J. Eq. 8, 149 Atl. 589; Chelsea Nat. Bank v. Our Lady Church *et al.* (1929), 147 Atl. 470 (where a gift to *some* Catholic institution without the appointment of a trustee was void, though charitable bequests in the same will were sustained); Kinnear v. Ballagh (1931), 109 N. J. Eq. 27, 156 Atl. 269 (where a bequest to purposes of permanent value to the Presbyterian Church was regarded as too indefinite); Brezinsky v. Breves (1931), 109 N. J. Eq. 206, 156 Atl. 429; New Jersey Title Guarantee and Trust Co. v. American Nat. Red Cross (1932), 160 Atl. 842 (where a bequest to an unincorporated "Jersey City Chapter of the American Red Cross" was held valid, though there was no limitation as to use).

The *cy pres* doctrine is also in effect in this State; Mackenzie v. Trustees of the Presbytery of Jersey City (1905), 67 N. J. Eq. 652, 61 Atl. 1027; Brown v. Condit (1905), 70 N. J. Eq. 440, 61 Atl. 1055 (where the court admitting the doctrine of *cy pres,* confined its application to the case where the bequest vests at death, that is, if the means are impracticable then, the doctrine will be employed; but if there is an expectancy, the court must bide its time).

Cf. also Rector of St. James Church v. Wilson (1913), 82 N. J. Eq. 546, 89 Atl. 519; Vineland Trust Co. v. Westendorf (1916), 86 N. J. Eq. 343, 98 Atl. 314 (where a bequest was valid when made for the furtherance of the broadest interpretation of metaphysical thought); Raque *et al.* v. City of Speyer *et al.* (1925), 97 N. J. Eq. 447, 129 Atl. 207 (where the court held that the *cy pres* doctrine can be employed only where there is no particular charitable institution designated and where there is no particular alternative object).

[137] The Statutes provide for the appointment of a trustee by the court; § 2590; and for the distribution *cy pres,* which is to be applied in a very wide signification if the heirs do not claim the bequest for failure of object; § 2593.

For the doctrine of *cy pres cf.* also *In re* Toner's Estate (1918), 260 Pa. 49, 103 Atl. 541; *In re* Mears' Estate (1930), 299 Pa. 217, 149 Atl. 157. For the general doctrine; *cf.* Wright's Estate (1925), 284 Pa. 334, 131 Atl. 188; *In re* Mears' Estate (1930), 299 Pa. 217, 149 Atl. 157 (where a bequest to Harvard University to establish courses in eugenics was valid and did not fail on the refusal of the trustee to serve); *In re* Archambault's Estate (1932), 308 Pa. 549, 162 Atl. 801 (where a direction to set aside income from trust property sufficient to pay pew rent for all time was valid). *Cf.* McGirr v. Aaron (1829), 21 Am. Dec. 361 (where a devise to a priest and his successors was invalid as tending to a perpetuity, but was sustained as having been intended rather for the unincorporated church, for the support of the priest).

[138] Hoeffer *et al.* v. Clogan *et al.* (1898), 171 Ill. 462, 49 N. E. 527; Burke *et al.* v. Burke *et al.* (1913), 259 Ill. 262, 102 N. E. 293; Easton v. Hall (1926), 323 Ill. 397, 154 N. E. 216; Morgan v. National Trust Bank (1928), 331 Ill. 182, 162 N. E. 888; Carlstrom v. Frackelton, 263 Ill. App. 250 (where a bequest in trust for the building of a memorial bridge was held to be a charitable trust, and where it was said that equity will not permit a trust like this to fail for want of a trustee where the appointed trustees are incompetent to act). The doctrine of *cy pres* is operative: *cf.* Webb v. Webb (1930), 340 Ill. 407, 172 N. E. 730. The State adopted the English statutes that had been enacted prior to 1606; Zollman, *l. c.*

[139] Farmers' and Merchants' Bank v. Robinson (1902), 96 Mo. App. 385, 70 S. W. 372; Methodist Episcopal Church v. Walters, 50 Fed. (2nd) 416 (where a bequest to a charity connected with the Methodist Episcopal Church was held to be too vague); Newton v. Newton Burial Park (1930), 34 S. W. (2nd) 118 (where the building of a chapel and the beautifying, ornamenting, and maintaining of a cemetery for the benefit of an indefinite number of the public of the white race were held to be public charities); Gosset v. Swinney (1931), 53 Fed. (2nd) 772, affirming the decree (D. C.) Irwin v. Swinney, 44 Fed. (2nd) 172, *cert den* Gosset v. Swinney, 52 S. Ct. 497 (where it is definitely stated that the English Statute of charitable uses is part of the common law of Missouri, and that discretionary power will be upheld in a trustee where the purpose expressed is extremely general). Missouri adopted the English statutes effective prior to 1606; Zollman, *l. c.*

[140] Dingwell v. Seymour (1928), 267 Pac. 327; *In re* Wood's Estate (1930), 292 Pac. 144; O'Hara v. Grand Lodge (1931), 2 Pac. (2nd) 21; *In re* Vance's Estate (1931), 4 Pac. (2nd) 977 (where a fund given to executors to be invested for Bibles to be distributed in missions to be determined by them, while a public trust, was not a charitable one); *In re* Bartlett's Estate (1932), 10 Pac. (2nd) 126 (where the court said that the indefiniteness of the beneficiary is one of the characteristics of a charitable bequest); *In re* McDole's Estate (1932), 10 Pac. (2nd) 75; *In re* Wirt's Estate (1932), 12 Pac. (2nd) 95. The *cy pres* doctrine is applied: O'Hara v. Grand Lodge (1931), 2 Pac. (2nd) 21 (where

Indiana;[142] Georgia, where the court is permitted to fill a vacancy in the office of trustee;[143] Kentucky;[144] Florida;[145] Alabama;[146] Ar-

the means failed to establish an orphan asylum, and the property was permitted to be sold and devoted to a cognate purpose). California adopted the common law; Zollman, *op. cit.*, 95, 96.

[141] *In re* Galland's Estate (1918), 103 Wash. 106, 173 Pac. 740; *In re* Peterson's Estate, 141 Wash. 619, 252 Pac. 139 (where a bequest to the poor people of Spokane was upheld); Hunter's Estate, 147 Wash. 216; 265 Pac. 466 (where the court said that when the testator appoints a trustee and thus provided the means for choosing the ultimate beneficiaries, the gift is sufficiently definite); *In re* Planck's Estate, 150 Wash. 301, 272 Pac. 972. The common law is adopted by statute, § 143.

[142] Ackerman v. Fichter (1913), 179 Ind. 392, 101 N. E. 493; Richards v. Wilson (1916), 185 Ind. 335, 112 N. E. 780; Reasoner v. Herman (1922), 191 Ind. 642, 134 N. E. 276 (where it is said that the machinery of administration will be treated as suggestions to be disregarded if impracticable or unlawful). By statute Indiana also adopted the English statutes effective prior to 1606; § 244.

[143] Thompson v. Hale (1905), 123 Ga. 305, 51 S. E. 383; Ford v. Thomas, 111 Ga. 493, 36 S. E. 841; Bolick v. Cox (1916), 145 Ga. 888, 90 S. E. 54; Egleston v. Trust Co. (1917), 147 Ga. 154, 93 S. E. 84; Eagan v. Commissioners of Internal Revenue (1930), 43 Fed. (2nd) 881. *Cy pres* permits approximation to the general intent as far as possible where the original plan becomes impracticable; Ford v. Thomas, 111 Ga. 493, 36, S. E. 841; but where it was feared the hospital would not be able to receive all the patients expected of it by the testator, it was held that this did not make his plans impossible; Reynolds v. Stanton (1932), 162 S. E. 783.

[144] Kentucky took over the laws of Virginia in its Constitution of 1792 (June 1), at which time Virginia still had the Statute of Elizabeth, though it was repealed in Virginia in November of the same year. In fact for a time Kentucky treated *cy pres* as existing in that State in its widest sense. But soon the courts regarded the ultra-judicial power as not re-enacted. *Cf.* § 317. *Cf.* Ford v. Ford (1891), 91 Ky. 572, 16 S. W. 451 (where a devise of the whole estate was made for a monument). The statutes provide for the appointment of a trustee where this is necessary by the court; § 318.

Cf. Coleman *et al.* v. O'Leary's Executor *et al.* (1902), 114 Ky. 388, 70 S. W. 108 (where gifts to the Bishop of Louisville were valid for rewards to poor pupils in parochial schools, and for a home for poor Catholic men, but not a gift to the Jesuits for education and religion because they were unincorporated, nor one to a trustee to be used for charity according to his own judgment); Kasey v. Fidelity Trust Co. (1909), 131 Ky. 609; Owens v. Owens' Executor, 236 Ky. 118, 32 S. W. (2nd) 731 (where an educational fund for the education

kansas;[147] Kansas;[148] Colorado;[149] Utah;[150] North Dakota;[151] New

of worthy American boys and girls was regarded as valid); Gooding v. Watson's Trustee, 235 Ky. 562, 31 S. W. (2nd) 919; Goode's Administrators v. Goode (1931), 238 Ky. 620, 38 S. W. (2nd) 691 (where the use of income from a trust fund for higher education of young people in certain churches and for the testator's church were sustained); Obrecht v. Pujos *et al.* (1925), 206 Ky. 751, 268 S. W. 564 (cited in *AER,* LXXXVIII, 1933, 176).

145 Montgomery v. Carlton (1930), 99 Fla. 152, 126 So. 135 (where it was said that devises for charitable uses to church officers, conferences, and associations are valid even though indefinite or uncertain as to the individual recipients). Florida has adopted the English statutes effective prior to 1606; Zollman, *op. cit.*, 91-94.

146 Henderson v. Henderson (1923), 210 Ala. 73, 97 So. 353; Tarver v. Weaver (1930), 221 Ala. 663, 130 So. 209 (where it was said that a charitable bequest is not void if it is given to an unincorporated association or if the selection of the beneficiaries is left to a trustee). The *cy pres* doctrine is not effective as such in this State, but approximation to the testator's wish in arranging the details of administration is permitted: Trustees of Cumberland University v. Caldwell, 203 Ala. 590, 84 So. 846; Lovelace v. Marion Institute, 215 Ala. 271, 110 So. 381; King v. Banks (1929), 220 Ala. 663, 124 So. 871 (where the court did not permit a modification that would permit a public school to benefit by a bequest to a denominational school); Dunn v. Ellison (1932), 141 So. 700 (which holds that where the fulfillment of the testator's wish is impossible because of changed conditions, the gift escheats to the heirs). Alabama is governed by the provisions of the common law, which is adopted by statute, exept where the statutes modify it; §§ 395, 396.

147 The common law statutes effective prior to 1606 are operative here; Zollman, *l. c.; cf.* Whitten v. Wegman (1930), 30 S. W. (2nd) 834 (where, however, it was held that a devise of property to go toward the building of a home for the city's dependent old women was too vague). But the *cy pres* doctrine operates when it can be conclusively proved that the wish of the testator can not be effected: McCarroll v. Grand Lodge (1922), 154 Ark. 376, 243 S. W. 870; Burel v. Grand Lodge (1924), 163 Ark. 131, 259 S. W. 369; Hecks Memorial Christian Assn. v. Locke, 178 Ark. 692, 12 S. W. (2nd) 866.

148 The statutes adopt the common law; § 77-109. *Cf.* Troutman v. De Boissiere Home, 64 Pac. 33, 5 L. R. A. (N. S.) 693; Bauer v. Mauers (1917), 244 Fed. 902; Treadwell v. Beebe (1920), 107 Kan. 31, 190 Pac. 768 (where it was held that a trust for fuel and food for the needy who were actual residents of the city is valid in the hands of the city); Clark v. Wilkins (1930), 130 Kan. 549, 287 Pac. 244 (where a Masonic lodge was adjudged capable of taking a bequest for charity).

149 Colorado has adopted the English statutes effective prior to 1606; Zoll-

Mexico;[152] Nevada;[153] Nebraska;[154] Wyoming;[155] Montana;[156] Oklahoma;[157] South Dakota;[158] Idaho and Arizona.[159]

641. The general conclusion that may be drawn as to the disabilities affecting the beneficiaries of charitable and religious bequests may be summarized in seven points. The first three points derive from the attitude of the courts towards charitable bequests. The last four, from the mortmain statutes, which divide themselves, as will be evident, into three different types. Some forbid religious and charitable institutions to hold property (as is suggested in the fourth deduction made herewith) or restrict the amount of property

man, *l. c.* The court says that the Statute of Elizabeth is the law of Colorado; St. Mary's Academy v. Solomon, 77 Colo. 463, 238 Pac. 22. *Cf.* Haggin v. International Co. (1917), 60 Colo. 135, 169 Pac. 138; *In re* Forrester's Estate (1929), 279 Pac. 721; Schleier's Estate (1932), 13 Pac. 273.

150 The English common law is adopted by statute; § 5838. Staines v. Burton (1898), 53 Pac. 1015 (where a residuary estate to a bishop for the benefit of the members of the Latter Day Saints was held valid).

151 The English common law is adopted by statute; § 4331. Hagen v. Sacrison (1909), 19 N. D. 160, 123 N. W. 518 (which decided that a charitable bequest is valid if it can be determined whom the testator wished to be trustee).

152 The common law governs; Zollman, *op. cit.*, 95, 96. Rhodes v. Yates (1921), 27 N. M. 489, 202 Pac. 698 (where it was held that a trust for the purposes of evangelization was not void for uncertainty as to object or beneficiary).

153 The common law is effective by statute; § 9021. See Nixon v. Brown (1923), 46 Nev. 439, 214 Pac. 524 (where a gift of a theater in trust for the use of the people of a small city was held valid as a charitable trust).

154 The English common law is adopted by statute, § 49-101. *Cf. In re* Nelson's Estate, 81 Neb. 809, 116 N. W. 971 (where it is said that there is no application of the *cy pres* doctrine in the State and that the Statute of Elizabeth is not in operation, but that the court of equity exercises original and inherent jurisdiction); Elliott v. Quinn (1922), 109 Neb. 5, 189 N. W. 173 (where it is stated that a gift for charitable uses will not be permitted to fail for the lack of an appointed trustee, for the court will appoint one).

155 The common law is operative; Zollman, *l. c.*

156 Common law holds by adoption under the statutes; § 4.

157 Common law adopted by statute; § 2.

158 Statutes approve common law; § 3. *Cf.* Havsgaard's Estate (1931), 238 N. W. 130.

159 The common law governs; Zollman, *l. c.*

that such institutions may hold (as the seventh deduction suggests). A second type places a restriction on the proportion of an estate which a testator may devise to charity or religion, when he has surviving statutory heirs (as is indicated in the sixth deduction). While a third type requires that a bequest to charity or religion be made prior to a fixed date antecedent to death (as is pointed out in the fifth deduction). The points of the general conclusion follow.

First, charitable and religious bequests can be so made that they can be sustained in all the States, except Mississippi, where only bequests of personalty can be made, and even these not to religious purposes; and Wisconsin, where *devises* can not be made except to charitable and religious *corporations*. Second, it is always preferable to name a religious or charitable chartered corporation as beneficiary. Third, a trustee should be appointed, though this procedure is not sufficient in Maryland; while in Virginia, the trustee must not be an unincorporated association. Fourth, the incapacities touching clergymen and churches must be considered in Maryland, Vermont, Delaware, and Louisiana. Fifth, attention must be paid to the nullifying period preceding death within which a valid charitable bequest can not be made in Pennsylvania, California, Montana, Idaho, Ohio, and Georgia. Sixth, the statutes limiting aggregate charitable bequests to a certain portion of the estate should be studied in California, Georgia, Idaho, Montana, Iowa, Louisiana, and New York. And seventh, the restrictions on the amount of property that may be held by religious and charitable institutions should be scrutinized in Pennsylvania, Massachusetts, New Hampshire, Louisiana, Arkansas, Kentucky, Tennessee, Virginia, West Virginia, and the District of Columbia.

642. Scholion I. The *Restatement of Trusts,* Tentative Draft No. 5, of the American Law Institute contains references to the various disabilities that have been indicated. First, it provides that statutory restrictions (mortmain statutes) on the amount of an estate disposable by will, on the time at which a charitable bequest must be made, and on the amount of property institutions may hold, shall be permitted to remain in full vigor.[160] It provides that indefiniteness of

[160] § 352.

beneficiary and perpetuity of purpose will not invalidate charitable trusts.[161] Charitable trusts, it states, were enforced in chancery prior to the Statute, 43 Elizabeth, and therefore failure to adopt that Statute does not affect the validity of a charitable trust in any State.[162] A trust established indefinitely "for the poor" or "for the worship of God" is valid.[163] If an unincorporated association has no right to hold for itself, it can not hold property as trustee.[164] A trust is valid even though by its terms the trustee is authorized to apply the trust property to any charitable purpose he may select; even though no trustee has been named; and even if the ultimate beneficiary is an unincorporated association or a corporation incapable of holding property. The court will appoint a trustee in the two latter cases.[165] The doctrine of *cy pres* is to be operative, *i. e.*, to the extent of effecting the general intention of the testator. But a bequest merely "to charity" will be enforced.[166]

[161] §§ 354, 355.

[162] § 358.

[163] §§ 359, 361.

[164] § 368.

[165] §§ 378, 386, 387.

[166] §§ 386, 387.

CHAPTER X

BEQUESTS FOR MASSES

643. Bequests for Masses have been sustained as charitable trusts in many of the States where they have been brought before the court for adjudication. They offer themselves for study here, then, with no small measure of insistence. For now that the nature of a charitable trust is rather well understood, it is the more readily comprehended what the courts mean when they speak of a Mass bequest as a public or charitable trust. Consequently, it should be possible now to pass better judgment on this view than would otherwise have been the case. But these bequests have not been considered as charitable bequests in all the courts. For the sake of clarity, an attempt will be made here to introduce a semblance of order into the almost chaotic state of the various opinions on this matter.

According to the divergent views of the various courts a bequest for Masses may be:

1—a charitable trust:

a—valid (this is the more general view); adopted also by the American Law Institute, where the bequest is not made to a specified priest (*cf. Restatement of Trusts*, Tentative Draft No. 5, § 361);

b—invalid because the beneficiary is too indefinite to be sustained (this was once the view in New York, Wisconsin and Minnesota);

2—a private trust, that is, a trust for the benefit of one or a few private persons; in this instance, for the repose of the soul of the decedent;

a—valid (this is the current view in Iowa);

b—invalid (this is the view in Alabama) on the ground that it offends against the laws on perpetuities or because there is no living beneficiary to enforce the trust;

3—not a trust, but when given to a specified priest, a valid gift to him (this is the view in Kansas, California, and Rhode Island; it was once held also in New York); this is the view of the American Law Institute in its Tentative Draft No. 5 of the *Restatement of Trusts*, § 361;

4—not a trust, but sustainable as funeral expenses (once held in the lower courts in New York).

One other opinion has been held, but not in the United States, viz., that such a bequest is a trust that fails because it is instituted for superstitious purposes.[1]

644. Classification of Mass Stipends. In the interests of clarity, too, it will be expedient to note the distinction made by the canons between the three kinds of Mass stipends.[2] Stipends for Masses which are handed to a priest to be said once for all are called *manual*, even when they are given him by the heirs of the testator out of a fund which they hold for the purpose under the latter's will. Mass stipends that come to a priest from a charitable foundation, when he is not the one obliged under the foundation to celebrate the Masses, are called *quasi-manual* or *ad instar manualium*. Finally, when they are celebrated out of the income of a foundation by one who is bound under the foundation, they are called *founded* Masses. In the latter case, there is really no stipend. The celebrant assumes the obligation as part of his office; though from the office he usually obtains at least a portion of his living.[3]

[1] *Cf. AER*, LXXXVIII (1933), 170.

[2] Canon 826, § 1. "Stipendia quae a fidelibus pro Missis offeruntur sive ex propria devotione, veluti ad manum, sive ex obligatione etiam perpetua a testatore propriis heredibus facta, *manualia* dicuntur."

§ 2. "*Ad instar manualium* vocantur stipendia Missarum fundatarum, quae applicari non possunt in proprio loco, aut ab iis qui eas applicare deberent secundum tabulas fundationis, et ideo de iure aut Sanctae Sedis indulto aliis sacerdotibus tradendae sunt ut iisdem satisfiat."

§ 3. "Alia stipendia quae ex fundationum reditibus percipiuntur, appellantur *fundata* seu *Missae fundatae*."

[3] *Cf.* De Meester, *op. cit.*, 1488; Benedict XIV, *De Synodo Dioecesana*, lib. 13, c. ult., n. 4; S. C. C., 11 May, 1904—*Fontes*, n. 4317; S. C. C. *in Causa Aliphana*, 19 December, 1904—*Fontes*, n. 4319.

645. The Question Adjudicated in Fifteen States. The States where the problem of bequests for Masses has reached the highest courts are few enough, fifteen only. The consequence is that considerable doubt must remain as to the view the remaining States would take, were such a bequest to be brought before their highest court for adjudication. This doubt remains in spite of any knowledge that might be possessed concerning the State's doctrine on charitable bequests, because it is possible that a bequest for Masses might be regarded as a private trust. If the court should view the bequest in that light, it is immediately beset with all the difficulties that can arise from the uncertainty of the beneficiary, the inability of the beneficiary to enforce the trust, and the statute against perpetuities.

However, be it said that in only two of the States where the question has been adjudicated has a bequest for Masses been regarded as a private trust; and in only one of those has it been deemed invalid. That State is Alabama, which, as has been indicated, sustains indefinite charitable bequests. Iowa holds it to be a private trust, but valid.

In only three other of the States where the question has arisen, has the validity of the bequest been questioned, and that was due to the peculiar doctrine which these States held as to charitable and religious trusts in general. These States were New York, Wisconsin, and Minnesota. The former two have since sustained bequests for Masses; while the latter should do so under its statutes of 1927, though the problem has not come before its highest court since that time.

Kansas, too, might be regarded as doubtful, but with the probability that it will continue to support these bequests. The case that was presented to the courts in that State was hardly typical, since the priest beneficiary was the grandson of the testatrix, and the bequest was regarded as a gift. It is not certain whether every Mass bequest would be so construed.

The remaining States where the issue has been tried offer no difficulty, viz., Pennsylvania, New Jersey, Massachusetts, Illinois, California, Rhode Island, New Hampshire, Indiana, and Kentucky.[4]

646. A bequest for Masses would not be defeated as a bequest

[4] *Cf. AER,* LXII (1920), 650, 651; LXIII (1920), 289.

to a superstitious use in the United States, but it was regarded as such in England until quite recent times. In 1897 the courts in Ireland had sustained Mass bequests as not tending to superstition [5] but England did not reach that decision until twenty years later. Although the Catholic Relief Acts of 1791 and 1829, and the Catholic Charities Acts of 1823 and 1860 would have warranted the courts in sustaining Mass bequests, it was not until 1919 that such a benign interpretation of the law was made. But that decision merely declared them to be valid as not tending to superstition. In 1933 a later decision decided that they are charitable and thus valid even when established in a perpetual foundation.[6]

647. **In New York,** a bequest for Masses has been regarded in every one of the views presented at the beginning of the discussion, except as a private trust.

648. **Nevertheless, it seems fairly consistently to have been regarded as a charitable bequest in the highest court of the State.** It was held to be such in the case of Holland v. Alcock (1888),[7] but it was regarded as invalid due to the peculiar interpretation which the courts at the time placed upon the statutes of the State touching charity in general. The court declared that, to be sustained, bequests for Masses should be given to incorporated societies, just as other charitable bequests.

649. This decision was followed in Gifford v. O'Connor (1889),[8]

[5] *Cf.* Hoeffer v. Clogan, 171 Ill. 462; in O'Hanlon v. Logue (1906), they were held to be charitable because they provide for public worship, support priests, and benefit the faithful; *cf.* Irish Reports at p. 247 (cited by *The Tablet,* CLXII (1933), 659.

[6] Bourne v. Keane (1919), Appeal Cases, L. R. 815. In this case the testator bequeathed two hundred pounds to Westmister Cathedral and a similar amount in addition to his residuary estate to the Jesuit Fathers, Farm Street. The bequests were for the celebration of Masses, and were sustained. *Cf. AER,* XX (1899), 167; LXII (1920), 646; LXXXVIII (1933), 170. *In re* Caus; Lindeboom v. Camille (1933); *cf. The Tablet, l. c.; The Month,* "The Final Victory of the Mass," CLXIII (1934), 345.

[7] 108 N. Y. 312, 16 N. E. 305; *cf.* § 601; *AER,* XX (1899), 168; *cf.* Dillon, *Bequests for Masses,* p. 49.

[8] 117 N. Y. 275, 22 N. E. 1036. It was originally in the Surrogate Court

in a case where no priest beneficiary was named.[9]

650. In 1918 the problem was again before the Court of Appeals, and this time it was again regarded as a charitable bequest, but valid.[10] The Court of Appeals reversed the decision of a lower court, which had reduced a residuary estate to an allowance of five dollars for Masses. The higher court held that the balance was a trust for a certain public charity, that is, for Masses, and that the testatrix had no desire to die partially intestate. This is now the law of the State.

651. Mass Bequests as Funeral Expenses. Prior to the decision in the case of Holland v. Alcock, it was held in Holland v. Smith (1886) that a provision in a will for Masses is valid and enforceable, seemingly on the theory that it is a provision for funeral expenses.[11] This is the theory also behind the decision in the lower court in the case, *In re* Backes (1894),[12] where the court held that a bequest for Masses to be celebrated in a German Catholic Church in the City of Buffalo was not indefinite. But this theory seems to have been abandoned in a decision of the intermediate court in 1906, which

of Westchester County and was known there as *In re* McEvoy's Estate (1888), 3 N. Y. Supp. 207; it was also in the Supreme Court, 3 N. Y. Supp. 337.

[9] The executor had already paid the bequest, but was indemnified by the court because the claim had not been made in due season.

[10] In the lower court, the Surrogate Court of Kings County, the case was the Petition of Seitz, 170 N. Y. Supp. 635, 103 Misc. Rep. 566; in the Court of Appeals it was the case, Morris *et al.* v. Edwards *et al.*, 227 N. Y. 141, 124 N. E. 724. The will bequeathed all the rest, residue, and remainder of the testator's estate to his executor to pay for funeral expenses, to have Masses said, and to have a tombstone erected over his grave. The lower court held this was a trust in the executors to be discharged in accordance with the testator's condition in life, and allowed only five dollars to comply with the provision for Masses.

[11] In the case *In re* Backes' Will (1894), the court quoted the statement of the court in a previous case, and said that the court in Holland v. Alcock also quoted it. The statement was said to have been made by Judge Cullen and quoted in the case, Holland v. Smith, 3 How. Prac. (N. S.) 106, 40 Hun. 372. The Judge said: "I think that a provision for Masses for the benefit of the testator's soul is exactly akin to a provision for his funeral or monument. While decent burial is given, by law, out of even an insolvent's estate, I think the monument is no more an adjunct or concomitant of burial than the Masses."

[12] 30 N. Y. Supp. 394, 9 Misc. Rep. 504.

nevertheless regarded the bequest valid.[13] But it was re-asserted by the same court in 1920.[14]

652. Mass bequests as a gift under New York decisions. The adverse decision in Holland v. Alcock led to similar decisions in Gifford v. O'Connor, in the highest court, and in Porter v. Carolin in the intermediate court, and *In re* Schwartz's Will, in the Surrogate Court.[15] However, the courts seemed to be unwilling to let these bequests fail, and so arose the theory of gift. Prior to the Holland v. Alcock decision, a bequest for Masses had been sustained in the Court of Appeals where it had been a gift *inter vivos*.[16]

The circumstances were these. The decedent had given a fund to the trustee with the obligation that he would support her and her husband during their lives; that he would pay all funeral expenses, erect a monument, and have Masses said for the repose of their souls. The lower court had held that she could have revoked the commission, and that the trust was invalid for the want of a beneficiary. But the Court of Appeals held that the commission was more than a mere agency, and consequently an irrevocable trust, a valid contract *de praesenti* to be executed after death, similar to one in which a man would hire a sculptor to make a statue of him after his death. Obviously in the latter case, no beneficiary would be needed.

A similar arrangement was held valid in 1904; but in 1905 the court while, admitting the validity of a trust established *inter vivos*, demanded evidence to show the intention of the testator to establish it. In 1906, however, a trust of this kind was again sustained, even where a priest was the trustee.[17]

[13] *In re* McAvoy's Estate, 98 N. Y. Supp. 437, 112 App. Div. 377. The reason for the reversal was probably that if the bequest were regarded as funeral expenses, it would have been exempt from the transfer tax.

[14] *In re* Dwyer, 182 N. Y. Supp. 64, 192 App. Div. 72 (where the court said that the lower court should not have treated a bequest for Masses as a legacy, but as an expense which should have been deducted in determining the net estate).

[15] Porter v. Carolin (1888), N. Y. Supp. 791; *In re* Schwartz's Will (1888), 3 N. Y. Supp. 134.

[16] Gilman v. McArdle (1885), 99 N. Y. 451, 2 N. E. 464.

[17] Morris v. Hughes (1904), 92 N. Y. Supp. 288, 45 Misc. Rep. 278 (where

Whether the courts arrived at this decision in an attempt to save bequests for Masses from the operation of the adverse decisions against charitable bequests must remain a matter of conjecture.

653. In any event in the very next year after the Holland v. Alcock decision, a bequest for Masses was sustained as a gift to a Catholic church named as trustee, along with bequests for poor students, and for the establishment of a Catholic newspaper. The court seems to have placed reliance on the word *ordination* used in the will instead of bequest.[18] And in the same year where a designated priest was named beneficiary, the bequest was sustained in a similar case.[19] The following year, bequests for Masses to several pastors and to the Bishop of Long Island were held to be gifts to individuals.[20] And on the same theory, Mass bequests were again sustained in 1893 and 1898.[21]

the circumstances were these: Five thousand dollars had been validly transferred by the decedent before death to the trustee with the obligation of supporting her, paying the expenses of her funeral, and giving one thousand dollars to a priest designated by name for Masses; this was held to be a valid trust *inter vivos*). Hoffman v. Union Dime Savings Institution (1905), 95 N. Y. Supp. 1045, 109 App. Div. 24 (where the agent was given power of attorney and attempted to show that it was irrevocable from certain statements made by his principal relative to having Masses said for her soul; but this was held to be insufficient evidence to prove the intent to establish a trust). Morris v. Wucher (1906), 100 N. Y. Supp. 878, 115 App. Div. 278 (where a decedent gave four thousand dollars to a priest for church decorations, who was to pay interest during the donor's life, and to dispose of the principal after death according to instructions in a private letter; in a letter found among the decedent's effects there was an instruction that one hundred dollars should be distributed for Masses).

18 Ruppel v. Schlegel *et al.*, 7 N. Y. Supp. 936.

19 *In re* Black's Estate, 5 N. Y. Supp. 452, 1 Con. 477.

20 Vandeveer v. McKane, 11 N. Y. Supp. 808. Cited in *AER*, XIX (1898), 542; XX (1899), 170. The purpose here seems to have been not only to save these bequests from the operation of adverse decisions against charitable bequests, but also to prevent them from being added to the total of charitable bequests, which might thus exceed the limit allowed. California courts rendered a similiar decision with a similar purpose.

21 *In re* Howard's Estate (1893), 25 N. Y. Supp. 1111, 5 Misc. Rep. 295 (where three hundred dollars was left to two priests, one of whom had died

654. The view that a Mass bequest is a *valid* charitable bequest, embraced by the Court of Appeals in 1918, was advanced in the Surrogate Court of Kings County as early as 1909, which applied to bequests for Masses the liberal statute adopted in 1893 as tc charitable bequests in general.[22]

655. This view seems now to be the unmistakable doctrine in New York as is evidenced by a number of decisions in the lower courts.[23] A very late decision in the lower court, after stating that Mass bequests are general legacies for charitable purposes and not necessarily part of the funeral expenses, thought that if the Masses were celebrated as part of the funeral services and the amount was reasonable, it might be allowed under the items of the funeral charges.

656. In conclusion as to New York, two points seem well established: first, that a trust for the celebration of Masses can be constituted in that State prior to death, if sufficient evidence is left to prove that a real trust was instituted; **second, that bequests will be regarded as public or charitable legacies** subject to deductions if the testator exceeds the legal amount which he was authorized to bestow upon charity and religion.

657. Mass Bequests are Charitable in Pennsylvania. In Pennsylvania the question seems first to have come before the courts when it was attempted to save a bequest for Masses from the operation of the statute prescribing that charitable bequests must be made at

prior to the testator; the bequest was held a valid gift on condition to the living priest; invalid, however, as to the deceased because he was incapable of fulfilling the condition); cited in *AER,* XIX (1898), 542; XX (1899), 170. *In re* Zimmerman's Will (1898), 50 N. Y. Supp. 395, 22 Misc. Rep. 411 (six hundred dollars bequeathed to a priest described as being stationed at a certain church was held a conditional gift to the priest and not a trust, inasmuch as it was not to the church nor for the benefit of the church).

[22] Now § 12 of the Personal Property Law and § 113 of the Real Propert} Law. The case was *In re* Eppig's Estate, 118 N. Y. Supp. 683, 63 Misc. Rep. 613.

[23] *In re* Welch (1918), 172 N. Y. Supp. 349, 105 Misc. Rep. 27; *In re* Beck's Estate (1927), 225 N. Y. Supp. 187; 130 Misc. Rep. 765 (where the bequests for Masses were reckoned among the charitable bequests in determining what proportion of the estate the decedent had given to charity); *In re* Werrick's Estate (1930), 239 N. Y. Supp. 740, 135 Misc. Rep. 876; *In re* Cunningham's Estate (1931), 249 N. Y. Supp. 439, 140 Misc. Rep. 91.

least thirty days prior to the testator's death.[24] In 1878 the Orphans Court of Philadelphia County had held a bequest for Masses not a charitable bequest but a private bequest for the benefit of the testator,[25] but two years later the Supreme Court decided that such a bequest was a charitable bequest, and such has been the rule ever since.[26]

658. The New Jersey courts are most favorable to bequests for Masses, basing their decisions on the ground that they are charitable bequests. Thus in 1898, where the priest appointed recipient of the bequest died prior to the testator, the court assumed to appoint another in his place. In 1900, a bequest for Masses to Woodstock College, in Howard County, Maryland, was ordered paid to

[24] Act of April 26, 1855, § 11; now § 8312.

[25] *In re* Dougherty, 12 Phila. 70.

[26] Rhymer's Appeal (1880), 93 Pa. 142; cited also in *AER,* XIX (1898), 542; Appeal of Seibert (1886), 6 Atl. 105 (where immediate payment of the full sum to the priest was ordered, minus the collateral inheritance tax; cited in *AER, l. c.*); *In re* O'Donnell's Estate (1904), 209 Pa. 63, 58 Atl. 120; Nead's Estate (1914), 55 Pa. Supp. 573 (where the court, while incidentally approving the prevailing doctrine, said it was not necessary to resort to the doctrine of charitable bequests to sustain the bequest before the court, because there was no indefiniteness as to amount, purpose, or trustee—the latter was to spend the money with power to choose whomsoever she might wish; but the bequest was subjected to the collateral tax).

A curious case connected with this problem arose under the will of Father Browers, who left his estate to "a Roman Catholic priest that shall succeed me in this said place, to be entailed to him and his successors, and so left by him who shall succeed me to his successors, and so in trust for the use herein mentioned in succession forever." It was argued that because there was an obligation of celebrating Masses attached to it, this was a bequest for Masses and that Father Fromm, who had taken possession of the parish by agreement with the executors, but without the authority of Bishop Carroll, and who, though interdicted and suspended, could not lose the power of saying Mass validly, was able to fulfill the requirements of the bequest and could not therefore be dispossessed. The court decided that Father Browers meant to establish a trust for the congregation and that the saying of the Masses was incidental. Since Father Fromm was not the lawful successor of Father Browers, he could not retain possession. *Cf.* Lessee of Executors of Theodorus Browers v. Franciscus Fromm—Westmoreland County, 1798. See also McGirr v. Aaron (1829), 21 Am. Dec. 361, where this same bequest was held to be a charitable gift to the congregation.

Woodstock College, of Baltimore County, as there is no other college of that name in Maryland. The court said that the absence of proof to show that Masses are not said at the College left no other course open than to award the legacy. As recently as 1929, a bequest for Masses bequeathed to a priest who never existed was invalid, but one hundred dollars of the bequest was ordered paid as funeral expenses, even though one charitable bequest in the same will was held invalid for want of a trustee and of definite beneficiaries (it was bequeathed to *some* Catholic institution).[27]

659. Illinois regards these bequests as valid charitable bequests. In the case, Gilmore v. Lee, where a priest who had been made beneficiary and had been given by the testatrix a deed for realty, a promissory note, and a certificate of deposit, he was held not entitled to the realty or the promissory note, even though he released the claim under the will and based his case only on the *donatio mortis causa*. But he was permitted to take the certificate of deposit, which had been given him for Masses. The court gave two reasons, saying that the gift was intended for charity and in support of a form of worship; and second, that the priest would be obliged to perform the religious services and thus would earn the money. The deed could not pass by manual delivery and the promissory note labored under the presumption of undue influence.[28]

660. Kentucky follows the decision in Hoeffer v. Clogan in the case, Coleman *et al.* v. O'Leary's Executor *et al.* (1902). The court, in rendering its opinion said, "a gift . . . for the establishment of a church would not . . . be avoided by a provision that the church should be called by the name of the testator." So a private benefit is consistent with a public trust. Consequently it sustained bequests of three thousand dollars to a Father Hayes and of one thousand dollars for Masses to be said in the Cathedral at Louisville.[29]

[27] Kerrigan v. Tabb *et al.* (1898), 39 Atl. 701; Kerrigan *et al.* v. Connelly *et al.* (1900), 46 Atl. 227; Moran v. Kelley *et al.* (1924), 95 N. J. Eq. 380, 124 Atl. 67 (affirmed in 100 N. J. L. 305, 126 Atl. 924); Chelsea Nat. Bank v. Our Lady Church (1929), 147 Atl. 470.

[28] Hoeffer *et al.* v. Clogan *et al.* (1898), 171 Ill. 462, 49 N. E. 527; Gilmore v. Lee (1908), 237 Ill. 402, 86 N. E. 568; Burke *et al.* v. Burke *et al.* (1913), 259 Ill. 262, 102 N. E. 293.

661. The same theory prevails in Massachusetts,[30] New Hampshire,[31] and Indiana.[32]

662. Wisconsin seems always to have regarded these bequests as charitable. But due to the peculiar theory in that State subjecting public trusts to the same requirements that were demanded of private trusts, bequests for Masses failed in the case, McHugh v. McCole *et al.* (1897).[33] Due to the modified attitude of the courts under the decision in Harrington v. Pier, a bequest for Masses was sustained in 1910, where the court, fearful still of enforcing devises offending against the statutes against perpetuities, decided that the real estate had been converted into personalty under the necessities of the will, and the bequests could be sustained. The concurring judge denied the necessity of relying on equitable conversion, arguing that devises of realty to public trusts are exempt from the statute against perpetuities. On the other hand, the dissenting judge said that the court could not compel the performance of a religious ceremony, and that consequently the trust must fail. But the court

[29] Coleman *et al.* v. O'Leary's Executor *et al.*, 114 Ky. 388, 70 S. W. 1068. *Cf.* also Obrecht v. Pujos (1925), 206 Ky. 751, 268 S. W. 564 (where a Trappist novice bequeathed three hundred dollars for Masses for his soul, and the bequest was regarded as for a public benefit as conducing to the promotion of public worship, and was held not to fail for the lack of a trustee or because there is no beneficiary to enforce the fulfillment of the trust, because the donee takes the bequest subject to a moral obligation and the next of kin may apply for enforcement; cited in *AER*, LXXXVIII, 1933, 176).

[30] *Ex parte* Schouler (1883), 134 Mass. 426.

[31] Webster v. Sughrow *et al.* (1898), 69 N. H. 380, 45 Atl. 139.

[32] Ackerman v. Fichter *et al.* (1913), 179 Ind. 392, 101 N. E. 493. Here the Masses were bequeathed for the repose of all poor souls. The court said that it was not a private trust, as it might be if the Masses were restricted in their application to the souls of designated persons. The Mass, it is said, is a public and general religious service, for the living as well as the dead; and those who are living, and the living kindred of those who are dead, have a direct interest in its observance, and can enforce the execution of the trust. Bread, wine and music cost something, it was added by the court.

[33] 97 Wis. 166, 72 N. W. 631 (where the court said that bequests for Masses in an amount of more than three thousand dollars in the particular case must fail because they were not personal gifts to the bishop; if they were, they would be sustained; instead, the trust failed because the object and purpose are indefinite and there is no beneficiary to enforce its fulfillment).

declared that it could compel the performance of a religious ceremony, not *per se*, but under the contractual aspect of the trust.[34]

663. **In the case, *In re* Shanahan's Estate (1903), Minnesota courts definitely included bequests of personalty under the trusts forbidden by the statutes of that State, even when the object was charity. It was this same case that regarded bequests for Masses invalid for the reason noted,** just as any other charitable bequest would be invalid. The court said that the bequests were not made outright to the bishop with motive expressed, as would be the case if they were made to a corporation. Since they were charitable trusts, ground is offered for believing that under the liberalizing statutes of 1927, bequests for Masses will be sustained in Minnesota. This is merely a forecast, as the problem has not come before the courts since those statutes were enacted.[35]

664. **Iowa, on the other hand, regards these bequests as private trusts.** In 1897 the court said that a bequest was valid for Masses when made to a priest who may be pastor at a definitely named church at the time of the execution of the will, even though the bequest contains no element of a charitable use.[36] It is said to be a private trust as much as the erection of a monument or any other act to perpetuate the memory of a testator. The court recognized the difficulty that caused the courts in Alabama to declare a private trust invalid, that is, the lack of a beneficiary. But it said that the court should not quibble about the technicalities of trusts and beneficiaries where it had before it a bequest for a known lawful purpose, where the power of execution is prescribed and available. On the other hand, the bequest was in the way of fulfilling the testator's hopes for happiness hereafter. Where promises and pledges made in life for the support of religious observances seek

[34] *In re* Kavanaugh's Estate, 143 Wis. 90, 126 N. W. 672 (cited in *AER*, LXXXVIII (1933), 172. The attorneys seeking to sustain the bequest developed a very thorough argument for the public character of the Mass, quoting from the Canon the prayers for superiors and for the living and the dead.

[35] *Cf.* §§ 623-625, supra.

[36] Moran v. Moran *et al.* (1897), 104 Ia. 216, 73 N. W. 617; cited in *AER*, XIX (1898), 542; XX (1899), 169. In a prior case, Seda v. Huble (1888), 75 Ia. 429, 39 N. W. 685, where property was given to a church with the obligation of an annual Mass, it was regarded as a charitable bequest.

the same end, they are valid. Why, then, should not this bequest be valid? The provision, it is repeated, differs little from one for the erection of a monument after the death of the testator, not intended for the benefit of the living, but capable of being procured by the testator, if he were alive, by contract. Such bequests, when definite enough for the intent to be known, are valid.

The decision, it must be said, rests on rather insecure ground. It is, however, the ruling opinion at the moment, for a similar decision was rendered in 1919, where a bequest for Masses was to be paid out of the proceeds of the sale of land and no priest beneficiary was named. The court sustained the bequest as being sufficiently definite in its beneficiaries, who were the testator and his wife, for the repose of whose souls the Masses were to be celebrated.[87]

665. Alabama, on the other hand, regarding these bequests as private trusts, refuses to sustain them, because there is no beneficiary to enforce due fulfillment.[88]

666. The final view remaining to be considered is that these bequests are personal gifts. Rhode Island and Kansas adopted this view in the same year, 1898. However, only one case has been decided by the highest court in Kansas, and there the priest was the grandson of the testatrix and the language was precatory.[89]

667. The court in Rhode Island had before it the various decisions rendered prior to 1898, and deliberately accepted the view that the bequest is personal to the priest. The gift takes effect at once as any other personal bequest. It is given to the priest him-

[87] Wilmes v. Tiernay (1919), 187 Ia. 390, 174 N. W. 271; cited in *AER*, LXXXVIII (1933), 175.

[88] Festorazzi *et al.* v. St. Joseph's Catholic Church *et al.* (1894), 104 Ala. 327, 18 So. 394; cited in *AER*, XX (1899), 168; LXXXVIII (1933), 174.

[89] Harrison v. Brophy *et al.* (1898), 59 Kan. 1, 51 Pac. 883, where the words of the testarix were: "I give and bequeath to Rev. James Collins, for Mass for his grandfather's and grandmother's soul." The court said that on the conscience of the donee alone is laid the duty of performing the sacred service. It distinguished the case from the bequests in Holland v. Alcock (the New York case), by saying that in the latter case the bequests were left to the trustees *eo nomine*, and that the court there recognized the distinction by admitting that its decision would be different if the bequests had been made to incorporated churches.

self, not for another, for his service in saying the Mass. The court compares the bequest to a mourning ring to be worn in memory of a deceased person. It confers a benefit on the deceased through a benefit to the beneficiary. Moreover, one can not be trustee for himself, which would be the conclusion to be drawn from the theory that a bequest for Masses is a trust.[40]

The argument was repeated when the same case was brought once more to the attention of the court in an attempt to resist abatement of the bequests for Masses. The court argued that the bequest was not to abate with the other legacies, for it is really a payment for the services of the priest, on the principle of a consideration arising after the testator's death.[41]

In 1923, a gift for Masses was sustained where the words of the bequest were that one hundred dollars is bequeathed "for religious services, in memory of me, my parents and relatives—I request that said sum be given to Rev. John Murry, of SS. Peter and Paul's Parish, in said Providence (if in the Diocese of Providence), or to such other priest as the executor decides." The executor had died without making any choice. The administrator was directed to pay the sum to the priest named.[42]

668. In 1907, California adopted this view, thus withdrawing bequests for Masses from the disabilities arising out of the statutes requiring that charitable bequests be made more than thirty days prior to the decease of the testator and limiting the amount of an estate that may be devoted to charity.[43] In 1918 a case came before the court where the trust was instituted during the life of the testatrix, and was to be paid after her death for Masses. It was attacked because it was given to a church and not to a priest. The court said that it was given to the pastor by implication.[44] In 1920, the courts, while still holding that bequests to pastors are gifts, agreed that they are charitable trusts when bequeathed to bishops, on the ground that

[40] Sherman v. Baker *et al.* (1898), 20 R. I. 446, 40 Atl. 11, cited in *AER*, XX (1899), 169.

[41] 20 R. I. 613, 40 Atl. 765.

[42] Slattery v. Ward (1923), 45 R. I. 54, 119 Atl. 755.

[43] *In re* Lennon's Estate (1907), 152 Cal. 327, 92 Pac. 870, cited in *AER* LXII (1920), 651; LXIII (1920), 289.

[44] Rutherford v. Ott (1918), 37 Cal. App. 47, 173 Pac. 490.

bishops must distribute the stipends to priests.[45] The decisions in the previous cases were followed *In re* Ward's Estate (1932), where a bequest for Masses given to a pastor was considered as a gift, not invalid because made within thirty days of the testator's death. It imposed an obligation on the priest, however, of saying the Masses. But the obligation is not to be conceived as attaching to the money or to the disposition which the pastor may make of it. The gift is absolute so far as the money is concerned.[46]

669. The California position seems to be the correct one. There is merit in the other views. The Mass is a public religious service, in which the living may participate actively; in the benefits of which they share even when not participating actively. On the other hand, there can be no doubt that in making bequests for Masses the testator usually is not prompted primarily by a desire to promote public worship. Bequests for that purpose are usually made to the church in a general way. The testator almost always desires that Masses be offered for the repose of his soul, sometimes joining the souls of his relatives in his intention. It is on this ground that Iowa and Alabama regard Mass bequests as private trusts.

670. The Various Plans by Which Testators Make Mass Bequests. To approach an analysis of the problem methodically, observe that Masses may be bequeathed to a priest, to a bishop, indefinitely to no one, to a church or institution, or they may be required of an incumbent of a founded institution. Moreover, when they are given to a church or an institution they may be granted in such a way that the capital is to be expended as soon as possible for the celebration of Mass or that only the income shall be expended annually for this purpose.[47]

671. First, consider Masses bequeathed to a priest by name. Such bequests are really gifts. While the bequest may be called a trust in the moral sense, it is not a trust in the legal sense. It is, as

[45] *In re* Hamilton's Estate (1920), 181 Cal. 758, 186 Pac. 587. The large amounts involved were sufficient to convince the court that the bishop was not expected to say all the Masses himself.

[46] *In re* Ward's Estate (1932), 14 Pac. 91.

[47] The question of stipends for the Masses on the occasion of the funeral is omitted. Such stipends usually do not appear in the will, and the courts seem to make no trouble about allowing them as funeral expenses.

the courts in Kansas, Rhode Island, and California say, a gift to the priest.

672. **That a Mass bequest to a priest is a gift will be evident from four arguments. First, from experience.** When a Catholic gives stipends to a priest for Masses, does he ever have the idea of reclaiming the money? Supposing, but not granting, that the Masses, in an unfortunate instance, would not be said, would the Catholic even think of demanding a return of the stipends? He would demand that the Masses be said, but no more.

673. **The second argument derives from the nature of the Mass.** A Mass can not be bought, because its infinite supernatural value transcends any equivalent in material wealth. The priest has the power to offer this sacrifice; the layman, not. The latter can not buy the favor, and the former can not sell it. But by accepting the gift of the latter, the former binds himself to bestow the favor on the donor rather than on some other man who has not shown benevolence to him. Take an illustration. A man can not usually pay a good woman to marry him. But he can make her well disposed to him by gifts. Supposing that by custom or by positive law, the woman who accepted such gifts were to be bound to enter into the marriage, at least if she had accepted gifts in a certain amount. That represents fairly well the position of the priest who has accepted a stipend. He is bound because the donor knows that from the gift there arises an obligation on him to say Masses for the donor's intention.

674. **The third argument is taken from the manner in which the priest takes the bequest.** He becomes not merely the trustee with legal title; but the owner with legal and equitable title. If the money is lost, he is not discharged. He is still bound to celebrate the Masses. Now, if a person becomes full owner of property before he has discharged an obligation arising out of the property, he is not a mere trustee. The obligation thenceforward rests on the priest, by a special claim residing in the donor, just as all the other duties of his state in life rest on him by the general claim residing in the faithful.[48]

[48] Canon 829. "Licet sine culpa illius qui onere celebrandi gravatur, Missarum eleemosynae iam perceptae perierint, obligatio non cessat." *Cf.* Prümmer,

675. Fourth, an argument is offered by the manner in which the obligation is discharged. When the testator has bequeathed stipends to a definitely mentioned priest, if the latter finds it necessary to have another priest say the Masses for him, he is obliged to send only the usual stipend established by the Ordinary, retaining the excess, if there be any. This seems to indicate that the bequest is a gift. At the very least, it shows that there is no essential connection between the duty to say the Masses and the receipt of the bequest.[49]

676. On the other hand, bequests for Masses given to a bishop would seem to be a trust, as it is decided in the courts of California. For the testator can hardly be presumed to have made a *gift* to one whose only means of complying with the condition on which the gift would be made is to convey it to another. Similarly, Masses bequeathed to no one in particular must be regarded as bequeathed

Theol. Mor., III, 265; Woywod, in *The Homiletic and Pastoral Review*, XXI (1921), 811.

[49] Vermeersch-Creusen, *op. cit.*, II, 108. This is true only of legacies given to the priest by name, on account of the presumed favor of the testator for the priest mentioned in the will. If the Masses were bequeathed to a church, the Sacred Congregation of the Council ordains that the whole stipend be sent to the priest who is to celebrate the Mass; 25 July, 1874—*Fontes*, n. 4228. A similar decision was handed down by the Sacred Congregation, including manual and quasi-manual stipends; S. C. C. *in Causa Bredae*, 25 February, 1905—*Fontes*, n. 4321; *ASS*, XXXVIII (1905), 15. Vermeersch-Creusen say that this decree applies *a fortiori* to Masses bequeathed without the designation of any priest beneficiary, *l. c.* In general, profiteering in Mass stipends is strictly forbidden under penalty of suspension; Benedict XIV, ep. encycl., *Quanta Cura*, 30 June, 1741—*Fontes*, n. 311; ep., *Pro eximia*, 30 June, 1741—*Fontes*, n. 312. The prohibition is repeated in the decree of the Sacred Congregation of the Council, 19 December, 1904—*S. C. P. F. Coll.*, n. 2210

On the other hand, if the founded Masses in any foundation can not be celebrated at the institution in any year, the excess income can be retained for the institution, because it would seem that the testator had two intentions and wished to benefit the institution as much as to have the Masses celebrated; Vermeersch-Creusen, *op. cit.*, II, 106; Prümmer, *Man. Iur. Can.*, 294; Bargilliat, *op. cit.*, 1120. *Cf. AER*, LXXXVII (1932), 32. And where a priest is invited to the institution to say the Mass, a certain amount may be deducted from his stipend for the benefit of the institution for heat, light, bread, wine, and candles; but the stipulated number of Masses must not be diminished; Vermeersch-Creusen, *op. cit.*, II, 108; *AAS*, XXI (1929), 301.

in trust, for it is implicitly laid upon the executor as a condition that he choose a priest who will say the Masses.

Even if such trusts be regarded as private trusts, there is no reason why they should fail for want of a beneficiary to enforce them. The executor or administrator is conceived to be capable of representing the decedent in enforcing obligations resulting from contracts made by the latter. Why can he not represent the decedent in enforcing the distribution of the stipends prior to his discharge as trustee? That is as far as the decedent wished the obligations of the trust to extend, not to the actual saying of the Masses. He desired that some one should make proper distribution in his place. For a trustee is conceived to be one who holds and manages a fund in the place of a person who establishes the trust. Now one who distributes the stipends performs such a task; but not the priest that says the Masses. The obligation of the one who receives the stipends is not to re-distribute the money, but to say the Masses. Where the courts of Alabama seem to go astray is in their notion that there must be some one able to see that the Masses are said by the person who received the stipend. In the nature of the case, no one can do this. The decedent could not have done it while he was alive. For it is a matter of internal intention on the part of the priest who says the Mass. Besides, no Catholic testator would make a bequest for Masses and then impose on his trustee the impossible obligation of checking on the actual celebration of the Masses. The extent of the obligation which he imposes is that the trustee give the stipends to a worthy priest. The trustee can do this before the executor discharges his task, under the compulsion of the executor, if need be.[50]

677. If the Masses are left to a church or to an institution with the understanding that they are to be celebrated as soon as reasonably possible, they are gifts to the priests who may be at the institution or the church, under the obligation of celebrating the Masses. The person in charge administers the fund. If the body is legally incorporated, the courts will probably accept this interpre-

[50] This solution also answers the objection that a court can not compel the performance of a religious ceremony. The testator did not wish the court to compel such a performance. All the testator desired was proper distribution of the stipends.

tation of the testator's wish. If it is not incorporated, the familiar problem of distribution by trustee arises once more. It can be solved by the plan suggested in the case where the bishop is trustee for distribution.[51]

678. **Finally, the obligation of saying Masses may be established for a long period of time,** either by depositing with the church or the institution a definite fund the income of which is to be used for stipends; or by annexing the obligation to the foundation of some charitable institution. If the obligation is established in the latter fashion, the bequest would probably be sustained in the courts, in view of the fact that the obligation of saying the Masses seems incidental to the general charitable purpose of founding a charitable institution.[52] If the obligation were established through the income of a fund, there would be set up a trust in the real and true sense of the term. This seems to be the only plan of providing for the celebration of Masses that deserves the name of trust. For, even the distribution of Mass stipends is really an act of administering the estate, and could be done by the executor (with the bishop's approval under the canons). But where a fund is entrusted to a church to be invested, so that the income can be collected annually and expended as stipends for annual Masses, there seems to be sufficient management of the fund to establish a trust. Of course, these trusts can be sustained as public trusts, fostering religious worship. And in any event, there is no good reason why such funds, if they are to be established at all, should not be instituted during the life of the founder.

[51] A solution of this kind was given in the *Ecclesiastical Review*, LX (1919), 703, where the testator bequeathed three thousand dollars to St. Ives' Church for Masses for one year. Three questions arose, viz., as to the persons who should say the Masses, the plan according to which they should be said, and the persons who should receive the stipends. The answer was that the pastor and the priests at the church may assume the burden. But if they do assume it, they share the whole amount *pro rata* with the obligation of saying all the Masses of the year for the decedent (except the pastor's Masses for the parish, *i. e., pro populo*). And any substitutes that are called in, are to be paid *pro rata*, too, for the testator was favoring no priest in particular.

[52] It was so regarded in Seda *et al.* v. Huble *et al.* (1888), 75 Ia. 429, 39 N. W. 685.

679. Suggestions for Testators. The whole problem could be solved best if provision were made by the decedent by contract during his life, or by his establishing a fund in the hands of a trustee to be distributed after his death. But if he will not do that, then at least he should make distribution in his will to definite priests, as he would make distribution to them during his life. In doing this, he should not bequeath too great a sum to any one priest, unless he wishes high Masses celebrated. In that case, he should specify that this is his wish. If he fears that the priests named may die before him, and he does not wish to make a codicil after such a death has ensued, he may name alternates. But the importance of having Masses celebrated for one's soul surely warrants the inconvenience involved in naming a new beneficiary in a codicil.

680. Scholion I. Should high Masses or low Masses be celebrated when the testator has not clearly indicated his preference? That is a question that insistently presents itself for recognition in any discussion of Mass bequests. No matter what answer is offered here, the matter will still remain dubious. There seems to be no definite official answer that would throw light on the problem. The solution seemingly must be thrown back on the conclusions of a few authors, and these, Americans.

681. The Presumption for High Masses. Keller, in his dissertation on *Mass Stipends,* relying on Woywod's opinion, holds that the presumption is that the testator desired high Masses to be celebrated, unless there be evidence to the contrary.[53] He argues that the Church prefers a high Mass to a low Mass, and that the stole fee or stipend is due the celebrant not from any extrinsic title of external splendor, but from the intrinsic right conferred on him by the celebration of the Holy Sacrifice according to the manner in which the Church would have him celebrate it. The substance of that argument would seem to be that the celebrant is always entitled to the stipend for a high Mass unless there is some restriction placed upon

[53] Keller, *Mass Stipends,* pp. 85, 86; Woywod, in *The Homiletic and Pastoral Review,* XXI (1921), 812; *cf.* Miller, *Founded Masses,* p. 62. Noldin simply says that where there is a doubt as to the number of Masses to be celebrated, the Ordinary is to be consulted or the fixed stipend of the place to be used as a guide; *op. cit.,* III, 187.

him. Consequently, Keller continues, if any person should give a priest fifty dollars for Masses, saying no more, the priest could celebrate two solemn high Masses, or ten high Masses, due regard being paid to other presumed intentions.

The *Ecclesiastical Review* adopted this view in 1931 in solving a case presented to it,[54] where the problem was this: a member of a certain parish had made a bequest of two thousand dollars for requiem Masses for himself and his wife, to be said in that particular church. The difficulty lay in this, that there was only one Mass celebrated in that church each week day, and during each week, two or three high Masses. Thus it would require many years to say two thousand low Masses in that very church. The answer made was that it may reasonably be presumed that the testator's intention was to have high Masses said, or at least that it can not be presumed that his intention was to have low Masses said.

This solution was criticized by a bishop who wrote to the *Review*, and whose argument appears in the *Review* some six months later.[55] In the course of his letter he speaks of a certain residuary estate bequeathed to him by a priest for Masses to be said in poor parishes. Friends of the decedent told the bishop that it had been the custom of the deceased to offer high Masses, and that they were quite certain that it was his intention to have high Masses sung. The bishop, though not entirely convinced by this line of argument, gave two hundred stipends for low Masses to priests in poor parishes, doubling the usual stipend. Then he decided to refer the matter to the Sacred Congregation of the Council, which, while absolving him from the obligation in regard to the stipends already distributed, instructed him to have as many Masses offered as there were ordinary stipends remaining.

To this the *Review* replied that the precise action of the bishop, which failed to receive the approval of the Sacred Congregation, was the raising of the stipend for a low Mass. It was not the act of assigning high Masses instead of low Masses. The action of raising the stipend was in contravention of Canon 830.[56]

[54] *AER*, LXXXIV (1931), 521.

[55] *AER*, LXXXV (1931), 525.

[56] Canon 830. "Si quis pecuniae summam obtulerit pro Missarum applica-

682. The Presumption for Low Masses. But in 1917, the *Review* had said that the decision as to preference is to be made from the presumed intention of the testator,[57] and in 1900, it had argued that *ex communiter contingentibus* low Masses are to be said.[58]

683. What is to be the conclusion from this argumentation? The solution seems to consist in the answer to the question, what presumption holds in the absence of evidence indicating a definite intention? No one would deny that if circumstance raise the presumption that high Masses are preferred, high Masses may safely be celebrated. Such presumptions probably existed in the case solved in the *Ecclesiastical Review* (1931),[59] where two thousand dollars was bequeathed for Masses to be celebrated in one particular church.

But is such a presumption raised by the line of argument adopted by the priest's friends who counseled the bishop in the case just noticed? [60] The argument was that because the decedent priest had offered high Masses, it was to be presumed that he would wish high Masses offered for the stipends he had left in his will. The argument is not convincing.

Under what circumstances did the decedent offer high Masses? On the occasion of Forty Hours' Devotion? When asked to offer them by persons who gave him a stipend for them? High Masses offered on such occasions would seem to afford no presumption of the deceased's preference for them. If it could be shown that when he remembered his deceased friends and relatives without a stipend he offered high Masses, that would seem to give sufficient ground for his preference.

684. Does the Church juridically prefer a high Mass to a low Mass? If so, would this official preference offer grounds for a general presumption that all decedents prefer high Mass unless they state otherwise? From a liturgical point of view, the Church indeed prefers

tione, non indicans earundem numerum, hic supputetur secundum eleemosynam loci in quo oblator morabatur, nisi aliam fuisse eius intentionem legitime praesumi debet."

[57] *AER,* LVI (1917), 302.

[58] *AER,* XXII (1900), 536.

[59] *Cf.* § 680, supra.

[60] *Cf.* § 681, supra.

the high Mass. But it is yet to be proved that she prefers it juridically. Nowhere in the course of the Church's present legislation, or, it would seem, in the legislation of the Church at any time, has a high Mass been commanded, except in the case of the conventual Mass. There the command arises not only from the liturgical preference of the Church for the high Mass, but also from juridical obligation attached to the benefice. The juridical obligation arises from a juridical office. On the other hand, it seems unwarranted to build a general juridical presumption on what is a liturgical preference.

685. Besides, there are four arguments which would indicate that the presumption is in favor of low Masses. The first is from the doctrinal concept of the relative importance of the low Mass and the high Mass when diminished income demands a reduction in the number. The second derives from the reply of the Sacred Congregation of the Council, just noted, to the bishop who had doubled the Mass stipend in the act of distribution. The third is taken from doctrinal decisions indicating that the testator's intention is to be interpreted strictly. And the fourth springs from the motives testators usually have in making these bequests.

686. The Argument from the Procedure in the Reduction of Mass Intentions. If it is permissible to argue from the principles which authors lay down for the procedure to be followed in reducing the obligations of saying Masses when the income from endowments is diminished, there seems to be some evidence in the plan they suggest which would indicate that juridically the Church does not have a preference for high Masses. Ordinaries are counseled to eliminate the obligations of high Masses first, in order that a greater number of Masses may remain to be said as low Masses. This suggestion seems to touch just the crux of the problem under discussion. The authors seem to think that the testator would prefer to have the high Masses omitted in order that he may benefit by the greater number of low Masses. On the same theory, the testator would be presumed to wish as great a number as possible of Masses to be said for the fund he leaves in his will, and consequently to prefer that low Masses be said.[61]

[61] D'Annibale, *op. cit.*, III, 76; Many, *De Missa*, p. 80. It is called the *praxis curiae* to change chanted Masses into low Masses where the poverty of the priests or the need of repairs on the church demand it; Vromant, *op. cit.*, 357.

687. The second argument derives from the reply of the Sacred Congregation of the Council to the bishop who doubled the stipend for low Masses. While the reply is not conclusive that the bishop could not have distributed the stipends for high Masses instead of low Masses, at least it indicates the practice of the *Curia* in procuring as many Masses as possible for the soul of the decedent. Remembering that the Sacred Congregation could have permitted the bishop to double the stipend without any injustice to the decedent, is it reasonable to conclude that it denied him this faculty in order that he might procure the celebration of even fewer Masses on the basis of a stipend not merely twice as great, but actually five times as great as that for a low Mass?

688. Doctrinal Decisions Favoring Strict Interpretation of the Testator's Will. The third argument is taken from certain doctrinal decisions that indicate that the strict interpretation is to be applied to the intention of the testator who makes these bequests. There are three such decisions rendered in the *Ecclesiastical Review*.

In one case, an old man had bequeathed five hundred dollars for Masses to a priest whom he had previously promised to remember in his will. The decision held that the Masses must be said. The only legal title that the priest has comes from the will. The attorney may have made a mistake in drafting the will; but, on the other hand, the testator may have forgotten his promise or even changed his mind.[62]

In another case, where the testator had bequeathed five hundred dollars for Masses, it was alleged that in life he had always offered five times the stipend. Surely, if presumptions count for anything, there would seem to be a presumption in this case that the testator would be consistent in the manner of providing for Mass intentions. Yet, the *Ecclesiastical Review* decided that the presumption can not be allowed, noting, however, that in cases of doubt it is the function of the Ordinary to make the decision.[63]

In a third case, there were two bequests of five hundred dollars for Masses in the same will. They were outright gifts, the purpose of the testator being to safeguard them from the operation of the

[62] *AER*, LI (1914), 736.
[63] *AER*, XXVII (1902), 201.

nullifying thirty-day limit statute. Now, in the case of one of these bequests, the priest beneficiary had been accustomed to receive gifts from the testator at Christmas time in the amount of twenty-five dollars, and to be requested, when those gifts were made, to say two Masses for the donor. He wanted to know if he could interpret the bequest as being made in the same frame of mind as the Christmas gifts. The decision was that he could not, but that the whole amount must be devoted to Miss stipends.[64]

All three cases, it is true, fail to touch exactly the point at issue, but they do indicate on what side presumptions lie. But there is a fourth argument that seems conclusive.

689. The Argument from the Motive of the Testator. The fourth argument derives from the motive which prompts decedents to leave bequests for Masses, a motive, by the way, which they do not so much conceive as accept from their accredited teachers. The motive is that their souls may be aided by the propitiatory power of the Holy Sacrifice. Since that is the motive, not benevolence to a church or to a priest, for this benevolence can be expressed by outright gifts with no obligations attached, it would seem that whatever presumption is to be recognized here should be in favor of that motive. By way of illustration, suppose that in a will there was a bequest for a certain number of Masses. The number has been written in numerals and those numerals are so indistinct as to admit interpretation as either one hundred or ten. The doubt arises in the given instance because the last nought in the series of numerals is blurred and so small that it might easily be a period. What would be the presumption in that case? It seems unquestionable that the presumption would be in favor of one hundred. The presumption, indeed, would be founded on the usual practice of testators as much as on the desire of the deceased to procure the celebration of a large number of Masses. Few would ask for ten Masses in their wills. But then the very practice of asking for a hundred results from nothing but the thought that since it is the testator's last opportunity to provide for the celebration of Masses, he should provide for a reasonably large number.

690. Scholion II. Must a priest accept a bequest for Masses?

[64] *AER,* LXIII (1920), 294.

Strictly speaking, he is under no obligation to do this. But since in the United States it is often necessary that he should accept it in order to prevent the bequest from failing, there is certainly an obligation in such cases deriving from charity and *per se gravis*. Even if there is no such danger, the consistent conduct observed by priests who understand the importance of providing for Masses for the deceased is that of offering whatever assistance they can in making such a provision. The fact that the priest may not be able to say the Masses himself implies some slight inconvenience in transmitting the obligation to some other priest, who, perhaps in poverty, may also have a claim in charity against his fellow priest who could thus bring him relief.

Indeed, as to Masses to be founded in a parish, while the Ordinary must be consulted and may refuse his consent, canonists hold that he may not reject such foundations without a just reason, under penalty of grave sin.[65]

691. **There are three opinions as to whether the bishop must make restitution for refusing either an inheritance or a bequest.** The first holds that to reject either, would be alienation of ecclesiastical property. The second distinguishes and says that a legacy vests at once, but an inheritance must be accepted. Therefore, to reject an inheritance is not alienation, but to reject a legacy is alienation. The third, adopted by Schmalzgrueber, is that neither vests automatically, and that neither is automatically church property. The importance of the opinions revolve about the question of restitution and censure under the penalties of Canons 2346 and 2347. If the property has once become the property of the Church, it can not be alienated without due formalities. That this is the central thought behind the distinctions is evident from Schmalzgrueber's contention that even though the property is not the property of the Church until accepted by the bishop,

[65] *AER*, LVIII (1918), 208. No one may reject a legacy without a proper and just cause under the rulings of the Sacred Congregation of the Council; S. C. C. *in Causa Rhegien.*, 11 March, 1843, § *Nullo*—Pallottini, XI, 509; *in Causa Romana*, 21 February, 1818, § *Haec*—Pallottini, *l. c.* Rejection by one of several beneficiaries does not prejudice the others; S. C. C. *in Causa Cremona*, 31 May, 1704, and 19 November, 1707—Pallottini, XI, 510.

the bishop who refuses to take it without just cause commits a grave sin. This is the milder opinion, and seems safe in practice.[66]

692. Scholion III. The Distribution of Bequests for Masses. Vermeersch-Creusen argue that because the distribution of an inheritance is a kind of payment due by the executor of a last will, he may even in bequests to the Church and to charity enjoy the benefit of the secular law as to the time interval within which he is obliged to make payment.[67] This seems to be valid reasoning, for the canons, while providing for the validity of bequests to charity and religion, and for the administration of such funds when they are paid, has made no explicit provision as to the time at which they should be paid. Ancient decisions of the Sacred Congregation of the Council would indicate that these bequests are to be paid at once, and that the order of the court is sufficient protection for the executor. By that very assigning of a reason, however, these decisions seem to leave the executor free to follow the provisions of secular law in this matter. For the court now will not give him an order to make distribution until the legal period set for the presentation of claims has expired. Besides, there seems to be implicit provision for the payment of these bequests in Canon 1529 where the canons accept the provisions of the secular law in matters of contract. The payment made by an executor is surely a matter of quasi-contract raised by his assuming his position under the law. The payment of bequests, as to him, is really the payment of creditors. On the other hand, it would seem that the executor's distribution of the funds is incidental to the administration of the will, to be governed, where pious bequests are concerned, by canon law and not by the secular provisions. But in any event it would seem that a reasonable time should be allowed the executor to make payment. As he was given one year to fulfill

[66] *Cf.* Schmalzgrueber, *op. cit.*, III, I, 13, 13-20. *Cf.* §§ 739-746 infra. Neglect by the bishop to accept the legacy within the time set in the will does not defeat the legacy, nor his actual rejection of it; S. C. C. *in Causa Urbevitana,* 10 March, 1742—Pallottini, XI, 510.

[67] *Op. cit.*, II, 850. The Sacred Congregation of the Council said that pious legacies are to be paid at once, because the order of the court protects the heir against claims; S. C. C. *in Causa Albinganen.*, 18 March, 1820—Pallottini, XI, 532; *in Causa Fanen.*, 19 July, 1828—Pallottini, XI, 515; *in Causa Hortana,* 24 August, 1844, § *Neque*—Pallottini, XI, 98.

his task under the canons of the Middle Ages, it may fairly be concluded that even under the canons he may be allowed a similar period for distribution now.[68]

But in the matter of bequests for Masses there seems to be an exception, for there is an explicit provision as to the distribution of Mass stipends in general, which seems to affect also Mass stipends in the hands of an executor of a last will. Canon 837 provides that Mass stipends be distributed as soon as possible.[69]

693. When a priest is designated the beneficiary of the sum stipulated for Mass stipends, he is to be guided by the expressed intention of the testator, and if he is authorized to say the Masses himself whenever he can, he need make no distribution, even at the end of one year after he has received them. But if there is no expression of such an intention, there is a presumption that the testator accepted the canons, and that the Masses are to be given to the Ordinary at the end of one year. If at the very beginning of the obligation, it is evident that the priest can not say all the Masses prescribed within one year, he must distribute at once the stipends which he foresees he can not satisfy within that time.[70] Prior to the end of the year he may distribute them himself to any priest he chooses, provided that the recipients are known to him.[71]

[68] *Cf.* §§ 722-724, infra.

[69] *Cf.* Keller, *op. cit.*, p. 122, Canon 837. "Qui Missas per alios celebrandas habet, eas quamprimum distribuat, firmo praescripto can. 841; sed tempus legitimum pro earundem celebratione incipit a die quo sacerdos celebraturus easdem receperit."

Canon 841, § 1. "Omnes et singuli administratores causarum piarum aut quoquo modo ad Missarum onera implenda obligati, sive ecclesiastici sive laici, sub exitum cuiuslibet anni, Missarum onera quibus nondum fuerit satisfactum, suis Ordinariis tradant secundum modum ab his definiendum."

§ 2. "Hoc autem tempus ita est accipiendum ut in Missis ad instar manualium obligatio eas deponendi decurrat a fine illius anni intra quem onera impleri debuissent; in manualibus vero, post annum a die suscepti oneris, salva diversa offerentium voluntate."

[70] Canon 835. "Nemini licet tot Missarum onera per se celebrandarum recipere quibus intra annum satisfacere nequeat."

[71] Canon 838. "Qui habent Missarum numerum de quibus sibi liceat disponere, possunt eas distribuere sacerdotibus sibi acceptis, dummodo probe sibi constet eos esse omni exceptione maiores vel testimonio proprii Ordinarii commendatos."

694. The Ordinary can not, even by a synodal decree, forbid the sending of Mass stipends out of the diocese to worthy priests, nor require that the priests sending them have the permission of the Ordinary to do so. Such provisions are beyond the powers also of a provincial council.[72]

695. The decrees of the Sacred Congregation of the Council, *Ut debita*,[73] and *Recenti decreto*,[74] required that Mass stipends that were sent out of the diocese should be sent through the Ordinary or the Provincial of the recipient, who was not to refuse them unless the celebrant was such as would not comply with the requirements of the decree, *Ut debita*. But Mass stipends sent to missions in the East were to be sent through the Sacred Congregation for the Propagation of the Faith. The latter provision, however, was not binding on the laity nor on regular Ordinaries when the latter were sending the stipend to missionaries of their own community. Now, however, neither obligation is repeated in the canons.[75]

696. But if the stipends have been given to a church rather than to a priest or to a religious community, the Ordinary in virtue of his

[72] Vermeersch-Creusen, *op. cit.*, II, 107; Prümmer, *Man. Iur. Can.*, 293.

[73] 11 May, 1904—*Fontes*, n. 4317; *Periodica*, I (1911), 44; *AER*, XXXI (1904), 162, 172.

[74] 22 May, 1907.

[75] *AER*, XXXVII (1907), 191, 436; LII (1915), 219; LXXIII (1925), 632. Stipends sent to priests of an Oriental Rite may also be sent directly to the priest provided he is known to be trustworthy, as the canons require. Under the decree, *Complures*, of the Sacred Congregation for the Propagation of the Faith, 15 July, 1908, stipends intended for such priests were ordered to be sent to the Apostolic Delegate in the respective countries. Under the decree, it was rite, not geography that determined what priests were to be considered as belonging to the Oriental Church. And stipends could be sent to the bishop under whose jurisdiction the priest lived, provided that the Apostolic Delegate was notified of the number of stipends that had been sent. It is a matter of doubt whether this decree still binds. Some canonists think it does in virtue of Canon 1, which leaves the Oriental Church unaffected by the Code; others hold that the decree did not affect the Oriental Church directly, but rather the priest of the Latin Rite who was sending stipends. Under the latter view, it would be superseded by the Code. Since the matter is doubtful, the persons sending stipends must be allowed liberty in the matter. *Cf. ASS*, XLI, 460; Keller, *op. cit.*, p. 129.

jurisdiction over the church can forbid the sending of those stipends outside the diocese.[76]

And as executor of all wills for charity and religion, the Ordinary may prohibit such transfers of Mass stipends as he deems imprudent, within or outside the diocese. He is prevented merely from making a general provision that Mass stipends must not be sent outside the diocese without his permission.

697. It should be observed, too, before the conclusion of this discussion is reached, that the sender is responsible for the stipends until they reach their destination. If they are lost, he is still bound to the obligation of saying the Masses.[77]

698. **Scholion IV. Various questions may arise as to the intention of the testator** besides that concerned with his preference for high or low Masses.

699. **The testator may in his will bequeath a certain sum to a church and then in a memorandum indicate that the sum is intended for Masses.** Should the secular court learn of the existence of such a memorandum, much would depend on whether the beneficiary knew of its existence. If he did not, the Pennsylvania decisions would regard it as free from any obligation under the memorandum, that is, so far as the external forum is concerned. But if he knew of the secret memorandum, he would probably be held to its terms.[78] But in Missouri, where such a memorandum was found, it was regarded as being outside the will, and the bequests made in the will were held to be indefinite because not completely expressed there, requiring the memorandum for explanation. That might be

[76] The Sacred Congregation of the Council in plenary session, 19 February, 1921, affirmed the decree of a provincial council forbidding the sending of Mass stipends outside the diocese without the permission of the Ordinary, but only as to Masses *ad instar manualium* (Masses to be said by priests other than those obliged by the terms of the foundation or in a different place from that named in the foundation), and as to manual stipends given for the benefit of the church or the institution; *AAS*, XIII (1921), 229 ff.; *Periodica*, X (1921), 294 E; *AER*, LXXIII (1925), 632; LXXXVII (1932), 32.

[77] *Cf.* § 674, supra.

[78] *Cf.* § 373, this treatise, for incorporation of memoranda. Flood v. Ryan (1908), 220 Pa. 450, 69 Atl. 908.

the fate of any bequest that was explained in a document that was not part of the will.[79] Under the canons, the memorandum is binding, if it can be proved to the satisfaction of the Ordinary that it was written by the testator, or at least signed by him.

700. Another problem may arise where the pastor believes that the sum bequeathed was meant for the construction of the church because the amount seems excessive if it is meant to be devoted exclusively to Masses. The solution in this difficulty seems to be no other than that which was offered in the case where the priest had been promised that he would be remembered in the decedent's will, only to discover that five hundred dollars was bequeathed to him for Masses.[80]

Testators sometimes really believe that in making a bequest for Masses, they are making a gift to the priest, as well as assisting their own souls. While it is a gift in a sense, it can not be retained by the priest if he can not say the Masses. So, testators may believe that in leaving Mass bequests they may also be assisting in the work of construction, not realizing that the stipends must be distributed to priests who can say the Masses.

But the only title that the priest or the church has to the bequest arises out of the will, and if there happens to be an obligation attached to the bequest, there seems no way of escaping it. It is difficult to know for certain that the testator wished to make a gift for construction purposes, if he explicitly stated that the bequest is for Masses. In addition to proving that the testator had definitely stated that he had made a will in which he had made such a gift to the church, it would have to be shown that the will at hand is the one to which he referred, and that he labored under no misconception as to the possibility of using a bequest for Masses for construction purposes with an obligation on the priests of the church to say the Masses. Of course, the pastor could take the gift for the church, if he and his assistants are willing to say the number of Masses due.

No presumption can arise from the previous actions of the testa-

[79] Leopold Schmucker's Estate v. John H. Reel, Executor, Appellant (1876), 61 Mo. 592.

[80] See § 688, supra.

tor, as is evident from the solution of the case where a decedent had been accustomed to give a rather generous Christmas present to a priest and request that a couple of Masses be said.[81] Consequently, if a testator had given one thousand dollars to a church for construction purposes in the past, it would not be presumed that a similar amount bequeathed in his will for Masses should be devoted to construction. If the amount bequeathed were very great, a presumption could probably be made out that he did not wish the full number of Masses said, but that he wished primarily to benefit the church, expecting in return that for his soul a number of Masses would be said equivalent to what persons in his station would usually be expected to provide.

701. Presumption That Testator Wished Only a Memento It might be said that what the testator really wishes in making such a large bequest is only a memento in the Mass. But that must be proved rather than merely asserted. Again in this connection, the habit of the individual affords no basis for a presumption. There usually is no positive evidence that the testator wished only a memento.[82]

702. Parol Evidence Where There Is Patent Ambiguity. It is hardly necessary to add that in the secular courts, parol evidence could not be introduced where the face of the will is clear and offers no patent ambiguity. The same rule holds in the ecclesiastical court. But the excessive amount of the bequest might afford a patent ambiguity which would permit the Ordinary to hear evidence as to the testator's real wish. His decision then should be rendered in accordance with the principles just explained.

[81] *Cf.* § 688, supra.

[82] *Cf.* § 765, infra.

CHAPTER XI

THE CHURCH'S EXECUTOR IN HISTORY

ARTICLE 1

PRIOR TO THE TWELFTH CENTURY

703. The bishop's position as executor derives from his authority as father and protector of the poor. From the infancy of the Church, as he was the recipient of the liberal donations of the wealthy, so he was charged by the canons with the burden of exercising solicitude and paternal care towards the unfortunate.[1] He was charged with the task of encouraging and collecting contributions for them.[2] Indeed, his exclusive right to distribute alms was rather clearly emphasized.[3] It followed as a matter of course that he should be the administrator of the contributions destined for charity and religion by the last wills of generous decedents. This canonical attitude was given considerable impetus when imperial law recognized the bishop as the administrator of all funds devoted to charity and religion.[4]

[1] Canons of the Apostles, cc. 26 and 40—Harduin, 1, 18 and 19; Council of Gangre, c. 8—Harduin, I, 535 C; Council of Antioch (341), c. 25—Harduin, I, 605 A; Council of Sardica (347), c. 10—Mansi, III, 26 B; Letter of Pope Gelasius to the Bishop Honorius—Mansi, VIII, 124 A; Letter of Pope Gelasius I to the Bishops Gerontius and Peter—Mansi, VIII, 136 C; cc. 1 and 4, Dist. LXXXVII; Council of Orléans (511), c. 16—Mansi, VIII, 354 B; *Capitula* of Hadrian (773), c. 37—Mansi, XII, 861 B; Third Council of Tours (813), cc. 10 and 11—Mansi, XIV, 84 E; Council of Worms (868), cc. 45 and 46—Mansi, XV, 877; Council of Aix-la-Chapelle (816), c. 10—Mansi, XIV, 63 E; Sixth Council of Paris (829), lib. 1, c. 14—Mansi, XIV, 548 D.

[2] Council of Nice, c. 75—Mansi, II, 1006 E; c. 6—Mansi, II, 1022 C; Council of Sardis, c. 12—Mansi, III, 15 D.

[3] Synod of St. Patrick (*circa* 450), cc. 4 and 5—Mansi, VI, 516 A; c. 25—Mansi, VI, 518 A; *Capitula* of Hadrian, c. 8—Mansi, XII, 864 A; *AER*, LXXXVII (1932), 561.

[4] C. 1, 2, 13 and 14; 1, 3, 41, 3 and 5; 1, 3, 41, 11 and 16; 1, 3, 28, 1 and 2; 1, 3, 48; *Nov.*, 131, 11, 1 and 2; 131, 13.

The bishop's duty of vigilance over charitable bequests is at first recognized by the imperial law, and then imposed on him as an obligation. Moreover, he is granted a secular action to enforce the fulfillment of charitable foundations of almost every kind.[5] He can not be excluded from this office of administrator, even though the testator should expressly attempt to do so. He is authorized to appoint subordinate administrators and to supplant them when they proscrastinate. He is to recognize, however, administrators appointed by the testator, though he may remove them, if they prove incompetent[6]. He is to compel the heir to complete the construction of a church which the latter's ancestor may have begun;[7] and when the testator has merely given instructions for the construction of a church or charitable institution, the heir is to complete the latter within one year; a church, within three years (changed to five years in the Novels). If the institution is not completed within a year, the bishop is to rent a house until the building is complete.[8] If the executor or heir fails to heed two warnings of the bishop or of the bishop's administrator as to the completion of buildings, he loses whatever accrued to him under the will of the testator. The bishop is authorized under these circumstances to become personal executor, to claim the estate along with the income accruing, and to distribute it according to the prescriptions of the decedent.[9]

If the heir complains that he has not received sufficient under the succession to fulfill the testator's wish, the bishop claims whatever there is in the estate, even the Falcidian twenty-five per cent, and gives it to the charity designated.[10] If legal suit became necessary to compel the heir to comply with the bishop's demand, he was assessed

[5]C. 1, 2, 15. This was enacted in the year 477. Even earlier Pope Celestine I had enlisted the aid of Theodosius the Younger to repress the rapacity of the administrators of a certain endowment in Asia, and to compel them to pay the rents to the beneficiaries as provided by the testator—*Epistola* XXIII—*MPL.* L, 546.

[6] C. 1, 3, 45; *Nov.*, 131, 10.

[7] C. 1, 2, 15; *Nov.*, 131, 7; Thomassin, *op. cit.*, III, 1, 19, 1.

[8] *Nov.*, 131, 10.

[9] Nov., 131, 11, 3 and 4; *ASS,* II (1866), 372.

[10] C. 1, 3, 45; *Nov.*, 131, 12.

twice the value of the bequest. In the usual case, the bequest was to be paid within six months.[11]

704. The Influence of Gregory the Great. But this position of the bishop was probably definitely established by the energetic, far-visioned, statesmanlike policy of Pope Gregory the Great, who seemed to be present everywhere in Christendom, directing social relief work through his bishops, reminding them of their duty, encouraging them, correcting them tactfully, demanding reports, and directing special commissions.[12]

As to the obligation of seeing that charitable bequests were fulfilled, he was especially solicitious, reminding bishops that there is a duty resting on them to insure the due performance of them.[13] If there is any one explanation more than another for the recognized authority of the bishop in executing bequests to charity, it was the zeal with which Gregory the Great supervised the fulfillment of them in obedience to the canonical tradition that had come down to him.

705. The Position of the African Church. In that tradition there was only the slightest trace of a discordant voice. That was

[11] C. 1, 3, 45.

[12] *Cf.* his letters on social relief in Mansi, IX, 1129 A; 1171 E; X, 4 A; 8 A; 21 A; 25 A; 62 A; 226 C; 231 C.

[13] *Cf.* his decrees in: c. 1, X, *de testamentis et ultimis voluntatibus,* III, 26 (*Ad Antonium Subdiaconum*); c. 2, X, *de testamentis et ultimis voluntatibus,* III, 26 (*Ad Januarium*—epistola 7, lib. 9, ind. 2—*MPL,* LXXVII, 945); c. 3, X, *de testamentis et ultimis voluntatibus,* III, 26 (Januario—*ASS,* II, 1866, 371); c. 4, X, *de testamentis et ultimis voluntatibus,* III, 26 (*Ad Petrum Subdiaconum—MPL.,* LXXVII, 569 B); c. 4, C. XVII, q. 4 (*Ad Sabinum*—Mansi X, 214 B); *Ad Januarium,* epistola 9, lib. 4, ind. 12—*MPL,* LXXVII, 677; *Ad Januarium,* epistola 8, lib. 4, ind. 12—*MPL,* LXXVII; *Ad Romanum Defensorem,* epistola 24, lib. 9, ind. 2—*MPL,* LXXVII, 963 (where Romanus was to determine whether the Diocese of Rome had become heir, as ordained in a last will, by failure of the appointed heirs to build a monastery within a year; and, if such be the case, to collect the funds and build the monastery); *Ad Vitalem Defensorem*—Mansi, X, 380 A; *MPL,* LXXVII, 1262; *Ad Scholasticum Defensorem—MPL,* LXXVII, 1133; *Ad Fantinum Defensorem—MPL,* LXXVII, 1068; c. 34, C. XVI, q. 7 (*Ad Secundinum—MPL,* LXXVII, 934); *Ad Romanum* Defensorem—Mansi, X, 218 B; *MPL,* LXXVII, 1075; *Ad Fantinum Defensorem*—Mansi, X, 315 E; *MPL,* LXXVII, 1225; *Ad Fantinum Defensorem*—Mansi, X, 317 D; *MPL,* LXXVII, 1227; *Ad Castorium Diaconum—MPL,* LXXVII, 754; *Ad Bonam Abbatissam—MPL,* LXXVII, 633.

the voice of St. Augustine. He wished that clerics should avoid litigation and every semblance of avarice and that they should show a du regard for the claims of the testator's dependents. The whole Africa Church was marked in some measure by this attitude.[14] Nevertheless, the African Church was at one with the rest of the Catholic worl in its willingness to permit the bishops to accept the free and untainted contributions of the faithful for the relief of the poor.[15] Indeed, Augustine admits that he is not without critics who are no pleased with his attitude in the matter, and would wish him to b more zealous for the welfare of the Church.[16] But he does not refus legacies that are free from sordid implications.[17] However, he woul not accept a bequest from a monk who had retained ownership of hi property,[18] or from a man who by endowing the Church had disinherited his son.[19]

706. The Tradition Among the Early Germanic Nations

[14] Second Council of Carthage (217)—Mansi, I, 735 B (where clerics we forbidden to accept appointment as executors of wills, or to confer such appointment on others); Fourth Council of Carthage (436), cc. 18, 19—Mans III, 952 E; Harduin, I, 980; Thomassin, *op. cit.*, III, 1, 17, 3; *Statuta Ecclesic Antiquae*, cc. 6 and 8—Mansi, VII, 893 B. In the two sources last mentione prohibitions are found against the acceptance by bishops of the obligation c procuring the due execution of wills or of sustaining court actions of any kin for the goods of this world.

Possidius described the desire of Augustine to have peace in this matte When a certain donor asked Augustine that the estate given to the dioces be returned to him and a small sum accepted in lieu of it, Augustine complie readily with the request, but refused even the substitute donation, warning th donor to be less vacillating in the future; Possidius, c. 24—*MPL*, XXXII, 53 Thomassin, *l. c.*

Augustine had a precedent for this conduct in the action of Aurelius, Bisho of Carthage, who had voluntarily returned a deed to a benefactor becaus heirs were born to the latter after the conveyance had been made; Augustin *De Diversis Sermonibus*, Sermo CCCLV, c. 4—*MPL*, XXXIX, 1570; Thomassin, *l. c.*, n. 5.

[15] Fourth Council of Carthage (436), c. 95—Mansi, III, 958 E.

[16] *Op. cit.*, c. 3—*MPL*, XXXIX, 1572.

[17] Possidius, *l. c.;* De Héricourt, *op. cit.*, H 181; Thomassin, *l. c.*, nn. 2 an 4; Augustine, *op. cit.*, c. 3—*MPL*, XXXIX, 1572.

[18] C. 43, C. XVII, q. 4; Augustine, *op. cit.*, c. 4—*MPL*, XXXIX, 1570.

[19] Augustine, *op. cit.*, c. 2—*MPL*, XXXIX, 1571.

Conscious of the precedents established by custom, by imperial constitutions, and by the zeal of Gregory the Great, canon law, in the period of barbarian colonization, kept bishops mindful of their duty of supervising the payment of charitable bequests. As Gregory the Great, in his untiring vigilance, was guided by the tradition of the Church more than by imperial constitutions, which, no doubt, he had at hand, so the councils of the period of colonization were guided principally by the same tradition, crystallized into a dynamic principle of canonical discipline by the great pontiff. The conciliar legislation, enacted before the end of Justinian's century, declaring wills valid even though they lacked the requirements of secular law, is significant of the content of similar legislation protecting charitable bequests. It becomes pertinent at this point to examine certain features of this legislation.

707. The Ordinary is given the assistance of the bishop of the delinquent in his attempt to collect bequests unlawfully detained.[20] They who retain or conceal bequests made to charity or religion are condemned as murderers of the poor.[21] Delay in fulfilling the bequest was forbidden as equivalent to a denial of faith,[22] even under penalty of excommunication.[23] The heirs were forbidden to reclaim gifts made to the Church.[24]

708. The Merovingians were generally well disposed towards

[20] Third Council of Paris (*circa* 557), c. 1—Mansi, IX, 743 D; Harduin, III, 337; *ASS,* II (1866), 372.

[21] Council of Agde (506), c. 3—Mansi, VIII, 324 D; Second Council of Vaison (442), c. 4—Mansi, VI, 453; *ASS,* II (1866), 372; Second Council of Arles, c. 47—Mansi, VII, 884 B; Third Council of Orléans (538), c. 1—Mansi, IX, 18 B; Third Council of Paris (*circa* 557), c. 1—Mansi, IX, 743 D; Second Council of Tours (567), c. 25—Mansi, IX, 804 D; Council of Macon (581), c. 4—Mansi, IX, 932 D; Council of Mayence (888), c. 6—Mansi, XVIII A, 66 B.

[22] First Council of Vaison under Julius I, c. 1—Mansi, III, 175 B (the genuineness of this Council is uncertain); Second Council of Vaison, *l. c.*

[23] *Cap. Coll. Can. Hibern.,* lib. 17, c. 6—Mansi, XII, 124 A; Wasserschleben, p. 52.

[24] Fourth Council of Orléans (541), c. 19—Harduin, II, 1438; Fifth Council of Orléans (549), c. 16—Mansi, IX, 116 E; Council of Auvergne, c. 15—Mansi, IX, 144 B; Council of Rheims, c. 10—Harduin, III, 572.

such gifts. Childebert founded a hospital in Lyons which was the object of the solicitude of the Fifth Council of Orléans (549);[25] and Clothaire proscribed by royal edict the unwarranted theft of charitable bequests.[26] On the other hand, Chilperic forbade the faithful to make charitable bequests, but his successor, Guntram, validated all the wills that were rendered void by this prohibition and made all such bequests valid for the future.[27] It was probably due to the nullifying influence of Chilperic's policy that the Third Council of Paris excommunicated those who appealed to the king to justify their defiance of the Church.[28] On the contrary, the Council of Pavia (850), ordained that heirs who seek to claim any portion of a bequest to a hospital should be denounced to the emperor.[29]

709. Due repairs are ordered made on hospitals.[30] In general, the bishop is sustained as the recipient of charitable bequests and the administrator of them according to the will of the testator.[31] The Third General Council of the Lateran visited failure to carry out the provisions of the will with forfeiture of the whole estate.[32] And Alexander III interfered in an unusual case where a decedent had bequeathed to a hospital a sum owed him by a monastery, demanding that the abbot notify the prior to fulfill the bequest.[33]

710. Wills of this period were formless in the main.[34] A will was largely a religious act inasmuch as the three beneficiaries were wife, children, and charity; towards all of these the decedent was

[25] Cc. 13, 15—Harduin II, 1466. The Council excommunicated any person who should be responsible for any loss of the hospital's endowment.

[26] Harduin, III, 343.

[27] Thomassin, *op. cit.*, III, 1, 21, 11; De Héricourt, *op. cit.*, H 183.

[28] C. 6—Mansi, IX, 746 B.

[29] C. 15—Mansi, XIV, 935 E.

[30] Council of Pavia (855), c. 5—Mansi, XV, 22 A; Council of Langeais (859), c. 14—Mansi, XV, 540 B.

[31] Synod of Rome (853), cc. 23, 24—Mansi, IV, 1006 C; Council of Rome (1059), c. 5—Mansi, IX, 898 C; (1063), c. 5—Mansi, XIX, 1025 D; Council of Fritzlar, Hesse (*circa* 1200, found in the Acts of the Synod of Mayence, 1540)—Mansi, XXII, 705 A; Council of Paris (1212), pars. 4, c. 19—Mansi XXII, 843 C; Council of Rouen (1212), pars. 3, c. 20—Mansi, XXII, 920 D.

[32] Pars. 43, c. 5—Mansi, XXII, 405 C.

[33] *Ad Abbatem S. Remigii*—Mansi XXI, 948 A.

[34] *Cf.* Chapter I, art. 4, supra.

conceived to have a religious obligation. The will was usually a commission given to a *salman* orally or on a card. Though nominally it was governed by the secular law, it was always under the actual supervision of the bishop. A rather remarkable evidence of this is the declaration of the Synod of Frankfort (794) that Charlemagne decreed that bishops should do justice in their diocese, and that the counts of the realm should be subject to the tribunal of the bishop.[35] Another unusual indication of it, prophetic of the doctrine that the bishop is the administrator of the estate of one who dies intestate, is the provision of the Council of Tribur, Germany, legislating for the payment of the *wergild* (the penalty or fine for murder) by the murderer of a priest, ordained that it should be paid one-half to the bishop for distribution among the poor, and the other half to the church with which the dead priest was associated.[36]

Article 2

After the Twelfth Century

711. The coming of feudalism and the revival of the formal will were probably as contemporaneous as two such diverse phenomena could well be expected to be. Feudalism was probably first on the world scene. But both conspired to disturb the practical system that had enabled the secular authorities to work out the public administration of charitable bequests through the bishops. Land was withdrawn from testamentary power under the tenets of feudalism. Under that regime, too, a network of private courts was set up in the castles of the lords. These courts were inclined to be more officious in their independence than the courts of the king had been. The ecclesiastical courts struggled to retain their jurisdiction over bequests to charity; indeed, over all wills, when it became apparent that the secular courts, that is, principally the courts of the barons, were not justly administering the estates of decedents. They insisted zealously that the faithful make wills, lest the barons regard the personalty of the intestate as escheating to themselves, as they

[35] *M. G. H.*, *Legum*, § II *Capitularia Regum Francorum*, tom. I, 74.
[36] C. 5—Mansi, XVIII A, 161 C.

were too prone to do. To prevent invalid wills and consequent intestacy, they strenuously asserted the principles as to formalities inserted by the Third General Council of the Lateran into the general law of the Church. On the Continent, it seems to have been a losing struggle. In England, on the contrary, it was successful. The consequence for England was that the law of wills follows substantially the canon law practice; and that testaments were subject to the ecclesiastical courts down to 1837.[37]

The details of this period of transition may be profitably examined. First the position of the ecclesiastical courts will be reviewed; second, the usurpations of the secular power; and third, the acts of the councils in resisting these usurpations.

712. The ecclesiastical courts were entitled to jurisdiction over bequests to charity and religion *iure cumulativo,* that is, by reason of jurisdiction over the beneficiary a right was acquired to insure that the beneficiary should obtain its bequest. The jurisdiction over other testaments was acquired *iure devolutivo,* that is, when the secular courts were negligent or incompetent, it devolved upon the ecclesiastical courts to secure the rights of widows and orphans under those wills.[38] It was under this right that jurisdiction was exercised in periods of civic unrest and turmoil, notably in the ninth, tenth, and eleventh centuries. But the disposition of the feudal lords to usurp the property of their vassals created a similar emergency. In this emergency the secular courts failed to do justice, and the ecclesiastical courts interfered in their place. But this jurisdiction was claimed with less success on the Continent than in England, though in Normandy, in 1190, it is conceded that the distribution of estates under wills and by intestacy belongs to the bishop.[39] But from the twelfth to the sixteenth century the secular courts on the Continent

[37] Cc. 10, 11, X, *de testamentis et ultimis voluntatibus,* III, 26; Pollock-Maitland, *op. cit.,* I, 122, 123; 128; 131; 133; II, 336, 337.

[38] Ottaviani, *Inst. Iur. Pub.* I, 155-159, cc. 3, 6, 9, X, *de testamentis et ultimis voluntatibus,* III, 26; c. 26, X, *de verborum significatione,* V, 40; Council of Salzburg (1420), c. 23—Harduin, VIII, 970; *ASS,* II (1866), 371, 372.

[39] Laws of Ecclesiastical Liberty (by the authority of Richard of Normandy, *i. e.,* Richard I of England), nn. 6 and 8—Mansi, XXII, 592 A; Selected Essays, III, 725; Blackstone, *op. cit.,* III, 7, 96.

seem to have disputed with the ecclesiastical as to the jurisdiction each should enjoy.[40]

713. The Bishop's Jurisdiction in England. It was not so in England. The earliest judiciary system in England differed from that on the Continent. The bishop sat with the secular sheriff or alderman in the court of the hundred under the Anglo-Saxon regime. Thus the sentence was at once ecclesiastical and secular. When William the Conqueror came, however, he complained that this manner of procedure was contrary to the canons, and so separated the ecclesiastical and the secular jurisdictions. Henry I attempted a reunion, but this was opposed by Archbishop Anselm, who ordained that no bishop should be present at the trial of secular suits. When Stephen ascended the throne, he promised under oath that spiritual causes and spiritual persons should be subject to the exclusive jurisdiction of the bishop. The divergence that then developed between the two systems soon became so great as to prevent coalition.[41]

It is probable that at that moment, with bequests for charity subject to them exclusively, the ecclesiastical courts sought no more than concurrent jurisdiction in the matter of wills in general. But by reason of its being exercised very frequently to prevent the failure of last wills due to the injustices of the barons' courts, the jurisdiction over all wills soon became exclusive.[42] Glanvil in the reign of Henry II recognizes the exclusive jurisdiction of the ecclesiastical courts;[43] *Magna Carta* provides that the chattels of a free man are to be distributed under the supervision of the Church;[44] and Bracton in the reign of Henry III says that testamentary causes belong to the exclusive jurisdiction of the ecclesiastical courts precisely as matrimonial

[40] Brissaud, *op. cit.*, p. 696. Philip of Valois complained (1329) that the bishops were executing wills and refusing to accredit wills made by his notaries. The Bishop of Augsburg replied that they were competent as executors; Thomassin, *op. cit.*, III, 1, 24, 12.

[41] *Cf.* Charter of William I—Mansi, XX, 605 A; Blackstone, *op. cit.*, III, 5, 61-64.

[42] Pollock-Maitland, *op. cit.*, II, 332, 333; Ottaviani says that the Decretals demanded no more than concurrent jurisdiction even where pious bequests were involved; *op. cit.*, I, 155, 156.

[43] Blackstone, *op. cit.*, III, 7, 96.

[44] Selected Essays, III, 727.

causes do.[45] But late in the century, the kin still claimed the right to participate in the distribution of the estate. Probably they were often appointed by the bishop in practice.[46]

714. But decedents' estates belonged to the jurisdiction of the ecclesiastical courts, even when there was an intestacy. Blackstone traces the time when the bishop's right to distribute such estates first appeared to the reign of Henry I, alleging that it was by the express concession of the king that it was granted, and citing canonists who justify the bishop's right on the ground that it was an ancient custom conceded by the king. Whatever its origin, it was still the law under Charles I.[47] The towns struggled to reject the intervention of the bishop, and it is probable that he was obliged to forego his rights there.[48]

715. This right to distribute an intestate's property seems not to have been accepted too widely outside of England. In Normandy, for instance, it seems that if a man died intestate after an illness of several days, his estate was forfeit to the duke.[49] And in a Conference under Philip of Valois (1329), the king's judges complained that bishops were making inventories of the estates of intestates. The Bishop of Augsburg replied that they do this only where custom warrants it.[50]

716. The Crown's Right to the Chattels of an Intestate. The origin of the bishop's right to distribute the property of intestates in England, if it came from a concession of the king would imply that the king had a right to the property of the intestate.[51] The Rolls of the twelfth and thirteenth centuries would possibly indicate that the crown did sometimes claim the goods of an intestate, but in these

[45] Bracton, *De Legibus Angliae,* 2, 26, 487.

[46] Pollock-Maitland, *op. cit.,* II, 359, 360.

[47] Blackstone, *op. cit.,* II, 32, 492; Council of London (1268), c. 24—Mansi XXIII, 1238; Council of London (1342), c. 7—Harduin, VII, 1661.

[48] Selected Essays, III, 734, 735.

[49] Pollock-Maitland, *op. cit.,* II, 359.

[50] Thomassin, *op. cit.,* III, 1, 24, 12.

[51] The Domesday Book says that in the time of Edward the Confessor, the king could claim the property of a citizen of Hereford who died intestate; Selected Essays, III, 726, 727.

cases the king was probably acting as feudal lord, rather than as sovereign.

Besides, it is not conceivable that, if the king understood that he had a right to the property of intestates, he would have applied to the Holy Father for permission to confiscate such property. Such an application in itself was an acknowledgment of a power over these estates superior to that of the prerogative of the crown. And two kings actually did make such application. Henry III (1256) asked and obtained this permission to defray the expenses of a crusade. Edward I (1284) asked for a similar permission, but was refused.[52]

717. The Second Problem, the Claim of the Feudal Lord. The question of the right of the crown suggests the problem of the right of the lords to usurp the property of their vassals. From the days of Canute to the reign of Edward I they struggled to obtain, or maintain, as they claimed, the right to confiscate the chattels of intestate vassals. A compromise seems to have been affected under the Constitution of Walter, Bishop of Worcester (1240), under which it was agreed that distribution should be made by the lord with the assistance of a delegate of the bishop. But in Wales, the lords claimed this right long after the time of Edward I; in fact, an attempt at such confiscation was made in that country as late as the reign of Edward VI.[53]

718. The ecclesiastical courts imposed their claim of jurisdiction on all decedents' estates in order to oppose this rapacity. The right to enter was granted as a franchise by the crown to many lords of manors. Even after feudalism had collapsed, many of them exercised the right by prescription to grant in their own courts intestate administration of the estate of their intestate tenants.[54] But these courts often lent color to the acts of usurpation. By the usurpation thus practised the wife and children of the deceased were often deprived of their lawful share and left destitute. It was often a case of brutal oppression under the guise of legal procedure. In time, the ecclesiastical courts were successful in getting control of the chattels

[52] Selected Essays, III, 726

[53] Selected Essays, III, 729.

[54] Blackstone, *op. cit.*, II, 32, 494.

of the intestate, which they then distributed according to the demands of justice.[55] It was only the soul's portion on which the courts exercised their judgment in making distribution, though the portions for the wife and the children also passed through their hands.[56]

719. The concern of ecclesiastical councils that due restitution be made by the testator provides ample assurance that the bishops paid the debts of the intestate in the course of the distribution of his personalty.[57]

720. The third phase of the problem is the reaction of the councils. They are emphatic in forbidding the disposal of the decedent's property contrary to his will.[58] The Council of Nantes (1127) speaks of the custom of the secular power to confiscate the chattels of decedents, and condemns it.[59] The Council of Anjou (1269) condemns the lords who prevent their subjects from making bequests to charitable causes.[60] The Council of Merton (1258) explicitly states that the feudal lords do not permit the chattels of an intestate to be used to pay the decedent's debts, to care for his wife and children, or to be distributed for his soul. It ordains that such intruders are to be warned to cease their usurpations under penalty of excommunication.[61] In general, the councils are concerned that there be no rapacious seizure, even temporary, of the deceased's property or of the benefice of which he had charge.[62]

[55] Morris, *Development of Law*, p. 225.

[56] Pollock-Maitland, *op. cit.*, II, 360; Blackstone, *op. cit.*, II, 32, 495.

[57] *Cf.* § 171, supra.

[58] First General Council of the Lateran (1123), c. 12—Mansi, XXI, 284 C; Council of Toulouse (1056)—Mansi, XIX, 849 A; Harduin, VI A, 1045; Council of Clermont (1095), c. 21—Mansi, XX, 818; Council of Nantes (1127)—Harduin, VI B, 1129.

[59] Harduin, VI B, 1129; *cf.* Council of Lambeth (1261)—Harduin, VII, 543.

[60] C. 1—Harduin, VII, 647.

[61] Mansi, XXIII, 982 C; *cf.* Council of London (1342), cc. 7 and 8—Harduin, VII, 1662; Provincial Council of England (1509)—Mansi, XXXI A, 401 A.

[62] Second General Council of the Lateran (1139), c. 5—Mansi, XXI, 527 B; Council of Rheims (1131), c. 3—Mansi, XXI, 458 C; Council of Merton (1258)—Mansi, XXIII, 981 A; Council of Nîmes (1284)—Mansi, XXIV, 543 E; Council of Würzburg (1287), c. 26—Mansi, XXIV, 861 B; Council of Reggio (1285), c. 18—Mansi, XXIV, 583 B.

They refer to this kind of misconduct on the part of patrons and benefices

721. Contemporaneous with these protests, the councils in England legislated for the due administration of wills under the supervision of the bishop. The Council of Lambeth (1261) excommunicates laymen who interfere with the exclusive jurisdiction of the ecclesiastical courts;[63] the Council of London (1268) forbade the bishop to admit any one to be testamentary executor until he had promised not to have recourse to the secular courts;[64] and the Synod of Oxford (1287) excommunicates those executors who refuse to be cited in the ecclesiastical court in order that for lack of proof they may defraud either the creditor or the estate of sums to which either had a claim.[65] The history revealed by these two later decrees indicates a further struggle between the ecclesiastical and the secular courts. The issue was the right of the executor to sue and be sued for debts. The secular courts held that this was not a testamentary issue, and consequently could not be tried in an ecclesiastical court. Before Edward I, the executor had no action for debts in the secular courts. If he entered his suit there, he lost it. In a similar way, the creditor of the estate was limited in the actions that he had in the secular courts. It was to prevent the injustices that would thus result from suing in the secular courts that these councils launched their decrees.

722. Probate in the Ecclesiastical Courts. Meanwhile the bishops under the guidance of the Supreme Pontiff, strengthened their position by practical legislation for the more efficient discharge of their duties as executors.[66] They require the probate of wills.[67] For

and decree the penalty of excommunication, to be lifted only upon restitution; Council of Magdeburg (1266), c. 14—Mansi, XXIII, 1164 C; Council of Vienne (1267), c. 10—Mansi, XXIII; Council of Buda (1279), c. 49—Mansi, XXIV, 292 E; Council of Salzburg (1281)—Mansi, XXIV, 401 D.

[63] Harduin, VII, 543; *cf.* Council of York (1518), c. 6—Mansi, XXXVI A, 193 D.

[64] C. 15—Mansi, XXIII, 1232.

[65] C. 50—Harduin, VII, 1114; *cf.* § 171, supra.

[66] Constitutions of Simon, Bishop of Meath, c. 10—Mansi, XXII, 1102 E (forbidding archpriests to probate wills); the Scotch Council (1225); c. 25—Mansi, XXII, 1229 B (exempting the Cistercians from the obligation of account to the bishop); Council of the Isle of Man (1239)—Mansi, XXIII, 507 C; Gregory IX to the Bishop of Noyon (1235), (c. 17, X, *de testamentis et ultimis*

this purpose the cooperation of the pastor is frequently required, and he is commanded to procure a copy of all the charitable bequests in his parish and to keep a record of them in his parish register,[68] or to demand within fifteen days a transcript from the testator of all charitable bequests and to keep a record of them.[69] They who refuse to cooperate with the pastor after admonition are excommunicated.[70] The will is to be brought to the bishop or his official. If it was made orally, it is to be proved in the presence of the bishop by oath.[71] And the bishop is to be notified either by the notary,[72] or by

voluntatibus III, 26)—*ASS,* II (1866), 372 (*cf.* Benedict XIV, *op. cit.*, lib. 13, c. ult.); Gregory IX (1235) in c. 19, X, *de testamentis et ultimis voluntatibus* III, 26 (inculcating the necessity of paying the decedent's debts; this decision was rendered in the case of a will where no charitable bequests were involved, indicating the Holy Father's conviction that the ecclesiastical authority enjoyed at least concurrent jurisdiction with the secular courts in the matter of wills)

[67] There seems to be little of the probate of wills in England prior to the thirteenth century. The prior history of probate is difficult to ascertain. Pollock-Maitland, *op. cit.*, II, 341.

[68] Council of Cahors (1289)—Mansi, XXIV, 1023 A; Council of Mexico, lib. 3, tit. 9, c. 1—Harduin, X, 1678; Council of Avignon (1594), c. 56—Harduin, X, 1868; Council of Avignon (1725), tit. 37, c. 9—*Coll. Lacensis,* I 556 c.

[69] Council of Albi (1254), c. 39—Harduin, VII, 464; Council of Arles (1275), c. 9—Mansi, XXIV, 149 A; Council of L'isle (1288), c. 8—Mansi, XXIV, 955 D; Council of Milan (1311)—Mansi, XXV, 502 A.

[70] Council of Nîmes (1284)—Mansi, XXIV, 543 C.

[71] No specification of period within which the will is to be brought to the bishop is found in: Council of Lambeth (1261)—Harduin, VII, 543; Council of London (1268), c. 15—Mansi, XXIII, 1232 B (if the decedent had property in two dioceses, even though it be realty, the will is to be probated in the diocese where he died); Synod of Oxford (1287), c. 50—Harduin, VII, 1114; Council of Florence (1573), rub. 54, c. 1—Mansi, XXXV A, 795 B.

The will is to be presented to the bishop within eight days of the testator's death: Council of Avignon (1279), c. 14—Mansi, XXIV, 242 B; Council of Reggio (1285), c. 16—Mansi, XXIV, 582 D; Council of Constance (1300), c. 63—Mansi, XXV, 53 E; Council of Avignon (1326), c. 20—Harduin, II, 1503; Council of Beziers (1357), c. 10—Mansi, XXVI, 249 B; Council of Lavaur (1368), c. 62—Harduin, VII, 1830. Within ten days: Council of Tours (1236), c. 7—Harduin, VII, 264; Council of Le Mans (1247)—Mansi, XXIII, 758 E; Council of Bourges (1286), c. 27—Harduin, VII, 959 (provision is made that the bishop's deputy may receive probate); Council of Florence (1517)—Mansi XXXV A, 265 B. Within fifteen days: Council of Ferrari (1332), c. 49—

the pastor, who in that case, informs the bishop of the notary's name;[73] or by both the pastor and the notary.[74] And the estate is ordered sequestered until the will is probated.[75]

Mansi, XXV, 926 C; Council of Milan (1311)—Mansi, XXV, 502 A; Council of Fermo, tit. 11, c. 11—Mansi, XXXVII, 635.

Within a month: Council of Clermont (1268)—Mansi, XXIII, 1206 E; Council of Milan (1287), c. 20—Mansi, XXIV, 878 E; Council of Ravenna (1311), c. 31—Harduin, VII, 1378; Council of Perugia (1320)—Mansi, XXV, 642 E; Council of Benevento (1331), c. 15—Mansi, XXV, 941 D; Council of Aquileia (1339)—Mansi, XXV, 1122 B (within two months outside the city); Council of Padua (1350)—Mansi, XXVI, 230 B; Council of Arezzo (1350), c. 68—Mansi, XXVI, 220 B; Council of Benevento (1378), c. 17—Mansi, XXVI, 627 A; Council of Cologne (1536), pars. 13, c. 10—Mansi, XXXII, 1289 A (as to the wills of priests): Council of Sipontino (1575)—Mansi, XXV B, 890 C; Council of Naples (1576), c. 45—Mansi, XXV B, 850; Council of Capua (1577)—Mansi, XXV B, 902 D; Council of Cosenza (1579), sess. 4—Mansi, XXXV B, 950; Council of Trani-Salpi (1589)—Mansi, XXXVI B, 882 B; Council of Salerno (1596), c. 25—Mansi, XXXV B, 1013 D; Council of Benevento (1599), tit. 40, c. 1—Mansi, XXXVI B, 450 C; Council of Sancta Severina (1597)—Mansi, XXXV B, 1053.

Within forty days: Council of Treves (1310), c. 73—Mansi, XXV, 266 D. Within two months: Council of Saintes (1282), c. 5—Harduin, VII, 884; Council of Naples (1699), tit. 13, 2—*Coll. Lacensis,* I, 241 b. Within three months: Second Council of Milan (1569), tit. 3, dec. 17—Harduin, X, 754; Council of Toulouse (1590), pars. 4, c. 15—Harduin, X, 830; Council of Avignon (1594)—*l. c.*

[72] Council of Ravenna (1311), c. 31—Harduin, VII, 1378; Council of Beziers (1357), c. 10—Mansi, XXVI, 249 B; Second Council of Milan (1569), tit. 3, dec. 17—Harduin, X, 754; Council of Toulouse (1590), pars. 4, c. 15—Harduin, X, 1830; Council of Avignon (1594)—*l. c.*

[73] Council of Perugia (1320)—Mansi, XXV, 642 E; Council of Ferrari (1332), c. 49—Mansi, XXV, 926 C; Council of Tarragona (1691)—*Coll. Lacensis,* VI, 901 c.

[74] Council of Benevento (1331), c. 15—Mansi, XXV, 941 D; Council of Arezzo (1350), c. 68—Mansi, XXVI, 220 B; Council of Benevento (1378), c. 17—Mansi, XXVI, 627 A; Council of Lavaur (1368), c. 62—Harduin, VII, 1830.

The notaries are allowed a fee for making their transcript: Council of Naples (1576), c. 45—Mansi, XXXV B, 850; Council of Cosenza (1570), sess. 4—Mansi, XXXV B, 950; Council of Fermo (1726), tit. 11, c. 11—Mansi, XXXVII, 635.

[75] Constitution of the Archbishop of Canterbury (1416)—Mansi, XXVIII, 962 A.

723. The bishop administered the estate through an executor. This procedure developed probably with the Germanic custom of disposing of the soul's portion through a *salman,* who was obliged under the custom to convey the bequest to the beneficiary within a year. On the mainland, the heir was consequently at first the representative of the testator, and the executor represented the beneficiary; but gradually the executor came to be the personal representative of the testator. This was especially true in England where the heir had absolutely no concern with the personalty. The personalty descended to the executor named in the will, or to the administrator appointed by the bishop.[76] Now since the executor superseded the heir as the personal representative of the testator, the councils came to apply to him the legislation of Gregory the Great when he commanded that Januarius take over the building of a monastery within one year after he had admonished the heir to do so.[77]

But in the beginning there seems to have been considerable reliance on the bishop's judgment as to the time within which the testator's will should be fulfilled. In England it seems that the bishop was always required to administer the estate through other executors, whom, however, he might remove for incompetence. The bequests to charity, however, he could distribute by his own hand.[78]

[76] Pollock-Maitland, *op. cit.,* II, 336, 337; Huebner, *op. cit.,* pp. 740, 754; Brissaud, *op. cit.,* p. 692; *cf.* Chapter I, art. 4, supra.

[77] This decision or command became a part of the Decretals, c. 3, X, *de testamentis et ultimis voluntatibus,* III, 26. It will be remembered that Justinian also required the heir to comply with the provisions of the will and to construct a charitable institution within one year of the testator's death; C. 1, 3, 45, and that he authorized the bishop to become executor if the heir failed to comply after two warnings; *Nov.,* 131, 11, 3 and 4.

[78] Inquisition is to be made by the bishop as to the fulfillment of charitable bequests when he makes his diocesan visitation: *v. gr.* Q. I for the Bishop of Girone's visitation—Mansi, XXIII, 943 D; Council of Lavaur (1368), c. 60—Harduin, VII, 1829 (summary trial to be established for the inquisition wherever necessary); Council of Narbonne (1609), c. 25—Harduin, XI, 26; Council of Tarragona (1292), c. 13—Mansi, XXIV, 1112 C; Council of Tarragona (1329), c. 55—Mansi, XXV, 864 C.

Worthy men are to be appointed executors; Council of Paris (1248), c. 22—Mansi, XXIII, 768 C. Competent executors are to be substituted for incompetent with the consent of the decedent's relatives; Council of Worcester (1240), c.

The specification of one year as the time limit within which the executory task was to be fulfilled seems to originate in the middle of the thirteenth century. The first clear mention of it is found in the Synodal Constitutions of the Bishop of Valencia (1261).[79] As late as 1416, the Archbishop of Canterbury sets this term as a limit, but adds, *si possibile fuerit,* that is, if fulfillment within that time was possible.[80] The Council of Le Mans (1247) determines the time within which the work of execution is to begin, without specifying when it is to be completed.[81] But the Synod of Oxford (1287) regards an executor negligent enough to be removed if he has failed to complete execution within a year.[82] This sort of failure sometimes subjects the executor to excommunication,[83] renders his prior acts null and void,[84] and incapacitates him for this office in the future.[85]

The bishop is burdened with the responsibility of enforcing execution within a year [86] and often of taking over the task of execu-

49—Harduin, VII, 345; Pollock-Maitland, *op. cit.,* II, 343. Negligent executors are to be removed by the bishop; Council of Norwich (1257)—Mansi, XXIII, 972. The deans are to assume the office of negligent executors; Council of Le Mans (1247)—Mansi, XXIII, 758 E. The bishop is to take over the administration when the executors are negligent; Council of Bourges (1286), cc. 27-29 —Harduin, VII, 959, 960.

[79] Mansi, XXIII, 1052 C.

[80] Mansi, XXVIII, 962 A.

[81] Mansi, XXIII, 758 E.

[82] C. 50—Harduin, VII, 1114.

[83] Council of Lucania (1308), c. 51—Mansi, XXV, 187 E; Council of Lucania (1351), c. 49—Mansi, XXVI, 275 B; Constitutions of the Bishop of Valencia (1261)—Mansi, XXIII, 1052 C.

[84] Council of Lucania (1351), c. 49—Mansi, XXVI, 275 B.

[85] Council of Ravenna (1311), c. 31—Harduin, VII, 1378.

[86] Council of Avignon (1270), c. 2—Mansi, XXIII, 16 D; Council of L'isle (1288), c. 4—Mansi, XXIV, 953 D; Council of Constance (1300), c. 62—Mansi, XXV, 54 E; Council of Mayence (1310)—Mansi, XXV, 322 A; Council of Beziers (1310)—Mansi, XXV, 364 D (adds a month of grace); Council of Prague (1346)—Mansi, XXVI, 87 B; Council of Prague (1355)—Mansi, XXVI, 393 E; Council of Magdeburg (1489)—Mansi, XXXIII, 458 B; Council of Seville (1512), c. 9—Mansi, XXXII, 589 E; Council of Rouen (1522), c. 4—Mansi, XXXII, 1073 C; Council of Cologne (1536)—*l. c.;* Council of Edinburgh (1559), c. 20—Mansi, XXXV A, 541 D; Second Council of Milan (1569), tit. 3, dec. 16—Harduin, X, 753; Council of Petrokow (1577)—Mansi, XXXVI B, 719 D; Council of Tarragona (1691)—*Coll. Lacensis,* VI, 901 c.

tion.[87] However, he is to await the period appointed by the testator in the will.[88]

724. Inventory. Executors are forbidden to assume their office without the permission of the bishop [89] or without an inventory [90] to be made in the presence of honest and qualified appraisers [91] within

Within two months: Council of Ravenna (1568)—Mansi, XXXV A, 642 B; Council of Urbino (1569)—Mansi, XXXV A, 700 B. Time period indefinite: Council of Mayence (1549), c. 97—Mansi, XXXII, 1436 A. The bishop is to be notified if the work of execution is not completed within a year: Council of Mexico (1585), lib. 3, tit. 9, c. 1—Harduin, X, 1678; Council of Mechlin (1607), tit. 17, c. 9—Mansi, XXXIV B, 1462 D; Council of Cambrai (1631), tit. 17, c. 16—Mansi, XXXVI C, 185 C.

87 Left to his discretion when he shall take over the task: Council of Tours (1236), c. 7—Harduin, VII, 264; Council of Bourges (1286), c. 29—Harduin, VII, 960; Council of Sancta Severina (1597)—Mansi, XXXV B, 1053 C. After six months: Council of Lavaur (1368), c. 62—Harduin, VII, 1830; Council of Narbonne (1609), c. 25—Harduin, XI, 26; Council of Mexico (1585), *l. c.*, c. 4 (clerics are to say the Masses and fulfill the other charges in the will within six months unless otherwise specified).

After a year: Council of Treves (1310), c. 13—Mansi, XXV, 251 E; Council of Ravenna (1311), c. 31—Harduin, VII, 1378; Council of Etruria (1327)—Mansi, XXV, 823 E; Council of Benevento (1331), c. 15—Mansi, XXV, 941 D; Council of Aquileia (1339)—Mansi, XXV, 1122 B; Council of Florence (1346)—Mansi, XXVI, 46 C; Council of Arezzo (1350), c. 68—Mansi, XXVI, 220 B; Council of Padua (1350)—Mansi, XXVI, 230 A; Council of Beziers (1357), c. 10—Mansi, XXVI, 249 B; Council of Benevento (1378), c. 15—Mansi, XXVI, 626 B; Council of Mexico (1585)—*l. c.;* Council of Utrecht (1565)—Mansi, XXXV A, 575 E; Council of Cambrai (1586), tit. 15, c. 16—Mansi, XXXIV B, 1462 D. After a second executor proves negligent: Benedict XIV, *l. c.;* Ferraris, *op. cit.*, *s. v.* *"Testamentum,"* III, 49.

88 Council of Florence (1346)—Mansi, XXVI, 46 C.

89 Council of Reggio (1285), c. 16—Mansi, XXIV, 582 D; Council of Perugia (1320)—Mansi, XXV, 642 E.

90 Council of Clermont (1268)—Mansi, XXIII, 1206 E; Council of Cahors (1289)—Mansi, XXIV, 1023 A; Council of Treves (1310), c. 13—Mansi, XXV, 251 E; Council of Mayence (1310)—Mansi, XXV, 322 A; Council of London (1342), c. 7—Harduin, VII, 1661.

91 Council of Lambeth (1261)—Harduin, VII, 543; Council of London (1268), c. 15—Mansi, XXIII, 1232 B; Council of Prague (1346)—Mansi, XXVI, 87 B; Council of Prague (1355)—Mansi, XXVI, 393 E; Council of Magdeburg (1489)—Mansi, XXXII, 458 B; Council of Dublin (1518), c. 4—Harduin, IX, 1889.

fifteen days, and the inventory is to be fortified with the seals of the executors and the witnesses.[92] But the Councils of Cologne (1300) and Liége (1287) order the inventory to be made by the pastor with two synodal officials, and the pastor's seal is to be affixed; if the pastor is executor, the dean is to make the inventory in his place.[93] Should new property be acquired by the estate, the executor may not attempt to administer it until he has submitted a new inventory. On assuming office, he is obliged to make affidavit that he will make the inventory within the specified time.[94]

725. At the completion of his task, the executor is to render an account to the bishop[95] even under penalty of censure.[96] He is not to be discharged in any event without rendering his account.[97] He is not permitted to purchase the property of the testator or to take it on any title by his own authority.[98] If he does so he is penalized

[92] Synod of Oxford (1287), c. 50—Harduin, VII, 1114; Pollock-Maitland, *op. cit.*, II, 343. The inventory is to be made in the presence of a notary and two witnesses under the provisions of the following councils; Council of Mayence (1549)—*l. c.;* Council of Edinburgh (1549)—Mansi, XXXV A, 448 D; Council of Petrokow (1577)—*l. c.*

[93] Council of Cologne, c. 10—Mansi, XXV, 19 D; Council of Liége, c. 34—Mansi, XXIV, 939 D.

[94] Constitution of the Archbishop of Canterbury (1416)—Mansi, XXVIII, 962 A.

[95] C. 1, *de testamentis et ultimis voluntatibus,* III, 6, in Clem.; Council of Lambeth (1261)—Harduin, VII, 543 (within the option of the bishop to demand it); Council of Cologne (1280), c. 17—Harduin, VII, 834; Synod of Oxford (1287), c. 50—Harduin, VII, 1114; Council of Constance (1300), c. 63—Mansi, XXV, 54 E; Council of London (1342), c. 7—Harduin, VII, 1661; Council of Padua (1350)—Mansi, XXVI, 230 A; Council of Lavaur (1368), c. 62—Harduin, VII, 1831; Constitution of the Archbishop of Canterbury (1416)—Mansi, XXVIII, 962 A; Council of Cologne (1536)—*l. c.;* Council of Mayence (1549)—*l. c.;* Council of Edinburgh (1559) (as to the property of an intestate) —*l. c.;* Council of Narbonne (1609)—*l. c.*

[96] Council of Cologne (1280), c. 17—Harduin, VII, 834.

[97] Council of London (1321), c. 1—Mansi, XXV, 670 E; Council of London (1399), c. 20—Mansi, XXVI, 925 D; Provincial Council of England (1509)—Mansi, XXXI A, 400 E.

[98] Council of Norwich (1257)—Mansi, XXIII, 972; Council of Langeais (1278), c. 5—Harduin, VII, 760; Council of Bourges (1286), c. 27—Harduin, VII, 959; Constitution of the Archbishop of Canterbury (1416)—Mansi, XXVIII, 962 A.

twice the value of the property so appropriated.[99] And he can not rely on the pretext that the property was due him under an old debt.[100] On the other hand, he seems to be permitted to be a legatee [101] and to take donations that he can prove the testator had given him.[102] He is forbidden to contract debts against the estate except in the presence of witnesses [103] or to subtract, without the permission of the bishop,[104] any portion of the estate as a fee for execution.

726. Registration and Publication. The bishop preserved the inventory in the diocesan register,[105] which was kept by a special registrar.[106] The Bishop of Valencia (1261) appointed a special attorney to supervise the execution of wills, and imposed an oath on him by which he promised that he would enter into no pacts with the executors for the purpose of delaying prompt and honest execution.[107] The Fifth Council of Milan (1579) required the appointment of a diocesan procurator of wills, prescribing also a weekly meeting between the bishop, the general procurator, and the procurators of all charitable institutions.[108]

727. For greater security, a table of the legacies due the institu-

[99] Council of Langeais (1278), c. 5—Harduin, VII, 760.

[100] Council of Tours, c. 7—Harduin, VII, 264.

[101] Council of Clermont (1268)—Mansi, XXIII, 1206 E; Council of Treves (1310), c. 77—Mansi, XXV, 268 A; Synod of Oxford (1287), c. 50—Harduin, VII, 1114.

[102] Council of Worcester (1240), c. 49—Harduin, VII, 345; Council of Lambeth (1261)—Harduin, VII, 544.

[103] Council of Liége (1287)—Mansi, XXIV, 939 D; Council of Cologne (1300), c. 10—Mansi, XXV, 19 D.

[104] Third Council of Milan (1573), c. 16—Mansi, XXXIV A, 167 A.

[105] Council of Clermont (1268)—Mansi, XXIII, 1206 E; Council of Florence (1517)—Mansi, XXXV A, 265 B; Council of Florence (1573), rub. 54, c. 2—Mansi, XXXV A, 795 B; Third Council of Milan (1573), c. 16—Mansi, XXXIV A, 166 E; Council of Cosenza (1579), sess. 4—Mansi, XXXV B, 949; Council of Trani-Salpi (1589)—Mansi, XXXVI B, 882 B; Council of Narbonne (1609), c. 25—Harduin, XI, 26; Council of Benevento (1693), tit. 27, c. 2—*Coll. Lacensis,* I, 54 b; Council of Toulouse (1590), pars. 4, c. 15—Harduin, X, 1830; Council of Avignon (1594), c. 56—Harduin, X, 1868; Council of Naples (1699), tit. 13, 2—*Coll. Lacensis,* I, 241 b.

[106] Council of Avignon (1594)—*l. c.*

[107] Mansi, XXIII, 1052 C.

[108] C. 11—Mansi, XXXIV A, 473 D.

tion and of obligations to be fulfilled under legacies was to be kept in a public place.[109] The pastor was commanded to announce publicly the bequests made by the deceased,[110] and to invite creditors to present their claims.[111] Parishioners were to be constantly reminded by him of their duty to report when pious bequests had been made.[112]

728. Distribution. If the testator designated no objects under his charitable bequest, the executor was not permitted to distribute it without the consent of the bishop.[113] Where the testator owed restitution, but did not know to whom, the bishop took over the amount and distributed it to the poor. It seems, however, that canonists were not unanimous in granting him the right to do this. For the Council of Benevento (1331) notes the adverse opinion but repudiates it.[114] It is the bishop's right also to distribute the whole estate of persons who die intestate.[115] But this right seems not to be too widely granted him outside of England.[116]

109 Council of Cosenza (1579)—*l. c.*

110 Council of Albi (1254), c. 40—Harduin, VII, 464; Council of Clermont (1268)—Mansi, XXIII, 1206 E; Council of Arles (1275)— Mansi, XXIV, 149 A.

111 Council of Cologne (1300), c. 10—Mansi, XXV, 19 D.

112 Council of Arezzo (1350), c. 68—Mansi, XXVI, 220 B; Third Council of Milan (1573), c. 16—Mansi, XXXIV A, 166 E.

113 Council of Arles (1234), c. 21—Harduin, VII, 239; Council of Avignon (1326), cc. 20, 21—Harduin, VII, 1503; Council of Lavaur (1368), c. 62—Harduin, VII, 1830; Council of Avignon, (1594)—*l. c.*

114 Council of Reggio (1285), c. 16—Mansi, XXIV, 582 D; Council of Avignon (1326), c. 20—Harduin, VII, 1503; Council of Benevento (1331), c. 20—Mansi, XXV, 944 A; Council of Ferrari (1332), c. 50—Mansi, XXV, 926 D; Council of Avignon (1337), c. 24—Mansi, XXV, 1094 C; Council of Padua (1350)—Mansi, XXVI, 230 B; Council of Lavaur (1368), c. 62—Harduin, VII, 1830; Council of Benevento (1378), c. 20—Mansi, XXVI, 628 C; Council of Cologne (1536) (orders distribution by the bishop of foolish bequests)—*l. c.*

115 Council of London (1257), c. 25—Mansi, XXIII, 957 E; Council of London (1268), c. 24—Harduin, VII, 631 B; Synod of Oxford (1287), c. 50—Harduin, VII, 1114; Council of London (1342), c. 7—Harduin, VII, 1661; Provincial Council of England (1509)—Mansi, XXI A, 401 A.

116 The Council of Constance (1300), c. 63, has this provision—Mansi, XXV, 53 E. The Council of Bayeux (1300) punishes with suspension the failure of a pastor to notify the bishop of the death of an intestate, c. 57—Mansi, XXV, 70 B. As late as 1725 the Council of Rome refers to this practice as the custom of the Kingdom of Naples, and expresses a desire that it be made universal, tit. 20, c. 2—*Coll. Lacensis*, I, 382 b.

729. Following the Protestant revolt, secularism gradually interfered with the bishop's prerogative, though the bishops of the Established Church in England succeeded to the rights of their Catholic predecessors.

730. The most notable modification of discipline in the matter of ecclesiastical control of wills is observed in the manner in which the property of an *intestate* is henceforth distributed. For example, now the relatives are to come to an agreement upon an executor whose appointment is subject to the bishop's confirmation. But in case the relatives can not be found, the bishop is to make the appointment himself.[117] The property is to be given to the heirs, if they can be found, and only when they can not be discovered is the bishop to make the traditional distribution.[118] But a small portion of the estate is to be devoted to charity, unless the estate is very small; the relatives, however, are to be consulted about the objects of charity that are to be beneficiaries.[119]

731. **As to bequests in wills, following the Protestant revolt, the attention of the canons centers on bequests to charity.** While regulations touching probate, inventory, and account are repeated, as already indicated in the respective footnotes, they are concerned principally with bequests to charity. These bequests fall under the jurisdiction of the ecclesiastical court exclusively; the others, only *iure devolutivo*. But the Councils of Besancon (1571) and Petrokow (1577) raise their voices to defend the concurrent jurisdiction of the ecclesiastical courts over all wills.[120] The Council of York (1518) excommunicates all who impede the bishop in realizing

[117] Council of Edinburgh (1559)—*l. c.*

[118] Council of Capua (1569)—Mansi, XXXV A, 720 C; Council of Naples (1576), c. 45—Mansi, XXXV B, 850 (unless the custom permits distribution by the bishop in any case).

[119] Council of Naples (1576), c. 45—Mansi, XXXV B, 850; Council of Benevento (1599), tit. 40, c. 2—Mansi, XXXVI B, 450 C; Decree of the S. C. EE. RR., 19 April, 1641, cited in Council of Benevento (1693), tit. 27, c. 2—*Coll. Lacensis*, I, 54 c; S. C. EE. RR., 19 August, 1678—*Coll. Lacensis*, I, 104 d; Council of Rome (1725), tit. 20, c. 2—*Coll. Lacensis*, I, 381 (praises the custom and urges other dioceses to adopt it).

[120] Council of Besancon—Mansi, XXXVI B, 45 B; Council of Petrokow, *l. c.*

his claim to execute all wills without exception.[121] And in some instances the period of one year for the execution of wills seems to be applied to all bequests without distinction.[122]

732. Scholion I. Clerics and Religious as Executors. Towards the end of the thirteenth century, a movement arose to prevent religious from being executors of wills.[123] Pope Boniface VIII required that they have the permission of their superior,[124] and this provision was repeated by Pope Clement V in the Council of Vienne (1311); but the latter also demanded that when a religious performs the duty of an executor, he must render an account to the bishop, even if he is otherwise exempt, and no matter what dignity he enjoys in his community.[125] Clement V also forbade the Friars Minor to accept this responsibility inasmuch as it involves the administration of pecuniary assets and frequently also contention and litigation.[126] Under the present law clerics are forbidden to exercise

[121] C. 6—Mansi, XXXVI A, 193 D.

[122] Council of Rouen (1522)—*l. c.;* Council of Edinburgh (1559)—*l. c.;* Council of Petrokow (1577)—*l. c.*

[123] Council of Lambeth (1261)—Harduin, VII, 543; Synod of Oxford (1287), c. 50—Harduin, VII, 1114; Council of London (1342), c. 7—Harduin, VII, 1661; Provincial Council of England (1509)—Mansi, XXI A, 400 C.

[124] C. 2, *de testamentis et ultimis voluntatibus,* III, 11, in VI°; Wernz, *op. cit.,* III, 283; Santi, *op. cit.,* III, 26, 73. *Cf.* also Council of Cahors (1289)—Mansi, XXIV, 1024 B.

[125] C. 1, *de testamentis et ultimis voluntatibus,* III, 6, in Clem.; Wernz, *l. c.;* Santi, *l. c.;* Schmalzgrueber, *op. cit.,* I, IV, 31, 11. Wernz says that the permission of the local superior suffices, except that the Jesuits need the permission of the higher superior; and that the Franciscans require the permission of the Holy See.

[126] C. 1, *de verborum significatione,* V, 11, in Clem.; Santi, *l. c.* De Héricourt says that in France the religious could never be an executor, for the secular law regarded him as civilly dead; *op. cit.,* D, III, 126.

Two councils of Benevento demanded that religious give bond to the bishop before undertaking their task: (1331), c. 19—Mansi, XXV, 943 D; and (1378), c. 19—Mansi, XXVI, 628 A. In Cyprus this provision was extended to all clerics who were thus required to guarantee faithful performance; they needed also the permission of the bishop to act (1253)—Mansi, XXVI, 321 C; and (1340), c. 7—Mansi, XXVI, 379 A.

The Sacred Congregation of the Council held that the Guardian of the Capuchins is incapable of being an executor and declared that the Ordinary

acts of administration of property belonging to lay persons or to assume any secular office that carries with it the obligation of rendering an account. The cleric's Ordinary may give him permission, however, to act in both capacities. Under the prohibition, he would not be permitted to act as executor of a will. However, the counsel of the Third Plenary Council of Baltimore directing priests to name some priest as executor of their wills provides sufficient warrant for a priest's acting in this capacity for a decedent priest in the United States.[127]

733. Scholion II. The Bishop's Visitatorial Power. The Council of Vienne also required that bishops should compel non-exempt religious by their ordinary power and exempt religious by delegated power, to reclaim all bequests due them and to keep all foundations in good repair. The bishop was also to demand an inventory and an annual account from both.[128] The Council of Trent adopted the decree of the Council of Vienne by name,[129] repeating the right of bishops, as delegates of the Holy See, to be executors of all legacies to charity,[130] and placing on all administrators the obligation of making an annual accounting to the bishop, whether they be laymen or ecclesiastical persons, and whether the institution be a church, a hospital, a confraternity, or a charitable foundation. The obligation of the account binds them even though they are obliged, by privilege or by custom, to render an account also to some other persons, unless the terms of the foundation excuse them from rendering an account to the bishop.[131]

The Council also gives bishops the right of visiting, as delegates of the Holy See, all hospitals, schools, and charitable and religious

should take his place as executor of all pious bequests; *in Causa Montis Cassinen.*, 24 September, 1729—*Fontes*, n. 3355; 14 and 28 January, 1730—*Fontes*, n. 3360.

[127] *Cf.* Canon 139, § 3; Third Plenary Council of Baltimore, n. 277.

[128] C. 2, *de relig. dom.*, III, 11, in Clem.; *ASS*, II (1866), 370; Council of Cosenza (1579), sess. 4—Mansi, XXXV B, 948; Blat, *op. cit.*, 426. This decree states, however, that it does not apply to the hospitals of the military orders or of other religious.

[129] Sess. VII, *de ref.*, c. 15.

[130] Sess. XXII, *de ref.*, c. 8.

[131] Sess. XXII, *de ref.*, c. 9.

foundations, even though they are under the care of a layman or of a religious who is otherwise exempt, unless such institutions are directly under the supervision of the king; even then they may visit them with the king's permission. In the visitation they have the right to scrutinize every phase of the work which is connected with divine service, the salvation of souls, and the work of charity.[132] The bishop can compel even by censure all administrators, except those subject to regulars provided that they are living under rule, to fufill their task, and he may remove them and impose on them the obligation of restitution in the degree in which they have been negligent. In any event, the administrator is not to hold office for more than three years.[133] He is to visit benefices and monasteries every year and to report to the superiors of the exempt religious whatever he finds deficient; and whenever negligence has been found, a visit is to be made six months afterwards to determine whether due amendment has ensued.[134]

As to the subject matter of the account, whatever regulars own as religious, that is, whatever is devoted to the support of the community and its members, is exempt from the annual account, but whatever they administer *intuitu missionis* must be accounted for each year.[135] And the substance of this decree of the Sacred Congregation for the Propagation of the Faith Pope Leo XIII repeated for England,[136] while the Third Plenary Council of Baltimore requires that bishops exact this annual accounting *ad normam Constitutionis, Romanos Pontifices*.[137]

[132] Sess. XXII, *de ref.*, c. 8; *ASS*, II (1866), 370.

[133] Sess. XXV, *de ref.*, c. 8; *ASS*, II (1866), 370.

[134] Sess. XXI, *de ref.*, c. 8.

[135] S. C. P. F., 19 April, 1869 (for England)—*AAS*, XIII (1881), 494.

[136] Const., *Romanos Pontifices*, 8 March, 1881—*ASS*, XIII (1881), 494. The decree was extended to Canada by the decree of the Sacred Congregation of the Council, 14 March, 1911—*AAS*, III (1911), 183.

[137] N. 272.

These regulations are quite in accord with the spirit of the canons of rather early times. In the first place, Justinian imposed the duty of supervision on bishops; C. 1, 3, 45; *Nov.*, 131, 10. As early as the seventh century, Pope Gregory the Great suggested to the Bishop of Cagliari that he demand a regular accounting from the charitable institutions in his diocese. The Capitulary of the Causes of the Kingdom of Italy (893) demanded that the administrators of

734. Following the Council of Trent, a series of particular councils embodied its legislation with various modifications. The Council of Avignon (1594) prescribed that all administrators of charitable institutions should take an oath in the presence of the bishop that they would discharge the obligations of their office faithfully.[138] The Council of Mechlin (1607) provided that the bishop should make a complete survey of the property of such institutions every ten years, and that the archpriest should make a visit to them each year.[139] As to the interval within which the report must be made, the councils repeat the term laid down by the Council of Trent, *i. e.*, one year.[140] The duty of the bishop to visit the institutions is re-enacted;[141] and the three-year term for administrators.[142] And the Council of Rouen repeats that a lay administrator is to be removed at any time the bishop thinks him negligent.

charitable institutions should govern with the counsel of the bishop, c. 1—Mansi, XIII, 863 A. In 1237, the Bishop of Coventry commanded in his Constitutions that no one should be admitted to the hospice without his permission; Mansi, XXIII, 432 E.

[138] C. 50—Mansi, XXXIV B, 1360 E.

[139] Tit. 17, c. 10—Mansi, XXXIV B, 1462 D.

[140] Council of Augsburg (1548), c. 27—Mansi, XXXII, 1319 E; Council of Cambrai (1586), tit. 15, c. 9—Mansi, XXXIV B, 1245 E; Council of Toulouse (1590), part 3, c. 6, n. 3—Mansi, XXXIV B, 1299 D; Council of Avignon (1594), c. 50—Mansi, XXXIV B, 1360 E; Council of Utrecht (1565)—Mansi, XXXV A, 575 E; Council of Ravenna (1568)—Mansi, XXXV A, 639 A; Council of Salerno (1596), c. 25—Mansi, XXXV B, 1012 C; Council of Salzburg (1569), const. 61, c. 3—Mansi, XXXVI A, 299 B; Council of Besancon (1571)—Mansi, XXXVI B, 73 B; Council of Benevento (1599), tit. 44, c. 1—Mansi, XXXVI B, 454 A; Council of Trani-Salpi (1589)—Mansi, XXXVI B, 882 A; Council of Fermo (1590), c. 26—Mansi, XXXVI B, 908 D; Council of Benevento (1693), part 3, tit. 10, n. 223—*Coll. Lacensis*, VI, 72 d.

But the Council of Cambrai (1631) specifies no particular period; tit. 17, n. 7—Mansi, XXXVI C, 184 D. The Council of Rouen (1581) specifies a two-year period—Mansi, XXXIV A, 638 B.

[141] Council of Cologne (1549), part 4, c. 4—Mansi, XXXII, 1378 E; Council of Milan (1576), part 3, c. 12—Mansi, XXXVI A, 326 D; Council of Fermo (1590), c. 26—Mansi, XXXVI B, 908 D.

[142] Council of Rouen (1581)—Mansi, XXXIV A, 638 B; Council of Ravenna (1568)—Mansi, XXXIV A, 639 A; Council of Salerno (1596), c. 25—Mansi, XXXV B, 1012 C (assigns a two-year term).

CHAPTER XII

THE ORDINARY'S PRESENT DUTIES AS EXECUTOR

ARTICLE 1

THE DUTY OF FULFILLMENT

735. The Formal Statement of the Duty. That the bequests which are given to charity and religion should be devoted to the purpose intended by the testator and in the manner intended by him has been the burden of most of the conclusions at which this discussion has already arrived. Canon 1514 enshrines it as a definite precept of the law.[1] This precept is so traditionally an ordinance of the canons as hardly to have needed re-statement. It appears in the Decree of Gratian,[2] in the Decretals,[3] in the Council of Trent,[4] in Proposition 43 of the Jansenists condemned by the Sacred Congregation of the Holy Office, viz., "*Annuum legatum pro anima relictum non durat plus quam per decem annos*";[5] and in the various responses of the Sacred Congregation of the Council.[6]

[1] Canon 1514. "Voluntates fidelium facultates suas in pias causas donantium vel relinquentium, sive per actum inter vivos, sive per actum mortis causa, diligentissime impleantur etiam circa modum administrationis et erogationis bonorum, salvo praescripto can. 1515, § 3.

[2] Cc. 4 and 9, C. XIII, q. 2: the former canon warning that it is a sacrilege to retain bequests to charity; and the latter ordering restitution of thefts from the Church.

[3] Cc. 3, 4, 6, 17, 19, X, *de testamentis et ultimis voluntatibus*, III, 26; c. un., *de testamentis et ultimis voluntatibus*, III, 6, in Clem.; c. 2, *de relig. dom.*, III, 11, in Clem. (*Cf.* § 733, supra.)

[4] *Cf.* § 733.

[5] 18 March, 1666—Denzinger, *Enchiridion*, n. 1143.

[6] V. gr., *in Causa Venusina,* 15 November, 1704—Pallottini, XI, 524 (where a plan made by the bishop and approved by the administrators was overruled because it was at variance with the plan of the testator). *Cf. In Causa Forosempronien.*, 8 May, 1824—Pallottini, XI, 517; *in Causa Novarien.*, 18 September, 1824, § *Servanda*—Pallottini, XI, 599; *in Causa Tolentinaten.*, 22 April, 1826, § *Verum*—Pallottini, XI, 599; *in Causa Camerinen.*, 17 May, 1828, §

736. The Sanctions. The precept of this canon is fortified with the sanction of Canon 2348.[7] But the punishment is *ferendae sententiae*. It would seem that it is not to be inflicted until the Ordinary has exhausted every other means by which the heir might be persuaded to make due payment. But when payment can not otherwise be obtained the Ordinary would seem to be bound to inflict the censure. And the obligation resting on him is *per se gravis*. But the obligation seems to bind him only in the case of bequests contained in wills valid in secular law.[8]

737. Canon 2346. The question arises whether they who refuse to pay a bequest due the charitable or religious institution fall under the excommunication decreed in Canon 2346 against those who convert the property of the Church to their own uses or prevent the Church from obtaining the proper income from that property.[9]

738. Here it is pertinent to recall that canonists are not agreed as to the moment at which bequests vest. One opinion seems to be that the church obtains only a *ius ad rem* and that the bequest does not vest in the beneficiary until he accepts it.[10]

Hisce—Pallottini, *l. c.; in Causa Ferrarien,* 20 November, 1830, § *Oratorum*—Pallottini, *l. c.; in Causa Firmana,* 1 February, 1834, § *Sancte*—Pallottini, *l. c.*

Cf. Vermeersch-Creusen, *op. cit.*, II, 835; Cocchi, *op. cit.*, VI, 193; Bargilliat, *op. cit.*, 1481; Mothon, *op. cit.*, 2610; Vromant, *op. cit.*, 157.

[7] Canon 2348. "Qui legatum vel donationem ad causas pias sive actu inter vivos sive testamento, etiam per fiduciam, obtinuerit et implere negligat, ab Ordinario, etiam per censuram, ad id cogatur."

[8] *Cf.* § 495, supra.

[9] Canon 2346. "Si quis bona ecclesiastica cuiuslibet generis, sive mobilia sive immobilia, sive corporalia sive incorporalia, per se vel per alios in proprios usus convertere et usurpare praesumpserit aut impedire ne eorundem fructus seu reditus ab iis, ad quos iure pertinent, percipiantur, excommunicationi tandiu subiaceat, quandiu bona ipsa integre restituerit, praedictum impedimentum removerit, ac deinde a Sede Apostolica absolutionem impetraverit; quod si eiusdem ecclesiae seu bonorum patronus fuerit, etiam iure patronatus eo ipso privatus exsistat; clericus vero, hoc delictum committens vel, in eodem consentiens, privetur praeterea beneficiis quibuslibet, ad alia quaelibet inhabilis efficiatur et a suorum ordinum exsecutione, etiam post integram satisfactionem et absolutionem, sui Ordinarii arbitrio suspendatur."

[10] Vermeersch-Creusen, *op. cit.*, II, 834; Cocchi, *op. cit.*, VI, 189; Vromant, *op. cit.*, 148-150. Wernz holds the opposite opinion—*op. cit.*, III, 286; so, Schmalzgrueber, *op. cit.*, III, I, 13, 13-20. *Cf.* § 691, supra.

739. Moreover, property belonging to an institution or society that has not been canonically erected by the authority of the church is not to be regarded as ecclesiastical property.[11] Nor stipends for Masses in the hands of a priest. But a foundation for the celebration of Masses would be ecclesiastical property.

740. The penalties of Canon 2346 attach, however, to crimes against any kind of ecclesiastical property, whether or not it be sacred or of great value.[12] Persons who purchase the property or receive it on any title for their own use, whether it is acquired mediately or immediately, whether for perpetual use or only temporarily, are bound by the same excommunication.[13] Those who hold this property even by lease suffer the same penalty.[14]

[11] *Cf.* §§ 518-522.

[12] Cappello, *De Censuris,* 330, 333; Cipollini, *De Censuris,* p. 148; Cerato, *Censurae,* 62; Chelodi, *Ius Poenale,* 78; Vromant, *op. cit.,* 28.

Genicot holds that the property must be of great value; *op. cit.,* II, 600. But though this was a probable opinion prior to the Code under the penalty imposed by the Council of Trent (Sess. XXII, *de ref.,* c. 11), it seems that it can no longer be regarded as such because of the general language of Canon 2346, *cuiuslibet generis.*

[13] Vromant, *op. cit.,* 29; Cappello, *op. cit.,* 336; Cipollini, *op. cit.,* p. 150; Genicot, *l. c.*

Genicot says this opinion is the more probable, and Cappello says that the opposite opinion lacks probability, though Cerato claims that the Constitution, *Apostolicae Sedis,* left the matter in doubt and the legislator in the Code made no attempt to settle it; *op. cit.,* 62. *Cf.* const., *Apostolicae Sedis,* 12 October, 1869, Art. 11—*ASS,* V (1869), 291. *Cf.* Sebastiani, *Theol. Mor.,* 611.

But the opinion of Cappello is supported by four documents issuing from the Holy See. First, the Allocution of Pope Pius IX, 25 July, 1873—*ASS,* VII (1873), 337. This bound even buyers of the property. Second, the Decree of the Holy Office (8 July, 1874—*S. C. P. F. Coll.,* n. 1420), which explained that delinquents of this kind fell under two excommunications: viz., the one *speciali modo reservata* in the Constitution, *Apostolicae Sedis,* and the other *simpliciter reservata* in the decree of the Council of Trent (Sess. XXII, *de ref.,* c. 11); and that buyers incur the second, even if not the first, even when they purchase from persons who in turn had purchased from the government. Third, an identical response given by the Sacred Penitentiary, 21 May, 1897—Boudinhon, *Biens d'Eglise,* 92 and Appendix, 139. Fourth, the Constitution, *Si umquam,* of Pope Pius XI (15 July, 1924, ad 5um—*AAS,* XVI [1924], 311), in which the Holy Father regards as censured all who have acquired ecclesiastical property without permission.

741. But the crime must be presumptuous before the censure is incurred. Consequently even crass ignorance of the law or of the penalty can be invoked in excuse.[15]

742. But it is controverted whether this penalty is incurred by those who do not surrender what has been bequeathed to the Church. There is no doubt that they would incur it, if the property had ever passed into the hands of the Church. But the precise question turns about the property that has been bequeathed to charity or religion, but has never been transmitted to the beneficiary. Moreover, it is certain that the penalty would not be incurred by those who withheld bequests from lay associations not formally established by the proper ecclesiastical authority.[16]

As to the precise problem at hand, Vromant believes that the penalty is not incurred, and he bases this view on the ground that the property has not yet vested in the beneficiary. Cappello, however, Cerato, and Cipollini hold the opposite view, because they think the property vests at once unless suspended by a condition.[17]

The opinion of Vromant is probably correct. If it were otherwise, Canon 2348 would be superfluous. If the delinquent has already incurred the censure of Canon 2346, it would seem futile to oblige the Ordinary to inflict censures on him.

In any event, there is a *dubium iuris,* and in such a situation, the penalty is not incurred. Thus, persons who might buy such property, while they would be bound to restitution, would not incur the penalty. Nor would they who sold it incur the penalty under Canon 2347 directed against those who with full knowledge and without the necessary permission dispose of ecclesiastical property.

743. As to commutation by the bishop or the administrator, the problem is solved once it is understood that before either can change the destination of the fund, he must have accepted it. His acceptance

[14] S. Penitentiary, 5 August, 1907—Boudinhon, *op. cit.,* Appendix, 149; Vromant, *op. cit.,* 29; Chelodi, *op. cit.,* 78; NRT, 1922, p. 208.

[15] *Cf.* Canon 2229; Vromant, *op. cit.,* 31; Cappello, *op cit.,* 341; Cerato, *op. cit.,* 62.

[16] Cappello, *op. cit.,* 339; Cipollini, *op. cit.,* p. 148.

[17] Vromant, *op. cit.,* 30; Cappello, *op. cit.,* 331; Cerato, *op. cit.,* 62; Cipollini, *op. cit.,* p. 148; *cf.* S. C. C. *in Causa Fanen.,* 21 June, 1828—Pallottini, XI, 509.

makes it ecclesiastical property, subject to all the penalties imposed by the law for the abuse of it.

744. Cappello says that persons who divert property bequeathed to one pious use and bestow it on another more probably do not incur the censure of Canon 2346. The censure is directed not only against those who take ecclesiastical property away from ecclesiastical uses, but also against those who take such property away from any person entitled to the use of it. For it subjects to the penalty any one who "praesumpserit . . . impedire ne eorundem fructus seu reditus ab iis, ad quos iure pertinent, percipiantur." Now, even under the opinion that the bequest does not become ecclesiastical property until it is accepted by the pious institute, to divert a fund to one pious use is to deprive the other of its income. However, since again there is a *dubium iuris,* the censure would not be incurred.

745. Canon 2347. Alienation. If the property is in the hands of the Church for one instant, it is ecclesiastical property, even if it is reclaimed by the heir. And in any event, the bishop or ecclesiastical administrator can perform no acts of alienation in regard to it; for such an act implies acceptance. They are bound by the canons touching the alienation of ecclesiastical property and subject to the penalties of Canon 2347, should they violate them.[18] And these penalties

[18] Canon 2347. "Firma nullitate actus et obligatione, etiam per censuram urgenda, restituendi bona illegitime acquisita ac reparandi damna forte illata, qui bona ecclesiastica alienare praesumpserit aut in iis alienandis consensum praebere contra praescripta can. 534, § 1, et can. 1532:

1°. Si agatur de re cuius pretium non excedit mille libellas, congruis poenis a legitimo Superiore ecclesiastico puniatur;

2°. Si agatur de re cuius pretium sit supra mille, sed infra triginta millia libellarum, privetur patronus iure patronatus; administrator, munere administratoris; Superior vel oeconomus religiosus, proprio officio et habilitate ad cetera officia, praeter alias congruas poenas a Superioribus infligendas; Ordinarius vero aliique clerici, officium, beneficium, dignitatem, munus in Ecclesia obtinentes, solvant duplum favore ecclesiae vel piae causae laesae; ceteri clerici suspendantur ad tempus ab Ordinario definiendum.

3°. Quod si beneplacitum apostolicum, in memoratis canonibus praescriptum, fuerit scienter praetermissum, omnes quovis modo reos sive dando sive recipiendo sive consensum praebendo, manet praeterea excommunicatio latae sententiae nemini reservata.

Cf. c. 12, X, *de rebus eccl. alienandis,* III, 13; c. 4, X, *de relig. dom.,* III, 36.

attach to every presumptuous transaction by which the church or charitable institution is placed in a less advantageous position, and includes consequently acts of sale, gift, lease, exchange, mortgage, pledge, as well as the making of promissory notes with the church responsible and the permission of servitudes.[19]

746. The refusal to accept a bequest, however, does not subject the person who refuses to the penalties of Canon 2347, for the property more probably does not vest in the Church until it has been accepted.[20] A subordinate, however, may not refuse such a bequest without the permission of the Ordinary. If he does the corporation has an action for *restitution in integrum* and for indemnification.[21] Even the Ordinary may not refuse without a just cause. And if he refuse in favor of a third party, he falls subject to Canon 2347, for that act implies acceptance with a gift to the new beneficiary.[22] Consequently, it would seem that diversion of property from one charitable institution to another would subject the delinquent to at least the penalties of Canon 2347.

747. But if the testator ordered the realty to be sold and the proceeds to be applied to a definite purpose, Schmalzgrueber reasons correctly, it seems, that the formalities required in Canon 1532 for

[19] This is the view of Cerato (*op. cit.*, n. 43) and Cipollini (*op. cit.*, p. 187). Cocchi agrees with the view, holding that both the *dominium utile* and the *dominium directum* are included under the term "alienation," forbidden under the penalties of Canon 2347. Cocchi admits that there are other authors who maintain that the censure is incurred only when the *dominium directum* is transferred; *cf.* Cocchi, *op. cit.*, VIII, 195. Ayrinhac (*Penal Legislation*, n. 301) argues that while the same formalities are required for every transaction "by which the condition of the Church can be impaired," nevertheless the Code treats in separate canons of the various transactions. Consequently, the penalty prescribed for alienation is not to be extended to the other transactions. Chelodi (*op. cit.*, n. 79) excludes loans, leases, and mortgages from the transactions for which the penalty is incurred. Vermeersch-Creusen agree (*op. cit.*, III, 547), except as to mortgage and leases for long periods (*locatio diuturna*). On the other hand, Sole (*op. cit.*, n. 387) and Augustine (*Canon Law*, VI, 593), agree with the rigorous view.

[20] *Cf.* §§ 690, 691, supra.

[21] *Cf.* Canon 1536, §§ 2 and 3; Cipollini, *op. cit.*, p. 187; Cerato, *op. cit.*, 43; Schmalzgrueber, *op. cit.*, III, I, 13, 13-20.

[22] Schmalzgrueber, *l. c.*

alienation need not be observed. It really does not become the property of the Church until it has been converted into money, and the bishop is acting rather as the agent of the testator in that transaction than as the executor of a bequest.[23] He thinks the same conclusion probable if the testator simply granted permission for the sale of the property, unless the realty had been incorporated with other ecclesiastical property prior to the sale. For the testator could have given the bequest to a trustee, and the power of sale which could have been given to a trustee is given to the church instead.[24] Finally, if in the foundation it was required that the patron's consent should be obtained prior to sale, that condition must be met for the just disposal of the property.[25]

ARTICLE 2

THE DUTY OF SUPERVISION

748. The Duty Involves a Multitude of Functions. The duty of a bishop in supervising the fulfillment of charitable bequests is a complicated one, comprising a multitude of functions. A clear discussion of those functions is the aim of the present article.

749. Who is the Ordinary? First observe that though the bishop is usually the executor of these bequests, Canon 1515, § 1, speaks of the executor as the Ordinary, thus including the major superiors of exempt clerical religious orders,[26] as well as all who possess the jurisdiction of a bishop without the episcopal character, and all who may be styled the vicegerents of the bishop.[27] Therefore, the executor is, under diverse circumstances, the residential bishop, the Apostolic Administrator, the Vicar and the Prefect Apostolic, the Vicar General, Abbots and Prelates *nullius* and their Vicars

[23] *Op. cit.*, III, I, 13, 61.

[24] *L. c.*, nn. 141, 142.

[25] *L. c.*, n. 110.

[26] Vermeersch-Creusen, *op. cit.*, II, 836; Vromant, *op. cit.*, 158; De Meester, *op. cit.*, 1468. Blat says that religious superiors are excluded from this duty *ex natura rei, i. e.*, because the bequest is always one coming from the subject of a bishop; *op. cit.*, 427. Larraona holds that the canon includes the major superiors of even non-exempt clerical communities; *Comm. pro Rel.*, IV (1923), 119. But this view seems to contradict Canon 198, § 1.

[27] Cocchi, *op. cit.*, VI, 194; Prümmer, *Man. Iur. Can.*, 448, 2.

General,[28] the Cathedral Chapter, *sede vacante,* the Vicar Capitular and the Pro-Vicar or Pro-Prefect Apostolic when the Vicar or the Prefect are incapacitated.[29]

750. Pious foundations. That the duties of the Ordinary may be fully understood, something must be said here about pious foundations. Sufficient explanation of the nature and the method of establishment of non-collegiate persons has been given in Chapter VIII. The foundation to be observed at this place is neither collegiate nor non-collegiate. It is rather a fund entrusted to a collegiate corporation, for example, to a religious community.

751. Elements of a pious foundation. A pious foundation of this kind, it may be said by way of anticipation, is marked by five essential elements. First, there is temporal property, personalty or realty, given by donation or testamentary disposition. Second, a canonically established moral person is the beneficiary. Third, the purpose is religious or charitable. Fourth, there is an arrangement whereby the annual revenue of the endowment is to be devoted to a precise purpose, the income being derived from the capital fund invested for the period of the foundation. Fifth, the obligation is perpetual, or at least for a long period of time.[30]

752. There is no doubt among canonists that this property, once accepted, becomes ecclesiastical property. But the controversy has already been observed touching the reason upon which it can be predicated such. Vermeersch-Creusen hold with the old view that the connection between the property and the ecclesiastical institute makes the property ecclesiastical in itself. But De Meester thinks

[28] *Cf.* Canon 198, § 1.

[29] Nebraska, *Comm. pro Rel.,* VII (1926), 110.

[30] Cance, *op. cit.,* III, 172; Vromant, *op. cit.,* 345; Vermeersch-Creusen, *op. cit.,* II, 865; Prümmer, *Man. Iur. Can.,* 456, 1; Ferreres, *Insts. Can.,* II, 515; De Meester, *op. cit.,* 1499; Cocchi, *op. cit.,* VI, 227.

Canon 1544, § 1. "Nomine piarum fundationum significantur bona temporalia alicui personae morali in Ecclesia quoquo modo data, cum onere in perpetuum vel in diuturnum tempus ex reditibus annuis aliquas Missas celebrandi vel alias praefinitas functiones ecclesiasticas explendas, aut nonnulla pietatis et caritatis opera peragendi."

§ 2. "Fundatio, legitime acceptata, naturam induit contractus synallagmatici; *do ut facias.*"

that the property does not become ecclesiastical in itself, but only by reason of the ecclesiastical community with which it is connected.[31]

753. Perhaps the distinctive element of a foundation is its perpetuity. In this it differs from a mere gift or bequest. On the other hand, a foundation can be established for a limited period, provided that the period be long enough. Authorities differ as to the length of time required to establish a foundation. Prümmer requires at least a term of fifty years. Blat thinks that forty years is necessary; and he gives two reasons: first, the analogy with the establishing of a custom *contra ius;* and second, it was the accepted doctrine prior to the Code.[32]

Ten years seems a sufficiently long period to Vermeersch-Creusen, Vromant, and De Meester, if the secular law is silent as to the time necessary for prescription. Vromant argues that prior to the Code canonists thought this period sufficient for prescription and for the establishing of a custom. If the secular law, however, specifies a shorter time as sufficient for prescription, the same authors contend that the shorter period will suffice also as the time set in establishing a foundation. This conclusion they derive from the authority which Canon 1529 gives to the secular law in the matter of contracts. For a foundation is said to be a contract in Canon 1544. Cocchi admits that this concession to Canon 1529 possesses extrinsic probability.[33]

[31] *Cf.* §§ 520, 521; Vermeersch-Creusen, *op. cit.*, II, 812; De Meester, *op. cit.*, 1431; Miller, *op. cit.*, p. 33.

[32] Canon 6, § 2°. "Canones qui ius vetus ex integro referunt, ex veteris iuris auctoritate, atque ideo ex receptis apud probatos auctores interpretationibus, sunt aestimandi."

3°. "Canones qui ex parte tantum cum veteri iure congruunt, qua congruunt, ex iure antiquo aestimandi sunt; qua discrepant, sunt ex sua ipsorum sententia diiudicandi."

[33] Vermeersch-Creusen, *op. cit.*, II, 865; De Meester, *op. cit.*, 1499-1450; Vromant, *op. cit.*, 345 (citing correctly Reiffenstuel, *op. cit.*, I, 4, 96 and II, 26, 148, and Pirhing, *op. cit.*, I, 4, 35-39, as to the ten year term's sufficing for prescription and custom); Blat, *op. cit.*, 462; Prümmer, *Man. Iur. Can. l. c.*; *cf.* also Cocchi, *op. cit.*, VI, 192, 227; Cance, III, 172; *Periodica*, I (1911), 47; Miller, *op. cit.*, pp. 1, 2.

Benedict XIV notes the privilege of the Friars Minor of St. Francis de Paul, confirmed by himself, under which they were not bound more than fifty years

The argument from Canon 1529, however, seems invalid. Canon 1529 adopts the secular law governing contracts, the payments to be made under them, and the effects produced by the contract. Prescription would not be an effect *under* a contract, but an effect *contrary* to it. Consequently, it seems incorrect to argue from a law producing an effect *contrary* to a contract when the canons adopt only the law touching an effect *according* to a contract.

If the secular law had a provision stating that perpetuity would be induced by the prolongation of an agreement beyond a certain time, that would seem to be acceptable as governing the time required to classify a gift as a foundation. For then, at the very moment the agreement was made, the contract would be producing its permanent effect. Such an effect is conceived as the consequence of a foundation.

The period of time is to be determined rather from what authors regard as a *tempus diuturnum.* Since it seems that a sufficiently large number regard ten years as a period sufficiently long, an endowment established for that length of time would seem to meet the requirements of Canon 1544.

Nevertheless, it is sufficiently probable also that forty or more years must be set forth as the period for which the foundation is to endure. Consequently, that opinion can be followed in practice.

754. Since a foundation is a bilateral contract, acceptance of the obligation is required.[34] Vermeersch-Creusen believe the obligation imposed to be either a condition precedent or a condition subsequent. If it is meant to be a condition precedent, and there is no compliance, the foundation fails. If it is a condition subsequent, the provisions of the secular law are to be observed.[35] It would seem, however, that only a very small portion of the total obligation could be a condition precedent in a foundation that is to endure for years, unless one is to conclude that the fund *never* vests in the community.

The obligation could be regarded as the actual consideration of

by foundations for the celebration of Masses. But all persons who had made foundations with them were to be notified of this privilege, and a memento was to be made for the intentions *in genere;* Vromant, *l. c.;* Benedict XIV, *op. cit.*, lib. 13, c. ult., nn. 9-12.

[34] Cocchi, *op. cit.*, VI, 227.

[35] *Op. cit.*, II, 865.

the contract. The religious community offers fulfillment of the obligation in return for the foundation entrusted to it. This view justifies the conclusion of Blat, Vromant, Cocchi, Cance, and Ferreres, who maintain that restitution must be made if the obligation is not fulfilled. The same conclusion, however, would be justified if the obligation were a condition subsequent.[86] Failure to comply with the obligations of the contract would seem also to justify the founder in regarding the contract as broken, and demanding that his donation be returned and restitution made for the omissions.

755. Where a foundation is established in a will, the Ordinary provides that it shall be duly received and the obligation properly discharged. The Ordinary is the Ordinary of the place, except for foundations established in the houses and churches of exempt clerical religious when the house or church does not belong to the diocese. For these foundations, the Ordinary is the major religious superior.[87]

756. The actual establishing of the endowment may be viewed in two aspects: one, the substance of the endowment; the other, the act of acceptance.

As to the substance of the endowment the Ordinary has two rights. One is the establishing of a definite sum below which no one may accept an endowment validly or licitly.[88] The other is the establishing of a plan of distribution where the founder made no express disposition; for instance, in a case where the founder merely expressed a wish to have the endowment devoted to several charitable purposes.

Where the founder is establishing the endowment *inter vivos,* it is the Ordinary who determines the sum needed for the purpose he designates and the manner in which the revenue is to be employed. Consequently, the founder has no right to interfere with the admin-

[86] Blat, *op. cit.,* 462; Cocchi, *op. cit.,* 227; Cance, *op. cit.,* III, 172; Vromant, *op. cit.,* 346; Ferreres, *l. c.* Cance also holds that the contract can be repudiated when the obligations are not fulfilled, that is, that the foundation can be revoked.

[87] Canon 1550; *cf.* Miller, *op. cit.,* p. 56.

[88] Cocchi, *op. cit.,* VI, 228; Vromant, *op. cit.,* 348; Mothon, *op. cit.,* 2608; Ferreres, *op. cit.* II, 516; Benedict XIV, *l. c.,* n. 10; Innocent XII, const., *Nuper,* 23 December, 1697, § 15 ad 5—*Fontes,* n. 260.

istration of the endowment. And the patron of the church to which the endowment may be given has no right to interfere in any way with the transaction.[39] General or special rules for the establishing of endowments may be provided by the Ordinary in the diocesan synod or by proclamation in any other way. He may also make regulations for the individual case.[40]

Where the testator has failed to determine the number of Masses to be said, it does not become the right of the heirs to supply the omission. This is the duty of the Ordinary on the basis of the stipend fixed by diocesan statute or the custom of the place. And the stipend itself may be a special one for founded Masses.[41] When the founder determined the number of Masses and the income proves inadequate to provide the synodal stipend, the matter should be taken up with him. If he refuses to make the necessary accommodation, the Ordinary can refuse the endowment. Indeed, the Ordinary must constantly be vigilant lest the stipend implicitly established be so small that soon it will be difficult to find any one to assume the burden of saying the Masses; or lest the income be so slight that the moral person would soon be obliged to accept new burdens to provide for its sustenance. But the foundation is not invalid if a sum is accepted smaller than that established by the Ordinary.[42]

[39] Canon 1546, § 2. "In acceptatione, constitutione, et administratione fundationis patronus ecclesiae nullum ius habet."

[40] *Reg.* 80 in VI°: "In toto partem non est dubium contineri." This is evident also from the const., *Nuper,* § 2 ad 5.

[41] Blat, *op. cit.,* 463, 464; Vromant, *op. cit.,* 348; Miller, *op. cit.,* pp. 19, 22.

[42] Const., *Nuper,* § 2; Cocchi, *op. cit.,* VI, 228; Vromant, *op. cit.,* 348, 349; Blat, *op. cit.,* 464.

Canon 1545. "Loci Ordinarii est normas praescribere de dotis quantitate infra quam pia fundatio admitti nequeat et de eius fructibus rite distribuendis."

Canon 1550. "Si agatur de piis fundationibus in ecclesiis, etiam paroecialibus, religiosorum exemptorum, iura et officia Ordinarii loci, de quibus in can. 1545-1549, exclusive competunt Superiori maiori."

The major superior of regulars may fix the stipends for Masses to be founded in churches belonging to them, that is, in churches that are not diocesan; although as to manual stipends the religious are bound to the regulations established by the Ordinary of the place. Const., *Nuper,* §§ 7, 8, 14, 18, 19, 24; Vermeersch-Creusen, *op. cit.,* II, 869; Cance, *op. cit.,* III, 174; Prümmer, *op. cit.,*

757. **Acceptance is permitted** on three conditions: viz., that the consent of the Ordinary has been obtained; that the beneficiary is able to discharge the obligation; and that the fund is adequate.[43]

758. Vromant thinks the consent of the Ordinary is required for validity, in virtue of Canon 1527, § 1.[44] He exempts foundations made to religious, but probably without good reason. Aside from the fact that the legislator understood that quite a large proportion of foundations would be given to religious, there remains the pertinent fact that according to the common opinion of canonists, a non-exempt religious is obliged to account to the Ordinary of the place for all fiduciary administration.[45] Even exempt religious are similarly bound as to funds established for the promotion of a diocesan or parochial enterprise when it is not established in a house of their own. If they are obliged thus to account for trustee funds, it seems futile to argue that the property given to them as an endowment is not wholly under the jurisdiction of the Ordinary of the place. For exempt clerical religious the consent of the bishop is, of course, not required; but they need the consent of their Ordinary, who is their major superior.

The constitutions, *Nuper* and *Cum saepe,* prescribed this requirement prior to the Code. They did not contain an invalidating clause touching foundations established without the consent of the Ordinary. Moreover, Gasparri contends that the Sacred Congregation of the Council in times past has replied that the Ordinary's consent is demanded for only the licit, and not the valid, institution of a founda-

456, 2; Cocchi, *op. cit.,* VI, 230; Blat, *op. cit.,* 468; Benedict XIV; *l. c.,* n. 5; Miller, *op. cit.,* p. 21.

[43] Canon 1546, § 1. "Ut huiusmodi fundationes a persona morali acceptari possint, requiritur consensus Ordinarii loci, in scriptis datus, qui eam ne praebeat, antequam legitime compererit personam moralem tum novo oneri suscipiendo, tum antiquis ilam susceptis satisfacere posse; maximeque caveat ut reditus omnino respondeant oneribus adiunctis secundum cuiusque dioecesis morem."

[44] Canon 1527, § 1. "Nisi prius ab Ordinario loci facultatem impetraverint, scriptis dandam, administratores invalide actus ponunt qui ordinariae administrationis fines et modum excedant."

[45] In virtue of Canon 1516, § 1. *Cf.* Vermeersch-Creusen, *op. cit.,* II, 836; Cocchi, *op. cit.,* VI, 195; Blat, *op. cit.,* 428.

tion; though it added that the foundation thus unlawfully established can be repudiated by the Ordinary. Consequently, in virtue of Canon 6, the present law should impose the obligation for only the licit institution of a foundation.[46] But even Vromant concedes that the formality of a *written* permission is not necessary for the validity of the act.[47]

759. The capacity of the moral person to discharge the obligation is not required for the validity of the foundation, but incapacity gives the founder an action for the violation of the contract or for substantial error in the act of making it.[48] However, it may be provided in the articles of the foundation that the burdens annexed to it may be discharged by other persons in lieu of those primarily liable.[49]

760. The foundation requires acceptance because it is a bilateral contract, and as such is perfected only by the mutual consent of the donor and the beneficiary. Since the offer can be revoked at any time prior to acceptance, there should be no unnecessary delay before this formal act is performed.[50] The offer and the acceptance may be made orally, but the agreement should be set down in writing at once.[51]

[46] Vromant, *op. cit.*, 349; Gasparri, *De SS. Euch.*, 561; S. C. C., 16 January, 1664 (cited by Pignatelli, who also agrees with Gasparri's opinion—*Consultationes*, cons. 222, circa finem tom. IV.).

Cf. const., *Nuper*, § 7; Urban VIII, const., *Cum saepe—Fontes*, n. 2560; Miller, *op. cit.*, pp. 27-29.

[47] *Op. cit.*, 309, 349.

[48] Cance, *op. cit.*, III, 173.

Canon 104. "Error actum irritum reddit, si versetur circa id quod constituit substantiam actus vel recidat in conditionem *sine qua non;* secus actus valet, nisi aliud iure caveatur; sed in contractibus error locum dare potest actioni rescissoriae ad normam iuris."

[49] For the capacity of the moral person, *cf.* Cocchi, *l. c.;* Prümmer, *op. cit.*, 456, 3; Blat, *op. cit.*, 464; Vromant, *op. cit.*, 349; Mothon, *op. cit.*, 2609; Ferreres, *l. c.*

[50] Cocchi, *l. c.;* Vromant, *l. c.;* Bargilliat, *l. c.;* De Meester, *op. cit.*, 1500; Blat, *op. cit.*, 462.

[51] Canon 1548, § 1. "Fundationes, etiam viva voce factae, scripto consignentur."

Cf. Cance, *op. cit.*, III, 173; Mothon, *op. cit.*, 2615; Ferreres, *op. cit.*, II, 517.

761. Custody and Investment. Canon 1547 lays down special rules for the custody and the investment of the fund of the endowment.[52] Realty and chattels annexed to realty, as well as securities, are to be retained in the form given by the founder. If they are to be sold, it can only be with the permission of the Holy See or the proper Superior according to the provisions of Canons 534, 1530, and 1532. Other chattels, however, should be sold, and the proceeds devoted to the purposes of the fund.[53]

762. The money or movable property is to be placed in a safe place at once. A reliable bank would be safe enough in the United States as a temporary depositary. But it is to be invested as soon as possible in property that will make possible prompt payment of the annual income. The Ordinary passes final judgment on the investment of the fund, after taking counsel with the diocesan council of administration, the founder, the superior of the moral person, and all other persons interested.

763. Whether the consultation with persons interested is necessary for the validity of the investment depends on the opinion held under Canon 105, § 1.[54] Ojetti, Ferreres, Maroto, De Meester, Prümmer, and Ayrinhac hold that it is necessary to have the consultation in order that the act may be valid; Vermeersch-Creusen, that it is required only for lawful action.[55] But Vermeersch's opinion seems

[52] Canon 1547. "Pecunia et bona mobilia, dotationis nomine assignata, statim in loco tuto, ab eodem Ordinario designando, deponantur ad eum finem ut eadem pecunia vel bonorum mobilium pretium custodiantur et quamprimum caute et utiliter secundum prudens eiusdem Ordinarii arbitrium, auditis et iis quorum interest et dioecesano administrationis Concilio, collocentur in commodum eiusdem fundationis cum expressa et individua mentione oneris."

[53] Cance, *op. cit.*, III, 174; Vromant, *op. cit.*, 350; Blat, *op. cit.*, 465; const., *Nuper*, § 7.

[54] Canon 105. "Cum ius statuit Superiorem ad agendum indigere consensu vel consilio aliquarum personarum:

"1°. Si consensus exigatur, Superior contra earundem votum invalide agit; si consilium tantum, per verba, ex. gr.: *de consilio consultorum* vel *audito Capitulo, parocho,* etc., satis est ad valide agendum ut Superior illas personas audiat."

[55] Ojetti, *Commentarium,* III, 186-202; Ferreres, *op. cit.*, I, 229; De Meester, *op. cit.*, 333; Maroto, *op. cit.*, I, 471; Prümmer, *op. cit.*, 56; Ayrinhac, *Gen.*

to lack sufficient probability to be applicable in practice.[56]

764. Separate investment of funds. The fund should be divided where there are several distinct burdens, and there should be a separate and distinct investment of each subordinate fund. Nevertheless, Vermeersch-Creusen think that the whole fund could be invested as a unit, for instance, in a plot of ground. And Vromant thinks that mutual insurance could be provided if the fund should be invested in several kinds of securities, the total income of which was to be divided among the beneficiaries. But De Meester believes that the words of the canon are too explicit, and that each specific obligation must be protected by its own specific portion of the fund.[57]

De Meester seems to argue more correctly, otherwise it would seem that the canon specifies the division of the fund without reason. If investment of the funds *en masse* were to be allowed, it would have been superfluous to add that each subordinate fund should be segregated for a specific burden. It would seem that there is not sufficient probability in the other opinion to make the matter dubious.

765. Circumstances prescribed for the celebration of Founded Masses. If a foundation for Masses is contained in a will, the will of the founder determines the place where the Masses are to be celebrated, the time when they are to be celebrated, the stipend to be given, the person who is to be the celebrant, and the like. The place, where none is mentioned, is the church where the foundation has been established.[58] It is the duty of the rector to celebrate the Masses and fulfill such other obligations as the foundation imposes. If he is unable to do this, he must comply with the obligation through his vicars, though he need give only the ordinary stipend if the purpose

Legislation, n. 225; Vermeersch-Creusen, *op. cit.*, I, 194; *cf. Ius Pontificium,* X (1930), 136; VIII (1928), 29, 99.

[56] For the doctrine on the investment of these funds *cf.* const., *Nuper,* § 7; Cocchi, *op. cit.*, VI, 229; Cance, *l. c.;* Vromant, *l. c.;* Blat, *l. c.;* Mothon, *op. cit.*, 2608.

[57] Vermeersch-Creusen, *op. cit.*, II, 867; Vromant, *l. c.;* De Meester, *op. cit.*, 1501; *cf.* Cocchi, *l. c.*

[58] Cance, *op. cit.*, III, 175; De Meester, *op. cit.*, 1502; S. C. C. *in Causa Veglen.*, 23 February, 1907—*Fontes,* n. 4335; *in Causa Mutinen.*, 21 January, 1905—*Thesaurus,* 164, 91; *in Causa Mediolanen.*, 19 December, 1904—*Coll. S. C. P. F.*, n. 2210.

of the foundation is to support the benefice.[59] If the testator expressed no intention as to the purpose for which the Masses are to be celebrated, they are to be offered for him, for that is most probably his intention, unless very grave presumptions are present to the contrary.[60] Vromant says the stipend from the income may be so small as to indicate that the testator did not wish the application of the Mass, but only to insure the celebration of the Mass.[61]

766. The articles of foundation are to be consigned to writing by the administrator of the institute that is beneficiary, and in them should be expressed the amount of the funds, the burdens to be fulfilled, the manner in which they are to be fulfilled, the person who is to fulfill them, the provisions to be made if the income is diminished or the capital lost, and the fate of the fund should there be a dissolution of the moral body to which the fund is entrusted.[62] Blat thinks that the document should be consigned to writing by the chancellor or a notary for its validity.[63] But his opinion does not seem probable. The language of Canon 1548, § 1, seems too general to warrant such a restrictive conclusion.

767. Two copies of the articles are to be made, one to be kept in the archives of the Chancery and the other in the safe of the institute.[64] Both copies should be subscribed by the administrator as the acceptor of the obligation.[65]

[59] De Meester, *op. cit.*, 1502; Bargilliat, *op. cit.*, 1518.

[60] Cocchi, *op. cit.*, VI, 230; Ferreres, *op. cit.*, II, 516; Bargilliat, *op. cit.*, 1514, 1518; S. C. C. *in Causa Osnabruck*, 22 May, 1875—*Thesaurus*, 134, 465.

[61] *Op. cit.*, 348; *cf.* Miller, *op. cit.*, p. 32.

[62] *Cf.* Vermeersch-Creusen, *op. cit.*, II, 868; Cocchi, *op. cit.*, VI, 230; Cance, *op. cit.*, III, 173, 174; Prümmer, *op. cit.*, 456, 5; Mothon, *op. cit.*, 2615.

[63] *Op. cit.*, 465.

[64] Vermeersch-Creusen, *op. cit.*, II, 868; Cocchi, *l. c.;* Vromant, *l. c.;* Mothon, *op. cit.*, 2615. If the foundation is made in a church belonging to an exempt clerical community, one copy is to be sent to the Provincial instead of the Chancery; Prümmer, *op. cit.*, 456, 5. The execution of similar articles is recommended in the establishing of a non-collegiate person; Cocchi, *op. cit.*, VI, 162; Prümmer, *op. cit.*, 441, 1; Cance, *op. cit.*, III, 123.

[65] Cance, *op. cit.*, III, 174. It would be wise to attach a copy of the bishop's permission to the copy kept by the institute.

Canon 1548, § 2. "Alterum tabularum exemplar in Curiae archivo, alterum in archivo personae moralis, ad quam fundatio spectat, tuto asservetur."

768. Obligations of the Administrator. The rector of the institute must preserve three documents in order to discharge his burden in compliance with the canons. In addition, he is obliged to make an annual report to the Ordinary.

The first of the three documents which must be carefully guarded has just been noticed, *i. e.*, the copy of the articles of foundation. The second is a complete inventory of all the obligations resting on the foundation. In the inventory the obligations are listed as they are accepted. The third is a book of account, a current book, distinct from the book in which the account of manual Masses is recorded. In this book for founded obligations, the rector opens an account for each obligation, in which he enters the date on which the items of income are received and the respective amounts, as well as the date on which the recurrent obligation was discharged with the amount given to the benefice on such occasions.[66]

769. When foundations are given exempt clerical communities, it is the major superior who has complete authority over them, even though they be established in parish churches, if the churches belong to the community and not to the diocese, or if they have been surrendered to the community for the community's benefit, though not in ownership, even when the object of the foundation is the promotion of divine service or the exercise of charitable works in the very place where the house is located.[67] But foundations in other churches are governed by the Ordinary of the place, even though they be churches that have been assigned to the care of an exempt clerical community for an indefinite period, and even though a religious is appointed in a stable fashion as pastor by an agreement between the Ordinary of the place and the major superior.[68]

[66] Vermeersch-Creusen, *l. c.;* Cocchi, *l. c.;* Cance, *l. c.;* Vromant, *op. cit.*, 352; Prümmer, *op. cit.*, 456, 7; Mothon, *op. cit.*, 2630; Blat, *op. cit.*, 467; const., *Nuper*, §§ 18, 19.

[67] Vromant, *op. cit.*, 354; *Pont. Comm.*, 25 July, 1926, *AAS*, XVIII (1926), 393.

[68] This latter situation is of frequent occurrence, for in spite of Canon 1442, by force of which secular benefices are to be conferred only on secular priests, it happens that because of a shortage of priests, Ordinaries are able to obtain the faculty to appoint religious priests to secular parishes; Vromant, *op. cit.*, 354; decree of S. C. P. F., 9 December, 1920, ad 3um; *AAS*, XIII (1921), 18.

When the foundation is established in a parish church over which the religious have been placed by the appointment of the bishop, the Ordinary of the place controls it also if it is meant for the works of charity in the parish, for the schools, and for the poor. Foundations made for the more brilliant exercise of the functions of the altar seem to be given to the community, rather than to the parish; consequently they would be subject to the major superior rather than to the Ordinary.[69] This conclusion is disputed where the exempt community is not an Order with solemn vows, but a *congregation* with simple vows. Indeed, the dispute covers any gift or bequest given a community of the latter type whenever the amount is to be expended in the very place where the community is located.[70] For, Canon 533, § 1, n. 3, binds all congregations to administer such bequests subject to the vigilance of the Ordinary of the place. It makes no distinction. Nevertheless, because the privilege of exemption, which has been specially granted some, withdraws them from the jurisdiction of the Ordinary of the place, it is maintained that they are to be compared to the Orders in this matter. This is the view of Vermeersch-Creusen, De Meester, and Schäfer; but it is opposed by Cocchi, Prümmer, and Chelodi.[71]

770. However, if the foundation is given not to a house, but to the community in general, for work in any given parish, or diocese, the community assumes the relation of a fiduciary, and even if it be an exempt clerical community, it is the Ordinary of the place who has complete control of the articles of foundation, the investment of funds, and the rendering of accounts.[72] **As to non-exempt communities, the last conclusion is valid even when the foundation is made in the interests of a particular house;** for example, in the case of a bed founded in a hospital; a burse in a college; a fellowship for

[69] Vromant, *op. cit.*, 355; *Pont. Comm.*, 25 July, 1926—*AAS*, XVIII (1926), 393. *Cf.* Canons 615; 533, § 1, n. 3; 535, § 3, n. 2.

[70] *Cf.* Canon 533, § 1, n. 3.

[71] Vermeersch-Creusen, *op. cit.*, I, 606; De Meester, *op. cit.*, 980; Schäfer, *op. cit.*, 197; Cocchi, *op. cit.*, II, 54; Prümmer, *op. cit.*, 194; Chelodi, *De Personis*, 260.

[72] Vromant, *l. c.;* Nebreda, in *Comm. pro Rel.*, VII (1926), 198, 266; *cf.* Canon 1516, § 3.

professors; a light for the tabernacle. It supposes in the Ordinary of the place the right of supervision, visitation, and account.[73]

771. But if the foundation to a non-exempt community *iuris pontificii* is made for the accomplishment of the objects of the community without specification, it is exempt from the intervention and supervision of the Ordinary of the place; for instance, a foundation for the education of its own members, or for any other work that is non-diocesan in the sense that the religious are free to interrupt it on their own motion and the Ordinary of the place at the same time is free of any obligation to carry on the work they might thus interrupt.[74] And the same exemption occurs in the case of a foundation granted a religious community for foreign missions in general provided that the missions are within the scope of the community's activities.[75]

772. Communities *Iuris Dioecesani,* Non-Collegiate Institutions and Lay Associations. The Ordinary of the place has full control over foundations granted to communities or to particular houses of communities *iuris dioecesani.* The same conclusion applies to independent non-collegiate institutions,[76] and to lay associations that have been canonically established.[77]

[73] Vromant, *op. cit.*, 165, 356; Goyeneche, *Comm. pro Rel.*, III (1922), 269; Prümmer, *op. cit.*, 195.

[74] Vromant, *op. cit.*, 347; Goyeneche, *Comm. pro Rel.*, III (1922), 269; Nebreda, *Comm. pro Rel.*, VII (1926), 324; Mothon, *op. cit.*, 2617.

[75] But note that alms collected by the Franciscan Missionary Union are subject to the vigilance and the visitation of the Vicars Apostolic under a response of the Sacred Congregation for the Propagation of the Faith, 28 July, 1932—*Periodica,* XXII (1933), 162; *cf.* Vromant, *op. cit.*, 356; Nebreda, *Comm. pro Rel.*, VII (1926), 267.

[76] *Cf.* Canon 1491, § 1. "Loci Ordinarius omnia huiusmodi instituta, etiam in personam moralem erecta et quovis modo exempta, visitare potest et debet."

§ 2. "Imo licet in personam moralem non sint erecta et domui religiosae concredita, si quidem agatur de domo religiosa iuris dioecesani, iurisdictioni Ordinarii loci penitus subduntur; si de domo religiosa iuris pontificii, episcopali vigilantiae subsunt quod spectat ad religionis magisteria, honestatem morum, exercitationes pietatis, sacrorum administrationem."

[77] Canon 690, § 1. "Omnes associationes, etiam ab Apostolica Sede erectae, nisi speciale obstet privilegium, iurisdictioni subsunt et vigilantiae Ordinarii loci, qui ad normas sacrorum canonum eas invisendi ius habet et munus."

773. The Council of Trent in most general terms placed all charitable institutions under the supervision of the Ordinary of the place,[78] giving him the right to visit them, to supervise administration, and to receive an account from the administrators, whether they be laymen or ecclesiastics. It seems, however, that the Council did not mean to include religious with solemn vows.[79]

On the other hand, it seems still to be the mind of the Holy See that pious institutions dedicated to the service of diocesans should be subject to the Ordinary of the place even when the administrators are exempt clerical religious, unless the latter have a privilege by which it is specially exempt as to visitation or account or both. For Pope Leo XIII in his Constitution, *Romanos Pontifices* (1881), exemplified the distinction between institutions subject and institutions not subject to the control of the Ordinary of the place by giving an illustration in the case of a cemetery. If the cemetery is devoted to the burying of religious, it is exempt from the control of the Ordinary of the place; but if diocesans are buried in it, it is subject to the bishop's control.[80] And the principle that he illustrates he applies

Canon 691, § 1. "Associatio legitime erecta, nisi aliud expresse cautum sit, bona temporalia possidere et administrare potest sub auctoritate Ordinarii loci, cui rationem administrationis saltem quotannis reddere debet, ad normam can. 1525, minime vero parochi, licet in eius territorio erecta sit, nisi aliud Ordinarius ipse statuerit."

[78] *Cf.* § 733, supra.

[79] Melo says that the authors generally concede that regulars were not included in this decree. Reiffenstuel says, "Ibidem solum de saecularibus, non de regularibus, loquitur (Concilium), prout declaravit S. C. ap. Fagnanum." Reiffenstuel, III, 36, 7; Melo, *De Exemptione*, p. 130; Fagnanus, *op. cit.*, III, 36, 47. But the reply to which Fagnanus refers seems to indicate that the monastery itself, or a house similarly independent, is what the Sacred Congregation regards as exempt. However, the decree of Clement V (c. 2, *de relig. dom.*, III, 11, in Clem.), on which the legislation of the Council of Trent seems to be based, expressly excluded the hospitals of the military orders and of other religious.

[80] The Holy Father says, "Officium curationis animarum sedulitati Regularium commissum alias etiam dubitationes gignit; eaeque loca spectant finibus comprehensa missionum quae ab ipsis reguntur. Coepit enim ambigi utrum coemeteria et pia loca, intra fines illarum sita, Episcopus visitare possit. Ast in coemeteriis facilis ac prona suppetit distinctionis adeoque finiendae controversiae ratio. Nam si de coemeteriis agatur quae solis religiosis familiis reservantur, ea plane ab Episcopi iurisdictione, proindeque a visitatione exempta sunt;

to all pious institutions, asserting the application to be in conformity with the sacred canons and the Apostolic constitutions.

The attitude of the Holy See is further manifested by Pope Leo's reference to colleges, made in the same document. He holds them as exempt from the jurisdiction of the bishop well enough, but not in virtue of the universal law but rather by reason of special privileges granted them by the Holy See.[81] This was evidently understood to be the attitude of the Holy See by the Fathers of the Third Plenary Council of Baltimore when they commanded that the bishops of the country should demand an accounting from the administrators of pious institutions, whether they be secular or *regular,* in accordance with the Constitution, *Romanos Pontifices.*[82]

774. The Bishop's Present Duty of Supervising Charitable Institutions. With this traditional background, it seems not difficult to understand the bishop's duties under Canons 1491 [83] and 1492, § 1.[84] The former authorizes him to visit all charitable institutions

cetera vero fidelium multitudini communia, quum uno ordine haberi debeant cum coemeteriis paroecialibus, iurisdictioni Ordinariorum subsunt indubitate, ac propterea optimo iure ab Episcopo visitantur . . . Haud absimili distinctione de locis piis quaestio dirimitur, ea secernendo quae exempta sunt ab iis quibus praeest Episcopus sive ordinario iure, sive delegato. De utrisque igitur, tum coemeteriis tum piis locis, sententiam Nostram paucis complectimur pronunciantes: sacrorum canonum et constitutionum Apostolicarum praescripta esse servanda." *ASS,* XIII (1881), 494.

[81] "Alia profecto causa est [quam causa scholarum paroecialium] ceterarum scholarum et collegiorum, in quibus religiosi viri secundum ordinis sui praescripta iuventuti catholicae instituendae operam dare solent; in hisce enim et ratio postulat, et Nos volumus firma atque integra privilegia manere quae illis ab Apostolica Sede collata sunt, prout aperte est declaratum . . . a sacro Concilio christiano nomini propagando"—*l. c.*

[82] N. 272: "Mandamus itaque ut quilibet Episcopus nostrarum provinciarum a rectoribus missionum, et saecularibus et regularibus (ad normam Const. Romanos Pontifices), locorum piorum praepositis aliisque rei ecclesiasticae curatoribus plenam et perspicuam administrationis rationem singulis annis districte exigat."

[83] *Cf.* n. 76, this chapter.

[84] Canon 1492, § 1. "Etiamsi fundatione, praescriptione, aut privilegio apostolico pium institutum a iurisdictione et visitatione Ordinarii loci exemptum fuerit, ius tamen Ordinario est redditionem rationum exigendi, reprobata contraria consuetudine."

whether established as independent corporations by ecclesiastical authority, under the control of a lay association, or conducted by religious. If conducted by religious, he scrutinizes the manner in which religious life flourishes as well as the way in which the corporal and spiritual works of mercy are exercised (*exercitationes pietatis*). The latter canon entitles him to an accounting from every such institution, no matter what kind of a privilege it enjoys, unless that privilege actually include exemption from rendering an account. Consequently, he is entitled to such an account from every school, hospital, asylum, and home in his diocese, unless the religious can show a privilege accorded them by the Holy See exempting them not only from the jurisdiction of the Ordinary of the place and from his visitation, but also from the obligation of rendering the account.[85] *A fortiori*, the Ordinary of the place has complete right of supervision over foundations established in these institutions. But his right over foundations would stand, even though his control over all charitable institutions serving his diocesans were to be denied.[86]

775. The bishop is the executor of bequests to charity even though the will should attempt to exclude him, and any clause attempting this is regarded as invalid.[87] But he should not execute the will himself, unless there is no other way of giving it effect. He should not change the executor designated by the testator unless he prove unworthy.[88] The executor appointed in the will is thus preferred to all others.[89]

776. The delegated executors rest under the obligation of rendering an account to the Ordinary at the completion of their task, even though the Ordinary was excluded in the will itself, and whether the

[85] *Cf.* Vermeersch-Creusen, *op. cit.*, II, 835, 836, 815; Cocchi, *op. cit.*, VI, 163, 194; Cance, *op. cit.*, III, 124, 147; Vromant, *op. cit.*, 159, 160; Prümmer, *op. cit.*, 441, 3 and 448, 2; De Meester, *op. cit.*, 1468; Blat, *op. cit.*, 401, 427; Mothon, *op. cit.*, 2625.

[86] *Cf.* § 769, supra.

[87] Canon 1515, § 3. "Clausulae huic Ordinariorum iuri contrariae, ultimis voluntatibus adiectae, tanquam non appositae habeantur."

[88] Cance, *op. cit.*, III, 147; Vromant, *op. cit.*, 159; Vermeersch, *Theol. Mor.*, II, 558; D'Annibale, *op. cit.*, II, 369.

[89] Cocchi, *op. cit.*, VI, 194.

executor was designated by the testator or the Ordinary, whether he is a religious, a cleric, or a layman.[90]

777. The vigilance of the Ordinary is to be manifested with paternal insistence and, if need be, with penalties to be imposed on heirs, executors, and administrators, as the case may require.[91]

778. **The fiduciary, or trustee, differs from the executor** in that the former actually takes title to the property to be paid out by him; while the executor has the ministry of execution without title. A trustee can be appointed by will or by a contract *inter vivos*.[92] His obligations are set forth in Canon 1516.[93]

779. **A trust is constituted** whenever any commission is entrusted to the integrity of another. Thus a precious article given in pledge is given in trust. This is especially true of a bequest made to one person with the obligation of employing it for a pious use or of conveying it to some charitable enterprise.[94] However, if the act to be performed is merely one of purchase, the commission is not a

[90] Cc. 6 and 17, X, *de testamentis et ultimis voluntatibus,* III, 26; Litt. Ap., Pius VII, 24 August, 1822—*Fontes,* n. 480; Vermeersch-Creusen, *op. cit.,* II, 836; Cance, *op. cit.,* III, 147; Vromant, *op. cit.,* 157; Prümmer, *op. cit.,* 448, 2; Cocchi, *op. cit.,* VI, 194.

[91] Benedict XIV states that the bishop is given a year within which to bring about the fulfillment of the will, after which the *Fabrica Sancti Petri in Vaticano* interferes; if the latter does not act, then either it or the bishop has the right of precedence, accordingly as one or the other first sets hand to it; *op. cit.,* lib. 13, c. ult., ad 3um. *Cf.* Blat, *op. cit.,* 427.

[92] Vromant, *op. cit.,* 153; Wernz, *op. cit.,* III, 283.

[93] Canon 1516, § 1. "Clericus vel religiosus qui bona ad pias causas sive per actum inter vivos, sive ex testamento fiduciarie accepit, debet de sua fiducia Ordinarium certiorem reddere, eique omnia istiusmodi bona seu mobilia seu immobilia cum oneribus adiunctis indicare; quod si donator id expresse et omnino prohibuerit, fiduciam ne acceptet."

§ 2. "Ordinarius debet exigere ut bona fiduciaria in tuto collocentur et vigilare pro exsecutione piae voluntatis ad normam can. 1515."

§ 3. "Bonis fiduciariis alicui religioso commissis, si quidem bona sint attributa loci seu dioecess ecclesiis incolis aut piis causis iuvandis, Ordinarius de quo in §§ 1, 2, est loci Ordinarius; secus, est Ordinarius eiusdem religiosi proprius."

[94] Vermeersch-Creusen, *op. cit.,* II, 836; S. C. C., 23 April, 1927—*AAS,* XX (1928), 362, where a private letter was held binding on a trustee.

trust, but an agency. In this case, the title to the property does not vest in the agent.[95]

780. As pointed out elsewhere,[96] a bequest to a definite priest for Masses is a gift, and not a trust. Therefore, a priest, though the bequest can be properly called a bequest to a religious purpose, is not a trustee as to the Masses he is obliged to say.

781. **The obligation of probating a trust with the Ordinary** and of providing him with an inventory of assets and liabilities rests only on clerics and religious.[97] The notification can be made orally or by writing. It may also be made by separate account entries in the parish report, but in this case, no portion of it can be employed until the report has been approved.[98]

782. Canon 1516 is derived substantially from the reply of the Sacred Congregation of the Council to the Bishop of Beauvais.[99] That decree, of course, binds only those to whom the rescript was sent.[100] In the present law, the decree of 1909 is modified in five noteworthy particulars. First the present law is not binding on laymen, except to oblige them to tender account and to permit visitation by the Ordinary. It would seem wise, however, that confessors should advise laymen to notify the Ordinary at once of their charge, lest in case of their death it should be defeated.[101] Second, the former decree did not include donations *inter vivos* within the scope of its provisions; the present law does. Third, the present law adds a prohibition against accepting a trust where the supervision of the Ordinary is prohibited. Fourth, the requirement of an inventory of all assets and liabilities is new. Fifth, the present law clarifies the

[95] Cocchi, *op. cit.*, VI, 195; Prümmer, *op. cit.*, 448, 3.

[96] *Cf.* §§ 669-679, supra.

[97] Vermeersch-Creusen, *op. cit.*, II, 836; Augustine, *op. cit.*, VI, 573; Cance, *op. cit.*, III, 147; Vromant, *op. cit.*, 161, 162; De Meester, *op. cit.*, 1469; Bargilliat, *op. cit.*, 2616; *Comm. pro Rel.*, VII (1926), 326; *Le Canoniste Contemporain*, XLV (1922), 119; Miller, *op. cit.*, p. 43. A trust need not be a secret commission, as Vermeersch-Creusen show in answering Bondini, who held that it is; *Ius Pontificium*, VI (1926), p. 87 ff.

[98] *Le Canoniste Contemporain*, XLVIII, 1926, 359.

[99] 7 August, 1909—*AAS*, I (1909), 766.

[100] Canon 17, § 3.

[101] Vromant, *op. cit.*, 161.

problem as to which Ordinary is to exercise supervision in the respective case.[102]

783. If the Ordinary hears that a cleric or a religious has been entrusted with a *fiducia,* he can summon witnesses. If the trust is proved by two reliable witnesses,[103] he can compel proper discharge of it even by censures.[104] But if there are no witnesses who can submit proof, the Ordinary can put the cleric or the religious on oath, and then let the matter to the conscience of the one making the affidavit.[105]

784. Though Mass bequests are not strictly a trust when given to a definite priest, still the Ordinary has the right of scrutinizing the priest's record of manual Mass stipends to discover whether the Masses have been duly celebrated.[106]

785. The Ordinary to whom the inventory is to be sent is either the Ordinary of the place and his *vices gerens* [107] or the major superior of an exempt clerical community.

But sometimes a bequest is not really a *fiducia,* and consequently implies no obligation of inventory to any Ordinary. What is today the rule in Maryland [108] assists in the explanation of the distinction of which a hint has just been given. It will be recalled that the Maryland rule is that a bequest is valid if given to a corporation for the works of the corporate body but not if given to a trustee. It happens in the present problem that where a bequest is left to a community for the works which it conducts under its constitutions, there is no need to make a report by inventory to any Ordinary, provided that no place has been designated where the bequest must be spent and

[102] Doheny, *Church Property,* p. 100; Blat, *op. cit.,* 428.

[103] Canon 1791, § 2.

[104] Canon 2348.

[105] Vromant, *op. cit.,* 165; Bondini, *Ius Pontificium,* VI (1926), 87 ff.

[106] Canon 842. "Ius et officium advigilandi ut onera Missarum adimpleantur, in ecclesiis saecularium pertinet ad loci Ordinarium; in religiosorum ecclesiis, ad eorum superiores."

Canon 843, § 1. "Rectores ecclesiarum aliorumque piorum locorum sive saecularium sive religiosorum in quibus eleemosynae Missarum recipi solent, peculiarem habeant librum in quo accurate notent Missarum receptarum numerum, intentionem, eleemosynam, celebrationem."

[107] *Cf.* § 740, supra, for the list of persons who come within this category.

[108] *Cf.* §§ 592-596, supra.

provided that the community is not one *iuris dioecesani*. For a bequest of this kind is really a gift to the community to be administered under the direction of the superiors, and there is strictly speaking no question of a trust. This conclusion is valid, for instance, when a bequest is made to the community for the work of educating the scholastics of the community, for the missions of the community, or for the education of a priest for such missions.[109]

786. **As to works of piety and charity foreign to the constituted purposes of the community, the common opinion holds that in the case of a *non-exempt* community,** the religious must report the inventory to the Ordinary of the place, even if the work is named generally and without any specification of place;[110] and even as to the works of the community, this report must be made when a particular place or diocese is named as beneficiary, for then the religious become a fiduciary for that place.[111] This last conclusion is valid, for instance, in the case of a bequest made for a definite foreign mission of the community, or for Masses to be celebrated in a definite church of the community.

787. **Who is the Ordinary of the place, that is, by what place is the proper Ordinary to be determined?** Nebreda thinks that the place where the bequest is to be fulfilled determines the Ordinary, not the place where the trustee lives.[112] But, on the other hand, it seems clear enough that it must be the Ordinary of the domicile of the trustee in the case where a bequest is left without specification of place for works foreign to the purposes of the community. For there is no other place by which the Ordinary may be determined. Indeed, Blat says that the Ordinary for a ***non-exempt*** religious is the Ordinary of the place where the trustee resides. And Vermeersch-Creusen and Cocchi agree in effect.[113] Nevertheless, the place when it is specified

[109] Vromant, *op. cit.*, 160, 164; Goyeneche, *Comm. pro Rel.*, III (1922), 266 ff.; Nebreda, *Comm. pro Rel.*, VII (1926), 324; De Meester, *op. cit.*, 980; Vermeersch, *Theol. Mor.*, I, 606; Vermeersch-Creusen, *op. cit.*, II, 836; Cocchi, *op. cit.*, VI, 195; Blat, *op. cit.*, 428.

[110] Vromant, *l. c.;* Vermeersch-Creusen, *l. c.;* Blat, *l. c.*

[111] Vromant, *l. c.;* Nebreda, *Comm. pro Rel.*, VII (1926), 324.

[112] *Comm. pro Rel.*, VII (1926), 328.

[113] Vermeersch-Creusen, *l. c.;* Cocchi, *l. c.;* Blat, *l. c.*

for the fulfillment of the bequest would seem, as Nebreda thinks, to determine the Ordinary to whom inventory must be made by every fiduciary, exempt, non-exempt, or secular. The whole spirit of the Code seems to entrust the supervision of bequests and foundations to the Ordinary of the place where they are to be fulfilled.[114]

788. **In the case of exempt clerical communities,** it is only when the bequest is meant for a definite work of religion or charity not connected with a house of the community or with the purposes of the community, that the inventory must be made to the Ordinary of the place where the bequest is to be fulfilled. Therefore, there are four possible situations in which the Ordinary for an exempt religious is his *major superior,* viz., first, when the bequest is given for the works of the community in general; second, when given to a definite house of the community for its work in that house; third, when given for any other house or for any definite work of the community; fourth, when the bequest is indefinitely for religion and charity. In the first instance, as has already been pointed out, there is really not so much a trust as a gift to the community, but the religious is responsible to his major superior according to the requirements of the constitutions of the community.

789. What has been said of the obligations and duties of bishops in the matter of vigilance, visitation, account, and inventory, applies to the major superior of an exempt clerical community in all matters where his subjects are exempt as to foundations, trusts, bequests, and charitable, religious, and educational institutions.

Article 3

The Task of Commutation

790. **Commutation in Disfavor.** Prior to the sixteenth century, the stress in the canons is found to have been laid upon the exact fulfillment of the will of the testator, as has been indicated in the commentary on Canon 1514, where expression is given in the New Code to the same demand.[115]

[114] *Cf.* Canon 533, § 1, n. 3; Canon 535, § 3, n. 1; Canons 1491, 1492; Canons 1545-1547.

[115] *Cf.* § 735, supra; *cf.* also c. 2, *de relig. dom.*, III, 11 in Clem., where Clement V forbade the changing of a charitable institution into a benefice for

791. Early Examples of Commutation. But Justinian had permitted that a legacy to a charitable institution might be traded for some other property if a profit was made for the charitable institution of not less than twenty-five per cent, provided that the distance at which the property lay made it inconvenient to prosecute the specific transfer.[116] And while Pope Gregory the Great refused to commute a legacy granted to an orphan asylum [117] and insisted on the payment of a bequest to a monastery even though there were no monks attached to it,[118] nevertheless he permitted a monastery to be erected on a site other than that determined by the will, to be determined by the prudent judgment of the bishop; and this decree was incorporated in the Decretals.[119] And where a decedent had been indebted to the Church, Pope Gregory allowed the children to take their inheritance and renounced the Church's claim.[120]

792. A departure from the expressed will of the testator was countenanced in the particular Council of Tarragona (1329), which forbade Ordinaries to distribute legacies to Franciscans, because they had a vow not to be proprietors even as a community. The Council provided that the heirs be consulted as to distribution which was to be made to other pious works with their advice.[121]

793. The law as it stands today is found in Canon 1517, touching the commutation of wills in general, and Canon 1551, touching bequests for Masses specifically.[122]

secular clerics, but permitted the ancient custom whereby priests were attached to these foundations for the purpose of administering the sacraments to the poor and vindicated the authority of the Holy See to make commutations.

116 C. 1, 3, 45; *Nov.*, 131, 12.

117 *Ad Philippum Presbyterum—MPL,* LXXVII, 1280.

118 *Ad Januarium—MPL,* LXXVII, 1135.

119 C. 3, X, *de testamentis et ultimis voluntatibus,* III, 26; *Ad Januarium,* ep. 8, lib. 4, ind. 12—*MPL,* LXXVII, 674; *Ad Januarium,* ep. 15, lib. 4—*MPL,* LXXVII, 684.

120 Letter to Paschal and others—Mansi, IX, 1125; *MPL,* LXXVII, 620.

121 C. 57—Mansi, XXV, 866 A.

122 Canon 1517, § 1. "Ultimarum voluntatum reductio, moderatio, commutatio, quae fieri ex iusta tantum et necessaria causa debent, Sedi Apostolicae

794. The Right of the Supreme Pontiff. The first paragraph of Canon 1517 expresses the right of the Holy See to make changes in the wills of persons leaving gifts to charity and religion. The Supreme Pontiff does this in virtue of his sovereign power over the property of the Church, a power similar to that of eminent domain enjoyed by temporal sovereigns. But the act of modifying the apparent directions of a will is rather an act of interpretation, the supplying of a deficiency due to changed circumstances. Consequently the modification must be made to approach as closely as possible to the known wishes of the testator, and to provide as far as possible what he would wish in the changed situation.[128]

795. As to the nature of the various acts mentioned in the canons, observe that reduction respects the number of acts specified; moderation means the simplification of the plan or the restriction of its proportions made necessary by the lack of resources or the nature

reservantur, nisi fundator hanc potestatem etiam Ordinario loci expresse concesserit."

§ 2. "Si tamen executio onerum impositorum, ob imminutos reditus aliamve causam, nulla administratorum culpa, impossibilis evaserit, tunc Ordinarius quoque, auditis iis quorum interest, et servata, meliore quo fieri potest modo, fundatoris voluntate, poterit eadem onera aeque imminuere, excepta Missarum reductione quae semper Sedi Apostolicae unice competit."

Canon 1551, § 1. "Reductio onerum quae pias fundationes gravant, uni Sedi Apostolicae reservatur, nisi in tabulis fundationis aliud expresse caveatur, et salvo praescripto can. 1517, § 2."

§ 2. "Indultum reducendi Missas fundatas non protenditur nec ad alias Missas ex contractu debitas nec ad alia onera piae fundationis."

§ 3. "Indultum vero generale reducendi onera piarum fundationum ita intelligendum est, nisi aliud constet, ut indultarius potius alia onera, quam Missas reducat."

[128] De Luca, *op. cit.*, disc. 72, n. 14; Wernz, *op. cit.*, III, 283, Barbosa, *De off. episcopi*, III, 83, 1; Schmalzgrueber, *op. cit.*, III, III, 26, 213; S. C. C. *in Causa Nullius Piscien.*, 13 July, 1720, § *Supplicationis*—Pallottini, XI, 637; *in Causa Nullius Piscien.*, 21 June, 1721—*Thesaurus*, 2, 37; in *Causa Arianen.*, 7 February, 1733—Richter, 161; *in Causa Cassanen.*, 26 November, 1763—*Thesaurus*, 32, 181 and 188; *in Causa Santandrien.*, 1 February, 1766, § *De*—Pallottini, XI, 602; *in Causa Albintimilien.*, 25 January, 1772, § *Haec*—Pallottini, XI, 641; *in Causa Fanen.*, 21 June, 1828, § *Ceterum*—Pallottini, XI, 637; *in Causa Senogallien.*, 7 September, 1833, § *Verumtamen*—Pallottini, *l. c.; in Causa Lucana*, 22 May, 1841, § *Quod*—Pallottini, *l. c.*

of the terrain; commutation is the substitution of a new beneficiary for the gift.[124]

796. Even the Supreme Pontiff requires a just and necessary cause to modify a will in any of the ways enumerated; for instance, to divert funds intended for church ornaments to the building of a church in a town where the churches are in ruins,[125] or of a necessary catechumenate or seminary.[126] Consequently, a modification obtained by the allegation of falsehoods is void.[127] However, the Supreme Pontiff does not require a just cause if the new plan fulfills the wishes of the testator more perfectly than the latter's own plan.[128] But if any right under the will has already vested, not only a just and necessary cause is required, but one that is also public, that is, one that affects the common welfare.[129]

[124] Vromant, *op. cit.*, 166; Cocchi, *op. cit.*, VI, 196; Blat, *op. cit.*, 429; De Meester, *op. cit.*, 1470; Cance, *op. cit.*, III, 147.

[125] Barbosa, *l. c.*, n. 13.

[126] Vromant, *op. cit.*, 167.

Cf. Coll. S. C. P. F., 689; Blat, *op. cit.*, 429; Cocchi, *l. c.;* Vermeersch-Creusen, *l. c.;* Bargilliat, *op. cit.*, 1521; Mothon, *op. cit.*, 2627; S. C. C. *in Causa Taurinen.*, 20 December, 1732, § *Sed*—Pallottini, XI, 611; *in Causa Albintimilien.*, 25 January, 1772, § *Notum*—Pallottini, *l. c.; in Causa Hipporegien.*, 17 September, 1791, § *Applicationi*—Pallottini, *l. c.; in Causa Tridentina,* 15 September, 1804, § *Ex*—Pallottini, *l. c.; in Causa Civitatis Castelli,* 19 December, 1807, § *Verum*—Pallottini, *l. c.; in Causa Civitatis Castellanae,* 13 January, 1816, § *Stricte*—Pallottini, *l. c.; in Causa Savonen.*, 22 March, 1823, §§ *Deest* and *Certum*—Pallottini, *l. c.; in Causa Camerinen.*, 23 December, 1826, § *Verum*—Pallottini, *l. c., in Causa Camerinen.*, 17 May, 1828, § *Hisce*—Pallottini, *l. c.*

[127] Cance, *op. cit.*, III, 148.

[128] S. C. C. *in Causa Tolentina,* 13 June, 1744, § *Urget*—Pallottini, XI, 646; *in Causa Albintimilien.*, 25 January, 1772, § *Addunt*—Pallottini, *l. c.*

[129] S. C. C. *in Causa Nucerina,* 15 March, 1794, § *Suam*—Pallottini, XI, 602.

The Sacred Congregations within the province of which this matter falls are: *in foro externo,* the Sacred Congregation of the Council; *in foro interno,* the Sacred Penitentiary; for missions, the Sacred Congregation for the Propagation of the Faith; for religious, the Sacred Congregation of Religious; *cf.* Cance, *l. c.;* Vromant, *l. c.;* De Meester, *l. c.* Vermeersch-Creusen think that for the *mensa episcopalis,* the Sacred Consistorial Congregation is to be consulted; and for seminaries, the Sacred Congregation of Seminaries and Studies. He bases this conclusion on the declaration of December 7, 1922—*Periodica,* XII (1923), 43 ff.; *AAS,* XV (1923), 39.

797. The rights of a bishop in this matter must be regarded under two subdivisions, viz., his right to modify charitable bequests in general, and his right to reduce the number of Masses established by foundation. It is convenient to consider first his right to modify charitable bequests in general.

From the second paragraph of Canon 1517, it is evident that his right is operative only when it becomes impossible to fulfill the testator's wishes and when the administrators are not to blame.

The Council of Trent had extended a privilege which was practically the same as this. It said that when there are so few cases of charity of the kind which the testator had in mind as to make his bequests impractical, the bishop with two skilled capitulars could make that modification which would most nearly comply with the testator's design. But he dare not do this if the testator had forbidden any modification.[130] From the language of the Council it is evident that moral impossibility of fulfillment sufficed to justify modification by the bishop; not, however, if the impediment could be removed. If there existed a legal impossibility of fulfillment, arising out of either canon or secular law, the bishop was competent. For instance, he might change the site prescribed for the erection of a monastery because the Council of Trent forbade the building of a monastery on a public street.[131] On the other hand, the Sacred Congregation of Rites and Ceremonies replied in a given case (1630) that where a foundation is established contrary to the rubrics or to the laws and decrees of the Holy See, recourse may be had to the Holy See for modification. This rescript, however, was a particular decree. Moreover, it did not command recourse to the Holy See. Its problem was not precisely to solve where the authority to modify resided but whether the rubrics or the requirements of the foundation were to be sustained. The remark touching the person who had power to modify was on a matter not in issue.[132]

[130] Sess. XXV, *de ref.*, c. 8.

[131] Barbosa, *l. c.*, nn. 3, 7-9, 11; Wernz, *op. cit.*, III, 283; S. C. C. *in Causa Ariminen.*, 30 January, 1779—Pallottini, XI, 644.

[132] Decree, 23 March, 1630—*Decreta Authentica*, 528.

Barbosa holds that bishops, and Cardinals in churches committed to their

But if it is only a condition that is impossible of fulfillment, it is considered as *non-adiecta*.[133] The same conclusion is valid as to conditions the fulfillment of which is substantially illicit; for instance, if the bequest is granted on condition that the testator be avenged. Whatever is legal and moral in the bequest is valid; the whole is valid, if it can stand by ignoring the unlawful elements.[134]

798. Where it is impossible to ascertain what the obligation is, the bishop is competent to name the persons to be benefited or the purpose to be promoted. This conclusion is based on four arguments. First, this designation of beneficiaries is not an act of commutation, but one of fulfillment. Second, nothing is more certain than the constant tradition evinced in the councils that the distribution of the soul's portion, that is, the naming of beneficiaries to receive it, was the function of the bishop, as well as the distribution of the estate of an intestate. Third, the councils following the Council of Trent adopt this view. Fourth, it is approved by the decisions of the Sacred Congregation of the Council.[135]

care, could make modifications in wills even when there was no impossibility of fulfillment, whether *de iure* or *de facto; l. c.*, n. 5. And Schmalzgrueber agrees with him, saying that this is the more common and received opinion. But this conclusion he reaches by extending beyond proper limits the delegation of the Council of Trent which merely empowered bishops to hold a summary process to ascertain whether a just and necessary cause existed. The findings were then to be sent to the Holy See. Schmalzgrueber may have been influenced in some measure also by various texts in the *Decretum* referring to the bishop's position as executor of wills and as custodian of contributions to charity; *cf.* Council of Trent, sess. XXII, *de ref.*, c. 6; Schmalzgrueber, *op. cit.*, I, V, 35, 31; III, III, 26, 213. Wernz disagrees with this view and it would seem correctly; *l. c.*

[133] Schmalzgrueber, *op. cit.*, III, 1, 9, 33.

[134] D'Annibale, *op. cit.*, II, 365.

If the bequest is made to a hospital belonging to a community that both conducts the hospital and teaches school, the gift may be applied to the schools if the Holy See should later deprive the community of its right to conduct hospitals, unless the gift was intended primarily for hospital work and only secondarily for the benefit of the community; Vromant, *op. cit.*, 170.

[135] Where a bequest was refused by the original beneficiary, the Sacred Congregation of the Council ordered commutation to be made in the discretion of the bishop; *in Causa Fanen.*, 19 July, 1828—Pallottini, XI, 515. *Cf.* also Barbosa, *l. c.*, n. 16; Council of Urbino (1596)—Mansi, XXXV A, 696 D; Council

799. To grasp the significance of commutation, it is well to remember the distinctions in the application of the *cy pres* doctrine as it is employed in the United States.[186] There are two degrees of modification which are adopted in the courts of the United States. First, there is the change of object when the intended object becomes incapable of being realized. Second, there is the change merely in the plan of distribution. Though some canonists maintained that both these powers reside in the Ordinary,[187] the better view is that the prerogative power of substituting one object for another belongs to the Holy See. It will be remembered that some of the courts in the United States refuse to employ that power because they allege that it resides in the legislature and not in the judiciary, the legislature being the sovereign power in each State.

800. Commutation Reserved to the Holy See. The Sacred Congregation of the Council has repeatedly taught that commutation in its strict sense can be effected only by the prerogative power of the Holy See, and has declared null and void all commutations made without such intervention.[188] Moreover, it has definitely stated that the Ordinary has the right merely to determine by a summary process whether there is a just and reasonable cause for the commutation,

of Salerno (1596)—Mansi, XXXV B, 1012 D; S. C. C. *in Causa Viterb.*, 14 December, 1754—*Thesaurus*, 18, 108; *in Causa Vicen.*, 20 November, 1762—*Thesaurus*, 31, 240; *in Causa Faenza*, 22 February, 1823—*Thesaurus*, 83, 47; *in Causa Conimbricen.*, 21 August, 1717—Pallottini, XI, 571; *in Causa Elboren.*, 3 September, 1718—*Thesaurus*, 1, 98; *in Causa Forosempronien.*, 8 February, 1823—*Thesaurus*, 83, 47 and 49.

Certain rules of distribution are given by Barbosa for the bishop's guidance. If the bequest is for the poor, it is not to be given to one person: the poor relatives of the testator are to be preferred to others, but not a spurious son; then the more needy are to be preferred, provided they are worthy of help. The relatives of the bishop and the executor may participate in the bequest, if they are really in need. Barbosa, *l. c.*, nn. 17-21.

[186] *Cf.* §§ 576, 577, supra.

[187] *Cf.* n. 132, this chapter.

[188] S. C. C. *in Causa Maturanen.*, 25 January, 1738, § *Tertio*—Pallottini, XI, 600; *in Causa Santandrien.*, 1 February, 1766, § *De*—Pallottini, XI, 602; *cf.* the decree of the Sacred Congregation for the Propagation of the Faith, delegating the power of commutation but requiring a report of every commutation—*Coll. S. C. P. F.*, n. 689.

but not to proceed to the actual modification.[139] Consequently, the Ordinary can not transfer a bequest from one charitable institution to another, nor prolong the time for the payment of a bequest, except as heretofore indicated.[140]

801. Recourse to Rome is required even if the legacy is so small that it will be entirely consumed in the process;[141] but the Sacred Congregation of the Council grants a *sanatio* where the commutation was made in good faith or under stress of necessity.[142]

802. However, the Ordinary may exercise the equivalent of the prerogative power if it has been conceded to him in the will or if he has been specially delegated by the Holy See.[143]

803. The faculty as it now exists under Canon 1517, paragraph 2, arises from the bishop's right to be the executor and the interpreter of the will of the testator.[144] Blat says it is personal to the Ordinary, though incorrectly;[145] as the power to be executor of the will is not personal to him.

804. Augustine maintains that the Ordinaries of religious do not possess this faculty,[146] but he seems to be misled in this opinion by the fact that the Ordinary of the place is authorized expressly to exercise power of commutation when the testator makes provision for this in the will. But it is futile to argue that because the Ordinary of religious is excluded in one portion of a Canon, he is omitted also from the other portion where he is not expressly mentioned.

Two reasons seem to indicate that both Ordinaries are meant by

139 S. C. C. *in Causa Imolen.*, 26 February, 1820, § *Quatenus*—Pallottini, XI, 600; *in Causa Faenza*, 22 February, 1823—*Thesaurus*, 83, 47; Council of Trent, Sess. XXII, *de ref.*, c. 6; Barbosa, *l. c.*, n. 5.

140 *Cf.* § 692, supra.

141 Innocent XII, const., *Nuper*, s. 15, as lum.—*Fontes*, n. 260.

142 *In Causa Faenza*, 22 February, 1823—*Thesaurus*, 83, 49.

143 Cance, *op. cit.*, III, 148; *cf.* Blat, *op. cit.*, 429.

144 Cocchi, *op. cit.*, VI, 196; De Meester, *l. c.*

145 Blat, *l. c.* Barbosa held that the Vicar General could not act under the faculties granted by the Council of Trent, unless he had a special mandate; *l. c.*, n. 16. Both he and Schmalzgrueber held that the cathedral chapter could act *vacante sede;* Barbosa, *l. c.;* Schmalzgrueber, *op. cit.*, III, I, 9, 33. *Cf.* § 747, this chapter.

146 *Op. cit.*, VI, 576.

the second paragraph of Canon 1517. First, the second paragraph omits the word *loci* when that very word was certainly in the mind of the legislator, inasmuch as it was used by him only a few clauses previously. This omission would seem to indicate a deliberate intent on the part of the legislator to use the word *Ordinarius* in its fullest extent in paragraph 2. Second, the root of the power of diminishing the burden when it becomes incapable of being fulfilled is to be sought in the power enjoyed by the Ordinary as executor of wills. But Canon 1515, § 1, includes the Ordinary of religious as the executor of wills. Therefore, Canon 1517, § 2, seems to include him also.[147]

805. Conditions Under Which the Ordinary May Commute. The act of commutation which the Ordinary is authorized to perform under Canon 1517, § 2, is limited by four definite conditions: the impossibility of fulfillment of the original plan; the lack of fault on the part of the administrators; a hearing granted all interested parties; and the fulfillment of the testator's will as nearly as may be. Each condition must be verified if the act is to be valid. The reason is that the Holy See has constantly regarded commutations null and void when made by any power below that of the Sovereign Pontiff. Consequently, all are invalid except such as are validated by the law. Now only those are validated which comply with the conditions established under Canon 1517, § 2. Cance and Vromant, however, say that the two latter conditions are required only for the lawfulness of the act.[148] As to the third condition, Canon 105 seems clear on the point that whenever the canons require that any persons be heard prior to the performance of an action, the action is invalid if that formality is omitted. There is an opinion that maintains this sort of condition is required only for the lawfulness of the action, and though it is advanced by Vermeersch-Creusen, it seems to lack sufficient probability for practice.[149]

806. The first condition, the impossibility of fulfillment,

[147] Barbosa and Schmalzgrueber included inferior prelates among those enjoying the power to commute wills under the faculty granted by the Council of Trent; Barbosa, *l. c.;* Schmalzgrueber, *op. cit.*, III, V, 41, 137.

[148] Cance, *l. c.;* Vromant, *op. cit.*, 169.

[149] *Cf.* § 763, supra.

may be brought about by the inadequacy of the original fund, or by a reduction in its value: for example, if the amount bequeathed is sufficient to maintain only one bed instead of two.[150]

The persons to be given a hearing are the pastor, the founder, the heir, the beneficiary, and all others who have an interest in the fund.

807. To what act is the Ordinary limited? The act itself may be one of reduction, moderation, or commutation. Cance and De Meester think that under the second paragraph of this Canon, the Ordinary is empowered merely to reduce or moderate, but not to substitute another object for the bequest.[151]

Vromant, however, believes that commutation is included for two reasons: first, the impossibility of fulfilling the original design of the testator is given as the motive on which the power of the Ordinary is granted him, and that power is not restricted, under the canon, to the circumstances where the impossibility arises from the diminution in the value of the fund, but would seem to extend even to the case where the object itself can not be the beneficiary of the bequest. The second reason is that commutation is practically the same act as moderation, so far as the will of the testator is basically concerned. That will is being fulfilled approximately in any case. Finally, Vromant calls upon Canon 20 which states that where there is an omission in the law, the principles of the law set down for similar matters are to be applied to the case where no provision has been made.[152]

Two other arguments, not noticed by Vromant, may be suggested. One argument is based on the nature of the permission granted bishops by the Council of Trent, which included commutation.[153] Since the present law is practically a repetition of the former permission, a

[150] Vermeersch-Creusen, *l. c.;* Cocchi, *op. cit.*, VI, 196; Cance, *l. c.;* Prümmer, *op. cit.*, 448.

[151] De Meester, *l. c.;* Cance, *l. c.*

[152] Vromant, *l. c.* Bargilliat admits that commutation is permitted the Ordinary when the general intent can not be fulfilled in any other way; *op. cit.*, 1521.

[153] Sess. XXV, *de ref.*, c. 8. *Cf.* § 797, supra.

change in the law is not to be presumed without clear evidence to the contrary.

The second argument derives from the use of the words, "*meliore quo fieri potest modo,*" in Canon 1517, § 2, which imply more than mere reduction or moderation of the burden. They clearly indicate the substitution of a plan different from that of the testator, but as nearly like it as possible.

808. **May Canon 81 be invoked?** If the fulfillment of the original plan has not become impossible *de iure* or *de facto,* it would seem that the Ordinary can not invoke Canon 81 to justify commutation where it would prove useful, even though recourse to Rome means the passing of an opportunity for great gain. This seems to be a conclusion warranted by the Constitution, *Nuper,* of Innocent XII, which requires recourse to Rome even when the fund is so small as to be consumed in the process.[154]

809. **The transition from Canon 1517 to Canon 1551** becomes necessary when the question of reducing the burden of celebrating Masses is reached. The Council of Trent had authorized a reduction of such burdens, saying that often there are so many Masses that must be said by reason of foundations in churches and monasteries that there are not enough priests stationed there to comply with the obligation or the income is so small that no adequate stipend is available for them. So bishops were authorized to make a practical arrangement in the diocesan synod, and abbots in the general chapter, by which the commemoration of all the souls involved would be assured.[155]

Wernz holds that this privilege was granted for only the first synod to be held after the Council and for foundations established

[154] *Cf.* § 801, supra.

[155] Sess. XXV, *de ref.*, c. 4.

The provincial councils then ordered that synods be held where it was necessary to make this reduction: viz., Council of Avignon (1594), c. 33—Mansi, XXXVI B, 1343 D; Council of Toledo (1582), dec. 10—Mansi, XXXVI B, 168 B (where it was also decreed that the synod should set a standard stipend adequate to meet the economic demands of the time). The council of Trani-Salpi decreed that one Mass was to be celebrated each day for all anniversaries, excepting Sundays, Mondays, and feast days, on which occasions Masses were ordered to be celebrated for all poor souls—Mansi, XXXVI B, 891 B.

prior to that time.[156] And this was the answer which the Secretary of the Sacred Congregation of the Council was uniformly instructed to give to all *dubia* on the point.[157]

The Sacred Congregation of the Council also indicated early that the privilege was not to be exercised to reduce the burden of Masses attached to the endowments of churches, chapels,[158] and benefices.[159] It forbade the reduction of the number of Masses to be celebrated, if the heir was obliged to make up the deficiency in income;[160] and decreed that the reduction in any case could not be made without the convocation of a synod, even though it was alleged that the bishop had this power independently of the delegation granted by the Council of Trent.[161]

810. Moreover, in 1625 the Sacred Congregation by express and universal decree authoritatively interpreted the decree of the Council of Trent. It forbade the reduction of Mass burdens imposed by foundation or bequeathed since the Council of Trent.[162]

[156] *Op. cit.*, III, 207; *cf.* Miller, *op. cit.*, pp. 68, 69.

[157] *In Causa Florentina*, 15 December, 1629—*Fontes*, n. 2515.

[158] *In Causa Mediolanen.*, October, 1587—*Fontes*, n. 2189.

[159] *In Causa Lauden.*, 30 May, 1591—*Fontes*, n. 2232; *in Causa Ferrarien.*, 3 March, 1597—*Fontes*, n. 2305; *in Causa S. Agathae Gothorum*, 24 May, 1601—*Fontes*, n. 2339.

[160] *In Causa Cremonen.*, July, 1586—*Fontes*, n. 2161.

[161] *In Causa Hieracen.*, April, 1587—*Fontes*, n. 2175.

[162] Urban VIII, *Cum saepe contingat*, 21 June, 1625—*Bullarium Romanum*, XX, 807; *Fontes*, n. 2560. *Cf.* Innocent XII, const., *Nuper*,—*Fontes*, n. 260; Schmalzgrueber, *op. cit.*, III, V, 41, 154; Blat, *op. cit.*, 469; Many, *De Missa*, 74.

And the Sacred Congregation decreed in a rescript that the decree, *Cum saepe contingat*, and the Constitution, *Nuper*, were binding on the whole world; *in Congr. Passionis*, 16 December, 1693, ad 1um—*Fontes*, n. 4289.

Schmalzgrueber argues that the decree, *Cum saepe contingat*, had been abrogated by custom in Germany, and maintains that bishops and the prelates of churches and monasteries in Germany might still reduce the burden of Masses bequeathed since the Council of Trent. This they might do even without summoning a synod or a general chapter, if convocation proved difficult. However, superiors who were not prelates must convene the chapter, because they did not possess the right to make reduction prior to the time when it was conferred by the Council of Trent, and consequently they must abide by the conditions established by the Council for the valid use of it. Schmalzgrueber admits, however, that under the privilege granted by the Council, Mass burdens imposed

811. A faculty to make reduction in the burden of Masses was granted in 1724 by the Sacred Congregation of the Council[163] to the Abbot of the Cassinese Congregation to select with the counsel of his assistants one abbey in each province where a Mass should be celebrated each year within the Octave of All Souls for Masses which might have been omitted in the past. A commission was to be appointed in each province to determine the number of Masses to which the province was annually obliged, and to examine the state of the income from its foundations. The Abbot General was authorized to order that one Mass be celebrated for each sixty *scutata* of income. Perpetual foundations of Masses were forbidden for the future unless the permission of the provincial superior intervened.

812. This privilege was extended by Benedict XIII in the Council of Rome (1725) to all the bishops present at the Council whether in person or by proxy.[164]

A faculty similar to this had been conceded at various times, according to Benedict XIV,[165] by the Supreme Pontiffs who succeeded Urban VIII, *i. e.*, Alexander VII, Clement X, and Clement XI, to certain Orders of regulars. Because of great pressure that was brought to bear on the Sacred Congregation of the Council, he states that as secretary he counseled Pope Innocent XIII to extend the privilege to all Orders. The Holy Father agreed and granted the privilege for a period of three years. At the end of that time, it was granted for another three-year term and extended to bishops who had not attended the Council of Rome.

813. Cessation of obligations. Before reference is made to the indults that are enjoyed at the present time in this regard, observe that it is possible for the burdens of a foundation to cease without ac-

by *contract* could not be reduced. He asserts, moreover, that where the endowment for Masses has been merged with the funds of the monastery, no reduction can be made; *op. cit.*, III, V, 41; 145; 149-151; 152-154.

[163] 15 July, 1724—*Coll. Lacensis*, I, 369 d.

[164] Tit. 15, c. 8—*Coll. Lacensis*, I, 369 d; Pallottini, XI, 508. The Council also required that for the future it would not suffice to determine the amount of income necessary on the basis of the manual stipend, but that a greater income should be demanded according to the custom of the diocese or the province. *Cf.* Miller, *op. cit.*, p. 19.

[165] *Op. cit.*, lib. 13, c. ult., nn. 21, 22.

tive reduction on the part of the superior. If the income ceases without any fault of the administrator, the burdens also cease. If the receipt of the income is temporarily suspended, the burdens are similarly temporarily suspended.[166] Confiscation of the property of a foundation transfers the obligations attached to it to the persons who come into possession of it.[167]

814. Prescription never removes the burden of a foundation for charity or religion. The lapse of time so far from releasing the endowment from the obligation, imposes the obligation of restitution for the performance of the acts omitted in the interval.[168] Prescription can not operate as a release from the burdens for three reasons. First, prescription does not run against the founder, for he is unable to act; second, equity will not permit that a successor should obtain the endowment without the burden by reason of his predecessor's failure to comply with the burden; third, alms and the obligations of Masses are withdrawn by the canons from the operation of prescription.[169] But the obligations can be transferred to another person or another institution by prescription.[170]

815. Reduction Reserved to the Holy See. Under paragraph one of Canon 1551, in harmony with the decree, *Cum saepe contingat*, the burdens of Masses can not be reduced by the Ordinary, this act being reserved to the Holy See as a *causa maior*, unless the Ordinary is authorized in the articles of foundation to make such an accommodation.[171]

[166] Badii, *Insts. Iur. Can.*, II, 648; Cocchi, *op. cit.*, VI, 232; Bargilliat, *op. cit.*, 1520; Cance, *op. cit.*, III, 176; Vromant, *op. cit.*, 358.

[167] S. C. de Negotiis Extraord., 1906—*Periodica*, III (1911), 43; Cocchi, *l. c.*; Cance, *l. c.*

[168] De Meester, *op. cit.*, 1503.

[169] *Cf.* Canon 1509, n. 5; S. C. C. *in Causa Mariannen.*, 20 December, 1879—*Thesaurus*, 138, 534; *in Causa Romana*, 21 June, 1879—*Thesaurus*, 138, 261; Many, *op. cit.*, 72; Cance, *l. c.*; Wernz, *op. cit.*, III, 206.

[170] De Meester, *op. cit.*, 1462; Wernz, *op. cit.*, III, 300.

[171] Pontifical Commission for the Authoritative Interpretation of the Canons of the Code, 14, July, 1922—*AAS*, XIV (1922), 529; *Periodica*, XI (1922), 165. *Cf.* Innocent XII, const., *Nuper*, 23 December, 1697—*Fontes*, n. 260; the decree, *Cum saepe contingat*, 21 June, 1625—*Fontes*, n. 2560; Blat, *op. cit.*, 469, 429; Vromant, *op. cit.*, 169, 357; De Meester, *op. cit.*, 1470; Cocchi, *op. cit.*, VI, 231;

816. Judicial declarations as to cessation of obligation. However, it is the reduction of the burdens that is forbidden, not declarations of fact or judicial declarations of respective rights. Consequently, Benedict XIV admits that a reduction of the burden is not to be found in such declarations and that the Ordinary is competent to perform them: v. gr., declarations that the income has ceased, that there is no more capital, or that the founder sold the property intended for an endowment. These decrees may be issued by the Ordinary in virtue of his ordinary power. But if there is a judicial suit, the usual procedure must be followed as outlined in the Fourth Book of the Code.[172]

817. Reduction prior to acceptance. It would be a reduction of the burden, however, and beyond the bishop's ordinary competence, to accommodate the number of Masses to the income prior to the acceptance of the endowment by the institution. Of course, if the founder is still living, the Ordinary can make the necessary arrangement with him. This, however, is impossible where the endowment is made by will.[173]

818. Power to reduce implied by the manner of foundation. There are at least two cases, however, where the power of reducing the burdens of Masses is granted the Ordinary by the founder by implication. The first is where the founder did not mention the number of Masses or the stipend. In this case the Ordinary can accommodate the number to the income on the basis of the current stipend for founded Masses. The second case is where the founder indicated the stipend but not the number of Masses. Here the Ordinary can divide the income into the number of stipends based on the figure set by the founder.[174]

819. Partial diminution. If the income ceases or is suspended, all authorities agree that the burdens cease or are suspended.[175] But

Cance, *op. cit.*, III, 175, 176; Prümmer, *op. cit.*, 456, 8; Bargilliat, *op. cit.*, 1521; Benedict XIV, *l. c.*, nn. 17-19.

[172] *Cf.* Benedict XIV, *l. c.*, nn. 8, 9; Many, *op. cit.*, 75, 79; De Meester, *op. cit.*, 1503.

[173] Benedict XIV, *l. c.*, n. 19; Many, *op. cit.*, 74.

[174] Many, *op. cit.*, 76.

[175] *Cf.* § 813, supra; Vermeersch-Creusen, *op. cit.*, II, 836; Vromant, *op. cit.*, 171; De Meester, *l. c.*

there is a controversy as to whether a partial diminution of the income without the fault of the administrator works a partial diminution of the burdens of Masses. Many offers four reasons why it should. First, the decree, *Cum saepe contingat,* had in mind only those churches which, *iam oneratae et gravatae missis fundatis, adhuc in dies novas missarum fundationes acceptabant, quocumque stipendio,* that is, which accepted new burdens with a low stipend, hoping that the Ordinary would soon make the necessary reduction to make the burden fit the stipend. Many reasons that it is fair to interpret the dispositive part of the law from this narrative part, and that as the decree was aimed at a specific evil it should not be extended to include situations not affected by that evil.

His second reason derives from the cessation of the whole burden when the whole income ceases. He fails to see why a proportional loss should not imply a proportional diminution of the burden. Even the Ordinary's interference he conceives to be necessary only to determine whether there has in fact been a diminution of income and whether there has been any fault on the part of the administrator.

His third reason takes him back to the decree, *Cum saepe contingat,* the general words of which might seem to indicate that though it aimed at a specific evil, it reached beyond the situations affected by the evil. He says that in spite of the general language of the decree, it does not extend to the case where the income has been partially lost. He thinks this to be evident on four grounds. First, there is in this case no question of reduction, which the decree contemplates, but rather of partial extinction. Second, in spite of the general language of the decree, it permits other exceptions, for all agree that it does not extend to the burdens of Masses incurred by reason of contract, for over these the Ordinary has power of judicial investigation and decree. Third, the language is not so general as to prevent the Ordinary from using his ordinary power of interpreting the will of the testator and determining whether the fulfillment of the trusts is possible. Fourth, whatever restriction of the Ordinary's power the decree contains must be strictly interpreted in spite of the general language, for it is an infringement on the Ordinary's rights.

Finally, he argues that the granting of indults to bishops for the reduction of the burdens of Masses does not provide an argument *e converso* to prove that the Ordinary otherwise has no power without such a faculty. This is evident from three considerations. First, the indult prescinds from the previous state of the capital and income, makes no reference to the relative state of past and present, and refers only to the present situation in an attempt to harmonize it with the necessities of the Church. Second, an indult may be given for tranquillity of conscience as well as for an objective need. Third, it enables the Ordinary to reduce the burdens imposed by wills prior to their acceptance by the institution.

He cites as holding this view with him the following authors: Fagnanus, Schmalzgrueber, St. Alphonse, D'Annibale, Icard, and Gennari; and as opposed: Benedict XIV, Tamburini, Lucidi, Gasparri, Passerini, and Ferrari.[176]

There is clearly a *dubium iuris* in this case, and it still remains, inasmuch as Canon 1551 repeats the old law which is consequently to be interpreted according to the opinions of the doctors prior to the Code.[177] Since the opinion of St. Alphonse is entirely probable, it seems that the Ordinary can declare a reduction in the burden of Masses, if it be established that the income has partially been lost without any fault on the part of the administrator. While the authors seem to speak only of the bishop as enjoying this right, it should be extended, it would seem, by the whole spirit of the canons to the major superiors of exempt clerical communities, who are now given the same jurisdiction over bequests and foundations within their provinces as the bishop has within his diocese.

820. Moreover, in virtue of his ordinary power, and in case of grave inconvenience, the Ordinary can change the altar, the hour, and

[176] Many, *op. cit.*, 76; Fagnanus, *op. cit.*, I, 12, 25; Schmalzgrueber, *op. cit.*, III, V, 3, 139; St. Alphonse, lib. 6, n. 331, d. 1; D'Annibale, *op. cit.*, III, 75; Gennari, *Consultazioni,* II, cons. 2, 8; Benedict XIV, *l. c.*, nn. 17-19; Lucidi, *De visitatione,* c. 7, 78, 79, 106; Gasparri, *op. cit.*, 588. St. Alphonse and Gennari understand their opinion in the sense that the income was once adequate. D'Annibale says that this power of the Ordinary is operative even if the inadequacy of the income arises from the increase in the amount of the stipend and not from a decrease in the amount of the income; for he says that if the income does not increase with the stipend, there is a case of decreased income. Schmalzgrueber calls the opinion the common one.

[177] *Cf.* Canon 6, n. 2.

the day for the celebration of the founded Masses, provided that the modification is proportionate to the inconvenience. But according to the more probable opinion, the Holy See must be consulted for permission to transfer the celebration of the Masses to another church, unless the original church is destroyed, or it becomes otherwise impossible to comply with the founder's will as to the particular church. But if the foundation was meant primarily to benefit the religious body, it seems that they may say the Masses in a new location without consulting the Holy See.[178]

821. Interpretation of Indults. The Holy See, as has been indicated, is accustomed to grant faculties to bishops to moderate the burdens of Masses; [179] but recourse against the bishop's action is reserved to the Holy See, that is, to the Sacred Congregation of the Council.[180] These indults are to be interpreted strictly.[181] Consequently if the language of the indult includes only founded Masses it is not to be extended to burdens established by contract.[182] So it may not be extended to manual Masses or to Masses *ad instar manua-*

[178] De Meester, *op. cit.*, 1502; Many, *op. cit.*, 83; Schmalzgrueber, *op. cit.*, III, III, 41, 133; Miller, *op. cit.*, p. 77.

[179] Vermeersch-Creusen, *l. c.;* De Meester, *op. cit.*, 1470; 1503; Many, *op. cit.*, 77; Benedict XIV, *l. c.*, n. 20.

[180] Benedict XIV, *l. c.*

[181] Vermeersch-Creusen, *op. cit.*, II, 870.

[182] Vromant, *op. cit.*, 357; Cance, *op. cit.*, III, 176; Prümmer, *op. cit.*, 456, 8; Ferreres, *Insts. Can.*, II, 520; Mothon, *op. cit.*, 2632; Benedict XIV, *l. c.*, n. 25.

But where the burden of Masses has been established by contract, the Ordinary, as judge, can investigate whether the diminution in the income is so great as to justify the rescinding of the contract or the conforming of the burden to the demands of equity; Benedict XIV, *l. c.*, n. 26.

Cf. S. C. C. *in Causa Vallisolitana,* 22 May, 1784—*Fontes,* n. 3837 (where a daily Mass established by contract was held not included in a *general* reduction of Mass burdens); *in Causa Placentina,* 21 July, 1792—*Fontes,* n. 3881 (where a family, having assumed the trust imposed on another family, sought reduction of the burden on account of the expenses of litigation involved in obtaining the property from a third party, but was refused on account of the contractual assumption of the obligation); *in Causa Sutrina,* 18 April, 1795—*Fontes,* n. 3894 (where a cleric had taken over a chaplaincy by contract, with the obligation of having Masses said, and consequently could not obtain a reduction of the burden); *in Causa Novarien.,* 5 and 27 August, 1780—*Fontes,* nn. 3810 and 3812 (where after the lapse of one hundred and seventy-five years a

lium.[183] Nor to the burdens of Masses arising out of a bequest carrying with it the obligation of saying Masses; nor to any other burdens that may be concomitant with the burden of celebrating Masses. But only to those Masses for which a founder established a definite endowment with a definite institution which was to enjoy the income on condition that a certain number of Masses be celebrated by the persons responsible for the administration of the institution thus benefited.

But Benedict XIV says that an indult for founded Masses permits a complete condonation of such burdens unfulfilled in the past with an obligation of saying a Mass on All Souls' Day for the omissions,[184] but it seems that at present the faculty is not included in the general indult if it be not expressly mentioned.[185] Moreover, the ordinary faculty does not grant the right to reduce the burdens of universal and solemn Masses.[186]

822. In making the reduction, the Ordinary should observe that it is the practice of the Roman Curia to reduce first chanted Masses to low Masses, and to let the process rest there, if thus the income can be made to meet the obligation as to number.[187] He should moreover be conversant with the reasons that justify reduction; viz., the partial destruction or loss of the capital; the infertility of the soil; the increased cost of living; an increased stipend; higher rate of taxation on the endowment; and in fact any circumstance that destroys

congregation could not find a chaplain to say three Masses a week which it had agreed by contract to have celebrated, but was nevertheless refused a reduction of the burden); *in Causa Montis Regalis,* 30 April, 1729—Pallottini, XI, 557 (where a woman who had been given a legacy with the obligation of leaving one-half of it at death to a certain community of nuns, but made a contract instead, the nuns agreeing to have two Masses said each week, the nuns were bound by their contract and could not obtain a reduction of the burden).

[183] *Cf.* § 644, supra, for a description of the different kinds of stipends.

[184] *L. c.,* n. 34.

[185] De Meester, *op. cit.,* 1503; Many, *op. cit.,* 81; Wernz, *op. cit.,* III, 207; S. C. C. *in Causa Dioecesis H.,* 20 November, 1915—*AAS,* IX (1917), 17.

[186] Benedict XIV, *l. c.,* n. 25.

[187] Vromant, *op. cit.,* 357; Many, *op. cit.,* 80; D'Annibale, III, 76.

the proportion between the income and the number of Masses as established by the founder.[188]

823. Contribution by the Heir. If the obligation of supplying for the deficiency of the income has been placed by the founder on any heir or trustee, the number of Masses must not be reduced. The proper person must be compelled to make due contribution. That there may be no doubt as to whether any person is liable to this obligation, the founder should be asked at the very moment when the foundation is being established whether he prefers, in the event of a diminution of income, that contribution should be made by his heirs or that the number of Masses should be reduced. His preference should be noted in the articles of foundation. If he wishes the number of Masses to remain undiminished in any event, his presumed wish is that the heirs be compelled to make the necessary contribution. In the absence of any expressed preference the decision should follow certain rules laid down by the Sacred Congregation of the Council.[189]

824. The first rule is that if the fund is set down in the first place, this is to be regarded as the sole source whence the income for the obligations is to be derived, and no contribution is to be sought from the heirs. Second, if the number of Masses is set down first, contribution is to be sought. Third, if the founder told the heir to give a definite and specific farm to the institution, the heir can not be asked to contribute, because the farm loses its value to the detriment of the owner, which happens to be the institution. If the diminution in value had occurred before the heir had transferred it, the heir would be obliged to make up the deficiency. Fourth, contribution is to be sought if the fund remained with the heir who was obliged under the terms of the testator's will to provide that a certain number of Masses be said each year. Fifth, contribution is also due if the heir by his own wish and on his own motion transferred the farm to the institution, when under the terms of the will he should have kept it himself and arranged each year that the Masses be said. Sixth, contribution also is due if the testator in general terms directed that a quantity of land be given the institution sufficient to provide an income for the

[188] De Meester, *op. cit.*, 1503; S. C. C. *in Causa Romana*, 13 April, 1904—*ASS*, XXXVII (1904), 181; Benedict XIV, *l. c.*, n. 28.

[189] Benedict XIV, *l. c.*, nn. 29-33; *cf.* Miller, *op. cit.*, p. 73.

celebration of a definite number of Masses, for the number of Masses is all important and the heir must see to it that a sufficient amount of land is always in the hands of the institution to provide for that number.

825. A general indult for the reduction of obligations imposed in pious foundations means that Masses are to be reduced last. This is the law under paragraph three of Canon 1551. It is also the practice of the Roman Curia. This conclusion is valid whether the indult is general in the sense that it is given to many Ordinaries; or to one Ordinary for many foundations; or even for the general works of one institution.[190] Exceptions to this rule occur when the founder decreed otherwise, or when the fund that has suffered diminution is recognizable as the fund set aside for the burden of Masses. But in either case Benedict XIV says that the Holy See must be consulted even by a bishop who has faculties to reduce the burden of Masses.[191]

826. Scholion I. Examples of faculties granted by the Sacred Congregation of the Council touching the administration of Mass obligations are given by Vermeersch-Creusen in Appendix III of Volume I of the *Epitome*. Ordinaries in the United States should consult their quinquennial faculties to discover the extent to which they are empowered to act in this matter. The faculties cited by Vermeersch-Creusen are taken from Formula Three. They are as follows:

> 1. Reducendi per quinquennium, ob diminutionem redituum, perpetua missarum onera ad rationem eleemosynae in dioecesi legitime vigentis, quoties nemo sit qui de iure teneatur et utiliter cogi queat ad eleemosynae augmentum, et sub lege ut de missarum ita reductarum satisfactiones a singulis celebrantibus Curia dioecesana quovis anno legitime doceatur;
>
> 2. Transferendi per quinquennium intra fines dioecesis onera missarum in dies, ecclesias vel altaria alia a fundatione

[190] Vermeersch-Creusen, *op. cit.*, II, 870; S. C. C. *in Causa Cremonen.*, July, 1586—*Fontes*, n. 2161; Cocchi, *op. cit.*, VI, 231; Cance, *l. c.;* Prümmer, *l. c.;* Vromant, *l. c.;* Blat, *l. c.;* Mothon, *l. c.;* Many, *l. c.;* D'Annibale, *l. c.;* Benedict XIV, *l. c.*, n. 23.

[191] *L. c.*, nn. 23, 24.

statuta, dummodo adsit vera necessitas nec divinus cultus idcirco minuatur aut populi commoditati praeiudicium inferatur, exceptis tamen legatis quae in certis locis adimpleri facile possunt per eleemosynae augmentum, et cauto ut de translatarum missarum satisfactione quovis anno Curia dioecesana a singulis celebrantibus legitime doceatur;

3. Transferendi per quinquennium exuberantia missarum onera etiam extra dioecesim, cauto tamen ut quam maximus missarum numerus intra fines dioecesis celebretur atque adamussim serventur praescripta Codicis iuris canonici circa cautelas adhibendas in missis committendis.

BIBLIOGRAPHY

Sources

Acta Apostolicae Sedis (*AAS*), Romae, 1909—

Acta et Decreta Conciliorum Recentiorum (*Collectio Lacensis*), 7 vols., Friburgi Brisgoviae, 1870-1890.

Acta Sanctae Sedis (*ASS*), 41 vols., Romae, 1865-1908.

Bullarium Romanum, Bullarium Diplomatum et Privilegiorum Sanctorum Romanorum Pontificum, Taurinensis Editio, 24 vols., Augustae Taurinorum, 1857.

Canones et Decreta Concilii Tridentini, 19 ed., Taurini, 1913.

Codex Iuris Canonici Pii X Pontificis Maximi iussu digestus Benedicti Papae XV auctoritate promulgatus, Romae, 1918.

Codex Theodosianus, Theodosiani Libri XVI cum Constitutionibus Sirmondianis et Leges Novellae ad Theodosianum Pertinentes, ed. P. Krueger, T. Mommsen, P. M. Meyer, 3 vols., Berolini, 1905.

Codicis Iuris Canonici Fontes (*Fontes*), cura Emi. Petri Card. Gasparri editi, 6 vols., Romae, 1925—

Collectanea S. Congregationis de Propaganda Fide, 2 vols., Romae, 1907.

Collectanea in Usum Secretariae Sacrae Congregationis Episcoporum et Regularium Edita (Bizzarri), Romae, 1885.

Concilii Plenarii Baltimorensis II, Acta et Decreta, 2 ed., Baltimorae, 1877.

Concilii Plenarii Baltimorensis III, Acta et Decreta, Baltimorae, 1886.

Constitutiones Apostolorum, ed. F. X. Funk, 2 vols., Paderborn, 1895.

Corpus Iuris Canonici, Editio Lipsiensis II (Richter-Friedberg), 2 vols., Lipsiae, 1922.

Corpus Iuris Civilis: I.—*Institutiones,* quas recognovit P. Krueger; D.—*Digesta,* quae recognovit T. Mommsen et retractavit P. Krueger, Vol. I, Berolini, 1928; C.—*Codex Iustinianus,* quem recognovit et retractavit P. Krueger, Vol. II, Berolini, 1929; *Nov.*—*Novellae,* quas recognovit R. Schoell, et absolvit G. Kroll, Vol. III, Berolini, 1928.

Corpus Scriptorum Ecclesiasticorum Latinorum, 65 vols., Vindobonae, 1866.

Decreta Authentica Congregationis Sacrorum Rituum, 6 vols., Romae, 1898.

Denzinger, Henricus, *Enchiridion Symbolorum,* 10 ed., Friburgi Brisgoviae, 1908.

Gai Institutiones, ed. E. Poste, 4 ed., Oxford, 1894.

Harduin, J., *Acta Conciliorum et Epistolae Decretales ac Constitutiones Summorum Pontificum,* 12 vols., Parisiis, 1715.

Iurisprudentiae Ante-Iustinianae Reliquiae, ed. E. Seckel and B. Kuebler, 6 ed., 2 vols., Leipzig, 1908.

Lex Romana Visigothorum, ed. G. Haenel, Berolini, 1849.

Mansi, Joannes, *Sacrorum Conciliorum Nova et Amplissima Collectio,* 53 vols., 1901—

Monumenta Germaniae Historica (MGH), Legum Sectio Secunda, Capitularia Regum Francorum, Hanover-Berlin, 1826-1890.

Migne, Jacques, *Patrologiae Cursus Completus Series Latina (MPL)*, 221 vols., Parisiis, 1858-1864.

Moyle, J. B., *Institutionum Iustiniani Libri Quatuor*, 2 ed., 2 vols., Oxford, 1890.

Pallottini, Salvator, *Collectio Omnium Conclusionum et Resolutionum quae in causis propositis apud S. Cong. Cardinalium S. Concilii Tridentini Interpretum prodierunt ab anno 1564 ad annum 1860*, 17 vols., Romae, 1868-1893.

Richter, Aemilius, *Canones et Decreta Concilii Tridentini*, Lipsiae, 1853.

Thesaurus Resolutionum Sacrae Congregationis Concilii, 167 vols., Romae, 1718-1908.

Ulpian, *Iurisprudentiae Ante-Iustinianae Reliquiae*, ed. E. Seckel and B. Kuebler, 6 ed., 2 vols., Leipzig, 1908.

AUTHORS

Abbas Panormitanus, *Commentaria in Libros Decretalium*, 8 vols., Venetiis, 1588.

Alphonse, de Liguori, *Theologia Moralis*, 4 vols., Augustae Taurinorum, 1827.

Ayrinhac, H. A., *General Legislation in the New Code of Canon Law*, New York, 1930.

Ayrinhac, H. A., *Penal Legislation in the New Code of Canon Law*, New York, 1920.

[Bachofen], Charles Augustine, *A Commentary on the New Code of Canon Law*, 8 vols., St. Louis, 1918-1922.

Badii, C., *Institutiones Iuris Canonici*, 2 ed., 3 vols., Florentiae, 1922.

Ballerini, Antonius-Palmieri, Dominicus, *Opus Theologicum Morale*, 7 vols., Prati, 1893.

Barbosa, A., *Collectanea Doctorum in Ius Pontificium Universum*, Lugduni, 1666.

Barbosa, A., *De Officio et Potestate Episcopi*, Lugduni, 1656.

Bargilliat, M., *Praelectiones Iuris Canonici*, 37 ed., 2 vols., Parisiis, 1923.

Bartlett, Chester J., *The Tenure of Parochial Property in the United States of America*, Washington, 1926.

Benedict XIV, *De Synodo Dioecesana*, 2 vols., Rome, 1806.

Benedict XIV, *Institutiones Ecclesiasticae*, 3 vols., Louvanii, 1762.

Blackstone, Sir William, *Commentaries on the Law of England*, ed. George Sharswood, 4 vols., Philadelphia, 1870.

Blat, Albertus, *Commentarium Textus Iuris Canonici*, 6 vols., Romae, 1921-1927. Liber III, *De Rebus*, tom. 2.

Boudinhon, A., *Biens d'Eglise et Peines Canoniques*, Parisiis, 1909.

Bouuaert, F.-Simenon, G., *Manuale Iuris Canonici*, 3 ed., 3 vols., Leodii, 1931.

Bracton, Henry, *De Legibus et Consuetudinibus Angliae*, 6 vols., London, 1878.

Brissaud, Jean, *History of French Private Law*, translated by R. Howell, Boston, 1912.

Brown, Brendan, *The Canonical Juristic Personality with Special Reference to its Status in the United States of America*, Washington, 1927.

Bry, Georges, *Principes de Droit Romain*, 6 ed., 2 vols., Parisiis, 1927.

Buckland, W. W., *A Text Book of Roman Law*, Cambridge, 1921.

Cance, Adrien, *Le Code de Droit Canonique*, 4 ed., 3 vols., Parisiis, 1930.

Cappello, Felix M., *Tractatus Canonico-Moralis de Censuris*, 2 ed., Taurini, 1925.

Cappello, Felix M., *Summa Iuris Publici Ecclesiastici*, 2 ed., Romae, 1928.

Catholic Encyclopedia, The, 16 vols., New York, 1912.

Cavagnis, Felix, *Institutiones Iuris Publici Ecclesiastici*, 3 vols., Romae, 1896.

Cerato, Prosdocimus, *Censurae Vigentes Ipso Facto a Codice Iuris Canonici Excerptae*, 2 ed., Patavii, 1931.

Chelodi, Ioannes, *Ius de Personis*, 2 ed., Tridenti, 1927.

Chelodi, Ioannes, *Ius Poenale*, 3 ed., Tridenti, 1920.

Cipollini, A., *De Censuris Latae Sententiae*, Taurini, 1925.

Cocchi, Guidus, *Commentarium in Codicem Iuris Canonici ad Usum Scholarum*, 8 vols., Augustae Taurinorum, 1925-1927.

Creusen, J., *Religieux et Religieuses*, 3 ed., Louvain, 1924.

D'Annibale, Ioseph, *Summula Theologiae Moralis*, 3 ed., 3 vols., Romae, 1891.

De Héricourt, L., *Les Lois Ecclésiastiques de France*, Parisiis, 1771.

De Luca, Ioannes, *Theatrum Veritatis et Iustitiae*, 16 vols., Coloniae Agrippinae, 1706.

De Meester, A., *Iuris Canonici et Iuris Canonico-Civilis Compendium*, 4 vols., Brugis, 1921-1928.

Dictionnaire Encyclopedique de la Théologie Catholique, 26 vols., Parisiis, 1859.

Dignan, Patrick J., *A History of the Legal Incorporation of Catholic Church Property in the United States (1784-1932)*, Washington, 1933.

Dillon, W., *Bequests for Masses*, Chicago, 1896.

Doheny, William J., *Church Property: Modes of Acquisition*, Washington, 1927.

Duchesne, L., *Early History of the Christian Church*, translated from 4 ed., New York, 1909.

Fagnanus, Prosperus, *Commentaria in V Libros Decretalium*, 4 vols., Venetiis, 1696.

Fanfani, L. I., *De Iure Religiosorum*, 2 ed., Romae, 1925.

Ferraris, F. L., *Bibliotheca Prompta*, 8 vols., Parisiis, 1858.

Ferreres, Ioannes, *Compendium Theologiae Moralis*, 14 ed., 2 vols., Barcinone, 1928.

Ferreres, Ioannes, *Institutiones Canonicae*, 2 ed., 2 vols., Barcinone, 1920.

Ferrini, C., *Manuale di Pandette*, 3 ed., Milano, 1917.

Gasparri, Petrus, *De Sanctissima Eucharistia*, 2 vols., Parisiis, 1897.

Gasparro, F. M., *Institutiones Iuris Civilis*, Venetiis, 1741.

Genicot, E.-Salsmans, I, *Institutiones Theologiae Moralis*, 11 ed., 2 vols., Bruxellis, 1927.

Gennari, C.-Boudinhon, A., *Consultations de Morale, de Droit Canonique, et de Liturgie,* Parisiis, 1907.

Glanvell, V. W. von, *Die letztwilligen Verfügungen nach gemeinem Kirchlichen Rechte,* Paderborn, 1900.

Heineccius, J. G., *Elementa Iuris Civilis,* Genevae, 1749.

Hefele-Leclercq, *Histoire des Conciles,* 9 vols., Parisiis, 1907-1930.

Hilling, Nicholas, *Das Personenrecht des Codex Iuris Canonici,* Paderborn, 1924.

Huebner, Rudolf, *A History of German Private Law,* translated by F. S. Philbrick, Boston, 1918.

Ilg, John, *An Explanation of the Rule of the Friars Minor,* Chicago, 1927.

Keller, C. F., *Mass Stipends,* Washington, 1925.

Kenrick, F. P., *Theologia Moralis,* 2 ed., 2 vol., Mechlin, 1866.

Lehmkuhl, Augustinus, *Theologia Moralis,* 9 ed., 2 vols., Friburgi Brisgoviae, 1898.

Leo XIII, *Rerum Novarum,* official translation of the International Catholic Truth Society.

Lucidi, A., *De Visitatione Sacrorum Liminum,* 3 vols., Romae, 1866.

Maine, Henry Sumner, *Ancient Law,* 3 ed., New York, 1875.

Mansi, J. D., *Epitome Doctrinae Moralis et Canonicae,* Mechlin, 1824.

Many, S., *Praelectiones de Missa,* Parisiis, 1903.

Maroto, Philippus, *Institutiones Iuris Canonici,* 3 ed., 2 vols., Romae, 1921.

Martindale-Hubbell, *Law Directory,* 2 vols., New York, 1932.

Marucchi, H., *Elements d'Archeologie Chretienne,* Parisiis, 1900.

Melo, Antonius, *De Exemptione Regularium,* Washington, 1921.

Miller, N. T., *Founded Masses According to the Code of Canon Law,* Washington, 1926.

Moore, Thomas Verner, *Dynamic Psychology,* 2 ed., Philadelphia, 1926.

Morris, M. F., *An Introduction to the History of the Development of Law,* Washington, 1911.

Mothon, Joseph, *Institutions Canoniques,* 3 vols., Bruges, 1924.

Noldin, H., *Summa Theologiae Moralis,* quam recognovit A. Schmitt, 19 ed., 3 vols., Oeniponte, 1928.

Ojetti, B., *Commentarium in Codicem Iuris Canonici,* 2 vols., Romae, 1928.

Ottaviani, A., *Institutiones Iuris Publici Ecclesiastici,* 2 vols., Romae, 1925.

Phillips, H., *Compendium Iuris Ecclesiastici,* Ratisboniae, 1875.

Pichler, V., *Candidatus Iurisprudentiae Sacrae,* 5 vols., Augsburg, 1723.

Pignatelli, I., *Consultationes Canonicae,* Coloniae Allobrogum, 1700.

Pirhing, Henricus, *Ius Canonicum,* 5 vols., Dilingae, 1722.

Pistocchi, M., *De Re Beneficiali,* Turin, 1928.

Pius XI, *Quadragesimo Anno,* translation of the National Catholic Welfare Conference, Washington, 1931.

Plato, *Laws,* ed. George Grote, F.R.S., 3 vols., London, 1867.

Pollock, F.-Maitland, F. W., *History of English Law Before the Time of Edward I,* 2 vols., Cambridge, 1895.

'othier, R. J., *Oeuvres de Pothier,* 10 vols., Parisiis, 1861.

'rümmer, Dominicus, *Manuale Iuris Canonici,* 3 ed., Friburgi Brisgoviae, 1922.

'rümmer, Dominicus, *Manuale Theologiae Moralis,* 4 and 5 ed., 3 vols., Friburgi Brisgoviae, 1928.

'ufendorf, S., *De Iure Naturae et Gentium Dissertationes,* ed. Ludwig von Bar, Washington, 1916.

ledfield, I. F., *The Law of Wills,* 4 ed., 3 vols., Boston, 1876.

leiffenstuel, Anacletus, *Ius Canonicum Universum,* 7 vols., Parisiis, 1864-1870.

lood, J. R., *A Treatise on the Law of Wills,* Chicago, 1904.

lubei, L., *Resolutiones Practicabiles circa Testamenta Aliasque Dispositiones ad Pias et non Pias Causas,* Lugduni, 1676.

ianti, Franciscus, *Praelectiones Iuris Canonici,* 2 ed., 5 vols., Ratisboniae, 1892.

iavigny, F., *Sistema del Diritto Romano Attuale,* translated by V. Scialoja, 7 vols., Torino, 1888.

Schäfer, T., *De Religiosis,* Münster, 1931.

Schmalzgrueber, Franciscus, *Ius Ecclesiasticum Universum,* 12 vols., Romae, 1844.

Schouler, J., *A Treatise on the Law of Domestic Relations,* 3 ed., Boston, 1882.

Sebastianelli, G., *Praelectiones Iuris Canonici,* 2 ed., 2 vols., Romae, 1905.

Sebastiani, N., *Summarium Theologiae Moralis,* 3 ed., Augustae Taurinorum, 1919.

Selected Essays in Anglo-American Legal History, 3 vols., Boston, 1909.

Slater, Thomas, *A Manual of Moral Theology,* 2 vols., London, 1928.

Sohm, Rudolph, *The Institutes,* translated by J. C. Ledlie, 3 ed., Oxford, 1926.

Soglia, J., *Institutiones Iuris Privati,* 3 vols., Parisiis.

Sole, J., *De Delictis et Poenis,* Romae, 1920.

Suarez, Franciscus, *Opera Omnia,* ed. Carolo Berton, 26 vols., Parisiis, 1866.

Tacitus, C., *Germania,* ed. D. Lallemant,, Lugduni, 1842.

Tanquerey, Ad., *Synopsis Theologiae Moralis et Pastoralis,* 3 ed., 2 vols., New York, 1907.

Thomas Aquinas, *Opera Omnia, ed. Frette,* Parisiis, 1873-1879.

Thomassin, L., *Vetus et Nova Disciplina Ecclesiae circa Beneficia et Beneficiarios,* Venetiis, 1773.

Turner, S. J., *The Vow of Poverty,* Washington, 1929.

Vermeersch, Arthur, *Theologiae Moralis Principia, Responsa, Consilia,* 2 ed., 4 vols., Romae, 1926.

Vermeersch, A.-Creusen, J., *Epitome Iuris Canonici,* 4 ed., 3 vols., Mechlin, 1930.

Vromant, G., *Ius Missionariorum,* Vol. III: *De Fidelium Associationibus,* Louvain, 1932.

Vromant, G., *Ius Missionariorum,* Vol. VI: *De Bonis Temporalibus Ecclesiae,* Louvain, 1927.

Wasserschleben, Herrmann, *Die Irische Kanonensammlung,* 2 ed., Leipzig, 1885.

Weber, N. A., *The Christian Era,* 2 vols., Washington, 1919.

Wernz, F. X., *Ius Decretalium,* 6 vols., Romae, 1908-1913.

Woerner, J. G., *A Treatise on the American Law of Administration,* 2 vols., Boston, 1889.

Woywod, Stanislaus, *Canonical Decisions of the Holy See,* New York, 1933.

Zallinger, J. A. *Institutiones Iuris Ecclesiastici Maxime Privati,* 5 vols., Romae, 1823.

Zallinger, J. A., *Institutiones Iuris Naturalis et Ecclesiastici Publici,* 5 vols., Romae, 1823.

Zollman, Carl, *American Law of Charities,* Milwaukee, 1924.

Periodicals

American Ecclesiastical Review, The (*AER*), Philadelphia, 1889—

Commentarium pro Religiosis, Rome, 1920—

Homiletic and Pastoral Review, The, New York, 1900—

Irish Ecclesiastical Record, The, Dublin, 1864—

Ius Pontificium, Romae, 1921—

Le Canoniste Contemporain, Paris, 1878—

Month, The, London, 1865—

Nouvelle Revue Theologique, Louvain, 1873—

Perfice Munus, Turin, 1926—

Periodica de Morali, Canonica Liturgica, Romae et Brugis, 1912—

Tablet, The, London, 1840—

Theologisch-praktische Quartalschrift, Linz, 1832—

American Legal Sources

(Unless specially noted, citations for California are from the Probate Code; for Louisiana, from the Civil Code; for New York, from the Decedent's Estate Law.)

Alabama Code of 1928, edited under the direction of A. Hewson Michie, Charlottesville, Va., 1929.

Alaska, Compiled Laws of the Territory of, Washington, 1913.

Arizona, Revised Code of 1928, edited by F. C. Struckmeyer, Phoenix, 1930.

Arkansas, Digest of the Statutes of, edited by T. D. Crawford and Hamilton Moses, Little Rock, 1921.

California, Probate Code of 1931, Appendix to *Code of Civil Procedure,* edited by James H. Deering, San Francisco, 1931.

Statutes (no editor), Sacramento, 1931.

Civil Code, edited by James H. Deering, San Francisco, 1931.

Colorado, Compiled Laws 1921 (no editor), Denver, 1922.

Connecticut, General Statutes of, Revision of 1930 (no editor), 3 vols., Orange and New Haven, 1930.

Delaware, Revised Statutes of the State of, 1915 (no editor), Wilmington, 1915.
District of Columbia, Code of (no editor), Washington, 1930.
Florida, Compiled General Laws of, 1927, compiled by Harry B. Skillman, Atlanta, 1929.
General Statutes of 1932, edited by Benjmin W. Dart, 4 vols., Indianapolis, 1932.
Georgia Code of 1926, edited under the direction of Thomas Johnson Michie, Charlottesville, Va., 1926.
Hawaii, Revised Laws of (no editor), Honolulu, 1925.
Idaho Code Annotated, 1932, edited by T. Bailey Lee, C. Ben Ross and Fred E. Lukens, Indianapolis, 1932.
Illinois, Revised Statutes of the State of, 1931, edited by Basil Jones, Chicago, 1931.
Indiana, Annotated Statutes, edited by Harrison Burns, Indianapolis, 1926.
Iowa, Code of, 1931, compiled by U. G. Whitney and Nancy M. Conlee.
Kansas, Revised Statutes of, Annotated, 1923, edited by Chester I. Long, F. Dumont Smith and Hugh P. Farrelly, Topeka, 1923.
Kentucky, Carroll's Statutes of, 1930, revised by William Edward Baldwin, Louisville, 1930.
Louisiana, Civil Code of the State of, revision of 1870, edited and annotated by Benjamin W. Dart, Indianapolis, 1932.
Maine, Revised Statutes of (no editor), Augusta, 1930.
Maryland, Annotated Code of the Public General Laws of, edited by George P. Bagby, Baltimore, 1924.
Massachusetts, Tercentenary Edition of the General Laws of, edited by William E. Dorman and Henry D. Wiggin, 2 vols., Boston, 1932.
Michigan, Compiled Laws of the State of, 1929, edited by Wilbur B. Brucker, Oscar K. Riopelle and John Kaminski, 4 vols., Lansing, 1930.
Minnesota, Mason's Statutes of 1927 (no editor), 2 vols., St. Paul, 1927.
Mississippi Code of 1930 (no editor), 2 vols., Atlanta, 1930.
Missouri, Revised Statutes of the State of, 1929 (no editor), 3 vols., Jefferson City, 1930.
Montana, Revised Code of, 1921, compiled by I. W. Choate, 4 vols., San Francisco, 1921.
Nebraska, Compiled Statutes of, 1929, compiled by William C. Dorsey, Lincoln, 1930.
Nevada, Compiled Laws, 1929, compiled and annotated by Curtis Hillyer, 6 vols., San Francisco, 1930.
New Hampshire, Public Laws of, 1926.
New Jersey, Compiled Statutes of, 1910 (no editor), 5 vols., Newark, 1911.
New Mexico Statutes Annotated, 1929, compiled by William H. Courtright, Denver, 1929.
New York, Cahill's Consolidated Laws of, 2 ed., edited by Basil Jones, Chicago, 1930.

North Carolina Code of 1931, edited by A. Hewson Michie and Beirne Skedman, Charlottesville, Va., 1931.

North Dakota, Compiled Laws of the State of, 1913 (no editor), 2 vols., Rochester, 1914.

Ohio, Throckmorton's 1929 Annotated Code of, Cleveland, 1930.

Oklahoma Statutes 1931, edited by Frank O. Eagin and C. W. Van Eaton, 2 vols., Oklahoma, 1932.

Oregon, Code 1930 (no editor), 4 vols., Indianapolis, 1930.

Pennsylvania, Digest of the Statute Law, 1920 (no editor), St. Paul, 1921.

Porto Rico, Compilation of Revised Statutes and Codes of, Washington, 1913.

Rhode Island, General Laws of (no editor), 2 vols., Pawtucket, 1923.

South Carolina, Code of the Laws of, 1932 (no editor), 4 vols., Charlottesville, 1932.

South Dakota, Compiled Laws, 1929 (no editor), 2 vols., Pierre, 1930.

Tennessee, Code of, 1932, edited by Samuel C. Williams, Robert T. Shannon and George Harsh, Kingsport, Tenn., 1931.

Texas, Revised Civil Statutes of, 1928 (no editor), Kansas City, 1928.

Utah, Revised Laws of, 1933 (no editor), Kaysville, Utah, 1933.

Vermont, Public Laws of, 1933 (no editor), Montpelier, 1934.

Virginia, Code of, 1930 (no editor), Charlottesville, 1930.

Washington, Remington's Compiled Statutes, 1932.

West Virginia, Code of 1932 (no editor), Charlottesville, 1932.

Wisconsin, Statutes, 1931, edited by E. E. Brossard, Fort Atkinson, 1931.

Wyoming, Revised Statutes, 1931, edited by William H. Courtright, Cheyenne, 1931.

Foreign Legal Codes

Les Codes et Les Lois Speciales Les Plus Usuelles en Vigeur en Belgique, 18 ed., Bruxelles, 1929.

Das Allgemeine bürgerliche Gesetzbuch, edited by Joseph Schey, 21 ed., Wien., 1926.

Codigo Civil Español, edited by D. Victor Covian y Junco, 18 ed., Madrid, 1932.

French Civil Code, translated by E. Blackwood Wright, London, 1908.

The Civil Code of the German Empire, translated by Walter Loewy, Boston, 1909.

Il Codice Dei Codici, Torino, 1928.

Nuevo Codigo Civil, annotated by F. J. Santamaria, Mexico, 1933.

Swiss Civil Code (English Version), translated by Ivy Williams, Oxford, 1925.

Universitas Catholica Americae

WASHINGTON, D. C.

Facultas Juris Canonici

No. 86

1934

TOPICAL TEXT

(The figures in this index refer to the sections of the text. Roman Law references will be found in this index, *s. v.*, "Roman Law.")

BIOGRAPHICAL NOTE

Jerome Daniel Hannan was born on November 29, 1896, in Pittsburgh. He was educated in the parochial schools of that city and at Duquesne University, where he was graduated with the degree of A.B. in 1916. He began the study of theology as a student for the Diocese of Pittsburgh in September, 1916, at Saint Vincent's Seminary, Latrobe, Pa., where he was given the degree of A.M. in June, 1918, and S.T.B., in September of that year. A year later he received the degree S.T.L. and in 1920 the degree S.T.D. He was ordained to the priesthood May 22, 1921. After serving two years in parochial work, he became secretary to the Bishop of Pittsburgh in September, 1923. During his incumbency in that office, he studied law at Duquesne University and was graduated in 1931 with the degree, LL.B. In September of that year he enrolled in the School of Canon Law at the Catholic University of America, where in 1932 he received the degree, J.C.L.

CANON LAW STUDIES

1. Freriks, Rev. Celestine A., C.PP.S., J.C.D., Religious Congregations in Their External Relations, 121 pp., 1916.
2. Galliher, Rev. Daniel M., O.P., J.C.D., Canonical Elections, 117 pp., 1917.
3. Borkowski, Rev. Aurelius L., O.F.M., De Confraternitatibus Ecclesiasticis, 136 pp., 1918.
4. Castillo, Rev. Cayo, J.C.D., Disertacion Historico-canonica sobre la Potestad del Cabildo en Sede Vacante o Impedida del Vicario Capitular, 99 pp., 1919 (1918).
5. Kubelbeck, Rev. William J., S.T.B., J.C.D., The Sacred Penitentiaria and Its Relations to Faculties of Ordinaries and Priests, 129 pp., 1918.
6. Petrovits, Rev. Joseph J. C., S.T.D., J.C.D., The New Church Law on Matrimony, X-461 pp., 1919.
7. Hickey, Rev. John J., S.T.B., J.C.D., Irregularities and Simple Impediments in the New Code of Canon Law, 100 pp., 1920.
8. Klekotka, Rev. Peter J., S.T.B., J.C.D., Diocesan Consultors, 179 pp., 1920.
9. Wannenmacher, Rev. Francis, J.C.D., The Evidence in Ecclesiastical Procedure Affecting the Marriage Bond, 1920. (Not Printed.)
10. Golden, Rev. Henry Francis, J.C.D., Parochial Benefices in the New Code, IV-119 pp., 1921. (Printed 1925.)
11. Koudelka, Rev. Charles, J., J.C.D., Pastors, Their Rights and Duties According to the New Code of Canon Law, 211 pp., 1921.
12. Melo, Rev. Antonius, O.F.M., J.C.D., De Exemptione Regularium, X-188 pp., 1921.
13. Schaaf, Rev. Valentine Theodore, O.F.M., S.T.B., J.C.D., The Cloister, X-180 pp., 1921.
14. Burke, Rev. Thomas Joseph, S.T.B., J.C.D., Competence in Ecclesiastical Tribunals, IV-117 pp., 1922.
15. Leech, Rev. George Leo, J.C.D., A Comparative Study of the Constitution "Apostolicae Sedis" and the "Codex Juris Canonici," 179 pp., 1922.
16. Motry, Rev. Hubert Louis, S.T.D., J.C.D., Diocesan Faculties According to the Code of Canon Law, II-167 pp., 1922.
17. Murphy, Rev. George Lawrence, J.C.D., Delinquencies and Penalties in the Administration and the Reception of the Sacraments, IV-121 pp., 1923.
18. O'Reilly, Rev. John Anthony, S.T.B., J.C.D., Ecclesiastical Sepulture in the New Code of Canon Law, II-129 pp., 1923.
19. Michalicka, Rev. Wenceslas Cyrill, O.S.B., J.C.D., Judicial Procedure in Dismissal of Clerical Exempt Religious, 107 pp., 1923.

20. Dargin, Rev. Edward Vincent, S.T.B., J.C.D., Reserved Cases According to the Code of Canon Law, IV-103 pp., 1924.
21. Godfrey, Rev. John A., S.T.B., J.C.D., The Right of Patronage According to the Code of Canon Law, 153 pp., 1924.
22 Hagedorn, Rev. Francis Edward, J.C.D., General Legislation on Indulgences, II-154 pp., 1924.
23. King, Rev. James Ignatius, J.C.D., The Administration of the Sacraments to Dying Non-Catholics, V-141 pp., 1924.
24. Winslow, Rev. Francis Joseph, A.F.M., J.C.D., Vicars and Prefects Apostolic, IV-149 pp., 1924.
25. Correa, Rev. Jose Servelion, S.T.L., J.C.D., La Potestad Legislativa de la Iglesia Católica, IV-127 pp., 1925.
26. Dugan, Rev. Henry Francis, M.A., J.C.D., The Judiciary Department of the Diocesan Curia, 87 pp., 1925.
27. Keller, Rev. Charles Frederick, S.T.B., J.C.D., Mass Stipends, 167 pp. 1925.
28. Paschang, Rev. John Linus, J.C.D., The Sacramentals According to the Code of Canon Law, 129 pp., 1925.
29. Piontek, Rev. Cyrillus, O.F.M., S.T.B., J.C.D., De Indulto Exclaustrationis necnon Saecularizationis, XIII-289 pp., 1925.
30. Kearney, Rev. Richard Joseph, S.T.B., J.C.D., Sponsors at Baptism According to the Code of Canon Law, IV-127 pp., 1925.
31. Bartlett, Rev. Chester Joseph, A.M., LL.B., J.C.D., The Tenure of Parochial Property in the United States of America, V-108 pp., 1926.
32. Kilker, Rev. Adrian Jerome, J.C.D., Extreme Unction, V-425 pp. 1926
33. McCormick, Rev. Robert Emmett, J.C.D., Confessors of Religious, VIII-266 pp., 1926.
34. Miller, Rev. Newton Thomas, J.C.D., Founded Masses According to the Code of Canon Law, VII-93 pp., 1926.
35. Roelker, Rev. Edward G., S.T.D., J.C.D., Principles of Privilege According to the Code of Canon Law, XI-166 pp., 1926.
36. Bakalarczyk, Rev. Richardus, M.I.C., J.U.D., De Novitiatu, VIII-20[illegible] pp., 1927.
37. Pizzuti, Rev. Lawrence, O.F.M., J.U.L., De Parochis Religiosis, 1927 (Not Printed.)
38. Bliley, Rev. Nicholas Martin, O.S.B., J.C.D., Altars According to the Code of Canon Law, XIX-132 pp., 1927.
39. Brown, Brendan Francis, A.B., LL.M., J.U.D., The Canonical Juristic Personality with Special Reference to its Status in the United States of America, V-212 pp., 1927.
40. Cavanaugh, Rev. William Thomas, C.P., J.U.D., The Reservation of the Blessed Sacrament, VIII-101 pp., 1927.
41. Doheny, Rev. William J., C.S.C., A.B., J.U.D., Church Property: Modes of Acquisition, X-118 pp,. 1927

42. Feldhaus, Rev. Aloysius H., C.PP.S., J.C.D., Oratories, IX-141 pp., 1927.
43. Kelly, Rev. James Patrick, A.B., J.C.D., The Jurisdiction of the Simple Confessor, X-208 pp., 1927.
44. Neuberger, Rev. Nicholas J., J.C.D., Canon 6 or the Relation of the Codex Juris Canonici to the Preceding Legislation, V-95 pp., 1927.
45. O'Keeffe, Rev. Gerald Michael, J.C.D., Matrimonial Dispensations, Powers of Bishops, Priests, and Confessors, VIII-232 pp., 1927.
46. Quigley, Rev. Joseph, A.M., A.B., J.C.D., Condemned Societies, 139 pp., 1927.
47. Zaplotnik, Rev. Ioannes Leo, J.C.D., De Vicariis Foraneis, X-142 pp., 1927.
48. Duskie, Rev. John Aloysius, A.B., J.C.D., The Canonical Status of the Orientals in the United States, VIII-196 pp., 1928.
49. Hyland, Rev. Francis Edward, J.C.D., Excommunication, Its Nature, Historical Development and Effects, VIII-181 pp., 1928.
50. Reinmann, Rev. Gerald Joseph, O.M.C., J.C.D., The Third Order Secular of Saint Francis, 201 pp., 1928.
51. Schenk, Rev. Francis J., J.C.D., The Matrimonial Impediments of Mixed Religion and Disparity of Cult, XVI-318 pp., 1929.
52. Coady, Rev. John Joseph, S.T.D., J.U.D., A.M., The Appointment of Pastors, VIII-150 pp., 1929.
53. Kay, Rev. Thomas Henry, J.C.D., Competence in Matrimonial Procedure, VIII-164 pp., 1929.
54. Turner, Rev. Sidney Joseph, C.P., J.U.D., The Vow of Poverty, XLIX-217 pp., 1929.
55. Kearney, Rev. Raymond A., A.B., S.T.D., J.C.D., The Principles of Delegation, VII-149 pp., 1929.
56. Conran, Rev. Edward James, A.B., J.C.D., The Interdict, V-163 pp., 1930.
57. O'Neil, Rev. William H., J.C.D., Papal Rescripts of Favor, VII-218 pp., 1930.
58. Bastnagel, Rev. Clement Vincent, J.U.D., The Appointment of Parochial Adjutants and Assistants, XV-257 pp., 1930.
59. Ferry, Rev. William A., A.B., J.C.D., Stole Fees, X-107 pp., 1930.
60. Costello, Rev. John Michael, A.B., J.C.D., Domicile and Quasi-Domicile, VII-201 pp., 1930.
61. Kremer, Rev. Michael Nicholas, A.B., S.T.B., J.C.D., Church Support in the United States, VI-136 pp., 1930.
62. Angulo, Rev. Luis, C.M., J.C.D., Legislación de la Iglesia sobre la intención en la applicación de la Santa Misa, VII-104 pp., 1931.
63. Frey, Rev. Wolfgang Norbert, O.S.B., A.B., J.C.D., The Act of Religious Profession, VIII-174 pp., 1931.
64. Roberts, Rev. James Brendan, A.B., J.C.D., The Banns of Marriage, XIV-140 pp., 1931.

65. RYDER, REV. RAYMOND ALOYSIUS, A.B., J.C.D., Simony, IX-151 pp., 1931.
66. CAMPAGNA, REV. ANGELO, PH.D., J.U.D., Il Vicario Generale del Vescovo, VII-205 pp., 1931.
67. COX, REV. JOSEPH GODFREY, A.B., J.C.D., The Administration of Seminaries, VI-124 pp., 1931.
68. GREGORY, REV. DONALD J., J.U.D., The Pauline Privilege, XV-165 pp., 1931.
60. DONOHUE, REV. JOHN F., J.C.D., The Impediment of Crime, VIII-110 pp., 1931.
70. DOOLEY, REV. EUGENE A., O.M.I., J.C.D., Church Law on Sacred Relics, IX-143 pp., 1931.
71. ORTH, REV. CLEMENT RAYMOND, O.M.C., J.C.D., The Approbation of Religious Institutes, 171 pp., 1931.
72. PERNICONE, REV. JOSEPH M., A.B., J.C.D., The Ecclesiastical Prohibition of Books, XII-267 pp., 1932.
73. CLINTON, REV. CONNELL, A.B., J.C.D., The Paschal Precept, IX-108 pp., 1932.
74. DONNELLY, REV. FRANCIS B., A.M., S.T.L., J.C.D., The Diocesan Synod, VIII-125 pp., 1932
75. TORRENTE, REV. CAMILO, C.M.F., J.C.D., Las Processiones Sagradas, V-145 pp., 1932.
76. MURPHY, REV. EDWIN J., C.PP.S., J.C.D., Suspension Ex Informata Conscientia, XI-122 pp., 1932.
77. MACKENZIE, REV. ERIC F., A.M., S.T.L., J.C.D., The Delict of Heresy in its Commission, Penalization, Absolution, VII-124 pp., 1932.
78. LYONS, REV. AVITUS E., S.T.B., J.C.D., The Collegiate Tribunal of First Instance, XI-147 pp., 1932.
79. CONNOLLY, REV. THOMAS A., J.C.D., Appeals, XI-195 pp., 1932.
80. SANGMEISTER, REV. JOSEPH V., A.B., J.C.D., Force and Fear as Precluding Matrimonial Consent, V-211 pp., 1932.
81. JAEGER, REV. LEO A., A.B., J.C.D., The Administration of Vacant and Quasi-Vacant Episcopal Sees in the United States, IX-229 pp. 1932.
82. RIMLINGER, REV. HERBERT T., J.C.D., Error Invalidating Matrimonial Consent, VII-79 pp., 1932.
83. BARRETT, REV. JOHN D. M., S.S., J.C.D., Comparative Study of the Third Plenary Council and the Code, IX-221 pp., 1932.
84. CARBERRY, REV. JOHN J., PH.D., S.T.D., J.C.L., The Juridical Form of Marriage, 1934.
85. DOLAN, REV. JOHN L., A.B., J.C.L., The Defensor Vinculi, 1934.
86. HANNAN, REV. JEROME D., A.M., S.T.D., LL.B., J.C.L., The Canon Law of Wills, 1934.
87. LEMIEUX, REV. DELISLE A., A.M., J.C.L., The Sentence in Ecclesiastical Procedure, 1934.
88. O'ROURKE, REV. JAMES J., A.B., J.C.L., Parish Registers, 1934.

89. TIMLIN, REV. BARTHOLOMEW, O.F.M., A.M., J.C.L., Conditional Matrimonial Consent, 1934.

90. WAHL, REV. FRANCIS X., A.B., J.C.L., The Matrimonial Impediments of Consanguinity and Affinity, 1934.

91. WHITE, REV. ROBERT J., A.B., LL.B., S.T.B., J.C.L., Canonical Ante-Nuptial Promises and the Civil Law, 1934.

www.ingramcontent.com/pod-product-compliance
Lightning Source LLC
LaVergne TN
LVHW041117090826
844660LV00060B/668
* 9 7 8 0 8 1 3 2 2 2 7 5 2 *